Macroeconometrics

RECENT ECONOMIC THOUGHT SERIES

Editors:

Warren J. Samuels
Michigan State University
East Lansing, Michigan, USA

William Darity, Jr.
University of North Carolina
Chapel Hill, North Carolina, USA

Other books in the series:

Macroeconometrics

Developments, Tensions, and Prospects

Edited by
Kevin D. Hoover
University of California
Davis, California

Kluwer Academic Publishers
Boston / Dordrecht / London

Distributors for North America:
Kluwer Academic Publishers
101 Philip Drive
Assinippi Park
Norwell, Massachusetts 02061 USA

Distributors for all other countries:
Kluwer Academic Publishers Group
Distribution Centre
Post Office Box 322
3300 AH Dordrecht, THE NETHERLANDS

Library of Congress Cataloging-in-Publication Data

Macroeconometrics: developments, tensions, and prospects / edited by
   Kevin D. Hoover.
       p.   cm.—(Recent economic thought series)
   Includes index.
   ISBN 0-7923-9589-1
   1. Macroeconomics—Econometric models.   2. Econometrics.
I. Hoover, Kevin D., 1955-   II. Series.
HB172.5.M325   1995
339—dc20   95-16697
                                                                     CIP

Printed on acid-free paper.

Printed in the United States of America

Contents

CONTENTS vii

Contributing Authors

Anindja Banerjee, Wadham College and the Institute of Economics and Statistics, Oxford University, Oxford, England.

Charles W. Calomiris, Department of Finance, University of Illinois, Champaign, Illinois, U.S.A.

Fabio Canova, Department of Economics, University of Pompeu Farra, Barcelona, Spain; Department of Economics, University of Catania, Catania, Italy.

Francis X. Diebold, Department of Economics, University of Pennsylvania, Philadelphia, Pennsylvania, U.S.A.; National Bureau of Economic Research, Cambridge, Massachusetts, U.S.A.

Steven N. Durlauf, Department of Economics, University of Wisconsin, Madison, Wisconsin, U.S.A.

Neil Ericsson, International Finance Division, Board of Governors of the Federal Reserve System, Washington, D.C., U.S.A.

Jon Faust, Department of Economics, Massachusetts Institute of Technology, Cambridge, Massachusetts, U.S.A.

Clive W.J. Granger, Department of Economics, University of California, San Diego, California, U.S.A.

James D. Hamilton, Department of Economics, University of California, San Diego, U.S.A.

Christopher Hanes, Department of Economics, University of Pennsylvania, Philadelphia, Pennsylvania, U.S.A.

Kevin D. Hoover, Department of Economics, University of California, Davis, U.S.A.

Beth Fisher Ingram, Department of Economics, University of Iowa, Iowa City, Iowa, U.S.A.

John Irons, International Finance Division, Board of Governors of the Federal Reserve System, Washington, D.C., U.S.A.

Finn E. Kydland, University of Texas, Austin, Texas, U.S.A.

Eric Leeper, Department of Economics, Indiana University, Bloomington, Indiana, U.S.A.

Stephen F. LeRoy, Carlson School of Management, University of Minnesota, Minneapolis, Minnesota, U.S.A.

Jose A. Lopez, Department of Economics, University of Pennsylvania, Philadelphia, Pennsylvania. U.S.A.

Grayham E. Mizon, Department of Economics, European University Institute, Florence, Italy; Department of Economics, Southampton University, Southampton, England.

Masao Ogaki, Department of Economics, Ohio State University, Columbus, Ohio, U.S.A.

Adrian Pagan, Research School of Social Science, Australian National University, Canberra, Australia.

Simon M. Potter, Department of Economics, University of California, Los Angeles, California, U.S.A.

Edward C. Prescott, Department of Economics, University of Minnesota, Minneapolis, Minnesota, U.S.A.; Research Department, Federal Reserve Bank of Minneapolis, Minneapolis, Minnesota, U.S.A.

William T. Roberds, Research Department, Federal Reserve Bank of Atlanta, Atlanta, Georgia, U.S.A.

Glenn D. Rudebusch, Research Department, Federal Reserve Bank of San Francisco, San Francisco, California, U.S.A.

Daniel E. Sichel, Brookings Institution, Washington D.C., U.S.A.

Gregor W. Smith, Department of Economics, Queen's University, Kingston, Ontario, Canada.

Douglas G. Steigerwald, Department of Economics, University of California, Santa Barbara, California, U.S.A.

Charles H. Whiteman, Department of Economics, University of Iowa, Iowa City, Iowa, U.S.A.

Eric Zivot, Department of Economics, University of Washington, Seattle, Washington, U.S.A.

Acknowledgments

Assembling and editing a volume of individually commissioned papers was substantially more work than I could have imagined before I started. To make this volume possible I have relied on the goodwill, help, and cooperation of a number of people. I should first note the twenty-eight authors of papers and commentaries, without whom there would be no volume at all. Of these, I would especially like to thank Adrian Pagan, Gregor Smith, and Neil Ericsson for giving me invaluable advice on other economists to tap for various chapters and commentaries. I thank Catherine Whitney Hoover for expert preparation of the index and for proofreading the entire text. I thank the staff of the Department of Economics of the University of California at Davis, especially Marlene Baccala, Kathy Miner, and Donna Raymond, for diverse bits of assistance. I would also like to acknowledge Warren Samuels, the general editor of this series, and Zachary Rolnick, senior editor at Kluwer Academic Publishers, for giving me the opportunity to undertake this project and for helping it along the way.

Chapter 5, "The Econometrics of the General Equilibrium Approach to Business Cycles," by Finn E. Kydland and Edward C. Prescott was originally published in the *Scandinavian Journal of Economics* 93(2), pp. 161–178, 1991, copyright © 1991, and is reproduced here by kind permission of the editors and publisher of the *Scandinavian Journal of Economics*.

1 THE PROBLEM OF MACROECONOMETRICS

Kevin D. Hoover

Macroeconometrics and the Macroeconomist

This volume contains twelve chapters that discuss important topics in recent macroeconometrics. The presumed audience is the practicing macroeconomist or the student of macroeconomics who has some knowledge of econometrics but who is not a specialized econometrician. Each chapter is written by respected econometricians with the aim of providing information and perspectives useful to those who wish to reflect on fruitful ways to use econometrics in macroeconomics in their own work or in macroeconomics generally. The chapters are all written with clear methodological perspectives and aim to make the virtues and limitations of particular econometric approaches accessible to a general audience in applied macroeconomics. Because each chapter also represents the considered methodological views of important practitioners, I hope that they will also be of substantial interest to technical macroeconometricians as well as to the intended audience of macroeconomists. In order to bring out more fully the real tensions in macroeconometrics, each chapter is followed by a critical comment from another econometrician with an alternative perspective. The full chapters on competing methodologies in Part I further highlight these tensions.

Macroeconometrics in Perspective

Macroeconomics and econometrics are more closely joined than microeconomics and econometrics, and it seems always to have been so. Where much of microeconomics is the working out of the deductive consequences of principles of rational choice, much of macroeconomics is the consequence of broad empirical generalizations about aggregate variables. In the earliest macroeconomic theories —long before the term *macroeconomics* had currency—reasonable conclusions were drawn from first principles to be sure, but the urge to check these against the data was irresistible. David Hume and David Ricardo propounded versions of the quantity theory; but, in short order, Thomas Tooke and William Newmarch were at work on their *History of Prices* (1838–1857)—a six-volume compendium of data all aimed at testing, and ultimately disproving, the quantity theory. William Stanley Jevons, in his empirical studies of the gold standard and of business cycles, is sometimes regarded as the first modern econometrician (see Morgan, 1990, ch. 1, sec. 1). At the turn of the century the detailed statistical studies that accompany Irving Fisher's investigations of interest rates (Fisher 1930) and, once again, the quantity theory of money (Fisher 1911/1931), as well as Henry Moore's investigations of business cycles, stand out as illustrations of the close connection between macroeconomics and statistical investigation (Morgan, 1990, ch. 1, sec. 2).

For all the close connection between macroeconomics and econometrics, econometrics had its own independent development. In her history of econometrics, Mary Morgan (1990) identifies two distinct strands of econometric thinking that persist to this day. On the one hand, statistical methods were applied to characterizing business cycles. This was largely an atheoretical approach aimed at learning facts about the cycle. On the other hand, statistical methods were applied to estimating demand curves. Here the theory of the downward-sloping demand curve was taken as given, the statistics aimed only to measure the relevant elasticities. On the eve of the birth of modern macroeconomics, Ragnar Frisch (1933) began investigating yet another strand of econometrics. Frisch assigned reasonable values to the parameters of a simple theoretical model of the business cycle in order to examine its simulated behavior and to compare that behavior to the actual economy.

In 1936 the macroeconomic world changed with the publication of John Maynard Keynes's *General Theory of Employment, Interest and Money*. Although Keynes himself had little use for the econometrics that he found in, for example, Tinbergen's early models of the business cycle, the practical Keynesian revolution was as much an econometric revolution as a revolution in economic theory or policy (Keynes, 1939, 1940). The early interpretations of Keynes's macroeconomics in the models of John Hicks (1937) and Franco Modigliani (1944) provided the necessary frameworks for econometric elaboration. The macroeconomic and the econometric meet most notably in Lawrence Klein. Klein's (1947) book *The Keynesian Revolution* provides a formal interpretation of the *The General Theory*. Hard on its heels, Klein became the foremost developer of large-scale macro-econometric models—in his case, the FRB-Penn-SSRC model that is used by the Federal Reserve among others for policy analysis.

Models such as Klein's were important for many reasons. As was clear in the formalizations of Hicks and Modigliani, the Keynesian system was, despite its appeal to aggregates, intrinsically a general equilibrium system. Consumption, investment, and the demand for money depended on national income and interest rates; but income and interest rates in turn depended on consumption, investment, and the demand for money. As systems of interdependent equations, macroeco-nometric models could be seen as relatives of the Walrasian general equilibrium models, interest in which was growing in the twenty-five years after the mid-1930s. Once formalized the Keynesian model appeared to replicate on an aggre-gate level the structural characteristics of microeconomic equations. In them, the econometrics of the business cycle could be joined to the structural econometrics of demand measurement. The Cowles Commission program in econometrics aimed at synthesizing these two strands of earlier econometrics.

As in any synthesis, new problems arose. The most important were the problems of simultaneous equation bias (Haavelmo, 1943) and identification (Koopmans, 1949; Hood and Koopmans, 1953). The simultaneous equations problem led to the development of new systems estimators, while the identification problem encour-aged the elaboration of theory that would underwrite the *a priori* restrictions that the Cowles Commission program regarded as its solution.

The search for *a priori* restrictions, for the true structure underlying macroeco-nomic relations, motivated the program of microfoundations for macroeconomics. Keynes had already provided informal microeconomic rationales for consumption, investment, and portfolio behavior in *The General Theory*. Klein (1947) made a first attempt at deriving the principal components of the Keynesian model from first principles. Subsequent work included derivations by Baumol (1952) and Tobin (1956, 1958) of money-demand functions; Modigliani and Brumberg (1954) and Friedman (1957) of consumption functions; Lipsey (1960) of the Phillips curve (a component of the postwar Keynesian model not actually found in *The General Theory*); Jorgenson (1963) of the investment function; and so forth. Each of these was an attempt to provide microfoundations for a part of the Keynesian model, and each was to some degree successful theoretically and empirically.

Their empirical success, however, was imperfect. Typically, theoretical purity was compromised through the use of *ad hoc* lag distributions to improve the em-pirical fit and predictive ability of such microfoundational macroeconomic rela-tions. What is more, the equation-by-equation approach treated each aspect of the Keynesian model as a separate optimization problem and did not integrate them in accordance with the strictures of microeconomic general equilibrium. As early as 1936, Leontief criticized Keynes's system for its supposed incompatibility with individual optimization in general equilibrium. Patinkin (1956) provides perhaps the first systematic attempt to render a Keynesian model into a general-equilibrium framework. The decisive break with the piecemeal approach to microfoundations was Clower's (1965) article "The Keynesian Counterrevolution." Clower argued that microfoundations were unsatisfactory without a general-equilibrium approach and that, if such an approach were to have Keynesian features, the assumption of smoothly adjusting prices would have to be abandoned. After Clower, macro-economics could go two ways: give up the search for Keynesian features and adopt wholeheartedly the implications of the Walrasian model, which is essentially the new classical approach, or attempt to provide microfoundations for the impediments to smooth price adjustment that would justify Keynesian features, which became the new Keynesian approach.

The implications of general equilibrium for econometric models was first felt in in the estimation of demand systems. Here it was recognized that Walras's law imposed cross-equation restrictions that both posed a challenge for estimators and a cross-check of the model specification. The Yale School first applied the same ideas to macroeconomics in its general equilibrium models of financial inter-mediation (Tobin, 1969, 1980).

The macroeconometric models in widespread use in commercial forecasting and government policy analysis circa 1970 were an uneasy compromise between the drive for deep microfoundations and the exigencies of empirical reality. The models did not acquit themselves well in the face of the inflation, unemployment, and oil and commodity price shocks of the late 1960s to mid-1970s. A first response to the failure of the large macroeconometric models was to incorporate the expectations-augmented Phillips curves of Friedman (1968) and Phelps (1967) to improve the manner in which they modeled the inflation process. This was an example of the old style equation-by-equation microfoundations at work. Lucas and Rapping (1969a, 1969b) took another tack. Rather than treating the relationship between employment (unemployment) and inflation as freestanding, they sought to model the labor market as an integral part of a general equilibrium system. The expectations-augmented Phillips curve was imbedded into their model. Like Friedman, they continued to model expectations of inflation according to an adaptive scheme that extrapolated from past inflation rates.

The new classical macroeconomics was born in Lucas and Rapping's general equilibrium microfoundations.[1] It left its infancy when Lucas (1972a, 1972b) replaced extrapolative expectations with Muth's (1961) rational expectations hypothesis. Muth argued that extrapolative expectations were irrational because they led economic agents to make systematic, and therefore easily correctable, errors in forming their expectations. In their place Muth suggested that people should be modeled as expecting precisely what the model itself predicts. Rational expectations are therefore model-consistent expectations and should be accurate up to a serially uncorrelated error (that is, up to an unsystematic error). From the point of view of the new classical macroeconomics, the important thing about Muth's hypothesis was that it modeled expectations as part of the scheme of general-equilibrium microfoundations.

Two aspects of the new classical macroeconomics are especially worthy of notice. First, Lucas (1972a) shifted the analysis of policy away from single policy actions to policy rules. Because of rational expectations, any policy, whether or not it is intentionally based on a rule, may be divided into a systematic component and a random component. Expectations are based on the systematic component, and the random component is simply noise. Noise can lower the efficiency of the economic system, but it cannot be used for policy because it is unsystematic. The systematic component can be accounted for in the optimizing decisions of economic agents. Policymakers cannot ignore the interaction between their policy rules and the behavior of rational agents. They must design their policies taking that interaction into account.

Second, Lucas (1972a) undermined the structural interpretation of estimated econometric models. Despite the attempt to provide equation-by-equation microfoundations, Lucas demonstrated that rational expectations alone was enough to force the econometrician to pay attention to general equilibrium interactions between equations. "Keynesians" had, for example, regarded the Phillips curve as a structural relationship. Lucas showed, however, that the coefficients on lagged inflation depend on the policy rule in place. When the rule changes, so must the coefficients. This is Lucas's earliest statement of the so-called Lucas critique, the classic and more general statement of which is found in Lucas's (1976) "Econometric Policy Evaluation: A Critique."

Developments, Tensions, and Prospects

Lucas's (1976) paper is perhaps the most influential and most cited paper in macroeconomics in the last twenty-five years (or even the last fifty years). It plays a key role in the organization of the current volume. Part I of the current volume consists of four chapters presenting the four dominant macroeconometric methodologies of the present day. Each has roots that predate the Lucas critique, yet each can be seen as encapsulating a particular reaction to the Lucas critique.

Beth Fisher Ingram's Chapter 2 reports on the current state of econometric thinking with regard to structural modeling. In some sense, this is the natural extension of the Cowles Commission program to seek out models that could be identified on the basis of *a priori* economic theory. The Lucas critique could be viewed as asserting that large-scale macroeconometric models embody unstable relationships between aggregate data because they have not taken the economy apart at its joints: they do not represent the optimization problems of agents in general equilibrium with rational expectations. Thomas Sargent (1981) and Lars Peter Hansen and Sargent (1980) are early proponents of the program that seeks, in effect, to render macroeconometric models immune to the Lucas critique by grounding their equations in the bedrock of given tastes and technology. The implementation of this program required the full development of the implications of new classical microfoundations and innovations in the econometric techniques for dealing with nonlinear constraints among different equations in a system. Ingram's chapter reviews these developments and assesses their future prospects.

A different response to the Lucas critique was developed in the context of a generalization of the old atheoretical tradition of time-series econometrics applied to business cycles. In "Macroeconomics and Reality" (1980), Christopher Sims argues that the Cowles Commission program was a failure when it comes to large-scale macroeconometric models. According to Sims, econometricians imposed large numbers of restrictions that were "incredible" in the sense that they did not arise from sound economic theory or institutional or factual knowledge, but simply from the need of the econometrician to have enough restrictions to secure identification. Sims proposed that macroeconometrics give up the impossible task of seeking identification of structural models and instead ask only what could be learned from macroeconomic data without imposing restrictions. Sims's constructive alternative was the program of vector autoregressions (VARs)—that is, systems of reduced form equations that were used in innovation-accounting exercises and to generate impulse response functions.

Sims appears at first glance to answer the Lucas critique by studiously ignoring it. But in fact his response is more subtle. Sims (1982, 1986) proposes that the Lucas critique is correct in principle but that genuine changes in regime are rare. This is because agents with rational expectations understand the choices facing policymakers and so form probability distributions over the range of possible policy stances. Thus, what appear to be regime changes are, in fact, particular draws from probability distributions that have already been integrated into the optimization problems of individual agents. A true regime change might be the change of the entire distribution. But not only are such changes rare, the range of possible distributions might itself be governed by an even higher-order distribution.

Sims's program of vector autoregressions was attacked by Cooley and LeRoy (1985) and Leamer (1985). They demonstrated that, without making implicit structural assumptions, there could be no unique innovation accounting or interpretation of impulse response functions. Sims (1986) effectively concedes the point and considers VARs in which weak identifying assumptions, usually specifications of permissible contemporaneous correlations, give enough structure to justify sensible interpretations of the VARs (see also Bernanke, 1986). These are *structural VARs* (SVARs). In Chapter 3, Fabio Canova reports on the current state of the VAR program and relates it to competing methodologies.

In Chapter 4, Grayham Mizon provides a detailed account of the history and nature of the time-series econometric methodology associated with the work of Dennis Sargan and his students, notably David Hendry, at the London School of Economics. The LSE methodology in many ways stands apart from the other methodologies presented in this volume. It was developed outside of the United States and therefore reacts less directly to the American macroeconomic debate. Even more than the VAR methodology, it represents a direct development from the earliest time-series tradition in business-cycle econometrics. In some ways, the LSE methodology seeks a middle ground between structural estimation and the VAR program. The emphasis is on dynamic econometric models. Theory, it is argued, speaks mainly to static or long-run characteristics but has little to say practically about short-run dynamics. The emphasis is therefore on models in which statistical testing is used to choose dynamic specifications that are designed to be compatible with general, theoretically based long-run characteristics. The Lucas critique is acknowledged in principle, but proponents of the LSE methodology look for models that are stable in the face of interventions, suggesting the practical irrelevance of the Lucas critique in the particular case. Rigorous statistical testing and comparative standards for competing specifications are stressed.

In contrast to the LSE methodology, which finds the Lucas critique of little practical importance, the proponents of the so-called calibration approach believe that the Lucas critique, properly interpreted, undercuts the case for structural estimation at the macroeconomic level altogether. Chapter 5 by Finn Kyland and Edward Prescott reprints the classic methodological defense of the calibration approach.[2] Kydland and Prescott trace their methodology back to the early work of Frisch (1933) (see Hoover, 1995, however, for some caveats on the historicity of their claims). They are at great pains to establish the credentials of calibration as an *econometric* methodology despite the fact that they eschew macroeconometric estimation. They argue that structural estimation may be implementable and useful at the microeconomic level and that macroeconomic estimation may be useful in summarizing the actual behavior of data that a theoretical model must emulate. Macroeconomic estimation cannot, however, measure structural parameters directly. In other words, the Cowles Commission program applied to macroeconomics is a mistake. Instead, they propose that stylized (or idealized) models be derived from microfoundational macroeconomics models. The parameters of these models are then to be calibrated—that is, their values are supplied from microeconometrics, accounting identities, or institutional facts, or they are chosen informally to secure a good match between the behavior of the actual macrodata and simulated data from the model along limited dimensions of interest. Calibrated models are then used for policy analysis. The Lucas critique is answered, in Kydland and Prescott's view, because up to the limits of the idealization the models have identified the bedrock of tastes and technology that constrain individuals' optimization.

While Part I of the current volume presents competing econometric methodologies that are conditioned by the Lucas critique, the five chapters of Part II address the Lucas critique directly. Chapters 6 and 7 by Stephen LeRoy are a pair. The Lucas critique is fundamentally about the extent to which macroeconometric models capture causal structure. LeRoy argues that there is substantial confusion in macroeconometrics about the very notion of causal structure, and in Chapter 6 he seeks to clarify the issues. Chapter 7 is an application of some of the lessons of Chapter 6 to the problem of econometric policy analysis. In a line of argument related to early work of his own (Cooley, LeRoy, and Raymon, 1984) as well as to Sims's interpretation of the Lucas critique reported above, LeRoy argues that most formulations of the Lucas critique misunderstand the notion of a change of regime and the proper interpretation of the rational expectations hypothesis.

Writing in the tradition of the LSE econometrics (see Chapter 4), Neil Ericsson and John Irons examine the question of whether the Lucas critique matters in practice. In Chapter 8, they provide a wide-ranging survey of the influence of Lucas's article on the profession as well as concrete econometric illustrations of cases in which the Lucas critique appears not to be practically important.

Starting from a premise similar to that of Sims, that policy regimes are governed by a probability distribution, James Hamilton in Chapter 9 discusses procedures for modeling time-series in the face of regime switches. This is principally a time-series, data-oriented approach. In contrast, Charles Calomiris and Christopher Hanes argue in Chapter 10 that to take regime switching and structural change seriously, it is critical to have a fuller structural understanding of the economy. Such an understanding can be derived from a more explicitly historical approach. On the one hand, historical macroeconomics draws on a variety of sources of information that help to make econometric approaches to time-series data more informative. On the other hand, history provides us with examples of alternative regimes and clear structural change that might allow us to ascertain the importance of the Lucas critique or the relevance of particular macroeconomic theories in practice.

While the first two parts of the current volume are motivated by the aftershocks of the Lucas critique, the third part looks to the future. Some of the most important developments in econometrics have yet to percolate fully to the typical applied macroeconomist. Each of the developments reported in the three chapters in this part involve departures from the standard assumptions of traditional econometrics.

Econometricians have usually been content to assume that the true errors in their estimated equations are homoscedastic or capable of being made so through a straightforward transformation of the data. They have then concentrated on estimating the means of economic processes. For many macroeconomic issues— such as the cost of inflation or the behavior of financial markets—the error variance may well be an endogenous process and may itself influence the behavior of other variables. The econometrics of such processes, called *Auto*Regressive *C*onditional *H*eteroscedasticity (*ARCH*) was first investigated by Robert Engle (1982). In Chapter 11, Francis Diebold and Jose Lopez review developments in the ARCH literature since Engle's early work and illustrate their application to macroeconometrics.

Traditional econometric theory presumed that data were stationary—that their characteristics were, in a specific sense, not time dependent. Clearly, when data grow or trend over time, this is not correct. Typically, data were rendered stationary through differencing or fitting deterministic trends. The literature on the macroeconometrics of nonstationary processes, which Anindja Banerjee reviews and evaluates in Chapter 12, suggests that this is usually inappropriate. Variables such as GNP may be random walks (that is, their dynamic processes may have unit roots). Two nonstationary time-series may be related in such a way that a linear combination of their levels is itself stationary. These data are then said to be *cointegrated*. Failure to account for cointegration in effect throws away information about the long run that is relevant to short-run behavior. Banerjee reviews the recent literature on the estimation of cointegrated processes and shows how to make effective use of the information available in nonstationary time-series.

The linearity of econometric relationships is generally presumed for tractability. Yet a number of recent theoretical developments in macroeconomics cry out for nonlinear models: for example, asymmetrical models of business cycles in which booms and slumps represent different regimes with different transition probabilities or econometric models of chaotic economic behavior. In the final chapter, Chapter 13, Simon Potter presents an overview of nonlinear macroeconometrics, giving examples of its empirical applicability and suggestions for future developments.

Notes

1. The history of the new classical macroeconomics and of econometrics in a new classical framework is discussed in detail in Hoover (1988).

2. This chapter is the only one that reprints previously published work. The strategy in compiling this volume was to include new and up-to-date statements of the various points of view. To my surprise, however, I could not persuade any of at least twenty prominent practitioners of the calibration methodology to contribute a new account of calibration to the volume. Gregor Smith's commentary on Kydland and Prescott's paper is, however, published here for the first time.

References

Baumol, William J. (1952). "The Transactions Demand for Cash: An Inventory Theoretic Approach." *Quarterly Journal of Economics* 66, 545–556.

Bernanke, Ben S. (1986). "Alternative Explanations of the Money-Income Correlation." In Karl Brunner and Allan H. Meltzer (eds.), *Real Business Cycles, Real Exchange Rates and Actual Policies* (Vol. 25) (pp. 49–100). Carnegie-Rochester Conference Series on Public Policy. Amsterdam: North Holland.

Clower, Robert. (1965). "The Keynesian Counter-revolution: A Theoretical Appraisal." In Frank Hahn and F.P.R. Brechling (eds.), *The Theory of Interest Rates*. London: Macmillan.

Cooley, Thomas F., Stephen LeRoy, and Neil Raymon. (1984). "Econometric Policy Evaluation: Note." *American Economic Review* 74, 467–470.

Cooley, Thomas F., Stephen LeRoy. (1985). "Atheoretical Macroeconometrics: A Critique." *Journal of Monetary Economics* 16, 283–308.

Engle, Robert F. (1982). "Autoregressive Conditional Heteroscedasticity with Estimates of the Variance of United Kingdom Inflation." *Econometrica* 50, 987–1007.

Fisher, Irving. (1911/1931). *The Purchasing Power of Money*. New York: Macmillan.

Fisher, Irving. (1930). *The Theory of Interest*. New York: Macmillan.

Friedman, Milton. (1957). *A Theory of the Consumption Function*. Princeton, NJ: Princeton University Press.

Friedman, Milton. (1968). "The Role of Monetary Policy." *American Economic Review* 58, 1–17.

Frisch, Ragnar. (1933). "Propagation Problems and Impulse Response Problems in Dynamic Economics." In *Economic Essays in Honour of Gustav Cassel: October 20th, 1933*. London: George Allen and Unwin.

Haavelmo, Trgve. (1943). "The Statistical Implications of a System of Simultaneous Equations." *Econometrica* 11, 1–12.

Hansen, Lars Peter, and Thomas J. Sargent. (1980). "Estimating and Formulating Dynamic Linear Rational Expectations Models." Reprinted in Robert E. Lucas, Jr. and Thomas J. Sargent (eds.), *Rational Expectations and Econometric Practice*. London: George Allen and Unwin, 1981.

Hicks, John R. (1937). "Mr. Keynes and the Classics." Reprinted in *Critical Essays in Monetary Theory*. Oxford: Clarendon Press, 1967.

Hood, W.C., and Tarjalling Koopmans (eds.). (1953). *Studies in Econometric Method*. Cowles Commision Monograph 14. New York: Wiley.

Hoover, Kevin D. (1988). *The New Classical Macroeconomics: A Sceptical Inquiry*. Oxford: Blackwell.

Hoover, Kevin D. (1995). "Facts and Artifacts: Calibration and the Empirical Assessment of Real-Business-Cycle Models." *Oxford Economic Paper* 47, 24–44.

Jorgenson, Dale W. (1963). "Capital Theory and Investment Behavior." *American Economic Review* 53(2), 247–259.

Keynes, John Maynard. (1939). "Professor Tinbergen's Method." *Economic Journal* 49, 558–568.

Keynes, John Maynard. (1940) "Comment." *Economic Journal* 50, 141–156.

Klein, Lawrence R. (1947). *The Keynesian Revolution.* New York: Macmillan.

Koopmans, Tarjalling. (1949). "Identification Problems in Economic Model Construction." *Econometrica* 17, 125–144.

Leamer, Edward E. (1985). "Vector autoregressions for causal inference?" In Karl Brunner and Allan H. Meltzer (eds.), *Understanding Monetary Regimes.* Carnegie-Rochester Conference Series on Public Policy, vol. 22. Amsterdam: North-Holland.

Leontief, Wassily. (1936). "The Fundamental Assumptions of Mr. Keynes's Monetary Theory of Unemployment." *Quarterly Journal of Economics* 51, 92–197.

Lipsey, Richard G. (1960). "The Relationship between Unemployment and the Rate of Money Wage Changes in the United Kingdom, 1862–1957: A Further Analysis." *Economica* NS, 27, 1–31.

Lucas, Robert E., Jr. (1972a). "Econometric Testing of the Natural Rate Hypothesis." Reprinted in *Studies in Business Cycle Theory.* Oxford: Blackwell, 1981.

Lucas, Robert E., Jr. (1972b). "Expectations and the Neutrality of Money." Reprinted in *Studies in Business Cycle Theory.* Oxford: Blackwell, 1981.

Lucas, Robert E., Jr. (1976). "Econometric Policy Evaluation: A Critique." In Karl Brunner and Allen H. Meltzer (eds.), *The Phillips Curve and Labor Markets.* Carnegie-Rochester Conference Series on Public Policy, Vol. 1. Amsterdam: North-Holland.

Lucas, Robert E., Jr. and Rapping, Leonard A. (1969a). "Real Wages, Employment and Inflation." *Journal of Political Economy* 77, 721–54.

Lucas, Robert E., Jr. and Rapping, Leonard A. (1969b). "Price Expectations and the Phillips Curve." *American Economic Review* 59, 342–350.

Modigliani, Franco. (1944). "Liquidity Preference and The Theory of Interest of Money." *Econometrica* 12, 44–88.

Modigliani, Franco and Brumberg R. (1954). "Utility Analysis and the Consumption Function: An Interpretation of Cross-section Data." In K. Kurihara (ed.), *Post-Keynesian Economics.* New Brunswick, NJ: Rutgers University Press.

Morgan, Mary. (1990). *The History of Econometric Ideas.* Cambridge: Cambridge University Press.

Muth, John F. (1961). "Rational Expectations and the Theory of Price Movements." Reprinted in Robert E. Lucas, Jr. and Thomas J. Sargent (eds.), *Rational Expectations and Econometric Practice.* London: George Allen & Unwin, 1981.

Patinkin, Don. (1956). *Money, Interest and Prices*, 1st edition; 2nd edition 1965. New York: Harper and Row.

Phelps, Edmund S. (1967). "Phillips Curves, Expectations of Inflation and Optimal Unemployment Over Time." *Economica* NS, 34, 254–281.

Sargent, Thomas (1981). "Interpreting Economic Time Series." *Journal of Political Economy* 89, 213–48.

Sims, Christopher A. (1980). "Macroeconomics and Reality." *Econometrica* 48, 1–48.

Sims, Christopher A. (1982). "Policy Analysis with Econometric Models." *Brookings Papers on Economic Activity* 13(1), 107–152.

Sims, Christopher A. (1986). "Are Forecasting Models Usable for Policy Analysis?" *Federal Reserve Bank of Minneapolis Quarterly Review* 10, 2–15.

Tobin, James. (1956). "The Interest Elasticity of the Transactions Demand for Cash." *Review of Economics and Statistics* 38, 241–247.

Tobin, James. (1958). "Liquidity Preference as Behaviour Towards Risk." *Review of Economic Studies* 25, 65–86.

Tobin, James. (1969). "A General Equilbrium Approach to Monetary Theory." *Journal of Money, Credit and Banking* 1, 15–29.

Tobin, James. (1980). *Asset Accumulation and Economic Activity*. Oxford: Blackwell.

Tooke, Thomas, and William Newmarch. (1838–1857). *A History of Prices: and of the State of the Circulation from 1792–1856* (Vols. I–VI). Introduction by T.E. Gregory. New York: Adelphi.

I ALTERNATIVE ECONOMETRIC METHODOLOGIES

2 RECENT ADVANCES IN SOLVING AND ESTIMATING DYNAMIC, STOCHASTIC MACROECONOMIC MODELS

Beth F. Ingram

Two of the major objectives of macroeconomic research are to explain the behavior of aggregate economic data and to predict the effects of policy interventions. Within the macroeconomics literature, there are two identifiable approaches to these issues. The reduced-form method[1] involves specifying a *statistical* model for the variables of interest, estimating the parameters of the model, and answering the underlying question by analyzing the estimated values of the parameters or some function of the parameters. The coherence between the model and the data is of primary concern; theory, in general, plays a subordinate role. The structural approach, on the other hand, entails describing a *theoretical* model for the relevant macroeconomic variables and analyzing the relationships implied by the model to answer the questions of interest. An important feature of the theoretical model is that the parameters of the model be policy invariant; the parameters are *structural*, remaining fixed under hypothetical interventions. The magnitude of the roles that measurement and observation play in the structural approach have varied greatly over time, being central in the work of the Cowles Commission and, more recently, subsidiary in the real business-cycle (RBC) literature. The point of this essay is to discuss the second approach—the structural program in macroeconomics.

Structural analysis grew in importance through the work of the members of the Cowles commission in the 1940s and 1950s. In criticizing the alternative approach, the reduced-form methods exemplified at that time by Burns and Mitchell (1946), Koopmans (1947) indicated his reasons for favoring structural modeling: the centrality in macroeconomics of questions about the effects of policy interventions, and the importance of using both theory and measurement to analyze cyclical fluctuations. The contributions of the Cowles group, including the advocacy of a probabilistic viewpoint about economic phenomenon and of using systems of equations to describe behavior, provided the impetus for the development of the simultaneous-equation model (SEM), which obtained widespread acceptance among academics and policy makers during the 1960s and early 1970s.

A simultaneous-equation model is composed of a set of (usually linear) equations, derived from economic theory, which describe the behavior of various sectors of the economy. Observed data are used to assign values to the parameters of the model, given that the parameters are uniquely identified. Once the parameters of the model are estimated, the model can be used to explain behavior (why does consumption rise when income rises?) or to forecast behavior (by how much will consumption rise if the income tax rate falls by 10 percent?). As emphasized by Hurwicz (1962), the latter question can be answered reliably only under the assumption that the parameters of the model are structural—invariant—with respect to the proposed intervention (the change in the tax rate).

Two events precipitated a decline in academic interest in linear simultaneous-equation models: the empirical failure of SEMs to capture the high inflation and high unemployment of the early 1970s, and the publication of Lucas's theoretical critique of econometric policy evaluation in 1976. Simply stated, Lucas argued that the simultaneous equation models in use at the time were not structural in the sense of Hurwicz. The parameters of the specified equations could be expected to vary with changes in policy rules, thus invalidating the policy conclusions derived from the model. More specifically, given that agents are forward looking, the parameters of their decision rules will change with alterations in the stochastic environment that they face. Lucas maintained that the most reasonable way to model a fiscal or monetary policy shift was as a change in the stochastic behavior of policy. Hence, if the researcher had estimated the parameters of decision rules under one stochastic policy environment, then those estimates could not be used to analyze alternative policy environments.

An outgrowth of the Lucas critique was the development of the rational expectations structural modeling approach to policy analysis. As outlined by Lucas and Sargent (1981), a *model* is a description of the economic environment facing the agents in the economy, including the system for producing goods, the preferences of the agents, and the behavior of the policy authorities. Parameters of the model have explicit economic interpretations; in addition, they are presumed to be structural with respect to any proposed policy interventions. Agents are assumed to maximize utility subject to a set of constraints. In most cases, today's decisions are contingent on what the agents expect to occur in the future. Agents form expectations of future variables rationally, using all information available to them and making use of the correct statistical distribution function.[2] This leads to a set of restrictions among the equations of the model that must be accommodated in the solution and estimation algorithms.

The mechanics of the post-Keynesian macroeconomic paradigm were first given expression in two related papers written by Hansen and Sargent (1980). In the first paper, the authors outlined a model of labor demand in which a competitive firm chooses the amount of labor to hire to maximize the discounted value of expected future profits. The model had a linear-quadratic setup so that the (linear) decision rule for labor demand can be derived explicitly. Since labor demand depends on a random shock to the productivity of labor, the labor-demand schedule is stochastic. The shock is observed by the firm but not by the econometrician; statistical methods can be used to estimate the parameters of the demand function.[3] The companion paper (1981) described how to extend the method to a multiple equation framework.

Lucas and Sargent maintained that the key features of this approach were the assumptions that agents are rational optimizers and that markets clear, but both of these assumptions have been relaxed in various applications. The unifying feature of modern macroeconomic models is the detailed specification of the behavior of agents (including the information sets of the agent and the econometrician) and of the institutional structure of the economy.

The goal of this essay is to outline the post-Keynesian approach to structural modeling, as envisioned in the new classical economics of Lucas and Sargent, and to discuss the evolution of this program over the past decade. Specifically, I discuss extensions to nonlinear models and various estimation methods. It is probably fair to say that the methods exemplified in Hansen and Sargent have not enjoyed, in the ensuing period, the same success that the SEM framework did in the 1950s and 1960s. One objective of this essay is to comment on possible explanations.

Hansen and Sargent's model

The features of the Hansen-Sargent implementation can be illustrated in the following version of their model. A competitive firm rents capital, k_t, to maximize the present value of profits:

$$E_0 \sum_{t=0}^{\infty} \beta^t \left[(\gamma_0 + a_t - r_t)k_t - \frac{1}{2}\gamma_1 k_t^2 - \frac{1}{2}\delta(k_t - k_{t-1})^2 \right],$$

where E_0 represents the expectation conditioned on information available at time zero. An exogenous shock a_t shifts the level of capital productivity. The stochastic sequence of rental rates, r_t, is taken as given by the firm. The production function is quadratic; the parameters γ_0 and γ_1 control the shape of the function. The term $(k_t - k_{t-1})^2$ reflects the cost of adjusting the size of the capital stock; its importance in capital adjustment is determined by δ. The initial endowment of capital, k_{-1}, is given. The rate at which the firm discounts the future is determined by β, $0 < \beta < 1$.

To complete the specification of the model, we need to describe how the stochastic processes $\{a_t\}_{t=0}^{\infty}$ and $\{r_t\}_{t=0}^{\infty}$ evolve. For simplicity, assume that each is an independent AR(1) process:

$$a_t = \rho_a a_{t-1} + \varepsilon_{at}, \qquad \varepsilon_{at} \sim N(0, \sigma_a^2)$$

$$r_t = \mu + \rho_r r_{t-1} + \varepsilon_{rt}, \qquad \varepsilon_{rt} \sim N(0, \sigma_r^2),$$

with $E(\varepsilon_{rt}\varepsilon_{at}) = 0$ for all t, and ρ_a and ρ_r constrained to lie in the interval $(0, 1)$. The firm is assumed to have rational expectations: it bases its decisions on all currently available information and uses the correct probability distribution for the variables that it needs to forecast. Here, we assume that the firm's information set at t contains current and past values of the shocks and decision variables, $I_t = \{a_s, r_s, k_{s-1}, s \leq t\}$.

A solution to this model can be characterized as a decision rule for the capital stock such that the firm maximizes the present discounted value of its profits; the rule will be a function of the variables in I_t, and its functional form will depend on the stochastic processes, $\{a_t\}_{t=0}^{\infty}$ and $\{r_t\}_{t=0}^{\infty}$. Given the first-order nature of the driving processes in this example, the current capital stock, k_t, will depend on the current value of r_t and a_t and one lagged value of capital, k_{t-1}.

Solving the Model

The decision rule for capital that characterizes optimal behavior for the firm can be obtained analytically in this model. The first-order condition for the firm's maximization problem is a second-order stochastic difference equation in the capital stock:

$$\delta\beta E_t k_{t+1} - [\delta(\beta + 1) + \gamma_1]k_t + \delta k_{t-1} + \gamma_0 + a_t - r_t = 0.$$

Dividing both sides of the expression by $\delta\beta$, we can write

$$\left[1 - \left(1 + \frac{1}{\beta} + \frac{\gamma_1}{\delta\beta}\right)B + \frac{1}{\beta}B^2\right]E_t k_{t+1} = \frac{(r_t - a_t - \gamma_0)}{\delta\beta},$$

where B is an operator such that $BE_t k_{t+j} = E_t k_{t+j-1}$. To solve this difference equation, we factor the polynomial in B:

$$(1 - \lambda_1 B)(1 - \lambda_2 B) \equiv 1 - [1 + 1/\beta + \gamma_1/(\delta\beta)]B + (1/\beta)B^2. \qquad (2.1)$$

Note that $\lambda_1 \lambda_2 = 1/\beta$. Now apply this factorization to the difference equation:

$$(1 - \lambda_1 B)(1 - \lambda_2 B)E_t k_{t+1} = \frac{(r_t - a_t - \gamma_0)}{\delta\beta}.$$

Given the values assigned to the underlying parameters of the model, Hansen and Sargent show that $\lambda_1 < 1 < \lambda_2$.

To find a unique solution to the difference equation, we need two boundary conditions. One is provided by the specification of the initial value of the capital stock, k^{-1}. The other is provided by the transversality condition, which requires that the capital stock not grow too quickly. In order to guarantee that the transversality condition is satisfied, the effect of the unstable root in the difference equation that governs the capital stock, λ_2, must be eliminated. Mechanically, the forward expansion of $(1 - \lambda_2 B)$ is applied to both sides of the difference equation. The optimal decision rule for capital derived by Hansen and Sargent is[4]

$$k_t = \lambda_1 k_{t-1} - \frac{\lambda_1}{\delta} \sum_{s=0}^{\infty} (\beta\lambda_1)^s E_t[r_{t+s} - a_{t+s} - \gamma_0]$$

$$= \lambda_1 k_{t-1} - \frac{\lambda_1}{\delta}\left[\frac{r_t}{1 - \beta\lambda_1\rho_r} - \frac{a_t}{1 - \beta\lambda_1\rho_a} - \frac{\gamma_0}{1 - \beta\lambda_1} \qquad (2.2) \right.$$

$$\left. + \frac{\beta\lambda_1\mu}{(1 - \beta\lambda_1)(1 - \beta\lambda_1\rho_r)} \right].$$

The rule has this simple form because of the $AR(1)$ assumption for the exogenous driving processes and the simple form for the capital-adjustment-cost term. The persistence of the capital stock is determined by λ_1, which depends on β, δ, and γ_1 through equation (2.1). As expected, the current capital stock responds negatively to an increase in the current rental rate and positively to a favorable technology shock.

To understand the Lucas critique in this context, contrast the effect on current and future capital of an upward movement in r_t due to a large positive shock, ε_{rt}, to that of a rise in r_t due to an increase in its persistence (an increase in ρ_r). The two changes can be rigged so that the effect of each on the current capital stock is the same. However, the effect on the future capital stock is quite different. The effect of a higher than normal shock, ε_{rt}, on the capital stock, k_{t+s}, dissipates as s becomes large. A shift in ρ_r permanently alters the relationship of the capital stock to rental rate shocks and results in a permanent decrease in the stock of capital. Lucas argued that the sorts of experiments in which macroeconomists were interested were similar to the second experiment—a change in the parameter ρ_r. In this case, we need to know the structure of the model: the reduced form is not sufficient.

The solution that we have derived provides us with a mapping from the exogenous shocks that drive the economy to the endogenous choice variables. The researcher will likely have available a data set that includes a subset of these variables. This data set, in conjunction with the equilibrium mapping, allows the researcher to estimate the parameters of the model. This is the subject of the next section.

Estimation of the Model

The parameters of the model can be estimated using the decision rule in conjunction with the known form for the data generating process for the rental rate. Multiply both sides of equation (2.2) by $(1 - \rho_a L)$ and substitute the equality $(1 - \rho_a L)\, a_t = \varepsilon_{at}$ into the resulting expression. Then we have the system of equations:

$$
\begin{bmatrix} 1 & \dfrac{\lambda_1}{\delta}\dfrac{1}{1-\beta\lambda_1\rho_r} \\ 0 & 1 \end{bmatrix}
\begin{bmatrix} k_t \\ r_t \end{bmatrix}
=
\begin{bmatrix} \lambda_1 + \rho_a & \dfrac{\lambda_1}{\delta}\dfrac{\rho_a}{1-\beta\lambda_1\rho_r} \\ 0 & \rho_r \end{bmatrix}
\begin{bmatrix} k_{t-1} \\ r_{t-1} \end{bmatrix}
-
\begin{bmatrix} \rho_a\lambda_1 & 0 \\ 0 & 0 \end{bmatrix}
\begin{bmatrix} k_{t-2} \\ r_{t-2} \end{bmatrix}
$$

$$
+
\begin{bmatrix} \dfrac{\lambda_1}{\delta}\dfrac{1}{1-\beta\lambda_1\rho_a} & 0 \\ 0 & 1 \end{bmatrix}
\begin{bmatrix} \varepsilon_{at} \\ \varepsilon_{rt} \end{bmatrix}
+
\begin{bmatrix} K \\ \mu \end{bmatrix}
$$

where $K = -\dfrac{\gamma_0}{1-\beta\lambda_1} + \dfrac{\beta\lambda_1\mu}{(1-\beta\lambda_1)(1-\beta\lambda_1\rho_r)}$.

To derive a reduced form for this system, invert the matrix on the left side of the equation, implicitly defining K' and μ':

$$
\begin{bmatrix} k_t \\ r_t \end{bmatrix}
=
\begin{bmatrix} \lambda_1 + \rho_a & (\rho_a - \rho_r)\dfrac{\lambda_1}{\delta}\dfrac{1}{1-\beta\lambda_1\rho_r} \\ 0 & \rho_r \end{bmatrix}
\begin{bmatrix} k_{t-1} \\ r_{t-1} \end{bmatrix}
-
\begin{bmatrix} \rho_a\lambda_1 & 0 \\ 0 & 0 \end{bmatrix}
\begin{bmatrix} k_{t-2} \\ r_{t-2} \end{bmatrix}
+
$$

$$
\begin{bmatrix} \dfrac{\lambda_1}{\delta}\dfrac{1}{1-\beta\lambda_1\rho_a} & -\dfrac{\lambda_1}{\delta}\dfrac{1}{1-\beta\lambda_1\rho_r} \\ 0 & 1 \end{bmatrix}
\begin{bmatrix} \varepsilon_{at} \\ \varepsilon_{rt} \end{bmatrix}
+
\begin{bmatrix} K' \\ \mu' \end{bmatrix},
$$

with the obvious definition for the matrices A_1, A_2, and the constants K' and μ' we can write

$$\begin{bmatrix} k_t \\ r_t \end{bmatrix} = A_1 \begin{bmatrix} k_{t-1} \\ r_{t-1} \end{bmatrix} + A_2 \begin{bmatrix} k_{t-2} \\ r_{t-2} \end{bmatrix} + \begin{bmatrix} v_{kt} \\ v_{rt} \end{bmatrix} + \begin{bmatrix} K' \\ \mu' \end{bmatrix}. \qquad (2.3)$$

The error terms in this expression are related to ε_{at} and ε_{rt} through the expressions

$$v_{kt} = \frac{\lambda_1}{\delta} \frac{1}{1 - \beta\lambda_1\rho_a} \varepsilon_{at} - \frac{\lambda_1}{\delta} \frac{1}{1 - \beta\lambda_1\rho_r} \varepsilon_{rt},$$

$$v_{rt} = \varepsilon_{rt}.$$

Equation (2.3) forms the basis for a likelihood function (given some assumption about the distribution of the shocks) that can be used to estimate the reduced-form parameters A_1, A_2, K', and μ', and the variance-covariance matrix of $[v_{kt}\ v_{rt}]$.[5] Estimating the structural parameters entails confronting two problems: the cross-equation restrictions and identification.

A hallmark of the assumption of rational expectations is that the structure often imposes nonlinear cross-equation restrictions on the reduced form, in addition to the more familiar zero restrictions. Examples of the latter include the restriction that the coefficients on the k_{t-1} and k_{t-2} terms in the rental rate equation be zero and that only two lags of capital appear in the capital stock equation. In this example, the single nonlinear cross-equation restriction can be derived analytically. Let V represent the variance-covariance matrix of $[v_{kt}\ v_{rt}]$, let $V[i, j]$ represent the entry in the ith row and jth column of V, and let $A_1[i, j]$ represent the entry in the ith row and jth column of A_1. Define $A_2[i, j]$ similarly. Then, once A_1 and A_2 are estimated, the elements $A_1[1, 1]$ and $A_2[1, 1]$ can be used to solve for ρ_a and λ_1. The quantity ρ_a, which must lie between zero and one by assumption, will satisfy

$$A_1[1, 1] - \rho_a - A_2[1, 1]/\rho_a = 0, \qquad (2.4)$$

and $\lambda_1 = A_1[1, 1] - \rho_a$.

Under the assumption that ε_{at} and ε_{rt} are uncorrelated, the variance-covariance matrix of the vector v is related to the structural parameters as follows:

$$V[1, 1] = \left(\frac{\lambda_1}{\delta(1 - \beta\lambda_1\rho_a)} \right)^2 \sigma_a^2 + \left(\frac{\lambda_1}{\delta(1 - \beta\lambda_1\rho_r)} \right)^2 \sigma_r^2,$$

$$V[1, 2] = - \frac{\lambda_1}{\delta(1 - \beta\lambda_1\rho_r)} \sigma_r^2,$$

$$V[2, 2] = \sigma_r^2.$$

The nonlinear cross-equation restriction is written

$$A_1[1, 2] + \frac{V[1, 2]}{V[2, 2]}(\rho_a - A_1[2, 2]) = 0,$$

with ρ_a a solution to equation (2.4). The reduced-form parameters, A_1, A_2, and V must be estimated so that this equation holds and $0 < \rho_a < 1$. The cross-equation restriction stems directly from the assumption that the ε's are uncorrelated. If this assumption is relaxed, then an additional term appears in the matrix V and the model imposes no cross-equation restrictions on the reduced form.

An examination of the reduced form makes it clear that several of the parameters are not separately identified: β, δ, γ_1, and σ_a. Evidently, rational expectations does not *guarantee* identification. In this application, the value of one of these parameters must be specified *a priori* in order to identify the other three. In more complicated models, the restrictions needed for identification may not be so clear, and the issue is often sidestepped.

Several features of the problem were of particular importance in solving and estimating the model. The quadratic-linear setup, the nature of the capital adjustment cost term, the incorporation of a single decision variable, and the simple form for the data-generation process for the exogenous shock ensured that the decision rule for capital could be derived analytically. More specifically, in a linear-quadratic model, only first moments of stochastic variables appear in the first-order conditions so that conditional moments of nonlinear functions of the variables of the model do not need to be evaluated. These particular assumptions also produced a low-order difference equation for the decision variable that could be factored analytically in order to obtain the decision rule. As a result, explicit expressions were available for the mapping between the structure and the reduced form, allowing for the derivation of the nonlinear cross-equation restrictions that must be imposed during estimation and for the explicit analysis of the identification problem.

The desirability of moving beyond these assumptions seems clear, but there is a lack of consensus about which direction to take. Nonlinear models allow for the incorporation of higher-order moments into the decision-making process of the agent. If risk aversion is important, or if agents respond to the conditional variance of variables, then the linear-quadratic setup will not be adequate. Some authors have pointed out that several different kinds of shocks impinge on macroeconomic variables, implying that a single-shock model is not an adequate characterization of the stochastic structure of the economy. Recently, there has been a move toward increasing the complexity of models through the incorporation of more sectors, the modeling of heterogeneity across agents, or the assumption that agents use a more limited information set than is commonly assumed in the rational expectations literature.

Researchers attempting to analyze more complicated models face problems on two fronts: finding solution algorithms that will deliver the decision rules for the agents' choice variables and finding estimation strategies that are feasible. In the following sections, I outline the approaches that have been suggested for solving nonlinear stochastic rational-expectations models and for estimating these models.

Moving Away from the Linear Framework

To put the discussion in context, consider the following standard growth model. A representative agent chooses consumption, c_t, and the capital stock, k_t, to maximize lifetime utility subject to a resource constraint:

$$E_0 \sum_{t=0}^{\infty} \beta^t \ln(c_t).$$

$$s.t. \ c_t + k_t = A_t k_{t-1}^{\alpha} + (1 - \delta)k_{t-1}, \ k_0 \text{ given}. \tag{2.5}$$

The technology shock, A_t, is governed by a particular data-generating process, $f(A_t; \phi)$. The rate of time preference is determined by β, the rate of capital depreciation by δ, and the marginal productivity of capital by α.

We are interested in deriving solution paths for the choice variables in this model and comparing the paths for c_t and k_t to an observed data set. Given a data-generating process for the random shock in the model, $f(A_t; \phi)$, solution paths for consumption and the capital stock are characterized by the resource constraint, (2.5), the following first-order condition:

$$\frac{1}{c_t} - \beta E_t \left\{ \frac{1}{c_{t+1}} [1 - \delta + \alpha A_{t+1} k_t^{\alpha-1}] \right\} = 0 \tag{2.6}$$

and a transversality condition:

$$\lim_{s \to \infty} E_t \beta^s \frac{k_{t+s}}{c_{t+s}} = 0.$$

The transversality condition is a necessary condition for optimality and requires that the expected value of the capital stock not grow too quickly.

An alternative form for the Euler equation is given by

$$\frac{1}{c_t} - \beta \left\{ \frac{1}{c_{t+1}} [1 - \delta + \alpha A_{t+1} k_t^{\alpha-1}] \right\} = \eta_{t+1}, \tag{2.7}$$

with the requirement that the forecast error have conditional mean zero, $E_t(\eta_{t+1}) = 0$. Suppose that $f(A_t; \phi)$ is given by

$$\ln(A_t) = \rho\ln(A_{t-1}) + \varepsilon_{At}, \qquad \varepsilon_{At} \sim N(-\sigma^2/2, \sigma^2). \tag{2.8}$$

The equations (2.5), (2.6), and (2.8) comprise a set of nonlinear stochastic difference equations that jointly determine the evolution of the shocks to the economy and the decision variables. The state of the system at time t is the vector $s_t = [k_{t-1} \; A_t]$. Given values for the parameters of the model, the solution to the system can be characterized by a decision rule for the capital stock that depends on the state of the system and a parameter vector: $k_t = g(s_t; \psi)$. The difficulty in finding the decision rule is that we must guarantee that both the Euler equation and the transversality condition are satisfied.

Most algorithms for finding solutions to nonlinear stochastic models involve approximating the decision rule by some function $\tilde{g}(s_t; \psi)$, then finding a ψ that ensures that (2.6) holds. Judd (1991) and Taylor and Uhlig (1990) discuss the various methods in more detail; here, I show how to apply them to this specific problem. The appendix contains a partial listing of papers appearing in the economics literature that are concerned with solution methods.

Maximizing a quadratic function subject to linear constraints is a relatively straightforward procedure, even when the problem is stochastic. This suggests transforming the nonlinear problem into an appropriate linear-quadratic form and using solution methods akin to those outlined in Hansen-Sargent. The procedure is to calculate a first-order Taylor expansion of the first-order conditions and constraints in either the levels of the variables or the logs of the variables of the model. Since the stochastic steady state is not known, the expansion is performed around the deterministic steady state.

In this application, I log-linearize the system around the nonstochastic steady state using a first-order Taylor expansion, taking derivatives of each equation with respect to the log of the decision and state variables. This results in the following linear difference equation (using the second form for the Euler equation):

$$
\begin{bmatrix} c & k & -k^a \\ 1 & 0 & -\dfrac{\alpha k^{\alpha-1}}{1-\delta+\alpha k^{\alpha-1}} \\ 0 & 0 & 1 \end{bmatrix}
\begin{bmatrix} \hat{c}_t \\ \hat{k}_t \\ \hat{A}_t \end{bmatrix}
+
\begin{bmatrix} 0 & -\alpha k^a - (1-\delta)k & 0 \\ -1/\beta & \dfrac{-\alpha(\alpha-1)k^{\alpha-1}}{1-\delta+\alpha k^{\alpha-1}} & 0 \\ 0 & 0 & -\rho \end{bmatrix}
\begin{bmatrix} \hat{c}_{t-1} \\ \hat{k}_{t-1} \\ \hat{A}_{t-1} \end{bmatrix}
=
\begin{bmatrix} 0 \\ \eta_t \\ \varepsilon_{At} \end{bmatrix},
$$

$$\tag{2.9}$$

where I define $\hat{c}_t = \ln(c_t/c)$, $\hat{k}_t = \ln(k_t/k)$, and $\hat{A}_t = \ln(A_t/A)$. The steady state in this model is $A = 1$, $k = ((1/\beta - 1 + \delta)/\alpha)^{1/(\alpha-1)}$, $c = k^\alpha - \delta k$. The error vector includes η_t, the Euler equation forecast error, and e_{At}.

Implicitly defining M_0 and M_1, I can invert the first matrix on the left side of (2.9) and write

$$
\begin{bmatrix} \hat{c}_t \\ \hat{k}_t \\ \hat{A}_t \end{bmatrix} = M_0 \begin{bmatrix} \hat{c}_{t-1} \\ \hat{k}_{t-1} \\ \hat{A}_{t-1} \end{bmatrix} + M_1 \begin{bmatrix} 0 \\ \eta_t \\ \varepsilon_{At} \end{bmatrix}.
\tag{2.10}
$$

The system of equations in (2.10) summarizes the first-order conditions and resource constraint. To use (2.10) to generate data on consumption, capital, and the technology shock, I require three boundary conditions, a realization of the shocks, $\{\varepsilon_{At}, t = 1, \ldots, T\}$, and the mapping from ε_{At} to η_t. The boundary conditions are provided by the initial values of capital and total factor productivity, k_0 and A_0, and the transversality condition.

This behavior of this difference equation is governed by the eigenvalues of M_0. This matrix can be decomposed into the product of three matrices: Λ, a diagonal matrix with the eigenvalues of M_0 on the diagonal, C, the matrix of left eigenvectors of M_0, and C^{-1}: $M_0 = C\Lambda C^{-1}$. For an arbitrary initial level of consumption, c_0, an eigenvalue that exceeds $(1/\beta)^{1/2}$ will cause the variables of the system to grow too quickly, violating the transversality condition. If there is only one such eigenvalue,[6] its effect on the system may be eliminated by choosing the correct initial level of consumption and the correct mapping from ε_{At} to η_t. Let $C^{-1}[i,.]$ denote the row of C^{-1} associated with the unstable eigenvalue. Then c_0 must satisfy $C^{-1}[i,.][\hat{c}_0 \, \hat{k}_0 \, \hat{A}_0]' = 0$ and the random elements must be related according to $C^{-1}[i,.]M_1[0 \, \eta_t \, \varepsilon_{At}]' = 0$. Given a realized time series for $\varepsilon_{At}, t = 1, \ldots, T$, these two relationships in conjunction with (2.10) can be used to generate artificial data from the model. Equivalently, the expression $C^{-1}[i,.][\hat{c}_t \, \hat{k}_t \, \hat{A}_t]' = 0$ can be substituted for the middle equation in (2.9), which can then be used to generate data. The decision rule for capital, $g(s_t; \psi)$, is derived by using the resource constraint to eliminate c_t from the previous expression.

The linearization method has enjoyed widespread use in macroeconomics. In models that are more complicated than this example model, the eigenvalues and decision rule must be calculated numerically and can be obtained only after values are assigned to the parameters of the model. The outcome is only an approximate solution to the original nonlinear model; it is difficult, if not impossible, to evaluate the quality of the approximation. If the nonlinearities are important, or if the problem is one in which higher-order moments of the stochastic shocks play a role, the linear approximation is not appropriate. This is true of asset-pricing models, for example, in which risk aversion plays a role. It is also true of models in which complicated transactions costs terms appear.

A second strategy focuses on finding a nonlinear decision rule by approximating the function $k_t = g(s_t; \psi)$ within a specified class of nonlinear functions. Judd (1991) discusses these methods in detail. These methods rely on functional approximation theory—the ability to approximate a continuous function arbitrarily well by using series of functions belonging to a certain class. Consider again the initial formulation of the model: the resource constraint, equation (2.5), and the Euler equation, equation (2.6). Substitute the expression for capital into the resource constraint, and substitute the resource constraint into the Euler equation to obtain the following expression:

$$
\frac{1}{A_t \tilde{g}(s_{t-1}, \psi)^\alpha + (1 - \delta)\tilde{g}(s_{t-1}, \psi) - \tilde{g}(s_t, \psi)} -
$$

$$
\beta E \left\{ \frac{1 - \delta + \alpha A_{t+1}\tilde{g}(s_t, \psi)^{\alpha-1}}{A_{t+1}\tilde{g}(s_t, \psi)^\alpha + (1 - \delta)\tilde{g}(s_t, \psi) - \tilde{g}(s_{t+1}, \psi)} \Bigg| s_t \right\} = 0. \qquad (2.11)
$$

The goal is to find an approximate policy function, $\tilde{g}(s_t; \psi)$, such that this equation is satisfied for a subset of possible states, $s_t \in S$. (Since $s_t \in R_+^2$, it is not possible for us to check, in finite time, whether this equation is satisfied at every point in the state space.)

Given a functional form $\tilde{g}(s_t; \psi)$, such as

$$
\tilde{g}(s_t; \psi) = \psi_0 + \psi_1 k_{t-1} + \psi_2 A_t + \psi_3 k_{t-1} A_t,
$$

the objective will be to choose ψ so that (2.11) holds at a chosen set of grid points, $k_i \in [k_L, k_H]$, $i = 1, \ldots, N_i$ and $A_j \in [A_L, A_H]$, $j = 1, \ldots, N_j$. Recall that $s_t = [k_{t-1} A_t] = [\tilde{g}(s_{t-1}; \psi) A_t]$, implying that $s_{t+1} = [k_t A_{t+1}] = [\tilde{g}(s_t; \psi) A_{t+1}]$, and

$$
\begin{aligned}
\tilde{g}(s_{t+1}; \psi) &= \tilde{g}(\tilde{g}(s_t; \psi), A_{t+1}; \psi) \\
&= \tilde{g}(\tilde{g}(s_t; \psi), A_t^\rho \exp(\varepsilon_{t+1}); \psi).
\end{aligned}
$$

If we substitute this expression into the Euler equation, we obtain an expression solely in terms of s_t and $\tilde{g}(s_t; \psi)$. For a given value of ψ, we calculate

$$
g(s_{i,j}; \psi) = \psi_0 + \psi_1 k_i + \psi_2 A_j + \psi_3 k_i A_j \qquad (2.12)
$$

and a residual value at each grid point using the following expression:

$$
\frac{1}{A_j k_i^\alpha + (1 - \delta)k_i - \tilde{g}(s_{i,j}; \psi)}
$$

$$
- \beta E \left\{ \frac{1 - \delta + \alpha(A_t^\rho \exp(\varepsilon_{t+1}))\tilde{g}(s_{i,j}; \psi)^{\alpha-1}}{A_t^\rho \exp(\varepsilon_{t+1}))\tilde{g}(s_{i,j}; \psi)^\alpha + (1 - \delta)\tilde{g}(s_{i,j}; \psi) - \tilde{g}(\tilde{g}(s_{i,j}; \psi), (A_t^\rho \exp(\varepsilon_{t+1})); \psi)} \Bigg| s_{i,j} \right\} = r_{i,j}.
$$

Since we know the distribution of the shock, ε_{t+1}, we use numerical integration to calculate the expectation of the term in brackets.

For the correct decision rule, the residual, $r_{i,j}$, is zero at all the selected grid points. More generally, the projection of the residual error function should be zero in all directions; this property can be used to find values for ψ. One possibility is to fix a number of directions equal to the number of elements in ψ and to choose ψ so that the projection of the residual function in each of those directions is zero.

In our example, ψ has four elements, so we choose four weighting functions w_p, $p = 1, \ldots, 4$, and find the vector ψ that sets the following set of four equations equal to zero:

$$\sum_{i=1}^{N_i} \sum_{j=1}^{N_j} r(s_{i,j}; \psi) w_p(s_{i,j}) = 0, \qquad p = 1, \ldots, 4.$$

For example, if $w_1(s_{i,j}) = 1/(N_i N_j)$, the average residual will be zero for the derived ψ.

To implement this procedure, we need a method for choosing the functional form for $\tilde{g}(s_i; \psi)$ and the grid points. In order to minimize numerical errors, the most efficient procedure is to use a class of orthogonal polynomials and choose the grid points to be the zeros of $N + 1^{th}$ degree polynomial in this class. For example, one possible class of polynomials is the Chebychev polynomials, which are defined as

$$T_n(x) = \cos(n \cos^{-1}(x)), \qquad x \in [-1, 1]$$

or, recursively:

$$T_0(x) = 1,$$

$$T_1(x) = x,$$

$$T_{n+1}(x) = 2xT_n(x) - T_{n-1}(x), \; x \in [-1, 1].$$

Here, if $N_i = N_j = 2$, use of first-order Chebychev polynomials results in expression (2.12) with

$$k_i = \pm[\; ^2\!/_{\sqrt{2}} - (k_h + k_l)\,]/(k_h + k_l), \qquad i = 1, 2,$$

$$A_j = \pm[\; ^2\!/_{\sqrt{2}} - (A_h + A_l)\,]/(A_h + A_l), \qquad j = 1, 2,$$

which are the zeros of the second-order Chebychev polynomial. One means of proceeding is to choose ψ_0, ψ_1, ψ_2, and ψ_3 to solve the following set of equations:

$$P_0(\psi) = \sum_{j=1}^{2} \sum_{i=1}^{2} r_{i,j} = 0,$$

$$P_1(\psi) = \sum_{j=1}^{2} \sum_{i=1}^{2} r_{i,j} k_i = 0,$$

$$P_2(\psi) = \sum_{j=1}^{2} \sum_{i=1}^{2} r_{i,j} A_j = 0,$$

$$P_3(\psi) = \sum_{j=1}^{2}\sum_{i=1}^{2} r_{i,j} k_i A_j = 0.$$

As the fineness of the grid increases, this method becomes increasingly accurate; we are guaranteed arbitrary accuracy as we add higher-order terms to the approximation of the decision rule and refine the grid. In this simple problem, the method is also rapid. However, the accuracy is obtained at the cost of computational intensity and speed. For example, given two state variables and ten grid points for each variable, the residual function must be evaluated at 100 points. If the function is approximated using the tensor product of polynomials of degree two, a set of nine nonlinear equations must be solved with respect to nine parameters.[7] To evaluate the conditional expectation, Gaussian quadrature can be used to evaluate the double integral that appears in the stochastic Euler equation. Increasing the state space by one variable expands the number of times the residual must be calculated tenfold, and twenty-seven nonlinear equations must be solved with respect to twenty-seven parameters. The method becomes computationally expensive very quickly. In addition, the method depends heavily on the accuracy of available minimization algorithms since a system of nonlinear functions must be solved with respect to a large number of parameters.

Albert Marcet and Christopher Sims have suggested techniques that avoid the computational burden of the previous method. Parameterizing expectations, outlined in Marcet (1989), also uses functional approximation theory. Marcet's idea is to find a function $h(s_t; \psi)$ that approximates the conditional expectation that appears in equation (2.6) and estimate ψ by nonlinear regression. More specifically, suppose we assume a function $h(s_t; \psi)$ such that

$$h(s_t; \psi) = E_t \left\{ \frac{1}{c_{t+1}} [1 - \delta + \alpha A_{t+1} k_t^{\alpha-1}] \right\}.$$

With a given setting for ψ, ψ_0, we can generate a data series for k_t and c_t from the resource constraint and the Euler equation:

$$\frac{1}{c_t} = \beta h(s_t; \psi_0).$$

Once we have a long data series, $\{c_t, k_t, t = 1, \ldots, T\}$, we estimate a new ψ, ψ_1, by regressing the following quantity:

$$\frac{1}{c_{t+1}} [1 - \delta + \alpha A_{t+1} k_t^{\alpha-1}]$$

on $h(s_t; \psi_0)$ using nonlinear regression methods. Given this new ψ, ψ_1, generate a new set of data; generate another ψ by running the nonlinear regression with the new data set. We iterate until the change in ψ is less than some predetermined tolerance level.

Marcet notes that, in some applications, the sequence of ψ's can become explosive unless the starting ψ, ψ_0, is close to the correct value. Marcet suggests the following updating scheme for situations in which good initial values are unavailable:

$$\psi_t = \lambda \hat{\psi} + (1 - \lambda)\psi_{t-1},$$

where λ is a fraction chosen beforehand by the investigator, ψ_{t-1} is the parameter vector used in the previous iteration, and $\hat{\psi}$ is the parameter estimate obtained from the nonlinear regression. A utilitarian approach is to be taken in choosing the parameter λ; the researcher should find the value that works.[8]

Finally, Sims (1984) has suggested a technique called "backsolving" that decreases the complexity of the problem by avoiding the need to evaluate the conditional expectation in the stochastic Euler equation. The method is most easily understood in a linearized model.[9] Recall the methodology for obtaining a solution to the model by linear-quadratic approximation. After the system is linearized, the researcher stabilizes the linear difference equation by imposing a set of constraints that eliminate the effect of any explosive roots in the system. The constraint also imposes a relationship between the fundamental errors that define the distribution of the exogenous shocks and the forecast error in the Euler equation. Data for the decision variables and the forecast error in the Euler equation is generated by drawing realizations of the exogenous shocks and generating the endogenous data from the derived specification of the linear difference equations.

However, we could just as well generate a realization of the Euler equation shock, η_t, use the mapping *in reverse* to generate ε_{At}, then use the remaining equations to generate the exogenous shock and decision variables. We will obtain the same realization of $\{A_t, c_t, k_t, t = 1, \ldots, T\}$ either way. This is the intuition behind the method, which can be extended to the nonlinear version of the model. First, generate a series of Euler equation errors which have conditional mean zero. Then use equations (2.5) and (2.7) and a version[10] of the constraint $C^{-1}[i,.][\hat{c}_t, \hat{k}_t, \hat{A}_t]' = 0$ to generate the data on consumption, the capital stock and the technology shock. Then (2.8) can be used to calculate $\{\varepsilon_t\}$, if desired, although there is no reason to believe that this series will be serially uncorrelated or even have mean zero. Since $\{A_t\}$ is not generated according to (2.8), the solution that we have derived is no longer a solution to the model as originally formulated.

"Backsolving" does not lend itself well to exercises in which the researcher wishes to conduct a policy experiment. As the parameters of the model are changed, the statistical properties of the backed-out shocks change. Controlling these properties is usually very important when interpreting the outcomes of perturbations to the model. For example, if we were interested in the effect on the capital stock of a higher rate of time discount, we would want to ensure that the persistence of the technology shock was constant as we decreased β.

Overall, the solution techniques that are meant to be used in the nonlinear context have not been widely adopted. For most researchers, the gain that is expected to be obtained by using one of these methods is probably outweighed by either the presumed technical or computational cost. Abandonment of the linear-quadratic approximation will take place only when there is a demonstration that this approximation leads to an incorrect analysis of the model.

Model Estimation and Evaluation

In order to generate data from the model or to answer particular policy questions within the context of the model, values must be assigned to its free parameters. Few authors in the 1980s actually used Hansen-Sargent's recommended method—maximum likelihood—to estimate structural business-cycle models.[11] Two other methods, both easier to implement and less computationally intensive, became the techniques of choice for assigning values to parameters in stochastic general equilibrium models: generalized method of moments (GMM), introduced by Hansen (1982) (see also Hansen and Singleton, 1982), and calibration, initially used in the computable general equilibrium literature (Johansen, 1960) and applied in the real business-cycle literature in early papers by Kydland and Prescott (1982) and Long and Plosser (1983). Recent techniques that have been added to the toolbox are the method of simulated moments (Lee and Ingram, 1991; Kwan and Tierens, 1992; Duffie and Singleton, 1993) and Bayesian methods (Canova, 1993; Kwan, 1991; and DeJong, Ingram, and Whiteman, 1994). Finally, Ingram, Kocherlakota, and Savin (1994) suggest an alternative framework for approaching models with data. In this section, I contrast the various methods.

Maximum Likelihood Estimation

Maximum likelihood is a full-information method; it requires a complete specification of the data-generating process for the exogenous stochastic processes in the model. In addition, the researcher must derive the mapping from the exogenous stochastic processes to the endogenous observable variables. Consider, as an example, the linearized version of the growth model presented in the previous section. The form of the likelihood is determined by the assumption that ε_{At} is normally distributed with mean $-\sigma^2/2$ and variance σ^2. The mapping between observables and shocks is given by

$$
\begin{bmatrix} c & k & -k^\alpha \\ C^{-1}[i, 1] & C^{-1}[i, 2] & C^{-1}[i, 3] \\ 0 & 0 & 1 \end{bmatrix} \begin{bmatrix} \hat{c}_t \\ \hat{k}_t \\ \hat{A}_t \end{bmatrix}
$$

$$
+ \begin{bmatrix} 0 & -\alpha k^\alpha - (1 - \delta)k & 0 \\ 0 & 0 & 0 \\ 0 & 0 & -\rho \end{bmatrix} \begin{bmatrix} \hat{c}_{t-1} \\ \hat{k}_{t-1} \\ \hat{A}_{t-1} \end{bmatrix} = \begin{bmatrix} 0 \\ 0 \\ \varepsilon_{At} \end{bmatrix}. \tag{2.13}
$$

Suppose that the data set consists of a time series on aggregate consumption. Manipulate the previous equation system to derive an expression for ε_{At} solely in terms of consumption; find the moving average representation for A_t,

$$
\hat{A}_t = (1 - \rho L)^{-1} \varepsilon_{At},
$$

and substitute this into the expression for capital:

$$
\hat{k}_t = -(C^{-1}[i, 1]\hat{c}_t + C^{-1}[i, 3]\hat{A}_t)/C^{-1}[i, 2]
$$
$$
= -(C^{-1}[i, 1]\hat{c}_t + C^{-1}[i, 3] (1 - \rho L)^{-1}\varepsilon_{At})/C^{-1}[i, 2].
$$

Finally, replace the relevant parts of the top equation in (2.13) with these expressions to obtain a fairly complicated (linear) formula involving ε_{At} and c_t,[12] which forms the basis for a likelihood function under the assumption that ε_{At} is normally distributed. Note that the structural parameters will enter this expression in a highly nonlinear fashion, so that the likelihood function must be maximized numerically, subject to constraints on feasible values for the parameters (such as, $0 < \beta < 1$). Identification of the parameters may be difficult to assess.

Suppose, now, that the data set includes measures of both consumption and the capital stock. Since the model has only one shock, the likelihood can be formed in terms of consumption *or* capital. Both consumption and capital are linear functions of the same shock, implying that there is some exact linear relationship between capital and consumption; presumably, this restriction would be rejected if tested in available data sets. The implication, of course, is that the model is misspecified: we are trying to model a two-dimensional stochastic process (the joint distribution of consumption and capital) by use of a model that involves a one-dimensional shock. The resolution of this problem is to supplement the stochastic elements of the model, either by the addition of measurement error to the capital or consumption series or by the inclusion of additional exogenous shocks.

The first route was taken by Altug (1989) and McGrattan (1994). In the example model, the error vector in (2.13) would be augmented to include a second random element that, presumably, had classical measurement error properties: it would be i.i.d. and uncorrelated with ε_{At}. Leeper and Sims (1994), on the other hand, incorporate enough exogenous shocks in their model to avoid the implication that the observable variables form a stochastically singular system.

Maximum likelihood, as implemented by Hansen and Sargent, required that the researcher derive the mapping from the distribution of the exogenous shocks to the distribution of the observable variables analytically. As noted earlier, this is not possible in most multivariate, nonlinear macroeconomic models. However, we do have methods that allow us to generate simulated data from these models. Kwan and Tierens (1992) suggest making use of the simulated data to estimate parameters by using a partial likelihood function.

Maximum likelihood estimation requires the imposition of a significant amount of structure on the problem in the form of restrictions on the exogenous shocks. In general, we do not observe these shocks, nor does economic theory deliver much information about their behavior. In addition, MLE can be difficult to implement in complicated models, since it involves finding the parameter vector that minimizes a set of highly nonlinear equations, subject to side constraints on the parameter vector. These considerations have motivated many researchers to adopt limited-information estimation methods such as calibration and generalized method of moments (GMM). The following section discusses some of these methods.

Limited-Information Estimation Methods

One common thread links the methods discussed in this section: each uses a subset of the restrictions available from the theoretical model in estimating the model's parameters. GMM and calibration are probably the most widely used and criticized of the methods (see Kim and Pagan, 1994). GMM and calibration do not require specification of the form of the data-generating process of the shocks,[13] nor do they require the user to find the decision rule that is the solution to the agent's optimization problem. All of the methods discussed in this section allow researchers to assign values to the parameters of the model based on particular features of the model, while neglecting other specifics of the model or the data.

Calibration.   Calibration is discussed elsewhere in this volume, but I will briefly indicate where it fits into the structural estimation program. Calibration involves informally setting the parameters of the model so that some chosen statistical properties of the model match the pertinent properties of microeconomic data or the long-run implications of macroeconomic data. In the example above, δ might be calibrated to correspond to the average depreciation rate of different kinds of capital in the post-war period. The parameter α is equal to the share of income going to capital in an expanded production function and is usually set to 0.42. The rate of time preference, β, is related to the rate of return on capital and is usually set equal to the inverse of the mean of some long-term interest rate. The list of papers that use calibrated parameter values is lengthy, with the advantage of the method being its simplicity. Calibration allows researchers to gain insight into the range of behavior that is possible in a particular model without completing a complicated estimation exercise. The technique is not given a formal statistical foundation; standard errors are not usually calculated for the estimated parameters. Testing the fit of the model in this framework involves a visual comparison of first- and second-moment properties of the data of the model to an observed data set.

Calibration, as initially implemented, had little foundation in formal statistics. Authors using this technique do not seem to think of the assigned values as "estimates" in a statistical sense. In addition, the testing stage of the procedure is informal, and an overall metric measuring the fit of the model is not presented. This poses several problems. First, the features of the historical record that are used to calibrate the parameter values are chosen based on the tastes of the author. There is no objective criterion for deciding whether a particular parameter value is reasonable or not. The calibration literature has developed in such a way that, often, the parameters of a model will be calibrated by simply borrowing the values used in another, perhaps very different, modeling exercise. Second, the *ad hoc* nature of the testing procedure makes it difficult to decide whether a modification of a model in a certain direction does or does not lead to improvement. Third, in many instances, several different data sets are used to assign values to various parameters. There is no guarantee that the data sets are consistent with each other or with the variables of the model.[14] Finally, if we want to take the policy conclusions that we derive from a model seriously, we want that model to be connected in some rigorous fashion to the real world. It is of interest to know, for example, the welfare cost of an expansion in the money supply for various rates of time discount. In the end, however, we would like to know the welfare cost of inflation under the parameterization of the model that is relevant for the country under study.

Several authors have attempted to ground calibration on a firmer statistical footing. Gregory and Smith (1989, 1991) and Christiano and Eichenbaum (1992) treat calibration as a method-of-moments estimator. For example, a researcher may calibrate δ so that it is consistent with the behavior of depreciation in observed U.S. data. Since real depreciation is not constant across different types of capital, the average rate of depreciation (the sample first moment) would be used to estimate δ. Then uncertainty about the calibrated value of δ arises from sampling error in estimating the mean rate of depreciation across different types of capital. As a second example, consider the parameter α, the share of income flowing to capital, which is often calibrated to be equal to the *mean* (the sample first moment) of the historical share of income going to capital in postwar U.S.

data; the mean, of course, has a sampling distribution that exhibits some degree of dispersion. As noted by Gregory and Smith and Christiano and Eichenbaum, method-of-moments procedures offer a procedure for calculating standard errors for the estimates. Reporting a standard error for α is the prototypical method used in empirical work for conveying the amount of uncertainty a researcher has about a parameter value to the reader.

One reason to calculate standard errors for the parameters of a model is to provide a guide for performing sensitivity analysis. When we ask a policy question within the context of the model, we would like know whether the answer produced by the model is sensitive to perturbations in the parameters. Standard errors give us an idea of the range of values that are reasonable to consider. For example, we might estimate a rate of depreciation of 0.025 in quarterly data with a standard error of 0.005. Based on this, we might evaluate the robustness of our conclusions to a range of values for depreciation—say, for $\delta \in [0.010, 0.04]$—under the assumption that values lying more than three standard deviations from the mean are unreasonable from the perspective of our data set.

Calibration exercises usually conclude with an informal testing phase in which statistics calculated in a real data set are compared to statistics implied by the theoretical model. The point of this part of the exercise is diagnostic—along which dimension is the model failing? As noted by Kydland and Prescott (1990), there is little point in simply rejecting a model. We would like the test of the model to produce information about how the model can be improved.

Both Gregory and Smith and Christiano and Eichenbaum suggest classical testing procedures designed to evaluate the statistical significance of differences between predicted and empirical moments in sets of data. These are very similar to the tests of overidentifying restrictions developed in the GMM literature, described below. However, in both cases, the estimation phase is separated from the testing phase. The parameters of the model are estimated by equating one set of model moments to data moments, and the model is tested by measuring the distance between a second set of model and data moments; uncertainty about the parameter estimates is not accounted for in the testing stage. In other words, the test is conditional on the given parameter setting. One can interpret procedures that separate the estimation of the parameters from the testing of the model as performing GMM with an inefficient weighting matrix.

Watson (1993) suggests a classical framework for model evaluation based on second-moment properties of the data. Rather than focusing on parameter uncertainty, his approach involves augmenting the variables of the model with stochastic error in order to match empirical second moments; the larger the amount of error required for a match, the poorer the fit of the model. The size of the error is measured by it second-moment properties, which can be calculated only under particular assumptions about the cross-covariance generating function of the model data and the observed data. Assuming that this is the zero function, Watson's method provides an upper bound on the variance of the error that will be necessary to match model and data statistics. If the upper bound is small, the model fits well. If the upper bound is large, we reach no conclusion.

As an alternative to the classical approach, a number of authors have suggested using Bayesian methods to analyze structural models. An important characteristic of a standard calibration exercise is that the researcher usually displays a fair amount of uncertainty regarding parameter values; oftentimes, the researcher will conduct a sensitivity analysis in which the model is analyzed over a range of parameter values. As noted in Canova (1993), DeJong, Ingram, and Whiteman (1994), and Kwan (1991), Bayesian methods are uniquely suited for incorporating this prior uncertainty into the analysis. The procedure involves the specification of prior distributions over the parameters of the model under investigation, which in turn induces prior distributions over the statistical properties of artificial data generated from the model. The prior distribution over model parameters can be specified based on information derived from microeconomic data, the long-run properties of macroeconomic data, or individual intuition. The plausibility of the model is evaluated by a comparison of the distributions of statistical moments induced by the model to their empirical counterparts. In Canova, empirical moments are estimated with time averages of functions of the data, which has been filtered to induce stationarity. Uncertainty about these moments arises from sampling variability in the data set. DeJong, Ingram, and Whiteman, on the other hand, take a more symmetric view of the model and data and base inference about the properties of the actual data on a statistical model (a likelihood function); uncertainty about the statistical properties of the data arises from uncertainty about the parameters of the likelihood function.

Generalized Method of Moments. Generalized method of moments, described in Hansen (1982), is a more formal limited-information estimation technique that makes use of an important property of models in which agents have rational expectations: the forecast error in the Euler equation, η_{t+1}, should be uncorrelated with information available in period t. Let z_t represent a $p \times 1$ vector of variables observable at time period t. Then, under the null hypothesis that the model is true, $E(\eta_{t+1} z_t) = 0$. A strategy for estimating the parameters of the model, then, is to find the parameter vector that sets the sample counterpart to $E(\eta_{t+1} z_t)$ equal to zero in the observed data set. In the example in this paper, this translates into finding values for the parameters such that

$$\frac{1}{T}\sum_{t=1}^{T}\left\{\frac{1}{c_t} - \hat{\beta}\left[\frac{1}{c_{t+1}}\left(1 - \hat{\delta} + \hat{\alpha}\, y_{t+1}/k_t\right)\right]\right\} z_t = 0 \qquad (2.14)$$

for a data set of length $T + 1$ consisting of consumption, c_t, the capital stock, k_t, and output, y_t. Obviously, the length of the instrument vector, p, must equal or exceed the number of parameters to be estimated. Note that only three of the five parameters to be estimated appear in this expression; two parameters, ρ and σ, cannot be estimated using (2.14).

Define $f_t(\psi)$ to be the term in brackets in (2.14), where we have suppressed the dependence of this function on the data set, and $\psi = [\alpha \; \beta \; \delta]$. Suppose that z_t, $t = 1, \ldots, T$, are vectors of length three, so that the number of instruments equals the number of parameters to be estimated. The estimates are obtained by finding the value of ψ that minimizes the following function:

$$\left[\frac{1}{T}\sum_{t=1}^{T}\mathbf{f_t}(\psi)z_{1t} \;\; \frac{1}{T}\sum_{t=1}^{T}\mathbf{f_t}(\psi)z_{2t} \;\; \frac{1}{T}\sum_{t=1}^{T}\mathbf{f_t}(\psi)z_{3t} \right]$$

$$\times W \left[\frac{1}{T}\sum_{t=1}^{T}\mathbf{f_t}(\psi)z_{1t} \;\; \frac{1}{T}\sum_{t=1}^{T}\mathbf{f_t}(\psi)z_{2t} \;\; \frac{1}{T}\sum_{t=1}^{T}\mathbf{f_t}(\psi)z_{3t} \right]'$$

where W is a (3×3) positive definite weighting matrix. Given certain regularity conditions, Hansen shows that the estimator, $\hat{\psi}$, has an asymptotic normal distribution with mean ψ_0 and variance-covariance matrix $(B'WB)^{-1}$ $B'W\Omega WB(B'WB)^{-1}$, where

$$B = E[\partial \mathbf{f}(\psi_0)/\partial \psi \otimes z_t],$$

$$\Omega = E[\, \mathbf{f}(\psi_0)\mathbf{f}(\psi_0)'].$$

The weighting matrix that yields the smallest asymptotic variance is $W = \Omega^{-1}$, reducing the covariance matrix to $(B'\Omega^{-1}B)^{-1}$. Since the weighting matrix depends on the unknown parameter vector, ψ_0, a two-step procedure can be employed: obtain an initial estimate of ψ by minimizing the criterion function with $W = \mathbf{I}$, employ this estimate to evaluate B and Ω, then reminimize using $W = \Omega^{-1}$.

If we expand the instrument vector so that the number of instruments exceeds the number of parameters to estimate, the overidentifying restrictions provide a test of the fit of the model. In that case, the minimized value of the criterion function has an asymptotic χ^2 distribution with degrees of freedom equal to the difference between the dimension of the instrument vector and the parameter vector. Lack of fit, in this case, indicates that there is information contained in the instrument vector that is relevant for forecasting the Euler equation shock.[15]

It may not be possible to use GMM to estimate all of the parameters of a general-equilibrium model: the parameters that appear in the stochastic Euler equations may not comprise the entire vector of model parameters, or the parameters may not be identified. In addition, the method depends on having an observed data set that corresponds to the variables appearing in the stochastic Euler equation. This will not be the case if, for example, the model includes a preference shock or certain types of agent heterogeneity or unobserved transactions costs. Finally, as pointed out by Kocherlakota (1990) and Kim and Pagan (1994), the quality of the asymptotic distribution of the GMM estimator depends crucially on the correlation between the instrument vector, z_t, and $(\partial \mathbf{f}/\partial \psi)$. Lack of an adequate instrument vector can entail a substantial departure from the asymptotic distribution in the small samples typically available in macroeconomic applications.

Method of Simulated Moments. A second version of the method of moments estimator, suggested in Lee and Ingram (1991), relies on the ability to quickly generate artificial data from the model for arbitrary parameter settings. Given this technical capacity, the method of simulated moments (MSM) consists of finding the parameter vector for which the statistical properties of the simulated data match most closely the statistical properties of the observed data set. More specifically, let $y_n(\psi)$, $n = 1, \ldots, N$, represent a $k \times 1$ data vector generated from an artificial model parameterized by a $q \times 1$ vector ψ. Let x_t, $t = 1, \ldots, T$, represent a vector of real data and $m(\cdot)$ represent an $r \times 1$ vector of functions. If the model is true, $E\{m(y_n(\psi_0))\} = E\{m(x_t)\}$ for the value of ψ, ψ_0, that generated the observed data. The estimation strategy is to pick ψ so that the following function is minimized, given a fixed, positive definite weighting matrix, W:

$$\Xi = \left[\frac{1}{T}\sum_{t=1}^{T} m(x_t) - \frac{1}{N}\sum_{n=1}^{N} m(y_n(\psi)) \right] W \left[\frac{1}{T}\sum_{t=1}^{T} m(x_t) - \frac{1}{N}\sum_{n=1}^{N} m(y_n(\psi)) \right]'.$$

Using an argument similar to Hansen's, Lee and Ingram show that the estimator has an asymptotic normal distribution with mean ψ_0 and covariance matrix:

$$(B'WB)^{-1}B'W(1 + 1/n)\Omega WB(B'WB)^{-1},$$

where

$$n = N/T,$$

$$B = E[\partial m(y_j(\psi))/\partial \psi],$$

$$\Omega = Var\left[\frac{1}{T}\sum_{t=1}^{T} m(x_t) \right].$$

Choosing $W = [(1 + 1/n)\Omega]^{-1}$ produces the smallest asymptotic covariance matrix. As the length of the simulated series expands relative to the length of the data series, $n \to \infty$, the term $1/n$ becomes negligible and the asymptotic variance is reduced.

If the number of statistics chosen exceeds the number of parameters to be estimated, then $T*\Xi$ has an asymptotic χ^2 distribution with $r - q$ degrees of freedom, providing a test of fit of the model. In this procedure, the test of fit will give us information about how well the model replicates a set of statistics calculated in a real data set. By altering the set of statistics, the researcher can gather information about the dimensions along which the model is performing poorly.

This estimation procedure is straightforward, and allows the researcher to concentrate attention on the parts of the model that are relevant for the question at hand. However, it depends crucially on being able to simulate data from the model quickly. For every candidate parameter vector analyzed in the minimization algorithm, the model must be solved and simulated. If a gradient method is used for minimization, the model must be solved and simulated an additional number of times in order to evaluate the gradient in q (the number of parameters) directions.

Lee and Ingram provide no guidance in choosing the set of moments to be used for estimation; different sets of moments will lead, presumably, to different point estimates. Gallant and Tauchen (1994) propose a systematic method for determining which moments to employ in a simulated-moments estimation exercise. The idea is to make use of reliable and well-developed statistical models of the target data set and to use moments derived from the statistical model to estimate the parameters of the theoretical model. The statistical model need not necessarily correspond to the likelihood function that is implied by the theoretical model. The procedure involves using the score—the derivative of the log density—of the statistical (or auxiliary) model. The set of moments is then the expectation of the score under the structural model. Gallant and Tauchen show that if the auxiliary model nests the structural model, then the estimator is as efficient as the maximum likelihood estimator. The Gallant and Tauchen moments estimator is motivated by statistical considerations (which empirical model provides the best statistical description of the data?) rather than economic considerations (is the forecast error in the stochastic Euler equation zero?) as in GMM and MSM.

Bayesian Methods

The (classical) estimation methods discussed above involve the use of a data set for the estimation and evaluation of a theoretical model. In contrast, DeJong, Ingram, and Whiteman (1993, 1995) develop an approach, based on Bayesian principles, in which a theoretical model is used to aid in the estimation of a reduced form, statistical model. The theoretical model plays the role of prior information, which is formally combined with the statistical model—characterized by the likelihood function—via Bayes's rule. Hence, the approach enables the formal incorporation of theoretical restrictions (such as cross-equation or identifying restrictions) into the estimation of reduced form models.

The procedure involves specifying a prior distribution over the parameterization of the theoretical model, then mapping the prior into the parameter space of the reduced-form model under investigation. After combining the prior with the likelihood function, posterior analysis over functions of interest (correlation patterns, impulse response functions, and so on) is straightforward. In addition, it is possible to generate numerically posterior distributions over the structural parameters of the theoretical model. Unlike classical procedures, the Bayesian posterior distributions will reflect prior information that the researcher possesses about the values of the parameters of the model.

Ingram and Whiteman (1994) use the method in the context of a forecasting exercise, demonstrating that a particular real business-cycle model carries information that is useful for predicting movements in consumption, output, hours, and investment. DeJong, Ingram, and Whiteman (1993) examine the impulse response functions generated by a VAR that had been estimated subject to the restrictions imposed by a monetary general equilibrium model.

Rational Expectations Shock Estimation

With the exception of GMM and, to some extent, backsolving, all of the methods of solution and estimation outlined above require that we specify the nature of the exogenous shocks in the model *a priori*. In most applications, the number of exogenous shocks is relatively small, and the data-generating process for vector shock process is simple, perhaps AR(1). Model shocks, however, are unobservable; they represent the unmeasurable parts of the model. Theory tells us little about their behavior *a priori*. Hence, there is little justification for imposing structure on these processes except as a necessary prerequisite for many methods of model analysis.

A few authors have begun to use the structure of the model and the observed data to make inferences about the exogenous shocks (Ingram, Kocherlakota, and Savin, 1993, 1994; Burnside, Eichenbaum, and Rebelo, 1993; Baxter and King 1991; Parkin, 1988). The technique can be illustrated in the growth model described above, under the assumption that $\alpha = 1$ (making production linear in capital). A solution to this optimization problem is given by

$$c_t = (1 - \beta)(1 - \delta + A_t)k_{t-1},$$

$$k_t = \beta(1 - \delta + A_t)k_{t-1},$$

$$y_t = A_t k_{t-1}.$$

Suppose that we have data on consumption, c_t, and output, y_t. Then a series for the technology shocks, A_t, can be obtained from

$$A_t = \frac{y_t(1 - \delta)(1 - \beta)}{c_t - y_t(1 - \beta)}.$$

Given a series for A_t, the researcher can analyze its behavior and estimate various parametric forms for its data-generating process.

The reader probably has noticed that there is another, equally valid, expression for A_t:

$$A_t = \frac{y_t(1 - \beta)}{c_{t-1}\beta}.$$

In general, it will not be the case that both of these expressions produce the same series for A_t. The problem is that the model is stochastically singular: one single shock, A_t, drives fluctuations in both consumption and output. This assumption implies that there is an exact, nonstochastic relationship between c_t and y_t:

$$c_t = \beta y_t + (1 - \beta)(1 - \delta)c_{t-1}.$$

We would be quite surprised if this equation held in our data set for any values of the structural parameters β and δ.

Most macroeconomists would acknowledge that variables such as consumption, output, labor hours, and wages are not driven by a single stochastic shock. A model that incorporates this assumption is misspecified and will be rejected when subjected to a test of fit. The solution proposed by some authors has been to simply reject formal statistical estimation and testing of models. Ingram, Kocherlakota, and Savin (1994) argue that this resolution of the problem ignores much of the useful information available in the data set. They propose that models be augmented by additional shocks, until the number of shocks in the model equals the number of observed variables in the data set. In the example, suppose that δ were random. Then the solution to the model is essentially the same:

$$c_t = (1 - \beta)(1 - \delta_t + A_t)k_{t-1},$$
$$k_t = \beta(1 - \delta_t + A_t)k_{t-1}.$$

Now the equation that ties consumption to output and lagged consumption is

$$c_t = \beta y_t + (1 - \beta)(1 - \delta_t)c_{t-1}.$$

Unless we have restricted $\{\delta_t, t = 1, \ldots, T\}$ *a priori*, for any β, we can always find a sequence for depreciation such that the previous equation holds. The parameter β is unidentified in this model. To identify β, we require some additional assumptions about the behavior of the stochastic process, $\{\delta_t\}$. An assumption about the data generating process for $\{\delta_t\}$ imposes a restriction on the relationship between current consumption, current output, and lagged consumption. This restriction can be used to estimate β.

If we are unwilling to impose structure on the exogenous process but are willing to restrict the possible values of β, the model can be used "in reverse" to back out some information about the exogenous shocks. Given a value for β and data on consumption and output, we can derive the following expressions for the shocks:

$$A_t(\beta) = (1 - \beta)y_t/(\beta c_t),$$

$$\delta_t(\beta) = 1 + (1 - \beta)y_t/(\beta c_{t-1}) - c_t/(\beta c_{t-1}).$$

In other words, we can use the information contained in the data set to derive some information, in the form of a realized series, for the exogenous shocks. These backed-out shocks can then be analyzed in order to determine their relative importance in driving certain movements in consumption or output.

Ingram, Kocherlakota, and Savin have successfully applied this method in two problems. However, in more complicated models, the mapping from observable variables to exogenous shocks cannot be derived analytically. In addition, a researcher might be interested in conducting policy experiments with the model. This requires knowledge of the data-generating process for the shocks. This method does not deliver this information directly, and it is not clear that there are enough observations in available data sets to uncover this process nonparametrically.

Concluding Remarks

The rational expectations modeling paradigm developed as a response to what was viewed as a defect in the Cowles commission approach. Linear simultaneous equations models, loosely tied to the behavior of households and firms, were replaced by models in which there was explicit recognition of optimizing and forward-looking behavior on the part of agents.

The intent of the Hansen-Sargent paper was to apply rigorous statistical methods to rational expectations models. The characteristics of their model, however, that made this possible also seemed unrealistic from a theoretical standpoint. Authors who subsequently relaxed the assumptions of quadratic utility and linear budget constraints discovered the difficulties in applying maximum likelihood estimation to more realistic models. Limited information methods for estimation, such as GMM, proved to be more workable in the subsequent generation of models.

Much of the energy of the profession focused on theory: developing models with more realistic institutional frameworks and agent behavior and finding methods for solving these complicated models. Many of these solution algorithms became feasible with the advent of high-speed desktop computers.

Many authors avoided formal statistical analysis of models, arguing that macroeconomic models are inherently misspecified and formal statistical proof of that fact did not add to our knowledge (Prescott, 1986; Kydland and Prescott, 1990). It was not until the end of the 1980s that the profession again turned its attention to estimation and testing. By then, GMM had fostered a set of methods for estimation: estimation by simulation, Bayesian methods, and a rigorous interpretation of calibration. The methods outlined in this paper enhance our understanding of our models and their relationship to the real economy in two ways. First, calculating a standard error for a parameter estimate can aid in sensitivity analysis by informing us about the empirically relevant range of the parameter. Second, analyzing the fit of the model can tell us about the dimensions along which the model fails and the dimensions along which the model performs well.

Acknowledgments

This essay benefited from the suggestions and comments of Charles Whiteman, Narayana Kocherlakota, N. Eugene Savin, Adrian Pagan, and Eric Leeper. The financial support of NSF grant SES92-23257 is gratefully acknowledged.

Notes

1. Examples include the VAR, ARCH, and ECM frameworks discussed in Chapters 3, 4, 8, and 11 in this volume.

2. As noted in Kim and Pagan (1994), one feature that distinguishes the rational expectations structural modeling approach from the SEM approach is this informational assumption. In the former, agents use all available information; in the latter, agents use a subset of the available information.

3. If the shock was observable by the econometrician, the model would imply an exact relationship between a set of observable variables. In that case, formal estimation of the parameters is trivial. However, unless this exact relationship were satisfied in the data for some parameter vector, the model would be rejected.

4. This derivation is also available in Sargent (1979). Whiteman (1983) addresses the solution to more general linear difference equations.

5. This requires an assumption about the distribution of the ε's. Hansen and Sargent recommended quasi-maximum likelihood estimation, which involves using a normal likelihood in the presence of possibly non-Gaussian errors.

6. If the number of eigenvalues that exceed $(1/\beta)^{1/2}$ is greater than one, then there is no solution to the model that satisfies the transversality condition; if the number is less than one, there are multiple solutions each indexed by the initial level of consumption.

7. If x and y represent the variables, we have the constant term in addition to the terms x, y, xy, x^2, y^2, xy^2, x^2y, and x^2y^2.

8. Judd (1991) presents a critique of this method, to which Marcet (1993) responds.

9. There is no reason to backsolve a linear model; I use this example for pedagogic purposes.

10. We can add any function of c_t, k_t, and A_t for which $f(c_t, k_t, A_t) = 0$ and such that the first-order Taylor expansion is equal to $C^{-1}[i,.][\hat{c}_t \ \hat{k}_t \ \hat{A}_t]' = 0$.

11. The exceptions of which I am aware are Altug (1989), McGrattan (1994), and Leeper and Sims (1994).

12. If the available data was the capital stock instead of the consumption series, we could use the same steps to derive an equality involving k_t and ε_{At}.

13. However, if a researcher is planning to perform a policy experiment in which the model is simulated, or if the researcher is going to examine the statistical properties of the series in the model, this form will need to be specified.

14. This point was made by Singleton (1988).

15. A more thorough discussion of this material is contained in Hamilton (1994).

References

Altug, Sumru. (1989). "Time-to-Build and Aggregate Fluctuations: Some New Evidence." *International Economic Review* 30, 889–920.

Baxter, Marianne, and Robert King. (1991). "Productive Externalities and Cyclical Volatility." Manuscript, University of Rochester.

Burns, Arthur, and Wesley Mitchell. (1946). *Measuring Business Cycles*. New York: Columbia Free Press for the NBER.

Burnside, C. M. Eichenbaum, and S. Rebelo. (1993). "Labor Hoarding and the Business Cycle." *Journal of Political Economy* 101, 245–273.

Canova, Fabio. (1993). "Sensitivity Analysis and Model Evaluation in Simulated Dynamic General Equilibrium Models." Manuscript, University of Rochester.

Christiano, Lawrence, and Martin Eichenbaum. (1992). "Current Real Business Cycle Theories and Aggregate Labor Market Fluctuations." *American Economic Review* 82, 430–450.

DeJong, David, Beth Ingram, and Charles Whiteman. (1993). "Beyond Calibration." Journal of Business Economics and Statistics, forthcoming.

DeJong, David, Beth Ingram, and Charles Whileman. (1993). "Analyzing VARs with Monetary Business Cycle Model Priors." *Proceedings of the American Statistical Association, Bayesian Statistical Science Section* (pp. 160–169).

Duffie, Darrell, and Kenneth Singleton. (1993). "Simulated Moments Estimation of Markov Models of Asset Prices." *Econometrica* 61, 929–952.

Gallant, R., and G. Tauchen. (1994). "Which Moments to Match?" Manuscript.

Gregory, Allan, and Gregor Smith. (1989). "Calibration as Estimation." *Econometric Reviews* 9, 57–89.

Gregory, Allan, and Gregor Smith. (1991). "Calibration as Testing: Inference in Simulated Macroeconomic Models." *Journal of Business and Economic Statistics* 9, 297–303.

Hamilton, James. (1994). *Time Series Analysis*. Princeton, NJ: Princeton University Press.

Hansen, Lars. (1982). "Large Sample Properties of Generalized Method of Moments Estimators." *Econometrica* 50, 1029–1054.

Hansen, Lars, and Thomas Sargent. (1980). "Formulating and Estimating Dynamic Linear Rational Expectations Models." *Journal of Economic Dynamics and Control* 2, 7–46.

Hansen, Lars, and Thomas Sargent. (1981). "Linear Rational Expectations Models for Dynamically Interrelated Variables." In Robert Lucas and Thomas Sargent (eds.), *Rational Expectations and Econometric Practice* (pp. 127–158). Minneapolis: University of Minnesota Press.

Hurwicz, Leonid. (1962). "On the Structural Form of Interdependent Systems." In Ernest Nagel et al. (eds), *Logic and Methodology in the Social Sciences* (pp. 232–239). Stanford, CA: Stanford University Press.

Ingram, Beth, Narayana Kocherlackota, and N. Eugene Savin. (1993). "What's the Culprit? Letting the Data Tell Us About the Great Productivity Slowdown." Manuscript, University of Iowa.

Ingram, Beth, Narayana Kocherlakota, and N. Eugene Savin. (1994). "Explaining Business Cycles: A Multiple Shock Approach." *Journal of Monetary Economics* 34, 415–428.

Ingram, Beth, and Charles Whiteman. (1994). "Supplanting the 'Minnesota' Prior: Forecasting Macroeconomic Times Series Using Real Business Cycle Model Priors." *Journal of Monetary Economics* 34, 497–510.

Johansen, L. (1960). *A Multi-sectoral Study of Economic Growth.* Amsterdam: North Holland.

Judd, Kenneth L. (1991a). "Minimum Weighted Residual Methods for Solving Aggregate Growth Models." Discussion Paper 49, Institute for Empirical Macroeconomics.

Judd, Kenneth L. (1991b) "Numerical methods in Economics." Manuscript.

Kim, K., and Adrian Pagan. (1994). "The Econometric Analysis of Calibrated Macroeconomic Models." Manuscript, Economics Program RSSS, Australian National University.

King, Robert, Charles Plosser, and Sergio Rebelo. (1988). "Production, Growth and Business Cycles: I. The Basic Neoclassical Model." *Journal of Monetary Economics* 21, 195–232.

Kocherlakota, Narayana. (1990). "On Tests of Representative Consumer Asset Pricing Models." *Journal of Monetary Economics* 26, 285–304.

Koopmans, Tjalling. (1947). "Measurement Without Theory." *Review of Economic Statistics* 29, 161–172.

Kwan, Yum-Keung. (1991). "Bayesian Calibration and Estimation of Business Cycle Models." Manuscript, Graduate School of Business, University of Chicago.

Kwan, Yum-Keung, and Ingrid Tierens. (1992). "Estimating Non-Linear Rational Expectations Models by Simulated Method of Partial Likelihood.' Manuscript, University of Chicago.

Kydland, Finn, and Edward Prescott. (1982). "Time to Build and Aggregate Fluctuations." *Econometrica* 50, 1345–1370.

Kydland, Finn, and Edward Prescott. (1990). "The Econometrics of the General Equilibrium Approach to Business Cycles." Staff Report No. 130, Federal Reserve Bank of Minneapolis Research Department.

Lee, Bong-Soo, and Beth Ingram. (1991). "Simulation Estimation of Time Series Models." *Journal of Econometrics* 47, 197–205.

Leeper, Eric, and Christopher Sims. (1994). "Towards a Modern Macroeconomic Model Useable for Policy Analysis." Manuscript, Yale University.

Long, J., and Charles Plosser. (1983). "Real Business Cycles." *Journal of Political Economy* 91, 39–69.

Lucas, Robert E., Jr. (1976). "Econometric Policy Evaluation: A Critique." In Karl Brunner and Alan Meltzer (eds.), *The Phillips Curve and Labor Markets*. Amsterdam: North-Holland.

Lucas, Robert E., and Thomas Sargent. (1981). "After Keynesian Macroeconomics." In Robert Lucas and Thomas Sargent (eds.), *Rational Expectations and Econometric Practice*. Minneapolis: University of Minnesota Press.

Marcet, Albert. (1989). "Solving Nonlinear Models by Parameterizing Expectations." Manuscript, Carnegie Mellon Graduate School of Industrial Administration.

Marcet, Albert. (1993). "Simulation Analysis of Dynamic Stochastic Models: Applications to Theory and Estimation." Working Paper No. 6, Universitat Pompeu Fabra Economics.

McGrattan, Ellen. (1994). "The Macroeconomic Effects of Distortionary Taxation." *Journal of Monetary Economics* 33, 573–601.

Parkin, Michael. (1988). "A Method for Determining Whether Parameters in Aggregative Models Are Structural." *Carnegie-Rochester Conference Series on Public Policy* 29, 215–252.

Prescott, Edward. (1986). "Theory Ahead of Business Cycle Measurement." *Carnegie-Rochester Series on Public Policy* 25, 11–44.

Sims, Christopher A. (1984). "Solving Stochastic Equilibrium Models 'Backwards.'" Discussion Paper No. 206, Center for Economic Research, University of Minnesota.

Singleton, Kenneth. (1988). "Econometric Issues in the Analysis of Equilibrium Business Cycle Models." *Journal of Monetary Economics* 21, 361–386.

Taylor, John, and Harald Uhlig. (1990). "Solving Nonlinear Stochastic Growth Models: A Comparison of Alternative Solution Methods." *Journal of Business and Economic Statistics* 8, 1–18.

Watson, Mark. (1993). "Measures of Fit for Calibrated Models." *Journal of Political Economy* 101, 1011–1041.

Appendix to References

The following papers deal with methods of solution for nonlinear stochastic general-equilibrium models. The list is not exhaustive.

Baxter, Marianne, Mario Crucini, and K.G. Rouwehorst. (1990). "Solving the Stochastic Growth Model by a Discrete State Space Euler Equation Approach." *Journal of Business and Economic Statistics* 8, 19–22.

Christiano, Lawrence. (1990). "Solving the Stochastic Growth Model by Linear-Quadratic Approximation and by Value-Function Iteration." *Journal of Business and Economic Statistics* 8, 23–28.

Coleman, W. John III. (1990). "Solving the Stochastic Growth Model by Policy Function Iteration." *Journal of Business and Economic Statistics* 8, 27–30.

den Haan, Wouter. (1991). "An Introduction to Numerical Methods to Solve Stochastic Dynamic Models." Carnegie-Mellon Graduate School of Industrial Administration.

den Haan, Wouter, and Albert Marcet. (1990). "Solving the Stochastic Growth Model by Parameterizing Expectations." *Journal of Business and Economic Statistics* 8, 31–34.

Gagnon, Joseph. (1990). "Solving the Stochastic Growth Model by Deterministic Extended Path." *Journal of Business and Economic Statistics* 8, 35–36.

Ingram, Beth. (1990). "Solving the Stochastic Growth Model by Backsolving with an Expanded Shock Space." *Journal of Business and Economic Statistics* 8, 37–38.

Judd, Kenneth L. (1991a). "Minimum Weighted Residual Methods for Solving Aggregate Growth Models." Discussion Paper 49, Institute for Empirical Macroeconomics.

Judd, Kenneth L. (1991b). "Numerical Methods in Economics." Manuscript.

Labadie, Pamela. (1990). "Solving the Stochastic Growth Model by Using a Recursive Mapping Based on Least Squares Projection." *Journal of Business and Economic Statistics* 8, 39–40.

Marcet, Albert. (1989). "Solving Nonlinear Models by Parameterizing Expectations." Manuscript, Carnegie Mellon Graduate School of Industrial Administration.

Marcet, Albert. (1993). "Simulation Analysis of Dynamic Stochastic Models: Applications to Theory and Estimation." Working Paper No. 6, Universitat Pompeu Fabra Economics.

McGrattan, Ellen R. (1993). "Solving the Stochastic Growth Model with a Finite Element Method." Working Paper 514, Federal Reserve Bank of Minneapolis Research Department.

McGrattan, Ellen. (1990). "Solving the Stochastic Growth Model by Linear-Quadratic Approximation." *Journal of Business and Economic Statistics* 8, 41–44.

Sims, Christopher A. (1984). "Solving Stochastic Equilibrium Models 'Backwards.'" Discussion Paper No. 206, Center for Economic Research, University of Minnesota.

Sims, Christopher. (1990). "Solving the Stochastic Growth Model by Backsolving with a Particular Nonlinear Form for the Decision Rule." *Journal of Business and Economic Statistics* 8, 45–48.

Tauchen, George. (1990). "Solving the Stochastic Growth Model by Using Quadrature Methods and Value-Function Iteration." *Journal of Business and Economic Statistics* 8, 49–52.

Taylor, John, and Harald Uhlig. (1990). "Solving Nonlinear Stochastic Growth Models: A Comparison of Alternative Solution Methods." *Journal of Business and Economic Statistics* 8, 1–18.

Commentary on Chapter 2

Adrian Pagan

Beth Ingram has produced a very good account of methods for solving and estimating small models that feature rational-expectations or intertemporal-optimization constraints. My discussion here will not provide much in the way of new techniques but rather is intended to raise a number of questions. Some of these have a bearing on estimation and solution procedures, while others aim to highlight my perception that an important "tension" in macroeconometrics is that academics are paying insufficient attention to the needs of those who must utilize macroeconometric models. Indeed, the latter fact has resulted in a separate literature that seeks to utilize theoretical insights but yet retain practical relevance.

Let me begin with the issue of solution. Beth's survey demonstrates very clearly that difficulties in this arena stem from two characteristics of the class of models she considers: nonlinear relations and the fact that the forcing variables of these models are taken to be stochastic rather than deterministic, meaning that an expectation has to be evaluated. As she observes, the most popular approach has been to work with linearized models, a strategy for which good arguments can be made. Foremost among these is the fact that any solution method must be approximate and reflect a tradeoff between the accuracy available from the approximation and the specification errors created by oversimplification of the model. There is little point in being highly accurate if the degree of simplification needed to attain this accuracy means that the model is of little use. As she points out in her survey, even when there are only two state variables, many of the "contraction mapping" type procedures become computationally infeasible, and it is hard to imagine many realistic models possessing only two state variables. In this context it is interesting to reflect on the interchange a few years ago at the Santa Fe Institute between physicists and economists; the former were amazed at the desire of the latter for exact solutions as they were more than happy with approximations. Given the versatility of the linear approximation in handling large models, my feeling is that we should be paying more attention to improving it, and to understanding its limitations, rather than seeking greater accuracy with algorithms that apply only in very restricted circumstances.[1]

The computational general-equilibrium (CGE) literature faced a similar challenge in the 1980s. Following Johansen (1960) one strand of this literature, represented in Dixon et al. (1982), linearized around equilibrium solutions and then solved for the changes in output variables caused by movements in control variables

47

such as tariff rates. Such an approximation is only valid in the neighborhood of the original equilibrium, implying that large changes in the control variables are likely to give rise to effects that are not well predicted by the linearized model. Nevertheless, the exact solution could be found by engaging in a sequence of linear approximations. Using the original equilibrium position, the linearized model was first solved and then relinearized around this new solution. The process was iterated until the transition was made to the new level of the control variable (see Dixon et al., 1991, for a more precise description). Generally what is involved at each step is a recomputation of factor and demand shares using the solution data. The success of this method suggests that something can be learned from it about the stochastic general equilibrium (SGE) models that Ingram concentrates on. For example, one might use the linear approximation around the steady-state solution, along with a simulated path for the forcing variables, to produce a sequence of Euler equation errors, η_t. These can then be inserted into the original set of nonlinear equations and $E(k_t)$ and $E(c_t)$ found numerically. Subsequently, these expectations replace the deterministic steady-state solutions as the point around which the linearization is performed, and the process is repeated.

Equally important is the need to understand circumstances in which the approximation will break down. Dotsey and Mao (1991) made a good start to answering this question. One of their conclusions was that the approximation was poorer the larger the variance of the innovations into the process driving the system. A surprising result from their work was that the approximation by a finite-state Markov chain was better the greater the degree of persistence of shocks into the system—that is, if the forcing variables were integrated, then the approximation would be better than if they were stationary. This is surprising since the deviations from the steady-state deterministic growth path will now have an unbounded variance and one would therefore expect poorer performance by the approximation. One possible explanation is that the method of computing the "true solution" breaks down as the approximation of a near-integrated process by a finite-state Markov chain becomes problematical. Following King, Plosser, and Rebelo (1988), it might be expected that the best approximation would be in terms of deviations from the sum of both the deterministic and stochastic trends rather than the deterministic trend line alone. When there is a single stochastic trend in the data, as in King, Posser, and Rebelo, deflation can be easily done in this way, but if there are multiple trends, the situation is less clear. What is needed is an expression for the predicted trend component in the endogenous variables. As this will be a combination of the underlying common trends, it is the determination of the weights to be applied to these variables that needs to be studied.

The possibility of integrated forcing processes raises challenging issues of estimation and inference as well. Instead of the linear approximation being a VAR, one would now have a vector error-correction model, and inferences from this system are unlikely to be of the standard type—that is, some of the asymptotic distributions of coefficient estimators will be nonnormal. If such processes are in evidence, the application of GMM would need to be done with some care. Consider, for example, the moment conditions used in her equation (2.7), writing the population restriction as $E[z_t \eta_{t+1}] = 0$. Following the argument in Hall (1978) and, as evident from her equation (2.9), c_t will have an AR root that is close to unity— that is, be near integrated. GMM applied to the estimation of, say, β using (2.7) effectively involves the application of an instrumental variables estimator with z_t as instrument and $\partial \eta_{t+1}/\partial \beta = (1 - \hat{\delta} + \alpha k_t^{-1} y_{t+1})/c_{t+1}$ as regressor, and the latter is likely to inherit the near-integrated properties of c_{t+1}. An approach that seeks to obviate this problem is to recognize that c_t is in the information set and therefore the moment conditions might be alternatively set up as $E_t [z_t \{1 - \beta(c_t/c_{t+1})$ $(1 - \hat{\delta} + \alpha k_t^{-1} y_{t+1})\}] = 0$; in this incarnation all regressors will be $I(0)$. However, it is not clear that this really represents a solution. To understand why, replace the conditional expectation by the observed value, producing

$$z_t \left[1 - \frac{c_t}{c_{t+1}} \beta(1 - \delta + \alpha k_t^{-1} y_{t+1}) \right] = z_t \varepsilon_{t+1}.$$

Thus the GMM estimator using these moment conditions can be regarded as coming from a regression with error term $\varepsilon_{t+1} = c_t \eta_{t+1}$. Consequently, a question that arises is, what are the properties of ε_t and η_t? If η_t was $i.i.d.(0, \sigma^2)$ then, although ε_t would be a martingale difference with respect to the information set, it would possess very strong dependence in the second moment, due to the fact that the conditional variance of ε_t depends on a near-integrated process c_t. Such a process would not fit easily into the conditions imposed by Hansen (1982) in his proof of the asymptotic properties of GMM. Oddly enough, there has been very little discussion of which type of moment condition is likely to be the best to use. Fundamentally the problem is that rational expectations only impose requirements such as $E_t(\varepsilon_{t+1}) = 0$, and nothing else about the nature of the random variable is known.

Some insight is available by simulating values for ε_t, using the method described in Ingram's paper.[2] I fixed $\delta = .25$ and $\alpha = .4$ and tried a number of values for $\sigma = std (\varepsilon_{At})$ and ρ. In general the $var(\eta_t)$ depends on c_{t-1}, e.g. when $\rho = .95$ and $\sigma = .007$ the regression of 2000 values of η_t^2 against unity and c_{t-1} yields a t ratio for the coefficient of c_{t-1} of -2.6. Conditional heteroskedasticity is present in ε_t as well, but it is considerably muted, with a t-ratio of -2.14. Across a range of parameter values it seemed that ε_t was a better-behaved random variable than η_t, pointing to the desirability of formulating the Euler equation restrictions in terms of changes in variables. Nevertheless, the conditional heteroskedasticity in ε_t tended to remain, and might therefore might cause some concern, owing to the fact that c_t is close to an $I(1)$ process. The most extreme case I encountered was when $\sigma = .015$ and $\rho = 1$. In this instance the t ratio for the regression that has η_i^2 as dependent variable was -18.48, and a plot of $\tau^{-1}\sum_{t=1}^{\tau}\eta_t^2$, a quantity used in Pagan and Schwert (1990) and Mandelbrot (1963) to assess the existence of moments, showed no signs of stabilizing even when $\tau = 2000$.

There are other problems with employing GMM, as the correlation of instruments with regressors in these models is frequently very low (see Pagan and Jung's 1993 analysis of the RBC model of Mao, 1990). When the correlation is identically zero, Phillips (1989) pointed out that the distribution of the IV estimator departed substantially from the normal distribution, and Staiger and Stock's (1993) analysis of the near-zero correlation case showed that these effects can persist in quite large samples. Consequently, it is not clear that estimating parameters from the Euler equation is as attractive as it looks.

Such reservations hint at the desirability of using maximum likelihood, but there are other difficulties associated with this estimation option that need to be appreciated. Ingram points to the fact that most linearized stochastic general equilibrium (SGE) models reduce to a VAR (see equation (2.9) of her paper for example). Such a VAR might be represented as

$$z_t^* = A z_{t-1}^* + \Gamma \varepsilon_t, \tag{1}$$

assuming that the system is only a first-order one. An immediate problem is that the number of shocks ε_t is generally smaller than the number of variables in z_t^*. Ingram mentions that one way to handle this difficulty is to "supplement the stochastic elements of the model, either by the addition of measurement error to the capital or consumption series or by the inclusion of additional exogenous shocks," thereby differentiating between the actual, z_t, and latent, z_t^*, random variables. Definitionally, $z_t = z_t^* + v_t$, where v_t represents some "error in variable." Substituting this out in equation (1) produces a relation in observables:

$$z_t = A z_{t-1} + \varepsilon_t + v_t - A v_{t-1}. \tag{2}$$

Ingram then outlines how MLE can be applied to this equation.

The main objection to this procedure is that some assumption needs to be made about the nature of v_t. Mostly, this is that v_t is normally and independently distributed, but that would seem to be an heroic assumption for many of the SGE models Ingram mentions. These are extremely stylized and almost certainly exclude variables that are important to actual realizations. In particular, this feature makes it likely that v_t will be correlated with z_{t-1}^* (and hence z_{t-1}), thereby invalidating standard estimation and inference measures. As an example of this phenomenon, take Ingram's addition of a stochastic depreciation shock δ_t to the system—say, $\delta_t = \delta + \varepsilon_{\delta t}$. Suppose that the modeler treats the depreciation rate as fixed at δ but agents correctly set it to the random value when optimizing. This means we would have

$$c_t = \beta y_t + (1 - \beta)(1 - \delta)c_{t-1} + (1 - \beta)(1 - \varepsilon_{\delta t})c_{t-1},$$

$$= c_t^* - (1 - \beta)\varepsilon_{\delta t}(k_{t-1}^* + v_{k t-1}),$$

where c_t^* and k_t^* are the solutions from the model setting the depreciation rate to δ—that is, $\varepsilon_{\delta t} = 0$ and $v_{kt} = k_t - k_t^* = -\beta\varepsilon_{\delta t}(k_{t-1}^* + v_{k t-1})$. Hence, $v_{ct} = c_t - c_t^* = -(1 - \beta)\varepsilon_{\delta t}(k_{t-1}^* + v_{k t-1})$, and this will be correlated with k_{t-1}^*.

In such circumstances doubt is cast on the simulation methods for estimation and inference outlined in Ingram's paper, and as practiced for example by Smith (1993), as these simulate z_t^* from (1) and then compare the implied moments with those of the data, z_t. The problem is that a wedge exists between these two variables, potentially creating a wide variety of relations between the two sets of moments depending on the nature of v_t, a point made in Ingram, Kocherlakota, and Savin (1993), Kim and Pagan (1994), and Watson (1993). In particular, it needs to be emphasized that the popular strategy of comparing $var(z_t)$ with $var(z_t^*)$ is meaningless unless accompanied by some statement about what is being assumed regarding v_t.

How do we deal with this quandary? One way to pose the question is to ask how one should perform estimation and evaluation in the presence of specification error of unknown form. Watson (1993) advanced the suggestion that bounds on the moments for z_t predicted by (1) be found that allow for v_t and z_t^* to have maximal correlation. Of course, this procedure produces only a measure of fit akin to an R^2 and does not provide any information on how likely it is that the upper bound will be encountered. For the latter one needs to have some idea of the data-generating process (DGP) for z_t. To gain this, one might fit a VAR to the data—effectively making the assumption that v_t can be represented as a linear function of the past history of variables entering the VAR—and then treat that as the DGP. As theoretical work on estimation and inference in the presence of specification error shows, knowledge of the DGP leads to the ability to correct for the impact of specification errors. Practically, the procedure requires that data be simulated from the estimated VAR, and the properties of whatever estimators have been used are then constructed from the empirical density function found by applying the estimator to the generated data.

Finally, I want to address the question of the relation between the type of model building described by Ingram and what has been the revealed preference of those engaged in the practical application of macroeconometric models. One sometimes has the impression that many academics in this area perceive that the problem is simply one of getting the right parameters into the model. However, the models Ingram describes are best thought of as useful for engaging in theoretical exercises, specifically those that concentrate on examining what would happen within an hypothetical economy as various shocks are administered to it. Their concern is with the "big picture," and they rarely produce an understanding of the dynamics of actual economies, a fact clearly seen in those instances where their predictions regarding dynamics are matched up with the VAR's describing an actual economy, such as Canova, Finn, and Pagan (1994). Nevertheless, there are certain features of these models that make them attractive, and the following four are of particular importance.

- They have a steady-state solution (either in levels or along a growth path), and any deviations from it are transitory.
- Producers and consumers optimize expected expected profits or utility using complete information on the economy.
- Dynamic adjustments that ensure a return to the steady state stem from both flow and stock disequilibrium.
- The forces driving the economy, such as productivity or terms of trade variations, are inherently stochastic and generally modeled as autoregressive processes.

There was a time when macroeconometric models in use failed to possess almost all of the above features. When simulated, they rarely converged to any point or path as the horizon lengthened; little in the way of optimizing behavior was assumed; and the interaction of flows and stocks was ignored. Wren-Lewis (1992) argues that this is because those models were invariably judged by the degree of their short-term forecasting prowess and that militated against incorporating such characteristics into a model. Within what I might refer to as the American school of macroeconometrics, it still seems to be believed that the choice set, when dealing with macroeconomic issues, is between this older style of model and those set out in Ingram's paper. Therefore, it is important to acknowledge that there is now a literature that is concerned with building useful macroeconomic models and that embodies the four features above but is a far cry from the caricature of macroeconometric models offered by prominent members of the American school such as Kydland and Prescott (1991).

Some of the early examples of this alternative style of model were Bergstrom and Wymer (1976), Jonson, Moses, and Wymer (1977) and Rose and Selody (1985). Since those early examples a distinctive style for building such models has emerged, as seen in the Murphy model (Murphy (1992), the TRYM model (Taplin et al., 1993), MULTIMOD (Masson et al., 1988), the CORE model (Laxton and Tetlow, 1993), the MSG2 model (McKibbin and Sachs, 1991), and the COM-PACT model of Wren-Lewis et al., (1993). It is interesting to observe that most of the models cited above are used more for policy simulations than for forecasting and that this division has become possible as consistency of forecasts can be achieved by properly designed spreadsheets. Although these models incorporate the first three of the features described above, they differ from the stylized models dealt with by Ingram in ways that are hard to describe in my limited space but that stem from the fact that they aim to replicate actual economies. Examples might be that agents are not endowed with full information, and there is concern about allowing for inertia or costs of adjustment when decisions are made. Rational expectations are always found in some markets, such as those for financial assets, but perhaps not in the short run for labor markets. Total factor productivity is viewed as deterministic rather than stochastic, although they could almost certainly be moved in that direction if it was thought desirable. Choices on these matters are model specific rather than universal. Because these models are in use, it is important that academics be involved in scrutinizing them, and it seems timely to draw attention to them and not to limit macroeconometrics to the type of models set out by Ingram.

Notes

1. It is assumed by Ingram that one can write the system as in her (2.9)—that is, the matrix attached to the contemporaneous variables $\hat{c}_t$, $\hat{k}_t$, and $\hat{A}_t$ is nonsingular. Preston and Pagan (1982, pp. 298–308) discuss rational expectations models for which this assumption fails and outline a "shuffle" algorithm that may be applied to transform the system into one in which the matrix is nonsingular.

2. I would like to thank Beth Ingram for providing her GAUSS program for this task.

References

Bergstrom, A.R., and C.R. Wymer. (1976). "A Model of Dis-equilibrium Neo-classical Growth and Its Application to the United Kingdom." In A.R. Bergstrom (ed.), *Statistical Inference in Continuous Time Econometric Models*. Amsterdam: North Holland.

Canova, F., M. Finn, and A.R. Pagan. (1994). "Evaluating a Real Business Cycle Model." In C. Hargreaves (ed.), *Nonstationary Time Series Analyses and Co-integration*. Oxford: Oxford University Press.

Dixon, P.B., B.R. Parmenter, A.A. Powell, P.J. Wilcoxen, and K.R. Pearson. (1991). *Notes and Problems in Applied General Equilibrium Economics*. Amsterdam: North Holland.

Dixon, P.B., B.R. Parmenter, J.M. Sutton, and D.P. Vincent. (1982). *ORANI: A Multisectoral Model of the Australian Economy*. Amsterdam: North Holland.

Dotsey, M., and C.S. Mao. (1991). "How Well Do Linear Approximation Methods Work? Results for Suboptimal Dynamic Equilibria." *Journal of Monetary Economics* 29, 25–58.

Hall, R.E. (1978). "Stochastic Implications of the Life-Cycle Permanent Income Hypothesis: Theory and Evidence." *Journal of Political Economy* 86, 971–987.

Hansen, L.P. (1982). "Large Sample Properties of Generalized Method of Moments Estimators." *Econometrica* 50, 1029–1054.

Ingram, B., N. Kocherlakota, and N.E. Savin. (1993). "Explaining Business Cycles: A Multiple Shock Approach." Mimeo, University of Iowa.

Johansen, L. (1960). *A Multi-sectoral Study of Economic Growth*. Amsterdam: North Holland.

Jonson, P.D., E.R. Moses, and C.R. Wymer. (1977). "The RBA Model of the Australian Economy." In *Conference in Applied Economic Research*. Reserve Bank of Australia.

Kim, K., and A.R. Pagan. (1995). "The Econometric Analysis of Calibrated Macroeconomic Models." In M.H. Pesaran and M.R. Wickens (eds.), *Handbook of Applied Econometrics*. Blackwell.

King, R.G., C. Plosser, and S. Rebelo. (1988). "Production, Growth and Business Cycles II: New Directions." *Journal of Monetary Economics* 21, 309–341.

Kydland, F., and E.C. Prescott. (1991). "The Econometrics of the General Equilibrium Approach to Business Cycles." *Scandanavian Journal of Economics* 93, 161–178.

Laxton, D., and R. Tetlow. (1993). "Government Debt in an Open Economy." Bank of Canada Discussion Paper.

Mandlebrot, B. (1963). "The Variation of Certain Speculative Prices." *Journal of Business* 36, 394–419.

Mao, C.S. (1990). "Hypothesis Testing and Finite Sample Properties of Generalized Method of Moments Estimators: A Monte Carlo Study." Mimeo, Federal Reserve Bank of Richmond.

Masson, P., Symansky, R. Haas, and M. Dooley. (1988). "Multimod: A Multi-region Econometric Model Part II." IMF Staff Studies for the World Economic Outlook.

McKibbin, W.J., and J. Sachs. (1991). *Global Linkages: Macroeconomic Interdependence and Co-operation in the World Economy*. Washington, DC: Brookings Institution.

Murphy, C.W. (1988). "An Overview of the Murphy Model." In M.E. Burns and C.W. Murphy (eds.), *Macroeconomic Modelling in Australia*, supplementary conference issue of *Australian Economic Papers*, 61–68.

Pagan, A.R., and Y. Jung. (1993). "Understanding the Failure of Some Instrumental Variable Estimators." Mimeo, Australian National University.

Pagan, A.R., and G.W. Schwert. (1990), "Testing for Covariance Stationarity in Stock Market Data." *Economics Letters* 33, 165–170.

Phillips, P.C.B. (1989). "Partially Identified Models." *Econometric Theory* 5, 181–240.

Preston, A.J., and A.R. Pagan. (1982). *The Theory of Economic Policy*. Cambridge: Cambridge University Press.

Rose, D.E., and J.G. Selody. (1985). "The Structure of the Small Annual Model." Technical Report No. 40, Bank of Canada, Ottawa.

Smith, A.A. (1993). "Estimating Non-linear Time Series Models Using Simulated Vector Autoregressions." *Journal of Applied Econometrics* 8, S63–S84.

Staiger, D., and J.H. Stock. (1993). "Instrumental Variables Regression with Weak Instruments." Mimeo, Kennedy School of Government, Harvard University.

Taplin, B., P. Jilek, L. Antioch, A. Johnson, P. Parameswaran, and C. Louis. (1993). *Documentation of the Treasury Macroeconomic (TRYM) Model of the Australian Economy*. TRYM Paper No. 2, Australian Treasury. Canberra.

Watson, M.W. (1993). "Measures of Fit for Calibrated Models." *Journal of Political Economy* 101, 1011–1041.

Wren-Lewis, S. (1992). "Macroeconomic Theory and U.K. Econometric Macromodels: Another Failed Partnership?" Paper presented at the ESRC Conference on the Future of Macroeconomic Modelling in the United Kingdom.

Wren-Lewis, S., O. Ricchi, J. Ireland, and J. Darby. (1993). "Fiscal and Monetary Policy in an Econometric Model with Consumption Smoothing, Vintage Production, Nominal Inertia and Rational Expectations." Mimeo, University of Strathclyde.

3 THE ECONOMICS OF VAR MODELS

Fabio Canova

Theraption the monk would frequently interrupt his prayers to follow tenderly the love-making games of the swallows, because that which is forbidden to the nymphs is allowed to the swallows.

—Marguerite Yourcenar

Introduction

In the minds of some economic theorists and traditional econometricians, the vector autoregressive (VAR) approach to time-series data is unscientific, obscure, confusing, or simply wrong. Since the publication of Sims's original contributions (1972, 1980a, 1980b, 1982), the methodology has spurred endless debates. Critics claim that the methodology has very little relationship with economic theory, relies on a set of unsustainable assumptions, and is fundamentally flawed, being subject to the well known Lucas's critique. But despite the controversies surrounding the use and interpretation of VAR models throughout the 1980s, they appear to have found a permanent position in the tool kit of applied time-series and macro-economic analysts. VARs are currently used as a tool to summarize data inter-dependences, to test generically formulated theories, to conduct policy analyses, and, more recently, as a way to compare actual data with the time series generated by artificial economies with calibrated parameters.

The purpose of this chapter is to describe the salient aspects of the original VAR methodology and of its current extensions, discuss the validity of policy analyses conducted with VAR models and their meaning, and compare the methodology with other competing approaches for applied research. Because of this choice we will only tangentially touch other matters that are of interest to VAR practitioners (such as forecasting or simulation comparisons with theoretical models). We will try to separate and distinguish as much as possible statistical from economic issues in order to highlight the stages where crucial assumptions are made. Therefore the next section begins by discussing questions concerning the specification and estimation of VAR models. There we present the approach followed by users of unrestricted VAR models and contrast it with the approach followed by rational expectation econometricians. We also discuss the so-called Bayesian VAR (BVAR) approach to specification and estimation and relate the methodology to the index models literature.

Section 3 deals with inference and with issues of interpretation of the results. In this section we provide a discussion of four important issues. First, we highlight the major features of what we call semistructural approach to policy analysis and contrast its philosophy with the one of rational expectation or generalized method of moment (GMM) econometricians and with the one of calibrators. Second, we discuss in detail the economic issues concerning the identification of a generic model of economic behavior from unrestricted VAR models. Third, we argue that the range of economic questions that are well posed within the context of the type of generic models of economic behavior that can be recovered from the VAR is sufficiently thick and does not necessarily violate the dictates of the Lucas's critique. Finally, we explain how innovation accounting exercises conducted on the generic structural model that is recovered via identification can be used to study questions of interest to macroeconomists and policymakers.

The fourth section examines three problems that may arise with the interpretation of the results obtained from semistructural VAR analyses. The first has to do with the correct number of shocks buffeting the system. The second with the recoverability of structural shocks. The third with time aggregation. A simple example highlights some of these problems.

The final two sections briefly examine some issues concerning the characterization of data interdependencies and unconditional forecasting exercises and conclude by stressing where critics of VAR models have pointed their guns and suggesting a possible avenue for future developments.

Specification and Estimation

It is well established by now that either the exact or the approximate solution of many stochastic dynamic-equilibrium models comes in the form of a restricted VAR (see Hansen and Sargent, 1980; King, Plosser, and Rebelo, 1988). Many of these models are in the neoclassical tradition, but examples of models that deliver dynamic solutions in the form of VARs also appear in the recent new Keynesian literature (see Taylor, 1980). One approach to the specification of a VAR, outlined, for example, in Hansen and Sargent (1980), is to tie down its parameterization to the underlying theory, estimate the unknown parameters of the model via maximum likelihood techniques, and examine the validity of the restrictions imposed by the theory using standard techniques such as likelihood ratio tests. Apart from the issue of estimation of the unknown parameters, the idea of tying down the parameters of the VAR to the theory and the testing apparatus developed by Hansen and Sargent can also be applied to the problem of evaluating dynamic economic models whose parameters are calibrated (see Canova, Finn, and Pagan, 1993).

Despite the fact that the VAR parameters are tied down to the "deep" parameters of the theory, there are at least two elements of arbitrariness that remain in specifying the empirical VAR corresponding to the theory. First, economic theory does not usually provide indications regarding the lag length of the VAR model. One can take two approaches in this respect: either *a priori* choose a lag length and verify that the results are independent of this auxiliary assumption or let the data choose the correct lag length using some optimal statistical criteria (such as Akaike, 1974, or Schwartz, 1978). Second, many dynamic models deliver solutions for the vector of endogenous variables whose covariance matrix is singular because there is a larger number of endogenous variables than shocks, so in order to undertake a meaningful estimation one must probabilistically complete the model by adding other sources of disturbance. These new sources of disturbance may come, for example, from measurement errors. In general, it is assumed that agents have an information set that is larger than the one of the econometrician. In this case the estimated VAR is nonsingular because important sources of dynamics are omitted from the model. Within this approach the econometrician must therefore choose which variables are either measured with error or not observable, and these choices must be verified and substantiated before the results are discussed.

The specification of a VAR model, however, need not to be tied down to any particular parameterization of the theory. Sims (1980a) suggested using an unrestricted VAR approach that is not linked to any particular theory. The major building block of the unrestricted VAR methodology is the Wold theorem. Complete technical details of the mathematics needed are contained in Rozanov (1967) or Quah (1992), while a simple and thorough presentation of the theory appears in Sargent (1986, ch. 11) or Canova (1994).

The Wold theorem states that one can decompose any vector stochastic process x_t of dimension m at every point in time t into the sum of two orthogonal components: one that is predictable based on the information available at time $t - 1$ and one that is unpredictable. Since the above decomposition holds at each t, repeated application of this decomposition to the vector x_t yields

$$x_t \equiv P_t[x_t \mid F_t] = P_t[x_t \mid F_{-\infty}] + \sum_{j=0}^{\infty} P_t[x_t \mid \varepsilon_{t-j}] \tag{3.1}$$

where F_t is the information set available at t, $F_{-\infty}$ is the information set available in the infinite past, ε_{t-j} is the set carrying the new information at each $t - j$, and P_t is an operator that geometrically projects x_t onto various information sets. The first component appearing on the right side of (3.1) is the deterministic part of x_t—that is, the part that is predictable given information contained in the infinite past, and the second component is the "regular" part, the part of x_t carrying the new information that becomes available at each t. While it is not necessary for the theory to be applied, it is typical to restrict the projection to be linear, so that it possible to write $P_t[x_t \mid F_{-\infty}] = H_{jt}d_{t-j} = H_t(\ell)d_t$, $P_t[x_t \mid \varepsilon_{t-j}] = C_{jt}e_{t-j} = C_t(\ell)e_t$ $\forall j$, where $H(\ell) = H_0 + H_1\ell + \ldots + H_q\ell^q$, $C(\ell) = C_0 + C_1\ell + \ldots + C_p\ell^p$ and ℓ is the lag operator, H_{jt} and C_{jt} are matrices of coefficients, d_t a set of deterministic variables and $e_{t-j} = x_{t-j} - P_{t-j}[x_{t-j} \mid F_{t-j-1}]$. By construction the sequence $\{e_{t-j}\}_{j=0}^{\infty}$ is a zero mean process that is uncorrelated with all of its past—that is, e_t represents the "news" or the "innovations" in x_t and therefore should be unpredictable using past information. The coefficients C_{jt} satisfy two conditions: (1) the elements of x_t are contemporaneously uncorrelated—that is, $C_{j0} = I$, and (2) the sequence of x_t defined by (3.1) is bounded—that is, $\Sigma_{j=0}^{\infty}C_{jt}^2 < \infty$. If this condition did not hold, news that occurred infinitely far in the past would have a nonnegligible effect on the process at t.

It is also typical to assume that x_t is covariance stationary—that is, the autocovariance function of x_t depends on the distance between two elements not no their position in time ($Ex_t x_{t-s}'$ depends on s but not on t), so H_{jt} and C_{jt} become independent of t. This restriction is made purely for convenience and is not needed for the theory to be applied. Because economic time series often do not satisfy this assumption, transformations of the data are usually required to induce this property.

When the restrictions (1) and (2) on the C_j coefficients are satisfied there exists an autoregressive representation that expresses e_t as a linear combination of current and past x_t's of the form

$$x_t = Gd_t + \Gamma^*(\ell)x_{t-1} + e_t \tag{3.2}$$

where $\Gamma(\ell) = (I - \Gamma^*(\ell)) = C(\ell)^{-1}$ and $G = H(\ell)C(\ell)^{-1}$. Therefore unrestricted VAR models are natural representations for vectors of time series and emerge from very mild regularity conditions on x_t and from the simple geometric principle of orthogonality.

In selecting a particular specification for an unrestricted VAR an empirical researcher must address four issues:

- Decide what variables should enter the model,
- Choose the lag length of the autoregression,
- Select the type of deterministic components to be included in d_t, and
- Know what to do if nonstationary or explosive roots appear in the $\Gamma(\ell)$ matrix.

In choosing the variables that enter the VAR, one can appeal to economic theory, empirical observations, or experience. In principle, one would like to include all variables that are likely to have important interdependencies. In practice, small-scale models are used because of the limited size of existing data sets. Implicit in the choice of variables is therefore a process of marginalization—that is, the joint probability density of the selected VAR has been marginalized with respect to all other potentially relevant variables (see Clements and Mizon, 1991). This assumption has raised some controversy. Some (see McNees, 1986; Fair, 1988; Kirchgassner, 1991) consider it dubious and a potential source of incorrect inference in small-scale VAR models. Others considers it innocuous as long as the statistical model is well specified.

In general, the polynomial $\Gamma(\ell)$ appearing in equation (3.2) will have an infinite number of elements for any reasonable specification of the polynomial $C(\ell)$. That is to say, under the regularity conditions we have outlined, an unrestricted VAR will approximate arbitrarily well any vector stochastic process x_t when the lag length of the model gets arbitrarily large. However, because of data limitations, one is forced to use a finite-order VAR model in the analysis. In this case, one can either consider the selected VAR as the true data-generating process (DGP) for the actual data, as a finite-order approximation to an underlying infinite-order linear model, or as a first-order Taylor approximation of a (in)finite order nonlinear model. Which of these three approaches is taken is essentially irrelevant in practice for two reasons. First, nonlinearities are typically of marginal interest in the VAR context, since monthly and quarterly macroeconomic variables are usually well approximated by linear time series processes (see Brock and Sayers, 1988). Second, except in the case of the computation of asymptotic standard errors and in determining the finite sample properties of estimators of functions of the VAR parameters, it will not matter which of the first two points of view is taken (see Lutkepohl, 1991).

In choosing the lag length of a finite-order unrestricted VAR model one must weigh two opposing considerations: the "curse of dimensionality" and the correct specification of the model. Since the number of parameters to be estimated quickly increases with the number of lags of the system, systems of moderate size become highly overparametrized relative to the total number of observations. This leads to poor and inefficient estimates of the short-run features of the data. A lag length that is too short, on the other hand, leaves unexplained information in the disturbance term, generating a statistical model where only a subset of the existing information is used to characterize the data and inducing spurious significance in the coefficients. The tradeoff between overparameteization and oversimplification is at the heart of almost all statistical selection criteria designed to choose the lag length of the autoregression (see Akaike's AIC, 1974; Schwarz's, 1978 SIC criteria; the modified likelihood ratio (MLR) procedure of Sims, 1980a; or the selection criteria suggested by Lutkepohl, 1991). While all these procedures are asymptotically equivalent, their small sample properties differ significantly and may depend on the true lag structure of the data generating process (see Nickelsburg, 1985; Lutkepohl, 1986).

One advantage of choosing the lag length of the VAR according to one of the above criteria is that the resulting model can be estimated using very simple tools. Because only predetermined variables and deterministic functions of time appear as right-side variables, and because the disturbances e_t are serially uncorrelated, OLS estimates of the VAR coefficients are consistent. In addition, because of the unrestricted nature of the model, single equation methods are (asymptotically) efficient. This is because a VAR model is a dynamic seemingly unrelated model (see Judge et al., 1980). Such a model has the property that the same right-side variables appear in each equation. Under this condition Zellner (1962) showed that single-equation methods are as efficient as systemwide methods no matter what the contemporaneous correlations among the disturbances are. In addition, when the e's are normal, OLS is efficient.

One drawback of choosing the lag length of the model using these selection procedures is that all the variables entering the system have identical lag lengths, which need not be a valid economic or statistical restriction, may reduce the efficiency of the estimates and, in some cases, even bias the results. To overcome this problem Hsiao (1981) suggested an approach that starts from univariate autoregression and sequentially adds lags and variables using predictive criteria. According to this criteria an additional variable should enter a univariate autoregression with a certain number of lags if it helps to improve the forecast of the endogenous variables—that is, if it Granger causes the left-side variable. Two drawbacks of this approach should also be mentioned. First, since the results of the predictive tests are treated as exact, the successive examination of hypothesis with economic content may be sensitive to type I errors committed at the specification stage.

Second, since the same variables do not appear in all equations, systemwide methods (such as full-information maximum likelihood (FIML)) are needed for efficient estimation. An alternative procedure to selection of the length of the VAR, which goes in the opposite direction of Hsiao's specific-to-general approach, has been popularized in the works of Hendry and Mizon (1990) and Clements and Mizon (1991), and it is thoroughly discussed in Chapter 4 of this book.

The idea that macroeconomic time series are stationary around, say, a deterministic polynomial function of time has come under debate in the last decade (see the original study by Nelson and Plosser, 1982). However, recent work by Perron (1989) and DeJong and Whiteman (1991) suggests that the evidence in favor of unit roots is not so overwhelming. While covariance stationarity is not needed to derive the Wold theorem, any estimation and testing procedure requires time invariance of the parameters of the model. Therefore, in specifying an unrestricted VAR model, a researcher has to take a stance on the sources of nonstationarity (deterministic or stochastic) and on the possible presence of shifts that may occur from time to time in economic time series. The choice made has implications for estimation and testing. For example, Phillips (1988) shows that knowledge of the order of integration of the variables of a regression and of the nature of deterministic components can be important in designing optimal inference. This is because testing hypotheses on coefficients of integrated variables requires nonstandard asymptotic theory. These considerations suggest that the appropriate modeling strategy to determine the long-run properties of each variable of the VAR model should be based on univariate unit roots tests (such as Dickey-Fuller, 1979; Phillips and Perron, 1986; Stock and Watson, 1989). However, as Engle and Granger (1987) have indicated, univariate unit root procedures may generate too many unit roots in a VAR. The solutions proposed to deal with this problem differ. Engle and Granger suggest writing the model in a vector error-correction form and use a two-step least-square procedure to estimate the parameters of interest. Johansen (1988) and Johansen and Joselius (1990) suggest jointly estimating cointegrating vectors, if they exist, and the coefficients of the VAR model by full-information maximum likelihood under rank restrictions on the matrix of long-run coefficients. Sims, Stock, and Watson (1990) suggest using an unrestricted VAR in levels and checking the order of integration of the variables and the number of cointegrating restrictions in order to know which asymptotic distribution applies.

To summarize, the classical approach to specification and estimation of VAR models involves two steps. First, one chooses a model that is dynamically well specified (in terms of variables included, lag length, noncorrelation, and, possibly, normality of the residuals), extracts as much information as possible from the data and tests for the order of integration of the data, taking into account the possibility of regime shifts, segmented trends, and so forth. Second, one can either transform the system and estimate the VAR coefficients using the two-step procedure of Engle and Granger, estimate the original VAR model under rank restrictions using the maximum-likelihood approach of Johansen, or estimate the coefficients of the untransformed, unrestricted model by OLS, equation by equation. In the first two cases testing of hypotheses on the coefficients of the transformed system can be undertaken using standard asymptotic theory. In the third case, the results of Sims, Stock, and Watson must be applied to test hypotheses of interest. As an intermediate step, it is possible to reduce the dimensionality of the system by eliminating either variables or lags that appear to be unimportant in explaining variations of the endogenous variables in one or more equations while maintaining a dynamically well-specified system. If this intermediate step is taken, single-equation methods of estimation of the second-step regression in Engle and Granger's procedure or of the untransformed system are no longer efficient.

An alternative strain of literature, originating from Litterman (1980, 1986) and described in Todd (1984), takes a Bayesian perspective to the specification of unrestricted VAR systems. The starting point of the approach is that in specifying econometric models one attempts to filter as much information as possible from the data. However, instead of relying on classical hypothesis testing or economic theory to decide whether a particular variable or lag should enter the VAR, these authors use a symmetric "atheoretical" prior on all variables to trade off overparametrization with oversimplification. The reason for taking an alternative route to the specification problem is that there is a very low signal-to-noise ratio in economic data and economic theory leaves a great deal of uncertainty concerning which economic structures are useful for inference and forecasting. Because highly parametrized unrestricted VAR models include many variables in each equation, the extraction filter is too wide and the noise obscures the relatively weak signal present in the data. The prior these authors employ is characterized by a small number of parameters and acts as an orientable antenna that, when appropriately directed, may clarify the signal. A specification search à-la Leamer (1978) over the parameters of the prior tunes up the filter for an optimal extraction of the information contained in a given data set. This approach to specification has two advantages over classical specification approaches. First, it avoids strong restrictions on which lags should enter the autoregression and refrains from specification testing procedures that may bias the examination of economic hypotheses. Second, it is flexible enough to allow different lag lengths to enter in different equations.

The prior typically appended to VAR models is nonstandard from the point of view of Bayesian analysis; it is objective in the sense that it is based on experience and reflects accepted rules in the forecasting community and is, in most cases, atheoretical because the restrictions implied by the prior have no economic interpretation. There are three basic observations underlying the specification of the prior. First, univariate random walks well represent the features of many series.

Second, the information contained in the far past of the series, has, in general, little importance in predicting current movements in the series. Third, both the conditional and the unconditional distribution of many variables seem to be shifting over time.

Because an unrestricted Bayesian VAR (BVAR) is nothing more than a state space-time-varying coefficient model, techniques developed for that framework can be used to estimate the unknown parameters of the model. In particular, maximum-likelihood estimates of the parameters of the model can be obtained by passing through the sample recursively with the Kalman filter algorithm (see Doan, Litterman, and Sims, 1984). In addition, in the special case considered by Litterman (1986)-a BVAR model is simply a VAR with a dummy observation appended to the system. In this special case the estimation of the model parameters can be carried out with a mixed-type estimation (see Theil, 1971). The result is a restricted estimator that shrinks the data toward the information contained in the prior.

Contrary to the classical approach previously discussed, the presence of trending variables in the system does not cause particular problems to this or any generic Bayesian approach (see Sims, 1988b; Sims and Ulhig, 1991). Inference in BVAR models is based, in fact, on the likelihood principle. The approach requires normal residuals, which may not always be a reasonable assumption, and good priors, which are not always easy to obtain, but is entirely invariant to the size of the dominant root of the system. As a consequence, no pretesting is need to determine which asymptotic distribution applies (the standard or the unit root one), and inferential procedures are considerably simplified.

It should be finally noted that a BVAR model is flexible enough to include as special cases several models that have been used to characterize the properties of macro and financial time series. Apart from the direct links with time varying coefficient (TVC) models (see Nicholls and Quinn, 1982), ARCH (Engle, 1982), ARCH-M (Engle, Lilien, and Robbins, 1987) models, bilinear models (Granger and Anderson, 1978), discrete regime shift models (Hamilton, 1989), and subordinated models (see Gallant, Hsieh, and Tauchen, 1991) can be nested and tested within a general BVAR specification (see Canova, 1993).

A final approach to specifying VAR's is linked to the observable index model literature (see Sargent and Sims, 1977; Quah and Sargent, 1993). The idea is to start from a completely unrestricted VAR model and examine whether an m-dimensional process x_t can be explained or predicted by past values of an index series η_t of dimension $r < m$. The economic rationale behind the scheme is that there is a low dimensional vector of variables (the states of the economy) that is responsible for most of the dynamic interdependencies of the economy. With these lenses, observable index models can be simply seen as providing an alternative focus to the overparametrization/oversimplification tradeoff. But there is also an alternative interpretation that may shed some light on the links between this approach and others. If we assume that one of the indices is a nonstationary process that is common to all series, this approach amounts to specifying and estimating a vector error-correction model or a common trend model (as in Stock and Watson, 1988) so that all the tools developed for these frameworks apply here as well. For the case in which all indices are stationary, Reinsel (1983) describes selection procedures for these models together with the theory for identification of the parameters, their estimation by maximum likelihood, and one approach to test the cross-equation restrictions implied by the index structure.

Semistructural Analyses with Unrestricted VARs

The Basic Philosophy

The previous section dealt with the specification and the estimation of VAR models. While these are important issues from a statistical point of view, and model selection is of crucial importance for forecasting purposes, the specification and estimation of an unrestricted VAR are only preliminary steps in undertaking economic analyses of the data. Because an unrestricted VAR is a reduced-form model, it is uninterpretable without reference to theoretical economic structures even when it is correctly specified and efficiently estimated. In other words, economic theory cannot simply be kept in the background during the analysis and used only as an organizing principle for the empirical research, as, for example, is the case when producing "stylized facts" in the empirical real business cycle literature. Instead, it must be employed (either in a weak or strong sense) in order to extract economically relevant information from the reduced form VAR innovations and moving average coefficients. This does not necessarily mean that one must have a well-specified economic model in mind to undertake the analysis (as is the case, for example, for Hansen and Sargent, 1980, 1991). In order to extract information about the behavior of agents in the economy one can appeal to a class of models that impose very generic restrictions on the data (such as long-run neutrality or superneutrality) or simply use informational constraints that are linked to the flow of information in the economy (see also Quah, 1991).

The issue of providing an economic interpretation of unrestricted VAR results is therefore linked to the question of the identification of a structural model from reduced form estimates. The terms *structure* and *structural* have many meanings in the economic literature. Some economists label *structural* a model where all parameters have economic interpretations in terms of preferences and technologies (Hansen and Sargent, 1980). Others claim that a model is structural if the consequence of a specific class of actions can be predicted by modifying part of the model (see Koopmans, 1963), if it is invariant to a specific class of actions (see Sargent and Lucas, 1980), or if it refers to the use of economic *a priori* hypothesis (Hendry and Mizon, 1990). Finally, some claim that a model is structural if it is in a particular mathematical form (see Harvey, 1985). Within the VAR literature, it is typical to term a model *structural* if it is possible to give distinct behavioral interpretations to the stochastic disturbances of the model. An example here may clarify our terminology. Consider a bivariate VAR with output and money. Then a structural model is obtained when it is economically meaningful to name the disturbances of the model—say, aggregate demand shocks, money supply shocks, and so on. From the perspective of identification, VARs are not dramatically different from those macroeconometric models that Sims criticized in his original (1980a) article. There is, however, a subtle difference in the approaches that concerns the style of identification employed. Traditional macroeconometric models typically were of large scale and attempted to identify and recover a structural model making frequent and extensive use of exclusion restrictions on the lags of some variables. Users of this type of models had in the back of their minds the dictates of the Cowles Commission that variables can be classified into endogenous and exogenous, where exogenous were those variables that were determined outside of the system and could be manipulated independently of the remaining variables. Exclusion restrictions on the lags of some variables were the practical tools to achieve this distinction.

Sims, echoing Liu (1960), criticized this procedure on the basis that there was no economic justification for the massive amount of exclusion restrictions employed to identify models and that these restrictions were routinely imposed without too much attention to the underlying economic structure. Given that economic theory placed very weak restrictions on the reduced-form coefficients and was essentially silent in deciding which variables must enter a reduced-form model, empirical research ought to be based on small-scale models that required a small number of constraints to be interpreted. In addition, and more important, users of unrestricted VAR models typically refrain from imposing restrictions on lag structure and, instead, attempt identification via restrictions on the contemporaneous or the long-run effects of behavioral shocks or on both. One reason for this choice is that the classification of variables in exogenous and endogenous is meaningless from the point of view of modern dynamic general equilibrium theory. In addition, theory has typically little to say about the time response of the variables of the system to shocks, while it has somewhat stronger predictions on lag time needed for the response to take place—for example, theory may have something to say on how monetary policy shocks affect the real side of the economy or on their long-run effects but not much to say regarding the magnitude of the responses three periods after a monetary shock has occurred. Interesting restrictions on the contemporaneous or the long-run impact of behavioral shocks are not numerous, but they are typically sufficient to just identify the disturbances of a small system of variables.

It is useful at this point to stress that the scope of economic analysis undertaken with VARs is not philosophically different from the analyses undertaken under the rational expectations econometric program pioneered by Hansen and Sargent (1980, 1991). Also, in this case, the objects of interest are various sources of innovations to an agent's information set and their effect on the endogenous variables of the system. However, the way these objects are recovered from the reduced-form VARs is different. Rational expectations models typically involve an extensive set of cross-equation restrictions that, when imposed on the VAR, allow the recovery of the so-called deep parameters of agents' preferences, technologies, and constraints. Because of the interrelationship between forcing variables and variables determined in equilibrium by agents' behavior, there are typically more constraints than reduced-form parameters, so a rational expectation econometrician can give additional content to the theory by testing the validity of these additional restrictions.

A VAR econometrician can be thought of as a rational expectation econometrician who is skeptical of many of the restrictions that a particular formulation of dynamic economic theory imposes on the VAR coefficients. Therefore, in order to produce a structural interpretation of the VAR model, he uses only a limited number of these constraints and "lets the data speak" regarding certain policy questions. A rational expectation econometrician, on the other hand, uses all the restrictions that a particular formulation of the theory imposes in order to produce refutable structures from the reduced-form VAR model. The main difference here is therefore on the extent of the economic restrictions employed, not on their merit or their usefulness. To put the argument in another way, the number of restrictions needed to identify behavioral disturbances is substantially smaller than the number of restrictions that a rational expectation econometrician imposes on the VAR to identify structural parameters and validate the model. It is also clear that, because a VAR econometrician uses only a subset of the theoretical restrictions, he can undertake only a limited set of interesting economic experiments. For example, he cannot undertake experiments that change the probability distributions of the behavioral disturbances. In this case, the famous Lucas's critique applies, and the exercise are meaningless. However, Sims (1982, 1988a) claims that although theoretically appropriate, the Lucas's critique should be nothing more that a cautionary footnote for skilled users of unrestricted VAR models. There are two reasons for this. First, the normal course of policy actions does not involve changes in the probability distribution of policy disturbances but instead can be seen as drawing different innovations from the existing distribution of disturbances. Second, forecasting the results of regime changes that have never been experimented with in the past or of situations that involve dramatic changes in the pattern of shocks may be dangerous in any model and should be avoided by anybody interested in providing policy advice. In other words, regime changes are rare events compared with everyday policymaking exercises, and because they are rare events, their effects can be predicted only with large errors, making prediction efforts somewhat hazardous.

It is also useful to compare the philosophy underlying identification and the economic analyses of unrestricted VAR models with the generalized method of moment (GMM) approach originated in Hansen (1982) and Hansen and Single-ton (1983). The GMM approach constitutes the most commonly used limited-information method of estimation and testing of fully specified general-equilibrium models. Because GMM procedures are typically applied to the Euler equations of dynamic models, an explicit final form for the endogenous variables of the system in terms of the exogenous shocks is not needed for estimation and testing. In this procedure, estimates of the parameters are obtained using the sample counterpart of the first-order condition of agents' optimization problems. Hence, while GMM is useful to test theories via the set of overidentifying restrictions that they impose on the data, the procedure is unable to recover structural shocks to agents' infor-mation set or to study their impact on the endogenous variables of the system.

Finally, it is useful to note that the scope of the so-called calibration approach to econometrics (see Kydland and Prescott, 1991; Danthine, 1992) shares com-mon features with economic analyses conducted with VARs. First, many of the models used in this literature have a restricted VAR representation where both cross-equation and exclusion restrictions appear (see Kydland and Prescott, 1982; King, Plosser, and Rebelo, 1988). Second, in both cases, econometricians are interested in the response of the variables of the system to well-identified shocks to agents' information set. However, because calibrators use completely specified general-equilibrium models and they match the deep parameters of preferences and technologies to sample averages of the data (what is typically termed *realistic parameterization* of the model), they can directly study the impact of shocks on the system without having to disentangle mongrel reduced-form coefficients. One way of contrasting the VAR and the calibration approaches is to note that a VAR econometrician obtains estimates of the objects of interest from reduced form coefficients—that is, given the data, he examines weakly restricted theoretical structures that are consistent with them. A calibrator imposes theoretical assump-tions on the structural coefficients that imply precise constraints for the reduced from coefficients—that is, given a theoretical structure, he examines whether a given set of parameters implies reduced-form evidence that is consistent with the data (see King, Plosser, and Rebelo, 1988, and Canova, Finn, and Pagan, 1993, among others for this interpretation).

From the above discussion it is clear that the philosophical approach of calibrators is similar to the one of rational expectation econometricians. The major difference is that calibrators directly estimate the deep parameters of the model while a rational-expectation econometrician estimates reduced-form coefficients subject to the identifying restrictions imposed by the theory. One additional difference should also be noted. Calibrators estimate parameters imposing economic restrictions on the error of the model (for example, they assume that the model's parameters are chosen so that it exactly fits the steady-state properties of the actual economies) while a RE econometrician estimates parameters imposing statistical assumptions on the error of the model (for example, normality).

Identification

The starting point of the identification process is the assumption that there is a class of dynamic theoretical models that deliver a solution for the endogenous variables of the model of the form

$$B(\ell)x_t = Fd_t + Su_t \tag{3.3}$$

where ℓ is the lag operator, the matrix polynomial $B(\ell)$ has all its roots not inside the unit circle, $B_0 \neq I$ and where $E(u_t u'_t)$ is a full-rank matrix and where the elements of $B(1) = \Sigma_j B_j$ may be, in principle, different from zero. The u's are primitive exogenous forces not directly observed by the econometrician that buffet the system and cause oscillation. Because the u's are among the primitives of the model, they are typically assumed to be contemporaneously and serially uncorrelated and can be given fairly specific behavioral interpretation. Models of this type can be found in Keynesian macro literature (see Taylor, 1980; Blanchard, 1989), in the rational-expectations literature (see Quah, 1990; Hansen, Roberds, and Sargent, 1991) and in the real business cycle literature (see King, Plosser, and Rebelo, 1988).

We assume that an econometrician investigates the properties of an unrestricted VAR model of the form

$$\Gamma(\ell)x_t = Gd_t + e_t, \tag{3.4}$$

where $\Gamma_0 = I$ and $E(e_t e'_t) = \Sigma_e$. If some of the components of x_t are nonstationary, we assume that both $B(\ell)$ and $\Gamma(\ell)$ can be decomposed as $B(\ell) = (I - \ell)\hat{B}(\ell)$, $\Gamma(\ell) = (I - \ell)\hat{\Gamma}(\ell)$. If some of the components are nonstationary but cointegrated, then the two above matrices have the form $B(\ell) = [(I - \ell)\hat{B}(\ell) - \tilde{B}\ell]$, $\Gamma(\ell) = [(I - \ell)\hat{\Gamma}(\ell) - \tilde{\Gamma}\ell]$ where $\tilde{B} = -B(1)$ and $\tilde{\Gamma} = -\Gamma(1)$. VAR users are generally interested in the u_t's from (3.3) since they are the primitives they want to examine and manipulate for policy analyses and not in the e_t's, which do not have an clear economic interpretation.

The moving average representation for the theoretical model and the data are, respectively,

$$y_t = M(\ell)d_t + N(\ell)B_0^{-1}Su_t$$

$$= M(\ell)d_t + N(1)B_0^{-1}Su_t + N^*(\ell)B_0^{-1}S\Delta u_t \tag{3.5}$$

$$y_t = H(\ell)d_t + C(\ell)e_t$$

$$= H(\ell)d_t + C(1)e_t + C^*(\ell)\Delta e_t \tag{3.6}$$

where y_t is a stationary inducing transformation of x_t, such as $y_t = (I - \ell)x_t$, $\Delta u_t = u_t - u_{t-1}$, $\Delta e_t = e_t - e_{t-1}$, $M(\ell) = F * \hat{B}(\ell)^{-1}$, $H(\ell) = G * \hat{\Gamma}^{-1}(\ell)$, $N(\ell) = \hat{B}^{-1}(\ell)$, $C(\ell) = \hat{\Gamma}^{-1}(\ell)$, and where $N^*(\ell) \equiv \dfrac{N(\ell) - N(1)}{1 - \ell}$ and $C^*(\ell) \equiv \dfrac{C(\ell) - C(1)}{1 - \ell}$.

Matching the coefficients of the moving average representations (3.5) and (3.6), we have

$$M(\ell) = H(\ell), \tag{3.7}$$

$$N(\ell)B_0^{-1}Su_t = C(\ell)e_t. \tag{3.8}$$

An alternative formulation of the second restriction, which can be derived from the second equality appearing in (3.5) and (3.6), is in terms of the long-run multipliers $N(1)$ and $C(1)$ and of innovations the theoretical and VAR model:

$$N(1)B_0^{-1}S = C(1), \tag{3.9}$$

$$B_0^{-1}Su_t = e_t. \tag{3.10}$$

The question of identification can then be posed in the following way: under what conditions is knowledge about the reduced-form VAR parameters and innovations sufficient to recover objects that may be of interest to the economic analyst? Clearly, unless the restrictions imposed by modern dynamic macroeconomic models are not taken into account, there is little hope of disentangling the "deep" parameters of preferences and technologies from the VAR coefficients and, as a consequence, little hope of recovering a model which is structural according to Lucas's terminology. Sims (1986), however, has argued that there is no need to recover the deep parameters of preferences and technologies to predict the consequences of specific policy actions. In other words, with meaningful economic restrictions it is possible to extract from a VAR a generic structure, which may not satisfy Lucas's criteria for policy intervention but is still useful to indicate the impact of policy actions that fall within the realm of historical experience. And this may be everything that an econometrician is interested and entitled to do.

To distinguish the analyses that originated from Sims's ideas from the structural analyses based on Lucas's critique, I will call these activities *semistructural analyses*. Semistructural VAR analyses require the identification of behavioral shocks and predicting the effect of a particular shock or a particular path of behavioral shocks on the endogenous variables of the system. For example, one may be interested in disentangling a monetary policy shock from the VAR disturbances in order to study the effect of a once-and-for-all one standard error monetary policy impulse or the effect of a particular path of monetary policy shocks on prices, output, and interest rates (see Sims, 1986; Canova, 1991; Leeper and Gordon, 1992). Alternatively, one may be interested in disentangling generic aggregate demand or supply disturbances and in studying the contribution of each of them to the variability of output or whether one of these shocks generates a particular historical episode (see Shapiro and Watson, 1989; Blanchard, 1989; Blanchard and Quah, 1989; Gali, 1992). To undertake such analyses, given estimates of e_t and of Σ_e, an investigator must commit himself to a particular class of theoretical structures to obtain an estimate of u_t from (3.7) and (3.8).

Giannini (1992) describes in great detail necessary and sufficient statistical conditions needed for the process of semistructural identification to be meaningful and provides a way to estimate and test VAR models that are overidentified. In essence, the statistical conditions for identification require that either rank or order conditions must be imposed on the theoretical model for the VAR coefficients and disturbances to convey information about theoretical coefficients and behavioral innovations. The order condition simply involves counting the number of free parameters and the number of restrictions imposed by (3.7) and (3.8) and checking whether the number of restrictions is larger or smaller than the number of parameters to be recovered. If the dimension of x_t is m, identification of all the behavioral shocks of the system requires $m \times m$ restrictions. The rank condition involves checking whether the space defined by the restrictions (3.7) and (3.8) has a full column rank. Roughly speaking, this condition implies that for identification to be meaningful the restrictions must be "correctly" placed on the system.

The question of interest in this section is, however, different from simple accounting of the conditions needed for identification. We are interested in the following problem: does theory impose enough meaningful economic restrictions for the identification process to be fruitful? In other words, can we justify the identifying restrictions we impose on the VAR from an economic point of view? It is clear that this question is very similar to the question raised by large-scale macro modelers or even by users of VARs that follow the so-called LSE style of analysis (see Hendry and Mizon, 1990).

As we already mentioned, the main difference with large-scale macro models is that in our case x_t is of small dimension so that the number of economic restrictions required to go from the VAR to the structural model is not overwhelming. In addition, for any given dimension of x_t, if we can demonstrate that components of x_t are nonstationary and cointegrated, the number of economic restrictions needed to achieve identification is smaller. This is an important point for the weakly restricted style of identification described here. Users of unrestricted VAR models who attempt semistructural identifications are typically skeptical of the usefulness of many of the constraints imposed by economic theory and believe that the set of uncontroversial restrictions is generally small. The presence of nonstationary components therefore lightens the burden of the VAR econometrician in terms of finding interesting economic restrictions to impose on the system. As compared with the Hendry and Mizon methodology, described in Chapter 4 of this volume, a semistructural VAR econometrician typically places restrictions on contemporaneous or long-run multipliers, not on lagged relationships or interim multipliers of the model. But this division need not be clear cut because, as discussed in Quah (1991), a semistructural VAR econometrician may be interested in studying the effect of a disturbance—say, a monetary shock—that leaves real wages unchanged over the adjustment path of other variables, in which case identification requires restrictions over the rows of $C(\ell)$ and $N(\ell)$, not on short-run or long-run impacts.

Hence the distinction between a semistructural VAR, a parsimonious VAR that is congruent with economic theory (see Hendry and Mizon, 1990), and a standard dynamic simultaneous equation model is a matter of degree, not of content. The two basic questions are (1) whether prior information should be imposed at the stage of construction or estimation of the model or if one should wait to extract as much information as possible from the data and use the *a priori* information at a later stage of the analysis and (2) whether economic restrictions are more sensibly paced on lagged relationships or on contemporaneous or long-run correlations.

Practical Details

For many models of interest, the relationship between a particular structure and the reduced-form VAR model holds at all lags. Therefore, one is free to choose restrictions for contemporaneous correlations, for long-run correlations, or for both. Initial users of VAR models (see Sims, 1980b, 1982) were not concerned with nonstationarities. Therefore the long-run multipliers $C(1)$ and $N(1)$ were assumed to be zero, and the restrictions used to identify the system were of the form (3.7) and (3.8). Within this class of restrictions, a typical choice was to assume that the unobservable behavioral disturbances contemporaneously impacted on one equation only—that is, $S = I$—and that the observables had a particular contemporaneous structure—that is, B_0 lower triangular (see Sargent, 1979; Sims, 1980b; Litterman and Weiss, 1985). This choice was originally proposed as a mechanical instrument to avoid data mining and to reduce the investigator's discretion in imposing unjustified restrictions (see Sims, 1980a). The approach is very simple since it involves only the computation of the Choleski decomposition of the covariance matrix of the VAR residuals. To see this note that, for $S = I$, (3.10) implies that $var(u_t) = B_0^{-1} \Sigma_e B_0^{-1\prime}$. If, in addition, we assume that $var(u_t) = I$, as we have done in the previous subsection, then B_0 is the Choleski decomposition of Σ_e—that is, B_0 is a lower triangular orthogonal matrix. Once these restrictions are imposed, the behavioral shock i does not contemporaneously affect variable k if the index k precedes index i in the list of the elements of x_t. The semistructural model is then said to be in Wold causal chain form. One implication of this choice is that if i and k are the only two variables in the system, then shock i fails to instantaneously Granger cause variable k (see Geweke, 1982).

One problem immediately noted by early VAR users was that the Choleski decomposition is unique up to a premultiplication by an orthonormal matrix—that is, $\Sigma_e = B_0 B_0' = B_0 A A' B_0$ where $A' = A^{-1}$. This implies that the space of mechanical transformations is equal to the number of possible permutations of the variables of the system—that is, the dimension is $m!$—and selecting one of the many transformations imposes a particular causal ordering on the variables of the system. Since there is no *a priori* reason to believe that economic variables can be ranked according to a particular causal ordering, identification achieved in this way contains an element of arbitrariness. Therefore, for the results to be considered meaningful, a researcher must show that the conclusions are robust to the choice of ordering. Robustness analysis is typically done by trying alternative orderings of the variables of the system (see the RATS manual: Doan, 1994). If the covariance matrix of the VAR innovations is approximately diagonal, the ordering of the variables is unimportant for the essence of the results. A Wold causal chain is a reasonable approximation in such an occasion, and the economic interpretation of the results is independent of the ordering chosen. However, if Σ_ε has large off-diagonal elements, different orderings of the variables will give different approximations, and results must be interpreted with caution, even after robustness analysis is carried out.

A second problem—noted, for example, by Cooley and Leroy (1985) and Leamer (1985)—has to do with the economic interpretation of the exercise. As we noted, the scope of the identification is to link the VAR to an interpretable economic model. The objection raised by these authors can be cast in these terms: how many economic models come in a contemporaneously recursive form—that is, have a structure where variables on the top of the triangle contemporaneously feed into all the other variables, and the variables on the bottom of the triangle contemporaneously affect only themselves? The above two papers claim that the class of such models is very thin and that, lacking such models, this style of identification leads to uninterpretable results. In other words, the disturbances recovered with a mechanical Choleski decomposition are linear combinations of the true behavioral shocks driving the system and as such uninterpretable. As we observed, dynamic structural economic models may place restrictions on the correlation among observables (the B_0 matrix), on the correlation among unobservables (the S matrix), or on both. In choosing one of these structures one ends up selecting a particular model for the correlation among variables. As emphasized by Blanchard (1989), absent meaningful economic motivation, such a choice is arbitrary.

The answer to this important objection has been to impose more economic structure on the restrictions employed to identify the system. The restrictions however, still remain generic, in the sense that they are generated by a large class of models that cover most of the existing camps. Four major approaches have been proposed. The first one, which emerges in the work of Bernanke (1986), Blanchard and Watson (1986), Blanchard (1989), Evans (1989), and Gali and Hammour (1991), maintains the basic identification style of earlier works but places restrictions on both the B_0 and S matrices and provides explicit economic justification for each choice. The second one, contained in the work of Sims (1986) and Canova (1991), instead of employing both debatable and scarce economic restrictions, uses knowledge about the flow of information in the economy to restrict the matrices B_0 and S and to recover generic semistructural models. The third one, pioneered by Blanchard and Quah (1989), Shapiro and Watson (1989), and King et al. (1991) exploits the nonstationarity of the data to impose restrictions on the long-run multipliers of the structural model—that is, the $N(1)$ matrix. A fourth approach, suggested by Gali (1992), mixes aspects of the first and the third approaches to achieve identification.

The first approach is sufficiently self-explanatory and does not require further comment. Because identification achieved via the second approach does not typically involve restrictions derived from economic theory, a simple example may clarify the usefulness and the limits of this approach. Suppose two of the variables of the system are nominal GNP and money and that a VAR econometrician is interested in studying whether monetary policy has effects on nominal GNP. Because of lags in data collection, it is known that GNP data becomes available only once every three months. Given this informational delay, it is reasonable to suppose that within a month, GNP is not a variable in the reaction function of the monetary authorities. This informational lag therefore provides identifying information that can be used to recover a behavioral rule used by the monetary authority. It is important to stress that the above identification procedure does not imply that over longer horizons (even a quarter) the monetary authorities do not use information contained in GNP data in setting targets for the growth rate of the money supply. There are two advantages of this approach. First, because this approach is less theoretically bound, it can be more useful in investigating controversial relationships that may otherwise require stringent assumptions on the nature of the behavioral shocks impinging on the system. Second, because informational delays are very common, there are often more than enough restrictions to identify particular shocks or, in some cases, the entire vector of behavioral shocks.

The use of long-run restrictions to identify a VAR has been motivated as a way of generating an unrestricted "permanent-transitory" decomposition for time series with unit roots that overcomes the lack of interpretability of traditional decompositions such as those of Beveridge and Nelson (1981) or Watson (1986). A VAR identified with long-run restrictions imposes an arbitrary but specific structure on the permanent and transitory components of the series and provides a useful measure of the relative importance of permanent components in explaining cyclical fluctuations in the system. However, while the use of long-run restrictions to identify the system has appealing features from the point of view of economic theory, the number of meaningful and uncontroversial long-run restrictions is limited, so for systems of medium size one hopes to have, at best, enough constraints to be able to just identify the model. In addition, disturbances identified via long-run restrictions cannot be in general related with interpretable economic news to agents information set. For example, a shock that has long-run effects can be classified as a supply disturbance (such as a technology shock) or a demand disturbance (a fiscal shock). Alternatively, a shock that has only transitory impact could be either real or monetary. In other words, disturbances recovered via long-run restrictions are indices comprising linear combinations of "economically meaningful disturbances" with no immediate behavioral interpretation.

As already mentioned, when the variables of the VAR are nonstationary but cointegrated, the burden of finding identifying restrictions is lighter, since the presence of cointegration implies that the number of shocks driving the system (the so-called common trends) is of smaller dimension than the vector x_t. In practical terms, the fact that the variables of the systems are nonstationary but cointegrated means that $N(1)$ is a matrix of reduced rank. If the dimension of x_t is m and there are p common trends, then the rank of $N(1)$ is $m - p$. This means that there are only $m - p$ independent sources of disturbances that have long-run effects. Hence, if cointegration is present, we need only $m \times m - p$ restrictions instead of $m \times m$ to be able to identify all the behavioral disturbances of the model. King et al. (1991), Quah (1991), and Wickens (1992) examine this situation in detail. Two points regarding the usefulness of cointegration restrictions to identification can be made. First, because unit root and cointegration tests appear to have very little power against the trend stationary alternative, the results may be very sensitive to the treatment of trends, and identification schemes that condition the economic analysis on weak statistical findings should be taken with great care. Second, although the imposition of cointegration restrictions helps identification by decreasing the number of restrictions needed to undertake a semistructural analysis, it helps, in a somewhat uninteresting way, by shifting the burden of finding an underlying structure away from economic theory onto the characterization of the statistical properties of economic time series. In other words, the relevant question becomes one about the existence of unit roots and cointegration rather than of economic behavior.

Summarizing the Results

If the statistical conditions for identification are satisfied and the restrictions are placed either on B_0 or on S or $N(1)$, one can employ either an indirect least-squares (ILS) procedure as in Sims (1986) or a two-stage least-squares procedure (2SLS) as in Blanchard (1989) to estimate the free parameters of the model. The first procedures involves first the computation of unrestricted VAR coefficients and of the variance covariance matrix of the VAR shocks. Then, given a particular theoretical structure, one manipulates these quantities to obtain estimates of the free parameters of the model. A 2SLS procedure imposes the identifying restrictions directly on the VAR system and obtains estimates of the free parameters using an instrumental variable procedure. When a system is just identified the two procedures yield the same estimators (see Shapiro and Watson, 1989). If the restrictions are placed on both the B_0 and the S matrices or both B_0 and $N(1)$, the ILS and 2SLS procedures are inapplicable, in which case one could employ a method of moments approach as suggested (Bernanke, 1986). For systems that do not have a special recursive structure or zeros appropriately placed and for overidentified systems, Giannini (1992) develops a full-information maximum-likelihood (FIML) estimator of the structural parameters and a formal test for overidentifying restrictions. Canova (1991) obtains estimates of the free parameters of the model using a latent variable procedure.

Once behavioral economic disturbances are recovered from reduced-form VAR innovations, summary statistics for interesting economic exercises can be collected. In the semistructural VAR tradition, the typical summary statistics reported are based on innovation accounting exercises. For example, one may be interested in the matrix of structural MA coefficients $N(\ell)$ since it gives information about the effects of behavioral shocks on the variables of the system in the short and long runs. Each N_j, $j > 1$ in fact describes the response of the vector x_t to innovations in a behavioral disturbance that occurred j-periods ago. The k-row of each N_j measures the responses of x_{kt} to innovations in the system that occurred j periods ago, $j = 0, 1, \ldots$. Finally, the hth element of the kth row of $N(1)$ measures the cumulative effect on x_{kt} of the behavioral innovation with index h that occurred j-periods ago, where $j \to \infty$. Operationally, the coefficients of the structural MA representation can be obtained by setting recursively each behavioral shock of the system equal to 1 at time $t - j$ and zero afterwards and simulating the responses of the components of x_{t-j+r}, $r = 1, \ldots, R$.

An alternative way of summarizing the information contained in an innovation accounting exercise is via the variance decomposition. To compute the variance decomposition of x_t note that from (3.5)

$$var(x_t) = N(\ell)B_0^{-1}SEu_tu_t'S'B_0^{-1'}N(\ell^{-1})'. \tag{3.11}$$

To see exactly what the above expression entails, consider the case where $m = 2$. Then, the variance of x_{1t} has two components: one due to the impact of its own innovations from time $t - j$ to time t, $j = 1, 2, \ldots$ and one due to innovations in x_{2t} from time $t - j$ to time t. If x_{2t} is shocked at time $t - j$ and left unperturbed afterward, we can examine how much of the variability of x_{1t} at time t is due that structural innovation, for all j. As (3.11) makes it clear, the variance decomposition does not add new information to the impulse response analysis but, instead, presents it in an alternative form.

The variance decomposition and the impulse response function are, essentially, in-sample forecasting exercises. They describe the effect on the system of a behavioral disturbance of typical size, where by *typical* one usually means either a shock or a sequence of behavioral disturbances that, on average, have occurred during the sample period. One alternative way of summarizing the results of the analysis is to perform a historical decomposition of x_t—that is, examine the contribution of each of the behavioral disturbances to the level of x_t. For example, if the dimension of x_t is $m = 2$ and x_t is stationary, then $x_{1t} = x_{1t}^0 + x_{1t}^1 + x_{1t}^2$ is the historical decomposition of x_t where the first element is due to the deterministic components, $x_{1t}^1 = N_{11}^\dagger(\ell)u_{1t}$ and $x_{2t}^2 = N_{12}^\dagger(\ell)u_{2t}$ where $N_{ij}^*(\ell)$ is the i, j element of the matrix $N^\dagger(\ell) = N(\ell)B_0^{-1}S$. This type of analysis may be very useful when a researcher is interested in attributing an historical episode to one particular behavioral or policy disturbance. For example, if the VAR includes money and output and a stock price index, it may be of interest to know if the monetary contraction of 1929, which could be represented by a series of large negative disturbances to a monetary policy equation, is responsible for the great depression, as Friedman and Schwartz (1963) claim, or if instead, it is due to an outlier disturbance in, say, an equation representing the behavior of financial markets.

Initial users of VAR models reported point estimates of the impulse responses and of the variance decomposition. As in a simple regression framework, the presentation of point estimates of the MA coefficients is not very useful unless standard errors are also provided. This is particularly important when the scope of the economic analysis is to investigate the long-run response of endogenous variables to behavioral shocks. Runkle (1987) shows that the N_j matrices for moderately large j tend to be very imprecisely estimated, with the measure of dispersion around the point estimate increasing with the lag length p of the VAR and the size m of the system. Blanchard (1987) and Watson (1987) consider possible ways to reduce the uncertainty around the point estimates of these statistics. They both find that meaningful economic restrictions (such as homogeneity of real variables with respect to nominal shocks or common trends in the variables) do not seem to help in reducing the size of the standard errors of the estimated impulse responses and variance decompositions. Watson, however, conjectures that constraints on the lag polynomials may be useful and presents a simple example where this is the case. These constraints may come from Granger causal orderings of the variables, uncertain restrictions like those imposed by BVAR models or fully Bayesian priors. The results contained in Canova (1991) confirm Watson's conjecture.

Because of the complicated structure of the N_j matrices, the asymptotic distribution of estimators of N_j has been worked out only relatively recently. Baillie (1987) derived a general form for the asymptotic distribution of maximum likelihood (ML) estimators of the impulse response function. Lutkepohl (1991) provides a simpler expressions for the asymptotic covariance matrix of ML estimators of the impulse-response function under alternative assumptions about the underlying data-generating process.

Since the asymptotic distribution of the impulse responses and of the variance decomposition was impossible to compute analytically until very recently, Runkle (1987) suggested using either a bootstrap technique and an approximate Monte Carlo approach to calculate standard errors of the statistics of interest. Sims (1987) argues that neither procedure is appropriate even as an approximation and suggests basing inference on posterior standard errors computed using full-fledged Monte Carlo methods. A comparative study of the small sample properties of different procedures appears in Griffiths and Lutkepohl (1990). They find that the asymptotic theory works well in small samples when near unit roots are present and even when the normality assumption is violated. They also find that among bootstrap, Monte Carlo simulation, and asymptotic procedures there is no clear winner for all lags and all parameter configurations.

Some Problems with the Interpretation of the Results

Number of Shocks and Semistructural VARs

One important issue, often neglected in all the semistructural VAR literature, is the correct number of behavioral disturbances buffeting the system. In many cases analysts investigate the properties of bivariate systems and identification is limited, say, to one source of supply and one source of demand disturbances. Alternatively, one assumes that existing variables have been marginalized with respect other potential sources of structural disturbances so that there is a one-to-one matching of endogenous variables and shocks generating them. Both of these approaches are obvious simplifications, and it should be clear that a misspecification of the number of shocks driving the structural system is likely to create problems. For example, if there are two sources of supply disturbances and one demand disturbance and an investigator uses a bivariate model where only one source of supply disturbance is identified, he is likely to confuse the impact of different structural disturbances and bound to produce uninterpretable impulse responses. Blanchard and Quah (1989) provide an example where these issues are thoroughly discussed. In essence, correct identification of at least one "type" of shock is possible if and only if the distributed lag responses of the variables of the system are sufficiently similar across types of behavioral disturbances—that is, all supply disturbances and all demand disturbances.

While the above problem is typical of small-scale VAR models, users of semistructural VAR models may also face the opposite problem. For example, a semistructural VAR researcher may have in mind the implications of a RBC model when imposing identification restrictions. However, existing RBC models are typically driven by no more than one or two shocks, so that the vector of endogenous variables may have a theoretical covariance matrix that is singular. This observation is also relevant if a semistructural VAR researcher has in mind the implications of a class of linear quadratic rational expectation models when imposing identifying restrictions. It is clear that in these situations, without further assumptions, the behavioral disturbances are not identified. And note that the typical assumptions used in this case, such as measurement errors or omitted variables, may not be sufficient to recover the true sources of behavioral disturbances unless the variables measured with error or omitted are serially and contemporaneously uncorrelated with the true disturbances.

A further but related problem emerges if, instead of structural models with shocks that have a generic behavioral interpretation, one is interested in relating VAR disturbances to general equilibrium shocks. Because of the general equilibrium assumption, shocks to agents information set have both a supply-type of effect and a demand-type effect. This is the case for example of technology or government expenditure shocks that directly affect agents utility, which may both increase output and demand because of the wealth effect of the shock. Structural disturbances that represent generic aggregate demand and supply shocks may therefore have very little relationship with these shocks and the analyses conducted on the basis of these identification schemes have dubious general equilibrium interpretations.

Fundamentalness and Semistructural VARs

As already mentioned, many dynamic rational expectations economic models deliver solutions for the endogenous variables that come in the form of VARs.

There are situations however, when a VAR econometrician, observing current and past realizations of the endogenous variables, is unable to recover the behavioral shocks and their effects on the system. This occurs, in general, when agents in computing their decision rule have an information set that is larger than the one available to the econometrician. Typically, the fact that econometricians have smaller information sets than economic agents is the rule rather than the exception, and in many instances this is not a problem as endogenous variables are fully revealing. That is, studying the behavior of available endogenous variables allows a VAR researcher to discover the correct relationship between "the news" and the endogenous variables even though the researcher never observes the news directly. Technically speaking, the endogenous variables are fully revealing of their relationships with unobserved news when the structural moving average representation linking the endogenous variables to the behavioral shocks is fundamental— that is, the space spanned by current and lagged x's is the same as the space spanned by the behavioral innovations (see Quah, 1992). Among the class of equivalent Wold MA representations, a semistructural VAR econometrician *always* recovers the MA that is "fundamental" (see Hansen and Sargent, 1980). This fact has been used by West (1988) and Campbell and Deaton (1989) in rejecting explanations of excess smoothness of consumption based on agents having larger information sets than econometricians.

Leeper (1989), Quah (1990), Hansen, Roberds, and Sargent (1991), Hansen and Sargent (1991), and Lippi and Reichlin (1993), however, have constructed theoretical models where the solution for the endogenous variables are not fully revealing of their relationship with the unobserved news. In their models the theoretical representation of the decision rule of agents has a nonfundamental moving average representation—that is, the space spanned by current and lagged x's is smaller than the space spanned by behavioral innovations. In this case, a semistructural VAR econometrician following the procedures described in this chapter fails to recover the objects of interest of his analysis.

There does not appear to be one unifying explanation for how this phenomenon may appear. In Leeper, nonfundamentalness is induced by the policy-reaction function of the fiscal authority. Because tax decisions are made through a legislative process that evolves slowly, economic agents may know next-period fiscal variables when making current consumption and saving decisions. An econometrician who lacks data on unobservable tax shocks and naively identifies tax news with the innovations in the tax process will be unable to uncover the correct relationship between taxes and other endogenous variables because his VAR will not be fully revealing of the relationship between news and endogenous variables. Quah generates nonfundamentalness by assuming that agents in the economy react to two types of shocks to labor income (permanent and transitory) while the econometrician simply observes the realization of the process for labor income.

When using a bivariate VAR process on consumption and labor income, the VAR econometrician will not be able to recover either the permanent and transitory shocks or their effect on consumption and labor income using current and past values of these variables. Hansen and Sargent describe a simple linear quadratic rational-expectations model of demand and supply, which under certain choices of the parameters leads to a theoretical decision rule for prices and quantities that displays a nonfundamental MA representation. They also explicitly show how the innovations and the impulse responses recovered by the econometrician are related to the true demand and supply shocks and their true effects on prices and quantities. Hansen, Roberds, and Sargent show the theoretical conditions under which a bivariate VAR model on deficit and debt can give information about present value budget constraint relationships. Finally, Lippi and Reichlin add technological diffusion to Blanchard and Quah's (1989) model. This addition implies that the theoretical representation for the bivariate process for unemployment and output displays nonfundamentalness.

These examples all show that the class of theoretical models that may generate decision rules for the endogenous variables that have a nonfundamental representation is not thin in any sense. Blanchard and Quah (1993) argue that any theoretical model with fundamental representation can be transformed into a model with nonfundamental representation without changing the underlying economic structure, by simply making use of particular orthogonal transformations (the Blaschke factors) of their MA representation. They note that nonfundamental representations can be obtained by appropriately renormalizing the system and these renormalizations are observationally equivalent to fundamental ones from the point of view of the autocovariance function of x_t. An example can be informative here. Suppose $d_t = 0$, $m = 2$, $\forall t$ and the theoretical MA has the form

$$\begin{pmatrix} x_{1t} \\ x_{2t} \end{pmatrix} = \begin{pmatrix} (1 + 4\ell) & 0 \\ 0 & (1 + 5\ell) \end{pmatrix} \begin{pmatrix} \varepsilon_{1t} \\ \varepsilon_{2t} \end{pmatrix}, \tag{3.12}$$

with $E(\varepsilon_{1t}\,\varepsilon'_{2t}) = I * \sigma_i^2$. The roots of the MA polynomial are -0.25 and -0.2, which are both less than 1 in modulus. In this case it is not possible to express ε_t's as a *convergent* linear combination of current and past x_t's. Therefore the above system is not in a fundamental MA form because the space spanned by the ε's is larger than the space spanned by the x's. It is easy to check that the x's generated from (3.12) and the x's generated by

$$\begin{pmatrix} x_{1t} \\ x_{2t} \end{pmatrix} = \begin{pmatrix} (1 + 0.25\ell) & 0 \\ 0 & (1 + 0.2\ell) \end{pmatrix} \begin{pmatrix} u_{1t} \\ u_{2t} \end{pmatrix}, \tag{3.13}$$

have the same autocovariance function. Now however, the u_t's and the x_t's span the same space, so that there exists an AR representation where current innovations can be expressed in terms of current and past x_t's with coefficients which are square summable—that is, if $\Sigma_j a_j x_{t-j} = u_t$ the coefficients a_j satisfy $\Sigma_j a_j^2 < \infty$. The system (3.13) is in a fundamental (Wold) MA form. Note that to go from (3.12) to (3.13) we have postmultiplied the MA coefficients by matrices like $\tilde{B} =$ diag $\left[\dfrac{(\ell - \alpha_i)}{1 - \overline{\alpha}_i \ell} \right]$ where α_i is the ith root of the original model and $\overline{\alpha}_i$ its complex conjugate, which have the property that $\hat{B}\hat{B}' = I$. Despite this generic observationally equivalent result, Lippi and Reichlin (1992) observe that there are less trivial nonfundamental transformations than the one obtained by Blanchard and Quah (1993). These transformations, which still have the same autocovariance function for x_t, have economic meaning and can be obtained by slightly changing the economic structure of the theoretical model.

The implications of these findings are, at the present, not fully explored. It is clear, however, that when the theoretical model delivers nonfundamental representations, VAR analysis fails to capture the news to economic agents and the their impact on the endogenous variables. One implication of these results is that one should at least check whether the results are sensitive to the assumption of fundamental representation implicit in the VAR analysis.

Aggregation and Semistructural VARs

Another difficulty that a VAR econometrician encounters in attempting to recover behavioral disturbances from the reduced-form VAR evidence has been pointed out by Hansen and Sargent (1991) and concerns the effects of time aggregation. Hansen and Sargent start from formulating an economic model in continuous time and show that a VAR econometrician has little hope of recovering innovations to agents' information set and of making sense of the discrete-time version of the MA coefficients recovered with standard innovation accounting exercises. They point out that when the continuous time MA coefficients are continuous functions of time, discrete-time innovations at t need not reflect the behavior of continuous time innovations near t, that the components of the discrete-time innovation vector are mixtures of the vector of continuous time innovations (a result that implies that Granger causality in discrete time may emerge even though in continuous time the components of vector processes are contemporaneously and serially uncorrelated among each other), and that the discrete-time MA coefficients will look like the sampled version of the continuous-time coefficients if and only if the equilibrium processes for the endogenous variables in continuous time is a VAR where only the coefficient on the first lag is different from zero.

These results have several implications for standard practice. First, discrete-time innovations tend to be distributed lags of the innovations in continuous time with memory that can go arbitrarily far in the past. This feature therefore implies that discrete-time "news" are weighted averages of the news hitting agents' information set over a possible large interval of time and, as such, need not to have much relationship with the true innovations at each t. Second, evidence of Granger causality in discrete-time data need not bear a relationship with the Granger causality existing in continuous time, unless the VAR econometrician finds no evidence of causality. Third, and as a consequence of the above, the impulse response analysis conducted in discrete time may have little relationship with the true continuous time impulse responses.

An Example

To demonstrate in practice some of the problems that may emerge with identification and interpretation of the results, I next present an example where it is possible to quantify the significance of certain assumptions and to measure the distortions implied by particular identification schemes.

I consider a version of the bivariate model studied by Quah (1990) where disposable income is a random process that has two components and agents take it as given. I assume that agents hold rational expectations and that they are interested in choosing the best possible path for consumption over time. Depending on the assumptions I will make, the two components of income have different interpretations.

The first one, suggested by Quah (1990), is that one component represents the permanent part of income and the second one the transitory part. The two components are theoretically identified by the assumption that the disturbances are uncorrelated and that, by definition, the transitory part is a process that has no long-run effects on the level of income. Note that in this interpretation, the two components are simply indices that need not have a unique economic interpretation. They can be identified with supply and demand shocks (as, for example, in Blanchard and Quah, 1989) or with real and monetary shocks (as in Robertson and Wickens, 1992).

The second interpretation identifies the first component with the result of private agents' behavior and the second component with policy behavior. For example, the second component of income may be driven by a shock that can be called the *stochastic income tax rate* while the first component can be driven by technology shocks. A model with this type of interpretation is provided by Leeper (1989). These two components may be contemporaneously uncorrelated if government policy is exogenous to the economy, contemporaneously correlated if the policy authority reacts to the current state of the economy or correlated with a lag if, within the unit of time of the model (such as the quarter), the policy authority does not see the current state of the economy.

Within these two interpretations we will consider two cases—one where the theoretical model generates a moving average representation that is fundamental for the joint consumption-income process and one where the representation is not fundamental.

Formally speaking, the process for income will be of the form

$$y_t = y_{1t} + y_{2t},$$
$$y_{1t} = a_1(\ell)u_{1t},$$
$$y_{2t} = a_2(\ell)u_{2t}. \tag{3.14}$$

$a_j(\ell)$ are polynomials in the lag operator and $E(u_t u_t') = \Sigma$ where $u_t' = [u_{1t}, u_{2t}]'$. In Model I, I assume that $a_1(0) \neq 0$, that $a_2(0) = 0$ where $a_j(0) \equiv a_{j0}$, and that $\Sigma = \text{diag}(\sigma_1, \sigma_2)$ so that u_{2t} does not instantaneously Granger cause u_{1t}. In Model II, I will assume that $a_1(1) \neq 0$ and that $a_2(1) = 0$ where $a_j(1) \equiv \Sigma_j a_j$ and that $\Sigma = \text{diag}(\sigma_1, \sigma_2)$ so that y_{1t} has a unit root but y_{2t} does not.

Following Quah (1990), if agents have rational expectations and maximize utility using a fixed interest rate to compute future annuities, the resulting theoretical bivariate moving-average representation for income and consumption will be of the form

$$\begin{pmatrix} \Delta y_t \\ \Delta c_{2t} \end{pmatrix} = \begin{pmatrix} a_1(\ell) & a_2(\ell)(1-\ell) \\ a_1(\beta) & a_2(\beta)(1-\ell) \end{pmatrix} \begin{pmatrix} u_{1t} \\ u_{2t} \end{pmatrix}, \tag{3.15}$$

where β is the agents' discount factor and $a_j(\beta) \equiv a_j(\ell = \beta)$. Note that if $\beta < 1$, Models I and II generate a nonfundamental MA representation, while if $\beta > 1$, both models generate fundamental representations (so that in total we have four different data-generating processes (DGP)). For all the experiments with Model I $a_1(\ell) = 0.6 - 0.3\ell + 0.2\ell^2$ and $a_2(\ell) = 0.0 + 0.2\ell - 0.5\ell^2$. For all the experiments with Model II $a_1(\ell) = 0.6 - 0.3\ell + 0.2\ell^2$ and $a_2(\ell) = 1.0 + 0.2\ell - 0.5\ell^2$. The discount factor beta can take two values $\beta = 0.96$ or $\beta = 1.04$ where the last value is selected following the considerations contained in Kocherlakota (1990).

We simulate data out (3.15) assuming that the time interval of the model is a quarter. For each of the four bivariate processes generated, we estimate a VAR(4), apply two identification schemes, and attempt to interpret the "structural innovations" and the corresponding structural impulse responses. The first identification scheme is the same as Blanchard and Quah (1989), where one of the shocks has no long-run effect on the variables of the system. The second is one where one of the shocks has no contemporaneous impact on the variables of the system. Figures

3.1 and 3.2 present the results. The first and the third rows of both figures report the responses of Δy, while the second and the fourth rows the responses of Δc for each of the two processes. In Figure 3.1 $\beta = 1.04$, in Figure 3.2 $\beta = 0.96$. The first column presents the theoretical responses; the second the responses generated with an identification scheme that places zeros on the contemporaneous correlation among shocks; the third the responses generated with a Blanchard and Quah decomposition. The solid line in each box is the response to shock 1, and the dashed line is the response to shock 2.

The results of the simulation exercise display some interesting features. First, when the DGP is a fundamental MA process, even when the choice of identification is correct (as it is the case of identification 1 when DGP1 is the true process and identification 2 when DGP2 is the true process), there may be some error in determining the size of the initial impact of the shocks (there is a downward bias of about 50 to 80 percent), in detecting the overall size of the total multipliers, and, in the case of DGP2 even, in recovering the overall shape of the responses. For example, when we use DGP2 and identification 2, the initial impact of u_{1t} on Δy and Δc (the solid line) has an incorrect sign and the shape of the responses do not correspond to the true ones. There are several reasons for why these results may emerge. First, we have used a VAR(4) to approximate a VAR(∞) so the model is misspecified. Second, the sample size may be too small to recover the correct responses. Third, since the size of the responses is in many cases close to zero, it may be, that once standard errors are taken into account, some sign reversal may not be significant. When the identification scheme is incorrect, several problems can be noted. The most evident problem is that the effect of the two shocks is reversed for both variables so that if one uses the wrong identification scheme he is likely to confuse the correct source of disturbances.

When the DGP is a nonfundamental MA, regardless of the exact DGP and identification scheme used, substantial errors emerge. First, in many cases shocks hitting consumption are incorrectly identified and their effect reversed. Second, especially when DGP2 is the true process and identification 2 is used, the sign of the initial response is incorrect. Third, even when the sign is correct, the magnitude of the impact is often 80 percent smaller than the true one. Finally, the shape of the responses to the two shocks is often incorrect.

Two conclusions can be drawn from the above exercise. First, when the DGP is a fundamental MA process, the use of an incorrect identification scheme may lead a researcher to confuse sources of disturbance, to underestimate the impact of the shocks, and, in some cases, to have an incorrect picture of the propagation of shocks over time. Second, when the DGP is a nonfundamental MA, both identification schemes provide a very distorted picture of the propagation mechanism of shocks in a bivariate system. This may lead a researcher to draw incorrect conclusions regarding the sources of shocks and their impact over time.

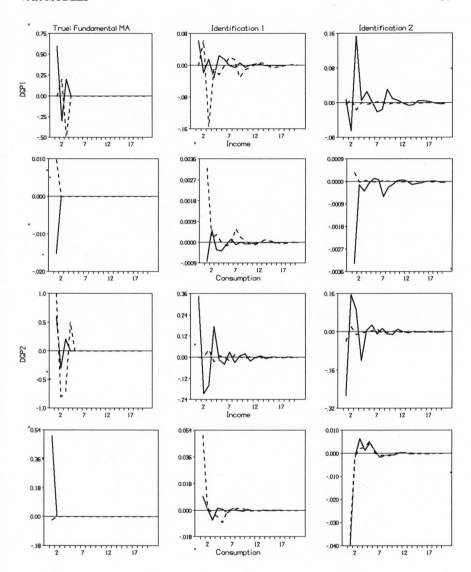

Figure 3.1

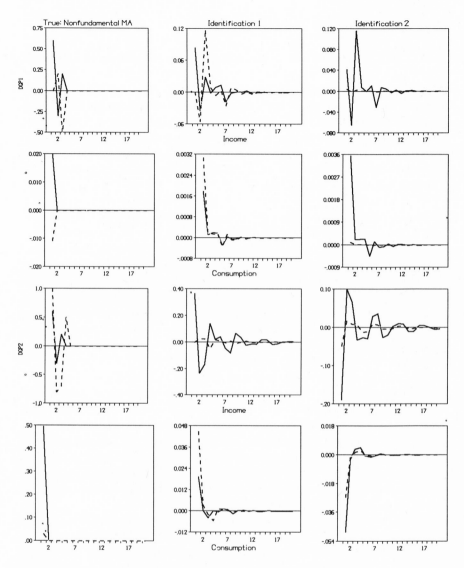

Figure 3.2

Data Characterization and Forecasting

Despite the emphasis we put in this chapter on the philosophy of unrestricted VARs and on semistructural analyses that can be undertaken with them, it should be mentioned that unrestricted VARs (or BVARs) are also extensively used simply as summary statistics to characterize data interdependencies and for unconditional forecasting purposes. Because of the many interpretations that the term *unconditional* has in forecasting, it is useful to define exactly what it is meant by this terminology. In this section I will call unconditional forecasts those exercises computed without interventions on the innovations or on the parameters of the estimated unrestricted VAR processes.

The popularity of VARs for these tasks stems primarily from their simplicity and the fact discussed in the second section, that under certain regularity conditions they are "good" representations of the data. For forecasting purposes, however, Litterman (1986) lists two additional advantages of VARs over standard simultaneous-equation systems. Unrestricted VARs give an objective summary of the uncertainty surrounding the data and the forecasts in the sense that they are only very weakly contaminated by the modeler's judgmental decisions and, because of this, they provide realistic multivariate probability distributions for current and future paths of the economy.

Unrestricted VAR models that are selected so as to satisfy the white-noise assumption for the disturbances typically forecast very poorly. To ensure that the disturbances are white-noise innovations one must include, in principle, a large number of lags. Because the number of parameters to be estimated may be large for a fixed sample size, the precision of the estimates is very dubious (see Litterman, 1980, or Todd, 1984, for this type of argument). In other words, although the in-sample fit of the model as measured, for example, by the R^2 coefficient may be extremely good, the out-of-sample performance can be very poor because of very poor parameter estimates. In comparison with parsimoniously parametrized univariate ARIMA models, standard out-of-sample measures (like the root mean square error) generally discard unrestricted VAR models.

One solution to this problem is to select the lag length of the model, bearing in mind that the specification will be used for forecasting. Information criteria such as the AIC or the SIC are helpful here because they measure adequacy by trading off in a nonlinear way the divergent considerations of accuracy in the forecasts and the "best" approximation to reality. Although the resulting model may inaccurately describe reality, it may turn out to be useful for forecasting. An alternative solution to this problem is the BVAR approach of Litterman (1986) previously discussed.

The literature studying the unconditional forecasting performance of VAR models is at this point very large (see Litterman, 1986; McNees, 1986; Sims,

1989b; McNees, 1990). Researchers have documented three basic regularities concerning the forecasting performance of VAR models. First, relative to large-scale structural models, unrestricted VARs are superior in long-run forecasting. Relative to other time-series models the evidence for long-run forecasting is more mixed. Second, BVARs are, at least, competitive with large-scale structural models and outperform univariate ARIMA models in forecasting real variables. For the most recent experience, however, McNees (1990) notes a deterioration of the forecasting ability of BVAR models that is especially evident for monetary variables. Third, both unrestricted VARs and BVARs usually contain information that is not present in the forecasts of large-scale models. This indicates that neither specification is totally adequate and that a pooling of the forecasts from different model specifications may improve the quality of the predictions.

Within the VAR methodology, while it is typical to prefer BVAR models over VAR's for forecasting purposes, Luppoletti and Webb (1986), demonstrated that shrewdly chosen unrestricted VAR models may be as good as more elaborate BVAR models in forecasting key macro variables.

Conclusions

The purpose of this chapter was to describe the main features of the unrestricted VAR approach to macroeconometrics and of semistructural exercises conducted with VARs and to discuss their meaning and interpretation. The emphasis was primarily on the economic aspects and on the interpretation of the results of the procedure rather than on statistical issues surrounding the approach (which are more thoroughly discussed in Lutkepohl (1991); Hamilton, 1994; Canova, 1993; and Watson, 1994). We have attempted to compare and contrast different approaches to specification and testing and have discussed differences with other existing methodologies for applied research.

Criticisms of the unrestricted VAR methodology discussed here appeared at two levels: at the stage of describing data interdependences and at the stage of undertaking useful policy analyses. Some authors (see Runkle, 1987; Ohanian, 1988; Spencer, 1989) have raised doubts about the usefulness of the methodology to robustly characterize the dynamics of the data (a result contradicted by the recent findings of Todd, 1990). In addition Maravall (1993) stressed that VAR models fit to seasonally adjusted data are unable to capture the dynamics of the data because seasonal adjustment procedures induce noninvertible MA components in the data.

The major bulk of the criticisms has focused, however, on the meaning and on the limitations of hypothesis testing and policy analysis with VARs. Attacks were mounted against its "atheoretical" underpinning (see Cooley and Leroy, 1985;

Leamer, 1985; Blanchard and Watson, 1986), on the type of policy interventions that were reasonable in light of the Lucas critique, on the way they were engineered (see Cooley and Leroy, 1985), and, in general, on the usefulness of providing policy advice with VARs (see Sargent, 1984). We argued that semistructural VAR analyses do have theoretical links, even though they are generic and refer to a large class of models. We have also argued that they can be used to provide answers to some questions that are of interest for policy makers and economists, but we also discuss their major limitations. We show that there are circumstances where the semistructural VAR econometrician cannot recover relevant news to agents' information sets and describe their impact on the variables of the system. These problems, however, are not unique to the methodology described in this chapter. Instead, they are typical of all the procedures that do not heavily rely on economic theory to put structure on the data and instead "let the data speak." Unfortunately, and in addition to the above problems, in many situations the data does not speak loud enough for the evidence presented to be conclusive. This, however, should not be regarded as a failure of the methodology but instead must be regarded as a weakness of the data. More precise models of economic behavior can overcome most of the deficiencies faced by the semistructural VAR analysis. However, very few economists really believe that our highly stylized economic models can be taken to be the true data-generating process for the actual data, and it is symptomatic that detailed models of economic behavior are almost always rejected by formal statistical testing. When nonrejections occur, it is often because of small samples or inefficient estimation techniques.

Whether the unrestricted semistructural VAR approach is more or less fruitful than approaches that rely on strongly formulated, and possibly false, theoretical models is still an open issue that deserves further study. We conjecture that the answer will not be univocal and will depend on the questions the researchers are interested in asking.

Acknowledgments

The financial support of the European Community through a European University Institute Grant is gratefully acknowledged. Part of this paper was written when the author was also associated with the European University Institute, Florence. Comments from Kevin Hoover are gratefully acknowledged. Conversations with Eric Leeper, Marco Lippi, Adrian Pagan, Danny Quah, Lucrezia Reichlin, and Mike Wickens were instrumental in forming the ideas contained in this chapter. Thomas Sargent and Christopher Sims provided an intangible but crucial input in the production process.

References

Akaike, H. (1974). "A New Look at the Statistics Model Identification." *IEEE Transactions on Automatic Control* AC-19, 716–723.

Baillie, R.T. (1987). "Inference in Dynamic Models Containing Surprise Variables." *Journal of Econometrics* 35, 101–117.

Bernanke, B. (1986). "Alternative Explorations of the Money Income Correlation." *Carnegie Rochester Conference in Public Policy* 25, 49–100.

Beveridge, S., and C. Nelson. (1981). "A New Approach to Decomposition of Economic Time Series into Permanent and Transitory Components with Particular Attention to Measurement of Business Cycle." *Journal of Monetary Economics* 7, 151–174.

Blanchard, O. (1987). "Comment to Runkle's Vector Autoregression and Reality." *Journal of Bussiness and Economic Statistics* 5, 449–451.

Blanchard, O. (1989). "A Traditional Interpretation of Macroeconomic Fluctuations." *American Economic Review* 79, 1146–1164.

Blanchard, O., and D. Quah. (1989). "The Dynamic Effects of Aggregate Demand and Supply Disturbances." *American Economic Review* 79, 655–673.

Blanchard, O., and D. Quah. (1993). "Fundamentalness and the Interpretation of Time Series Evidence: A replay to Lippi and Reichlin." *American Economic Review* 83(3), 653–658.

Blanchard, O., and M. Watson. (1986). "Are Business Cycles all Alike?" In Gordon, R. (ed.), *The American Business Cycle*. Chicago: University of Chicago Press.

Brock, W., and C. Sayers. (1988). "Is the Business Cycle Characterized by Deterministic Chaos?" *Journal of Monetary Economics* 22, 71–90.

Campbell, J., and A. Deaton. (1989). "Why Is Consumption so Smooth?" *Review of Economic Studies* 56, 357–373.

Canova, F. (1991). "The Sources of Financial Crises: Pre and Post Fed Evidence." *International Economic Review* 32, 689–713.

Canova, F. (1993). "Modelling and Forecasting Exchange Rates with Bayesian Time Varying Coefficient Model." *Journal of Economics Dynamic and Control* 17, 233–261.

Canova, F. (1994). "VAR Models: Specification, Estimation, Inference and Forecasting." In H. Pesaran and M. Wickens (eds.), *Handbook of Applied Econometrics*. Oxford: Basil Blackwell.

Canova, F., M. Finn, and A. Pagan. (1993). "Evaluating a Real Business Cycle Model." In C. Hargreaves (ed.), *Nonstationary Time Series Analysis and Cointegration*. Oxford: Oxford University Press.

Clements, M.P., and G.E. Mizon. (1991). "Empirical Analysis of Macroeconomic Time Series: VAR and Structural Models." *European Economic Review* 35, 887–917.

Cooley, T., and S. Leroy. (1985). "Atheoretical Macroeconometrics: A Critique." *Journal of Monetary Economics* 16, 283–308.

Dickey, D., and W. Fuller. (1979). "Distribution of the Estimators for a Autoregressive Time Series with a Unit Root." *Journal of the American Statistical Association* 74, 427–431.

Danthine, J.P. (1992). "Calibrated Macro Models: What and What For?" Manuscript, University of Lousanne.

DeJong, D., and Whiteman, C. (1991). "Reconsidering Trends and Random Walks in Macroeconomic Time Series." *Journal of Monetary Economics* 28(2), 221–254.

Doan, T. (1994). *RATS Manual, Version 4.10*. Evanston, II.

Doan, T., R. Litterman, and C. Sims. (1984). "Forecasting and Conditional Projections Using Realist Prior Distributions." *Econometric Reviews* 3, 1–100.

Engle, R. (1982). "Autoregressive Conditional Heteroskedasticity with Estimates of the Variance of the UK Inflation." *Econometrica* 50, 987–1006.

Engle, R., and C. Granger. (1987). "Co-Integration and Error Correction: Representation, Estimation and Testing." *Econometrica* 55, 251–276.

Engle, R., D. Lilien, and R. Robbins. (1987). "Estimating Time Varying Risk Premia in the Term Structure: The ARCH-M Model." *Econometrica* 55, 391–408.

Evans, G. (1989). "Output and Unemployment Dynamics in the United States: 1950–1985." *Journal of Applied Econometrics* 4, 213–237.

Fair, R. (1988). "VAR Models as Structural Approximations." Discussion Paper 856, Cowles Foundation.

Friedman, M., and A. Schwartz. (1963). *A Monetary History of the United States, 1867–1960*. Princeton, NJ: Princeton University Press.

Gali, J. (1992). "How Well Does the ISLM Model Fit Postwar U.S. Data?" *Quarterly Journal of Economics* 107, 709–735.

Gali, J., and M. Hammour. (1991). "Long Run Effects of Business Cycles." Manuscript, Columbia University.

Gallant, R., D. Hsieh, and G. Tauchen. (1991). "On Fitting Recalcitrant Series: The Pound/ Dollar Exchange Rate, 1974–1983." In W. Barnett, J. Powell and G. Tauchen, (eds.), *Nonparametric and Semiparametric Methods in Econometrics and Statistics*. Proceedings of the fifth International Symposium in Economic Theory and Econometrics. Cambridge: Cambridge University Press.

Geweke, J. (1982). "The Measurement of Linear Dependence and Feedback Between Multiple Time Series." *Journal of the American Statistical Association* 77, 304–313.

Giannini, C. (1992). *Topics in Structural VARs*. Berlin: Springer and Verlag.

Granger, C., and Anderson. (1978). *Introduction to Bilinear Time Series*. Gottingen, Germany: Vandenhoeck and Ruprecht.

Griffiths, W., and H. Lutkepohl. (1990). "Confidence Interval for Impulse Responses from VAR Models: A Comparison of Asymptotic Theory and Simulation Approaches." Manuscript, University of New England.

Hamilton, J. (1989). "A New Approach to Economic Analysis of Nonstationary Time Series and the Business Cycles." *Econometrica* 57, 357–384.

Hamilton, J. (1994). *Applied Time Series Analysis*. Princeton, NJ: Princeton University Press.

Hansen, L. (1982). "Large Sample Properties of Generalized Methods of Moment Estimators." *Econometrica* 50, 1029–1054.

Hansen, L., W. Roberds, and T. Sargent. (1991). "Time Series Implications of Present Value Budget Balance and of Martingale Models of Consumption and Taxes." In L. Hansen and T. Sargent (eds.), *Rational Expectations Econometrics*. Boulder, Co: Westview Press.

Hansen, L., and T. Sargent. (1980). "Formulating and Estimating Linear Rational Expectations Models." *Journal of Economic Dynamics and Control* 2, 1–46.

Hansen, L., and T. Sargent. (1991). "Two Difficulties in Interpreting Vector Autoregressions." In L. Hansen and T. Sargent (eds.), *Rational Expectations Econometrics*. Boulder, Co: Westview Press.

Hansen, L., and K. Singleton. (1983). "Stochastic Consumption, Risk Aversion and the Temporal Behavior of Asset Returns." *Journal of Political Economy* 91, 249–265.

Harvey, A.C. (1985). "Trends and Cycles in Macroeconomics." *Journal of Business and Economic Statistics* 3, 216–227.

Hendry, D., and G. Mizon. (1990). "Evaluating Dynamic Econometric Models by Encompassing the VAR." In P.C.B. Phillips and V.B. Hall (eds.), *Models, Methods and Applications of Econometrics: Essays in Honor of Rex Bergstrom*. Oxford: Oxford University Press.

Hsiao, C. (1981). "Autoregressive Modelling and Money-Income Causality Detection." *Journal of Monetary Economics* 7, 85–106.

Johansen, S. (1988). "Statistical Analysis of Cointegrating Vectors." *Journal of Economic Dynamics and Control* 12, 231–254.

Johansen, S., and K. Juselius. (1990). "Maximum Likelihood Estimation and Inference on Cointegration—with Application to the Demand for Money." *Oxford Bulletin of Economics and Statistics* 52, 169–210.

Judge, G., W. Griffith, R. Hill, H. Lutkepohl, and T. Lee. (1980). *The Theory and Practice of Econometrics* (2nd ed.). New York: Wiley.

Keating, J. (1990). "Identifying VAR Models under Rational Expectations." *Journal of Monetary Economics* 25, 453–476.

Kirchgassner, G. (1991). "Comments on M.P. Clements and G.E. Mizon: Empirical Analysis of Macroeconomic Time Series: VAR and Structural Models." *European Economic Review* 35, 918–922.

King, R., C. Plosser, and S. Rebelo. (1988). "Production, Growth and Business Cycles, I." *Journal of Monetary Economics* 21, 309–342.

King, R., C. Plosser, J. Stock, and M. Watson. (1991). "Stochastic Trends and Economic Fluctuations." *American Economic Review* 81, 819–840.

Kocherlakota, N. (1990). "On the Discount Factor in Growing Economies." *Journal of Monetary Economics* 25, 43–48.

Koopmans, T. (1963). "Identification Problems in Economic Model Construction." In W. Hood and T.J. Koopmans (eds.), *Studies in Econometric Methods*. New Haven, CT: Yale University Press.

Kydland, F., and E. Prescott. (1982). "Time to Build and Aggregate Fluctuations." *Econometrica* 50, 1345–1370.

Kydland, F., and E. Prescott. (1991). "The Econometrics of the General Equilibrium Approach to Business Cycles." *Scandinavian Journal of Economics* 93, 161–178.

Leamer, E. (1978). *Specification Searches and ah-Hoc Inference with Nonexperimental Data*. New York: Wiley.

Leamer, E. (1985). "Vector Autoregression for Causal Inference?" *Carnegie Rochester Conference Series on Public Policy* 22, 255–304.

Leeper, E. (1989). "Policy Rules, Information and Fiscal Effects in a 'Ricardian' Model." International Finance Discussion Paper 360, Board of Governors of the Federal Reserve System.

Leeper E., and R. Gordon. (1992). "In Search for the Liquidity Effects." *Journal of Monetary Economics* 29, 341–371.

Lippi, M., and L. Reichlin. (1992). "VAR Analysis, Non-Fundamental Representation, Blaschke Matrices." Manuscript, OCFE.

Lippi, M., and L. Reichlin. (1993). "A Note on Measuring the Dynamic Effects of Aggregate Demand and Supply Disturbances." *American Economic Review* 83(3), 644–652.

Litterman, R. (1980). "Techniques for Forecasting Vector Autoregressions." Ph.D. thesis, University of Minnesota.

Litterman, R. (1984). "Forecasting and Policy Analysis with Bayesian Vector Autoregression Models." *Quarterly Review* (Federal Reserve Bank of Minneapolis) 8 (Fall), 30–41.

Litterman, R. (1986). "Specifying Vector Autoregressions for Macroeconomic Forecasting." In P. Goel and A. Zellner (eds.), *Bayesian Inference and Decision Techniques.* Amsterdam: North Holland.

Litterman, R., and L. Weiss. (1985). "Money, Real Interest Rates and Output: A Reinterpretation of Postwar U.S. Data." *Econometrica* 52, 129–156.

Liu, T. (1960). "Underidentification, Structural Estimation and Forecasting." *Econometrica* 28, 855–865.

Long, J., and C. Plosser. (1983). "Real Business Cycles." *Journal of Political Economy* 91, 1345–1370.

Luppoletti, W., and R. Webb. (1986). "Defining and Improving the Accuracy of Macroeconomic Forecasts: Contributions from a VAR Model." *Journal of Business* 59, 263–285.

Lutkepohl, H. (1986). "Comparison of Criteria for Estimating the Order of a Vector Autoregressive Process." *Journal of Time Series Analysis* 6, 35–52; and "Correction," 8, 373.

Lutkepohl, H. (1991). *Introduction to Multiple Time Series Analysis.* New York: Springer and Verlag.

Maravall, A. (1993). "Stochastic Linear Trends: Models and Estimators." *Journal of Econometrics* 56, 5–37.

McNees, S. (1986). "Forecasting Accuracy of Alternative Techniques: A Comparison of U.S. Macroeconomic Forecasts" (with comments). *Journal of Business and Economic Statistics* 4, 23–28.

McNees, S. (1990). "The Role of Judgement in Macroeconomic Forecasting Accuracy." *International Journal of Forecasting* 6, 287–299.

Nelson, and C. Plosser. (1982). "Trends and Random Walks in Macroeconomic Time Series." *Journal of Monetary Economics* 10, 139–162.

Nickelsburg, G. (1985). "Small Sample Properties of Dimensionality Statistics for Fitting VAR Models to Aggregate Economic Data." *Journal of Econometrics* 28, 183–192.

Nicholls, D.F., and B.G. Quinn. (1982). *Random Coefficient Autoregressive Models: An Introduction.* New York: Springer and Verlag.

Ohanian, L. (1988). "The Spurious Effect of Unit Roots on Vector Autoregressions: A Monte Carlo Study." *Journal of Econometrics* 39, 251–266.

Perron, P. (1989). "The Great Crash, the Oil Price Shock and the Unit Root Hypothesis." *Econometrica* 57, 1361–1401.

Phillips, P.C. (1988). "Optimal Inference in Cointegrated Systems." *Econometrica* 55, 277–301.

Phillips, P.C., and P. Perron. (1986). "Testing for Unit Roots in Time Series Regressions." *Biometrika* 70, 335–346.

Quah, D. (1990). "Permanent and Transitory Movements in Labor Income: An Explanation Based on Excess Smoothness in Consumption." *Journal of Political Economy* 98, 449–475.

Quah, D. (1991). "Identifying Vector Autoregressions: A Discussion of P. Englund, A. Vredin and A. Warne: Macroeconomic Shocks in Sweden 1925–1986." Manuscript, London School of Economics.

Quah, D. (1992). "Lecture Notes in Macroeconometrics." Manuscript, London School of Economics.

Quah, D., and T. Sargent. (1993). "A Dynamic Index Model for a Large Cross Section." In J. Stock and M. Watson (eds.), *New Research on Business Cycles, Indicators and Forecasting.* Chicago: University of Chicago Press.

Reinsel, G. (1983). "Some Results on Multivariate Autoregressive Index Models." *Biometrika* 70, 145–156.

Robertson, D., and M. Wickens. (1992). "Measuring Real and Nominal Macroeconomic Shocks and Their International Transmission Under Different Monetary Systems." Working paper, London Business School.

Rozanov, Y. (1967). *Stationary Random Processes.* San Francisco: Holden Day.

Runkle, D. (1987). "Vector Autoregression and Reality." *Journal of Business and Economic Statistics* 5, 437–454.

Sargent, T. (1979). "Estimating Vector Autoregressions Using Methods Not Based on Explicit Economic Theory." *Quarterly Review* (Federal Reserve Bank of Minneapolis), 3 (Summer), 8–15.

Sargent, T. (1984). "Autoregression, Expectations and Advice." *American Economic Review, Papers and Proceedings* 74, 408–415.

Sargent, T. (1986). *Macroeconomic Theory* (2nd ed.). New York: Academic Press.

Sargent, T., and R. Lucas. (1980). *Rational Expectations and Econometric Practice.* Minneapolis, MN: University of Minnesota Press.

Sargent, T., and C. Sims. (1977). "Business Cycle Modelling Without Pretending to Have Too Much *A Priori* Economic Theory." In C. Sims (ed.), *New Methods in Business Cycle Research.* Minneapolis, MN: Federal Reserve Bank of Minneapolis.

Schwarz, G. (1978). "Estimating the Dimension of a Model." *Annals of Statistics* 6, 461–464.

Shapiro, M., and M. Watson. (1989). "Sources of Business Cycle Fluctuations." *NBER Macroeconomic Annual* (pp. 111–148). Cambridge, MA: MIT Press.

Sims, C. (1972). "Money, Income and Causality." *American Economic Review* 62, 540–553.

Sims, C. (1980a). "Macroeconomics and Reality." *Econometrica* 48, 1–48.

Sims, C. (1980b). "A Comparison of Interwar and Postwar Business Cycles: Monetarism Reconsidered." *American Economic Review Papers and Proceedings* 70, 250–257.

Sims, C. (1982). "Policy Analysis with Econometric Models." *Brookings Papers of Economic Activity* 2, 107–152.

Sims, C. (1986). "Are Forecasting Models Usable for Policy Analysis." *Quarterly Review* (Federal Reserve Bank of Minneapolis), 10 (Winter), 2–16.

Sims, C. (1987). "Comment to Runkle's Vector Autoregression and Reality." *Journal of Business and Economic Statistics* 5, 443–449.

Sims, C. (1988a). "Identifying Policy Effects." In R. Bryant, D. Henderson, G. Holtman, P. Hooper, and A. Symansky (eds.), *Empirical Macroeconomics for Interdependent Economies* (pp. 305–321). Washington DC: Brookings Institution.

Sims, C. (1988b). "Bayesian Prospective on Unit Roots Econometrics." *Journal of Economic Dynamic and Control* 12, 436–474.

Sims, C. (1989b). "A Nine Variable Probabilistic Model of the U.S. Economy." Discussion Paper 14, Institute for Empirical Macroeconomics, Federal Reserve of Minneapolis.

Sims, C., J. Stock, and M. Watson. (1990). "Inference in Linear Time Series Models with Some Unit Roots." *Econometrica* 58, 113–144.

Sims, C., and H. Ulhig. (1991). "Unit Rooters: An Elicopter Tour." *Econometrica* 59(6), 1591–1600.

Spencer, D. (1989). "Does Money Matter? The Robustness of the Evidence from Vector Autoregressions." *Journal of Money, Banking and Credit* 21, 442–454.

Stock, J., and M. Watson. (1988). "Testing for Common Trends." *Journal of the American Statistical Association* 83, 1097–1107.

Stock, J., and M. Watson. (1989). "Interpreting the Evidence on Money-Income Causality." *Journal of Econometrics* 40, 161–181.

Taylor, J. (1980). "Aggregate Dynamics and Staggered Contracts." *Journal of Political Economy* 88, 1–24.

Theil, H. (1971). *Principles of Econometrics*. New York: Wiley.

Todd, R. (1984). "Improving Economic Forecasting with Bayesian Vector Autoregression." *Quarterly Review* (Federal Reserve Bank of Minneapolis), 8 (Fall), 18–29.

Todd, R. (1990). "Vector Autoregression Evidence on Monetarism: Another Look at the Robustness Debate." *Quarterly Review* (Federal Reserve Bank of Minneapolis), 14 (Spring), 17–37.

Watson, M. (1986). "Univariate Detrending Methods with Stochastic Trends." *Journal of Monetary Economics* 18, 49–75.

Watson, M. (1987). "Comment to Runkle's Vector Autoregression and Reality." *Journal of Business and Economic Statistics* 5, 451–453.

Watson, M. (1994). "VAR and Cointegration." In R. Engle and D. McFadden (eds.), *Handbook of Econometrics* (Vol. 4).

Wickens, M. (1992). "VAR Analysis in the Presence of Cointegration." Working paper, London Business School.

Zellner, A. (1962). "An Efficient Methods for Estimating Seemingly Unrelated Regressions and Tests for Aggregation Bias." *Journal of the American Statistical Association* 57, 348–368.

Commentary on Chapter 3

Masao Ogaki

Fabio Canova has provided us with an excellent discussion of the VAR methodology's relationship to economic models. In this comment, I focus on the identification issue. Canova defines the question of identification in the following way: under what conditions is knowledge about reduced-form VAR parameters and innovations sufficient to recover objects that may be of interest to economic analysis? Canova offers a general discussion on this issue.

In order to understand the relationship between conditions of identification and economic models, it is helpful to have a concrete example of an economic model. For this purpose, a simple linear rational expectations model that imposes restrictions on the VAR representation is presented here. Using this example, I discuss some important conditions for identification under the VAR methodology and compare the VAR methodology with other competing approaches.

Nonlinear Restrictions on the VAR Representation

Let us consider West's (1987) model as an example of a linear rational expectations model. Let p_t be the real stock price (after the dividend is paid) in period t and d_t be the real dividend paid to the the owner of the stock at the beginning of period t. Then the arbitrage condition is

$$p_t = E[b(p_{t+1} + d_{t+1}) \mid I_t], \tag{1}$$

where b is the constant real discount rate and $E(\cdot \mid I_t)$ is the mathematical expectation operator conditioned on the information set I_t economic agents in period t. Solving (1) forward and imposing the no bubble condition, we obtain the present-value formula:

$$p_t = E\left(\sum_{i=1}^{\infty} b^i d_{t+i} \mid I_t \right). \tag{2}$$

We now derive restrictions on the VAR representation for p_t and d_t implied by (1) and (2). We consider two cases, depending on whether d_t is assumed to be covariance stationary or unit root nonstationary.

Case 1: Stationary d_t

Assume that d_t is covariance stationary with mean zero, so that it has a Wold moving average representation

$$d_t = \alpha(L)v_t, \tag{3}$$

where $\alpha(L) = 1 + \alpha_1 L + \alpha_2 L^2 \ldots$ and where

$$v_t = d_t - E(d_t \mid H_{t-1}). \tag{4}$$

Here, $E(\cdot \mid H_t)$ is the linear projection operator onto the information set $H_t = \{d_t, d_{t-1}, d_{t-2}, \ldots\}$. We assume that the econometrician uses the information set H_t, which may be much smaller than the economic agents' information set, I_t. Assuming that $\alpha(L)$ is invertible,

$$\phi(L)d_t = v_t, \tag{5}$$

where $\phi(L) = 1 - \phi_1 L - \phi_2 L^2 \ldots$.

Using (2) and the law of iterated projections, we obtain

$$p_t = E\left(\sum_{i=1}^{\infty} b^i d_{t+i} \mid H_t \right) + w_t, \tag{6}$$

where

$$w_t = E\left(\sum_{i=1}^{\infty} b^i d_{t+i} \mid I_t \right) - E\left(\sum_{i=1}^{\infty} b^i d_{t+i} \mid H_t \right), \tag{7}$$

and $E(w_t \mid H_t) = 0$. Because $E(\cdot \mid H_t)$ is the linear projection operator onto H_t,

$$E\left(\sum_{i=1}^{\infty} b^i d_{t+i} \mid H_t \right) = \delta(L)d_t, \tag{8}$$

where $\delta(L) = \delta_1 + \delta_2 L \ldots$. Following Hansen and Sargent (1980, app. A), we obtain the restrictions imposed by (8) on $\delta(L)$ and $\phi(L)$:

$$\delta(L) = \frac{bL^{-1}(\alpha(L) - \alpha(b))}{1 - bL^{-1}}\phi(L) = \frac{bL^{-1}(1 - \phi^{-1}(b)\phi(L))}{1 - bL^{-1}}. \tag{9}$$

We now parameterize $\phi(L)$ as a qth order polynomial:

$$d_{t+1} = \phi_1 d_t + \ldots + \phi_q d_{t-q+1} + v_{t+1}. \tag{10}$$

Then (9) is used to show that $\delta(L)$ is a finite-order polynomial and to give a explicit formula for the coefficients for $\delta(L)$ (see West, 1987, for the formula, which is based on Hansen and Sargent, 1980, and on West, 1989, for deterministic terms when $d(t)$ has a nonzero mean). Thus

$$p_t = \delta_1 d_t + \ldots + \delta_q d_{t-q+1} + w_t, \qquad (11)$$

where δ_i's are functions of b and ϕ_i's.

For simplicity, we started out with an assumption that the econometrician's information set is $H_t = \{d_t, d_{t-1}, d_{t-2}, \ldots\}$. In order to obtain the VAR representation for (d_{t+1}, p_t), we need to assume that the econometrician's information set is $H_t^* = \{d_t, d_{t-1}, d_{t-2}, \ldots, p_{t-1}, p_{t-2}, p_{t-3}, \ldots\}$. For simplicity, we now assume that that H_t and H_t^* has the same informational contents for d_{t+1} and p_t: $E(d_{t+1} \mid H_t) = E(d_{t+1} \mid H_t^*)$, $E(p_t \mid H_t) = E(p_t \mid H_t^*)$, so that (10) and (11) are the VAR representation. Without this simplifying assumption, the only thing we would need to do is to apply Hansen and Sargent's (1980) formula to H_t^*. Then we would obtain very similar restrictions as (9) except that $\phi(L)$ and $\alpha(L)$ become 2 by 2 matrices and that both current and lagged d_t's and lagged p_t's appear in (10) and (11) as regressors. Hence the following discussions are not affected by this simplifying assumption. Thus (9) gives the restrictions on the VAR representation consisting of (10) and (11).

Case 2: Unit Root Nonstationary d_t

Assume that d_t is unit root nonstationary, so that $\Delta d_t = d_t - d_{t-1}$ is covariance stationary. In this case, let us generate H_t from $\{\Delta d_t, \Delta d_{t-1}, \ldots\}$ and define w_t by

$$\Delta p_{t+1} = E\left(\sum_{i=1}^{\infty} b^i \Delta d_{t+1+i} \mid H_t\right) + w_t. \qquad (6')$$

Then (2) implies that $E(w_t \mid H_t) = 0$. Let

$$\Delta d_{t+1} = \phi_1 \Delta d_t + \ldots + \phi_q \Delta d_{t-q+1} + v_{t+1}, \qquad (10')$$

and

$$\Delta p_t = \delta_1 \Delta d_t + \ldots + \delta_q \Delta d_{t-q+1} + w_t. \qquad (11')$$

Then as in the previous case with stationary d_t, (6') implies that δ_i's can be written as functions of b and ϕ_i's.

Econometric Methods

In this section, econometric methods that impose and test the nonlinear restrictions discussed in the previous section are described. I focus on Hansen and Sargent's

(1982) method that applies Hansen's (1982) generalized method of moments (GMM) to estimating linear rational-expectations models.

Case 1: Stationary d_t

Let z_{1t} be a vector of random variables in H_t. For example, $z_{1t} = (d_t, \ldots d_{t-q+1})$. The unknown parameters b and ϕ_i's can be estimated by applying the GMM to orthogonality conditions $E(z_{1t}v_{t+1}) = 0$ and $E(z_{1t}w_t) = 0$ in the econometric system consisting of (10) and (11).

Let z_{2t} be a random variable in I_t—say, d_t—and

$$p_t = b(p_{t+1} + d_{t+1}) = u_{t+1}. \tag{12}$$

Then (1) implies another orthogonality condition $E(z_{2t}u_{t+1}) = 0$. This orthogonality condition can be used to estimate b. West (1987) forms a specification test à la Hausman (1978) by comparing the estimate of b from (12) with the estimate of b from (10) and (11). For this purpose, West forms a Wald test in the system consisting of (10), (11), and (12) without the restrictions (9) imposed. Another method to form West's specification test is to form a Lagrange multiplier test or a likelihood ratio type test, which will require estimation constrained by the restrictions (9). This method may be preferable because of small sample problems with the Wald test for nonlinear restrictions (see Ogaki, 1993, sec. 7, for discussions about these tests).

Case 2: Unit Root Nonstationary d_t

In this case, the GMM can be applied to the econometric system consisting of (10′) and (11′) to estimate b and ϕ_i's. A complication exists for (12). It should be noted that u_t in (12) is stationary, so that (12) implies that p_t and $p_{t+1} + d_{t+1}$ are cointegrated with a cointegrating vector $(1, -b)$ in Engle and Granger's (1987) terminology. In order to see this, note that

$$p_t - (b/(1-b))d_t = E\left[\sum_{i=1}^{\infty} b^i(d_{t+i} - d_t) \mid I_t\right]. \tag{13}$$

Because $d_{t+i} - d_t$ is stationary for any i, the right side of (13) is stationary (as long as the stationary random variables in I_t are enough to form optimum forecasts for $d_{t+i} - d_t$). Hence p_t and d_t are cointegrated with a cointegrating vector $[1, -b(1-b)]'$ as shown by Campbell and Shiller (1987). This implies that P_t is unit root nonstationary and that

$$u_t = p_t - b(p_{t+1} + d_{t+1})$$

$$= \left(p_t - \frac{b}{1-b} d_t \right) - b \left(p_{t+1} - \frac{b}{1-b} d_{t+1} \right) - \frac{b}{1-b} (d_{t+1} - d_t) \qquad (14)$$

is stationary.

There exist at least three alternative methods to deal with (12). West (1987) notes that his instrumental variable estimator for b from (12) has an asymptotic normal distribution when d_t has nonzero drift (equation (10′) above ignores nonzero drift). This is because p_t and $p_{t+1} + d_{t+1}$ satisfy the deterministic cointegration restriction in Ogaki and Park's (1990) terminology and because there is only one regressor in (12). Hence West's (1988b) results apply to this case. West forms a Wald test that compares his estimate of b from (12) and his estimate of b from (10′) and (11′), using the joint normal distributions for the estimators from the system consisting of (10′), (11′), and (12).

Another method, which is used in Cooley and Ogaki (1995) for a different model, can be applied in more general cases. Because the estimator for b from (12) converges faster than GMM estimators from (10′) and (11′) because of the super consistency, a two-step procedure is possible. In the first step, b is estimated from (12) by a cointegrating regression. It is preferable to use one of asymptotic efficient estimators than OLS estimators. In the second step, the estimate of b from (12) is used as the true value for the GMM estimation of b and ϕ_i's from (10′) and (11′). Because the estimator of b from (12) converges faster than the GMM estimators, this two-step procedure does not affect asymptotic distributions of the GMM estimators.

Another method is to first difference (12)—

$$\Delta p_t = b(\Delta p_{t+1} + \Delta d_{t+1}) = \Delta u_{t+1} - \qquad (12')$$

and use the orthogonality condition $E(\Delta u_{t+1} \mid I_{t-1}) = 0$. This may be somewhat simpler, but we lose information from stochastic trends by first differencing. The econometrician needs to be careful because Δu_{t+1} is overdifferenced. For example, a constant is not a valid instrument because the resulting long run covariance matrix for the GMM disturbance would be singular.

Some remarks are in order.

- Hansen and Sargent's method described above does not require an assumption that d_t is exogenous. Relation (10) or (10′) is obtained from the assumption that d_t is covariance stationary and that its Wald representation is invertible.
- For the econometric system consisting of (10) and (11) (or (10′) and (11′)), random variables in H_t can be used as instruments, but the variables in I_t that are not in H_t are not valid instruments by construction.

- Because u_{t+1} in (12) is in I_{t+1} and v_{t+1} in (10) is in H_{t+1}, u_t and v_t are serially uncorrelated (see Ogaki, 1993, sec. 6, for related discussions). However, w_t in (11) is not necessarily in H_{t+1}. Hence w_t has unknown order of serial correlation.

Comparing Methods

Compared with a method that applies GMM directly to linear Euler equations (see Pindick and Rotemberg, 1983; Fair, 1989; Eichenbaum, 1990), Hansen and Sargent's method described above requires more assumptions about the stochastic law of motion of economic variables but utilizes more restrictions and is asymptotically more efficient when these assumptions are valid.[1]

The unrestricted VAR approach will consistently estimate the system consisting of (10) and (11) under the assumptions laid out above. It should be noted that what the unrestricted VAR approach uncovers as the shock for p_t is w_t, which is given by (7). As evident from (7), w_t is nothing but the difference between the forecast of the present value with all information available to the economic agents and the forecast of the present value with the econometrician's information set. Thus in this example, the unrestricted VAR approach fails to identify shocks.

Conclusions

In this comment, a linear rational expectations model was presented, so that the reader can compare the VAR approach with other competing methods. In the example, the unrestricted VAR approach fails to uncover shocks. This example is not meant to demonstrate that the VAR approach is inferior: of course, we can construct other examples in which other competing methods fail to estimate parameters consistently while the unrestricted VAR approach is more successful. However, the example emphasizes the fact that the disturbances in the VAR approach contain the difference between the economic agents' forecast and the linear forecast based on econometricians' information sets in general. Before interpreting the shocks uncovered by the VAR approach, the econometrician needs to think whether or not all important information available to the relevant economic agents is included in the VAR system and whether or not economic agents are using nonlinear forecasting rules in important ways.

Note

1. Maximum-likelihood estimation has been used more frequently for the Hansen-Sargent type linear rational expectations model than GMM (see Sargent, 1978, 1981a, 1981b; Eichenbaum, 1984;

Finn, 1989; Giovannini and Rotemberg, 1989) even though Hansen and Sargent's (1982) method can be applied to these models. Other related applications include West (1987, 1988a).

References

Campbell, J.Y., and P. Perron. (1991). "Pitfalls and Opportunities: What Macroeconomists Should Know About Unit Roots." In O.J. Blanchard and S. Fishcer (eds.), *NBER Macroeconomics Annual 1991*. Cambridge, MA: MIT Press.

Campbell, J.Y., and R.J. Shiller. (1987). "Cointegration and Tests of Present Value Models." *Journal of Political Economy* 95, 1062–1088.

Cooley, T.F., and M. Ogaki. (1995). "A Time Series Analysis of Real Wages, Consumption, and Asset Returns Under Optimal Labor Contracting: A Cointegration-Euler Equation Approach." *Journal of Applied Econometrics*, forthcoming.

Eichenbaum, M. (1984). "Rational Expectations and the Smoothing Properties of Inventories of Finished Goods." *Journal of Monetary Economics* 14, 71–96.

Eichenbaum, M. (1990). Some Empirical Evidence on the Production Level and Production Cost Smoothing Models of Inventory Investment." *American Economic Review* 79, 853–864.

Engle, R.F., and W.J. Granger. (1987). "Co-Integration and Error Correction: Representation, Estimation, and Testing." *Econometrica* 55, 251–276.

Fair, R.C. (1989). "The Production-Smoothing Model Is Alive and Well." *Journal of Monetary Economics* 24, 353–370.

Finn, M.G. (1989). "An Econometric Analysis of the Intertemporal General Equilibrium Approach to Exchange Rate and Current Account Determination." *Journal of International Money and Finance* 8, 467–486.

Giovannini, A., and J.J. Rotemberg. (1989). "Exchange-Rate Dynamics with Sticky Prices: The Deutsche Mark, 1974–1982." *Journal of Business and Economic Statistics* 7, 169–178.

Hansen, Lars Peter. (1982). "Large Sample Properties of Generalized Method of Moments Estimators." *Econometrica* 50 (July), 1029–1054.

Hansen, L.P., and T.J. Sargent. (1980). "Formulating and Estimating Dynamic Linear Rational Expectations Models." *Journal of Economic Dynamics and Control* 2, 7–46.

Hansen, L.P., and T.J. Sargent. (1982). "Instrumental Variables Procedures for Estimating Linear Rational Expectations Models." *Journal of Monetary Economics* 9, 263–296.

Hausman, J.A. (1978). "Specification Tests in Econometrics." *Econometrica* 46 (November), 1251–1271.

Ogaki, M. (1993). "Generalized Method of Moments: Econometric Applications." *Handbook of Statistics*. Vol. 11, *Econometrics*.

Pindick, R.S., and J.J. Rotemberg. (1983). "Dynamic Factor Demands and the Effects of Energy Price Shocks." *American Economic Review* 73, 1066–1079.

Sargent, T.J. (1978). "Rational Expectations, Econometric Exogeneity, and Consumption." *Journal of Political Economy* 86, 673–700.

Sargent, T.J. (1981a). "The Demand for Money During Hyperinflations Under Rational

Expectations." In R.E. Lucas, Jr, and T.J. Sargent (eds.), *Rational Expectations and Econometric Practice*. Minneapolis, MN: University of Minnesota Press.

Sargent, T.J. (1981b). "Estimation of Dynamic Labor Demand Schedules Under Rational Expectations." In R.E. Lucas, Jr, and T.J. Sargent (eds.), *Rational Expectations and Econometric Practice*. Minneapolis, MN: University of Minnesota Press.

West, K.D. (1987). "A Specification Test for Speculative Bubbles." *Quarterly Journal of Economics* 102, 553–580.

West, K.D. (1988a). "Dividend Innovations and Stock Price Volatility." *Econometrica* 56, 37–62.

West, K.D. (1988b). "Asymptotic Normality, When Regressors Have a Unit Root." *Econometrica* 56, 1397–1417.

West, K.D. (1989). "Estimation of Linear Rational Expectations Models in the Prescence of Deterministic Terms." *Journal of Monetary Economics* 24, 437–442.

4 PROGRESSIVE MODELING OF MACROECONOMIC TIME SERIES
The LSE Methodology
Grayham E. Mizon

Introduction

Econometric models, large and small, have played an increasingly important role in macroeconomic forecasting and policy analysis. However, there is a wide range of model types used for this purpose, including simultaneous-equation models in either reduced or structural form, vector autoregressive models (VAR), autoregressive distributed-lag models, autoregressive integrated moving-average models, leading-indicator models, and error-correction models (ECM). Hendry, Pagan, and Sargan (1984) discuss a typology for dynamic single-equation models for time-series variables, and Hendry (1994) presents a typology for the various types of dynamic model used in the analysis of systems of equations. There is also a wide range of views about the appropriate way to develop and evaluate models. Sims (1980, 1992) advocates the use of VAR models, which can accurately represent the time-series properties of data, while eschewing the reliance on "incredible dentifying restrictions" that characterizes the use of simultaneous equation models of the structural or Cowles Commission type. The potential value of structure (loosely defined) within the context of VAR models has led to the development of structural VAR models, and Canova (1995) provides a recent review of this literature. Leamer (1978, 1983), on the other hand, has been critical of the use of non-Bayesian models that do not analyze formally the role and value of *a priori* information, especially when there is no checking of model sensitivity. Summers (1991), though aware of the important developments made in theoretical statistics and econometrics in this century, argues that too much emphasis is placed on the technical aspects of modeling and not enough on the real issues that are concerned with the analysis of well-established and fundamental relationships between economic variables. One approach to modeling that does not overemphasize the role of model evaluation and statistical technique is that associated with real business cycle analysis and the calibration of economic theory, rather than its evaluation. Kydland and Prescott (1982, 1995) have been pioneers in this field, and Canova, Finn, and Pagan (1994) provide a critique.

The focus of this paper is an alternative approach to the modeling of economic time series that was originally developed at the London School of Economics (LSE), though contributions and extensions to this methodology have subsequently been made by econometricians who have had no direct connection with LSE as an institution. The essence of this approach is the recognition that potentially valuable information for the analysis of any economic problem can come from numerous sources, including economic theory, the available sample of observations on the potentially relevant variables, knowledge of the economic history of the period under study, and knowledge of the way in which the observed data are defined and measured and their relationship to the theory variables. In the development of econometric models it is therefore important that information from all these sources is exploited as fully as possible. Of course, the marginal return to the exploitation of information from each source will vary across the sources and the degree to which each source has been used already. However, attention here will be confined to consideration of the extent to which available information has been exploited and to the relationship between this and the evaluation and comparison of alternative models of the same phenomena.

The next section provides a brief history of the group of econometricians involved in the development of the LSE modeling methodology. This is followed by a section presenting the essential components of the LSE methodology, emphasizing the importance of evaluating and comparing alternative models within a statistically and economically coherent framework. This approach helps to ensure that econometric modeling is progressive by only abandoning models found to be inadequate in favor of models that have been demonstrated to be improvements. It is also progressive in the sense that it is not necessary to know the complete structure characterizing the relationship between economic variables prior to commencing an analysis of it. Rather, it is possible to discover incrementally parts of the underlying structure as a result of careful analysis (see Hendry, 1993b). The following section contains an analysis of the time-series relationship between wages, prices, and unemployment in the United Kingdom between 1965 and 1993, from both a single-equation and system perspective. It is found that single-equation analysis can yield misleading inferences relative to system analysis and that there appears to be an important change in structure, which may reflect a change in economic policy. The final section provides conclusions.

Brief History of the LSE Methodology's Development

A distinctive feature of the British tradition in statistics is the high quality of applied work implementing, developing, and stimulating theoretical research, with the early work of R.A. Fisher, J.B.S. Haldane, K. Pearson, and G.U. Yule and the later contributions of G.A. Barnard, M.S. Bartlett, G.P.E. Box, D.R. Cox, M.G. Kendall, D.V. Lindley, and E.S. Pearson being examples. That the LSE, as a leading university specializing in the social sciences, should follow and take advantage of this tradition was natural. Indeed, A.L. Bowley and R.G.D. Allen initiated the LSE's strength in statistics and economic statistics in particular, with Roy Allen teaching a course in econometrics as early as 1946–1947 and 1947–1948 (see Gilbert, 1989). From the 1950s the LSE fostered and enlarged its group of statisticians engaged in social science applications, when the statistical research in most other institutions was concerned with medical and biological applications. As a result, the Statistics Department at LSE became pre-eminent in its chosen field of statistical research. By the mid-1960s R.G.D. Allen, D.J. Bartholemew, D. Brillinger, J. Durbin, J. Hajnal, M.G. Kendall, M.H. Quenouille, C.A.B. Smith, and A. Stuart had been among its members. Throughout this period time-series analysis was an important area for research and teaching at the LSE, with Kendall, Quenouille, and then Durbin being the early leaders in this field. This tradition in the Statistics Department was later to play an important role in the development of the LSE econometric methodology.

Although the Statistics Department had been responsible for the early teaching of economic statistics and the newly emerging subject of econometrics, it was jointly with the Economics Department that the initiative was taken to expand the activities in econometrics. A.W.H. (Bill) Phillips, who had been in the Economics Department since the mid-1950s, used his knowledge of electrical engineering to study the dynamics of economic systems. This resulted in important research on continuous-time autoregressive moving-average models, an hydraulic model of the linkages between stocks and flows in the economy, introduction into economics of the concepts of integral, derivative, and proportional control mechanisms, and the development of the empirical relationship between aggregate wages and unemployment—the Phillips curve. Phillips was joined by fellow New Zealander Rex Bergstrom at the beginning of the 1960s, and he too developed statistical theory for the analysis of continuous-time models as well as building small continuous-time macroeconometric models (see Phillips, 1988, 1993b, for discussion of Bergstrom's contributions to econometrics). The major push in econometrics came in the period 1962–1965, which resulted in the appointment of J. Denis Sargan, Meghnad Desai, and Jan Tymes in the Economics Department and Kenneth F. Wallis in the Statistics Department and the introduction of taught M.Sc. courses in economics and econometrics. As an LSE student at the time I was aware that changes were taking place and gradually realized that they were very important developments for the LSE and for at least one generation of students to follow.

By 1965 the "new" M.Sc. courses in economics and the more specialized course in mathematical economics and econometrics were introduced to provide a thorough training for professional economists, and in the next few years there were further staff recruitments—Terence Gorman, Frank Hahn, Michio Morishima, and Amartya Sen in economics—and a considerable expansion in the number of Ph.D. students working in theoretical economics and econometrics. Within the field of econometrics the first few cohorts of students supervised by Denis Sargan included Ray Byron, Terry Charatsis, Emmanuel Dretakis, Toni Espasa, Tony Hall, David Hendry, Essie Maasoumi, William Mikhail, Grayham Mizon, Pravin Trivedi, Peter Phillips, Robin Rowley, Ross Williams, and Cliff Wymer (see the fuller list including later cohorts given in Maasoumi, 1988, vol. 1). The principal supervisor of most Ph.D. students in econometrics was Denis Sargan, and he had students working on an impressive range of topics: formulation, estimation, and testing of alternative dynamic model specifications; the use of the Lagrange multiplier testing principle for hypothesis testing in systems of equations; the treatment of missing observations in multivariate time-series models; semiparametric estimation of systems using FIML and spectral estimates of the error covariance matrix; the development and use of nonlinear estimation methods; inference with continuous-time models; the development of finite-sample distribution theory and higher-order asymptotic expansions to provide small sample approximations to distribution functions. A distinctive feature of much of the research conducted on these topics was the fact that it was embedded in applied econometric studies. Areas of application included models of wages and prices; aggregate durable and nondurable consumer demand; consumer demand equations; aggregate production and factor demand behavior, especially investment and inventory behavior; and import and export determination.

Another important part in the development of the methodology was played by the visitors to LSE. Jean-François Richard, beginning with the year he spent at LSE as a visitor in 1973–1974 but continuing through his collaboration in joint research with Hendry and Mizon, made major contributions in pointing out the important role of the joint distribution in the analysis of models of the relationship between observed variables, the role of the theory of reduction, and the formulation of precise definitions of exogeneity—Richard (1980) remains a tour de force in this area. The weekly Econometrics Workshop, associated with research programs funded by the Social Science Research Council, was a focus for the development and discussion of research ideas internally, but it also benefited from the participation of longer-term visitors such as Takeshi Amemiya, Ted Anderson (see his foreword to Maasoumi, 1988), Rob Engle, Alain Monfort, and Charles Nelson. Interaction with other econometricians came via periods of leave spent by members of the LSE econometrics group at the Australian National University, University of California at Berkeley, CORE, Yale, and particularly at University of California at San Diego. These visits provided valuable opportunities to prove and enrich ideas, and many lengthy, vigorous, and sometimes provocative conversations with Rob Engle, Clive Granger, Michel Mouchart, Adrian Pagan, Tom Rothenberg, and Hal White stimulated further developments and resulted in some joint papers.

By the end of the 1970s the LSE methodology was becoming more widely known as a result of journal publications, presentation of papers to conferences and in particular to the U.K. SSRC Econometrics Study Group, and via the expanding group of former students such as Gordon Anderson, Richard Blundell, Julia Campos, James Davidson, Neil Ericsson, Chris Gilbert, Mark Salmon, and Aris Spanos. Also many of the estimation and testing procedures developed as an integral part of the methodology were implemented in the computer program written by David Hendry—GIVE (generalized instrumental variable estimation), which was widely distributed and used. GIVE and other programs in the AUTOREG library (see Hendry and Srba, 1980) were the mainframe precursors of the programs PcGive and PcFiml (see Hendry, 1989; Doornik and Hendry, 1992, 1993, 1994) used in the empirical work reported in the fourth section below.

Also at the end of the 1970s some members of the LSE econometrics group took up positions at other universities in the UK: Wallis went to Warwick, Hendry to Oxford, and Mizon to Southampton. Following this and the later retirement of Denis Sargan the methodology was much less clearly identified with the LSE. Indeed, the LSE has via Andrew Harvey (Statistics Department) and Peter Robinson (Economics Department) fostered other important aspects of econometrics, and the subsequent development of the methodology, especially for the analysis of systems of integrated-cointegrated variables, has been greatly influenced by the contributions of Peter Phillips (Yale), Søren Johansen (Copenhagen), and Katarina Juselius (Copenhagen) initially, and more recently by those of Peter Boswijk (Amsterdam) and Jean-Pierre Urbain (Limburg). Further, the initial development of the theory of encompassing by Hendry, Mizon, and Richard (see Hendry and Richard, 1982, 1989; Mizon, 1984; Mizon and Richard, 1986) has been much extended and refined by the contributions of Jean-Pierre Florens (Toulouse), Neil Ericsson (Federal Reserve, Washington), and Maozu Lu (Southampton) among others. Gourieroux and Monfort (1995) provide a recent contribution. Hence there are many people who have contributed to the development of the LSE methodology, and many more now ensuring that it is refined, improved, and applied. The next section provides a brief description of its main components.

Components of the LSE Econometric Modeling Methodology

There have been many papers written on this topic (Ericsson, Campos, and Tran, 1990; Gilbert, 1986, 1989; Hendry, 1987; Hendry and Mizon, 1990; Hendry and Richard, 1982, 1983; Mizon, 1991; Pagan, 1987, 1989; Spanos, 1986; and other papers in Granger, 1990). Hendry and Wallis (1984), which contains contributions by some of Sargan's former colleagues and students to mark his retirement, also provides an insight into the LSE methodology. Hence only a brief discussion of the main components of the LSE methodology will be presented in this section, together with comments on the nature of models and their relationship with the data generation process (DGP).

By way of illustration consider an artificial situation in which it is known that observations on y_t, x_t, and z_t (which might be wages, prices, and unemployment, respectively) are independent drawings from a trivariate normal distribution with mean vector μ and covariance matrix Σ. Hence the DGP for y_t, x_t, and z_t is independent normal with mean vector μ and covariance matrix Σ with

$$\mu = \begin{pmatrix} \mu_y \\ \mu_x \\ \mu_z \end{pmatrix} \quad \Sigma = \begin{pmatrix} \sigma_{yy} & \sigma_{yx} & \sigma_{yz} \\ \sigma_{xy} & \sigma_{xx} & \sigma_{xz} \\ \sigma_{zy} & \sigma_{zx} & \sigma_{zz} \end{pmatrix}, \tag{4.1}$$

that is, the joint distribution of y_t, x_t, and z_t, denoted $D(y_t, x_t, z_t; \mu, \Sigma)$, has the form $D(y_t, x_t, z_t; \mu, \Sigma) = NI(\mu, \Sigma)$. However, this joint density can be reparameterized as the product of conditional and marginal densities:

$$D(y_t, x_t, z_t; \mu, \Sigma) = D(x_t \mid z_t, y_t; \theta_x, \omega_{11}) \times D(z_t \mid y_t; \theta_z, \omega_{22}) \times D(y_t; \theta_y, \omega_{33})$$

$$= NI(c_x + \beta y_t + \gamma z_t, \omega_{11}) \times NI(c_z + \alpha y_t, \omega_{22}) \times NI(c_y, \omega_{33})$$

This reparameterization is always possible, and yields an observationally equivalent representation of the DGP. Hence $NI(\mu, \Sigma)$ and $NI(\theta, \Omega)$ are observationally equivalent ways of presenting the trivariate normal distribution, when the mapping between the alternative parameterizations is given by

$$\begin{aligned} \theta_x' &= (c_x, \beta, \gamma) \\ \theta_z' &= (c_z, \alpha) \quad \Omega = \begin{pmatrix} \omega_{11} & 0 & 0 \\ 0 & \omega_{22} & 0 \\ 0 & 0 & \omega_{33} \end{pmatrix}, \\ \theta_y' &= c_y \end{aligned}$$

with

$$c_x = \mu_x - \beta\mu_y - \gamma\mu_z \qquad\qquad c_z = \mu_z - \alpha\mu_y \qquad c_y = \mu_y$$

$$\varphi\gamma = \sigma_{yy}\sigma_{zx} - \sigma_{zy}\sigma_{yx} \qquad\qquad \varphi\beta = \sigma_{zz}\sigma_{yx} - \sigma_{yz}\sigma_{zx} \quad \alpha = \sigma_{zy}\sigma_{yy}^{-1}$$

$$\omega_{11} = \sigma_{xx} - \beta^2\sigma_{yy} - 2\beta\gamma\sigma_{yz} - \gamma^2\sigma_{zz} \quad \omega_{22} = \sigma_{zz} - \alpha^2\sigma_{yy} \qquad \omega_{33} = \sigma_{yy}$$

and $\varphi = \sigma_{yy}\sigma_{zz} - \sigma_{yz}^2$. Adopting the (θ, Ω) parameterization the DGP can be described in the equations

$$x_t = c_x + \beta y_t + \gamma z_t + \upsilon_{1t},$$

$$z_t = c_z + \alpha y_t + \upsilon_{2t},$$

$$y_t = c_y + \upsilon_{3t},$$

$$\mathbf{v}_t = (\upsilon_{1t}, \upsilon_{2t}, \upsilon_{3t})' \sim NI(0, \Omega). \tag{4.2}$$

Now, let the equations (4.2) be the equations used to generate the data in a Monte Carlo simulation study, so that the investigator who writes down the model

$$M_1 : x_t = c_1 + \beta_1 y_t + \gamma_1 z_t + u_{1t} \tag{4.3}$$

with $u_{1t} \sim NI(0, \sigma_{u1}^2)$ is clearly seen to have chosen a "true" model since it corresponds exactly to an equation of the DGP, with $c_1 = c_x$, $\beta_1 = \beta$, $\gamma_1 = \gamma$, and $\sigma_{u1}^2 = \omega_{11}$. Indeed, M_1 corresponds to $D(x_t \mid z_t, y_t; \theta_x, \omega_{11})$, which is part of the DGP. Hence provided that the phenomenon of interest to the investigator can be analyzed solely in terms of the parameters of M_1, and y_t and z_t are weakly exogenous variables for the parameters of interest, no problems will arise for that investigator. The fact that $D(x_t \mid z_t, y_t; \theta_x, \omega_{11})$ is only part of the DGP so that M_1 is not exploiting all the information in the DGP, is the reason for requiring y_t and z_t to be weakly exogenous. If the parameters of interest to the investigator are denoted ϕ, then y_t and z_t will be weakly exogenous for ϕ provided that (1) ϕ can be recovered uniquely from θ_x and ω_{11}, and (2) the values of θ_x and ω_{11} in the DGP are chosen independently of the values of the other parameters of the DGP—namely, θ_z, θ_y, ω_{22} and ω_{33}. The requirement (2) is satisfied for the DGP being discussed here provided that there are no *a priori* restrictions linking (θ_x', ω_{11}) to $(\theta_z', \theta_y, \omega_{22}, \omega_{33})$ (for example, $\alpha = \beta$). Engle, Hendry, and Richard (1983) provide fuller definitions and discussion of this and other concepts of exogeneity.

Now consider another investigator who claims to be interested in the model

$$M_2 : y_t = c_2 + \alpha_2 x_t + \gamma_2 z_t + u_{2t}. \tag{4.4}$$

With $u_{2t} \sim NI(0, \sigma_{u2}^2)$ this investigator is clearly not considering the "true" model since M_2 does not correspond to any of the equations of the DGP as given in (4.2)! It is, though, part of other valid parameterizations of the DGP:

$$D(y_t, x_t, z_t; \mu, \Sigma) = D(y_t \mid x_t, z_t; \xi_y) \times D(x_t \mid z_t; \xi_x) \times D(z_t; \xi_z)$$

$$= D(y_t \mid x_t, z_t; \xi_y) \times D(z_t \mid x_t; \zeta_z) \times D(x_t; \zeta_x)$$

and thus "true". Further, the investigator who chooses to analyze the model

$$M_3 : y_t = c_3 + \alpha_3 x_t + u_{3t} \tag{4.5}$$

with $u_{3t} \sim NI(0, \sigma_{u3}^2)$ is clearly misguided in ignoring the influence of z_t on y_t and could be argued to be using a misspecified model, in addition to not having a "true" model. However, M_3 need be neither misspecified nor untrue. If the parameters of interest to the investigator are those of the distribution $y_t \mid x_t$ (that is, ς in $D(y_t \mid x_t; \varsigma)$), then M_3 is obtained as a reduction of the DGP given by $NI(\mu, \Sigma)$ and as such is both true and correctly specified when $c_3 = \mu_y - \alpha_3 \mu_x$ and $\alpha_3 = \sigma_{xx}^{-1}\sigma_{xy}$ with $\sigma_{u3}^2 = \sigma_{yy} - \alpha_3^2 \sigma_{xx}$. Alternatively, if M_3 is thought to be a statement about the distribution $D(y_t \mid x_t, z_t; \xi_y)$, then it will only be fully exploiting the available information if the conditional independence hypothesis $y_t \perp z_t \mid x_t$ (or $\gamma_2 = 0$ in M_2) is valid.

Two important points have been illustrated in this discussion. First, all models can be obtained as reductions of the DGP for the variables they involve, and therefore their properties are implied by the DGP. In fact, the parameters of any model are appropriately interpreted as the pseudo true values (derived under the DGP) of the maximum-likelihood estimators given the model specification. Second, it is important in all econometric studies to know what the parameters of interest are or, equivalently, what the relevant statistical distribution and information set are. Hence a model can be relevant only if it is defined with respect to an appropriate information set and if the parameters of interest can be uniquely derived from its parameters. But this is not sufficient for efficient inference on the parameters of interest. It is also important that the model be congruent with the available information. For example, a necessary condition for a model like M_3 to be congruent, when the parameters of interest are functions of ξ_y, is $\gamma_2 = 0$. This is a testable hypothesis, and it is important that it be tested as a part of the evaluation of the model.

The importance of testing and evaluating econometric models is central to the LSE methodology. This was clear in Sargan (1964), in which tests for functional form (natural logarithm ln versus level), for appropriate dynamic specification (the order of dynamics and common factor restrictions (COMFAC)), and for instrument validity were proposed and used. Subsequent papers that further developed this theme include Hendry and Mizon (1978), Hendry and Richard (1982, 1983), Mizon (1977a), and Hendry (1980), this last paper concluding with the recommendation to "test, test, and test." Hypothesis testing can be used both to assess the adequacy of the currently specified model (misspecification testing) and to explore the possibility for simplifying the current model without losing coherence with available information including the observed data (specification testing) (see Mizon, 1977b, for discussion of this distinction). Both these forms of testing play important roles in the evaluation of econometric models, an issue to which attention is now turned.

Criteria for Evaluation

If an econometric model is to be taken and used seriously, then its credentials must be established. Two important ways to do this are to demonstrate that the model is coherent with the available relevant information and that it is at least as good as alternative models of the same phenomena. Hence congruence and encompassing are central to the LSE methodology.

Congruence.   In assessing the coherence of a model with available information, it has to be recognized that there are many sources of information, which can usefully be divided into four categories: *a priori* theory, observed sample information, the properties of the measurement system, and rival models.

A Priori *Theory.*   That for econometric models the primary source for *a priori* theory is economics and economic theory is obvious and uncontentious. The relative importance of economic theory and statistical criteria in the development and evaluation of econometric models, though, has been the subject of much debate, with probably the most frequently cited example being the "measurement without theory" debate between Koopmans and Vining (see Hendry and Morgan, 1995, for a recent assessment of this debate). However, the tensions between VAR modeling and real business cycle and calibrated models are a current manifestation of the debate that still surrounds this issue. In crude terms the contrast is between data-driven modeling in the use of VAR's, and theory-driven modeling of either the structural type (á la Hansen and Sargent) or the calibrated real business cycle type. Canova (1995) presents a survey of VAR modeling, Ingram (1995) reviews structural modeling, Kydland and Prescott (1995) present the case for calibration methods applied to models of the real business cycle, and Kim and Pagan (1994) discuss ways in which this latter class of model can be evaluated. In this context the LSE approach draws on the strengths of each of these alternative approaches, though this is not the way that the LSE methodology evolved. Hence Hendry (1993b) argues that while it is desirable that econometric models be consistent with an economic theory, it is not essential. Indeed, if all models were required to have their origins in existing economic theory, then the scope for developing new theories and learning from observation would be greatly reduced. Further, there is nothing that endows an economic theory with veracity *a priori*, and so coherence

of an econometric model with an economic theory is neither necessary nor sufficient for it to be a good model. The practice of judging a model to be satisfactory
if all the signs and magnitudes of its estimated parameters are consistent with an
economic theory, and hence regarding the economic theory as being confirmed by
the evidence, has little to recommend it (see Gilbert, 1986, for a critique of this
approach). Not the least reason for this is the fact that it is possible for a number
of alternative models to share this property (see Mizon, 1989, for an illustration).

There is a sense, though, in which all econometric models result from the use
of economic considerations, such as the choice of variables to include in the
model, and of the functional forms to characterize the relationships between them.
Congruence with economic theory in this category (which is similar to what
Hendry, 1993b, calls *low-level theory*) is an essential feature for an econometric
model. However, theories that imply very tight and specific forms for econometric
models (such as models embodying rational expectations, intertemporal optimization, or Euler equation formulations) are higher-level theories that embody testable hypotheses rather than specifying essential characteristics for any econometric
model of the phenomena being studied. The value and feasibility of testing economic theory against empirical observation are also much debated issues, as are
the questions of what are appropriate interpretations and reactions to the results of
statistical hypothesis tests. In particular, if a statistical test of an hypothesis is
unfavorable, there are many reasons why this may not lead to the immediate rejection of the hypothesis or the model incorporating the hypothesis. For example,
(1) the statistical model providing the framework for the hypothesis test may yield
invalid or misleading inferences as a result of being noncongruent with the sample
information; (2) there may be doubts about the suitability of the statistical model
as an implementation of the economic theory; (3) the observed data may not
correspond closely with the latent variables of the economic theory or may be
subject to other measurement errors; or (4) there may be no alternative models that
dominate it.

Sample Information.   The requirement that an econometric model be congruent
with sample information is a necessary condition for statistical inferences based
on it to be valid. Since there are distinct concepts associated with a model's congruence with respect to past, present, and future sample information, each of these
types of sample information will be considered separately.

1. *Relative Past Sample Information*: Past sample information consists of observations on lagged values of the variables in the modeling dataset. Hence if the tth
observation on the N variables in the dataset is denoted by $\mathbf{x}_t$, this constitutes the
present (relative to the time index t) sample information, the relative past sample

information is $\{\mathbf{x}_1, \mathbf{x}_2, \ldots, \mathbf{x}_{t-1}\}$, and the relative future information is $\{\mathbf{x}_{t+1}, \mathbf{x}_{t+2}, \mathbf{x}_{t+3}, \ldots, \mathbf{x}_T\}$ when T is the final observation available in the sample.

A model that is not congruent with past sample information will have errors that are correlated with lagged values of $\mathbf{x}_t$, and hence the errors will be serially correlated and at least partially explainable in terms of $\{\mathbf{x}_1, \mathbf{x}_2, \ldots, \mathbf{x}_{t-1}\}$. For example, if the OLS estimator of δ in the static regression model,

$$y_t = \delta z_t + u_t, \tag{4.6}$$

is used to make inferences, and possibly policy recommendations, involving the long-run response of y_t to z_t when u_t is serially correlated, then invalid and misleading inferences are likely to be the result. In particular, let the appropriate model to capture the relationship between y_t and z_t, and distinguish between long-run and short-run responses, be an autoregressive-distributed lag model ($AD(1, 1)$) of the form

$$y_t = \alpha y_{t-1} + \beta z_t + \gamma z_{t-1} + \varepsilon_t, \tag{4.7}$$

with

$$z_t = \lambda z_{t-1} + v_t \tag{4.8}$$

when each of $\{\varepsilon_t\}$ and $\{v_t\}$ are identically independently distributed processes that are independent of each other with $|\alpha| < 1$, $|\lambda| < 1$, so that both y_t and z_t are stationary. Then in the static long run (that is, when $y_t = y^*$ and $z_t = z^*$ $\forall t$) the response of y_t to z_t is given by $\kappa = (\beta + \gamma)/(1 - \alpha)$, whereas the pseudo true value of the OLS estimator of δ is given by $\delta_0 = (\beta + \gamma\lambda)/(1 - \alpha\lambda)$. Hence inferences about the long-run response of y_t to z_t based on the static regression model (4.6) will be invalid unless $\kappa = \delta_0$. Note that $\kappa = \delta_0$ if and only if $\gamma = -\alpha\beta$, which is the common factor restriction that ensures that the autoregressive distributed lag model (4.7) takes the form

$$y_t = \beta z_t + \varepsilon_t,$$

$$\varepsilon_t = \alpha \varepsilon_{t-1} + \varepsilon_t, \tag{4.9}$$

so that all the dynamics is captured by a first-order autoregressive error process. Also note that although $\lambda = 1$ appears to be another condition for $\kappa = \delta_0$, this possibility is ruled out by the assumption that z_t is stationary. That the static regression model (4.6) is not congruent with past sample information would be revealed by testing for the absence of serial correlation in the model residuals. The fact that congruence with information from this source can be tested via serial correlation tests does not imply that when a model is found to have serially correlated residuals subsequent analysis should adopt estimation methods that allow for autoregressive (or even moving average) error processes since this will only be appropriate if $\gamma = -\alpha\beta$. Sargan (1964, 1980b) provides detailed discussion of this point, and further analysis is contained in Hendry and Mizon (1978), Hoover (1988), Mizon (1977a, 1993), Mizon and Hendry (1980), and Spanos (1988). Mizon (1995) points out that there are also serious drawbacks to imposing invalid common factor restrictions in models for nonstationary variables, in particular integrated-cointegrated variables. This is illustrated in the fourth section below. In short, testing for congruence with past sample information is a way of checking the adequacy of the dynamic specification of the model (see the typology of univariate dynamic models in Hendry, Pagan, and Sargan, 1984, and that for multivariate dynamic models in Hendry, 1993c), but such tests will also have power against wrong functional form, regime shifts, and other causes of parameter nonconstancy.

2. *Relative Present Sample Information*: A model with errors that are not homoscedastic innovations with respect to the set of all current dated variables in the modeler's databank of relevant variables is not congruent and can be improved by using information already available. For example, if a model's errors u_t are such that $E(u_t \mathbf{x}_t) \neq 0$ then there is still information in x_t that is unexploited. This could arise from erroneously omitting variables from the model or by conditioning on variables that are not weakly exogenous for the parameters of interest. Another form of this type of noncongruence is heteroscedasticity in the errors (that is, $E(u_t^2) = \sigma_t^2 \neq \sigma^2 \forall t$), which implies that the distribution of the errors has features that are potentially explainable as functions of the $\mathbf{x}_t$. The distribution of the errors may also be skewed, leptokurtic, or platykurtic, and to the extent that these features of the error distribution are explainable as functions of the available data the model is noncongruent. Tests for omitted variables, for weak exogeneity (see Engle, Hendry, and Richard, 1983; Ericsson, 1993; Richard, 1980), excess skewness or kurtosis in the error distribution (see Doornik and Hansen, 1994), and homoscedasticity (see Breusch and Pagan, 1980; White, 1980) are examples of ways in which a model's congruence with present sample information can be assessed.

3. *Relative Future Sample Information*: For a model to be congruent with future sample information it must not suffer from predictive failure or parameter nonconstancy. A model with characteristics that change with modest extensions to the estimation period is clearly failing to represent important features of the DGP and is thus likely to yield poor inferences, whether these be parameter estimates, tests of hypotheses, or predictions. One of the essential characteristics for a model to have if it is to be valuable for inference is that it captures fundamental invariants in the relationships between the variables that are under scrutiny —that is, represent the structure. A model with all its "parameters" transient is

itself ephemeral, and inferences based on it are likely to appear whimsical when judged against subsequent observation. Indeed, such a model could not be capturing underlying structure. A more durable model will have its parameter estimates approximately constant across varying estimation periods. Further, when a model is to be used for prediction of the likely effects of a change in policy (such as a change in tax rates, a move from fixed to floating exchange rates, or the introduction of a tight monetary policy), it is crucial that the model's parameters are invariant to the policy regime shift. Discussion of this issue has a long history, early contributors being Frisch and Haavelmo who in their analysis introduced the concept of autonomy (see Aldrich, 1989). Lucas (1976) presented a more recent view of the problem, which has spawned a large literature. Indeed, for many macroeconometricians the Lucas critique was sufficiently pernicious to have removed the credibility of much econometric modelling. However, if a model has conditioning variables that are weakly exogenous for the parameters of interest, and the latter are invariant to changes in the process generating the conditioning variables (the conditions for superexogeneity; see Engle, Hendry, and Richard, 1983), then the Lucas critique is rendered benign. An important implication of this statement is that the Lucas critique is brought into the realms of testable hypotheses as explained by Engle and Hendry (1993) and Favero and Hendry (1992) (see Ericsson, 1993, for a recent appraisal). The main instruments of such testing are analysis of variance type parameter constancy and Chow (1960) prediction test statistics, as well as recursive estimation (see Brown, Durbin, and Evans, 1975; Hansen, 1992; and Terasvirta, 1970).

Measurement System.   It is important to know how variables are measured and their specific properties. With this knowledge it is then possible to choose functional forms for models, or variable transformations, to ensure that the models will yield fitted and predicted values of the modeled variables that share these same properties. This is the requirement that the models be data admissible. For example, in modeling aggregate consumption, which is known never to be negative, it makes sense to consider modeling the logarithm of consumption rather than its level in order to avoid generating negative fitted or predicted values. Similarly, a logarithmic or logit transformation of a variable-like unemployment that is bounded between 0 and 1 (or equivalently between 0 and 100 percent) will guarantee that the model's fitted and predicted values share this property. Hence the congruence of a model with the measurement system requires it to be logically possible for the model to generate the observed and future data. This concept of congruence can be extended to incorporate the requirement that the model should be capable of representing empirically determined characteristics of the data such as stationarity, deterministic nonstationarity, integratedness, or seasonality. To choose models to be data admissible and hence congruent with this source of information is prudent rather than contentious, though the nature of the particular problem being analyzed will determine the price of imprudence.

Rival Models. The importance of ensuring that a model is congruent with the information contained in rival models is twofold. First, in economics there is usually no shortage of alternative theories for a given phenomenon. Second, it is possible for more than one model to be congruent with *a priori* theory, sample information, and the properties of the measurement system. The fact that economics is a rich source of theories and hypotheses is a tribute to the economics profession's ingenuity and imagination and a problem only if there is no serious attempt to discriminate between the competing models. Typically, alternative theories when implemented in econometric models use different information sets and possibly different functional forms and are thus separate or nonnested models. It is this nonnested feature that enables more than one model to be congruent with respect to sample information: each can be congruent with respect to its *own* information set. Ericsson and Hendry (1989) analyze this issue and show that the corroboration of more than one model can imply the inadequacy of each, and Mizon (1989) provides an illustration. Hence to have a model that is congruent with respect to its own information set is a necessary condition for it to be exploiting that information, but it is not sufficient for it to be a dominant or encompassing model. An encompassing model is one which can account for the previous empirical findings that were thought to be relevant and adequate for the explanation of the variables and parameters of interest and can explain the features of rival models being considered currently. The encompassing model renders other models inferentially redundant and so is a dominant model.

The comparison of alternative models for the same phenomenon can be achieved by using one of the many statistics for testing nonnested hypotheses (see Cox, 1961, 1962; Davidson and MacKinnon, 1981; and Pesaran, 1974), but it is important to note that the statistical (size and power) properties of these test statistics are derived in the context of an embedding model—a point made clear by the encompassing interpretation of these test statistics (see Hendry and Richard, 1989; Mizon, 1984; Mizon and Richard, 1986). Further, the use of nonnested test statistics in pairwise comparison of models can lead to apparent contradictions and is a nontransitive procedure. In particular, it is possible for the hypotheses $M_1 \varepsilon M_2$ and $M_2 \varepsilon M_3$ to be valid while the hypothesis $M_1 \varepsilon M_3$ is invalid. Since this nontransitivity of encompassing arises essentially because the embedding model implicit in each of the three pairwise comparisons is different (often $M_1 \cup M_2$, $M_2 \cup M_3$ and $M_1 \cup M_3$, respectively), the problem can be avoided by comparing all models relative to a general model that embeds or nests all of them. Letting M_c denote such an embedding model (that is, $M_i \subset M_c \forall i$), it is then possible to test the nested hypothesis that M_i is an acceptable simplification of M_c for each i. If there is a model (M_1, say) that is a valid simplification of M_c, then it parsimoniously encompasses M_c—denoted $M_1\varepsilon_p M_c$. In the population it is possible for more than one model to parsimoniously encompass an embedding or completing model M_c only if they are observationally equivalent, consequently, if $M_1\varepsilon_p M_c$, then $M_1\varepsilon M_j \forall j$. Therefore the requirement that a model be congruent with information contained in rival models is equivalent to that model parsimoniously encompassing a model that embeds all the rival models. This implies that the relevant sample information set for the determination of a congruent model is the union of the information sets of the models implementing each competing theory. Unsurprisingly, this entails that if empirical evidence is to be used to evaluate and compare models rather than naively corroborate them, a modeling strategy that starts from a congruent general model and tests for valid simplifications or reductions of it is likely to be an efficient way to find parsimonious yet durable representations of the salient features of the relationships between the variables of interest.

Finally, in this section on the evaluation of model congruence, note that testing for congruence with respect to sample information is misspecification testing, whereas testing for congruence with respect to rival model information is specification testing. In this context misspecification testing can be seen as a means of ensuring that there is a valid statistical basis for using specification testing to find a parsimonious encompassing model. Provided that the sample information set used ensures that all econometric models implementing relevant economic theories are nested within a general model that is congruent with the sample information (this is determined by misspecification testing or diagnostic checking of the general model), the model that parsimoniously encompasses the general model and is data admissible will be the dominant model that is congruent with information from all four sources (this is determined by specification testing or checking the validity of reductions from the congruent general model).

Encompassing.   If parsimonious encompassing is an essential part of congruence, what is the separate role for encompassing? As emphasized above, parsimonious encompassing is the property that a model be an acceptable reduction of a congruent embedding model and as such is specification searching within a common general model. If after completing a modeling exercise and having determined which model is preferred further information becomes available, this raises the question as to whether the existing results are robust to this extension of the information set. The further information may take the form of new *a priori* theories that imply an extension of the information set to embrace the empirical models implementing these new theories. Testing the preferred model's ability to encompass the newly available rival models (which can be done using nonnested test statistics) is a form of misspecification testing. Conversely, the requirement that a model encompass its rivals ensures that the information set used for modeling is general enough to enable the empirical implementation of all the models. Hence each model is evaluated with respect to an information set more general than the minimum one required for its own implementation, thus achieving robustness to extensions of its information set in directions relevant for competing models.

Modeling Strategies

The previous section discussed the evaluation of econometric models and emphasized the important roles of congruence and encompassing in this assessment. Indeed, the most important features of a model are its quality and suitability for its intended use, features that are assessed in the process of model evaluation and not endowed on it as a result of the process by which the model is developed. The route by which a model is discovered (including serendipity, brilliant intuition, and systematic application of a particular modeling strategy) does not determine model quality, though it does affect research efficiency) (see Hendry and Mizon, 1990, for further discussion of these points). Although a model with a good pedigree (for example, derived from high-quality economic theory by a leading practitioner) is more likely to be valuable than one without, such a pedigree is neither necessary nor sufficient for the discovery of a congruent and encompassing model. This is fortunate since otherwise there would be little or no scope for the discovery of new theories and classes of model.

While there is no unique way to find congruent and encompassing models, some modeling strategies are more likely to do so, and to do so efficiently, than others. Of the many strategies that might be adopted in modeling, attention here is confined to a contrast between specific-to-general and general-to-specific modeling. Granger (1990) contains discussions of other possibilities.

Specific-to-General Versus General-to-Specific Modeling. In specific-to-general modeling the starting model is both very specific and simple, often implementing a particular narrowly defined economic theory. This approach, it has been argued, has the twin advantages of avoiding unnecessary generality (which results in loss of efficiency and can result in models being too finely tuned to the sample data) and guaranteeing the coherence of the model with economic theory thus ensuring that the model has an economic interpretation and is related to the phenomena being studied. An important issue with such modeling is the extent and means of model evaluation adopted. The average economic regression approach described by Gilbert (1986) seeks corroboration of the underlying economic theory in terms of signs, magnitudes, and significance of estimated parameters and does not question the adequacy of the model as a whole relative to the available information. However, no matter how elegant and sophisticated an economic theory is, there is no guarantee that the model implementing it will be statistically well specified, and yet without this inferences drawn from the model will be invalid. In short, the essence of the argument against specific-to-general modeling is that *a priori* theory is not endowed with empirical veracity and so econometric models must be scrupulously evaluated for congruence with information from sources additional to *a priori* theory, but tests performed in a noncongruent framework are themselves invalid in general. Further, it is possible to find more than one congruent model when the congruence of each model is with respect to its own implicit or explicit information set (see Mizon, 1989, for an illustration).

Although it is possible to test the statistical adequacy of simple models, once a model is found to be inadequate, specific-to-general modeling is a seriously flawed strategy for discovering other models that retain economic theory consistency and also achieve coherence with the data. In this regard the alternative of a general-to-specific strategy has many advantages, such as those associated with the following arguments listed by Hendry and Doornik (1994): "directed versus directionless strategies; validly interpreting intermediate test outcomes by avoiding later potential contradictions; escaping the *non sequitur* of accepting the alternative hypothesis when a test rejects the null; determining the baseline innovation error process on the available information; and circumventing the drawbacks of correcting manifest flaws when these appear as against commencing from a congruent model." Further discussion of these points can be found *inter alia* in Hendry (1983) and Mizon (1977b, 1989). Hendry and Doornik (1994) provide ten further logical and methodological arguments in favor of general-to-specific modeling and for commencing econometric analyses by modeling the joint density of all relevant variables.

Mizon (1995), in the context of a DGP given by the partial adjustment model

$$y_t = \beta z_t + \alpha y_{t-1} + \varepsilon_t, \tag{4.10}$$

with z_t generated by (4.8), illustrated the failure of a specific-to-general search starting from a static regression as in (4.6) to find an adequate model, whereas a general-to-specific strategy involving reduction from the congruent general model given by an AD(1, 1) model of the form (4.7) easily led to the selection of the DGP as the only model that is congruent and parsimoniously encompasses (4.7). In addition to being an efficient way to find a congruent encompassing model, the general-to-specific modeling strategy applied in Mizon (1995) was shown to avoid the statistically anomalous result of an algebraically more general model (4.9) failing to encompass the static regression (4.6), which is apparently nested within it. The failure of (4.9) to encompass the simpler model (4.6) arises because (4.9) involves the auxiliary COMFAC hypothesis $\alpha\beta + \gamma = 0$, which is not entailed in the specification of (4.6). However, adopting a general-to-specific strategy and only testing for simplifications within a congruent general model avoids this anomaly since (4.9) is clearly revealed to be noncongruent in that the hypothesis $\alpha\beta + \gamma = 0$ is rejected and (4.9) has serially correlated errors. Hendry and Doornik (1994) also contains a discussion of this anomaly and the use of a general-to-specific modeling strategy to avoid it.

Much of the early research done by members of the LSE was concerned with single-equation analysis and in particular the choice of an appropriate dynamic specification. Single-equation models of necessity involve conditioning on some variables and hence weak exogeneity assertions. The necessity of ensuring that conditioning variables are weakly exogenous for the parameters of interest was always emphasized (see Hendry and Richard, 1982, 1983). The testing of weak exogeneity assertions also involves modeling from the general to the specific, and an important example of this point is provided by the analysis in Hendry (1993a). Case (d) of his analysis considered a situation in which a model of the conditional distribution $D(y_t \mid z_t, y_{t-1}, z_{t-1})$ corresponded exactly to an equation of the DGP. Indeed it embodied the conditional expectation $E[y_t \mid z_t, y_{t-1}, z_{t-1}] = \beta z_t$, and yet inference on β based on OLS estimation was inefficient as a result of z_t not being weakly exogenous for β. This came about because the parameters β and σ_1^2 of the conditional distribution $D(y_t \mid z_t, y_{t-1}, z_{t-1}; \beta, \sigma_1^2)$ were linked directly to the parameters of the marginal distribution $D(z_t \mid y_{t-1}, z_{t-1}; \beta, \rho, \sigma_2^2)$ when the DGP had the form

$$y_t = \beta z_t + \varepsilon_{1t},$$

$$\Delta z_t = \rho(y_{t-1} - \beta z_{t-1}) + \varepsilon_{2t}, \tag{4.11}$$

with

$$\begin{pmatrix} \varepsilon_{1t} \\ \varepsilon_{2t} \end{pmatrix} \sim NI \left[\begin{pmatrix} 0 \\ 0 \end{pmatrix} \begin{pmatrix} \sigma_1^2 & 0 \\ 0 & \sigma_2^2 \end{pmatrix} \right]. \tag{4.12}$$

This example, and others presented in Hendry (1993a) in the context of a bivariate cointegrated system, illustrate the crucial role of weak exogeneity in sustaining valid single-equation inference with cointegrated processes, despite the fact that the OLS estimator is superconsistent in that context. This example indicates that whether or not variables are weakly exogenous for the parameters of interest depends on the properties of the joint distribution of all variables. Hence it is not surprising that members of the LSE also paid attention to the issues of model congruence and encompassing, and the desirability of using a general-to-specific modelling strategy, in a systems context.

Although the importance of carefully considering the dynamic specification of single-equation econometric models had been a crucial part of the LSE methodology since Sargan (1964), its relevance for systems of equations was also realized. Discussions of dynamic specification in systems is contained in Hendry

(1971, 1974), Hendry and Anderson (1977), and Mizon (1977a). However, the challenge to the econometric modeling of macroeconomic time series provided by the work of Box and Jenkins (1970) and Granger and Newbold (1974) stimulated other contributions. In particular, Prothero and Wallis (1976) analyzed the univariate implications of systems of simultaneous equations, drawing attention to the particular form taken by the implied autoregressive integrated moving average (ARIMA) time-series models (also see Zellner and Palm, 1974). These and other contributions, for which see the discussion in Hendry, Pagan, and Sargan (1984), were concerned with the specification, estimation, and testing of multivariate econometric models with respect to their own information sets and did not raise the issue of one structural econometric model encompassing its rivals. Noting that the typical specification of a dynamic linear structural econometric model (SEM), based on the pioneering work of the Cowles Commission researchers (see Koopmans, 1950), has the generic form

$$B\mathbf{y}_t + C\mathbf{z}_t + D\mathbf{x}_{t-1} = \mathbf{u}_t,$$

$$\mathbf{u}_t \sim NI(0, \Omega), \tag{4.13}$$

when y_t are the endogenous variables being modeled, z_t are weakly exogenous variables that are not modeled, $x'_{t-1} = (y'_{t-1}, z'_{t-1})$ are the lagged values of both endogenous and exogenous variables, and u_t is the vector of unobserved errors, it is clear that the underlying distribution is $D(y_t \mid z_t, x_{t-1})$, which corresponds to the unrestricted reduced form that in conventional notation can be written

$$\mathbf{y}_t = \Pi_z \mathbf{z}_t + \Pi_x \mathbf{x}_{t-1} + \mathbf{v}_t,$$

$$\mathbf{v}_t \sim NI(0, \Sigma). \tag{4.14}$$

As is well known, the parameters of (4.13) are unidentified without *a priori* restrictions, and so assuming that the specification of (4.13) asserts more restrictions than are required to achieve identification, it follows that the specification of (4.13) implies the hypothesis

$$\Pi_z = -B^{-1}C, \ \Pi_x = -B^{-1}D,$$

$$\Sigma = B^{-1}\Omega(B^{-1})', \tag{4.15}$$

Which embodies the overidentifying restrictions. Hence an important part of the evaluation of a structural econometric model is a test of these overidentifying restrictions (see Anderson and Rubin, 1950; Sargan, 1988). Richard (1980) pointed out that the restrictions on Π_z and Π_x are equivalent to the following hypothesis concerning the conditional mean of y_t:

$$BE(\mathbf{y}_t \mid \mathbf{z}_t, \mathbf{x}_{t-1}) + C\mathbf{z}_t + D\mathbf{x}_{t-1} = 0 \ \forall t, \tag{4.16}$$

and Mizon (1984) provided an encompassing interpretation of these and the covariance restrictions as the restrictions required for (4.13) to parsimoniously encompass (4.14). However, the identification of (4.13) relative to (4.14), and the parsimonious encompassing hypothesis (4.15) or (4.16), evaluate the SEM (4.13) relative to its own information set.

For linear dynamic systems, when there is more than one structural econometric model, and it is desired to test the exogeneity status of some variables in the system, an appropriate framework for evaluation is the VAR for the union of all variables in the structural models, plus any further variables required to achieve a congruent VAR. For the variables $\mathbf{x}_t$, a kth-order VAR takes the form

$$\mathbf{x}_t = \sum_{j=1}^{k} A_j \mathbf{x}_{t-j} + \boldsymbol{\varepsilon}_t,$$

which has proved to be a valuable way to model the joint distribution of $\mathbf{x}_t$ conditional on its history $D(\mathbf{x}_t \mid \mathbf{x}_0, \mathbf{x}_1, \ldots, \mathbf{x}_{t-1})$. Monfort and Rabemananjara (1990) for stationary x_t illustrated the use of a VAR as a general model within which to test the exogeneity status of a subset of variables and to test particular structural hypotheses. Hendry and Mizon (1993) proposed the use of a congruent VAR when $\mathbf{x}_t$ is nonstationary ($\mathbf{x}_t \sim I(1)$ and/or the process-generating $\mathbf{x}_t$ has deterministic nonstationarities such as trends and regime shifts) as a general statistical framework within which to test hypotheses about the dimension of cointegrating space following Johansen (1988), as well as hypotheses concerning dynamic simplification (such as Granger noncausality), weak exogeneity, and the ability of particular structural econometric models to parsimoniously encompass the VAR. Note that in this framework the evaluation of each SEM is relative to the information set supporting the VAR and not just the SEM's own information set. Clements and Mizon (1991) and Hendry and Doornik (1994) contain applications of the general-'to-specific modeling strategy for $I(1)$ systems proposed by Hendry and Mizon (1993), and the next section provides an illustration using an updated databank for a subset of the variables modeled in Clements and Mizon (1991).

Just as the importance of evaluating models by checking their congruence and encompassing abilities is not confined to single-equation models, it is not limited to models for time-series variables. It is just as important for cross-section and panel data models that their congruence be tested and that the encompassing properties of alternative models are assessed, rather than simply using empirical analysis to calibrate and confirm particular economic theories. Research devoted to furthering the development of model evaluation criteria and test statistics for microeconometric models, analogous to those developed for macroeconomic time series models, could yield high returns in terms of deepening and putting on a firmer basis our understanding of microeconomic relationships. Since general tools for estimation and hypothesis testing are available, the need is for a taxonomy of information sets relevant for the evaluation of microeconometric models, and the development of frameworks sufficiently general to enable the comparison of alternative models. Similarly, general-to-specific modeling strategies can be expected to be valid, effective, and efficient ways to develop congruent and encompassing models in microeconometrics.

Though the description of the main components of the LSE methodology presented above is largely concerned with the theory of model evaluation and theoretical aspects of modeling strategies, it is important to note that a major part of the research that led to the development of the methodology was firmly embedded in applied econometric studies. Such empirical econometric studies, in addition to being valuable directly in tackling the issues on which they are focused (if they are successful) and providing a test bed to prove the worth of existing econometric techniques and modeling strategies, are a rich source of problems requiring new theoretical results. The next section contains an empirical study of the relationship between wages, prices, and unemployment in the UK that provides an illustration of LSE-style modeling and draws attention to problems concerning the interrelationship between the modeling of nonstationary variables, regime shifts, and forecasting.

An Illustration: Wages, Prices, and Unemployment in the United Kingdom

As a simple illustration of modeling (both single-equation and system) within the spirit of the LSE methodology, three variables are taken from an updated data set containing the same variables as Clements and Mizon (1991). Quarterly data for the three variables, ln wages w (strictly, this variable is defined as the ln of earnings per employee but will be referred to as *wages*), ln of the retail price index p, and ln of the percentage unemployment rate u, are available for the period 1965(1) to 1993(1) (see Figure 4.1). The data for w and u are seasonally adjusted, but data for p and hence the inflation rate Δp are not. Precise definitions and sources are given in the data appendix.

Visual inspection of these graphs indicates that both w and p have strong positive trends of a similar magnitude, so that they might be modeled well as stationary deviations from a linear trend, or alternatively as variables with stochastic trends within a cointegrated-integrated system (see the discussion below and Banerjee et al., 1993, for a fuller description). However, this is allowing the visually clear domination of trend in both w and p to dictate the choice of the potential components for analyzing the structure of the series. u also has a strong upward trend, but the deviations from this exhibit cyclical movements that it will be important to capture in the modeling of these variables. That cyclical features,

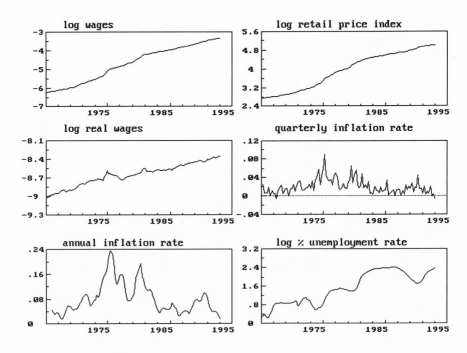

Figure 4.1. Data plots, 1965(1)–1993(1)

possible resulting from changes in economic policies (such as fixed or floating exchange rates and accommodating or tight monetary policies) and autonomous events (such as the movement in commodity prices, including the price of crude oil, in the late 1960s and early 1970s) may be important is also suggested by inspection of the graphs of the $\ln$ of real wages $(w - p)$ and the quarterly and annual inflation rates Δp and $\Delta_4 p$, respectively, when $\Delta = (1 - L)$ is the first difference operator and $\Delta_4 = (1 - L^4)$ is the fourth difference operator.

Inspection of the correlograms for the variables w, p, $(w - p)$, and u reveals high first-order serial correlation coefficients ($\cong 0.99$) with the higher-order coefficients declining extremely slowly, and correspondingly their spectra have peaks at the zero frequency (see Figure 4.2). This information is consistent with each of these series being nonstationary and probably integrated of order one (that is, $I(1)$), which means that it is necessary to difference the variables in order to remove their stochastic nonstationarity and render them $I(0)$. Indeed, the correlogram for Δp suggests that quarterly inflation is $I(0)$ but with a strong seasonal pattern. The correlogram for $\Delta_4 p$, on the other hand, exhibits no seasonal behavior and is consistent with this variable having a stationsary first-order autoregressive representation.

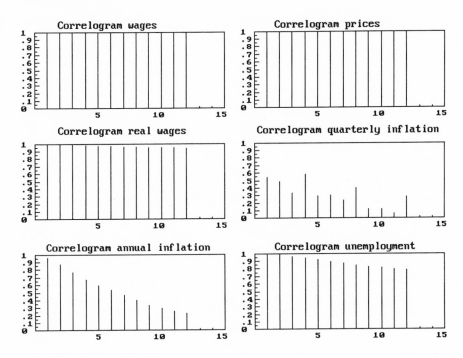

Figure 4.2.   Correlograms of data

As an illustration of the use of univariate test statistics for units roots, Table 4.1 provides the values of augmented Dickey-Fuller test statistics, which take the form of the t statistic for the hypothesis $\alpha = 0$ in the regression model for the generic variable y_t:

$$\Delta y_t = \alpha y_{t-1} + \mu + \sum_{j=1}^{m} \beta_j \Delta y_{t-j} + \xi_t \qquad (4.17)$$

Note that when $\alpha = 0$ equation (4.17) is a regression in the differences Δy_t corresponding to y_t being well modeled as a an $I(1)$ process and thus having a unit root in its autoregressive representation. The distribution of the t statistic when $\alpha = 0$ is nonstandard (that is, neither Student's t nor limiting normal), but tables of critical values were provided by Dickey and Fuller (1981). Although, as pointed out by West (1988), the limiting distribution of this t statistic is normal when there is drift in the series ($\mu \neq 0$), the small sample distribution is better approximated by the Dickey-Fuller distribution unless μ/σ_ξ is "large" (see Hylleberg and Mizon, 1989).

In calculating the statistics in Table 4.1, the maximum lag length m was 5, and the reported results are for the t statistic corresponding to the longest significant lag within this maximum. In the calculation of the statistics for p and Δp only

Table 4.1. Augmented Dickey-Fuller statistics

	t(ADF)	Lag length m
w	−1.27	2
u	−1.77	1
p	−1.31	1
(w − p)	−1.10	3
Δw	−3.30*	1
Δp	−3.83**	0
Δu	−4.95**	0

    * Significant at 5 percent.
    ** Significant at 1 percent.

seasonal dummy variables were included in the regression (4.17). On the basis of these augmented Dickey-Fuller statistics all three variables w, p, and u appear to be $I(1)$—the null hypothesis of $I(0)$ being rejected against the alternative of $I(1)$ and the null of $I(1)$ not being rejected against the alternative of $I(2)$ for each variable. In addition, the real wage $(w - p)$ is $I(1)$, and so w and p do not cointegrate as the real wage. In fact, the hypothesis that each of these variables has a unit root was not rejected when tested against the alternative of trend stationarity—that is, $\alpha = 0$ was not rejected even when a linear trend was added to the regression (4.17). Hence in the modeling of w, p, and u it will be important to choose models that can represent their nonstationarity, with the possibility that all three variables form a cointegrating relationship—that is, there is some linear combination of w, p, and u that is $I(0)$. Another characteristic of wages and prices is that they are nonnegative, so the use of linear models in the logarithmic transformations of them is data admissible—that is, cannot produce negative fitted or predicted values. Similarly, the unemployment rate is bounded between zero and 100 percent, so that a logit transformation might be appropriate for modeling it in a data admissible way. However, since all observations on the unemployment rate are below 13 percent, the use of its logarithm should be data admissible, and this is borne out by noting that the graphs of u and the logit transformation of U are essentially identical when adjusted for their different means.

Having briefly analyzed the univariate statistical properties of the variables to be analyzed, attention is now turned to a review of the Phillips curve literature in so far as it is relevant to the subsequent analysis.

Single-Equation Analysis

Noting the emphasis placed above on adopting a general-to-specific modeling strategy, an explanation of why single-equation analysis precedes system analysis is in order. First, given that the primary purpose of the empirical analysis is to illustrate the LSE methodology and that the methodology has important implications for system and single-equation modeling it is relevant to illustrate both. Second, there are pedagogical benefits to presenting the simpler case before the general, and the intention is to exploit these.

Many past and present members of the LSE Economics Department have analyzed models of wage and price determination (Desai, 1975, 1984; Espasa, 1975; Layard and Nickell, 1985; Lipsey, 1960; Nickell, 1984; Phillips, 1958; Sargan, 1964, 1980a; Vernon, 1970), and so it seems particularly appropriate to present the results of re-analysis of this relationship with the present dataset. The first and most influential piece of research in this area was that of A.W.H. Phillips, in which an empirical relationship representing a tradeoff between money wages and unemployment was described. As Desai (1984, p. 253) points out the Phillips curve "has been re-specified, questioned, rejected as being unstable and reinterpreted," and yet it is still evident in many models of aggregate labor market and wage and price behavior. The Colston paper of Sargan (1964), though primarily concerned with a number of methodological issues that had a major influence on LSE econometricians (see Hendry and Wallis, 1984), developed single-equation models of wage and price determination with the distinction between equilibrium and disequilibrium behavior explicit. Indeed, the foundations of the error-correction model, which is now so prevalent in the analysis of nonstationary-integrated data, were laid in this paper. An additional feature of Sargan's paper was the extension of the Phillips framework to allow for the impact of productivity. The results presented below, however, are confined to describing relationships between wages, prices, and unemployment. This is done in order to keep the empirical modeling as simple as possible, while still providing an illustration of many of the important points made in the previous discussion of the LSE methodology. In order to increase the economic and statistical credibility, as well as the applicability, of the model, it may well be necessary to enlarge the system to include productivity, hours of work, exchange rates, and interest rates. In addition, it may be important to pay detailed attention to the changes that have taken place in the U.K. labor market since 1979, such as the increase in part-time working, the increase in self-employed labor relative to employees, and the increased participation of women in the labor force. Thus the class of model considered in this section can be written in error correction form as

$$\sum_{j=0}^{k} \alpha_{1j} \Delta w_{t-j} = (\alpha_0 + \gamma \beta_0) + \sum_{j=0}^{k} (\alpha_{2j} \Delta p + \alpha_{3j} \Delta u)_{t-j}$$
$$- \gamma (w - \beta_1 p - \beta_2 u)_{t-1} + \lambda t + error, \qquad (4.18)$$

when k is the maximum lag and with the normalization $\alpha_{10} = 1$. A linear trend is included in (4.18) as a proxy for omitted variables such as average labor productivity that are dominated by trend. The steady-state solution of (4.18), in which Δw^*, Δp^*, and Δu^* are the constant quarterly growth rates in nominal wages, retail prices, and the unemployment rate respectively, is given by

$$E(w_t \mid p_t, u_t) = (\beta_0 + \beta_1 p_t + \beta_2 u_t)$$
$$+ (\lambda^* t + \alpha_1^* \Delta w^* - \alpha_0^* - \alpha_2^* \Delta p^* - \alpha_3^* \Delta u^*) \qquad (4.19)$$

when

$$\lambda^* = \lambda/\gamma \quad \alpha_0^* = \alpha_0/\gamma \quad \alpha_i^* = (\textstyle\sum_{j=0}^{k} \alpha_{ij})/\gamma, \; i = 1, 2, 3. \qquad (4.20)$$

The first term of (4.19) gives the static equilibrium response of w to the conditioning variables p and u and takes the form $E(ecm_t \mid p_t, u_t) = 0$ when ecm_t is the observed disequilibrium defined as

$$w_t - \beta_0 - \beta_1 p_t - \beta_2 u_t = ecm_t. \qquad (4.21)$$

Note that the defining characteristics of the static equilibrium are zero growth rates ($\Delta w^* = \Delta p^* = \Delta u^* = 0$) and no autonomous trend ($\lambda = 0$). When the growth rates are not zero, equation (4.19) can be rewritten as

$$E(w_t \mid p_t, u_t) = (\beta_0 + \beta_1 p_t + \beta_2 u_t) + \lambda^* t + (\alpha_1^* \lambda^* - \alpha_0^*)$$
$$+ (\alpha_1^* \beta_1 - \alpha_2^*) \Delta p^* + (\alpha_1^* \beta_2 - \alpha_3^*) \Delta u^* \qquad (4.22)$$

to ensure that the growth rate of nominal wages Δw^* is consistent with the equilibrium growth rate ($\Delta w^* = \beta_1 \Delta p^* + \beta_2 \Delta u^* + \lambda^*$) when for this single-equation analysis p_t and u_t are presumed to be weakly exogenous variables. In the case that the disequilibrium $ecm_t \neq 0$, equation (4.18) can be interpreted as an equilibrium correction mechanism. Indeed, w responds to the disequilibrium (equilibrium corrects) with adjustment coefficient γ. With the equilibrium correction interpretation of (4.21) it is expected that $\beta_1 > 0$, and the hypothesis that real wages respond to the strength of demand in the labor market as measured by the unemployment rate is given by $\beta_1 = 1$ (the real-wage hypothesis). Noting that w, p, and u are $I(1)$ and that $(w - p)$ also appears to be $I(1)$, the real-wage hypothesis can only hold if there is a cointegrating vector involving all three variables that has the sum of the coefficients of w and p equal to zero. The hypothesis that the strength of demand in the labor market has no effect on wages is given by $\beta_2 = 0$. This hypothesis does not preclude labor-market effects on wages altogether since changes in unemployment Δu will influence w provided that $\alpha_3^* \neq 0$.

For OLS inference applied to single equations such as (4.18) to be valid, it is important that the regressors are weakly exogenous for the parameters of interest, a point that was stressed by members of the LSE in their discussions of single-equation analysis (see, for example, Hendry and Richard, 1982, 1983). The importance of weak exogeneity as a necessary condition for efficient inference in this

Table 4.2. OLS estimates: general model for Δw_t, 1966(2)–1993(1)

$$\Delta w_t = -2.055 + 0.070\Delta w_{t-1} + 0.271\Delta w_{t-2} + 0.088\Delta w_{t-3} - 0.023\Delta w_{t-4} + 0.429\Delta p_t$$
$$\quad (0.53) \qquad (0.09) \qquad\quad (0.08) \qquad\quad (0.09) \qquad\quad (0.09) \qquad\quad (0.11)$$

$$\quad + 0.089\Delta p_{t-1} - 0.013\Delta p_{t-2} + 0.267\Delta p_{t-3} + 0.017\Delta p_{t-4} - 0.029\Delta u_t + 0.003\Delta u_{t-1}$$
$$\qquad (0.09) \qquad\quad (0.09) \qquad\quad (0.09) \qquad\quad (0.10) \qquad\quad (0.02) \qquad\quad (0.02)$$

$$\quad - 0.022\Delta u_{t-2} + 0.002\Delta u_{t-3} + 0.0001\Delta u_{t-4} - 0.240w_{t-1} + 0.204p_{t-1} + 0.004u_{t-1}$$
$$\qquad (0.02) \qquad\quad (0.02) \qquad\quad (0.02) \qquad\quad (0.06) \qquad\quad (0.05) \qquad\quad (0.01)$$

$$\quad + 0.002t + 0.038D745 - 0.028Policy$$
$$\qquad (0.0006) \qquad (0.005) \qquad\quad (0.006)$$

Diagnostic statistics:

$R^2 = 0.768$	$\sigma = 0.0099$	$V = 0.325$
$J = 2.581$	$AR(5, 82) = 0.712$	$ARCH(4, 79) = 0.642$
	$[p > 0.62]$	$[p > 0.63]$
$N = 0.042$	$H(40, 46) = 0.756$	$R(1, 86) = 0.851$
$[p > 0.98]$	$[p > 0.82]$	$[p > 0.36]$

context implies that the testing of it is crucial. However, it is necessary to specify more about the joint distribution of all variables in the analysis in order to be able to test the hypothesis that a subset of them are weakly exogenous for the parameters of interest. Hence this issue will be addressed in the next section where a model of the joint determination of all variables is developed.

Preliminary analysis using the full sample of data to estimate an autoregressive-distributed lag model for w in terms of p and u with eight lags on all variables (corresponding to $k = 7$ in the error-correction model (4.18)), plus a linear trend and seasonal dummy variables, revealed large outliers at the end of 1974 and beginning of 1975 when there was an explosion of wages following the relaxation of wage and price restraint. Including the dummy variables (1) $D745$ (which takes the value 1 in 1974(3) and 1974(4), 2 in 1975(1), and zero elsewhere) and (2) *Policy* (which takes the value 1 in 1968(2) and 1969(2), both of which were quarters when strong deflationary budgets were introduced, and the value -1 in 1980(3) and 1980(4) to capture the effects of the recession induced by the Thatcher government's tight monetary policy, and zero elsewhere) produced a congruent model for the full sample, which could be simplified by excluding the seasonal dummy variables and reducing the maximum lag length to 5. Table 4.2 gives the unrestricted estimates and their standard errors in parentheses for an ECM with $k = 4$.

The reported test statistics are $AR(5, .)$ a Lagrange multiplier (LM) test statistic for fifth-order serial correlation in the residuals, which under the null of no serial correlation has a $\chi^2(5)$ distribution that is presented in the form that has an approximate $F(5, .)$ null distribution; $ARCH(4, .)$ an LM statistic for testing fourth-order

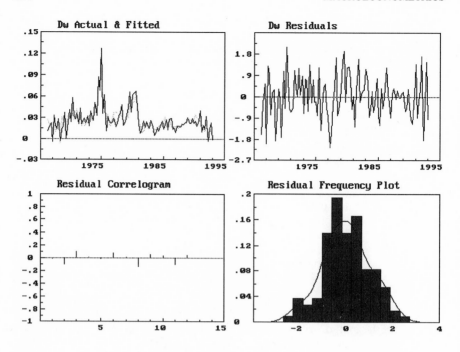

Figure 4.3.   OLS wage equation, 1966(2)–1993(1)

auto-correlated squared residuals, which under the null of no autoregressive conditional heteroscedasticity (no *ARCH*) has a $\chi^2(4)$ distribution that is presented in the form that has an approximate $F(4, .)$ null distribution; $R(1, .)$ the regression specification test (*RESET*) that tests the null of correct specification against the alternative that the residuals are correlated with the squared fitted values of the regressand and has an $F(1, .)$ null distribution; $H(., .)$ a statistic for testing the null hypothesis of unconditional homoscedasticity against the alternative that the residuals are correlated with the model's regressors and their squares, and has an approximate $F(., .)$ null distribution; N a new statistic (see Doornik and Hansen, 1994) for testing the null of normal skewness and kurtosis that has a $\chi^2(2)$ under the null that the residuals are normally distributed; V the residual variance instability and J the joint (variance and regression coefficients) instability test statistics based on the cumulative backward score statistics of Hansen, 1992. When appropriate the *p*-value is reported in [.] after a statistic. Doornik and Hendry (1994) give further details of these statistics.

On the basis of these statistics there is no evidence of misspecification. This is substantiated by the following graphs in Figure 4.3 of actual and fitted values, the

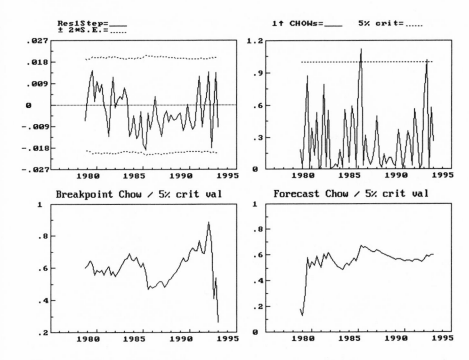

Figure 4.4.   Recursive graphics

residuals, the residual correlogram, and the residual frequency plot and density. Further, re-estimation of the model by recursive least squares, starting from an initial sample of 50 observations and sequentially increasing the sample from 50 to 108, revealed no serious indications of overall nonconstancy. The graphs of the recursively computed one-step ahead residuals bordered by ± twice their standard errors, and the one-step ahead Chow, breakpoint-F and forecast-F test statistics in Figure 4.4 confirm this, though there is a suggestion of some nonconstancy around 1984, which was the year of the miners' strike. Doornik and Hendry (1992, 1994) provide the definitions of these statistics, as well as discussing their role in modeling. However, the recursively computed estimates of the *constant* and the coefficients of w_{t-1}, p_{t-1}, and u_{t-1} show some evidence of change, starting in 1979 and stabilizing at new values after 1984.

Hence this general model appears to be reasonably congruent with the available information and so forms a valid basis for testing for further simplifications and testing other hypotheses. The real-wage hypothesis $\beta_1 = 1$ is rejected at 1 percent significance since the test statistic for the hypothesis that the coefficients of w_{t-1} and p_{t-1} sum to zero is $F(1, 87) = 5.00$ [$p > 0.028$]. However, the hypothesis that

Table 4.3.   OLS estimates reduced Δw model, 1966(1)–1993(1)

$\Delta w_t = 0.284\Delta w_{t-2} + 0.499\Delta p_t + 0.260\Delta p_{t-3} - 0.031\Delta u_t + 0.0017t - 1.80 - 0.210w_{t-1} +$
$\qquad\quad (0.07)\qquad\;\, (0.09)\qquad\;\, (0.08)\qquad\quad (0.02)\qquad\;\; (0.0004)\quad (0.37)\qquad (0.04)$

$\qquad\quad 0.181p_{t-1} - 0.0001u_{t-1} + 0.038D\,745 - 0.03Policy$
$\qquad\quad\; (0.04)\qquad\; (0.005)\qquad\;\; (0.004)\qquad\quad (0.005)$

Diagnostic statistics:

$R^2 = 0.753$	$\sigma = 0.0097$	$V = 0.299$
$J = 1.960$	$AR(5, 93) = 0.965$	$ARCH(4, 90) = 1.152$
	$[p > 0.44]$	$[p > 0.34]$
$N = 0.228$	$H(20, 77) = 1.345$	$R(1, 97) = 0.621$
$[p > 0.89]$	$[p > 0.18]$	$[p > 0.43]$

$\beta_3 = 0$ is not rejected ($F(1, 87) = 0.403$ [$p > 0.53$]), so that wages appear to be unaffected by the level of unemployment. For this model the solved ecm_t with autonomous growth added is

$$ecm_t = w_t + 8.57 - 0.85p_t - 0.02u_t - 0.008t,$$
$$\qquad\qquad (0.12)\quad\; (0.05)\quad\;\; (0.02)\quad\;\; (0.001)\qquad\qquad (4.23)$$

which describes a highly significant (the Wald test statistic for the hypothesis that all coefficients including those of the two dummy variables but excluding the constant are zero $\chi^2(5) = 47155$ has a p-value of zero) equilibrium correction mechanism between wages, prices, unemployment, and trend. However, unemployment u appears to have no role in the ecm_t, which also corresponds to a mechanism for determining nominal, rather than real, wages. The fact that $\beta_1 = 1$ is rejected but $\beta_3 = 0$ is not suggests that w and p might cointegrate when a linear trend and the dummy variables $D745$ and *Policy* are included in the modeling. If this is the case, though, the cointegrating vector would have the form $(1, -\kappa)$ with $\kappa \neq 1$ since the real wage hypothesis is rejected. However, these comments are predicated on the assumption that p and u are weakly exogenous variables for the parameters of interest in the wage equation, which the analysis in the following section shows to be doubtful.

The model reported in Table 4.2 clearly can be simplified, and the testing of a series of reductions from this congruent general model led to the following simple model that parsimoniously encompasses the general model ($F(10, 87) = 0.50$ [$p > 0.89$]). Not only does the model in Table 4.3 parsimoniously encompass that in Table 4.2, but it is congruent as indicated by the diagnostic statistics, and the graphical analysis in Figure 4.5. In addition, this reduced model still indicates that there is no role for the level of unemployment in the explanation of nominal wages, and so Table 4.4 presents the results for the final simplification, which

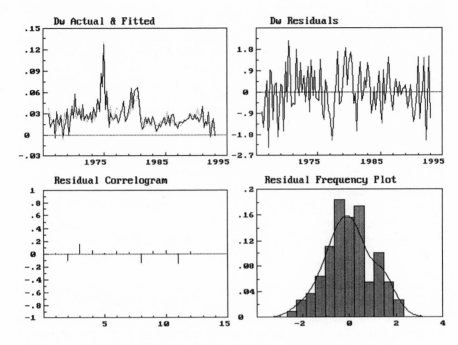

Figure 4.5.   OLS reduced-wage equation, 1966(1)–1993(1)

Table 4.4.   OLS estimates final Δw model, 1966(1)–1993(1)

$$\Delta w_t = 0.285\Delta w_{t-2} + 0.500\Delta p_t + 0.260\Delta p_{t-3} - 0.030\Delta u_t + 0.0017t - 1.801 - 0.210w_{t-1} +$$
$$\quad\;\;(0.07)\qquad\;\;(0.08)\qquad\;\;(0.08)\qquad\;\;\;(0.02)\qquad\;(0.0004)\quad(0.34)\qquad(0.04)$$

$$0.181p_{t-1} + 0.038D745 - 0.03Policy$$
$$(0.04)\qquad\;(0.004)\qquad\;(0.005)$$

Diagnostic Statistics:

$R^2 = 0.753$	$\sigma = 0.0096$	$V = 0.298$
$J = 1.680$	$AR(5, 94) = 0.941$	$ARCH(4, 91) = 1.161$
	$[p > 0.46]$	$[p > 0.33]$
$N = 0.233$	$H(18, 80) = 1.347$	$R(1, 98) = 0.608$
$[p > 0.89]$	$[p > 0.18]$	$[p > 0.44]$

eliminates u (but not Δu) from the model. Not surprisingly, this remains a congruent model, and the hypothesis that it parsimoniously encompasses the general model of Table 4.2 is not rejected since the relevant statistic is $F(11, 87) = 0.462$ $[p > 0.92]$. The long-run solution (with the dummy variables $D745$ and *Policy*, which were included in the estimation, omitted) of this final single-equation model takes the form

$$ecm_t = w_t + 8.573 - 0.852p_t - 0.008t.$$
$$(0.11)\quad (0.05)\quad (0.001) \qquad (4.24)$$

This equilibrium-correction mechanism is essentially the same as that estimated from the general model reported in Table 4.2 and has the same interpretation. In particular, the real-wage hypothesis is rejected, and in the longer term the level of the unemployment variable has no effect on wages. This latter result is surprising and will be investigated further in the following section. The estimated steady state corresponding to equation (4.22) for this model has the form

$$E(w_t \mid p_t, u_t) = -8.61 + 0.85p_t + 0.008t - 0.68\Delta p^* + 0.14\Delta u^*. \qquad (4.25)$$

By construction this steady-state equation is consistent with the growth of wages implied by the long-run equation (4.24). An implication of this steady-state equation for w is that the equilibrium value of nominal wages is smaller (larger) ceteris paribus the larger is the steady-state inflation rate when the latter is positive (negative). Since the rate of inflation is almost always positive, this finding is consistent with the view that higher rates of positive inflation are undesirable. The other implication of the steady-state equation is that the equilibrium value of nominal wages is larger (smaller) the larger is the growth rate of the percentage unemployment rate when it is positive (negative). Hence the equilibrium value of the nominal wage ceteris paribus is associated positively with increases in the unemployment rate.

Given the simplicity of this illustration there are not many sophisticated economic models that can be obtained from this data set and considered as alternative explanations of the determination of nominal wages. However, in the spirit of illustration the following models can used as examples of alternatives corresponding to four of the commonly used single equation model types:

$$M_{w1} \quad \Delta w_t = c_1 + \beta_1\Delta p_t + \gamma_1(w_{t-1} - \kappa_1 p_{t-1}) + v_{1t}$$
$$M_{w2} \quad \Delta w_t = c_2 + \gamma_2(w_{t-1} - \kappa_2 u_{t-1}) + v_{2t}$$
$$M_{w3} \quad (w_t - p_t) = c_3 + \lambda_3 t + v_{3t}$$
$$M_{w4} \quad \Delta w_t = c_4 + v_{4t} \qquad (4.26)$$

These models are: M_{w1}, a first-order error correction model with wages adjusting towards a static equilibrium that depends on prices only (that is, equation (4.18)

Table 4.5. Encompassing test statistics for M_{w2}, $M_{w4} \varepsilon M_{w3}$

	Cox	Ericsson	CPE
M_{w2}	$N(0, 1) = -0.82$	$N(0, 1) = 0.78$	$F(2, 105) = 1.53$
M_{w4}	$N(0, 1) = -0.78$	$N(0, 1) = 0.74$	$F(2, 106) = 0.33$

with $k = 0$ and $\alpha_{30} = \beta_2 = \lambda = 0$); M_{w2}, a first-order partial-adjustment model with target value of wages depending on unemployment only (that is, equation (4.18) with $k = 0$, and $\alpha_{20} = \alpha_{30} = \beta_1 = \lambda = 0$); M_{w3}, in which the logarithm of real wages is trend stationary (that is, equation (4.18) with $k = 0$, $\alpha_{20} = \beta_1 = 1$, and $\alpha_{30} = \beta_2 = 0$); and finally a random walk with drift model M_{w4} (that is, equation (4.18) with $k = 0$, $\alpha_{20} = \alpha_{30} = \gamma = \lambda = 0$). Hendry, Pagan, and Sargan (1984) and Hendry (1995) contain more discussion of these and other single-equation model types. With the exception of M_{w4}, which is nested in M_{w1} and M_{w2}, these are nonnested models in the sense than none can be obtained as restricted versions of any of the other models, though, of course, they are all special cases of (4.18). Therefore these models can be compared by using nonnested test statistics such as those of Cox (1960, 1961), Ericsson (1983), and the complete parametric encompassing (CPE) statistic of Mizon (1984) and Mizon and Richard (1986). However, as was emphasized in the previous section, when the alternative models to be considered are all special cases of the congruent general model, so that none of them imply an extension of the dataset or class of models being used, the principle of parsimonious encompassing provides an appropriate method for comparing the models. Further, the use of nonnested test statistics to make pairwise comparisons of rival models makes little sense unless each model is at least congruent with respect to its own information set (that is, the minimum information set needed to support the model). When the four models in (4.26) were estimated with the dummy variables $D745$ and *Policy* included in each, they all had serially correlated residuals and hence are probably dynamically misspecified, and models M_{w2}, M_{w3}, and M_{w4} had significant ARCH effects and nonnormality in their residuals, as well as having significant RESET test statistics. In addition, M_{w2} and M_{w3} exhibited signs of parameter nonconstancy in the variance and joint variance and regression coefficient stability test statistics V and J. Hence there is strong evidence that the four models in (4.26) are not coherent with their own information sets and so are inadequate. Despite this, M_{w2} and $M_{w4} \varepsilon M_{w3}$ in pairwise comparisons as the statistics in Table 4.5 indicate. This serves to illustrate the dangers of using such test statistics when the models being compared are noncongruent, for both M_{w2} and M_{w4} are inadequate models when evaluated relative to their own information sets and relative to that of the congruent general model (and neither model parsimoniously encompasses the reduced general model reported in Table 4.3).

Table 4.6. Parsimonious encompassing test statistics

M_{w1}	M_{w2}	M_{w3}	M_{w4}
$F(5, 98) = 9.15$	$F(6, 98) = 11.12$	$F(7, 98) = 10184.0$	$F(10, 98) = 29.86$

Given that each of the models in (4.26) is nested within the congruent model reported in Table 4.3 (this model rather than the final model of Table 4.4 is used in order to include u_{t-1} in the analysis), it is possible to test the validity of the implied reductions from that model, and the corresponding parsimonious encompassing test statistics are reported in Table 4.6. Hence each of the four models fails to parsimoniously encompass the general model (all the test statistics have p values of zero), and so they are each inadequate characterizations of the relationship between w_t, p_t, and u_t.

At this stage the model that performs most satisfactorily is that reported in Table 4.4, and so before turning to system analysis of the relationships between w_t, p_t, and u_t the forecasting ability of this model will be evaluated. Firstly, this model was re-estimated with sample data for 1966(1) to 1989(3) and then used to forecast Δw from 1989(4) to 1993(1). The outcome is reasonable as indicated by the graphs in Figure 4.6. In addition, the χ^2 prediction test statistic at $\chi^2(14) = 23.01$ [$p > 0.06$] and the Chow (1960) prediction test statistic at $F(14, 85) = 1.35$ [$p > 0.20$] do not reject the null of parameter constancy, though this result is very marginal for the χ^2 prediction test statistic. Indeed, Lu and Mizon (1991) showed that the implicit null hypothesis of the χ^2 prediction statistic is $(x_t'\Delta\beta)^2 + (\sigma_2^2 - \sigma_1^2) = 0 \; \forall \; t \in [(T+1), (T+H)]$, and that of the Chow statistic is known to be $X_2\Delta\beta = 0$, when for the generic linear regression model $y_t = x_t'\beta + u_t$, the data for the sample period ($t = 1, 2, \ldots, T$, which is denoted by subscript 1) and prediction period ($t = (T+1), (T+2), \ldots, (T+H)$, which is denoted by subscript 2) can be written as

$$\begin{pmatrix} y_1 \\ y_2 \end{pmatrix} = \begin{pmatrix} X_1 & 0 \\ X_2 & I_H \end{pmatrix} \begin{pmatrix} \beta_1 \\ X_2\Delta\beta \end{pmatrix} + \begin{pmatrix} u_1 \\ u_2 \end{pmatrix} \tag{4.27}$$

when $\Delta\beta = (\beta_2 - \beta_1)$ and with

$$E\begin{pmatrix} u_1 \\ u_2 \end{pmatrix} = \begin{pmatrix} 0 \\ 0 \end{pmatrix} \text{ and } V\begin{pmatrix} u_1 \\ u_2 \end{pmatrix} = \begin{pmatrix} \sigma_1^2 I_T & 0 \\ 0 & \sigma_2^2 I_H \end{pmatrix}. \tag{4.28}$$

Hence the χ^2 prediction test statistic is sensitive to both changes in the error variance and in the regression coefficients via changes in the conditional mean of y_t, whereas the Chow prediction statistic is powerful against changes in the conditional mean only: a constant error variance ($\sigma_1^2 = \sigma_2^2$) is part of the maintained

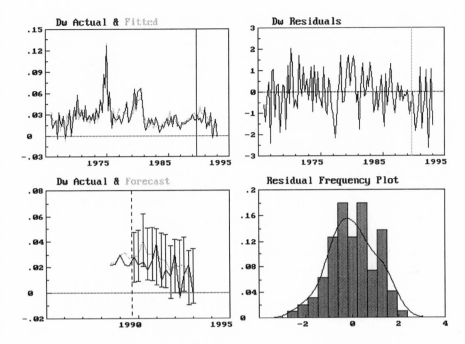

Figure 4.6.   Forecasts, 1989(4)–1993(1)

hypothesis for the Chow statistic. Clearly, though, if the error variance is not constant and/or the error distribution is otherwise nonstationary, the Chow statistic will not have a central $F(H, T + H - k)$ distribution under the hypothesis $X_2 \Delta \beta = 0$. Bearing in mind that 1989(4) saw the tightening of monetary policy following the United Kingdom joining the European Monetary Mechanism, the finding that there might have been a change in the model's error variance is not surprising, even though it is a clear limitation of the model. However, when secondly the model was re-estimated with data for the period 1966(1) to 1979(2), and then used to forecast Δw over the period 1979(3) to 1993(1) the result was much less satisfactory. The χ^2 prediction test statistic over this period takes the value $\chi^2(55) = 326.2 \ [p > 0.00]$, which strongly indicates parameter nonconstancy in the model. The Chow prediction statistic on the other hand takes the value $F(55, 44) = 0.962$ $[p > 0.56]$ and so still does not reject the null of parameter constancy—but there is evidence that the error does not have a stationary distribution throughout the period 1966(1) to 1993(1). Inspection of the graphs in Figure 4.7 does reveal the poor forecasting performance of the model for the period 1979(3) to 1993(1).

The estimates for the final model over the sample period 1966(1) to 1979(2) are given in Table 4.7, and these are noticeably different from those for the full sample

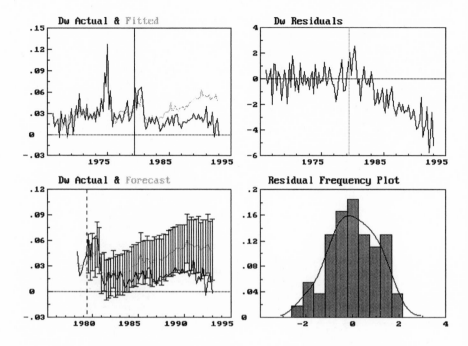

Figure 4.7.   Forecasts, 1979(3)–1993(1)

Table 4.7.   OLS estimates final Δw model, 1966(1)–1979(2)

$$\Delta w_t = 0.304\Delta w_{t-2} + 0.360\Delta p_t + 0.077\Delta p_{t-3} - 0.007\Delta u_t + 0.003t - 1.73 - 0.212w_{t-1} +$$
$$\quad\quad (0.08) \quad\quad\;\; (0.13) \quad\quad\;\; (0.12) \quad\quad\quad\; (0.02) \quad (0.0008) \;\; (0.52) \quad\;\; (0.06)$$

$$\quad\quad 0.145p_{t-1} + 0.039D745 - 0.03Policy$$
$$\quad\quad (0.05) \quad\quad\;\; (0.005) \quad\quad (0.007)$$

Diagnostic statistics:

$R^2 = 0.823$	$\sigma = 0.0097$	$V = 0.176$
$J = 0.759$	$AR(5, 39) = 2.599*$	$ARCH(4, 36) = 0.377$
	$[p > 0.04]$	$[p > 0.82]$
$N = 0.930$	$H(17, 26) = 1.210$	$R(1, 43) = 0.107$
$[p > 0.63]$	$[p > 0.32]$	$[p > 0.74]$

Table 4.8.   General model steady-state solutions

1966(2)–1993(1)

$E(w_t \mid p_t, u_t) = -8.57 + 0.851p_t + 0.016u_t + 0.008t + 1.19\Delta p^* - 0.23\Delta u^*$

1966(2)–1979(2)

$E(w_t \mid p_t, u_t) = -8.12 + 0.66p_t - 0.08u_t + 0.017t - 0.318\Delta p^* + 0.46\Delta u^*$

---

in Table 4.4. As a consequence the estimated steady-state solution of the model over the period 1966(1) to 1979(2) is

$$E(w_t \mid p_t, u_t) = -8.19 + 0.682p_t + 0.014t - 0.18\Delta p^*, \qquad (4.29)$$

which differs substantially from that obtained for the full sample (4.25). The coefficient of p_t is even further away from the real wage hypothesis value of unity, the response of w_t to the steady-state inflation rate Δp^* is a quarter of its full sample value, and there is no role for Δu^* since its estimated coefficient in the steady state solution is -0.03 and not significantly different from zero. Hence, although the full sample estimates of the general model (given in Table 4.2) appeared to be congruent, and the simplified model presented in Table 4.4 an acceptable reduction of it that also inferentially dominates the simple alternative models in (4.26), there is strong evidence that the simplified model is not constant pre- and post-1979(3). This is consistent with the suggestion that the recursively estimated constant and the coefficients of w_{t-1}, p_{t-1}, and u_{t-1} changed their values in the 1980s. In fact, when the general model is re-estimated for the sample 1966(2)–1979(2), it does indeed exhibit evidence of a change, as is indicated by its steady-state solutions for the full sample and the sample pre-1979(3) (see Table 4.8).

That there might be a change in the determination of wages within the class of linear regression models involving w_t, p_t, u_t, and t pre- and post-1980 is not a surprise. There have been important changes affecting the labor market such as the changes in labor productivity, the prevailing rate of unemployment, hours of work, the amount of part-time working, and the participation of women, as well as changes in the method of collection of some labor market statistics. In addition, there have been important changes in the rate of inflation, interest rates, and exchange rates often associated with changes in government economic policies. Indeed, the Thatcher government, which came into power in May 1979, encouraged small businesses and self-employment; encouraged the employment of cheaper labor, especially female labor, which led to more part-time working; and induced a severe recession with a very tight monetary policy. These aspects of policy are consistent with the observed data exhibiting a decrease in the rate of inflation Δp

and a rapid increase in unemployment. Both these features are clearly evident in Figure 4.1.

Therefore there appears to be evidence that the single-equation models developed above for the explanation of w_t in terms of p_t, u_t, and t have not captured a constant underlying structure. Note that this has arisen despite the fact that the full sample estimated models appeared to be congruent, with neither of the Hansen (1992) instability statistics V and J indicating any structural break around 1979–1980. Possible reasons for this include lack of cointegration between w_t, p_t, and u_t and the invalidity of the assumption that p_t and u_t are weakly exogeneous variables. These issues are related and best analyzed in the context of system modeling, to which attention is now turned.

System Analysis

A more comprehensive analysis of the relationships between the variables under scrutiny can be undertaken by modeling their joint distribution. In particular, this allows issues concerning the presence and nature of regime shifts and structural breaks and their links (if any) to changes in the exogeneity status of variables to be explored, and enables hypotheses about the precise form of the relationships between the variables to be tested.

The class of system to be considered in this section is a three-dimensional VAR of the form

$$\mathbf{x}_t = \sum_{j=1}^{k} A_j \mathbf{x}_{t-j} + \Phi D_t + \boldsymbol{\varepsilon}_t, \tag{4.30}$$

when $\mathbf{x}_t' = (w_t, p_t, u_t)$, D_t contains deterministic variables such as a constant, trend, seasonal, and other dummy variables, and $\boldsymbol{\varepsilon}_t$ is a three-dimensional error vector that is independently distributed with mean zero and covariance matrix Σ. It is assumed that the roots of det $(I - \sum_{j=1}^{k} A_j L^j) = 0$ lie on or outside the unit circle so that there are no explosive roots, and that k is finite so that moving average-error processes do not fall into the category of model being considered. The initial conditions $\mathbf{x}_{1-k}, \mathbf{x}_{2-k}, \ldots, \mathbf{x}_0$ are assumed fixed, and the parameters $(A_1, \ldots, A_k, \Phi, \Sigma)$ are required to be constant in order for the adopted inferential procedures to be valid. An observationally equivalent parameterization of (4.30) is provided by the following vector equilibrium correction model (VECM):

$$\Delta \mathbf{x}_t = \sum_{j=1}^{k-1} \Pi_j \Delta \mathbf{x}_{t-j} + \Pi \mathbf{x}_{t-k} + \Phi D_t + \boldsymbol{\varepsilon}_t, \tag{4.31}$$

in which $\Pi = (I - \sum_{j=1}^{k} A_j)$ is the static equilibrium response matrix, and $\Pi_j = (I - \sum_{i=1}^{j} A_i)$ for $j = 1, 2, \ldots, (k-1)$ are the interim multiplier matrices. In the case that $\mathbf{x}_t \sim I(1)$ the rank of Π is determined by the number of cointegrating vectors.

Letting the rank of Π be r and α and β be $3 \times r$ matrices of rank r such that $\Pi = \alpha\beta'$ yields the reduced rank VAR system:

$$\Delta\mathbf{x}_t = \sum_{j=1}^{k-1}\Pi_j\Delta\mathbf{x}_{t-j} + \alpha\beta'\mathbf{x}_{t-k} + \Phi D_t + \varepsilon_t, \qquad (4.32)$$

in which $\beta'\mathbf{x}_t$ are the r cointegrating vectors which are $I(0)$ and α contains the adjustment coefficients. The Johansen (1988) maximum-likelihood procedure, as modified in Johansen and Juselius (1990) to allow for dummy variables, enables the empirical determination of r provided that the systems in (4.30) and (4.31) are well specified and in particular have innovation homoscedastic errors and constant parameters.

In the light of the single equation analysis presented above an unrestricted VAR for w, p, and u with five lags on each variable (corresponding to (4.30) with $k = 5$) and D_t containing an unrestricted constant vector and linear trend was estimated for the full sample period 1966(2) to 1993(1). The results strongly indicated that this system was noncongruent, with each equation exhibiting serially correlated, heteroscedastic, and nonnormal residuals, with *ARCH* effects present as well. Inspection of the residuals revealed many apparent outliers, and recursive estimation showed many parameter estimates to be nonconstant. The sample period contains many important changes in economic policy and institutional arrangements, and so it may well be difficult to obtain a constant parameter VAR without some specific allowance for these events. For example, there were sharp movements in commodity prices generally in 1966 and in oil prices at the end of 1973, in 1979(3), and in 1986; there were pre-election booms 1972–1973, 1974, 1979, 1986–1987, and 1991; floating exchange rates were introduced in 1971 and exchange controls were abandoned in 1979; the rate of value added tax (VAT) was increased from 8 percent to 15 percent July 1979; periods of very tight monetary policy were introduced in 1980 and 1989, which had major effects on income, employment, and unemployment; in 1984 there was the year-long miners' strike; the introduction of the business expansion scheme in 1980 affected the ratio of self-employed to employees in the total employed; there were changes in the method of collection of some key statistics such as unemployment and the numbers self-employed. Noting that many of these changes affected the labor market and the rate of inflation suggests that the relationship between wages, prices, and unemployment may not be an easy one to capture without some allowance for their effect.

From inspection of the residuals for the unrestricted VAR with $k = 5$ and reference to the relevant economic history, it was decided to include the following four dummy variables: $D793$, which takes the value 1 in 1979(3) and 0 elsewhere to allow for the increase in value added tax and the second oil price hike; $D745$, which takes the value 1 in 1974(3) and 1974(4), the value 2 in 1975(1), and zero elsewhere to capture the wage explosion following the relaxation of wage and

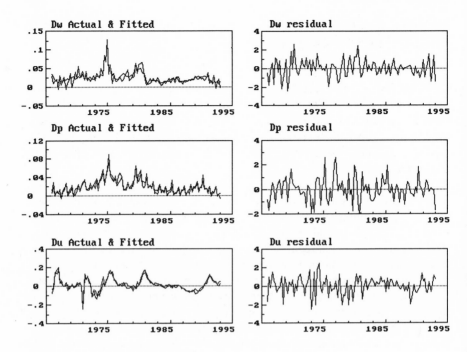

Figure 4.8.   System actual, fitted, and residual values

price controls; *Budget*, which takes the values 1 and −1 respectively in the second
and third quarters of every year and zero in all other quarters and represents fixed
seasonal effects and especially the changes in excise duties and other tax rates,
announced in the annual budget, on prices and the rate of inflation; and *Expansion*,
which takes the value 1 in 1966(3) −1 in 1967(2), 1972(3), and 1974(3), highlighting quarters in which fiscal policy was used to stimulate(+)/dampen(−) the economy,
and takes the values 2 in 1971(2) −2 in 1971(1) to represents the effect of the
announced cut of 50 percent in Selective Employment Tax. Since these four
dummy variables should not have a long-run effect on any of the modeled variables w_t, p_t, and u_t, they are entered unrestrictedly into the VAR when the reduced
rank maximum-likelihood procedure of Johansen (1988) is applied it. However,
there is no evidence of quadratic trend in any of the modeled variables and so the
linear deterministic trend is restricted to lie in the cointegration space.

    When an unrestricted VAR parameterized as (4.31) with $k = 4$, a constant and
the four dummy variables plus a linear trend entered as described above, was
estimated over the period 1966(1) to 1993(1) it produced a plausible and more-or-
less congruent system. Figure 4.8, which gives the graphs of the actual and fitted

Table 4.9.   System diagnostic statistics

	Δw_t	Δp_t	Δu_t
$\hat{\sigma}$	1.08%	0.72%	2.97%
$AR(5, 86)$	1.98	2.53*	0.68
$ARCH(4, 83)$	2.16	0.12	2.47
$H(26, 64)$	1.31	1.15	1.04
$N(2)$	1.67	3.08	2.58
	$vecAR(45, 220)$	1.59*	
	$vecH(156, 354)$	0.93	
	$vecN(6)$	7.20	

* Significant at

values for Δw_t, Δp_t, and Δu_t, and the corresponding residuals (scaled), illustrates this point. The system provides a high degree of explanation for the changes Δw_t, Δp_t, and Δu_t in the three modeled variables w_t, p_t, and u_t (it is, of course, even more impressive in terms of the levels of the variables), and there does not appear to be any strong heteroscedasticity or serial dependence in the residuals. Table 4.9 provides descriptive statistics for the estimated system: first single-equation residual standard deviations $\hat{\sigma}$, serial correlation AR, autoregressive heteroscedasticity $ARCH$, heteroscedasticity H, and normality N test statistics as defined for Table 4.2, and second test statistics for vector autoregressive residuals $vecAR$, vector heteroscedasticity $vecH$, and finally vector normality $vecN$ (see Doornik and Hendry, 1994, for more details of these test statistics). The only evidence of non-congruence comes from the AR test statistic for the Δp_t equation and the $vecAR$ statistic, both of which are significant at 1 percent. Further evidence on the approximate congruence of the system is provided by the residual correlograms and frequency plots given in Figure 4.9.

Though there is some evidence of residual serial correlation in the equations for Δw_t and Δp_t, it is not strong, and experimentation revealed that inappropriate lag length k does not appear to be the cause of this problem. In fact, inspection of the residual plots in Figure 4.8 suggests that the difficulty may still lie in the system's inability to represent the many changes in government policies towards wages and prices, interest rates and exchange rates, and unemployment during the sample period. However, rather than introduce more event specific dummy variables into the analysis, which would increase the risk of the system being too finely tuned to the particular sample data and hence even more likely to suffer from predictive failure, it was decided to continue with the present set of dummy variables. The other alternative of extending the information set to include interest and exchange

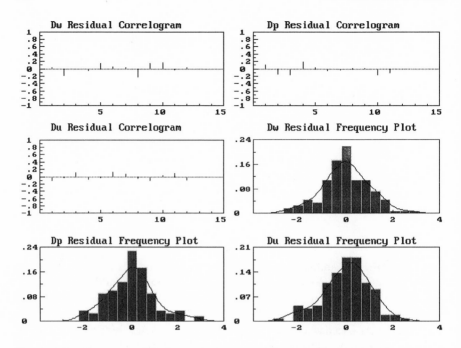

Figure 4.9. System residual correlograms and frequency plots

rates is not pursued here since the present modeling is intended to be illustrative rather than definitive, but it is the subject of further research.

Inspection of the residual correlations in Table 4.10 suggests that there is a modest correlation between w_t and p_t, but the correlations between w_t and u_t and p_t and u_t are negligible. The hypothesis that the order of lag required for each variable is i can be tested using the statistics $F_{k=i}$, and on the basis of these it appears that there is scope for simplifying the dynamics but that four lags are required for p_t consistent with it being seasonal. The estimated long-run matrix Π has eigenvalues whose moduli are given by $|\lambda_\pi|$, and these indicate that there are probably two zero eigenvalues suggesting that $r = 1$. This is confirmed by the results of applying the Johansen (1988) maximum-likelihood procedure to estimate the dimension of cointegrating space r, which are reported in Table 4.11.

The eigenvalues μ_i, which are involved in the maximization of the log-likelihood function with respect to β in order to obtain estimated cointegrating vectors (see Johansen, 1988, or Banerjee et al., 1993, for details), are small. However, the largest eigenvalue $\mu_1 = 0.28$ is significantly different from zero on the basis of the maximum eigenvalue $(Max = -T\log(1 - \mu_r))$ and trace $(Trace = -T\Sigma_{i=1}^r \log(1 - \mu_i))$ test statistics. r is the dimension of cointegrating space, and

Table 4.10. Residual correlations

	w_t	p_t	u_t
p_t	0.14	1.0	—
u_t	0.08	0.03	1.0

	System Dynamics		
	w_t	p_t	u_t
$F_{k=3}(3, 89)$	0.30	3.42*	1.08
$F_{k=2}(3, 89)$	1.79	1.32	2.89*
$F_{k=1}(3, 89)$	4.59**	3.25**	11.84**
$\mid \lambda_\pi \mid$	0.29	0.04	0.00

* Significant at
** Significant at

Table 4.11. Cointegration statistics

r	1	2	3
l	1438	1445	1446
μ	0.28	0.12	0.02
Max	36.17**	14.08	2.05
Trace	52.29**	16.13	2.05

** Significant at

l (which is defined as $-T/2\Sigma_{i=1}^{r} \log(1 - \mu_i)$) is the corresponding value of the log-likelihood function apart from a constant. Hence the value of 1445.87 for the unrestricted log likelihood function is reported as 1446 for $r = 3$. The Max and Trace test statistics are not adjusted for degrees of freedom as suggested by Reimers (1992), since the results in Kostial (1994) indicate a tendency for them to underestimate the dimension of cointegrating space even when unadjusted. The critical values used for the Max and Trace statistics are given in Osterwald-Lenum (1992). On the basis of the statistics in Table 4.11 it is concluded that there is one cointegrating vector ($r = 1$), and an estimate of it is given by $\hat{\beta}'_1$ in Table 4.12.

This cointegration analysis with the linear trend t restricted to be in the cointegration space yields an estimated cointegrating vector $\hat{\beta}'_1 \mathbf{x}_t = w_t - 0.88p_t - 0.017u_t - 0.008t$, which implies that wages in a long-run equilibrium ($E(\hat{\beta}'_1 \mathbf{x}_t) = 0$) increase by 3 percent per annum after the influence of prices and unemployment have been taken into account. Figure 4.10 gives the graphs of the disequilibria or cointegrating vectors $\hat{\beta}'_i \mathbf{x}_t$, the "actual" ($x_{it}$) and "fitted" ($\Sigma_{j\neq i} \beta_{ij} x_{jt}$) values for $\mathbf{x}'_t =$

Table 4.12.   Adjustment coefficients α_i and eigenvectors β_i'

$\hat{\alpha}_i$	$i = 1$	$i = 2$	$i = 3$	$\hat{\beta}_i'$	w	p	u	t
w	−0.16	−0.00	0.00	$i = 1$	1	−0.88	−0.017	−0.008
p	0.16	−0.00	0.00	$i = 2$	−14.85	1	7.57	0.29
u	−0.25	−0.01	−0.00	$i = 3$	−0.51	−1.11	1	0.007

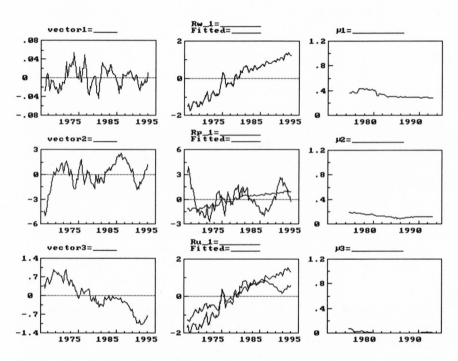

Figure 4.10.   Cointegrating vectors and recursive eigenvalues

(w_t, p_t, u_t), and the recursively estimated eigenvalues (see Hansen and Johansen, 1993) each after having partialled out the full-sample short-run dynamics and the unrestricted variables (that is, the constant and the dummies *Budget, Expansion, D*745, and *D*793). The first cointegrating vector appears to be $I(0)$, but the other two vectors are clearly nonstationary. There is a very close correspondence between the "actual" and the "fitted" values for w_t consistent with the disequilibrium rarely being over 4 percent. Note, though, that the estimated coefficient of u_t in the error correction has the opposite sign to that estimated by Clements and Mizon (1991), implying that ceteris paribus wages increase with increases in unemployment and so are counter cyclical! However, Clements and Mizon (1991) included average labor productivity in their analysis and found evidence of a long-run positive association between productivity and unemployment.

Note that these inferences concerning the integration-cointegration properties of the system require the system parameters to be constant if they are to be valid, whereas conventional test statistics for parameter constancy (such as system analogues of the analysis of variance and Chow statistics mentioned in the previous section) have known distributions for $I(0)$ rather than $I(1)$ systems. Although constancy tests for $I(1)$ variables are being developed, recursive estimation already provides a valuable check on parameter constancy. It is therefore reassuring that the recursive estimates of the eigenvalues are essentially constant. In particular, the largest μ_1 is approximately 0.4 for sample sizes 35 to 109, with only a suggestion of nonconstancy around 1979 and 1980. Of the other two eigenvalues, neither of which is significantly different from zero in the full sample, μ_2 take values declining from 0.2 to 0.1, and μ_3 is uniformly close to zero for all sample sizes. Therefore, it was decided to proceed to analyze the system further on the assumption that there is a single cointegrating vector.

Although the single cointegrating vector is already identified, it is of interest to test overidentifying restrictions on it such as (1) the absence of an unemployment effect on wages and prices ($\beta_{13} = 0$), (2) a long-run real wage equilibrium ($\beta_{12} = -1$), and (3) no long-run trend in wages and prices ($\beta_{14} = 0$). In addition, necessary conditions for p_t and u_t to be weakly exogenous for the parameters of the long-run wage-price equation—($\alpha_{21} = 0$) and ($\alpha_{31} = 0$), respectively—can be tested (see Boswijk, 1992; Hendry and Mizon, 1993; Johansen, 1992a, 1992b; Urbain, 1992). The test statistics are conventional likelihood ratio statistics, since the hypotheses are linear on an $I(0)$ parameterization of the system (N.B. if $\mathbf{x}_t \sim I(1)$, $\Delta \mathbf{x}_t$ and $\beta' \mathbf{x}_t \sim I(0)$ when there is cointegration), and so they have limiting χ^2 distributions with the degrees of freedom equal to the number of independent restrictions being tested.

The hypotheses that the long-run equilibrium is one for real wages ($\beta_{12} = -1$), that prices are weakly exogenous for a long-run wage equation ($\alpha_{21} = 0$), that wages are weakly exogenous for a long-run price equation ($\alpha_{11} = 0$), and that there is no trend in the long-run wage-price equation ($\beta_{14} = 0$) are all rejected. However, the hypotheses that u_t is weakly exogeneous for the parameters of the long-run wage-price equation ($\alpha_{31} = 0$), that there is no unemployment effect in the long-run wage-price equation ($\beta_{13} = 0$), and that the adjustment coefficient for wages is equal in magnitude but opposite in sign to that of prices ($\alpha_{11} + \alpha_{12} = 0$) are not rejected separately or jointly. Hence, the full-sample estimates of this system are reasonably congruent and consistent with the existence of a long-run wage-price equilibrium of the form

Table 4.13.   Overidentifying and weak exogeneity tests

Hypothesis	Statistic	p-value	Hypothesis	Statistic	p-value
$\beta_{13} = 0$	$\chi^2(1) = 0.57$	0.45	$\alpha_{11} = 0$	$\chi^2(1) = 9.31**$	0.00
			$\alpha_{21} = 0$	$\chi^2(1) = 14.49**$	0.00
$\beta_{14} = 0$	$\chi^2(1) = 17.23**$	0.00			
			$\alpha_{31} = 0$	$\chi^2(1) = 2.08$	0.15
$\beta_{12} = -1$	$\chi^2(1) = 5.46*$	0.02			
			$\alpha_{11} + \alpha_{21} = 0$	$\chi^2(1) = 0.01$	0.93

Hypothesis	Statistic	p-value
$\alpha_{31} = 0,\ \beta_{13} = 0$	$\chi^2(2) = 5.48$	0.07
$\alpha_{31} = 0,\ \beta_{12} = -1$	$\chi^2(2) = 12.92**$	0.00
$\alpha_{11} + \alpha_{21} = 0,\ \beta_{13} = 0$	$\chi^2(2) = 0.67$	0.72
$\alpha_{11} + \alpha_{21} = 0,\ \beta_{13} = 0,\ \alpha_{31} = 0$	$\chi^2(3) = 5.48$	0.14

$$E(w_t - 0.90p_t) - 0.008t = 0, \tag{4.33}$$

in which the p_t coefficient estimate of 0.9 is significantly different from unity. The estimated adjustment coefficient when the restrictions $\alpha_{11} + \alpha_{12} = 0$, $\alpha_{31} = 0$ and $\beta_{13} = 0$ are imposed is $\hat{\alpha}_{11} = -0.15$, which implies that both wages and prices adjust slowly to their equilibrium. Note that although u_t is weakly exogenous for the parameters of (4.33), it does not itself play a role in the long-run equilibrium. In fact, in this system u_t is determined independently of contemporaneous wages and prices, depending only on lagged values of wage and price inflation rates. This finding is consistent with u_t being a target of economic policy with at most weak links to the levels of wages and prices, instead being influenced by fiscal and monetary policies. Further, since the long-run wage-price disequilibrium is involved in the determination of both w_t and p_t, these variables require joint modeling in order to make efficient inferences. In particular, this casts doubt on the OLS results obtained in the previous section, though there is a remarkable similarity between (4.24) and (4.33).

The reduced rank ($r = 1$) system can be mapped from $I(1)$ to $I(0)$ space by adoption of the reparameterization

$$\Delta \mathbf{x}_t = \sum_{j=1}^{3} \Pi_j \Delta \mathbf{x}_{t-j} + \alpha \cdot ecm_{t-1} + \Phi D_t + \varepsilon_t \tag{4.34}$$

in which $ecm_t = w_t - 0.88p_t - 0.017u_t - 0.008t$ and the trend is excluded from D_t. Estimation and evaluation of (4.34) revealed the maintenance of the original system's congruence. This is illustrated by the graphs of actual and fitted values of

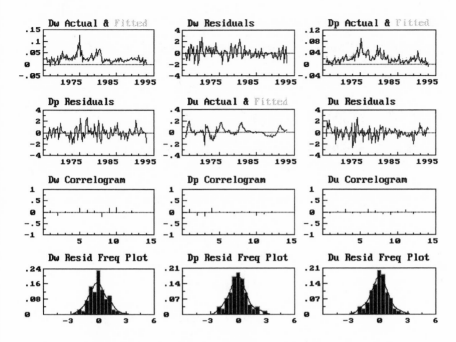

Figure 4.11. $I(0)$ system (PVAR) actual, fitted, and residual plots

Δw_t, Δp_t, and Δu_t, and the associated residual correlograms and frequency plots in Figure 4.11. As a result of imposing a rank of one on the cointegrating space (which the statistics in Table 4.11 indicated to be appropriate), and dropping the trend (other than its presence in the cointegrating vector ecm_t), the $I(0)$ system has nine fewer parameters than the original system and so will be referred to as a parsimonious VAR (PVAR). Although there is further scope for simplifying this PVAR since a number of the estimated coefficients do not appear to be significantly different from zero, the PVAR is retained in this form as a framework within which to compare alternative models by checking their ability to parsimoniously encompass the PVAR. The advantages of testing for simple models being able to parsimoniously encompass the PVAR are (1) reducing the risk of using models that are not robust to changes in the sample information (overparameterized models can be too finely tuned to the peculiarities of a particular sample), (2) increasing the chance that developed models are invariant to regime changes and thus capturing autonomous relationships rather than ephemeral occurrences, and (3) allowing the evaluation of models of particular interest (such as those implementing specific economic theories).

Table 4.14. Simplified model FIML estimates

$$\Delta w_t = 0.32\Delta p_t + 0.33\Delta w_{t-2} + 0.30\Delta p_{t-3} - 0.04\Delta u_{t-2} - 0.13ecm_{t-1} + 0.04D745 +$$
$$(0.14)\qquad(0.07)\qquad(0.08)\qquad(0.02)\qquad(0.06)\qquad(0.005)$$

$$0.03D793 - 1.10$$
$$(0.01)\quad\ (0.48)$$

$$\Delta p_t = 0.37\Delta p_{t-1} - 0.04\Delta u_{t-2} + 0.18ecm_{t-1} + 0.01Budget + 0.01D745 + 0.05D793 + 1.59$$
$$(0.06)\qquad(0.01)\qquad(0.02)\qquad(0.001)\qquad(0.003)\qquad(0.007)\qquad(0.21)$$

$$\Delta u_t = 0.76\Delta w_{t-1} + 0.79\Delta u_{t-1} + 0.12\Delta u_{t-2} - 0.14\Delta u_{t-3} + 0.13Expansion - 0.01$$
$$(0.17)\qquad(0.06)\qquad(0.06)\qquad(0.06)\qquad(0.01)\qquad(0.005)$$

$$ecm_t \equiv ecm_{t-1} + \Delta w_t - 0.88\Delta P_t - 0.017\Delta u_t - 0.008$$

Table 4.15. Simplified model diagnostic statistics

		Δw_t	Δp_t	Δu_t
$\hat{\sigma}$		1.08%	0.71%	3.10%
$AR(5, 89)$		3.85**	3.33**	2.04
$ARCH(4, 86)$		1.94	0.05	3.79**
$H(27, 66)$		0.93	1.34	1.10
$N(2)$		2.23	3.02	2.43

Vector Tests		*Residual Correlations*			
			w_t	p_t	u_t
$vecAR(45, 253)$	1.34				
$vecH(156, 413)$	1.04	p_t	−0.01	1.0	—
$vecN(6)$	7.45	u_t	0.11	0.07	1.0

The first model to be considered is an empirical simplification of the PVAR that retains the joint determination of w_t and p_t via the error correction ecm_t but simplifies the dynamics and restricts the presence of the dummy variables. Table 4.14 provides the FIML estimates of the simplified model. In the simplified model u_t is weakly exogenous for the parameters of the two equations that jointly determine w_t and p_t, and the long-run wage-price equilibrium is given by $E(ecm_t) = E(w_t - 0.88p_t - 0.017u_t) - 0.008t = 0$. The additional model information given in Table 4.15 provides further evidence that the simplified model, apart from increased serial correlation in the residuals for Δw_t and Δp_t and more $ARCH$ effects in those for Δu_t, performs just as well as the congruent system. The twenty-four restrictions implied by the simplified model relative to the PVAR are not rejected by a likelihood ratio test ($\chi^2(24) = 24.69$ [$p > 0.42$]), so that the simplified model parsimoniously encompasses the PVAR. Since there is evidence of serial correlation

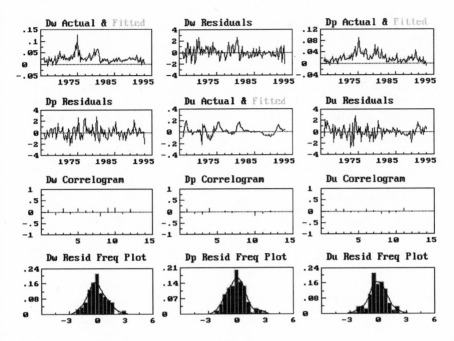

Figure 4.12.   Simplified model actual, fitted, and residual plots

and *ARCH* effects in the residuals the validity of this parsimonious encompassing test is called into question. However, comparison of Figure 4.12 with Figure 4.8 reveals the similarity between the congruent system and the simplified model and so lends some support (albeit weak support) to the use of this likelihood ratio test statistic.

The second model considered for encompassing comparison within the frame-work of the PVAR is a VAR for the differences Δw_t, Δp_t, and Δu_t (DVAR). This model corresponds to (4.34) with $\alpha = 0$ so that the disequilibrium ecm_t is ignored. As a system, a VAR in differences would be (4.31) with $\Pi = 0$ so that the long-run or zero-frequency information in the data is ignored and represents a class of model that has been popular in the time series analysis of nonstationary data particularly since the work of Box and Jenkins (1970). In addition to the three restrictions in $\alpha = 0$ there are a further six from restricting the number of dummy variables included in each equation as in the simplified model. The likelihood ratio test statistic takes the value $\chi^2(9) = 45.06$ [$p = 0.00$] so that the DVAR does not parsimoniously encompass the PVAR. Note that relative to the test statistics re-ported in Table 4.13 the present test is of the joint hypothesis $\alpha_{i1} = 0$, $i = 1, 2, 3$, plus the zero restrictions on the coefficients of the dummy variables. Hence, the

Table 4.16. System and model one-step-ahead forecast statistics, 1979(3)–1993(1)

VAR			PVAR		
$F_1(165, 37)$	$F_2(165, 37)$	$F_3(165, 37)$	$F_1(165, 40)$	$F_2(165, 40)$	$F_3(165, 40)$
8.45**	2.72**	1.05	1.08	0.90	0.85
$p = 0.00$	$p = 0.00$	$p > 0.45$	$p > 0.40$	$p > 0.69$	$p > 0.77$
Forecast error:	Δw_t	Δp_t Δu_t	Forecast error:	Δw_t	Δp_t Δu_t
Mean	−0.033	−0.002 0.032	Mean	−0.003	0.0001 −0.002
SD	0.035	0.010 0.041	SD	0.012	0.010 0.031
Simplified Model			DVAR		
$F_1(165, 48)$	$F_2(165, 48)$	$F_3(165, 48)$	$F_1(165, 43)$	$F_2(165, 43)$	$F_3(165, 43)$
0.92	0.85	na	1.10	0.93	na
$p > 0.66$	$p > 0.77$	na	$p > 0.37$	$p > 0.64$	na
Forecast error:	Δw_t	Δp_t Δu_t	Forecast error:	Δw_t	Δp_t Δu_t
Mean	−0.003	0.0001 −0.001	Mean	−0.003	−0.001 −0.001
SD	0.012	0.009 0.023		0.013	0.010 0.030

fact that the hypothesis $\alpha_{21} = 0$ was rejected contributes to, but does not entirely explain, the rejection of the DVAR model. The DVAR also fails to parsimoniously encompass the PVAR when the dummy variables are unrestricted—$\chi^2(3) = 33.86$ [$p = 0.00$] and so within-sample the zero frequency information contained in the cointegrating vector ecm_t has a valuable role in the modelling w_t, p_t, and u_t.

Recalling the evidence of a regime shift in 1979 for the single-equation modeling in the previous section, it is relevant to test the parameter constancy of the otherwise congruent system, the PVAR, the simplified model, and the DVAR. Table 4.16 presents the one-step ahead forecast test statistics from estimating the system and models with data up to 1979(2) and checking their ability to forecast over the fifty-five quarters in the period 1979(3)–1993(1). The three statistics are $F_i(165, T - k) = \mathbf{e}' \Psi_i^{-1} \mathbf{e}/165$, $i = 1, 2, 3$, when $\mathbf{e} = vec(E)$, E is a 55×3 matrix of forecast errors for the three modeled variables, the Ψ_i's are alternative estimates of the asymptotic covariance matrix of $\mathbf{e}$, $T (= 53)$ the sample size, and k the average number of estimated parameters per equation. Ψ_1 is the sample estimate of the innovation covariance matrix Σ, Ψ_2 is an estimate of the forecast error covariance matrix that allows for parameter uncertainty as well as the innovation variance, and Ψ_3 is an estimate of the forecast error covariance matrix that allows for innovation variance, parameter uncertainty, and the covariance between the forecast

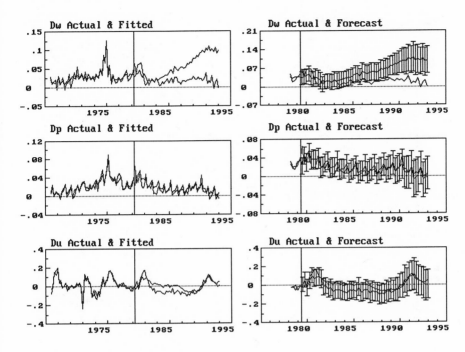

Figure 4.13. VAR actual, fitted, and forecasts

errors (see Doornik and Hendry, 1994 for details). The three statistics $F_i(165, 53 - k)$, $i = 1, 2, 3$, have approximate central F distributions with degrees of freedom 165 and $(53 - k)$ under the null hypothesis of parameter constancy.

The forecast performance of the VAR is poor (it is only $F_3(165, 37)$ that does not reject parameter constancy) as the graphs in Figure 4.13 make clear, especially for Δw_t, which has the actual and forecast values diverging disconcertingly, and the forecasts lying outside the confidence interval given by ± 2 forecast error standard deviations. The difficulties of the full-rank VAR are even more pronounced when the forecasts are presented for the levels of the variables w_t, p_t, and u_t. However, the PVAR, the simplified model, and the DVAR all forecast much better than the VAR, as evidenced by the statistics in Table 4.16. On the basis of the parameter constancy test statistics and the means and standard deviations of the forecast errors given in Table 4.16 the best overall performance is found in the simplified model, which is parsimonious and retains the zero frequency information in the disequilibrium ecm_t. The improved quality of these forecasts relative to those from the VAR is shown in Figure 4.14, which gives the actual, fitted, and forecast values for the simplified model.

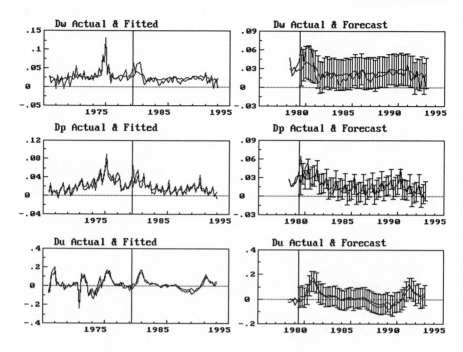

Figure 4.14.   Simplified model actual, fitted, and forecasts

Indeed, the difficulty lies in the different information used by the different models in forecasting the variables w_t, p_t, and u_t. The VAR uses the sample information on the levels of w_t, p_t, and u_t and their history, but wrongly treats the VAR as having full rank, and also ignores the regime shift in 1979. The DVAR uses sample information on the differences Δw_t, Δp_t, and Δu_t and their history but ignores sample information on the levels of these variables, the fact that the VAR has reduced rank, and that there is a regime shift. The PVAR (that is, the reduced-rank VAR mapped into $I(0)$ space) and the simplified model, on the other hand, implicitly use sample information on the levels of the variables and their history, as well as the fact that the VAR does not have full rank, but ignore the regime shift. However, the latter two models forecast well because they use a full sample estimate of ecm_t, which thus reflects the regime shift and so keeps the forecasts on track. If instead ecm_t were replaced by the estimate of the cointegrating vector using data from 1966(1) to 1979(2) only, the forecast performance of all the models (other than the VAR in differences) deteriorates to be similar to that of the VAR. Table 4.17 gives the split sample unrestricted (ecm_t) estimates of the cointegrating vector, plus restricted estimates (ecm_t^*) satisfying the nonrejected overidentifying restrictions discussed below.

Table 4.17. Split-sample estimates of the cointegrating vector

1966(1)–1993(1)	$ecm_t = w_t - 0.88p_t - 0.017u_t - 0.008t$
	$ecm_t^* = w_t - 0.90p_t - 0.008t$
1966(1)–1979(2)	$ecm1_t = w_t - 0.75p_t + 0.08u_t - 0.014t$
	$ecm1_t^* = w_t - 0.75p_t + 0.06u_t - 0.014t$
1979(3)–1993(1)	$ecm2_t = w_t - 0.94p_t + 0.06u_t - 0.006t$
	$ecm2_t^* = w_t - p_t - 0.006t$

Comparing $ecm1_t$ with ecm_t there is a 15 percent decrease in the coefficient of p_t, a 571 percent increase in the coefficient of u_t with a resultant change in sign (though neither estimate of this coefficient is significantly different from zero), and a 75 percent increase in the coefficient of the trend. Note that the response of wages and prices to unemployment in the period 1966(1)–1979(2) is procyclical, whereas that for the full sample and for the period after 1979(2) is countercyclical. Not surprisingly in view of this big difference between ecm_t and $ecm1_t$, the cointegrating vector estimated with data for the period 1979(3) to 1993(1) $ecm2_t$ is very different from $ecm1_t$ (see Table 4.17). In fact, though the Johansen *Max* and *Trace* statistics clearly indicated one cointegrating vector for the periods 1966(1)–1993(1) and 1966(1)–1979(2), they only marginally rejected the hypothesis of no cointegrating vectors for the period 1979(3)–1993(1). Therefore there is evidence of a fundamental change in the underlying relationship between w_t, p_t, and u_t pre- and post-1979(3). Indeed, there appears to have been a change in the exogeneity status of prices as the statistics in Table 4.18 indicate.

The restriction $\alpha_{31} = 0$ (a necessary condition for u_t to be weakly exogenous for the parameters of the long-run wage-price equation) is not rejected for any period, and so within this trivariate system unemployment appears to be weakly exogenous for the parameters of the one long-run equilibrium equation throughout the sample period. However, the corresponding hypothesis for prices ($\alpha_{21} = 0$), while being rejected for the full sample and for the period up to 1979(2), is not rejected for the post-1979(2) period. This result is consistent with prices and wages, while exhibiting autonomous growth, being jointly determined conditional on unemployment up to 1979(2), but with prices (and hence inflation) being a target of government policy after 1979(3) determined separately from contemporaneous wages and unemployment. Such an interpretation is coherent with the Conservative government elected in May 1979 adopting an economic policy aimed at reducing radically the rate of inflation, pursuant to which it introduced a tight monetary policy, instigated new labor market arrangements, and was willing to accept the attendant sharp changes in unemployment. Indeed, the pre-1979(3) error correction when estimated subject to the nonrejected restrictions $\alpha_{31} = 0$ and $\alpha_{11} + \alpha_{21} = 0$ (the test statistic for this joint hypothesis is $\chi^2(2) = 2.10$ $[p > 0.35]$) takes the form of $ecm1_t^*$

Table 4.18. Split-sample overidentifying and weak exogeneity tests

		1966(1)–1979(2)			
Hypothesis	*Statistic*	p-*value*	*Hypothesis*	*Statistic*	p-*value*
$\beta_{12} = 0$	$\chi^2(1) = 19.64$**	0.00	$\alpha_{11} = 0$	$\chi^2(1) = 5.78$*	0.02
$\beta_{13} = 0$	$\chi^2(1) = 7.48$**	0.01	$\alpha_{21} = 0$	$\chi^2(1) = 8.25$**	0.00
$\beta_{14} = 0$	$\chi^2(1) = 14.61$**	0.00	$\alpha_{31} = 0$	$\chi^2(1) = 1.69$	0.19
$\beta_{12} = -1$	$\chi^2(1) = 19.64$**	0.00	$\alpha_{11} + \alpha_{21} = 0$	$\chi^2(1) = 2.10$	0.15
		1979(3)–1993(1)			
Hypothesis	*Statistic*	p-*value*	*Hypothesis*	*Statistic*	p-*value*
$\beta_{12} = 0$	$\chi^2(1) = 6.40$*	0.01	$\alpha_{11} = 0$	$\chi^2(1) = 5.26$*	0.02
$\beta_{13} = 0$	$\chi^2(1) = 0.87$	0.35	$\alpha_{21} = 0$	$\chi^2(1) = 0.00$	0.98
$\beta_{14} = 0$	$\chi^2(1) = 2.29$	0.13	$\alpha_{31} = 0$	$\chi^2(1) = 2.52$	0.11
$\beta_{12} = -1$	$\chi^2(1) = 0.08$	0.78	$\alpha_{11} + \alpha_{21} = 0$	$\chi^2(1) = 4.07$*	0.04

  * Significant at
 ** Significant at

in Table 4.18, which is very different from the post-1979(2) error correction $ecm2_t^*$ estimated subject to the restrictions $\alpha_{31} = 0$, $\alpha_{21} = 0$, $\beta_{13} = 0$, and $\beta_{12} = -1$ ($\chi^2(4)$ = 8.40 [$p > 0.08$]). Hence there is evidence that u_t plays no role in the determination of the long-run equilibrium values of w_t and p_t after 1979(2) and that w_t adjusts fully to p_t and in addition has an autonomous trend. Finally, notice that ecm_t and $ecm2_t$ (ecm_t^* and $ecm2_t^*$) are very similar and noticeably different from $ecm1_t$ ($ecm1_t^*$). This helps to understand why the one-step-ahead forecasts for the period 1979(3)–1993(1) from the PVAR and the simplified model, both of which have ecm_t as an explanatory variable, are better than the corresponding forecasts from the VAR. In fact, if the single-equation model for wages is reparameterized to be in $I(0)$ space, it too has good one-step-ahead forecasts. In particular, if w_{t-1}, p_{t-1}, u_{t-1}, and t in the reduced model reported in Table 4.3, or w_{t-1}, p_{t-1}, and t in the final model reported in Table 4.4, are replaced by ecm_{t-1} the resulting forecasts for Δw_t are very similar to those for Δw_t of the simplified model shown in Figure 4.14. However, the fact that p_t is not weakly exogenous for the parameters of the long run equilibrium $E(ecm_t) = 0$ means that more efficient inferences should result from jointly modelling w_t and p_t, rather than using single equation OLS analysis. In fact, the forecasts for w_t from the system modeling should be preferable to those from the single-equation modeling. This is borne out in practice as can be seen from comparison of the forecast error mean and standard deviation from the single equation analysis (−0.0167 and 0.0168, respectively) with those for the simplified model reported in Table 4.16.

Although the above empirical analysis illustrates the importance of testing for weak exogeneity and modeling the joint distribution of variables in its absence, it is important to note that reasonable forecasts for the period 1966(1)–1993(1) were only obtained by using the full-sample estimate of the disequilibrium or error correction ecm_t, which would not be possible in practice for ex ante forecasting. The only model considered in this paper that would have been successful in ex ante forecasting is the DVAR. This highlights the fact that the presence of regime shifts in integrated-cointegrated systems for macroeconomic time series presents a substantial challenge to econometric modeling. Differencing time series that are subject to regime shifts does not account for the shifts even when they might be identifiable as changes in structure resulting from changes in government economic policies, but joint modeling of the differences in a VAR does enable the generation of multistep forecasts that converge on the unconditional means of the series (see Hendry and Clements, 1994). Forecasts from econometric models that include variables that have not been suitably differenced to transform regime shifts from step or trend changes into impulses or blips that have no duration (such as ecm_t in the above illustration) may require intercept corrections or other adjustments to keep them on track when there are regime shifts. Seen in this light the use of intercept corrections can be interpreted as a means of exploiting past forecast errors to keep present forecasts on track (see Clements and Hendry, 1994).

It is instructive also to note that the long run disequilibrium variable ecm_t, despite the fact that it is commonly called an error-correction mechanism, does not error-correct when it does not incorporate an explanation for regime shifts that are present in the system being modeled. Hence, ecm_t and $E(ecm_t) = 0$ have been referred to as long-run disequilibrium and long-run equilibrium, respectively. Ideally, econometric models should provide explanations for structural changes and account for autonomous shifts that affect the variables being modeled and thus avoid the necessity of differencing such changes out of the system in order to produce reliable forecasts. Although this statement describes an enormous challenge to econometric modelers, those who overcome the challenge are likely to develop econometric models with great potential for use in economic policy analysis and forecasting. To rise to this challenge in the modeling of wages, prices, unemployment, and other related variables such as productivity over the period 1966(1)– 1993(1) in the United Kingdom, it is likely that account will have to be taken of the important changes in the labor market structure, in exchange-rate regimes, and government policies toward inflation and unemployment. The fact that the models presented in this section have a single deterministic trend to approximate the effects of technical change, changes in productivity, and external factors and do not have long-run equilibria with price homogeneity (except for $ecm2^*_t$ in Table 4.17) indicates that there is ample scope for further modeling. This important task lies beyond the scope of the present paper, which has concentrated on the presentation of illustrative, rather than definitive, models of the relationship between wages, prices, and unemployment.

Conclusions

The LSE modeling methodology developed rapidly during the 1960s and 1970s and has had a significant effect on econometric modeling at large, as described in Gilbert (1986). However, no vital methodology is static but rather evolves with important developments. This is certainly true of the LSE methodology, and as suggested by Pagan (1992) a more accurate name today might be the LSE–Copenhagen–San Diego–Yale methodology—though even this ignores the valuable contributions of researchers in institutions in other geographical locations. The econometric modeling methodology associated with the LSE has achieved much, is still evolving and being refined, and provides a powerful tool for reaping the benefits of scientific econometric modeling. Though ultimately the model is the message, the system (that is, the congruent representation of the joint distribution of the observed variables of relevance) is the appropriate statistical framework for developing and evaluating such econometric models. The legacy of this methodology includes the widely accepted need to rigorously evaluate econometric models by checking their congruence with available information and their ability to encompass rival models, as well as the advocacy of the general-to-specific modeling strategy as an efficient and efficacious modeling strategy.

Econometric concepts that provide important objectives to be achieved in the LSE methodology are homoscedastic innovation error processes; weak, strong, and super exogeneity; encompassing; and parameter constancy. Failure to achieve these objectives in practice can result in econometric models that are likely to yield misleading conclusions from economic policy analyses and produce unreliable forecasts. Indeed one of the most important challenges in the econometric modeling of macroeconomic time series is to produce multistep forecasts that are at least as accurate as those generated from multivariate time-series models such as DVARs. This is a goal to which many of those espoused to the LSE methodology aspire. The simple illustration of empirical modeling presented above demonstrates the seriousness of this challenge but also suggests that there is hope of future success. In addition, the illustration highlighted the important effect changes in economic policy can have on the inter-relationships between macroeconomic variables, especially on the underlying equilibrating mechanisms and the exogeneity status of variables within them. The changes in economic policy from monitoring the rate of unemployment, to reducing radically the rate of inflation, had major effects on the U.K. economy post-1979.

Data Appendix

The quarterly data set runs from 1965(1) to 1993(1). The precise estimation periods used vary according to the number of lags in the specification. All series are seasonally adjusted except for the price series. The wage variable w is defined as log $(WS/EE*AVH)$, where WS is wages and salaries, EE is employees in employment, and AVH is a measure of average weekly hours in the manufacturing sector. The price variable p is the $\log(P)$ when P is the retail price index, so that Δp is the quarterly aggregate inflation rate. Finally, $u = \log(U)$, U being the percentage of unemployment rate.

The precise definitions and sources are as follows:

WS:

Wages, salaries and forces pay. £mn.	*ETAS*, 65:1 to 90:4
CSO mnemonic AIJB	*ET*, 91:1 to 93:1

EE:

Employees in employment 000's, whole UK	*ETAS*, 65:1 to 89:3
CSO mnemonic BCAJ	*ET*, 89:4 to 93:1

AVH:

Index of average weekly hours worked per operative in manufacturing (1980 = 100)	*EG*, 65:1 to 93:1

P:

Retail price index, all items (1987 = 100)	*ETAS*, 65:1 to 92:2
CSO mnemonics FRAG and CHAW	*ET*, 92:3 to 93:1

U:

Unemployment rate (UK) percent	*ETAS*, 65:1 to 91:1
CSO mnemonic BCJE	*ET*, 91:2 to 93:1

ETAS refers to *Economic Trends* (*Annual Supplement*) (1993 edition); *ET* refers to *Economic Trends* (August 1993 edition). Both were compiled by the Central Statistical Office (CSO). *EG* refers to the *Employment Gazette Historical Supplements* (No. 1, April 1985, Vol. 93, No. 4; No. 2, Oct. 1987, Vol. 95, No. 10) and various issues of the *Gazette* publised by the Department of Employment.

Acknowledgments

The views presented in this paper on the nature and role of econometric modeling are mine. However, since I am associated with what has become known as the LSE methodology (or sometimes Professor Hendry's methodology) (see Gilbert, 1986; Ericsson, Campos, and Tran, 1990), this is consistent with my brief to write a paper describing the LSE methodology. I should like to thank my many friends and colleagues of the "LSE School" for the intellectual stimulation they have provided over the last quarter of a century. In particular, I wish to thank Mike Clements, David Hendry, Maozu Lu, and Jean-François Richard for allowing me to draw on our joint research without wishing to hold them responsible for the result. I am also grateful to David Hendry for providing many valuable suggestions while the paper was in gestation and to Mike Clements and Kevin Hoover for providing detailed and constructive comments on an earlier version of the paper. Financial support for this research from the ESRC under grant R000231184 and from the EUI Research Council is gratefully acknowledged.

References

Aldrich, J. (1989). "Autonomy." *Oxford Economic Papers* 41, 15–34.

Anderson, T.W., and H. Rubin. (1950). "The Asymptotic Properties of Estimates of the Parameters of a Single Equation in a Complete System of Stochastic Equations." *Annals of Mathematical Statistics* 21, 570–582

Banerjee, A., J.J. Dolado, J.W. Galbraith, and D.F. Hendry. (1993). *Co-integration, Error-Correction, and the Econometric Analysis of Non-Stationary Data.* Oxford: Oxford University Press.

Boswijk, H.P. (1992). *Cointegration, Identification and Exogeneity.* Amsterdam: Thesis.

Box, G.E.P., and G.M. Jenkins. (1970). *Time Series Analysis Forecasting and Control.* San Francisco: Holden-Day.

Breusch, T.S. and Pagan, A.R. (1980). "The Lagrange Multiplier Test and Its Applications to Model Specification in Econometrics." *Review of Economic Studies* 47, 239–253.

Brown, R.L., J. Durbin, and J.M. Evans. (1975). "Techniques for Testing the Constancy of Regression Relationships Over Time." *Journal of the Royal Statistical Society* Series B, 37, 149–192.

Campos, J., N.R. Ericsson, and D.F. Hendry. (1993). "Cointegration Tests in the Presence of Structural Breaks." International Finance Discussion Paper No. 440, Board of Governors of the Federal Reserve System, February.

Canova, F. (1995). "The Economics of VAR Models." In K.D. Hoover (ed.), *Macroeconometrics: Developments, Tensions and Prospects* (ch. 3). Boston: Kluwer.

Canova, F., M. Finn, and A.R. Pagan. (1994). "Evaluating a Real Business Cycle Model." In C.P. Hargreaves (ed.), *Nonstationary Time Series Analyses and Cointegration* (pp. 225–255). Oxford: Oxford University Press.

Clements, M.P., and D.F. Hendry. (1994). "Towards a Theory of Economic Forecasting." In C.P. Hargreaves (ed.), *Nonstationary Time Series Analyses and Cointegration* (pp. 9–52). Oxford: Oxford University Press.

Clements, M.P., and G.E. Mizon. (1991). "Empirical Analysis of Macroeconomic Time Series: VAR and Structural Models." *European Economic Review* 35, 887–932.

Cox, D.R. (1961). "Tests of Separate Families of Hypotheses." In J. Neyman (ed.), *Pro-

ceedings of the Fourth Berkeley Symposium on Mathematical Statistics and Probability (pp. 105–123). Berkeley: University of California Press.

Cox, D.R. (1962). "Further Results of Tests of Separate Families of Hypotheses." *Journal of the Royal Statistical Society* Series B, 24, 406–424.

Davidson, R. and MacKinnon, J.G. (1981). "Several Tests for Model Specification in the Presence of Alternative Hypotheses." *Econometrica* 49, 781–793.

Desai, M.J. (1975). "The Phillips Curve: A Revisionist Interpretation." *Economica* 42, 1–19.

Desai, M.J. (1984). "Wages, Prices and Unemployment a Quarter of a Century After the Phillips Curve." In D.F. Hendry and K.F. Wallis (eds.), *Econometrics and Quantitative Economics* (pp. 251–273). Oxford: Basil Blackwall.

Dickey, D.A., and W.A. Fuller. (1981). "Likelihood Ratio Statistics for Autoregressive Time Series with a Unit Root." *Econometrica* 49, 1657–1672.

Doornik, J.A., and H. Hansen. (1994). "A Practical Test for Univariate and Multivariate Normality." Mimeo, Nuffield College, Oxford, March.

Doornik, J.A., and D.F. Hendry. (1992). *PC-GIVE Version 7: An Interactive Econometric Modelling System*. Oxford: Institute of Economics and Statistics, University of Oxford.

Doornik, J.A., and D.F. Hendry. (1993). *PC-FIML Version 7: An Interactive Econometric Modelling System*. Oxford: Institute of Economics and Statistics, University of Oxford.

Doornik, J.A., and D.F. Hendry. (1994). *PC-GIVE and PC-FIML Professional, Version 8: An Interactive Econometric Modelling System*. London: International Thomson.

Engle, R.F., and D.F. Hendry. (1993). "Testing Super Exogeneity and Invariance in Regression Models." *Journal of Econometrics* 56, 119–140.

Engle, R.F., D.F. Hendry, and J-F. Richard. (1983). "Exogeneity." *Econometrica* 51, 277–304.

Ericsson, N.R. (1983). "Asymptotic Properties of Instrumental Variables Statistics for Testing Non-nested Hypotheses." *Review of Economic Studies* 50, 287–303.

Ericsson, N.R. (1993). "Cointegration, Exogeneity, and Policy Analysis: Representation, Estimation and Testing." *Journal of Policy Modeling* 14, 251–280.

Ericsson, N.R., J. Campos, and H-A. Tran. (1990). "PC-GIVE and David Hendry's Econometric Methodology." *Revista de Econometria* 10, 7–117.

Ericsson, N.R., and D.F. Hendry. (1989). "Encompassing and Rational Expectations: How Sequential Corroboration Can Imply Refutation." International Finance Discussion Paper No. 354, Board of Governors of the Federal Reserve System, June.

Espasa, A. (1975). "A Wage-Earnings-Prices Inflation Model for the United Kingdom 1950–1970: Its Specification and Estimation by Classical and Spectral Methods." Ph.D. thesis, London School of Economics.

Favero, C., and D.F. Hendry. (1992). "Testing the Lucas Critique." *Econometric Reviews* 11, 265–306.

Gilbert, C.L. (1986). "Professor Hendry's Econometric Methodology." *Oxford Bulletin of Economics and Statistics* 48, 283–307.

Gilbert, C.L. (1989). "LSE and the British Approach to Time Series Econometrics." *Oxford Economic Papers* 41, 108–128.

Gourieroux, C., and A. Monfort. (1995). "Testing, Encompassing and Simulating Dynamic Econometric Models." *Econometric Theory* 11, 195–228.

Granger, C.W.J. (ed.). (1990). *Modelling Economic Series: Readings in Econometric Methodology*. Oxford: Oxford University Press.

Granger, G.W.J., and P. Newbold. (1974). "Spurious Regressions in Econometrics." *Journal of Econometrics* 2, 111–120.

Hansen, B.E. (1992). "Testing for Parameter Instability in Linear Models." *Journal of Policy Modeling* 14(4), 517–533.

Hansen, H., and S. Johansen. (1993). "Recursive Estimation in Cointegrated VAR Models." Discussion Paper, Institute of Mathematical Statistics, University of Copenhagen.

Hendry, D.F. (1971). "Maximum Likelihood Estimation of Systems of Simultaneous Regression Equations with Errors Generated by a Vector Autoregressive Process." *International Economic Review* 12, 257–272, with correction in 15, p. 260.

Hendry, D.F. (1974). "Stochastic Specification in an Aggregate Demand Model of the United Kingdom." *Econometrica* 42, 559–578.

Hendry, D.F. (1980). "Econometrics: Alchemy or Science?" *Economica* 47, 387–406.

Hendry, D.F. (1983). "Econometric Modelling: The Consumption Function In Retrospect." *Scottish Journal of Political Economy* 30, 193–220.

Hendry, D.F. (1987). "Econometric Methodology: A Personal Perspective." In T.F. Bewley. (ed.), *Advances in Econometrics* (pp. 29–48). Cambridge: Cambridge University Press.

Hendry, D.F. (1989). *PC GIVE: An Interactive Econometric Modelling System*. Oxford: Oxford Institute of Economics and Statistics.

Hendry, D.F. (1993a). "On the Interactions of Unit Roots and Exogeneity." *Econometric Reviews*, forthcoming.

Hendry, D.F. (1993b). "The Roles of Economic Theory and Econometrics in the Analysis of Economic Time Series." Unpublished paper, Institute of Economics and Statistics, Oxford. Presented to the European Meeting of the Econometric Society, Uppsala, September.

Hendry, D.F. (1994). "Typologies of Linear Dynamic Systems and Models." *Journal of Statistical Inference and Planning*, forthcoming.

Hendry, D.F. (1995). *Dynamic Econometrics*. Oxford: Oxford University Press.

Hendry, D.F., and G.J. Anderson. (1977). "Testing Dynamic Specification in Small Simultaneous Systems: An Application to a Model of Building Society Behaviour in the United Kingdom." In M.D. Intriligator (ed.), *Frontiers in Quantitative Economics* (Vol. 3a) (pp. 361–383). Amsterdam: North Holland.

Hendry, D.F., and M.P. Clements. (1994). "Can Econometrics Improve Economic Forecasting?" *Swiss Journal of Economics and Statistics* 130, 267–298.

Hendry, D.F., and J.A. Doornik. (1994). "Modelling Linear Dynamic Econometric Systems." *Scottish Journal of Political Economy* 41, 1–33.

Hendry, D.F., and G.E. Mizon. (1978). "Serial Correlation as a Convenient Simplification, Not a Nuisance: A Comment on a Study of the Demand for Money by the Bank of England." *Economic Journal* 88, 549–563.

Hendry, D.F., and G.E. Mizon. (1990). "Procrustean Econometrics: or Stretching and Squeezing Data." In C.W.J. Granger. (ed.), *Modelling Economic Series: Readings in Econometric Methodology* (pp. 121–136). Oxford: Oxford University Press.

Hendry, D.F., and G.E. Mizon. (1993). "Evaluation of Dynamic Econometric Models by Encompassing the VAR." In P.C.B. Phillips (ed.), *Models, Methods and Applications of Econometrics, Essays in Honor of Rex Bergstrom* (pp. 272–300). Oxford: Basil Blackwell.

Hendry, D.F., and M.S. Morgan (eds.). (1995). *The Foundations of Econometric Analysis.* Cambridge: Cambridge University Press.

Hendry, D.F., A.R. Pagan, and J.D. Sargan. (1984). "Dynamic Specification." In Z. Griliches and M.D. Intrilligator (eds.), *Handbook of Econometrics* (Vol. 2) (pp. 1023–1100). Amsterdam: North-Holland.

Hendry, D.F., and J-F. Richard. (1982). "On the Formulation of Empirical Models in Dynamic Econometrics." *Journal of Econometrics* 20, 3–33.

Hendry, D.F., and J-F. Richard. (1983). "The Econometric Analysis of Economic Time Series." *International Statistical Review* 51, 111–163.

Hendry, D.F., and J-F. Richard. (1989). "Recent Developments in the Theory of Encompassing." In B. Cornet and H. Tulkens (eds.), *Contributions to Operations Research and Econometrics. The Twentieth Anniversary of CORE* (pp. 393–440). Cambridge, MA: MIT Press.

Hendry, D.F., and F. Srba. (1980). "AUTOREG: A Computer Program Library for Dynamic Econometric Models with Autoregressive Errors." *Journal of Econometrics* 12, 85–102.

Hendry, D.F., and K.F. Wallis (eds.). (1984). *Econometrics and Quantitative Economics.* Oxford: Basil Blackwell.

Hoover, K.D. (1988). "On the Pitfalls of Untested Common Factor Restrictions: The Case of the Inverted Fisher Hypothesis." *Oxford Bulletin of Economics and Statistics* 50, 125–138.

Hylleberg, S., and G.E. Mizon. (1989). "A Note on the Distribution of the Least Squares Estimator of a Random Walk with Drift." *Economics Letters* 29, 225–230.

Ingram, B.F. (1995). "Recent Advances in Solving and Estimating Dynamic Macroeconomic Models." In K.D. Hoover (ed.), *Macroeconomics: Developments, Tensions and Prospects* (chap. 1). Boston: Kluwer.

Johansen, S. (1988). "Statistical Analysis of Cointegration Vectors." *Journal of Economic Dynamics and Control* 12, 231–254.

Johansen, S. (1992a). "Cointegration in Partial Systems and the Efficiency of Single Equation Analysis." *Journal of Econometrics* 52, 389–402.

Johansen, S. (1992b). "Testing for Weak Exogeneity and the Order of Cointegration in the U.K. Money Demand Data." *Journal of Policy Modeling* 14, 313–334.

Johansen, S., and K. Juselius. (1990). "Maximum Likelihood Estimation and Inference on Cointegration—with Applications to the Demand for Money." *Oxford Bulletin of Economics and Statistics* 52, 169–210.

Kim, K., and A.R. Pagan. (1994). "The Econometric Analysis of Calibrated Macroeconomic Models." Mimeo, Australian National University, March.

Koopmans, T.C. (ed.). (1950). *Statistical Inference in Dynamic Economic Models.* Cowles Commission Monograph No. 10. New York: Wiley.

Kostial, K. (1994). "The Role of the Signal-Noise Matrix in the Estimation of Cointegrated Systems." European University Institute, Economics Department Discussion Paper No. EC94/27. Presented to the European Meeting of the Econometric Society, Maastricht, September.

Kydland, F., and E. Prescott. (1982). "Time to Build and Aggregate Fluctuations." *Econometrica* 50, 1345–1370.

Kydland, F., and E. Prescott. (1995). "The Econometrics of the General Equilibrium Approach to Business Cycles." In K.D. Hoover (ed.), *Macroeconomics: Developments, Tensions and Prospects* (ch. 5). Boston: Kluwer.

Layard, R., and S.J. Nickell. (1985). "The Causes of British Unemployment." *National Institute Economic Review* 111, 62–85.

Leamer, E.E. (1978). *Specification Searches: Ad Hoc Inference with Non-Experimental Data.* New York: Wiley.

Leamer, E.E. (1983). "Let's Take the Con Out of Econometrics." *American Economic Review* 73, 31–44.

Lipsey, R.G. (1960). "The Relation Between Unemployment and the Rate of Change of Money Wage Rates in the United Kingdom 1862–1957: A Further Analysis." *Economica* 27, 1–31.

Lu, M., and G.E. Mizon. (1991). "Forecast Encompassing and Model Evaluation." In P. Hackl and A. Westlund (eds.), *Economic Structural Change: Analysis and Forecasting* (pp. 123–138). Vienna: Springer-Verlag.

Lucas, R.E. (1976). "Econometric policy evaluation: a critique." In K. Brunner and A.H. Meltzer (eds.), *The Phillips Curve and Labor Markets* (Vol. 1) (pp. 19–46). Carnegie-Rochester Conference Series on Public Policy. Amsterdam: North Holland.

Maasoumi, E. (1988). *Contributions to Econometrics: John Denis Sargan* (Vols. 1–2). Cambridge: Cambridge University Press.

Mizon, G.E. (1977a). "Model Selection Procedures in Dynamic Models." In M.J. Artis and A.R. Nobay (eds.), *Studies in Modern Economic Analysis* (ch. 4, pp. 97–120). Oxford: Basil Blackwell.

Mizon, G.E. (1977b). "Inferential Procedures in Nonlinear Models: An Application in a UK Cross Sectional Study of Factor Substitution and Returns to Scale." *Econometrica* 45, 1221–1242.

Mizon, G.E. (1984). "The Encompassing Approach in Econometrics." In D.F. Hendry and K.F. Wallis (eds.), *Econometrics and Quantitative Economics* (ch. 6, pp. 135–172). Oxford: Basil Blackwell.

Mizon, G.E. (1989). "The Role of Econometric Modelling in Economic Analysis." *Revista Española de Economia* 6, 165–191.

Mizon, G.E. (1991). "The Role of Measurement and Testing in Economics." In M. Bleaney, D. Greenaway, and I.M. Stewart (eds.), *Companion to Contemporary Economic Thought* (ch. 28, pp. 547–592). London: Routledge.

Mizon, G.E. (1995). "A Simple Message for Autocorrelation Correctors: DON'T." *Journal of Econometrics*, forthcoming.

Mizon, G.E., and D.F. Hendry. (1980). "An Empirical Application and Monte Carlo Analysis of Tests of Dynamic Specification." *Review of Economic Studies* 49, 21–45.

Mizon, G.E., and J-F. Richard. (1986). "The Encompassing Principle and Its Application to Non-Nested Hypothesis Tests." *Econometrica* 54, 657–678.

Monfort, A., and R. Rabemananjara. (1990). "From a VAR Model to a Structural Model: With an Application to the Wage-Price Spiral." *Journal of Applied Econometrics* 5, 203–227.

Nickell, S.J. (1984). "The Modelling of Wages and Employment." In D.F. Hendry and K.F. Wallis (eds.), *Econometrics and Quantitative Economics* (ch. 2, pp. 13–35). Oxford: Basil Blackwell.

Osterwald-Lenum, M. (1992). "A Note with Quantiles of the Asymptotic Distribution of the ML Cointegration Rank Test Statistics." *Oxford Bulletin of Economics and Statistics* 54, 461–472.

Pagan, A.R. (1987). "Three Econometric Methodologies: A Critical Appraisal." *Journal of Economic Surveys* 1, 3–24. Reprinted in C.W.J. Granger (ed.), *Modelling Economic Series: Readings in Econometric Methodology* (pp. 97–120). Oxford: Oxford University Press.

Pagan, A.R. (1989). "Twenty Years After: Econometrics, 1966–1986." In B. Cornet and H. Tulkens (eds.), *Contributions to Operations Research and Econometrics: The Twentieth Anniversary of CORE* (pp. 319–383). Cambridge, MA: MIT Press.

Pagan, A.R. (1992). "Three Econometric Methodologies: An Update." Mimeo, Australian National University.

Phillips, A.W.H. (1958). "The Relation Between Unemployment and the Rate of Change of Money Wages Rates in the United Kingdom 1861–1957." *Economica* 25, 283–299.

Phillips, P.C.B. (1988). "The *ET* Interview: A.R. Bergstrom." *Econometric Theory* 4, 301–327.

Phillips, P.C.B. (ed.). (1993a). *Models, Methods, and Applications of Econometrics: Essays in Honor of A.R. Bergstrom.* Cambridge: Basil Blackwell.

Phillips, P.C.B. (1993b). "Rex Bergstrom's Career and Research." In P.C.B. Phillips (ed.), *Models, Methods, and Applications of Econometrics: Essays in Honor of A.R. Bergstrom* (pp. 3–8). Cambridge: Basil Blackwell.

Pesaran, M.P. (1974). "On the General Problem of Model Selection." *Review of Economic Studies* 41, 153–171.

Prothero, D.L., and K.F. Wallis. (1976). "Modelling Macro-Economic Time Series (with discussion)." *Journal of the Royal Statistical Society* Series A, 139, 468–500.

Reimers, H.-E. (1992). "Comparisons of Tests for Multivariate Cointegration." *Statistical Papers* 33, 335–359.

Richard, J-F. (1980). "Models with Several Regimes and Changes in Exogeneity." *Review of Economic Studies* 47, 1–20.

Sargan, J.D. (1964). "Wages and Prices in the United Kingdom: A Study in Econometric Methodology." In P.E. Hart, G. Mills, and J.K. Whitaker (eds.), *Econometric Analysis for National Economic Planning.* London: Butterworths. Reprinted in D.F. Hendry and K.F. Wallis (eds.), *Econometrics and Quantitative Economics* (pp. 275–314). Oxford: Basil Blackwell.

Sargan, J.D. (1980a). "A Model of Wage-Price Inflation." *Review of Economic Studies* 47, 97–112.

Sargan, J.D. (1980b). "Some Tests of Dynamic Specification for a Single Equation." *Econometrica* 48, 879–897.

Sargan, J.D. (1988). *Lectures on Advanced Econometric Theory.* Oxford: Basil Blackwell.

Sims, C.A. (1980). "Macroeconomics and Reality." *Econometrica* 48, 1–48. Reprinted in C.W.J. Granger (ed.), *Modelling Economic Series: Readings in Econometric Methodology* (pp. 137–189). Oxford: Oxford University Press.

Sims, C.A. (1992). "Interpreting the Macroeconomic Time Series Facts: The Effects of Monetary Policy." *European Economic Review* 36, 975–1000.

Spanos, A. (1986). *Statistical Foundations of Econometric Modelling.* Cambridge: Cambridge University Press.

Spanos, A. (1988). "Error Autocorrelation Revisted: The AR(1) Case." *Econometric Reviews* 6, 285–294.

Summers, L.H. (1991). "The Scientific Illusion in Empirical Macroeconomics." *Scandinavian Journal of Economics* 93, 129–148.

Terasvirta, T. (1970). "Stepwise Regression and Economic Forecasting." Economic Studies Monograph No. 31. Helsinki: Finnish Economics Association.

Urbain, J.P. (1992). "On Weak Exogeneity in Error Correction Models." *Oxford Bulletin of Economics and Statistics* 54, 187–208.

Vernon, K. (1970). "An Econometric Study of Wage and Price Inflation in the United Kingdom in the Post War Period." Ph.D. thesis, London School of Economics.

West, K.D. (1988). "Asymptotic Normality When Regressors Have a Unit Root." *Econometrica* 56, 1397–1417.

White, H. (1980). "A Heteroskedastic-consistent Covariance Matrix Estimator and a Direct Test for Heteroskedasticity." *Econometrica* 48, 817–838.

Zellner, A., and F. Palm. (1974). "Time Series Analysis and Simultaneous Equation Econometric Models." *Journal of Econometrics* 2, 17–54.

Commentary on Chapter 4

Jon Faust
Charles H. Whiteman

Introduction

Over the past two decades or so, many approaches to the modeling of macro-economic time series have come and gone; one that has come and stayed is the LSE approach. Advocates of the approach have been prolific in asserting the virtues of their econometrics and the shortcomings of what Gilbert (1986) calls the average economic regression (AER) (Doornik and Hendry, 1994; Ericsson, Campos, and Tran, 1990; Gilbert, 1986, 1989; Hendry, 1987, 1995; Spanos, 1986). Despite these writings, the average econometrician may sympathize with a hotly-pursued Robert Redford (as the Sundance Kid), who repeatedly asked, "Who *are* those guys?"

Grayham Mizon approaches this question from several directions: he provides a general description of the methodology; he lists numerous contributors to the development of the methodology; he describes its main components; and he provides an example.

Having addressed the question, has Mizon answered it? We are not sure. Much of Mizon's discussion is couched in the special vocabulary of the LSE approach, making it difficult to determine what (other than language) distinguishes *those guys* from, say, the average econometrician reading this volume. Thus, we set out to distill from Mizon's paper what is unique about the LSE methodology.

The LSE Approach: Mizon's General Description

The place to begin trying to understand the LSE approach is at the beginning, Mizon's introduction. Therein, he states, "The essence of this [LSE] approach is the recognition that potentially valuable information for the analysis of any economic problem can come from numerous sources including, economic theory, the available sample of observations on the potentially relevant variables, knowledge of the economic history of the period under study, and from knowledge of the way in which the observed data are defined and measured, plus their relationship to the theory variables."

If this is true, then the LSE approach must share its essence with that of the

171

other approaches Mizon enumerates—the VAR approach, Leamer's approach, and calibration—as well as other approaches such as the Euler equation approach built on the generalized-method-of-moments (GMM) procedures of Hansen (1982), the rational-expectations approach to econometric practice (Lucas and Sargent, 1981; Hansen and Sargent, 1980), and the Bayesian approach (DeJong and Whiteman, 1991; DeJong, Ingram, and Whiteman, 1994). Indeed, Mizon claims that the LSE approach draws on the strengths of many of these approaches.

Would it be possible to identify the LSE approach as the common strengths of work as diverse as that of Sims, Hansen and Sargent, and Kydland and Prescott? Probably not. Each of the approaches pays attention in some way to the sources of information listed by Mizon; theory plays a more important role in the rational-expectations approach than in the VAR approach, and measurement issues are of greater concern to calibrators than to some others, but none of the camps displays a wholesale disregard for any type of information (except perhaps for survey information).

Surely the essence of the approach is not the *use* of information but the *way* the information is used. Thus there is hope that we can distinguish the LSE approach from the others by determining how the various types of information influence the course of analysis. One way to do this is to look at the common themes in the work of econometricians who have influenced the approach.

The LSE Approach: The Contributors

The LSE has been a center of tremendous productivity in econometrics, and the list of econometricians who have exited the tube at Holborn as faculty or visitors at the nearby LSE is a *Who's Who* of econometrics. Can one understand what is called the LSE approach by looking at the work of those individuals identified as having had important influence on it? No. There may be common features in the work of as diverse a group of eminent econometricians as James Durbin, Peter Phillips, Kenneth Wallis, Jean-Francois Richard, and Takeshi Amemiya, but those common features do not add up to the LSE approach. Many of those on Mizon's list do not even use the LSE methodology in their research. Of course, the LSE approach has benefitted from a large and diverse group of econometricians; perhaps it is more than the sum of its parts. To the parts we turn.

The LSE Approach: The Components

The goal of LSE econometrics, as described and applied in the third and fourth sections, seems to be to fit a *congruent, encompassing* model to the *DGP*;

undoubtedly, it is in the definitions of these terms that the distinguishing features of the approach will emerge.

DGP

The DGP is what other econometricians might refer to as the "likelihood function" or the "joint distribution." Mizon notes that there are many factorizations and observationally equivalent parameterizations of the likelihood. Though all factorizations are equal, some are more equal than others. To wit (third section) "Now consider another investigator who claims to be interested in the model: $[M_2]$ . . . this investigator is clearly not considering the 'true' model since M_2 does not correspond to any of the equations of the DGP as given in (2)! It is, though, part of other valid parameterizations of the DGP . . . and thus 'true.'"

It is clear that the nature of the LSE approach is tied to its users' interpretations of the meaning of words like *true* and *valid*, meanings that to us are not altogether clear. Meanwhile, our (not-so-clear) understanding of these statements and the ones surrounding them is that different factorizations and parameterizations of the likelihood may be of focal interest depending on the perspective and purpose. If we are correct, this point is not unique to the LSE approach.

Mizon's discussion does reveal one feature that distinguishes the LSE approach from some others: it is likelihood-based and pays great attention to what different factorizations of the likelihood imply for the properties of inferences. In this respect, the approach is founded in the statistical literature on the related concepts of sufficient and ancillary statistics, and admissibility and complete classes of procedures (see Barndorff-Nielsen, 1978; Basu, 1977; Lehmann, 1986). Engle, Hendry, and Richard (1983), for example, applied the notion of ancillarity in defining weak exogeneity.

Congruence

Being congruent means being consistent, in some sense, with information from four sources: *a priori* theory, sample information, the measurement system, and rival models.

Congruence with A Priori Theory

There is a spectrum of views in the profession on how big a role theory should play. Everything from nothing (VARs) to everything (RBC modelers are "ahead

of measurement," Prescott, 1986). Where does the LSE school fall? Mizon cites
Hendry as saying that under the LSE approach, consistency with economic theory
is a desirable but inessential property. Apparently, measurement without (much)
theory is permissible. Indeed, we do not know many economic theorists who
would find measurable comfort in Mizon's Table 4.14. Theory consistency is not
a particularly important component of congruence.

Congruence with Sample Information

In contrast with theory, congruence with sample information is essential. Indeed,
Mizon states that congruence with sample information is necessary for *valid* inference. Valid is not defined, however. From Mizon's description and, particularly, from the application, we learn that congruence requires satisfying a long list
of tests. Congruence with the relative past and the relative present, for example,
means having errors that are orthogonal to regressors and homoskedastic. But, of
course, these conditions are not necessary for inferences to be valid in the natural
sense of tests having the proper asymptotic size.

Ericsson, Campos, and Tran (1990) and Hendry (1995) define *valid* to mean
"without loss of information." While associating validity with such a strong condition distinguishes the LSE approach, the precise meaning remains elusive. The
phrase "without loss of information" has a clear meaning when discussing ancillary statistics; thus, it would be invalid, in the sense of Ericsson, Campos and
Tran (1990) and Hendry (1995), to condition on variables that are not weakly
exogenous. As we elaborate in the discussion of encompassing below, the *validity*
(usual sense) of the way the LSE school extends this notion to broader settings is
not so clear.

Congruence with the Measurement System

In principle, the model one uses should impose such things as accounting identities and nonnegativity constraints. Pragmatic application (or not) of this restriction
as advocated by Mizon seems common to most approaches.

Congruence with Rival Models

According to Mizon, "the requirement that a model be congruent with information
contained in rival models is equivalent to that model parsimoniously encompassing a model that embeds all the rival models."

Parsimonious Encompassing

The LSE has been at the forefront of advocating that new econometric models dominate those that preceded and has been instrumental in developing encompassing tests for evaluating the relative merits of econometric models (see Mizon, 1984). Comparing new models to old ones is surely part of any progressive approach, and the formal merits of encompassing tests seem well accepted.

Suppose one had a model that passed all the encompassing tests one had conducted. What would one have? Mizon claims that "an encompassing model is one that can account for the previous empirical findings that were thought to be relevant and adequate for the explanation of the variables and parameters of interest, and can explain the features of rival models being considered currently." Relevance to whom? adequate in what way? explain how? which features? Mizon elaborates that the encompassing model will be the "*dominant model* that is congruent with information from *all four sources*" (emphasis added). Since one of the four sources is *a priori* theory, which is inessential, this statement should probably read from "three of four sources." In what sense is the model *dominant*? Mizon explains that "the encompassing model renders other models inferentially redundant and so is a dominant model." Based on the discussion of validity above, we interpret this as a claim that restricting attention to the encompassing model involves *no loss of information* relative to considering a larger set of models or information. The literature on admissible procedures cited above provides a natural formal interpretation of this claim: an admissible decision procedure is, loosely speaking, one that is best under some loss function. One might say model A renders model B inferentially redundant if the set of admissible decision procedures based on model A contains all of the admissible procedures based on models A and B.

But parsimonious encompassing does not deliver a model that is dominant in this sense. For a simply exposited but trivial example, consider using standard tests as advocated by Mizon to select variables for two parsimonious models of the same data. For model A use 1 percent critical values; for model B use 10 percent critical values. Generally, model B will be nested in model A: it is harder to reject exclusion restrictions at the 1 percent level. Since it is nested and justified by 10 percent tests, model B will parsimoniously encompass the model A (at the 10 percent level). Decisions based on information in model A but not in model B will generally be admissible, however. Similar examples can be constructed for nonnested tests and tests of maintained restrictions. So sometimes one might want to use an encompassed model.

Very generally, parsimonious encompassing and dominance are like validity— Good Things. But it is the specifics about which we are unsure: a translation of LSE terms like *validity, no loss of information, dominance,* and *inferential redundance* in terms of more standard statistical concepts would be helpful. Though we quibble with this general-to-specific issue, there is another with which we will not—general-to-specific modeling.

General-to-Specific Modeling

Of all the elements of the approach, this final element of the LSE approach is the most clear. Start with a general model and obtain parsimony by applying and retaining restrictions that are not rejected in classical tests.

Having set out to distill the essence of the LSE approach, we think it is fair to say that our understanding of its distinguishing features has attained a clarity falling somewhere between that of Newcastle Brown and Old Milwaukee. We now turn to our opinion of this brew.

The LSE Approach: Summary and Evaluation

We have tried to specify some gross principles of the LSE approach that collectively set it apart from other approaches to modeling macroeconomic time series. Our brief list indubitably glosses over some important contributions of the approach, most notably, perhaps, the work cited by Mizon on dynamic specification, error correction, and cointegration.

The most general underlying principle seems to be, "If something is testable, test it," or simply "Test, test, and test" (Hendry, 1980). We see five guidelines filling out this dictum:

- *General-to-specific modeling*: To find a parsimonious econometric model for the data of interest, start with a general model and proceed to a parsimonious model by applying and retaining restrictions that are not rejected in classical tests.
- *Congruence with sample information*: Be sure that tests of all testable maintained restrictions are satisfied along the sequence of progressively simpler models.
- *Parsimonious encompassing*: Be sure that the final model is not dominated in model comparison tests by rival econometric models.
- *No loss of information*: The final model should involve no loss of information (in some sense) relative to the original data. Inferences should be considered invalid unless they are conducted within such a model.
- *Data versus theory*: A priori theory is a source of inspiration regarding possible restrictions but nothing more; impose restrictions from economic theory only if they are not rejected.

The general-to-specific methodology (the first guideline) is very attractive when compared to the specific-to-general approach in which work begins with a tightly specified equation and the equation is generalized to remove any symptoms of misspecification. A rejection of the null in any specification test can happen for many reasons, and the test provides no sound basis for choosing a particular alternative. The general-to-specific approach eliminates the need to make such choices.

The general-to-specific approach is, however, datamining in the same sense that Leamer applies to his own specification searches (Leamer, 1978; Hendry, 1995). Both Leamer and Hendry argue persuasively that such datamining is a necessity in econometrics, and we agree that when data must be mined, an explicit approach is best. While the LSE school's standard battery of tests is designed to minimize the dangers of fitting the peculiarities of the sample too closely (Campos and Ericsson, 1990), the efficacy of such testing is difficult to guarantee due to problems controlling test size along the sequence of tests. Pushing up critical values can provide a further safeguard (see Sargan, 1981), and this practice is sometimes followed. For example, all variables retained in the money demand equation of Baba, Hendry, and Starr (1992) have t-values of 3 or more. Nonetheless Hess, Jones, and Porter (1994) have recently claimed that the equation was overfit to the original sample. We agree with Amemiya's (1980) conclusion that no currently available criterion provides a clearly superior data-based route to parsimony and that *a priori* restrictions can provide a valuable alternative route.

The recommendation to test maintained assumptions (the second guideline) is very appealing and has been strongly advocated by the LSE school. In contrast, for example, inference in the GMM literature often proceeds from estimation to inference about economic questions of interest without testing the maintained assumption of constant parameters on which those inferences rest. Of course, as Mizon's example and recent papers in the GMM literature (Oliner, Rudebusch, and Sichel, 1995) remind us, the assumption of constant parameters is often not supported.

The valuable principle behind the third guideline is that a new model should be shown to be better, in some sense, than existing models. The LSE school has been at the forefront in developing and advocating a useful sense of *better* revealed in classical encompassing tests. Again, there are many other senses in which a model can dominate. Under a scheme that places more emphasis on *a priori* restrictions than that of the LSE school, the encompassing sense of better may not be of central interest: the encompassing test between an LSE-style model and a theory-constrained model may reveal little more than the different emphasis in modelling.

We have two reservations about the fourth guideline regarding loss of information. First, the sense in which the LSE approach delivers models involving no loss of information and the relation between the LSE sense of no loss and more familiar senses is unclear. Second, statistics, in our view, should be concerned with how best to use information, not with mandating its *full* use. Since using information can be difficult or costly, full use of information need not be (economically) efficient. In short, we question the goal of *no loss of information* and wonder how the LSE approach attains it.

We also find understanding the role of economic theory in the LSE approach problematic (the fifth guideline). As Mizon notes, Hendry has called consistency with theory inessential. Doornik and Hendry (1994) call theory essential but reach the conclusion that "overall, one can do little better than state the need for an econometric model to be theory consistent." In what sense?

Despite the fact that LSE econometricians have done considerable work on applying long-run homogeneity restrictions from theory using error correction models and cointegration (see Hendry, 1995; Bannerjee et al., 1993), it seems to us that evidence has the upper hand in the LSE approach. The general model with which one starts is supposed to nest, at least in some approximate sense, theories of interest, but the final model will retain a recognizable association with theory only if the theory is favored by the evidence as divined through the prescribed sequence of tests. This balance of theory and evidence makes perfect sense if one believes that there is no *a priori* or inductive reason to believe in theory. While this position is coherent and, perhaps, reasonable, very different ways of balancing theory and evidence are also coherent and reasonable.

Conclusion

The LSE school has made profound contributions to the progressive modeling of economic time series. In particular, the school stands out in its emphasis on general-to-specific modeling, its emphasis on testing maintained assumptions, and in its emphasis on new models dominating those that preceded. LSE econometricians have made a strong mark on econometric practice by advocating these principles and by developing tools and approaches for following them.

Given the difficulties faced in the modeling of economic time series—non-experimental data and short correlated samples—it is difficult to make a case that any single approach will foster the most progress in understanding the economy. The balance between *a priori* theory and data is at the heart of the differences among many of the popular approaches. It is clear to us that understanding of the economy may be enhanced by work involving the LSE approach and other approaches placing even less emphasis on constraints from theory, as well as work involving greater emphasis on theory. That there there are so many approaches being pursued and so little agreement about which is best is evidence that progress to date has not strongly favored a single progressive approach.

References

Amemiya, T. (1980). "Selection of Regressors." *International Economic Review* 21, 331–353.

Baba, Y., D.F. Hendry, and R.M. Starr. (1992). "The Demand for M1 in the U.S.A., 1960–1988." *Review of Economic Studies* 59, 25–61.

Banerjee, A., J. Dolado, J. Galbraith, and D. Hendry. (1993). *Co-integration, Error Correction, and the Econometric Analysis of Non-stationary Data.* Oxford: Oxford University Press.

Barndorff-Nielson, O. (1978). *Information in Exponential Families in Statistical Theory.* New York: Wiley.

Basu, D. (1977). "On the Elimination of Nuisance Parameters." *Journal of the American Statistical Association* 72, 355–366.

Campos, J., and N.R. Ericsson. (1990). "Econometric Modelling of Consumers' Expenditure in Venezuela." Manuscript, Federal Reserve Board.

DeJong, D.N., B.F. Ingram, and C.H. Whiteman. (1994). "A Bayesian Approach to Calibration." Manuscript, University of Iowa.

DeJong, D.N., and C.H. Whiteman. (1991). "Reconsidering 'Trends and Random Walks in Macroeconomic Time Series'." *Journal of Monetary Economics* 28, 221–254.

Doornik, J., and D.F. Hendry. (1994). *PcGive 8.0 An Interactive Econometric Modelling System.* New York: International Thomson.

Engle, R., D.F. Hendry, and J.-F. Richard. (1983). "Exogeneity." *Econometrica* 51, 277–304.

Ericsson, N.R., J. Campos, and H.-A. Tran. (1990). "PC-GIVE and David Hendry's Econometric Methodology." *Revista de Econometria* 10, 7–117.

Gilbert, C.L. (1986). "Professor Hendry's Econometric Methodology." *Oxford Bulletin of Economics and Statistics* 48, 283–307.

Gilbert, C.L. (1989). "LSE and the British Approach to Time Series Econometrics." *Oxford Economic Papers* 41, 108–128.

Hansen, L.P. (1982). "The Large Sample Properties of Generalized Method of Moments Estimators." *Econometrica* 50, 1029–1054.

Hansen, L.P., and T.J. Sargent. (1980). "Formulating and Estimating Dynamic Linear Rational Expectations Models." *Journal of Economic Dynamics and Control* 2, 7–46.

Hendry, D.F. (1980). "Econometrics: Alchemy or Science?" *Economica* 47, 387–406.

Hendry, D.F. (1987). "Econometric Methodology: A Personal Perspective." In T.F. Bewley (ed.), *Advances in Econometrics.* Cambridge: Cambridge University Press.

Hendry, D.F. (1995). *Dynamic Econometrics.* New York: Oxford University Press.

Hess, G.D., C.S. Jones, and R.D. Porter. (1994). "The Predictive Failure of the Baba, Hendry and Starr Model of the Demand for M1 in the United States." Working Paper, Federal Reserve Bank of Kansas City.

Lehmann, E.L. (1986). *Testing Statistical Hypotheses.* New York: Wiley.

Lucas, R.E. Jr., and T.J. Sargent. (1981). *Rational Expectations and Econometric Practice.* Minneapolis: University of Minnesota Press.

Mizon, G.E. (1984). "The Encompassing Approach in Econometrics." In D.F. Hendry and

K.F. Wallis (eds.), *Econometrics and Quantitative Economics* (pp. 135–172). Oxford: Basil Blackwell.

Oliner, S., G. Rudebusch, and D. Sichel. (1995). "The Lucas Critique Revisited: Assessing the Stability of Empirical Euler Equations for Investment." *Journal of Econometrics*, forthcoming.

Prescott, E.C. (1986). "Theory Ahead of Business Cycle Measurement." Federal Reserve Bank of Minneapolis *Quarterly Review* 10 (Fall), 9–22. Also in K. Brunner and A. Meltzer (eds.), *Real Business Cycles, Real Exchange Rates and Actual Policies* (pp. 11–45). Carnegie-Rochester Conference Series on Public Policy 25 (Autumn). Amsterdam: North-Holland.

Sargan, J.D. (1981). "The Choice Between Sets of Regressors." Manuscript, London School of Economics.

Spanos, A. (1986). *Statistical Foundations of Econometric Modelling*. Cambridge: Cambridge University Press.

5 THE ECONOMETRICS OF THE GENERAL EQUILIBRIUM APPROACH TO BUSINESS CYCLES*

Finn E. Kydland and Edward C. Prescott

I. Introduction

Early in this century American institutionists and members of the German histori-cal school attacked—and rightfully so—neoclassical economic theory for not being quantitative. This deficiency bothered Ragnar Frisch and motivated him, along with Irving Fisher, Joseph Schumpeter, and others, to organize the Econo-metric Society in 1930. The aim of the society was to foster the development of quantitative economic theory—that is, the development of what Frisch labeled *econometrics*. Soon after its inception, the society started the journal *Econometrica*. Frisch was the journal's first editor and served in this capacity for twenty-five years.

In his editorial statement introducing the first issue of *Econometrica* (1933), Frisch makes it clear that his motivation for starting the Econometric Society was the "unification of theoretical and factual studies in economics" (p. 1). This uni-fication of statistics, economic theory, and mathematics, he argues, is what is powerful. Frisch points to the bewildering mass of statistical data becoming avail-able at that time, and asserts that in order not to get lost "we need the guidance and help of a powerful theoretical framework. Without this no significant interpre-tation and coordination of our observations will be possible" (*ibid.*, p. 2).

181

Frisch speaks eloquently about the interaction between theory and observation when he says "theory, in formulating its abstract quantitative notions, must be inspired to a larger extent by the technique of observation. And fresh statistical and other factual studies must be the healthy element of disturbance that constantly threatens and disquiets the theorist and prevents him from coming to rest on some inherited, obsolete set of assumptions" (*ibid.*). Frisch goes on to say that

> this mutual penetration of quantitative economic theory and statistical observation is the essence of econometrics (*ibid.*, p. 2).

To summarize the Frisch view, then, econometrics is quantitative neoclassical theory with a basis in facts.

Forty years after founding the Econometric Society, Frisch (1970) reviewed the state of econometrics. In this review he discusses what he considers to be "econometric analysis of the genuine kind" (p. 163), and gives four examples of such analysis. None of these examples involves the estimation and statistical testing of some model. None involves an attempt to discover some true relationship. All use a model, which is an abstraction of a complex reality, to address some clear-cut question or issue.

It is interesting to note that, in his 1933 editorial statement, Frisch announced that each year *Econometrica* would publish four surveys of "the significant developments within the main fields that are of interest to the econometrician" (*ibid.*, p. 3). These fields are general economic theory (including pure economics), business cycle theory, statistical technique, and, finally, statistical information. We find it surprising that business cycle theory was included in this list of main fields of interest to econometricians. Business cycles were apparently phenomena of great interest to the founders of the Econometric Society.

Frisch's (1933) famous, pioneering work, which appears in the Cassel volume, applies the econometric approach he favors to the study of business cycles. In this paper he makes a clear distinction between sources of shocks on the one hand, and the propagation of shocks on the other. The main propagation mechanism he proposes is capital-starting and carry-on activities in capital construction, both of them features of the production technology. Frisch considers the implications for duration and amplitude of the cycles in a model that he calibrates using available micro data to select the numerical values for the parameters. Making the production technology with capital accumulation a central element of the theory has its parallel in modern growth theory.

There are many other papers dating from the 1930s that study business cycle models. In these papers, however, and in those of the 1940s and 1950s, little progress was made beyond what Frisch had already done. The main reason was that essential theoretical tools, in particular Arrow-Debreu general equilibrium theory, statistical decision theory, modern capital theory, and recursive methods had yet to be developed. The modern electronic computers needed to compute the equilibrium processes of dynamic stochastic model economies were also unavailable. Only after these developments took place could Frisch's vision be carried out.

In this paper, we review the development of econometric business cycle theory, with particular emphasis on the general equilibrium approach (which was developed later). Crucial to this development was the systematic reporting of national income and product accounts, along with time series of aggregate inputs and outputs of the business sector. Section II is a review of this important development in factual studies. In Section III we review what we call the system-of-equations approach to business cycle theory. With this approach, a theory of the business cycle is a system of dynamic equations which have been measured using the tools of statistics.

Section IV is a review of the general equilibrium approach to business cycle theory. General equilibrium models have people or agents who have preferences and technologies, and who use some allocation mechanism. The crucial difference between the general equilibrium and the system-of-equations approaches is that which is assumed invariant and about which we organize our empirical knowledge. With the system-of-equations approach, it is behavioral equations which are invariant and are measured. With the general equilibrium approach, on the other hand, it is the willingness and ability of people to substitute that is measured. In Section V we illustrate the application of this econometric approach to addressing specific quantitative questions in the study of business cycles. The final section contains some concluding comments.

II. National Income and Product Accounts

An important development in economics is the Kuznets-Lindahl-Stone national income and product accounts. Together with measures of aggregate inputs to the business sector, these accounts are the aggregate time series that virtually define the field of macroeconomics—which we see as concerned with both growth and business cycle fluctuations. The Kuznets-Lindahl-Stone accounting system is well matched to the general equilibrium framework because there are both household and business sectors, with measures of factor inputs to the business sector and of goods produced by the business sector, as well as measures of factor incomes and expenditures on products.

An examination of these time series reveals some interesting regularities—in particular, a number of ratios which remain more or less constant. These growth facts led Robert Solow (1956) to develop a neoclassical growth model which simply and elegantly rationalized these facts. Solow's structure was not fully neoclassical, however, because the consumption-savings decision was behaviorally determined rather than being the result of maximizing behavior subject to constraints. With the consumption-savings decision endogenized, Solow's growth model does become fully neoclassical, with agents' maximizing subject to constraints and market clearing. This structure can be used to generate time series of national income and product accounts.

Aggregate data present other features that are of interest to economists, such as the more volatile movements in the time series. During the 1950s and 1960s, neoclassical theory had not evolved enough to allow economists to construct computable general equilibrium models with fluctuations. Lacking the necessary tools, economists adopted an empirical approach and searched for laws of motion governing these variables. They hoped this research procedure would result in empirically determined laws which would subsequently be rationalized within the neoclassical paradigm. In the natural sciences, for example, empirically determined laws have often subsequently been rationalized at a deeper theoretical level, and it was hoped that this would also be the case in macroeconomics. In the following section we briefly review the econometrics of this approach to business cycle fluctuations.

III. The System-of-Equations Approach

Tjalling Koopmans, who was influenced by Frisch and might even be considered one of his students, argued forcefully in the late 1940s for what he called the econometric approach to business cycle fluctuations. At the time, it was the only econometric approach. The general equilibrium approach to the study of business cycles had yet to be developed. But since the approach Koopmans advocated is no longer the only one, another name is needed for it. As it is the equations which are invariant and measured, we label this approach the system-of-equations approach.[1]

In the 1930s, there were a number of business cycle models or theories. These logically complete theories were a dynamic set of difference equations that could be used to generate time series of the aggregate variables of interest. Notable examples include Frisch's (1933) model in Cassel's volume, Tinbergen's (1935) suggestions on quantitative business cycles, and Samuelson's (1939) multiplier-accelerator model. One problem with this class of models is that the quantitative behavior of the model depended upon the values of the coefficients of the variables included in the equations. As Haberler (1949) points out in his comment on Koopmans' (1949) paper, the stock of cyclical models (theories) is embarrassingly large. Give any sophomore "a couple of lags and initial conditions and he will construct systems which display regular, damped or explosive oscillation . . . as desired" (p. 85). Pure theory was not providing sufficient discipline, and so it is not surprising that Koopmans advocated the use of the statistics discipline to develop a theory of business fluctuations.

System-of-Equations Models

As Koopmans (1949, p. 64) points out, the main features of the system-of-equations models are the following: First, they serve as theoretical exercises and experiments. Second, the variables involved are broad aggregates, such as total consumption, the capital stock, the price level, etc. Third, the models are "logically complete, i.e., they consist of a number of equations equal to the number of variables whose course over time is to be explained." Fourth, the models are dynamic, with equations determining the current values of variables depending not only on current values of other variables but also on the values of beginning-of-period capital stocks and on lagged variables. Fifth, the models contain, at most, four kinds of equations, which Koopmans calls *structural equations*. The first type of equations are *identities*. They are valid by virtue of the definition of the variables involved. The second type of equations are *institutional rules*, such as tax schedules. The third type are binding *technology constraints*, that is, production functions. The final type are what Koopmans calls *behavioral equations*, which represent the response of groups of individuals or firms to a common economic environment. Examples are a consumption function, an investment equation, a wage equation, a money demand function, etc. A model within this framework is a system-of-equations. Another requirement, in addition to the one that the number of variables equal the number of equations, is that the system have a unique solution. A final requirement is that all the identities implied by the accounting system for the variables in the model hold for the solution to the equation system; that is, the solution must imply a consistent set of national income and product accounts.

Statistical Measurement of Equations

The behavior of these models depends crucially on the numerical magnitudes of the coefficients of the variables and of the time lags. This leads to attempts to estimate these parameters using time series of the variables being modeled. Given that the estimation of these coefficients is a statistical exercise, a probability model is an additional completeness requirement. For that purpose, a residual random disturbance vector typically is added, with one component for each behavioral equation. For statistical completeness, the probability distribution of this disturbance vector must be specified up to some set of parameters. Only then can statistical methods be applied to estimating the coefficients of the behavioral

equations and the parameters of the disturbance distribution. The crucial point is
that the equations of the macroeconometric model are the organizing principle of
the system-of-equations approach. What is measured is the value of the coefficients of the equations. The criterion guiding the selection of the values of the
coefficients is essentially the ability of the resulting system of equations to mimic
the historical time series. The issue of which set of equations to estimate is settled
in a similar fashion. The criterion guiding the selection of equations is in large part
how well a particular set can mimic the historical data. Indeed, in the 1960s a student of business cycle fluctuations was successful if his particular behavioral equation improved the fit of, and therefore replaced, a currently established equation.

The Rise and the Fall of the System-of-Equations Approach

With the emergence of a consensus on the structure of the system of equations that
best described the behavior of the aggregate economy, the approach advocated by
Koopmans became totally dominant in the 1960s. This is well-illustrated by the
following statement of Solow's, quoted by Brunner (1989, p. 197):

> I think that most economists feel that the short run macroeconomic theory is pretty well
> in hand. . . . The basic outlines of the dominant theory have not changed in years. All
> that is left is the trivial job of filling in the empty boxes [the parameters to be estimated]
> and that will not take more than 50 years of concentrated effort at a maximum.

The reign of this system-of-equations macroeconomic approach was not long.
One reason for its demise was the spectacular predictive failure of the approach.
As Lucas and Sargent (1978) point out, in 1969 these models predicted high unemployment would be associated with low inflation. Counter to this prediction, the
1970s saw a combination of both high unemployment and high inflation. Another
reason for the demise of this approach was the general recognition that policy-
invariant behavioral equations are inconsistent with the maximization postulate in
dynamic settings. The principal reason for the abandonment of the system-of-
equations approach, however, was advances in neoclassical theory that permitted
the application of the paradigm in dynamic stochastic settings. Once the neoclassical tools needed for modeling business cycle fluctuations existed, their application to this problem and their ultimate domination over any other method was
inevitable.

IV. The General Equilibrium Approach

A powerful theoretical framework was developed in the 1950s and 1960s that built
upon advances in general equilibrium theory, statistical decision theory, capital

theory, and recursive methods. Statistical decision theory provided a logically consistent framework for maximization in a dynamic stochastic environment. This is what was needed to extend neoclassical theory, with its maximization assumption, to such environments. Another crucial development was the extension of general equilibrium theory to dynamic stochastic models, with the simple yet important insight that commodities could be indexed not only by type, but also by date and event. This important insight was made by Arrow and Debreu (1954), who had important precursors in the work of Hicks (1939) and, particularly, in that of Lindahl (1929)—who had previously effectively extended competitive theory to dynamic environments. Subsequently, recursive methods, with their Markovian structure, were developed. These methods simplified the use of this dynamic framework and, in particular, its extension to stochastic general equilibrium analyses; see, for example, Stokey and Lucas (1989).

Perhaps just as important as the development of tools for carrying out aggregate equilibrium analysis was the access to better and more systematic national income and product accounts data. In his review of growth theory, Solow (1970) lists the key growth facts which guided his research in growth theory in the 1950s. These growth facts were the relative constancy of investment and consumption shares of output, the relative constancy of labor and capital income shares, the continual growth of the real wage and output per capita, and the lack of trend in the return on capital. Solow (1956), in a seminal contribution, developed a simple model economy that accounted for these facts. The key to this early theory was the neoclassical production function, which is a part of the general equilibrium language. Afterwards the focus of attention shifted to preferences, with the important realization that the outcome of the Cass-Koopmans optimal growth model could be interpreted as the equilibrium of a competitive economy in which the typical consumer maximizes utility and the markets for both factors and products clear at every date.

General Equilibrium Models

By general equilibrium we mean a framework in which there is an explicit and consistent account of the household sector as well as the business sector. To answer some research questions, one must also include a sector for the government, which is subject to its own budget constraint. A model within this framework is specified in terms of the parameters that characterise preferences, technology, information structure, and institutional arrangements. It is these parameters that must be measured and not some set of equations. The general equilibrium language has come to dominate in business-cycle theory, as it did earlier in public finance, international trade, and growth. This framework is well-designed for providing quantitative answers to questions of interest to the business cycle student.

One of these important questions, which has occupied business cycle theorists since the time of Frisch and Slutzky, is how to determine which sources of shocks give rise to cycles of the magnitudes we observe. To provide reliable answers to this and similar questions, abstractions are needed that describe the ability and willingness of agents to substitute commodities, both intertemporally and intratemporally, and within which one can bring to bear statistical or factual information. One of these abstractions is the neoclassical growth model. This model has proven useful in accounting for secular facts. To understand business cycles, we rely on the same ability and willingness of agents to substitute commodities as those used to explain the growth facts. We are now better able than Frisch was more than 50 years ago to calibrate the parameters of aggregate production technology. The wealth of studies on the growth model have shown us the way. To account for growth facts, it may be legitimate to abstract from the time allocation between market and nonmarket activities. To account for business cycle facts, however, the time allocation is crucial. Thus, good measures of the parameters of household technology are needed if applied business cycle theory is to provide reliable answers.

The Econometrics of the General Equilibrium Approach

The econometrics of the general equilibrium approach was first developed to analyze static or steady-state deterministic models. Pioneers of this approach are Johansen (1960) and Harberger (1962). This framework was greatly advanced by Shoven and Whalley (1972), who built on the work of Scarf (1973). Development was impeded by the requirement that there be a set of excess-demand functions, which are solved to find the equilibrium allocations. This necessitated that preference and technology structures have very special forms for which closed-form supply and demand functions existed. Perhaps these researchers were still under the influence of the system-of-equations approach and thought a model had to be a system of supply and demand functions. These researchers lacked the time series needed to estimate these equations. Given that they could not estimate the equations, they calibrated their model economy so that its static equilibrium reproduced the sectoral national income and product accounts for a base year. In their calibration, they used estimates of the elasticity parameters obtained in other studies.

Their approach is ill-suited for the general equilibrium modeling of business fluctuations because dynamics and uncertainty are crucial to any model that attempts to study business cycles. To apply general equilibrium methods to the quantitative study of business cycle fluctuations, we need methods to compute the equilibrium processes of dynamic stochastic economies, and specific methods for the stochastic growth model economy. Recursive competitive theory and the use of linear-quadratic economies are methods that have proven particularly useful. These tools make it possible to compute the equilibrium stochastic processes of a rich class of model economies. The econometric problem arises in the selection of the model economies to be studied. Without some restrictions, virtually any linear stochastic process on the variables can be rationalized as the equilibrium behavior of some model economy in this class. The key econometric problem is to use statistical observations to select the parameters for an experimental economy. Once these parameters have been selected, the central part of the econometrics of the general equilibrium approach to business cycles is the computational experiment. This is the vehicle by which theory is made quantitative. The experiments should be carried out within a sensible or appropriate model economy that is capable of addressing the question whose answer is being sought. The main steps in econometric analyses are as follows: defining the question; setting up the model; calibrating the model; and reporting the findings.

Question

To begin with, the research question must be clearly defined. For example, in some of our own research we have looked at quantifying the contribution of changes in a technology parameter, also called Solow residuals, as a source of U.S. postwar business cycles. But we refined it further. The precise question asked is how much variation in aggregate economic activity would have remained if technology shocks were the only source of variation. We emphasize that an econometric, that is, quantitative theoretic analysis, can be judged only relative to its ability to address a clear-cut question. This is a common shortcoming of economic modeling. When the question is not made sufficiently clear, the model economy is often criticized for being ill-suited to answer a question it was never designed to answer.

Model Economy

To address a specific question one typically needs a suitable model economy for addressing the specified question. In addition to having a clear bearing on the question, tractability and computability are essential in determining whether the model is suitable. Model-economy selection depends on the question being asked. Model-economy selection should not depend on the answer provided. Searching within some parametric class of economies for the one that best fits some set of aggregate time series makes little sense. Unlike the system-of-equations approach, no attempt is made to determine the true model. All model economies are abstractions and are by definition false.

Calibration

The model has to be calibrated. The necessary information can sometimes be obtained from data on individuals or households. An example of such information is the average fraction of discretionary time household members who are, or who potentially are, labor market participants actually spent in market activity. In many other cases, the required information easily can be obtained from aggregate nonbusiness-cycle information. The task often involves merely computing some simple averages, such as growth relations between aggregates. This is the case for inventory-output and capital-output ratios, and long-run fractions of the various GNP components to total output, among others.

In some cases, history has provided sufficiently dramatic price experiments which can be used to determine, with a great deal of confidence, an elasticity of substitution. In the case of labor and capital as inputs in the aggregate business production function, and also in the case of consumption and leisure as inputs to household production, the large real-wage increase over several decades in relation to the prices of the other input, combined with knowledge about what has happened to the expenditure shares on the respective inputs, provides this kind of information. Because the language used in these business cycle models is the same as that used in other areas of applied economics, the values of common parameters should be identical across these areas and typically have been measured by researchers working in these other areas. One can argue that the econometrics of business cycles described here need not be restricted to general equilibrium models. In fact it is in the stage of calibration where the power of the general equilibrium approach shows up most forcefully. The insistence upon internal consistency implies that parsimoniously parameterized models of the household and business sector display rich dynamic behavior through the intertemporal substitution arising from capital accumulations and from other sources.

Computational Experiments

Once the model is calibrated, the next step is to carry out a set of computational experiments. If all the parameters can be calibrated with a great deal of accuracy, then only a few experiments are needed. In practice, however, a number of experiments are typically required in order to provide a sense of the degree of confidence in the answer to the question. It often happens that the answer to the research question is robust to sizable variations in some set of parameters and conclusions are sharp, even though there may be a great degree of uncertainty in those parameters. At other times, however, this is not the case, and without better measurement of the parameters involved, theory can only restrict the quantitative answer to a large interval.

Findings

The final step is to report the findings. This report should include a quantitative assessment of the precision with which the question has been answered. For the question mentioned above, the answer is a numerical estimate of the fraction of output variability that would have remained if variations in the growth of the Solow residual were the only source of aggregate fluctuation. The numerical answer to the research question, of course, is model dependent. The issue of how confident we are in the econometric answer is a subtle one which cannot be resolved by computing some measure of how well the model economy mimics historical data. The degree of confidence in the answer depends on the confidence that is placed in the economic theory being used.

V. Two Applications to Business Cycle Theory

We illustrate the econometrics of the general equilibrium approach to business cycle theory with two examples. The first example, credited to Lucas (1987) and Imrohoroglu (1989), addresses the question of quantifying the costs of business cycle fluctuations. An important feature of the quantitative general equilibrium approach is that it allows for explicit quantitative welfare statements, something which was generally not possible with the system-of-equations approach that preceded it. The second example investigates the question of how large business cycle fluctuations would have been if technology shocks were the only source of fluctuations. This question is also important from a policy point of view. If these shocks are quantitatively important, an implication of theory is that an important component of business cycle fluctuations is a good, not a bad.

Costs of Business Cycle Fluctuations

The economy Lucas uses for his quantitative evaluation is very simple. There is a representative or stand-in household and a random endowment process of the single consumption good. The utility function is standard, namely, the expected discounted value of a constant relative risk aversion utility function. Equilibrium behavior is simply to consume the endowment. Lucas determines how much consumption the agent is willing to forgo each period in return for the elimination of all fluctuations in consumption. Even with an extreme curvature parameter of 10, he finds that when the endowment process is calibrated to the U.S. consumption behavior, the cost per person of business cycle fluctuations is less than one-tenth of a per cent of per capita consumption.

This model abstracts from important features of reality. There is no investment good, and consequently no technology to transform the date t consumption good into the date $t + 1$ consumption good. As the costs of fluctuation are a function of the variability in consumption and not in investment, abstracting from capital accumulation is appropriate relative to the research question asked. What matters for this evaluation is the nature of the equilibrium consumption process. Any representative-agent economy calibrated to this process will give the same answer to the question, so it makes sense to deal with the simplest economy whose equilibrium consumption process is the desired one. This is what Lucas does. Introducing the time-allocation decision between market and nonmarket activities would change the estimate, since the agent would have the opportunity to substitute between consumption and leisure. The introduction of these substitution opportunities would result in a reduction in the estimated cost of business cycle fluctuations as leisure moves countercyclically. But, given the small magnitude of the cost of business cycle fluctuations, even in a world without this substitution opportunity, and given that the introduction of this feature reduces the estimate of this cost, there is no need for its inclusion.

In representative-agent economies, all agents are subject to the same fluctuations in consumption. If there is heterogeneity and all idiosyncratic risk is allocated efficiently, the results for the representative and heterogeneous agent economies coincide. This would not be the case if agents were to smooth consumption through the holding of liquid assets, as is the case in the permanent income theory. Imrohoroglu (1989) examines whether the estimated costs of business cycle fluctuations are significantly increased if, as is in fact the case, people vary their holdings of liquid assets in order to smooth their stream of consumption. She modifies the Lucas economy by introducing heterogeneity and by giving each agent access to a technology that allows that agent to transform date t consumption into date $t + 1$ consumption. Given that real interest rates were near zero in the fifty-odd years from 1933 to 1988, the nature of the storage technology chosen is that one unit of the good today can be transferred into one unit of the good tomorrow. She calibrates the processes on individual endowments to the per-capita consumption process, to the variability of annual income across individuals, and to the average holdings of the liquid asset—also across individuals. For her calibrated model economy, she finds the cost of business cycles is approximately three times as large as that obtained in worlds with perfect insurance of idiosyncratic risk. But three times a small number is still a small number.

Technology Shocks as Source of Fluctuations

One source of shocks suggested as far back as in Wicksell (1907) is fluctuations in technological growth. In the 1960s and 1970s, this source was dismissed by many as being unlikely to play much of a role in the aggregate. Most researchers accepted that there could be considerable variation in productivity at the industry level, but they believed that industry-level shocks would average out in the aggregate. During the 1980s, however, this source of shocks became the subject of renewed interest as a major source of fluctuations, in large part supported by quantitative economic theory. The question addressed, then, was how much would the U.S. postwar economy have fluctuated if technological shocks were the only source of aggregate fluctuations?

Our selection of a model economy to address this question follows. First we extended the neoclassical growth model to include leisure as an argument of the stand-in household's utility function. Given that more than half of business cycle fluctuations are accounted for by variations in the labor input, introducing this element is crucial. Next we calibrated the deterministic version of the model so that its consumption-investment shares, factor income shares, capital output ratios, leisure-market time shares, and depreciation shares matched the average values for the U.S. economy in the postwar period. Throughout this analysis, constant elasticity structures were used. As uncertainty is crucial to the question, computational considerations led us to select a linear-quadratic economy whose average behavior is the same as the calibrated deterministic constant elasticity of substitution economy.

We abstracted from public finance considerations and consolidated the public and private sectors. We introduced Frisch's (1933) assumption of time-to-build new productive capital. The construction period considered was four periods, with new capital becoming productive only upon completion, but with resources being used up throughout its construction. Given the high volatility of inventory investment, inventory stocks were included as a factor of production. We found, using the variance of Solow residuals estimated by Prescott (1986), that the model economy's output variance is 55 per cent as large as the corresponding variance for the U.S. economy in the postwar period.

In the early 1980s, there was much discussion in the profession about the degree of aggregate intertemporal substitution of leisure. The feeling was that this elasticity had to be quite high in order for a market-clearing model to account for the highly volatile and procyclical movements in hours. This discussion may have started with the famous paper by Lucas and Rapping (1969). Realizing that the standard utility function implied a rather small elasticity of substitution, they suggested the possibility that past leisure choices may directly affect current utility. Being sympathetic to that view, we considered also a non-time-separable utility function as a tractable way of introducing this feature. When lags on leisure are considered, the estimate of how volatile the economy would have been if technology shocks were the only disturbance increases from 55 to near 70 per cent. But, until there is more empirical support for this alternative preference structure, we think estimates obtained using the economy with a time-separable utility function are better. Unlike the system-of-equations approach, the model economy that better fits the data is not the one used. Rather, currently established theory dictates which one is used.

Probably the most questionable assumption of this theory, given the question addressed, is that of homogeneous workers, with the additional implication that all variation in hours occurs in the form of changes in hours per worker. According to aggregate data for the U.S. economy, only about one-third of the quarterly fluctuations in hours are of this form, while the remaining two-thirds arise from changes in the number of workers; see Kydland and Prescott (1991, Table 1).

This observation led Hansen (1985) to introduce the Rogerson (1988) labor indivisibility construct into a business cycle model. In the Hansen world all fluctuations in hours are in the form of employment variation. To deal with the apparent nonconvexity arising from the assumption of indivisible labor, the problem is made convex by assuming that the commodity points are contracts in which every agent is paid the same amount whether that agent works or not, and a lottery randomly chooses who in fact works in every period. Hansen finds that with this labor indivisibility his model economy fluctuates as much as did the U.S. economy. Our view is that, with the extreme assumption of only fluctuations in employment, Hansen overestimates the amount of aggregate fluctuations accounted for by Solow residuals in the same way as our equally extreme assumption of only fluctuations in hours per worker leads us to an underestimation.

In Kydland and Prescott (1991), the major improvement on the 1982 version of the model economy is to permit variation both in the number of workers and in the number of hours per worker. The number of hours a plant is operated in any given period is endogenous. The model also treats labor as a quasi-fixed input factor by assuming costs of moving people into and out of the business sector. Thus, in this model there is what we interpret to be labor hoarding.

Without the cost of moving workers in and out of the labor force, a property of the equilibrium turns out to be that all the hours variation is in the form of employment change and none in hours per worker. In that respect, it is similar to Hansen's (1985) model. For this economy with no moving costs, the estimate is that Solow residuals account for about 90 per cent of the aggregate output variance. For this economy with moving costs, we calibrated so that the relative variations in hours per worker and number of workers matched U.S. data. With this degree of labor hoarding, the estimate of the fraction of the cycle accounted for by Solow residuals is reduced to 70 per cent.

A widespread and misguided criticism of our econometric studies, for example, McCallum (1989), is that the correlation between labor productivity and the labor input is almost one for our model economy while it is approximately zero for the U.S. postwar economy. If we had found that technology shocks account for nearly all fluctuations and that other factors were unimportant, the failure of the model economy to mimic the data in this respect would cast serious doubt on our findings. But we did not find that the Solow technology shocks are all-important. We estimate that these technology shocks account for about 70 percent of business cycle fluctuations. If technology shocks account for 70 percent, and some other shocks which are orthogonal to technology shocks account for 30 percent, theory implies a correlation between labor productivity and the labor input near zero. Christiano and Eichenbaum (1990) have established this formally in the case that the other shock is variations in public consumption. But the result holds for any shock that is orthogonal to the Solow technology shocks. The fact that this correlation for our model economy and the actual data differ in the way they do adds to our confidence in our findings.

The estimate of the contribution of technology shocks to aggregate shocks has been found to be robust to several modifications in the model economy. For example, Greenwood, Hercowitz, and Huffman (1988) permit the utilization rate of capital to vary and to affect its depreciation rate, while all technology change is embodied in new capital; Danthine and Donaldson (1990) introduce an efficient-wage construct; Cooley and Hansen (1989) consider a monetary economy with a cash-in-advance constraint; and Rios-Rull (1994) uses a model calibrated to life cycle earnings and consumption patterns. King, Plosser, and Rebelo (1988) have non-zero growth. Gomme and Greenwood (1993) have heterogenous agents with recursive preferences and equilibrium risk allocations. Benhabib, Rogerson, and Wright (1990) incorporate home production. Hornstein (1991) considers the implications of increasing returns and monopolistic competition. In none of these cases is the estimate of the contribution of technology shocks to aggregate fluctuations significantly altered.

VI. Concluding Remarks

Econometrics is by definition quantitative economic theory—that is, economic analyses which provide quantitative answers to clear-cut questions. The general equilibrium econometric methodology is centered around computational experiments. These experiments provide answers to the questions posed in the model economies whose equilibrium elements have been computed. The model economy selected should quantitatively capture people's ability and willingness to substitute and the arrangements employed which are relevant to the question. We base our quantitative economic intuition on the outcome of these experiments.

The dramatic advances in econometric methodology over the last 25 years have made it possible to apply fully neoclassical econometrics to the study of business cycles. Already there have been several surprising findings. Contrary to what virtually everyone thought, including the authors of this review, technology shocks were found to be an important contributor to business cycle fluctuations in the U.S. postwar period.

Not all fluctuations are accounted for by technology shocks, and monetary shocks are a leading candidate to account for a significant fraction of the unaccounted-for aggregate fluctuations. The issue of how to incorporate monetary and credit factors into the structure is still open, with different avenues under exploration. When there is an established monetary theory, we are sure that general equilibrium methods will be used econometrically to evaluate alternative monetary and credit arrangements.

Acknowledgments

We acknowledge useful comments of Javier Diaz-Giménez on an early draft. This research was partly supported by a National Science Foundation Grant. The views expressed herein are those of the authors and not necessarily those of the Federal Reserve Bank of Minneapolis or the Federal Reserve System.

Note

* Editor's note: This chapter reprints an article originally published in the *Scandinavian Journal of Economics*, vol. 93, no. 2, pp. 161–178. The authors have updated the references.

1. Koopmans subsequently became disillusioned with the system-of-equations approach. When asked in the late 1970s by graduate students at the University of Minnesota in what direction macroeconomics should go, Koopmans is reported by Zvi Eckstein to have said they should use the growth model.

References

Arrow, Kenneth J., and Gerard Debreu. (1954). "Existence of an Equilibrium for a Competitive Economy." *Econometrica* 22(3), 265–290.

Benhabib, Jess, Richard Rogerson, and Randall Wright. (1991). "Homework in Macroeconomics: Household Production and Aggregate Fluctuations." *Journal of Political Economy* 99(6), 1166–1187.

Brunner, Karl. (1989). "The Disarray in Macroeconomics." In Forrest Capie and Geoffrey E. Wood (eds.), *Monetary Economics in the 1980s*. New York: Macmillan.

Christiano, Lawrence J., and Martin Eichenbaum. (1990). "Current Real Business Cycle Theories and Aggregate Labor Market Fluctuations." DP 24, Institute for Empirical Macroeconomics, Federal Reserve Bank of Minneapolis and University of Minnesota.

Cooley, Thomas F., and Gary D. Hansen. (1989). "The Inflation Tax in a Real Business Cycle Model." *American Economic Review* 79(4), 733–748.

Danthine, Jean-Pierre, and John B. Donaldson. (1990). "Efficiency Wages and the Business Cycle Puzzle." *European Economic Review* 34, 1275–1301.

Frisch, Ragnar. (1933). "Propagation Problems and Impulse Problems in Dynamic Economics." In *Economic Essays in Honour of Gustav Cassel.* London.

Frisch, Ragnar. (1970). "Econometrics in the World of Today." In W.A. Eltis, M.F.G. Scott, and J.N. Wolfe (eds.), *Induction, Growth and Trade: Essays in Honour of Sir Roy Harrod* (pp. 152–166). Oxford: Clarendon Press.

Gomme, Paul, and Jeremy Greenwood. (1993). "On the Cyclical Allocation of Risk." *Journal of Economic Dynamics and Control,* forthcoming.

Greenwood, Jeremy, Zvi Hercowitz, and Gregory W. Huffman. (1988). "Investment, Capacity Utilization, and the Real Business Cycle." *American Economic Review* 78, 402–417.

Harberger, Arnold C. (1962). "The Incidence of the Corporation Income Tax." *Journal of Political Economy* 70(3), 215–240.

Haberler, Gottfried. (1949). "Discussion of the Econometric Approach to Business Fluctuations by Tjalling C. Koopmans." *American Economic Review* 39, 84–88.

Hansen, Gary D. (1985). "Indivisible Labor and the Business Cycle." *Journal of Monetary Economics* 16(3), 309–327.

Hicks, John R. (1939). *Value and Capital: An Inquiry into Some Fundamental Principles of Economic Theory.* Oxford: Clarendon Press.

Hornstein, Andreas. (1993). "Monopolistic Competition, Increasing Returns to Scale, and the Importance of Productivity Stocks." *Journal of Monetary Economics* 31(3), 299–316.

Imrohoroglu, Ayse. (1989). "Costs of Business Cycles with Indivisibilities and Liquidity Constraints." *Journal of Political Economy* 97, 1364–1383.

Johansen, Leif. (1960). *A Multi-sectoral Study of Economic Growth.* Amsterdam: North-Holland.

King, Robert G., Charles I. Plosser, and Sergio T. Rebelo. (1988). "Production, Growth and Business Cycles: II. New Directions." *Journal of Monetary Economics* 21, 309–341.

Koopmans, Tjalling C. (1949). "The Econometric Approach to Business Fluctuations." *American Economic Review* 39, 64–72.

Kydland, Finn E., and Edward C. Prescott. (1982). "Time to Build and Aggregate Fluctuations." *Econometrica* 50, 1345–1370.

Kydland, Finn E., and Edward C. Prescott. (1990). "Business Cycles: Real Facts and a Monetary Myth." *Federal Reserve Bank of Minneapolis Quarterly Review* (Spring) 3–18.

Kydland, Finn E., and Edward C. Prescott. (1991). "Hours and Employment Variation in Business Cycle Theory." *Economic Theory* 1(1), 63–81.

Lindahl, Erik. (1929). "Prisbildningsproblemets uppläggning från kapitalteoretisk synpunkt."

Ekonomisk Tidskrift 31, 31–81. Translated as "The Place of Capital in the Theory of Price," in *Studies in the Theory of Money and Capital* (pp. 269–350). New York: Farrar and Reinhart.

Lucas, Robert E., Jr. (1987). *Models of Business Cycles*. Yrjö Jahnsson Lectures. Oxford: Basil Blackwell.

Lucas, Robert E., Jr., and Leonard A. Rapping. (1969). "Real wages, Employment, and Inflation. *Journal of Political Economy* 77, 721–754.

Lucas, Robert E., Jr., and Thomas J. Sargent. (1978). "After Keynesian Macroeconomics." In *After the Phillips Curve: Persistence of High Inflation and High Unemployment* (pp. 49–72). Conference Series No. 19. Boston: Federal Reserve Bank of Boston.

McCallum, Bennett T. (1989). "Real Business Cycle Models." In R.J. Barro (ed.), *Modern Business Cycle Theory* (pp. 16–50). Cambridge, MA: Harvard University Press.

Prescott, Edward C. (1986). "Theory Ahead of Business Cycle Measurement." *Carnegie-Rochester Conference Series on Public Policy* 24, 11–44. Reprinted in *Federal Reserve Bank of Minneapolis Quarterly Review* 10(4), 9–22.

Rios-Rull, Jose Victor. (1994). "Life-Cycle Economies and Aggregate Fluctuations." Liminary draft, Carnegie-Mellon University, June.

Rogerson, Richard. (1988). "Indivisible Labor, Lotteries and Equilibrium." *Journal of Monetary Economics* 21, 3–16.

Samuelson, Paul A. (1939). "Interactions Between the Multiplier Analysis and the Principle of Acceleration." *Review of Economic Statistics* 21, 75–78.

Scarf, Herbert (with the collaboration of T. Hansen). (1973). *The Computation of Economic Equilibria*. New Haven: Yale University Press.

Schumpeter, Joseph. (1933). "The Common Sense of Econometrics." *Econometrica* 1, 5–12.

Shoven, John B., and John Whalley. (1972). "A General Equilibrium Calculation of the Effects of Differential Taxation of Income from Capital in the U.S." *Journal of Public Economics* 1 (3/4), 281–321.

Solow, Robert M. (1956). "A Contribution to the Theory of Economic Growth." *Quarterly Journal of Economics* 70(1), 65–94.

Solow, Robert M. (1957). "Technical Change and the Aggregate Production Function." *Review of Economics and Statistics* 39(3), 312–320.

Solow, Robert M. (1970). *Growth Theory: An Exposition*. Radcliffe Lectures. Oxford: Clarendon Press.

Stokey, Nancy, and Robert E. Lucas, Jr., with Prescott, Edward C. (1989). *Recursive Methods in Economic Dynamics*. Cambridge, MA: Harvard University Press.

Tinbergen, Jan. (1935). "Annual Survey: Suggestions on Quantitative Business Cycle Theory." *Econometrica* 3, 241–308.

Wicksell, Knut. (1907). "Krisernas gåta." *Statsøkonomisk Tidsskrift* 21, 255–270.

Commentary on Chapter 5

Gregor W. Smith

Finn Kydland and Edward Prescott argue persuasively that the development of dynamic, stochastic, general equilibrium theory has led to rich research possibilities in macroeconomics. Their case is particularly convincing because they are among the foremost scholars in the development and application of this research program. The methods outlined in their review have been applied to assessing the role of monetary and fiscal policy in business cycles, studying international cycles, evaluating macroeconomic policies, and other questions in addition to the examples they give.

The main theme in this discussion is a simple one: conventional statistics can be helpful in reporting the results of these modern macroeconomic investigations. There are now a number of studies making this general point and giving details in specific applications. Kim and Pagan (1995) provide a complete survey. I shall illustrate some uses of statistics with an artificial example. The notation will be simple and abstract—in the sense that I shall not refer to a specific model—but general enough to describe some of the ideas in the research cited below.

Imagine that a model consists of specifications of preferences, budget constraints, technologies, and market-clearing conditions. Suppose that the necessary (first-order) conditions can be written as

$$f(x_t, \varepsilon_t, \theta) = 0, \tag{1}$$

where x_t are endogenous variables, ϵ_t are shocks, and θ are parameters. In the case of the business-cycle model studied by Kydland and Prescott, x includes consumption, output, the capital stock, and so on, ε includes a technology shock and perhaps other shocks, and θ includes things such as the representative agent's intertemporal elasticity of substitution and the parameter of a Cobb-Douglas production function.

The researcher must deduce some of the model's implications in order to answer an economic question. Examples include gauging the welfare costs of business cycles or calculating the variance of output induced by a given sequence of shocks. If the question requires moments or sample paths of x_t, then the researcher must take two steps: describe the properties of the shocks ε_t and solve the equations for x_t.

A well-known example of describing the shocks is the stationary, first-order autoregression for technology shocks used in many business-cycle models. Its

199

moments are based on those of actual Solow residuals. For future reference, suppose that the shocks are modeled as

$$m(\varepsilon_t, \omega) = 0, \tag{2}$$

which is a probability law of motion describing the shocks, with parameters ω.

Next, solving a model usually requires approximation and numerical methods. Developing solution procedures has become an active area of research in macroeconomics. Approximation can begin with the first-order conditions in equation (1) or with the optimization problem itself. Taylor and Uhlig (1990) and Ingram (1995) review some solution methods and their properties.

Before outlining how statistics might be used to summarize the results of experiments with the solved model, I should note that preliminary tests of the theory usually can be undertaken, by the generalized method of moments (GMM), without either solving the model or describing the shocks. Typically the conditions in equation (1) can be summed over observations to yield moments. Those moment conditions may be used to estimate the parameters θ. If there are more moments than parameters (overidentification), then the ability of the same parameters to satisfy all the moment conditions may be used as a test of the theory. This method was pioneered by Hansen (1982) and Hansen and Singleton (1982). Davidson and MacKinnon (1993, ch. 17) and Ogaki (1993) outline the statistical theory and numerous applications.

Estimation and testing by GMM has weaker requirements than does solution of the model. The findings are consistent with a wide variety of shock processes, which need not be specified. These weak assumptions often are enough to make progress, for evidence against the necessary conditions in equation (1) may suggest some reformulation of the theory. Nevertheless, the results also are weaker in that this method cannot deliver predictions of future values of x or lead to calculations of unconditional moments of x. Still GMM is an important part of the econometrics of dynamic, general equilibrium models.

Returning to questions that do require a solution of the model, let us use the subscript t to index observations in the model and n to index observations in historical data. One can use actual, observed variables as shocks. For example, in the business-cycle model described by Kydland and Prescott, one could calculate x_t from the model for an historical sequence $\{\varepsilon_n\}$ of Solow residuals. This exercise would allow one to study the role of technology shocks (which the Solow residual is taken to measure) by seeing what time path for output the model would have generated under the actual shock history. This model-generated data then could be compared with the actual history x_n: $n = 1, \ldots, N$ to see whether other factors might have been important for certain elements of x. Hansen and Prescott (1993) use this method to assess the role of technology shocks in the 1990–1991 recession.

Most studies use a different method. They begin with a statistical description of the shocks ε_t parametrized so that some of its moments match those of the historical sequence $\{\varepsilon_n\}$. Then the research focuses on the moments of x_t, and a standard example is the variance of output in the model. The moments can be found by simulating a sequence $\{\varepsilon_t\}$, solving the model for a vector sequence $\{x_t\}$, and then averaging. Denote a set of such moments

$$G_T = \sum_{t=1}^{T} g(x_t;\ \varepsilon_t,\ \theta,\ \omega). \tag{3}$$

Population moments, denoted G, can be approximated by making T large.

Because these studies start with this weaker information on the shocks (as Andersen, 1991, notes), they focus on a similarly weaker property of the endogenous variables. The use of moments is weaker in the sense that one now cannot ask questions such as "Does the model predict cycle turning points close to those observed historically?" But it may also be more general in that the type of probability law used to simulate the shocks may apply over other time periods or for other countries, where the actual sequence naturally would not.

Two types of exercises are widespread once these moments are calculated. In type E (*Experiments*), described in Kydland and Prescott's review, the goal is to calculate something in the model economy. In their examples, one calculates welfare under various paths for consumption, or the variance of output under various paths for technology shocks. Other studies are of type M (*Moment-Matching*), in that they are concerned with matching moments implied by the theory with those of actual data (G_N) and perhaps with amending the basic model so as to improve the match. At some level a type M exercise seems necessary, for confidence in answers to questions of type E. Many macroeconomists proceed as if a model's fit in one direction is one criterion for confidence in its answers in another. Of course, other criteria, such as theoretical consistency, matter too, but they are not always very restrictive empirically.

In either type of exercise, it may be important to note that the moments G_T of x_t are random variables. The randomness arises for two reasons. First, there is sampling variability because the moments are calculated from short simulations. Second, there may be randomness from uncertainty about the parameter values θ and ω.

Sampling variability arises because the values of the simulated, sample moments may be sensitive to a specific draw of the ε_t sequence. Usually, researchers generate a small number of draws with $T = N$ and then average the moments across those draws, but standard statistical reasoning could improve the reporting of results. Sampling variability in the theoretical moments can be removed by making T large so that one calculates population moments.

However, the moments G usually are compared to G_N, and these historical moments retain sampling variability. This suggests a further use for simulations beyond their use in calculating population moments in the theory. One would like to gauge the sampling variability in G_N, but this may be difficult to do accurately with small numbers of observations on random variables x_n that have unknown distributions and that are far from i.i.d. But the standard error of G_T can be used to estimate the standard error of G_N. Suppose that one takes $r = 1, 2, 3, \ldots, R$ replications (Monte Carlo draws) of length $T = N$ from the statistical rule for the shocks in equation (2) and calculates model moments G_{Tr} at each draw. Keeping track of the calculated sample moments in each draw provides useful information on their dispersion which is lost in the averaging. For example, one could draw $R = 1,000$ replications indexed by r, and then construct a confidence interval by rank ordering the individual G_{Tr} and then taking an interquantile range.

Measuring sampling variability may be of interest for an exercise of type E. For example, it might be interesting to report some evidence of the variation in the sample variance of output. This measurement seems even more important for exercises of type M because the empirical density of experimental moments (or other statistics) can be used to compare the model moments G to the historical moments G_N and hence to establish goodness of fit. Of course, such findings may depend very much on the set of moments on which the investigator focuses. Watson (1993) and Kim and Pagan (1995) describe goodness-of-fit measures that allow for measurement error between x_t and x_n.

Consider a scalar case with G_N greater than G. For example, the variance of output in the data might exceed the variance of output implied by the theory. If we count the proportion of replications in which the moment from the theory exceeds the moment from the data, then we shall have calculated the exact (small-sample) p-value for the one-sided test of the hypothesis: H_0: $G = G_N$.

The general point here is simply that an exact match between G_T and G_N is not necessary for the theory to receive some support because both measures are random variables. Researchers who are concerned with moment matching sometimes present a table of moments from the theory and a similar table from the data. The method just described offers a simple way—based on repeated experiments with the theory—to judge whether the two are close or not. Cecchetti, Lam, and Mark (1990) and Gregory and Smith (1991) give some examples.

The second source of randomness in the moments (even if T is made large) is uncertainty about parameter values, as Kydland and Prescott mention in their discussion of computational experiments. For example, the model economy that they use to study technology shocks is calibrated so that its factor income shares match the average values for the United States in the postwar period. Simon (1990) shows considerable historical variation in "great ratios" such as labor's share of output, which may matter more in studying cycles than in studying growth. In many cases, the findings may not be sensitive to particular parameter settings such as the value of the labor share. But it still may be worthwhile to show that insensitivity concisely so that one has more confidence in the result.

In other cases, the properties of the theoretical model will be sensitive to the parameter settings. A good example arises when ω includes the first-order autocorrelation of the technology shocks, which may not be precisely estimated. Gregory and Smith (1990, 1993) describe some pitfalls in estimating parameters like this by informal moment matching and by using steady-state properties. Small variations in this parameter may have significant effects on the moments G. Kim and Pagan (1995) outline methods for sensitivity analysis. Canova (1994) has suggested that parameter uncertainty can be taken into account by drawing parameters from some distribution when calculating moments. For example, uncertainty about a parameter value might be summarized in a uniform density across a specific range. Moment calculations then would involve repeated draws from this density, in addition to draws of sequences of shocks. DeJong, Ingram, and Whiteman (1993) show how a prior distribution over parameter values θ and ω induces a distribution over the moments G. They also show how to compare that distribution with the estimated distribution of G_N and demonstrate the comparison for a business-cycle model. This use of priors may simplify reporting, for most researchers currently report results for several different, fixed parameter settings.

The variability in historical, sample moments may be estimated by repeated simulations of the theory, or it may be estimated directly from the data. Eichenbaum (1991) gives detailed examples of this second method, in which parameters θ and ω also are estimated by GMM. He finds that the estimated proportion of historical output volatility accounted for by technology shocks is particularly sensitive to the uncertainty in the first-order autocorrelation and innovation variance of detrended Solow residuals. The ratio of model output variance to historical output variance is estimated at 0.78, in a model with indivisible labor in which these two shock parameters are estimated. More strikingly, the standard error attached to this estimate is 0.64. Thus the question of what the variance of U.S. output would have been if technology shocks were the only source of aggregate fluctuations is answered imprecisely. This finding suggests that statistical evidence on experiments is not merely quibbling, as it may show that small changes in the theory may have large effects on the implications.

Several qualifications could be made to Eichenbaum's finding. First, Aiyagari (1992) and Englund (1991) argue that one cannot measure the contribution of technology shocks in a model that does not match the historical output variance. In other words, an experiment of type E also must be of type M. If the output variance in the model economy is less than that in the data, then a second shock may be missing. But adding that shock will affect the model's moments and hence conclusions about the importance of technology shocks. Perhaps because of this type of critique, a number of authors compare impulse-response functions in model and data in order to find properties that are not sensitive to omitted shocks.

The second qualification to this estimate of uncertainty is that the measured variability in the moments depends on the data sources and methods used to estimate parameters. The standard error attached to the model's output variance might be reduced by combining parameter estimates from other data sources with Eichenbaum's just-identified statistical model. If a model is calibrated using microeconometric estimates, then standard errors in those estimates can be carried through to standard errors in the model's implications (subject to aggregation), as Hoover (1995) notes. A strength and hallmark of the general equilibrium approach is its use of information from a variety of studies that have a common theoretical basis. Statistical methods thus seem especially worthwhile to keep track of the parameter uncertainty.

Some general equilibrium models are aimed at addressing business-cycle questions in that they do not include growth components or fluctuations at seasonal frequencies. To compare their implications with empirical evidence, one must isolate the cycle component by transforming data. However this is done, suppose that it involves a third set of parameters λ. Denote the untransformed data by X_n. Then the cycle component is

$$x_n = X_n - h(X_n; \lambda), \tag{4}$$

where h is a family of detrending filters. Some elements of λ might be intercept terms, so that the cycle components x_n have mean zero. Frequently it is necessary to remove a growth component. The notation in equation (4) is sufficiently abstract to allow this component to be a deterministic time trend, a stochastic trend (unit root), or some two-sided smoother, each of which involves some parameters.

The match between G and G_N may depend on how x_n is measured in equation (4). A number of studies have shown that some properties of x_n are sensitive to the particular scheme used. How should one choose the parameters λ, and hence the detrending scheme? There seem to be several possibilities. One is that the economic model includes a growth component endogenously, in which case its predictions for x_t may be compared to X_n, as both are trending. A second possibility is that the model produces growth from nonstationary, growing shocks (as in King, Plosser, and Rebelo, 1988a, 1988b), whose parametrization implies a detrending method.

A third possibility is that the economic model does not restrict trends but only describes cycles—in other words, that x_t is stationary. To compare these cycles with those in data, some researchers perform the trend-cycle decomposition in equation (4) by assuming that the trend $h(X_n; \lambda)$ is the conditional mean of the series X_n. In that case λ includes parameters of the conditional mean function, and the trend and cycle are uncorrelated by construction in the estimation of λ.

The orthogonality assumption involved in this decomposition may not be economically appealing. Fortunately, a macroeconomist can detrend, or measure cycles, using only the information in a business-cycle model. Business-cycle models restrict many moments and a detrending method can be chosen so that the measured cycles x_n have moments (or other properties) similar to those predicted in the theory. The theory describes cycles, so why not use it to measure them?

The simplest example is a method-of-moments estimation, in which one seeks to minimize the discrepancy:

$$\sum_{n=1}^{N} g\left(x_n - h(X_n; \lambda)\right) - \sum_{t=1}^{T} g(x_t; \varepsilon_t, \theta, \omega), \tag{5}$$

by varying λ. The value of T could be set very large so that one uses the population moments from the theory, removing sampling variability. And the free parameters of the shock process (ω) and of preferences and technology (θ) perhaps could be estimated at the same time, if they are identified.

This suggestion can be thought of as a formalization of the oft-used Hodrick-Prescott filter. In that filter the single parameter is set so that the resulting cycles appear to resemble the predictions of the theory. For example, they retain some autocorrelation, just as we think business cycles do. Gregory and Smith (1994) give a several examples of detrending in this way. Because this proposal uses some of the properties of a model to define cycles a close match between the predicted and measured properties obviously cannot be used as evidence in favor of the theory. However, general equilibrium models, as Kydland and Prescott note, often restrict a wide range of properties and have few free parameters so that some moments can be used to measure cycles while others remain to be used in testing the match between theory and evidence.

The discussion so far has outlined how statistics can be used to allow for sampling variability in moments, to allow for parameter uncertainty, and to measure cycles in a way consistent with business-cycle models. These uses of statistics in reporting results apply even in exercises of type E in which the aim is not to empirically match many features of the data.

In exercises of type M the aim, of course, is to reformulate the model in response to disparities between its predictions (in directions in which it is aimed to be informative) and some facts. It seems likely that the most interesting variations or perturbations are those to the *economics* of the theory (such as those collected by Cooley, 1994) rather than to its parameters or shocks. But research in equilibrium macroeconometrics typically proceeds by reformulating models in response to some mismatch between theory and evidence.

In certain cases the use of statistics in reporting results may show that mismatches are not significant. For example, certain consumption-based models of asset pricing may deliver mean equity premiums that are smaller than historical average premiums but not significantly so. Likewise, this formal reporting could supplement subjective statements such as "The model fits surprisingly well." In other cases this reporting style may simply strengthen results by convincing readers concisely that mismatches are significant so that a reformulation is necessary. The statistical issues may not be the most interesting or important, but that seems all the more reason to report them so as to clear the way forward.

It is sometimes argued that formal statistical tests will reject equilibrium models because the models are simple abstractions. Practitioners have tended to eschew formal hypothesis tests, as Hoover (1995) has noted. However, econometric testing can be used constructively to show in what directions a model may need to be reformulated in order for one to have more confidence in its implications. The test may be in a dimension with which the model is centrally concerned, so as not to discriminate against simple, illuminating models. Moreover, there are simple, optimizing models—such as the resilient, random-walk model of aggregate consumption—that are difficult to reject with statistical tests, even though (unlike the systems of equations approach) they are not fitted to the data as a design criterion.

Acknowledgments

I thank the Social Sciences and Humanities Research Council of Canada and the Foundation for Educational Exchange between Canada and the United States for research support.

References

Aiyagari, R. (1992). "A New Method for Determining the Contribution of Technology Shocks to Business Cycles." Working Paper 493, Research Department, Federal Reserve Bank of Minneapolis.

Andersen, T.M. (1991). "Comment on F.E. Kydland and E.C. Prescott, 'The Econometrics of the General Equilibrium Approach to Business Cycles.'" *Scandinavian Journal of Economics* 93, 179–184.

Canova, F. (1994). "Statistical Inference in Calibrated Models." *Journal of Applied Econometrics* 9, 123–144.

Cecchetti, S.G., P.-S. Lam, and N.C. Mark. (1990). "Mean Reversion in Equilibrium Asset Prices." *American Economic Review* 80, 398–418.

Cooley, T. (ed.). (1994). *Frontiers of Business Cycle Research*. Princeton, NJ: Princeton University Press.

Davidson, R., and J.G. MacKinnon. (1993). *Estimation and Inference in Econometrics*. Oxford: Oxford University Press.

DeJong, D.N., B.F. Ingram, and C.H. Whiteman. (1993). "Beyond Calibration." Mimeo, Department of Economics, University of Pittsburgh.

Eichenbaum, M. (1991). "Real Business-Cycle Theory: Wisdom or Whimsy?" *Journal of Economic Dynamics and Control* 15, 607–626.

Englund, P. (1991). "Comment on F.E. Kydland and E.C. Prescott, 'The Econometrics of the General Equilibrium Approach to Business Cycles.'" *Scandinavian Journal of Economics* 93, 175–188.

Gregory, A.W. and G.W. Smith. (1990). "Calibration as Estimation." *Econometric Reviews* 9(1), 57–89.

Gregory, A.W., and G.W. Smith. (1991). "Calibration as Testing: Inference in Simulated Macroeconomic Models." *Journal of Business and Economic Statistics* 9, 297–303.

Gregory, A.W., and G.W. Smith. (1993). "Statistical Aspects of Calibration in Macroeconomics." In G.S. Maddala, C.R. Rao, and H.D. Vinod (eds.), *Handbook of Statistics* (Vol. 11) (ch. 25, pp. 703–719). Amsterdam: North-Holland.

Gregory, A.W., and G.W. Smith. (1994). "Measuring Business Cycles with Business Cycle Models." Mimeo, Department of Economics, Queen's University.

Hansen, G.D., and E.C. Prescott. (1993). "Did Technology Shocks Cause the 1990–1991 Recession?" *American Economic Review* (P) 83, 280–286.

Hansen, L.P. (1982). "Large Sample Properties of Generalized Method of Moments Estimators." *Econometrica* 50, 1029–1054.

Hansen, L.P., and K.J. Singleton. (1982). "Generalized Instrumental Variables Estimation of Nonlinear Rational Expectations Models." *Econometrica* 50, 1269–1286.

Hoover, K.D. (1995). "Facts and Artifacts: Calibration and the Empirical Assessment of Real-Business-Cycle Models," *Oxford Economic Papers* 47, 24–44.

Ingram, B.F. (1995). "Recent Advances in Solving and Estimating Dynamic, Stochastic Macroeconomic Models." Chapter 2 in this volume.

Kim, K., and A.R. Pagan. (1995). "The Econometric Analysis of Calibrated Macroeconomic Models." In M. Wickens and M.H. Pesaran (eds.), *Handbook of Applied Econometrics.* Amsterdam: North-Holland.

King, R.G., C.I. Plosser, and S.T. Rebelo. (1988a). "Production, Growth, and Business Cycles I. The Basic Neoclassical Model." *Journal of Monetary Economics* 21, 195–232.

King, R.G., C.I. Plosser, and S.T. Rebelo. (1988b). "Production, Growth, and Business Cycles II. New Directions." *Journal of Monetary Economics* 21, 309–342.

Ogaki, M. (1993). "Generalized Method of Moments: Econometric Applications." In G.S. Maddala, C.R. Rao, and H.D. Vinod (eds.), *Handbook of Statistics* (Vol. 11) (ch. 17). Amsterdam: North-Holland.

Simon, J.L. (1990). "Great and Almost-Great Magnitudes in Economics." *Journal of Economic Perspectives* 4(1), 149–156.

Taylor, J.B., and H. Uhlig. (1990). "Solving Nonlinear Stochastic Growth Models: A Comparison of Alternative Solution Methods." *Journal of Business and Economic Statistics* 8, 1–17.

Watson, M.W. (1993). "Measures of Fit for Calibrated Models." *Journal of Political Economy* 101, 1011–1041.

II THE LUCAS CRITIQUE RECONSIDERED

6 CAUSAL ORDERINGS

Stephen F. LeRoy

Introduction

It is a commonplace of elementary instruction in economics that endogenous variables are not generally causally ordered, implying that the question "What is the effect of y_1 on y_2?" where y_1 and y_2 are endogenous variables is generally meaningless. The reason is that many possible interventions on the exogenous variables could have caused the hypothesized change in y_1 and these interventions generate different values of y_2. Therefore, if all one knows about a hypothetical intervention on the values of the exogenous variables is that it induced the change Δy_1 in y_1, one cannot generally characterize the effect of the intervention on y_2. Sometimes, however, it happens that all the interventions on exogenous variables consistent with a given change in y_1 induce the same change in y_2. If so, y_1 is said to *cause* y_2. Essentially, the idea of causal orderings is related to that of statistical sufficiency: y_1 causes y_2 if it aggregates the information contained in the exogenous variables that determine y_1 for the purpose of determining y_2.

The interpretation of causal orderings just summarized seems to correspond to the way the term is used in informal discussion among economists. Yet no formal characterization of causal orderings along these lines is available. Such a characterization is presented in the second and third sections of this paper. Related work by Simon and Leamer is discussed in the fourth section. Applications of this formal analysis are discussed in the fifth section, and the final section is the conclusion.

Causal Orderings

Structural Models

I distinguish variables and parameters that are structural from those that are nonstructural. *Structural* variables and parameters are those that the model builder is willing to specify to be either *exogenous* (determined outside the model and subject to direct and independent intervention) or *endogenous* (determined by the model and therefore not subject to direct intervention). *Nonstructural* variables and parameters are those for which the model builder does not make this classification. An example of nonstructural variables would be z_1 and z_2 in a model consisting of the specification that z_1 and z_2 are distributed as bivariate normal, and not including any specification of which variable causes the other, or whether instead their correlation can be ascribed to the common effect of a third variable. A *structural model*—that is, a model in which at least some of the variables are structural—is obviously the appropriate setting to analyze causal orderings.

This use of the terms *exogenous* and *endogenous* directly corresponds to their etymology. It differs from that of econometricians, who characterize observed variables as endogenous or exogenous according to whether or not they are correlated with certain unobserved variables. In general there is no connection between the two definitions.[1] The use here of the term *structural* differs from that in some analyses, particularly when applied to parameters. In the Cowles usage the term *structural parameter* means the same thing as *exogenous parameter* or *deep parameter* here. In the present usage, by contrast, a structural parameter may be either exogenous or endogenous, but by assumption the analyst is willing to specify which one.

In our usage it is not necessary that all the variables and parameters in a structural model be structural. For example, in vector autoregressions the coefficient matrices are treated as nonstructural: the analyst recognizes that the elements of these matrices of shallow parameters are in principle functions of deep parameters but leaves these functions unspecified. The coefficient matrices are, in effect, treated as constants. Taking the coefficient matrices as nonstructural does not prevent the analyst from treating the innovations as exogenous variables and the variables determined by the VAR as endogenous variables, implying the possible existence of causal orderings among the latter. An adjective like *semistructural* might be used to describe such model, but this seems like terminological overkill.

Causal Orderings

Assume for convenience that (1) the endogenous variables form a countable set and (2) equilibrium exists and is unique. For each endogenous variable y_n there exists a vector of exogenous variables $e(y_n)$ consisting of the smallest set needed to determine y_n. The vector $e(y_n)$ will be termed the *exogenous set* for y_n.[2] These exogenous sets will play a major role in the analysis of causal orderings.

Then the solution to any model consists of a sequence of functions f_n:

$$y_n = f_n(e(y_n)), \qquad n = 1, 2, \ldots.$$

The notation $y_1 \Rightarrow y_2$ is defined to mean that y_1 *causes* y_2.[3] We have $y_1 \Rightarrow y_2$ if three conditions—the strict inclusion condition, the composition condition, and the nonconstancy condition—are satisfied.[4] The *strict inclusion condition* is satisfied if $e(y_1) \subset\subset e(y_2)$ ($e(y_1)$ is a proper subset of $e(y_2)$). If the strict inclusion condition is satisfied, there exists at least one exogenous variable that affects y_2 but does not feed back onto y_1, guaranteeing the asymmetry of causations.

Define z_{2-1} as the vector of exogenous variables that appear in $e(y_2)$ but not in $e(y_1)$; satisfaction of the strict inclusion condition guarantees that z_{2-1} is nonempty. The *composition condition* consists of the requirement that the equation expressing the solution for y_2,

$$y_2 = f_2(e(y_2)),$$

be expressible as the composition of f_1 and g:

$$y_2 = g(f_1(e(y_1)), z_{2-1}) \tag{6.1}$$

for some function g.

For example, consider the model

$$n = \alpha_0 + \alpha_1 p + \alpha_2 r, \tag{6.2}$$

$$p = \beta_0 + \beta_1 n + \beta_2 c. \tag{6.3}$$

Equation (6.2) says that the number of nematodes on a farmer's land is determined by the amount of pesticides he applies and rainfall, while equation (6.3) says that the amount of pesticides the farmer applies is a function of nematodes and the cost of pesticides.[5] Here n and p are endogenous, while r and c are exogenous. For the present the parameters α_i and β_i are treated as nonstructural—that is, as constants. In the special case $\beta_1 = 0$ the model has the causation $p \Rightarrow n$. Failing the restriction $\beta_1 = 0$, the question "What is the effect of pesticides on nematodes?" is seen to be ambiguous: pesticide use is affected by both rainfall and pesticide cost, and the effect on nematodes depends on which caused the change in pesticide use (because rainfall affects nematodes directly as well as through its effect on pesticide use, whereas cost does not).

The *nonconstancy condition* requires that g in equation (6.1) cannot be specified to be a constant function of y_1. If g can be specified as a constant function of y_1 for some values of z_{2-1} and cannot be so specified for others, the interpretation is that y_1 causes y_2 for some values of z_{2-1} and not for others. To see the need for the nonconstancy condition, consider a model of a firing squad: the victim is killed if any of the bullets hits him and spared if all bullets miss. When can it be said that member i of the firing squad (whose bullet is assumed to have hit the victim) caused the victim's death? The ordinary-language usage would be that member i caused the victim's death only if all other members' bullets missed. Otherwise member i caused the victim's death jointly with the other executioners whose bullets also hit him (see the definition of joint causal orderings below) but did not do so individually, since the victim would have been killed anyway. Because of the nonconstancy condition, the definition of causal orderings proposed here (and that of joint causal orderings below) coincides with this usage: if any of the other members of the firing squad hit the victim, the victim is killed whether member i hit him or not. Formally, g can be taken to be a constant function of y_i (the variable corresponding to whether or not member i's bullet hit the victim) in this case, so the nonconstancy condition for a causal ordering fails.

For another example of causal orderings, consider the uninterpreted model

$$x_{11}y_1 = x_{10}, \tag{6.4}$$

$$x_{21}y_1 + x_{22}y_2 = x_{20}, \tag{6.5}$$

$$x_{31}y_1 + x_{32}y_2 + x_{33}y_3 = x_{30}, \tag{6.6}$$

where the x's are exogenous variables and the y's are endogenous variables. This model has $y_1 \Rightarrow y_2$ and $y_1 \Rightarrow y_3$: an intervention on the exogenous variables in $e(y_1)$—x_{10} and x_{11}—affects y_2 and y_3 only through its effect on y_1. Therefore the questions "What is the effect of y_1 on y_2?" and "What is the effect of y_1 on y_3?" are well posed: the questions presuppose an intervention on x_{10} and x_{11} with all other exogenous variables held constant, and all interventions on x_{11} and x_{10} resulting in a particular change in y_1 have the same effect on y_2 and y_3.

The model has no other endogenous variables that are causally ordered. In particular, it does not have $y_2 \Rightarrow y_3$ because of failure of the composition condition. Therefore the question "What is the effect of y_2 on y_3?" is not well posed: characterizing an intervention only by its effect on y_2 does not give enough information about the intervention to determine its effect on y_3. On the contrary, of the variables in $e(y_2)$—x_{10}, x_{11}, x_{20}, x_{21}, and x_{22}—the first two also affect y_3 through their effect on y_1.

Informally, it is obvious that exogenous variables and the endogenous variables that depend on them are also causally ordered: there is no ambiguity about the intervention if the variable being intervened on is itself exogenous. To take formal account of this fact we will extend the definition of causal orderings so as to have $x_i \Rightarrow y_j$ under exactly the same conditions as are required for $y_i \Rightarrow y_j$, with the specification that the exogenous set of an exogenous variable consists of that variable alone. Thus extended, for any model causality is a relation on the union of the set of the names of the exogenous and that of the names of the endogenous variables. It is easy to verify that the relation $\Rightarrow$ is irreflexive, asymmetric, and transitive, thus constituting a strict partial order, with the exogenous variables as minimal elements.

Extensions

Several related notions of causal orderings are useful in applications.

Joint Causal Orderings

It may be that the strict inclusion, composition, and nonconstancy conditions are satisfied for a nonsingleton set of endogenous variables b but not for any proper subset of b; in that case the variables b *jointly cause* y_2 (the exogenous set for a group of variables is taken to be the union of the exogenous sets of the individual variables). Causations in which b is a singleton will be referred to as *simple causations* when it is necessary to distinguish them from joint causations.[6] The most important example of joint causations is that between some subset of the parameters and any endogenous variable. By one definition of a parameter (see the discussion below) an intervention on variables leaves parameters unaffected, implying that parameters collectively are jointly causally prior to endogenous variables.[7] Of course, there may also exist causations among parameters: the distinction between "deep" and "shallow" parameters implies that some parameters are exogenous, creating the possibility that causations exist among endogenous parameters.

Conditional Causal Orderings

Suppose that the endogenous variables in the nonsingleton set b jointly cause y_2 and that $y_1 \in b$. Is there any sense in which y_1 by itself can be said to cause y_2? With $b \Rightarrow y_2$ there potentially is associated the *conditional causation* $y_1 \Rightarrow y_2 \mid (b - y_1)$. This definition and notation indicate that the intervention on $e(y_1)$ is understood to be restricted so that the variables in $b - y_1$ (the elements of b other than y_1) are held constant. Under the restriction on the domain of f_1 the strict inclusion and composition conditions for $y_1 \Rightarrow y_2$ are satisfied by definition. If under the domain restriction the nonconstancy condition is also satisfied, then the conditional causation obtains.

For example, consider the model

$$x_{11}y_1 + x_{12}y_2 = x_{10}, \tag{6.7}$$

$$x_{21}y_1 + x_{22}y_2 = x_{20}, \tag{6.8}$$

$$x_{31}y_1 + x_{32}y_2 + x_{33}y_3 = x_{30}. \tag{6.9}$$

This model has the joint causation $(y_1, y_2) \Rightarrow y_3$ but has no endogenous variables that are simply causally ordered. It also has the conditional causations $y_1 \Rightarrow y_3 \mid y_2$ and $y_2 \Rightarrow y_3 \mid y_1$. The first of these has the interpretation that all interventions on $e(y_1)$ that are associated with a particular change in y_1 and with no change in y_2 map onto a particular value of y_3.

The idea of conditional causal orderings has a serious drawback that impairs its usefulness in applications (in fact, I engage in the present discussion of conditional causal orderings only because having access to the concept of conditional causal orderings allows a compact statement below of the Lucas critique): postulating across-variable restrictions on the hypothesized interventions on exogenous variables implicitly presupposes the existence of functional relations among the exogenous variables. This is inconsistent with their exogeneity. Thus the idea of conditional causations conflicts with the attribute of exogenous variables that they vary independently.

There is also the problem that the existence of joint causations does not necessarily imply the existence of conditional causations. The restriction on the domain of f_1 may limit y_1 to a single value. In that case g can be chosen to be a trivial constant function of y_1, so there is no conditional causation. For example, consider the model

$$a_{11}y_1 + a_{12}y_2 = x_{10},$$

$$a_{21}y_1 + a_{22}y_2 = a_{20},$$

$$a_{31}y_1 + a_{32}y_2 + a_{33}y_3 = x_{30},$$

where the a's are constants. This model differs from the model (6.7) through (6.9) in that the coefficients of the y's and one of the intercepts are constants rather than exogenous variables. Here the exogenous sets for y_1 and y_2 each consist of the single exogenous variable x_{10}. In this model there exists the joint causation $(y_1, y_2) \Rightarrow y_3$ but not the conditional causations $y_1 \Rightarrow y_3 \mid y_2$ or $y_2 \Rightarrow y_3 \mid y_1$. The reason is that, in the first case, if y_2 is held constant a unique value for y_1 is implied, so g can be written as a constant function of y_1. If there exist conditional causations associated with a given joint causation, the joint causation is *separable*, following the terminology of Hicks's valuable (1979) discussion.

Causal Orderings Among Events

In the philosophy literature causal orderings are generally characterized as relating events rather than variables. Such questions as whether causes are necessary for effects, sufficient for effects, or both, are then debated. These issues are easily handled using the apparatus just laid out. Suppose that we have a model with the causation $y_1 \Rightarrow y_2$.

Then by definition there exists a nonconstant function g such that $y_2 = g(y_1, z_{2-1})$. The event Φ_1 (where $\Phi_1 \subset Y_1$) is a *sufficient cause* of the event Φ_2 (where $\Phi_2 \subset Y_2$) if $g(\Phi_1, z_{2-1}) \subset \Phi_2$. Here Y_1 and Y_2 are the spaces from which y_1 and y_2, respectively, are drawn. The idea is that for fixed values of z_{2-1} occurrence of the event Φ_1 (that is, taking $y_1 \in \Phi_1$) guarantees occurrence of the event Φ_2 (that is, $y_2 \in \Phi_2$). Similarly, Φ_1 is a *necessary cause* of Φ_2 if $g^{-1}(\Phi_2, z_{2-1}) \supset \Phi_1$, so that occurrence of Φ_2 guarantees occurrence of Φ_1.[8]

Finally, Φ_1 is a *necessary and sufficient cause* of Φ_2 if both conditions are satisfied, so that Φ_1 occurs if and only if Φ_2 occurs. Thus, contrary to assertions frequently found in the philosophy literature, the idea of causation has no particular link to either necessity or sufficiency. Of course, as the notation indicates the particular sets Φ_1 and Φ_2 such that Φ_1 is a necessary or sufficient cause of Φ_2 depend on z_{2-1}.[9]

Econometric Aspects of Causal Orderings

In models that are linear in variables, with every causation $y_1 \Rightarrow y_2$ there is associated a coefficient giving the effect of a unit change of y_1 on y_2. This coefficient is a parameter if it is structural or a constant if it is nonstructural. Having specified nothing about which variables are observable or about the probability distribution of unobserved exogenous variables, there is no presumption that the coefficients associated with causations are identified. However, there is an important special case in which the coefficients associated with causations are identified and easily estimated. Suppose that all exogenous variables are independently distributed random variables. Such a model will be called *complete* because it gives a complete account of the correlations among endogenous variables, assigning no role to uninterpreted correlations among exogenous variables. If a linear model with causation $y_1 \Rightarrow y_2$ is complete and if y_1 is observable, then the assumptions of the Gauss-Markov theorem are met and unbiased and consistent estimates of the coefficient associated with the causation can be obtained using ordinary least squares.

The contrapositive version of this result provides a convenient way of proving that two variables are not causally ordered, particularly in the hands of those familiar with econometric estimation theory. If in a complete model one knows that a particular regression coefficient is estimated with bias or inconsistency under ordinary least squares, it cannot be the case that the independent and dependent variables of the regression are causally ordered, with the parameter in question being that associated with the causation. Knowledge that estimation problems occur therefore indicates absence of causation.

For example, in the nematodes-pesticide example, if $\beta_1 \neq 0$, an OLS regression of nematodes on pesticides will result in an inconsistent estimate of α_1, even if r and c are independently distributed so that the model is complete. Therefore we cannot have the causation $p \Rightarrow n$, with α_1 as the associated parameter. However, under the restriction $\beta_1 = 0$ simultaneous equations bias is eliminated and α_1 is estimated consistently by OLS. This fact suggests that we may have $p \Rightarrow n$ with associated parameter α_1; independent investigation is required to confirm this (and does confirm it, as was seen above).

For another example, consider the model

$$x_t = \lambda x_{t-1} + u_t,$$

$$u_t = \rho u_{t-1} + e_t,$$

with the initial values x_0 and u_0 and the e_t as exogenous variables. Suppose also that the model is complete, so that x_0, u_0, and the e_t are distributed independently. Econometricians know that if λ is estimated by an ordinary least-square regression of x_t on x_{t-1}, bias will result in small samples because of the correlation between u_t and x_{t-1} induced by the autocorrelation of the error. Applying the above results, an econometrician could conclude immediately that the causation $x_{t-1} \Rightarrow x_t$ does not hold without bothering to verify that the formal conditions for a causal ordering are not satisfied.

Comparison with Simon and Leamer

Simon

According to Simon's (1953) definition, y_1 is exogenous with respect to y_2 if y_1 appears in the lowest-order self-contained subset of equations which contains y_2 and also in a self-contained subset of lower order (see Simon, 1953, for definitions of these terms). This condition is easily shown to coincide with the strict inclusion condition as defined above. Our characterization of causal orderings, by requiring in addition the composition and nonconstancy conditions, is thus seen to be more restrictive than Simon's.

If $y_1 \Rightarrow y_2$ according to Simon's definition of causal priority, it is possible according to the present definition either that (1) $y_1 \Rightarrow y_2$, (2) y_1 causes y_2 jointly with some other endogenous variables, or (3) y_1 does not cause y_2 either simply or jointly. For an example of (2), review model (6.7) through (6.9), which has the simple causation $y_2 \Rightarrow y_3$ according to Simon's definition and also the joint causation $(y_1, y_2) \Rightarrow y_3$ according to the present definition, but no simple causations according to the present definitions. For an example of (3) review model (6.4) through (6.6), which has the causation $y_2 \Rightarrow y_3$ according to Simon's definition but has neither the simple causation $y_2 \Rightarrow y_3$ under our definition nor the joint causation $(y_1, y_2) \Rightarrow y_3$ (the existence of the simple causation $y_1 \Rightarrow y_3$ means that y_2 is redundant as a cause of y_3).

Leamer

Leamer (1985, pp. 262 ff.) presented alternative definitions of terms corresponding to causal orderings as defined here:

Structural: A parameter is structural if it is invariant under any modification of the system selected from a specified family of modifications.[10]

Exogenous: If the observed conditional distribution of the variable y given a set of variables x is invariant under any modification of the system selected from a specified family of modifications that alter the process generating x, then the variables x are said to be *exogenous* to y.

What is noteworthy about Leamer's definitions is that they treat parameters and variables separately: the term *structural* is used for parameters, whereas *exogenous* is used for variables. Further, the definitions themselves differ: structuralness is directly related to invariance of parameters under intervention, whereas exogeneity is defined in terms of invariance of conditional distributions. In the present paper, in contrast, the characterization of causal orderings does not depend on any distinction between parameters and variables—for the purpose of defining causal orderings it is immaterial whether some or all of the variables of a system are treated as terms of families (that is, as elements of indexed sets).

It does not appear that the distinction between variables and parameters is used in any consistent sense in the economics literature: it is easy to find exceptions for the possible bases for such a distinction that come first to mind. For example, because Leamer's definition refers to probability distributions in connection with variables but not parameters, one might define variables as random and parameters as nonrandom. But that will not do: learning models have random parameters and all dynamic deterministic models have variables that are nonrandom. Alternatively, parameters might be defined as constant functions on an index set that is interpreted as time. This characterization will not do either: the capital-output ratio in a Solow growth model is constant in steady-state equilibrium, yet one would not call it a parameter. Similarly, in game-theoretic models with imperfect information it is common knowledge that players' types are unchanging over time, yet types would normally be classified as variables, not parameters. Finally, the term *parameter* might be used to connote structuralness or exogeneity. However, then the term *structural parameter* would contain a redundancy, and *shallow parameter* (as opposed to *deep parameter*) a contradiction.

It follows from this, not that the distinction between parameters and variables is meaningless but that it acquires different meanings in different contexts. For example, we often describe a model as linear, meaning linear in variables, with the coefficients being parameters, not variables. Here the distinction between parameters and variables derives from the assumption of linearity. For another example, we specify a model as incorporating rational expectations, meaning that agents are assumed to know all parameter values but not necessarily all variable values. For the meanings of *linear in variables* and *rational expectations* to be unambiguous, it is essential that the distinction between variables and parameters be specified clearly, but the distinction itself does not necessarily correspond to some preexisting difference between parameters and variables. The notation adopted in setting out a model is chosen to delineate the distinction between parameters and variables, usually without explicit discussion. The arbitrariness of the parameter-variable distinction means that it is inappropriate to distinguish, as Leamer did, structuralness of parameters from exogeneity of variables, at least in the absence of a clear characterization of the difference between parameters and variables and an explanation for the differing definitions of structuralness and exogeneity in terms of this characterization.

Rather than take the parameter-variable distinction as logically prior to the definition of causal orderings, it appears to make sense instead to use some of the conceptual apparatus of causal orderings to characterize the parameter-variable distinction. By calling something a *parameter* we (often) are implicitly committing to the assumption that its exogenous set consists only of exogenous parameters, not exogenous variables. Thus the definition of *parameter* would imply that an intervention on variables alone leaves endogenous parameters unaffected. This characterization of parameters corresponds to a parallel characterization of variables: by labeling a variable y_t we often are committing to the assumption that the exogenous set for that variable consists only of exogenous parameters and exogenous variables dated up to and including date t: exogenous variables dated after t cannot influence y_t. Like the alternative characterizations of the parameter-variable distinction reviewed above, the distinction proposed here is not universally employed—in deterministic dynamic models, for example, exogenous sets of endogenous variables include future-dated exogenous variables. It is, of course, entirely a matter of personal preference whether one finds it useful to construe the parameter-variable distinction in this rather than some other way.

Applications

The Cowles Program of "Structural" Estimation

Consider a dynamic version of the nematodes-pesticide example discussed above:

$$n_t = \alpha_{0t} + \alpha_1 p_t = \alpha_2 r_t,$$

$$p_t = \beta_{0t} + \beta_1 n_t = \beta_2 c_t.$$

If the model is complete, so that the exogenous α_{0t}, β_{0t}, r_t, and c_t are mutually independent, then the coefficient $\alpha_1 \beta_1/(1 - \alpha_1 \beta_1)$ associated with the causation c_t $\Rightarrow n_t$ can be estimated by a least-square regression of n_t on c_t. If r_t and c_t are not independent of each other but are observable, then the coefficient of c_t in a bivariate regression of n_t on c_t and r_t again gives a consistent estimate of the parameter associated with the causation.

The Cowles economists might have used a different (but equally valid) approach: find consistent estimates of α_1, β_1, and β_2 and combine these to derive a consistent estimate of $\alpha_1 \beta_2/(1 - \alpha_1 \beta_1)$. As is well known, two-stage least-square provides the requisite consistent estimates. Here the Cowles economists would have routinely characterized α_1, β_1, and β_2 as structural coefficients and $\alpha_1 \beta_2/(1 - \alpha_1 \beta_1)$ as a reduced-form coefficient. However, it is noteworthy that at no time in this exercise was it necessary to make any structural assumption about the parameters α_1 and β_2 stronger than the specification that the exogenous sets for these parameters do not include exogenous variables (so that an intervention on c_t leaves the parameters unaffected). In particular, the causation $c_t \Rightarrow n_t$ does not require us to assume that an intervention on any of the parameters leaves any or all of the other parameters unaffected. In other words, α_1 and $\alpha_1 \beta_2/(1 - \alpha_1 \beta_1)$ are on precisely the same footing: there is no sense in which α_1 is structural that does not apply equally to $\alpha_1 \beta_2/(1 - \alpha_1 \beta_1)$.

Vector Autoregressions

The analysis of causal orderings has a natural application in the interpretation of vector autoregressions. In VARs by definition the coefficient matrices are always interpreted as nonstructural. If the variables are also interpreted as nonstructural, as is adequate for forecasting exercises, analysis of causal orderings is impossible. However, sometimes VARs are used to determine the effects of hypothetical interventions on variables, particularly macroeconomic policy interventions, implying that variables are being treated as structural. The analysis of causal orderings can help to determine what assumptions are necessary to justify interpreting particular coefficients as corresponding to causations.

The analysis is most easily presented in the specific setting of a bivariate autoregression. Suppose that the money stock m_t and income y_t are related according to

$$m_t = \theta y_t + \beta_{11} m_{t-1} + \beta_{12} y_{t-1} + \varepsilon_{1t}, \tag{6.10}$$

$$y_t = \gamma m_t + \beta_{21} m_{t-1} + \beta_{22} y_{t-1} + \varepsilon_{2t}, \tag{6.11}$$

as in Jacobs, Leamer, and Ward (1979) and Cooley and LeRoy (1985). Here the exogenous variables m_0, y_0, ε_{1t}, and ε_{2t} are assumed to be contemporaneously and serially uncorrelated, so that the model is complete in the sense defined above.

First, we have the obvious point (obvious because ε_{1t} and ε_{2t} are directly specified to be exogenous variables) that the causations $\varepsilon_{1t} \Rightarrow m_t$, $\varepsilon_{1t} \Rightarrow y_t$, $\varepsilon_{2t} \Rightarrow m_t$, and $\varepsilon_{2t} \Rightarrow y_t$ obtain, with coefficients $1/(1 - \theta\gamma)$, $\gamma/(1 - \theta\gamma)$, $\theta/(1 - \theta\gamma)$ and $1/(1 - \theta\gamma))$, respectively. These coefficients are unidentified. Restrictions like $\theta = 0$ (so that realizations of ε_{2t} do not feed back to m_t) or $\gamma + \beta_{21} = 0$ (so that the steady-state effect of money on income is zero), however, identify all coefficients.

VARs are usually written in the triangular form

$$m_t = \rho_{11} m_{t-1} + \rho_{12} y_{t-1} + \eta_{mt}, \tag{6.12}$$

$$y_t = \delta m_t + \rho_{21} m_{t-1} + \rho_{22} y_{t-1} + \eta_{yt}, \tag{6.13}$$

where the innovations η_{mt} and η_{yt} are contemporaneously and serially uncorrelated. Because (1) the model (6.10) and (6.11) can be rewritten in the form (6.12) and (6.13) without any coefficient restrictions, (2) the coefficients θ, γ and the β_{ij} of (6.10) and (6.11) are not identified, and (3) the coefficients δ and the ρ_{ij} of (6.12) and (6.13) are just identified, it would be reasonable to guess that in the absence of parameter restrictions the parameters of (6.12) and (6.13) are not those associated with causations. This is correct. In particular, without restrictions we do not have any of the causations $\eta_{mt} \Rightarrow m_t$, $\eta_{mt} \Rightarrow y_t$, $\eta_{yt} \Rightarrow m_t$, or $\eta_{yt} \Rightarrow y_t$. In each case the strict inclusion condition is satisfied, but the composition condition is not. Failure of the composition condition occurs, for example, because the exogenous set for η_{mt} is $\{\varepsilon_{1t}, \varepsilon_{2t}\}$, and these exogenous variables influence m_t through η_{yt} as well as through η_{mt}. It follows that in the absence of prior parameter restrictions impulse response functions do not constitute the parameters associated with causation. Of course, under the restriction $\theta = 0$, equations (6.10) and (6.11) coincide with equations (6.12) and (6.13), so that $\delta = \gamma$, $\rho_{ij} = \beta_{ij}$ $(i, j = 1, 2)$, and in particular η_{mt} and η_{yt} equal ε_{1t} and ε_{2t}, respectively. Therefore the causations $\eta_{mt} \Rightarrow m_t$, $\eta_{mt} \Rightarrow y_t$, $\eta y_t \Rightarrow y_t$ (but not $\eta y_t \Rightarrow m_t$) now obtain. Further, under the restriction $\theta = 0$ the causations $\eta_{mt} \Rightarrow m_{t+j}$, $\eta_{mt} \Rightarrow y_{t+j}$, $\eta_{yt} \Rightarrow m_{t+j}$ and $\eta_{yt} \Rightarrow y_{t+j}$ $(j \geq 1)$ also obtain, with associated coefficients that are just identified.

The causation $m_t \Rightarrow y_t$ obtains only under extremely restrictive conditions; surprisingly, even the strong restriction $\theta = \beta_{12} = 0$, which assures that ε_{2t} does not feed back onto either current or future values of m_t, does not imply $m_t \Rightarrow y_t$. Therefore the question "What is the effect of money on income?" is ambiguous even under $\theta = \beta_{12} = 0$. However, the joint causation $(y_t, m_t, m_{t+1}, \ldots, m_{t+n} \Rightarrow y_{t+n})$ obtains under the restriction $\theta = \beta_{12} = 0$. This fact is useful in interpreting the "dynamic simulations" of Keynesian policy analysis, according to which the effect of changing the assumed future trajectory of some policy variable like the money stock is calculated by solving a macroeconomic model forward in time twice, once using the reference path for the policy variable and once using a perturbed path. We see that under the parameter restriction $\theta = \beta_{12} = 0$ the "dynamic multipliers" dy_{t+i+j}/dm_{t+i} $(i, j \geq 0)$ calculated from the exercise just described collectively give the effect of an alteration in the trajectory for the money stock on the trajectory for income. However, note that because $\theta = \beta_{12} = 0$ is not sufficient for the simple causation $m_{t+i} \Rightarrow y_{t+i+j}$, the dynamic multipliers individually cannot be interpreted as giving the effect of m_{t+i} on y_{t+i+j}.

It remains to ascertain the relation between Granger causation and causal orderings as defined in this paper. In the above model money is exogenous in the Granger sense if it is equally well predicted by its own lagged values as by these plus lagged values of income. This property implies and is implied by the parameter restriction $\theta \beta_{22} + \beta_{12} = 0$. It is seen that Granger noncausation of money is neither necessary nor sufficient for the causation $\eta_{mt} \Rightarrow y_{mt}$, since $\theta \beta_{22} + \beta_{12} = 0$ neither implies nor is implied by $\theta = 0$. However, rejection of Granger noncausation does imply rejection of $\theta = \beta_{12} = 0$, implying that the dynamic multipliers described in the preceding paragraph cannot be interpreted as corresponding to a joint causation.

Full Structural Models

I define a *full structural model* as a model in which a classification between variables and parameters is adopted, and in which both parameters and variables are treated as structural. That is, the classification into exogenous and endogenous applies to parameters as well as variables. The parameters characterizing preferences and technology are "deep," or exogenous, while the coefficients of the linearized version of a nonlinear model, for example, are "shallow," or endogenous.

Let Θ denote the set of names of the deep parameters and Ψ the set of the names of the shallow parameters. Then a full structural model (expressed in terms of its solution, as above) consists of

$$\Psi_i = f_i(e(\Psi_i)),$$

$$y_i = g_i(e(y_i)),$$

for $\psi \in \Psi$. Here $e(\psi_i) \subset \Theta$, while $e(y_i) \subset (\Theta \cup X)$, where X is the set consisting of the names of the exogenous variables. The fact that $e(\psi_i)$ is a subset of Θ alone rather than a general subset of $\Theta \cup X$ reflects the convention, discussed in the fourth section, that interventions on exogenous variables do not affect endogenous parameters.

As noted above, the argument just made implies that full structural models may have the joint causation $A \Rightarrow y_i$ for each y_i, where A is some subset of the shallow parameters Ψ. Suppose now that one treats the elements of A as exogenous variables and conducts interventions on them independently. Analytically this corresponds to treating a joint causation as a conditional causation. However, if there are fewer deep parameters than shallow parameters, as is virtually always the case, the requisite separability property does not obtain (see the third section), so the indicated conditional causation does not exist and the exercise is inadmissible. We have here one version of the Lucas (1976) critique: according to Lucas, Keynesian macroeconomists conducted policy analysis by treating the coefficients of linear equations as exogenous variables subject to independent intervention. In full structural models, however, these coefficients are shallow parameters that are linked by across-equation restrictions to the deep parameters of preferences and technology. Because there are few deep parameters and many shallow parameters, it is seldom possible to interpret the exercise of altering one shallow parameter and holding all others constant in terms of an intervention on the deep parameters.

Are Structural Models Needed for Policy Analysis?

The Lucas critique has persuaded many economists that policy evaluation can be conducted correctly only using full structural models: "Disentangling the parameters governing the stochastic processes that agents face from the parameters of their objective functions would enable the econometrician to predict how agents' decision rules would change across alterations in their stochastic environment. Accomplishing this task is an absolute prerequisite of reliable econometric policy evaluation" (Hansen and Sargent, 1981). However, contrary to the instruction of the Lucas critique, it is not the case that hypothetical alterations in agents' stochastic environments can be properly modeled only via parameter interventions (that is, as shifts in policy functions). Conditional distributions depend on the values taken on by conditioning variables as well as parameters, implying that alterations in agents' stochastic environments can be modeled by interventions on either parameters or variables. Which is appropriate depends on the question being asked. The definition of *rational expectations* is that agents know the values of parameters, where the meaning of parameters contains the implication that they do not change over time, and *know* contains the implication that this fact is the common knowledge of the agents whose behavior is being modeled. Therefore if one wants to analyze real-time policy change in a rational expectations setting—"regime change," in the parlance of new classical macroeconomics—one is restricted to variable interventions (LeRoy, 1993).

The convention that parameters are causally prior to endogenous variables means that interventions on variables leave parameters unaffected. This raises the possibility that parameters can be treated as nonstructural when analyzing variable interventions, so that policy change is analyzed via the causal orderings among endogenous variables. Whether this possibility can be realized in practice depends on whether the model under consideration has the requisite causal orderings when parameters are treated as nonstructural and whether the constants associated with these causations are identified. Advocates of the use of vector autoregressions for policy analysis answer both questions in the affirmative, at least implicitly. They are willing to treat orthogonalized innovations as exogenous variables; the parameters associated with interventions on the innovations (that is, the impulse response functions) are identified because of the assumed triangularity of the matrix of contemporaneous coefficients. It is recognized, of course, that these properties require parameter restrictions, but these restrictions are viewed as less onerous than the overidentifying restrictions implied by specification of full structural models along the lines of Hansen-Sargent.

Conclusion

The Cowles economists emphasized the econometric estimation of structural parameters because they were interested in analyzing interventions and needed to ensure that the structure being intervened on was invariant under intervention. They thought of the theory of causal orderings as related to this project but did not develop the theory to the point where they could state this relation clearly. In this paper the intention has been to develop the theory of causal orderings to the point where the analyst can give a completely explicit specification of what assumptions about structure are needed to justify any causal statement.

It was seen that an important shortcoming of the work of the Cowles economists was that they failed to characterize clearly the distinction between parameters and variables. I pointed out that, at least on one characterization of this distinction, if interventions on variables alone are contemplated, it is irrelevant whether parameters are structural or not. Thus at least in some settings some interventions of control can be analyzed without resorting to structural modeling (defined as formulating models that treat parameters as structural). This result goes contrary to the presumption of the Cowles economists and of current writers like Hansen-Sargent that the analysis of causal orderings is equivalent to that of the identification of parameters that are in some sense structural.

Advocates of the use of vector autoregressions for analysis of interventions find acceptable the assumptions needed to derive the causal orderings of interest in models that treat parameters as nonstructural and variables as structural. Critics of this use of vector autoregressions, on the other hand, believe that if parameters are treated nonstructurally the requisite causal orderings do not exist. Therefore, these argue, it is necessary to treat parameters as structural and include exogenous parameters in the intervention. Our purpose here is not to criticize or defend either modeling strategy but instead to provide analysts with a way to determine what assumptions justify particular causal interpretations.

Notes

1. However, in models that are complete in the sense defined below the two definitions are closely related.

2. It is evident that exogenous sets are unique. Suppose, on the contrary, that $e(y_n)$ and $e'(y_n)$ are exogenous sets for y_n. If these are distinct, for some exogenous variable x we have $x \in (y_n)$ but $x \notin e'(y_n)$. But this cannot occur: if the variables $e'(y_n)$ are held fixed, then y_n is fixed, implying that interventions on x do not affect y_n. However, then $e(y_n)$ contains a redundant element, contrary to the definition of exogenous sets.

3. Here we might instead read $y_1 \Rightarrow y_2$ as "y_1 is a cause of y_2" to emphasize that endogenous variables other than y_1 may also be causes of y_2. The chosen reading has the advantage of brevity.

4. Under the characterization here, the restrictions on the solution functions f_n implied by the existence of causal orderings are identical to those studied in functional structure theory (see, for example, Blackorby, Primont, and Russell, 1978). Therefore the formal theory of causal orderings is closely linked to such topics as demand theory and the theory of aggregation.

5. This example is drawn from the *SAS/ETS User's Guide* (Version 5 Ed.), p. 472. I am indebted to Mark Fisher for the reference.

6. Formally, joint causation is an ordering, not on the set of variable names but on the power set of that set.

7. Note that the term *variable* is used in different senses in this sentence and in the first sentence of this subsection. In the first sentence variables are distinguished from constants (constants are standins for particular numbers, whereas variables are interrelated via the functions of the model), while in this sentence they are distinguished from parameters, where the latter are not dated. Rather than weigh down the discussion by adopting special terminology that distinguishes the two senses of *variable*, I will rely on the context to make the meaning clear.

8. Here $g^{-1}(\Phi_2, z_{2-1})$ denotes $\{y_1 \in Y_1 \text{ such that } g(y_1, z_{2-1}) \in \Phi_2\}$.

9. In fact, changing z_{2-1} may result in $g(y_1, z_{2-1})$ becoming a constant function of y_1, invalidating the causation. This occurred in the firing squad example considered above: if all other members of the firing squad missed, then the event that member i hit the victim caused the event that the victim was killed. On the other hand, if any of the other members of the firing squad also hit the victim, the event that member i's bullet hit the victim did not cause the death of the victim, other things equal.

10. Leamer used the term *modification* with exactly the same meaning as *intervention* has here.

References

Blackorby, Charles, Daniel Primont, and R. Robert Russell. (1978). *Duality, Separability and Functional Structure: Theory and Applications*. New York: North-Holland.

Cooley, Thomas F., and Stephen F. LeRoy. (1985). "Atheoretical Macroeconometrics: A Critique." *Journal of Monetary Economics* 16, 283–308.

Hansen, Lars Peter, and Thomas J. Sargent. (1981). "Formulating and Estimating Dynamic Linear Rational Expectations Models." In Robert E. Lucas, Jr. and Thomas Sargent (eds.), *Rational Expectations and Econometric Practice*. Minneapolis: University of Minnesota Press.

Hicks, John. (1979). *Causality in Economics*. New York: Basic Books.

Jacobs, Rodney L., Edward E. Leamer, and Michael P. Ward. (1979). "Difficulties with Testing for Causation." *Economic Inquiry* 17, 401–413.

Leamer, Edward E. (1985). "Vector Autoregressions for Causal Inference." *Carnegie-Rochester Conference Series on Public Policy*.

LeRoy, Stephen F. (1993). "On Policy Regimes." Chapter 7 in this volume.

Lucas, Robert E., Jr. "Econometric Policy Evaluation: A Critique" (1976). In K. Brunner and A. Meltzer (eds.), *The Philips Curve and Labor Markets*. Carnegie-Rochester Series on Public Policy (Vol. 1). Amsterdam: North-Holland.

Simon, Herbert A. (1953). "Causal Ordering and Identifiability." In Wiliam C. Hood and Tjalling C. Koopmans (eds.), *Studies in Econometric Method*. New Haven: Cowles Foundation.

Commentary on Chapter 6

Clive W.J. Granger

Discussions of causality have been occurring for at least three thousand years, and the fact that they continue suggests both that the topic is a difficult one and that there is a continuing real demand for an acceptable definition. Anyone can propose their own definition of causality by emphasizing some aspect of causality that is considered to be of particular or obvious importance. For example, Hoover and Sheffrin (1992) equated causality with controllability and base a definition on that, whereas the definition that I have marketed and defended—for example, in Granger (1980)—emphasizes that the cause may occur temporally before the effect and contain special information about it, so that necessarily the cause can help forecast the effect.

Each definition, when considered formally, will be based on a number of assumptions, which may or may not be acceptable to potential users. From the definition there will be a number of consequences, which may or may not be thought to be sensible. It is virtually impossible to prove that one definition is inherently superior to another using just logical reasoning as, starting with the belief that one definition is correct, including that all its assumptions are true, will probably lead to an alternative definition producing "contradictory" results, or even results that seem lacking in common sense. The various definitions do not encompass each other, and one cannot be nested in another.

For LeRoy causality one has to be able to state a set of variables, denoted $e(y)$, which completely determine the variable y. If y is a random variable, the conditional distribution $F(y \mid e(y))$ is singular, so that $y = f(e(y))$ for some function of f, without any error or uncertainty. It is obviously an act of faith that such a set $e(y)$ exists, and that it is not uncountably infinite. To see the problem, suppose I note that at the age of fifty-nine I am six feet tall. I would need to list all of the reasons for or determinants of that fact. However, in the definition being considered a number of helpful assumptions are made, including that $e(y)$ consists of just a countable set of variables, that equilibrium exists and is unique and that some model is available that provides the function f.

Now suppose that the vector of variables under consideration can be decomposed into two distinct types, called *endogenous* and *exogenous*. This decomposition is performed by the researcher, and the two types of variables are not carefully defined, although the decomposition is very important for the paper. It is said that an exogenous variable is "determined outside the model *and* subject to direct and independent intervention" (my emphasis). Thus, the decomposition is relative to the model being considered. If one has an economic model, then sunspots would actually be thought of a being exogenous, but they are not subject to intervention by any economic agent and so are not classified here as being exogenous, presumably. Temperature, if one believes in global warming, may be exogenous, but not if there is an equation in the model explaining long-run changes in temperature. Money supply, traditionally thought of as being a policy variable under the control of some government agency, would be exogenous, but if one put in a government-reaction function in the model, then perhaps this variable would become endogenous, but not if this function did not fit perfectly. Similarly, endogenous variables are "determined by the model and not subject to direct intervention." If a variable P is such that its value cannot be known until the value of some other variable Q is known, it is unclear to me how it can be stated that P is exogenous to Y. However, in the formulation in the paper, in a model

$$Y_n = \beta X_n + e_n,$$

e_n, the residual, is thought of as an exogenous variable to the endogenous variable Y_n, even though in practice the value taken by e_n is not known until the value of Y_n is known. There appears to be some unnecessary confusion about exogeneity in the paper. In the second section it is stated that "econometricians . . . characterize variables as endogenous or exogenous according to whether or not they are correlated with certain unobserved variables," which is at least out-of-date and hardly reflects general attitudes. Further, in the fifth section a variable is said to be "exogenous in the Granger sense." I would like to make it clear that in my writings or lectures I have never equated non-(Granger) causality with exogeneity, even though some later writers incorrectly did do so. A substantial article clearing up these points is that by Engle, Hendry, and Richard (1983). It is a pity to see these earlier mistakes being perpetrated a decade after Engle, et al. have clarified them. In any case, if researcher A claims a causality from y_1 and y_2, then to accept this statement you have the decomposition of variables into exogenous and endogenous that A proposes, and this clearly can be controversial.

One endogenous variable y_1 can LeRoy cause another y_2 if three conditions are obeyed, as given in the second section, which is the core of the chapter. It is pointed out that a property of the definition is that feedback cannot occur. One cannot, for example, have both a change in the price of fertilizer causing a change in demand for the fertilizer and also a change in demand cause a change in price, within a two-variable model, because this model cannot be identified.

A particularly controversial property of the definition is that it appears to give deterministic causality, as emphasized in the third section, with an event occurring if and only if another event occurs. It has taken philosophers a very long time to get away from deterministic causality, the change largely happening because of quantum physics being widely accepted, and now they generally admit that causality can often be stochastic. If you smoke, you do not necessarily get cancer, but you do increase the probability of getting the disease. For a full discussion see Skyrms and Harper (1988). This has proved to be such a useful generalization, it would be a clear backward step to determinism, in my opinion, which follows from the assumption that all exogenous variables can be defined and listed.

One of the most curious and certainly controversial aspects of the new causal approach follows from the model given in the third section:

$$x_t = \lambda x_{t-1} + u_t,$$

$$u_t = \rho u_{t-1} + e_t,$$

where "x_o and u_o and the e_t are exogenous variables" and "the model is complete, so that x_o, u_o, and the e_t are distributed independently." It is pointed out that if λ is estimated by OLS it will usually be biased in small samples and so "x_{t-1} cannot cause x_t." This statement is made regardless of the true value of ρ. Is it true of $\rho = 0$, for example, or if $\rho = 1$? Is the bias result true if $| \rho |$ is less than one but the true λ is larger than one? Why should the existence of causation depend on the *method* of estimation used for a parameter: if a method can be found that produced an unbiased estimate of λ, is there then causation? Suppose that there is an estimator that produces a positive bias in the estimate of λ for sample sizes up to n_o, a negative bias for sizes over n_o, but no bias for a sample size exactly n_o. Can it really be possible that x_{t-1} causes x_t only for one particular sample size and no other? This is surely a confused argument between causal variables and unknown parameters. Most definitions of a deep concept such as causality would be based on the properties of populations, not on estimated models. The *tests* of causality may have to be based on data considerations, but one does not need to mix the question of definition with that of testing and thus of the estimation of models. The model given above can also be used to indicate a further weakness of the LeRoy definition, in that everything is conditional on the particular information set being considered. Thus, for example, the independence of x_o, u_o, and the ε_t may if one is just considering the x_t series and how it is generated but may not be true if it is embedded within a larger vector of variables. It is well known that a pair of Gaussian random variables x, y can be uncorrelated, and thus independent, within the set (x, y), but then their partial correlation corr $(x, y \mid z)$ need not be zero, so that they are not independent in the set (x, y, z). Independence is not a pervasive property, so that once found it is always present, but rather it depends on the context.

It seems that the new definition runs into logical problems when it tries to encompass all aspects of model generation, specification, and estimation, particularly when the models are dynamic. There is one area in which it can have a very useful impact—the possibility of giving causal order to contemporaneous relationships. To remove all of the complicating aspects of the discussion, suppose that one has a vector $\underline{x}_t$ which is an iid sequence of random vector variables with a covariance matrix $\underline{G}$. Thus, there is no dynamics, and the only parameters to be estimated are some means and those in $\underline{G}$, which can certainly be estimated consistently. Given this situation, can the LeRoy approach suggest a causal ordering of the variables? The researcher can, presumably, use outside knowledge to decide which variables are exogenous and which endogenous, using criteria that can be successfully communicated to others, hopefully convincingly so. An economic model or theory can then provide for each endogenous variable a function that determines it from the exogenous variables, and from these functions LeRoy causality can be determined. Presumably information about which are stocks and which are flows will be helpful in forming these functions, given that contemporaneous, discrete-time correlations are being considered, unless it is thought that the cause can occur after the effect, which seems to be generally unacceptable. The question that naturally arises is how these causal orderings can be verified. Presumably, if only linear models are being considered and as an endogenous variable is known completely from the exogenous variables, the matrix $\underline{G}$ will be found to be singular and the covariance will be found to obey certain linear restrictions. Even if some reality is allowed into the situation and "measurement errors" are considered on at least some of the variables, there should still be some inequality linear constraints on $\underline{G}$. It is interesting to ask if these will be similar to the "path-analysis" constraints analyzed by Glymour et al. (1987), Glymour and Spirtes (1988), and, in a more general framework, by Pearl and Verma (1991). If the present approach can be helpful, at least, in determining causal ordering in variables that are only contemporaneously related, such as reduced form or VAR residuals, then it will be extremely useful in filling a present gap in our abilities to interpret systems. Whether or not it is found acceptable will be determined by how wide a use it achieves in future economic research and whether it stands alone or is used in conjunction with alternative definitions.

References

Engle, R.F., D. Hendry, and J-F. Richard. (1983). "Exogeneity." *Econometrica* 51, 277–304.

Glymour, C., R. Scheimes, P. Spirtes, and K. Kelley. (1987). *Discovering Causal Structure* San Diego: Academic Press.

Glymour, C., and P. Spirtes. (1988). "Latent Variables, Causal Models and Overidentifying Constraints." *Journal of Econometrics* 39.

Granger, C.W.J. (1980). "Testing for causality: A Personal Viewpoint." *Journal of Economic Dynamics and Control* 2, 329–352.

Hoover, K.D., and S.M. Sheffrin. (1992). "Causation, Spending and Taxes: Sand in the Sand-box or Tax Collector for the Welfare State?" *American Economic Review* 82, 225–248.

Pearl, J., and T.S. Verma. (1991). "A Theory of Inferred Causation." In J.A. Allen, R. Filkes, and B. Sandewall (eds.), *Principles of Knowlege and Reasoning*: Proceedings of the Second International Conference. (San Mateo, CA: Morgan Kaufman).

Skyrms B., and W.L. Harper. (1988). *Causation, Chance and Credence* Dorchrecht: Kluwer.

7 ON POLICY REGIMES

Stephen F. LeRoy

Introduction[1]

Lucas's (1976) "Econometric Policy Evaluation: A Critique" is widely regarded as the most influential paper in macroeconomics of the 1970s. It is usually read as making the simple point that the Keynesian econometric models of the 1960s were not well founded on microeconomic principles and in particular that Keynesian model builders played fast and loose with agents' expectations (for example, Mankiw, 1990). On this conservative reading, Lucas was surely correct. Lucas, however, had more in mind than merely criticizing particular Keynesian macroeconomic models. He also argued that the entire mode of analyzing policy interventions employed in Keynesian policy analysis was in conflict with general equilibrium theory. Here Lucas was distinguishing the methodological question of how one analyzes policy using any macroeconomic model from the substantive question of whether Keynesian models are correct. That he considered the former problem the basic one is indicated by the fact that he contrasted the Theory of Economic Policy mode of policy analysis with his recommended mode within the context of an abstract functional representation of a generic macroeconomic model. Particular Keynesian and new classical models were considered only to develop the general argument.

The Theory of Economic Policy that Lucas criticized originated with Tinbergen (1952) and was developed by Cowles Commission economists (Simon, Marschak, and Klein) in the 1950s. The Cowles group contributed a variety of extremely important developments to economic and econometric theory: the theories of causal orderings, of econometric identification, and of simultaneous equations bias all were developed within the same broad project as the Keynesian mode of policy analysis. General equilibrium theorists of the stature of Debreu, Hurwicz, and Koopmans worked on related Cowles projects. Given the close association between macroeconomists and general equilibrium theorists, it is surprising to learn that the two traditions are in fundamental conflict.

In fact, there is no inconsistency between the Theory of Economic Policy as formulated by the Cowles group and general equilibrium theory. In this paper it will be argued that the Theory of Economic Policy as Lucas characterized and criticized it is substantially correct; the extension of the Cowles analysis to rational expectations does not alter the original analysis at any deep level. Rather, the conflict is between Lucas's recommended mode of policy analysis and a consistent application of rational expectations. I will argue that Lucas's preferred formulation of policy analysis via parameter interventions amounts to replacing the assumption of rational expectations with that of stationary expectations.

The Lucas critique is reviewed in the second section. In the third section the Lucas critique is contrasted with the received Cowles approach. The theme is that the two are diametrically opposed and that new classical economists confuse rational expectations with stationary expectations. Three examples are discussed in the fourth section. The discussion then deals with the consequences for such new classical doctrines as policy ineffectiveness of maintaining a consistent framework of rational expectations, and the sixth section concludes.

The Lucas Critique

Lucas (1976) began by juxtaposing two traditions of macroeconomic analysis: theoretical and econometric. The theoretical tradition, as reflected in the homogeneity of demand and supply functions and, later, the natural rate hypothesis, implies that there is no exploitable tradeoff between output and inflation. Therefore, expansionary fiscal and monetary policies designed to raise output by stimulating demand cannot succeed. The tradition of Keynesian econometric policy evaluation, on the other hand, implies that such a tradeoff exists, at least according to Keynesian models. Lucas's thesis was that the latter tradition is in fundamental error.

The "Theory of Economic Policy"

Lucas took the model characterizing the effect of policy variables on the economy to be

$$y_{t+1} = F(y_t, x_t, \theta, \varepsilon_t). \qquad (7.1)$$

Here y_t is a vector of endogenous state variables, x_t is a vector of exogenous forcing variables (including the policy variables), θ is a vector of parameters representing private agents' decision rules, technological constants and the like, and ε_t is a vector of random shocks. The difference between the ε_t and the x_t is that the former are characterized stochastically, whereas the latter are not. In Keynesian policy evaluation, policy makers are represented as choosing a sequence of x_t's to maximize a social objective function like the expectation of

$$\sum_t \beta^t u(y_t, x_t, \varepsilon_t)$$

subject to the past history of the system (represented by the current value of y_t) and to (7.1). This maximization takes the form of an optimal control problem. The optimal policy function

$$x_t = G(y_t, \theta) \qquad (7.2)$$

computed as the solution to the optimization problem provides the answer to the policy analysis question.

Lucas's criticism was that if the x_t are subject to change in the future but are not characterized probabilistically, then agents cannot be represented as maximizing utilities subject to well-defined constraints. Further, there can be no presumption that the parameters θ will be invariant to the interventions in the x_t, as assumed in the optimal control exercise.

Lucas's Representation of Policy Change

How, according to Lucas, can economists avoid these problems in conducting policy analysis? Lucas proposed replacing (7.2) as derived by optimal control theory with the policy rule

$$x_t = G(y_t, \lambda, \eta_t),$$

where λ parametrizes policy regimes and η_t is a vector of disturbances. The equations (7.1) describing the evolution of the economy are replaced by

$$y_{t+1} = F(y_t, \ \theta(\lambda), \ \varepsilon_t).$$

Here a policy is viewed as a specification of λ, so that a policy change is modeled as an altered value of λ. Private agents' decision rules depend on the chosen policy regime; this is represented by specifying θ to depend on λ. Lucas emphasized that if the dependence of θ on λ is ignored, erroneous policy analysis will result.

Several comments are in order. First, Lucas's advocacy that government policy be conducted according to fixed rules is reminiscent of Friedman's (1948) (and earlier, Mints' and Simons') proposal that central banks conduct monetary policy by implementing a constant growth rate rule for the money stock. However, the rationale in the two cases was different. Friedman opposed discretionary policy on substantive grounds: policy makers can be expected neither to diagnose the problem accurately enough nor to implement a policy response quickly enough to affect the macroeconomic environment in the right direction. Lucas, while agreeing with Friedman, based his objection to discretionary policy on methodological grounds: unless policy is conducted according to rules, so that policy change is modeled as a regime shift rather than as altered realizations of exogenous variables, economists cannot hope to succeed in modeling agents as solving well-posed optimizations. Therefore the prospects for successful economic analysis and policy recommendations are dim.

Second, in his critique Lucas was not primarily criticizing Keynesian models themselves; he cannot fairly be represented as arguing only the trivial point that misspecified models are likely to lead to bad policy analysis. It is not difficult, of course, to locate other papers in which Lucas took issue with Keynesian models, but his main purpose in the critique was to criticize a particular way of applying models, not the models themselves.

Third, Lucas cannot be represented as caricaturing Keynesian policy evaluation. A common criticism of Keynesian policy evaluation, and one that was justified prior to the late 1960s, was that intertemporal tradeoffs were not adequately recognized or incorporated in the analysis. Specifically, expansionary policy was too often advocated on the grounds that the costs were minor since inflation would not be greatly affected over the short run. By the late 1960s, however, the natural rate hypothesis was in the air, and Keynesian macroeconomists recognized the possibility that the consequences for GNP of sustained expansionary policies were temporary, while the implications for inflation, although delayed, were permanent. Optimal control methods were adopted precisely in order to allow analysis of such tradeoffs. By adopting the optimal control version of Keynesian policy evaluation as his target, however, Lucas foreclosed the line of criticism just outlined. Whatever reservations one has about the Lucas critique, one cannot fault him for knocking over a straw man.

Lucas on Policy Advice

Lucas's counsel to economists as model builders was that they represent policy choice by hypothetical parameter changes. This instruction had as its counterpart his injunction to economists as advice givers that they restrict themselves to advocating that policy be conducted according to simple rules. Lucas recognized that the transition to a regime of fixed rules can be done in many ways and that the argument for fixed rules gives no guidance in choosing among these. It appears to follow that economists have nothing to contribute by way of advice to policy makers in any setting in which the past conduct of policy is taken as given. Lucas (1980 p. 258) explicitly accepted this implication:

> To one with some responsibility for monetary policy in 1974, say, it is not very helpful to observe that monetary growth "should have" proceeded at a constant 4 percent rate for the 25 years preceding. . . . What advice, then, do advocates of rules have to offer with respect to the policy decisions before us *right now*?
>
> This question does have a practical, men-of-affairs ring to it, but to my ears, this ring is entirely false. It is a king-for-a-day question which has no real-world counterpart in the decision problems actually faced by economic advisors. . . .
>
> Economists who pose this "What is to be done, today?" question as though it were somehow the acid test of economic competence are culture-bound (or institution-bound) to an extent they are probably not aware of. They are accepting as *given* the entirely unproved hpyothesis that the fine-tuning exercise called for by the Employment Act [of 1946] is a desirable and feasible one.

Evaluation of the Lucas Critique

The Lucas Critique: Methodological or Substantive?

I noted in the previous section that Lucas made two points in his critique—that policy changes are to be modeled as parameter shifts and that policy should be governed by simple rules. The points are distinct and arguably unrelated. Even the intended audiences are different: the first is addressed to economists and concerns how to model policy; the second is addressed to government and concerns how to conduct policy. Yet Lucas argued them simultaneously. For example, consider his discussion of what happens when agents are confronted with arbitrary changes in their environment. This question came up twice in Lucas's paper: once in the context of his criticism of Keynesian policy evaluation and once in the context of his discussion of regime shifts under his preferred formalization of policy analysis. The essence of Lucas's criticism of Keynesian policy evaluation was that because the policy variables x_t are not characterized probabilistically, agents cannot be modeled as solving well-formulated optimization problems. Here the point is methodological: representing agents as subject to arbitrary shifts in their environment is a bad modeling strategy because it rules out application of economic theory.

Now, does not the same point come up in Lucas's preferred formalization of policy analysis when agents have been confronted with a recent unexpected regime shift? That is, does not the same line of reasoning used to criticize Keynesian policy evaluation apply under a regime shift? Here is Lucas's (1980, p. 125) discussion of regime shifts:

> A change in policy (in λ) affects the behavior of the system in two ways: first by altering the time series behavior of x_t; second by leading to modification of the behavioral parameters $\theta(\lambda)$ governing the rest of the system. Evidently, the way this latter modification can be expected to occur depends crucially on the way the policy change is carried out. If the policy change occurs by a sequence of decisions following no discussed or pre-announced pattern, it will become known to agents only gradually, and then perhaps largely as higher variance of "noise." In this case, the movement to a new $\theta(\lambda)$, if it occurs in a stable way at all, will be unsystematic, and econometrically unpredictable. If, on the other hand, policy changes occur as fully discussed and understood changes in *rules*, there is some hope that the resulting structural changes can be forecast on the basis of estimation from past data of $\theta(\lambda)$.

The perspective is seen to shift from methodological to substantive: the Keynesian practice of modeling a policy shift as an intervention on the x_t, where the x_t are not characterized probabilistically, is a bad idea because agents cannot be modeled as optimizers. It is to be remedied by a change in modeling strategy. A regime shift modeled as a nonpreannounced intervention on parameters, however, is a bad idea because it leads to a higher variance of noise. It is to be remedied by replacing discretionary changes in policy with policy changes which occur as fully discussed and understood changes in rules. The nonparallel treatment of parallel problems is evident.

Regime Changes as Parameter Interventions

The two points Lucas made—that policy changes should be modeled as parameter shifts rather than variable shifts and that policy should be governed by simple rules—are distinct and should be appraised separately. I take them in order. It is difficult to understand the basis for Lucas's distinction between policy evaluation defined as selection of an arbitrary sequence for a forcing variable, as under the theory of economic policy, versus policy evaluation as selection of a policy response function, as in his recommended mode of analysis. I have already observed that Lucas's characterization of Keynesian policy analysis implied that policy advice consists of recommending a response function derived from optimization of a control problem. Thus on Lucas's account Keynesian policy recommendation consists of choosing a function in exactly the same sense as under Lucas's own formulation.

Whether or not policy analysis should be represented as choice of a function is seen to be a false issue: it can always be so regarded and was so regarded both by Keynesians and by Lucas. The real issue is Lucas's claim that policy change should be modeled by altering the assumed value of a policy parameter λ. Under rational expectations agents are assumed to know all parameters, where *know* contains the implication that agents are assumed to be certain that these parameters will never change in the future. A regime shift as modeled by a parameter intervention consists of the assertion that parameters do change over time. Rational expectations therefore is inconsistent with regime shifts so modeled: the assertion that (certain classes of) policy changes should be modeled as regime shifts is equivalent to the assertion that (these classes of) policy changes are not subject to rational expectations.

In the received usage, modeling agents as assuming that the current value of some variable will persist forever, even when that variable changes over time, is characterized as assuming stationary expectations. The treatment in new classical economics is identical, except that the variable in question is referred to as a parameter despite the fact that it changes over time as policy rules are altered. The new classical term *rational expectations* seems less accurate than the received *stationary expectations* in describing this specification, and we will use the latter term henceforth.

Simple Rules

As has been seen, one of Lucas's major purposes, both in the "Critique" and elsewhere, was to argue that policy should be guided by preannounced simple rules, as opposed to either discretion or policy rules involving feedback. In the preferred new classical models of macroeconomic activity—those expressing equilibrium GNP as a function of the unexpected component of money or prices—the reduced form for GNP does not depend on the parameters of the policy rule. This is so because an intervention on the feedback parameters of the money supply process merely shifts the distribution of the money stock, implying that the distribution of the unexpected component of money is unaffected (see the discussion of Sargent-Wallace, 1976, below). Thus simple rules do just as well as feedback control rules.

In light of the discussion of the second and third sections, one may distinguish two versions of the foregoing argument for simple rules: the rational expectations version and the stationary expectations version. The rational expectations version argues that if agents in one country know that macroeconomic policy has been, is now, and always will be governed by a feedback control rule, and if in another otherwise identical country agents know that policy has been, is now and always will be governed by a simple rule, the two countries will have similar economic performances. This argument is correct, given the validity of the assumed model. In most discussions, however, the context of the discussion concerns real-time policy changes,[2] not hypothetical timeless comparisons, and the argument asserts that a fully understood change from one policy rule to another will not affect economic performance (again, see the discussion of Sargent-Wallace, 1976, below). Again the argument is correct, but it must be understood that now the setting is one of stationary expectations, not rational expectations: under both the old and new control rules agents are modeled as always being certain that the policy parameter will continue at its current value even though it changes over time as the policy regime shifts.[3]

Examples

We see that even though the Lucas critique is usually read as a criticism of Keynesians for not assuming rational expectations, in fact it is Lucas's own concept of policy regimes that is vulnerable to this criticism (if, indeed, it is a criticism). It is interesting to trace out this interplay in Lucas's paper. To do so I reconsider two of the examples discussed by Lucas, and also analyze the 1976 model of Sargent and Wallace.

The Permanent Income Hypothesis

Lucas's first example was based on the permanent income hypothesis of Friedman (1957). As is well known, the permanent-income hypothesis explains the slope of the observed consumption function in terms of the variances of the permanent and transitory components of income. Accordingly, Lucas observed, the effects of a policy consisting of a sequence of income supplements depend critically on whether the supplements are perceived as permanent or transitory. The Keynesian analytical practice, however, was the same for either case: simply add the supplement to the forecast of income and predict consumption by applying the estimated consumption function.

An analyst wishing to determine the effect of income supplements within the framework of the permanent income hypothesis would surely recognize that the permanent-income hypothesis specifies that agents can distinguish between the permanent and transitory components of their incomes. Accordingly, an intervention on income is not completely characterized until the analyst specifies how the income supplement is broken down into its permanent and transitory components. In the absence of an explicit specification, the use of the estimated consumption function to predict the effect of income on consumption can be construed as an implicit specification that the income supplement embodies the same mix of permanent and transitory income as prevailed for income as a whole in the past. If, however, the income supplement is perceived as completely temporary or completely permanent, it should be assumed that agents treat it as such. Ignoring this point is surely a slip, just as Lucas claimed, at least under the maintained framework of the permanent income hypothesis. However, it is far from clear that the Keynesian economists had committed themselves to the permanent income hypothesis, and in any case it is difficult to see why this example illustrates any of the general points which Lucas argued in his critique.

The Hall-Jorgenson Example

In his second example Lucas criticized Hall and Jorgenson's (1967) analysis of the effect of an investment tax credit on the level of investment. Hall and Jorgenson had treated the tax credit as a parameter, implying that any tax rate change is regarded as permanent. Lucas pointed out that if the tax rate is being used as a tool of countercyclical stabilization policy, however, then tax-rate changes are obviously not permanent. Lucas proposed modeling the tax rate not as a parameter but as a realization from a Markov process with transition probabilities approximating the real-world frequencies of tax rate changes.

The conclusion Lucas drew at the end of his section on Hall-Jorgenson was that the example illustrated the importance of modeling policy as generated by a fixed rule—in this case the stochastic process he proposed as a model for the tax rate—rather than characterizing policy by an arbitrary parameter. Correspondingly, Lucas argued by example, a change in tax policy should be represented as an altered realization of the random variable the probability distribution of which this policy rule consists. Yet in his conclusion at the end of the paper Lucas advocated modeling policy change as regime choice, precisely the opposite point. It was Hall and Jorgenson who modeled policy change as regime choice and Lucas who, in the Hall-Jorgenson section of his paper, proposed modeling a change in tax policy as an altered realization of a random variable. Hall and Jorgenson's analysis of tax rate changes appears to conform to the pattern advocated by Lucas in his conclusion; Lucas, by representing policy change as an altered realization of a variable, appears in his reformulation of Hall and Jorgenson to advocate doing policy analysis in exactly the way he criticized in his introduction and conclusion.

Lucas's third example dealt with the Phillips curve. It is essentially the same as the Sargent-Wallace model, to which I now turn.

The Sargent-Wallace Model

Sargent and Wallace's (1976) paper presented the argument for rules in the context of a linear-quadratic new classical macroeconomic model. Sargent and Wallace's purpose was to show that the general presumption in favor of feedback control implied by optimal control theory depends on the assumption that the structure generating GNP is constant over time as control rules change. If, however, as rational expectations appeared to them to imply, the structure changes as control rules change, then the presumption in favor of feedback control disappears.

Sargent and Wallace assumed that GNP y_t is related to the money stock m_t according to[4]

$$y_t = \lambda y_{t-1} + \beta m_t + u_t \tag{7.3}$$

and that the goal of policy is to minimize the variance of y_t. They began by reviewing the case for feedback control. The feedback control rule

$$m_t = g y_{t-1} \tag{7.4}$$

results in

$$V(y_t) = \frac{\sigma_u^2}{1 - (\lambda + \beta g)^2},$$

which, with $\lambda \neq 0$, is strictly lower under the optimal feedback rule $g = -\lambda/\beta$ than under the nonfeedback rule $g = 0$.

Sargent and Wallace observed that this argument in favor of feedback control depends on the assumption that λ and β can be taken to be independent of g. However, suppose that (7.3) is generated by the structural model

$$y_t = \xi_1(m_t - E_{t-1}(m_t)) + \xi_2 y_{t-1} + u_t, \tag{7.5}$$

$$m_t = g y_{t-1} + \varepsilon_t, \tag{7.6}$$

$$E_{t-1}(m_t) = g y_{t-1}. \tag{7.7}$$

The system (7.5) through (7.7) is consistent with (7.3) and (7.4): substituting (7.7) into (7.5) results in (7.3) with $\beta = \xi_1$ and $\lambda = \xi_2 - \xi_1 g$.

But Sargent and Wallace (1976, p. 203) argued that

suppose now that the monetary authority desires to design a feedback rule to minimize the variance of y . . . under the assumption that the public will know the rule it is using and so use the currently prevailing g in [7.7] in forming its expectations, rather than the old g that held during the estimation period. The public would presumably know g if the monetary authority were to announce [it]. Failing that, the public might be able to infer g from the observed behavior of the money supply and other variables. In any case, on the assumption that the public knows what g the authority is using, . . . λ . . . comes to depend on the authority's choice of g.

If so, Sargent and Wallace continued, in view of $\lambda = \xi_2 = \xi_1 g$ we cannot take λ in (7.3) to be the same for all values of g. Rather, the correct reduced form is derived by substituting (7.6) and (7.7) into (7.5) to obtain

$$y_t = \xi_1 \varepsilon_t + \xi_2 y_{t-1} + u_t,$$

which does not depend on g. Thus, contrary to the initial argument, a feedback control rule cannot lower the variance of y below that implied by a simple control rule. This is so because altering g leaves $m_t - E_{t-1}(m_t)$ unaffected.

The argument of the present paper implies that Sargent and Wallace have this exactly reversed. The assumption that λ is independent of g is consistent with rational expectations—in fact, is implied by rational expectations (if the intervention on g is interpreted as a variable intervention, as is appropriate given that the exercise concerns policy change over time)—rather than being inconsistent with rational expectations as Sargent and Wallace contended. If, as assumed, agents knew in the estimation period that the money stock was generated by (7.6) with a particular value of g, then rational expectations implies that they are certain that g will never change. Therefore when the monetary authority adopts the optimal feedback rule

$$m_t = -(\lambda/\beta)_t y_{t-1}, \tag{7.8}$$

agents interpret this as a sequence of interventions on the ε_t:

$$\varepsilon_t = -(\lambda/\beta + g)_t y_{t-1}. \tag{7.9}$$

To derive (7.9), equate the right sides of (7.8) and (7.6). Here the time subscript on $\lambda/\beta + g$ indicates that a variable intervention rather than a parameter intervention is intended, with the intervention involving only values taken on by ε_t after the policy change. No matter how long the monetary authority generates m_t according to (7.8), rational expectations implies that agents persist in attributing changes in the money stock to the idiosyncratic component of the money supply process, just as a gambler who bets on the toss of a coin he knows to be fair will continue to assume that the probability of heads on the next toss in one-half even after a long unbroken string of tails.

As noted above, it might be objected that this analysis is unrealistic since surely agents would eventually figure out that the average monetary growth rate had changed. If so, under rational expectations the conclusion is not that the parameter

g changed and eventually agents figured this out, but that a modeling error was made in specifying g to be a parameter in the first place. If it is believed that some evidence will convince agents that g has changed, then this belief should be incorporated in the model: g should be modeled as a variable rather than a parameter. One way to implement this alternative would be to replace (7.6) by a more complex specification in which agents attach some prior probability to the event of g changing, and then update their posterior distribution of g according to Bayes's law. Such a respecification would allow the analyst to avoid the implication that agents never revise their estimate of g if that specification is thought to be implausible.

Sargent and Wallace, in contrast, effectively proposed to replace rational expectations with stationary expectations: having "known" that g takes on a particular value in the estimation period, agents then come to "know" that g takes on a different value as policy changes.

Consequences of Rational Expectations

It was argued above that the treatment of policy regimes as parameters that vary over time is inconsistent with rational expectations. To summarize, the point is that if an analyst opts to model a regime as a parameter, rational expectations implies that he or she must be willing to assume both that its value never changed in the past and will never change in the future and further that the agents whose behavior is being modeled know this to be the case.[5] Correspondingly, to model regime change over time in a setting of rational expectations, one would assume that regimes are the values taken on by a stochastic process the parameters of which are known to agents. Lucas's reformulation of the Hall-Jorgenson model is a good example of a successful analysis of policy regimes; another is Flood and Garber (1983). Hamilton has several papers on stochastic regime switching, one in this volume. It is seen that under rational expectations a policy regime is properly modeled as a state of a stochastic process that has a small number of states and a low probability of state change at any date and not as a parameter that varies. There is no qualitative distinction between policy regimes and policy variables, and no harm would be done if the term *regime* were deleted.

How important is this point? Obviously the answer depends on the context. If policy change is infrequent, little harm is done by representing policy regimes by parameters. To insist on the distinction between rational expectations and stationary expectations in such settings would be excessively fastidious, since the two would have virtually identical implications in practice and stationary expectations is easier to implement analytically. But almost by definition most policy changes are of a type that occurs frequently, and when policy change is frequent the regime formulation is likely to lead to major error. Lucas, in fact, used exactly this observation to motivate his reformulation of the Hall-Jorgenson analysis of the investment tax credit, as was observed above. In any case, the purpose of the foregoing sections was not to argue that Lucas's preferred formulation of policy change can never be used fruitfully but instead to question his contention that the alternative formulation of the theory of economic policy is inherently flawed at a deep methodological level.

Policy Choice as a Variable Intervention

In this section we discuss further consequences of the foregoing analysis of consistently maintaining a framework of rational expectations. First, rational expectations implies that Lucas's criticisms of Keynesian policy analysis at a methodological level must be recognized as unjustified. Contrary to the Lucas critique, there is nothing wrong with representing policy by a sequence of arbitrary realizations of random variables. As we have seen, policy changes can be modeled either by parameter interventions or variable interventions, depending on the question being asked. Correspondingly, the policymaker's question, "What should we do here and now, taking the past as given?" is seen to be perfectly well posed; its answer is determined by analyzing the effect of a variable intervention. The fact that its answer may be "commit to a rule" does nothing to impugn the legitimacy of the question. Of course, Lucas's policy question, "What should we do now, given that we did the same in the past?," which is answered by analyzing a parameter intervention, is no less legitimate, although it is obviously of less applied interest since the policy maker cannot change the past. Contrary to the Lucas critique, there is no general flaw in the theory of economic policy as he represented it, nor is there any error in deriving optimal policy by solving an optimal control problem.

One encounters the objection that representing policy makers as choosing the values of random variables involves an inconsistency: if a variable is random, how can its value be chosen by policy makers (for example, Hoover, 1989)? For some reason this objection always arises in the context of modeling government behavior; however, it would seem that the same problem—if it is a problem—arises with consumption, investment, or unemployment, which equally are modeled both as variables the values of which are chosen by economic agents and as random variables. In fact there is no inconsistency: on the contrary, analysis of interventions under rational expectations always takes exactly the form of postulating an arbitrary realization or sequence of realizations for the variable being intervened on, while at the same time assuming that the agents being modeled situate these realizations as draws from a random population.

Policy Ineffectiveness

A second implication of rational expectations is that the policy effectiveness proposition of new classical macroeconomics fails, at least in the models customarily used to derive them. To see this, consider a linear new classical macroeconomic model in which the deviation of GNP from its natural rate is proportional to the unexpected component of the price level (as in, for example, Sargent-Wallace, 1976, discussed above). If a policy shift is modeled by a parameter intervention, a change in fiscal or monetary policy cannot affect GNP. This is so because, trivially, any change in policy that shifts the distribution of the price level affects its mean equally, implying that the unexpected component of the price level is unaffected by the change. But this familiar demonstration of the policy ineffectiveness proposition depends critically on the characterization of policy change over time by a parameter intervention. If instead an expansionary monetary policy is modeled as a sequence of higher-than-expected realizations of, for example, the money stock, then GNP will exceed its natural rate forever. The conclusion that "inflation can induce a permanent economic high" (Lucas, 1976, p. 104), from being an "obvious fallacy" is a derivable implication of the new classical models of GNP determination under rational expectations.

What are we to make of this? One response is to accept the conclusion. One would offer the reminder that the permanent economic high made possible by fiscal and monetary expansion is accompanied by permanent (and, in natural-rate models, accelerating) inflation, the costs of which, whether modeled or not, should figure in the policy decision. More interestingly, it could be objected that in the envisioned environment the agents being modeled would eventually draw inferences about the government's preferences and would revise their behavior so as to eliminate the possibility of a permanent economic high. This objection in effect questions the specification of new classical macroeconomists that government policy actions come out of a black box.[6]

Conclusion

Leo Rogin (1956) stressed that developments in economic theory can be understood only in relation to the economic problems and policy questions that these developments are intended to clarify. For example, Rogin observed, the extended Ricardo-Malthus controversy on various points of pure theory can be rendered intelligible only if it is situated relative to the differing positions the two took on the overriding policy question that engaged both: should the Corn Laws be repealed? In contrast to Rogin, new classical macroeconomists contend that, if anything, the opposite is true: controversy about ideological questions and policy issues represents the ephemera of economics generally, not its deepest meaning (for example, Lucas, 1980). The quality of economists' work as scientists, we are told, is limited primarily by the scope and sophistication of the intellectual tools at their disposal, and the enduring contribution of new classical macroeconomics owes to its development and use of powerful analytical tools not available to earlier macroeconomists.

The arguments of this paper support Rogin: policy questions, not technical issues, are at the heart of new classical macroeconomics. The energy of new classical macroeconomics springs from its rejection of the Keynesian mode of policy conduct and policy advice, not from such technical innovations as rational expectations, important as these are. The idea that technocrats in Washington can guide the economy toward a noninflationary full-employment equilibrium by implementing subtle adjustments in macroeconomic policy settings strikes new classical macroeconomists as antidemocratic, besides being implausible. It is difficult not to sympathize: the image of academic economists jetting down the coast to Washington to whisper in the ear of policy makers at congressional hearings appears elitist even to those entirely free of Midwestern populist leanings.

The central project of new classical macroeconomics was to discredit discretionary macroeconomic policy and the associated mode of policy advice by economists. Analytical developments in new classical macroeconomists are best understood when situated in relation to this project. The Lucas critique and the policy ineffectiveness proposition directly address policy questions; these therefore must be seen as the core propositions of new classical macroeconomics. Rational expectations, not being directly related to policy questions, is secondary. In fact, the theme of this paper is that the Lucas critique and policy ineffectiveness proposition are derived under stationary expectations, not rational expectations. The secondary role of rational expectations in new classical macroeconomics is amply demonstrated by the fact that it was sacrificed in favor of stationary expectations in arguing the Lucas critique and policy ineffectiveness proposition.

Macroeconomists were initially drawn to new classical macroeconomics because it appeared to provide a unified explanation for a series of perceived macroeconomic policy failures. Later the cost of embracing this explanation became evident: new classical doctrine failed to equip macroeconomists with analytical tools enabling them to think in a disciplined way about what policy response might be appropriate to current macroeconomic conditions. Not only this; the instruction of new classical macroeconomics was that the policy question framed this way is inherently misposed. Macroeconomists simply did not buy this argument. Culture-bound or not, most wanted to think about policy in relation to current economic conditions and were led shortly to look elsewhere for guidance about how to do so. The argument of this paper is that macroeconomists have displayed a sound instinct in rejecting the policy analysis of new classical macroeconomics: nothing about the equilibrium method or rational expectations should impede economists from trying to answer policy questions as they are posed by policy makers, nor does there exist any deep methodological argument favoring simple policy rules over policy rules that adapt the government's response to the macroeconomic environment.

Notes

1. The material in this paper was presented in Cooley, LeRoy, and Raymon (1984). See also Sims (1982), (1986), Grossman (1984), and Cooley (1985).

2. For example: "I shall argue . . . that simulations using [the major econometric] models can, in principle, provide no useful information as to the actual consequences of alternative economic policies. [This contention] . . . will be based not on deviations between estimated and "'true' structure prior to a policy change but on deviations between the prior 'true' structure and the 'true' structure prevailing afterwards" (Lucas, 1976, p. 105).

3. Another argument adduced in support of rules is that if policy rules are simple and if changes in policy are well understood, there is reason to hope that agents' decision environments will be rendered regular enough to be amenable to economic modeling. Complex policy rules and ambiguous changes in these rules result, it is held, in situations of Knightian uncertainty in which it is impossible for agents to act rationally and therefore difficult for economists to predict their actions. (Singell and I, 1987, have questioned the attribution of this idea to Knight; whether or not Lucas's citation of Knight is appropriate is irrelevant in the present context, however.) Here it is presumed that complex decision rules for the government translate directly into complex decision environments for private agents. This is assuming what needs to be demonstrated—namely, that there do not exist exogenous shocks that governments can succeed in offsetting. In the contrary case a successful feedback control rule would simplify agents' environment relative to that resulting from a simple control rule and would therefore presumably render their behavior easier to predict, not more difficult.

4. I have simplified by deleting constants throughout.

5. In a setting of asymmetric information, the corresponding assumption is that the fact that the parameter does not change over time is the common knowledge of the agents being modeled.

6. New classical macroeconomists, while insisting on the importance of explicitly modeled optimization in characterizing the behavior of private agents, have not applied the same reasoning to governments. This is a puzzling asymmetry. Surely the similarities between, say, the Federal Reserve Board and the General Motors Corporation outweigh their differences.

References

Blanchard, Olivier, and Danny Quah. (1989). "The Dynamic Effects of Aggregate Demand and Supply Disturbances." *American Economic Review* 79, 621–636.
Cooley, Thomas F. (1985). "Individual Forecasting and Aggregate Outcomes: A Review Essay." *Journal of Monetary Economics* 15, 255–266.
Cooley, Thomas F., Stephen F. LeRoy, and Neil Raymon. (1984). "Econometric Policy Evaluation: Note." *American Economic Review* 74, 467–470.

Flood, Robert P., and Peter M. Garber. (1983). "A Model of Stochastic Process Switching." *Econometrica* 51, 537–551.

Friedman, Milton. (1948). "A Monetary and Fiscal Framework for Economic Stability." *American Economic Review* 38, 245–264.

Friedman, Milton. (1957). *A Theory of the Consumption Function*. Princeton, NJ: Princeton University Press.

Grossman, Herschel I. (1984). "Counterfactuals, Forecasts and Choice-Theoretic Modelling of Policy." Mimeo, Brown University.

Hall, Robert E. Jr., and Dale W. Jorgenson. (1967). "Tax Policy and Investment Behavior." *American Economic Review* 57, 391–414.

Hoover, Kevin D. (1989). "The Logic of Causal Inference: Econometrics and the Conditional Analysis of Causation." Mimeo, University of California, Davis.

Keynes, John Maynard. (1936). *General Theory of Employment, Interest and Money*. New York: Harcourt, Brace & World.

LeRoy, Stephen F. (1991). "Causal Orderings." Chapter 6 in this volume.

LeRoy, Stephen F., and Larry J. Singell. (1987). "Knight on Risk and Uncertainty." *Journal of Political Economy* 95, 394–406.

Lucas, Robert E. Jr. (1976/1981). "Econometric Policy Evaluation: A Critique." In Robert E. Lucas, Jr., *Studies in Business-Cycle Theory*. Cambridge, MA: MIT Press.

Lucas, Robert E. Jr. (1980a/1981). "Methods and Problems in Business Cycle Theory." In Robert E. Lucas (ed.). *Studies in Business-Cycle Theory*. Cambridge, MA: MIT Press.

Lucas, Robert E. Jr. (1980b/1981). "Rules, Discretion and the Role of the Economic Advisor." In Robert E. Lucas, Jr., *Studies in Business-Cycle Theory*. Cambridge, MA: MIT Press.

Mankiw, N. Gregory. (1990). "A Quick Refresher Course in Macroeconomics." *Journal of Economic Literature* 28, 1645–1660.

Rogin, Leo. (1956). *The Meaning and Validity of Economic Theory*. New York: Harper.

Sargent, Thomas J. (1984). "Autoregressions, Expectations and Advice." *American Economic Review* 74, 408–415.

Sargent, Thomas J., and Neil Wallace. (1976/1981). "Rational Expectations and the Theory of Economic Policy." In Robert E. Lucas, Jr. and Thomas Sargent (eds.), *Rational Expectations and Econometric Practice*. Minneapolis: University of Minnesota Press.

Simon, Herbert A. (1953). "Causal Ordering and Identifiability." In William C. Hood and Tjalling C. Koopmans (eds.), *Studies in Econometric Method*.

Sims, Christopher J. (1982). "Policy Analysis with Econometric Models." *Brookings Papers on Economic Activity*.

Sims, Christopher J. (1986). "Are Forecasting Models Usable for Policy Analysis?" *Quarterly Review* (Federal Reserve Bank of Minneapolis) 10, 2–16.

Tinbergen, Jan. (1952). *On the Theory of Economics Policy*. Amsterdam: North Holland.

Commentary on Chapter 7

William Roberds

Introduction

The difference between my view of the Lucas critique and LeRoy's (1994) can perhaps best be described as a sort of cultural gap between two generations of economists. LeRoy sees the critique as a frontal attack on the validity of policy analysis as traditionally practiced by economists and particularly on the theory of economic policy advanced by Tinbergen and others. This was the view of the critique that was prevalent when I entered graduate school in 1978, and this view is still held by a large segment of the profession today.

However, the generation of economists trained since the publication of the Lucas critique has been forced to view the critique in less epic terms. After all, the publication of the critique did not spell the end of "life among the policy econ." Papers, dissertations, and memos containing policy analyses continue to be written by the truckload. Many of these analyses follow LeRoy's suggestion and ignore the critique completely, others strictly hew to the path outlined by Lucas, and still others fall between these two extremes. Yet it is safe to say that since 1976, the interpretation of all such analyses has been tempered by the arguments advanced by Lucas and by the counterarguments advanced in papers such as LeRoy's. While it is still unresolved whether the critique represents a stepping stone on the way to policy analysts' nirvana, no economist today can write as if the critique had never existed.

In what follows, I will try to present my own rather prosaic interpretation of the issues surrounding of the disagreement between the Lucas critique and the various papers that criticize it, including LeRoy's. It is my opinion that the essential disagreement can be quickly stated using an idea put forth in a 1971 paper by H.S. Witsenhausen—that is, the notion of causality as it applies to information structures.[1] Witsenhausen's idea of causality is also useful in explaining why neither the Lucas view nor the critics' view amounts to a wholly satisfactory approach to the problems of economic policy analysis.

The Macropolicy Game and Witsenhausen's Causality Property

Witsenhausen's (1971) *causality property* is a restriction on information available to players in a mathematical game. In issues of macroeconomic policy, some variant of the following game (virtually identical to the ones analyzed by Lucas and LeRoy) is commonly analyzed. In the typical macroeconomic policy game, both a policymaker and an agent representing the private sector[2] seek to maximize the time t expectation of their objectives

$$J_i \equiv \sum_j \beta^{t+j} u_i(y_{t+j}).$$

Above the vector y_t describes the state of the economy and evolves according to

$$y_{t+1} = F(y_t, x_t, \theta_t, \varepsilon_t).$$

Here x_t represents the decision variable(s) of the policy maker, θ_t the decision variable of the private sector, and ε_t a purely random shock. The decision variables x_t and θ_t are chosen on the basis of the information available to the policymaker and the private sector, respectively, available at time t. For analytical convenience, partition the policymaker and the private-sector representative agent into a sequence of policymakers $\{p_t\}$ and the representative agent into a sequence of representative agents $\{r_t\}$. The time t policymaker p_t chooses the value of x_t at time t, where x_t must depend on the information available:

$$x_t = G_t(I_t^p).$$

Similarly, the time t representative agent r_t chooses θ_t based on information available:

$$\theta_t = H_t(I_t^r).$$

The most natural definition of the information sets of the policymakers and the representative agents will include the (field generated by the) history of the game $\{(y_t, x_t, \theta_t, \varepsilon_t)\}$ up to time t. I assume that the policymaker will physically move first in every period.

   Most of the argument about the Lucas critique can be described as an argument over the appropriate specifications of information for the policymaker (or sequence of policymakers) I_t^p or the information for the representative agents I_t^r. In general it is difficult to interpret these specifications of a game's *information structure* unless they satisfy a condition similar to Witsenhausen's (1971) causality property. Intuitively, the causality property requires "that for any play of the game the actions of the agents can be ordered [so] that the information available to an agent may depend on the decisions of agents acting earlier but cannot depend upon the decisions of agents acting at concurrent or later times." In other words, the causality property formalizes the idea that agents may not condition their actions on things that have not yet happened. Mathematically, the causality property expresses conditions that are sufficient for a given mathematical game to be written down in extensive or "tree" form.

To illustrate the idea of causality, consider a simple variant of the policy game outlined above. In this simple game there is no uncertainty and a finite horizon of two periods.[3] To simplify things further, assume that the second period private agent r_2 has only one possible decision and that the other players (p_1, r_1, p_2) in the game have only two possible decisions: call these H and L for high or low inflation. Then the set of all possible outcomes of the game is given by the eight possible sequences for (p_1, r_1, p_2)—that is, the set $\Omega = \{LLL, LLH, LHL, HLL, LHH, HHL, HLH, HHH\}$. The set of all possible information about Ω is $\mathscr{F}$, the power set of Ω; agents' information sets will be subsets of $\mathscr{F}$. Under the most natural specification of the policy game, the information set of the first-period policy maker is $I_1^p = \{\phi, \Omega\}$, the information set of the first-period private agent is $I_1^r = \{\phi, \Omega, \{LLL, LLH, LHL, LHH\}, \{HLL, HHL, HLH, HHH\}\}$, and the information set of the second-period policy maker is $I_2^p = I_1^p \cup \{\{LLL, LLH\}, \{LHL, LHH\}, \{HLL, HLH\}, \{HHL, HHH\}\}$. Note that if the game is played in the order (p_1, r_1, p_2), then $I_1^p \subset I_1^r \subset I_2^p$, which for this example means that the causality condition is satisfied for that particular order of play.

In the context of this example, my interpretation of LeRoy's argument (the fifth section) is that the above specification of information sets is the natural and correct one for policy analysis. This specification corresponds to our commonsense notion of causality—that is, of time running in only one direction. More precisely, the assumed temporal order of play corresponds to the nesting of information sets that satisfies the causality restriction. However, Lucas evidently has a different specification in mind. In Lucas's formulation of the policy game, the policymakers p_1 and p_2 would make their decisions before the private agent r_1. Since $I_2^p \supset I_1^r$, however, the causality property would be not be satisfied by the ordering of players (p_1, p_2, r_1). On the other hand, if policy decisons are required to be time-invariant, then the second policy maker's information set can be respecified as $I_2^{p*} \equiv I_1^p$, and the causality condition will be satisfied for the order of play (p_1, p_2, r_1), since $I_1^p \subseteq I_2^{p*} \subset I_1^r$. Under this new specification of information sets, the causality condition is not satisfied for the order of play preferred by LeRoy—that is, (p_1, r_1, p_2).

Which Specification Is Correct?

Given the idea of causal information structures, a number of observations can be made concerning the Lucas-LeRoy debate. The first is that the debate is really a debate over information structures ("rules of play") of policy games, rather than any property of equilibria such as subgame perfection or time-consistency. Second, both Lucas's and LeRoy's preferred information structures formally satisfy the causality condition, although each satisfies causality through a different order of play. Third, by Witsenhausen's (1971) Theorem 1, both specifications are formally consistent with rational expectations. Witsenhausen's theorem states that if the causality property is satisfied (for some order of play), then it is possible to construct sequences of agents' decisions such that these are mutually consistent and such that all agents' expectations are well defined.

The essence of LeRoy's criticism of Lucas's approach is that it is counterintuitive. In terms of information structure in the Lucas version of foregoing example, LeRoy's criticism is manifested by the (1) the restriction of the second-period policy-maker's information set and (2) the changed order of play necessary to satisfy the causality property. The information structure preferred by LeRoy satisfies causality without requiring restrictions on future policymakers' ability to act on new information and without requiring a counterintuitive order of play.

On the other hand, LeRoy is correct to suggest that one of Lucas's purposes in formulating a policy game in this nonintuitive fashion was to argue the superiority of rules over discretion. This point was made more forcefully by Kydland and Prescott (1977). In the language of the preceding section, Kydland and Prescott showed that some policy games played by Lucas's rules would lead to more desirable outcomes than policy games played under the more intuitive specification preferred by LeRoy.

There is also a certain amount of intuitive support for the Lucas-Kydland-Prescott view. If one considers the real-world legal codes of most civilized societies, an important function of all such codes is to guarantee a degree of inertia in most governmental policy decisions. In matters of policy, continuity for continuity's sake evidently has a value that must be balanced against the current wisdom, no matter how compelling that wisdom may be.

While the causality property is not a necessary condition for the existence of rational expectations equilibria,[4] it is a defensible contention that policy rules be derived under some restriction that approximates the causality property. Optimal rules derived for noncausal information structures tend to have the following sort of character. Consider a dynamic optimal taxation problem of the sort analyzed by, for example, Sargent (1987, pp. 419–438). Given sufficient initial private wealth, then the unconstrained solution to such a problem is always a one-time tax tantamount to a confiscation of wealth sufficient to finance all future government expenditures. Such counterintuitive results can be avoided, to some degree, by restricting policies to be parametric—for example, by constraining tax policies to be invariant in the capital taxation example. A restriction to time-invariant policy rules that forces policy analysis into a causal framework can be understood as an attempt to back off from some of the counterintuitive implications of assigning complete credibility to policy makers.

Theoretical Ways Out of the Dilemma

LeRoy and allied papers make a valid point when they, in effect, argue that Lucas's methodology violates our commonsense notions of temporal order and causality. Yet Lucas and his supporters have a point when they argue that in a policy environment with rational agents, there is something to be gained by considering policy rules, which satisfy causality only under conditions that are implausible. An ideal theory of economic policy would be able to capture potential welfare gains associated with policy credibility, without elevating policy makers beyond the everyday constraints imposed by our physical notions of time and space.

Since the publication of the critique, several threads in the macroeconomic literature have attempted to formulate such a theory of economic policy, with mixed results. The most prominent such branch of the literature, typified by papers such as Barro and Gordon (1983), Rogoff (1987), and Chari, Kehoe, and Prescott (1989), has presented more refined versions of macropolicy games similar to the one described above. For example, Barro and Gordon (1983) describe a macropolicy repeated game with an information structure that satisfies the causality restriction in the natural way preferred by LeRoy. An equilibrium of this repeated game corresponds to a time-inconsistent equilibrium of a one-shot version of this game. The Barro-Gordon result suggests that certain time-inconsistent policies that are equilibria of games with counterintuitive information structures could be rationalized as equilibria of games with more intuitively appealing information structures.

Rogoff (1987) points out a major disadvantage associated with this approach, however. This drawback is familiar to even casual students of game theory as the problem of "too many equilibria." In most cases it is possible to write down many reasonable variants of a given macropolicy game, each with many reasonable equilibria. As Rogoff (1987, p. 165) notes, "it would seem premature to focus attention only on the most favorable equilibria."

Chari, Kehoe, and Prescott (1989) show that the Barro-Gordon type results can be derived for truly dynamic policy games involving play between a policy maker and a representative private agent, whose actions mirror potential conflicts of interests among private agents. Chari, Kehoe, and Prescott are careful to restrict the information structures of the games they consider to be causal along the lines preferred by LeRoy (in their words, strategies are history-contingent.) Once again they show that certain time-inconsistent equilibria can be at least closely approximated by the time-consistent equilibria of a more carefully specified game. However, such results provide insufficient guidance as to which of the many possible games or equilibria merit consideration as intuitively plausible models of the effects of policy.

It is difficult to assess the overall impact of the game-theoretic macro literature on the interpretation of the Lucas critique. Perhaps the largest contribution of this literature has been to illustrate how some of the results of Lucas-type policy-evaluation exercises are more intuitively appealing than the critique's opponents might suggest. However, the fact that such outcomes are plausible does not explain why such outcomes might be likely.

The ambiguity of these results does not offer support to economists such as LeRoy, who suggest that better policy analysis can be obtained simply by better econometric modeling. The problem of too many equilibria is really a problem derived from too many plausible information sets. While it is a possibility that an econometrician might make a good choice of information set,[5] the inevitability of such a choice is far from obvious.

This continuing impasse over policy analysis has helped to motivate some recent efforts to move away from rational expectations, and towards models where agents are boundedly rational—that is, where agents are in possession of desktop computers and of the latest algorithms from the cognitive science literature. As noted in Sargent (1993, pp. 26–28), the counterintuitive nature of a Lucas-type regime-change exercise stems not so much from the inherent nature of the exercise, as from the insistence that agents' information sets—that is, the information sets I_t in the game above—be constructed in a way that is consistent with the actual evolution of events—that is, with the field of events $\mathscr{F}$. As behaviorist critics of neoclassical economics have long complained, this is a higher degree of rationality than (most) economists are willing to ascribe to themselves.

Relaxation of rational expectations by use of models of bounded rationality evidently constitutes a quick way out of the paradox posed by a Lucas-type regime shift. However, there are at least two requirements that bounded-rationality models will likely have to meet before they are to be accepted by the profession as vehicles for policy analysis. The first requirement is that the new models will be able to deliver some specific, falsifiable predictions, particularly in cases where models constrained by rational expectations have failed to do so. The second requirement is the less rigorous but ultimately more important requirement that the boundedly rational agents be "rational enough." The concern over sufficient rationality can be illustrated by an anecdote from Sargent (1993, pp. 156–157). Sargent relates the performance of a boundedly rational computer program, designed by three distinguished researchers, playing against real participants in simulated double oral auctions. Over long periods of time the computer program was roundly outperformed by a simple trading strategy devised by a graduate student.

Such stories are not damning evidence against this new class for models, but at a minimum they point to the need for further refinement.

Conclusion

In the face of the theoretical ambiguity outlined above, how should policy analysis proceed? LeRoy (fifth section) suggests that correct approach is to just ignore the Lucas critique, as long as one's econometric model is capable of capturing some low-probability, low-frequency shifts in the nature of the stochastic processes that the being modeled. He argues that distinction between policy regimes and policy variables is an artificial one.

My conjecture is that LeRoy's prescription is for now probably the correct one for many of the marginal, short-term problems of policy analysis that are routinely faced by many macroeconomists and particularly for the large segment of the profession who work for governmental agencies. Economists in these positions are often called upon to construct multiple what-if scenarios on short notice. If the policy changes under consideration are marginal and the planning horizons are short-term, then there is no reason to expect that Lucas-type policy analyses with structural models would give more accurate answers.

However, many economists continue to see the old-fashioned, purely econometric approach to policy analysis as insufficient for predicting the longer-term consequences of major changes in policy. In such cases, the absolute accuracy of econometric projection is not so much the issue as an ability to interpret and defend the results. Along this dimension a Lucas-type policy analysis is likely to be at an advantage, any logical inconsistencies notwithstanding, over a more empirical approach.

My impression is that this ugly but pragmatic viewpoint is shared by the majority of economists trained since 1976, across the ideological spectrum. Despite LeRoy's contention that macroeconomists have rejected the policy analysis of the new classical macroeconomics, one sees more and more of the Lucas-type analysis in applied settings. For example, ten years ago policy discussions at Federal Reserve System meetings usually consisted of arguments over money-demand regressions, but now the same discussions often center on Lucas-type interventions in applied general equilibrium models. This trend is likely to continue given the diminishing costs of calculating and estimating rational expectations equilibria.

Certainly LeRoy and the other critics of the Lucas critique have advanced our profession's understanding of the critique and have done the profession a service by pointing out some of the unappealing features of Lucas's approach to policy analysis. In the view of a growing subset of the profession, however, these problems are not so great as to outweigh the insights gained by Lucas's approach. Until a new, more widely accepted paradigm emerges, however, little is to be gained by calls for a repeal of the critique. Given the current state of economic knowledge, the evidence points to 1976 as the date of a true regime change.

Acknowledgments

Thanks are due to Jerry Dwyer, Eric Leeper, and Chuck Whiteman for comments on earlier drafts, with the usual disclaimer. I am especially grateful to Mike Stutzer for making me aware of Witsenhausen's work. The opinions expressed are my own and not those of the Federal Reserve Bank of Atlanta or the Federal Reserve System.

Notes

1. It is unfortunate that Witsenhausen's concept shares the name *causality* with the econometric idea of *causality*. The two concepts are related but distinct.

2. For the purposes of the discussion below, it is not critical that the policy maker seeks to maximize any objective. The use of a representative agent for the private sector, though customary in the literature, glosses over some important issues. See Chari, Kehoe, and Prescott (1989) for a discussion.

3. As shown in Witsenhausen (1971), the applicability of the causality condition is quite general and is not restricted to such simple examples. Above I consider the simplest possible case due to space limitations.

4. Witsenhausen's (1971) Theorem 2 shows that if there are more that two players (or stages) in a game, solvability and measurability of a given solution of an information structure does not imply that the structure satisfies causality.

5. On this possibility see Sims (1988).

References

Barro, Robert J., and David B. Gordon. (1983). "Rules, Discretion and Reputation in a Model of Monetary Policy." *Journal of Monetary Economics* 12 (July), 101–121.

Chari, V.V., Patrick J. Kehoe, and Edward C. Prescott. (1989). "Time Consistency and Policy." In Robert J. Barro (ed.), *Modern Business Cycle Theory*. Cambridge, MA.: Harvard University Press.

Kydland, Finn E., and Edward C. Prescott. (1977). "Rules Rather Than Discretion: The Inconsistency of Optimal Plans." *Journal of Political Economy* 85 (June), 473–491.

Leroy, Stephen F. (1994). "On Policy Regimes." Chapter 7 in this volume.

Rogoff, Kenneth. (1987). "Reputational Constraints on Monetary Policy." In Karl Brunner and Allan H. Meltzer. (eds.), *Carnegie-Rochester Conference Series on Public Policy*, Vol. 26, *Bubbles and Other Essays*. Amsterdam: North-Holland.

Sargent, Thomas J. (1987). *Macroeconomic Theory*. New York: Academic Press.

Sargent, Thomas J. (1993). *Bounded Rationality in Macroeconomics*. Oxford: Oxford University Press.

Sims, Christopher A. (1988). "Projecting Policy Effects with Statistical Models." *Revista de Análisis Económico* 3 (November), 3–19.

Witsenhausen, H.S. (1971). "On Information Structures, Feedback, and Causality." *SIAM Journal on Control* 9 (May), 149–160.

8 THE LUCAS CRITIQUE IN PRACTICE

Theory Without Measurement

Neil R. Ericsson
John S. Irons

Introduction

Lucas (1976, p. 41) proposes an explanation for why coefficients in econometric equations might be nonconstant when policy rules change: "[G]iven that the structure of an econometric model consists of optimal decision rules of economic agents, and that optimal decision rules vary systematically with changes in the structure of series relevant to the decision maker, it follows that any change in policy will systematically alter the structure of econometric models." Lucas's critique of econometric models focuses on how parameters in policy rules may enter parametrically into economic agents' optimization rules. Lucas (1976) considers examples where agents' *expectations* of policy behavior enter into their optimization problem, and so parameters relating to policymakers' rules appear in the agents' first-order conditions. In essence, the issue is whether an econometric model isolates "invariants" of the economic process. Such invariance or autonomy is a topic with a lengthy and contentious history in the econometrics literature: see Haavelmo (1944) and Frisch (1948) for early discussions and Aldrich (1989) for an extensive historical perspective.

Lucas (1976, pp. 22–24) motivates his critique with four observations: "frequent and frequently important refitting of econometric relationships," intercept adjustments in forecasting, the empirically superior forecasts by models with randomly varying coefficients, and the exclusion (in modeling) of data prior to 1947, even though such data should be informative. All four observations could arise from empirical model misspecification of the sort described by Lucas.

While Lucas's (1976) paper has strongly influenced the course of the economics profession for nearly two decades, surprisingly little evidence exists to support the empirical applicability of the Lucas critique. As Fischer (1983, p. 271) noted: "It is indeed remarkable that the Lucas policy evaluation critique has triumphed without any detailed empirical support beyond Lucas's accusation that macroeconometric models in the 1960s all predicted too little inflation for the 1970s. The general [theoretical] point made by the critique is correct and was known before it was so eloquently and forcefully propounded by Lucas. That the point has been important empirically, however, is something that should have been demonstrated rather than asserted." By constructing a database of articles citing Lucas (1976), the current paper quantitatively documents the paucity of empirical evidence in favor of the Lucas critique. Further, using tests of super exogeneity, a growing literature empirically refutes the Lucas critique for the determination of specific macro-economic variables.

The following section defines the Lucas critique and discusses what constitutes evidence for and against it. The third section describes the methodology for constructing the database of articles citing Lucas (1976) and the strengths and shortcomings of that methodology. The fourth and fifth sections present the empirical evidence for and against the Lucas critique. The final section concludes.

Defining and Testing the Lucas Critique

This section considers the general economic structure postulated by Lucas, which a simple expectations model illustrates. The Lucas critique is empirically refutable as well as confirmable, this section also examines tests of the Lucas critique and then considers what constitutes empirical evidence for and against the Lucas critique.

The Lucas Critique Confirmed

Following Lucas, consider an economy characterized by an agent decision rule $F(\cdot)$ derived from optimizing behavior and a policy reaction function $G(\cdot)$:

$$y_{t+1} = F(y_t, x_t, \theta, \varepsilon_t), \tag{8.1}$$

$$x_t = G(y_t, x_{t-1}, \lambda, \eta_t), \tag{8.2}$$

where y_t is the endogenous variable at time t, x_t is the "exogenous" (policy or forcing) variable at time t, θ and λ are the parameters of $F(\cdot)$ and $G(\cdot)$, and ε_t and η_t are the corresponding independent, identically distributed shocks. For instance, y_t and x_t might be consumer expenditure and a government-supplied income supplement, $F(\cdot)$ and $G(\cdot)$ the empirical consumption function and the rule for providing supplements, and θ and λ the respective parameters. Through agent optimization, θ might depend on λ, in which case changes in the latter would alter the value of the former. Econometric models treating θ as a fixed parameter would then "break down" when policy changed λ, leading to (for example) Lucas's four confirmatory observations above. A "policy" is seen as "a specification of present and future values of some components of $\{x_t\}$" (Lucas, 1976, p. 21), so policy can be interpreted quite broadly to include tax law, a meteor striking the earth, and the oil prices set by OPEC *inter alia*. This broad interpretation of policy is central to the empirical analysis of super exogeneity in the fifth section below.

Lucas has models with forward-looking expectations explicitly in mind, and the following example illustrates how such expectations create difficulty for conditional econometric models. Suppose (8.1) and (8.2) are

$$y_{t+1} = \gamma \mathscr{E}(x_{t+1} \mid I_t) + \varepsilon_t, \tag{8.3}$$

$$x_t = \lambda x_{t-1} + \eta_t, \tag{8.4}$$

where γ is a "deep structural parameter" related to utility optimization, $\mathscr{E}(\cdot)$ is the expectations operator, and I_t is the information available to the agents at time t (when they decide on y_{t+1}). For $I_t = x_t$, then $\mathscr{E}(x_{t+1} \mid I_t) = \lambda x_t$ from (8.4), so (8.3) becomes

$$y_{t+1} = \theta x_t + \varepsilon_t, \tag{8.5}$$

where $\theta = \theta(\lambda) = \gamma \lambda$. If the econometrician estimates θ via (8.5), ignoring the dependence of θ on λ, then policy simulations based on (8.5) for alternative paths of $\{x_t\}$ (and so for alternative values of λ) will give misleading results. The estimated value of θ, which is used in simulation of (8.5), need not be the value implied by the agents' rule (8.3).

The Lucas Critique Refuted

Whether the Lucas critique applies for a specific economic relationship is thus an empirical issue. Specifically, two related properties of θ are of concern: its constancy (or lack thereof) as λ changes and its invariance to (or dependence on) λ.[1] As suggested by Gordon (1976, pp. 48–49) and Neftçi and Sargent (1978) and developed by Hendry (1988), Favero and Hendry (1992), and Engle and Hendry (1993), these properties provide two approaches to testing the Lucas critique:

- *Test 1:* Test for the constancy of θ in (8.1) and of λ in (8.2). If θ is constant but λ is not, θ is invariant to λ and so the Lucas critique could not apply. The Lucas critique could generate the three other combinations of constancy and nonconstancy for θ and λ, but those combinations also could arise from other sorts of misspecification.
- *Test 2:* Develop (8.2) until it is empirically constant. For instance, by adding dummies or other variables, model the way in which λ varies over time. Then test for the significance of those dummies or other variables in (8.1). Their insignificance in (8.1) demonstrates the invariance of θ to λ, whereas their significance shows the dependence of θ on λ.

The invariance of θ to λ implies the super exogeneity of x_t, provided that the parameters of interest to the investigator can be retrieved from θ alone.[2] The empirical presence of super exogeneity refutes the Lucas critique in practice. Under super exogeneity, models like (8.3)—(8.4) could not explain why θ remained constant while λ changed, and so could not be an adequate explanation of the data. Put somewhat differently, the Lucas critique as a *possibility theorem* is not empirically refutable; but through that theorem, its assumptions have testable implications. Empirical refutation of those implications invalidates the applicability of the Lucas critique in practice.

While tests for super exogeneity have been developed only relatively recently, several papers have found super exogeneity empirically. Hendry (1988), Hendry and Ericsson (1991a, 1991b), Favero and Hendry (1992), Baba, Hendry, and Starr (1992), and Engle and Hendry (1993) provide evidence of super exogeneity for U.S. and U.K. money demand functions. Brodin and Nymoen (1992) and the papers in Ericsson (1992a) *inter alia* demonstrate super exogeneity in a range of macroeconomic relations across developed and developing countries; see also Ericsson and Irons (1994). The fifth section below systematically discusses the empirical evidence on super exogeneity.

The Interpretation of Empirical Evidence

Several remarks are in order concerning tests of the Lucas critique. Specifically, clarification of what does and does not constitute empirical evidence on the Lucas critique is critical, since many of the articles in the literature survey below present evidence that is uninformative on the empirical applicability of the Lucas critique.

First, the empirical observations motivating Lucas's critique could arise from more mundane causes, such as dynamic misspecification, omitted variables, and incorrect functional form. Because those causes cannot be precluded *a priori*, nonconstancy of conditional models and vector autoregressions is uninformative about the Lucas critique. Such nonconstancy *could* arise from the Lucas critique applying.

Equally, nonconstancy could arise from, for example, an omitted variable bias, where that bias depended on a correlation with a policy variable and so would change when the associated policy rule changed.

Second, estimation of an expectations-based model is not evidence in itself for or against the Lucas critique, even if the implied cross-equation restrictions hold. The parameterization of a conditional-marginal representation could be such that those restrictions hold as well.

Third, and relatedly, modeling of expectations does not necessarily resolve the Lucas critique, even when the Lucas critique applies. If expectations are improperly modeled, policy analysis with the corresponding misspecification of (8.1) and (8.2) may well result in inaccurate and biased simulations. McCallum (1989, p. 230), a strong proponent of rational expectations models, emphasizes this point: "[U]sing models based on explicit optimization analysis of individual agents' choices . . . can provide no guarantee of success; explicit optimization analysis will not help if the agent's objective function or constraints are misspecified. The true message of the Lucas critique is simply that the analyst must be as careful as possible to avoid the use of equations that will tend, for plausible reasons, to shift with policy changes." To establish the empirical applicability of the Lucas critique, a researcher would require demonstrating that alternative explanations for the failure of a conditional model did not apply. Equally, the proposed expectations-based model would need to explain the data adequately—that is, be empirically congruent in the sense of Hendry and Richard (1982). For system-based expectational models, empirical congruence is required for (8.2) as well as (8.1): in particular, the changes in policy regime must be modeled. This contrasts with much of the empirical literature on rational expectations, where models are estimated assuming that λ is constant even though the Lucas critique assumes that λ is not.

Fourth, Sims's (1987) modification of Lucas's framework does not appear empirically relevant for a wide range of relationships examined through the literature searches in the third through fifth sections of this chapter or for the empirical example in the fifth section. Noting a potential logical inconsistency in Lucas's framework, Sims proposes allowing λ to be time-varying, with its distribution depending upon some fixed metaparameter. That implies that x_t and y_t are ergodic, coming from a distribution with constant parameters. Such a model is at odds with the observed nonconstancy of many empirical equations; see Judd and Scadding (1982) on money demand alone. Also, the potential logical inconsistency may vanish in the presence of information costs, as implied by Cochrane's (1989) analysis and the fifth section below.

Fifth, if the Lucas critique is empirically refuted by tests 1 or 2 above, the refutation is generic in the sense that a whole class of expectations-based models is inconsistent with the data evidence. This class includes typical rational expectations models and also a wide variety of expectations-based models where the information available to agents is limited or incomplete. Conceptually, generic rather than specific refutation is feasible because the null hypothesis associated with tests 1 and 2 excludes expectational models. If expectational models belonged to the null hypothesis and the null was rejected, only specific refutation could occur: other expectational models might belong to the alternative hypothesis. Hendry (1988), Ericsson and Hendry (1989), and Favero and Hendry (1992) provide further theoretical discussion, and the fifth section illustrates generic refutation with an empirically constant model of money demand.

Sixth, empirical refutation of the Lucas critique is specific to the economic relation and the class of changes in λ being considered. For instance, θ may be invariant to a temporary income supplement but not to a permanent one; the cause and magnitude of the supplement may affect invariance; and invariance may apply in one country but not another. For tests 1 and 2, the changes of λ occurring in sample may or may not belong to the same class of changes as do the policy simulations of interest to the economist. Resolution of this issue rests in part on determining the nature of the changes to λ in sample, which often entails a more detailed modeling of the policy reaction rule (8.2).

Seventh, and surprisingly, test 1 does not require a full specification of the policy reaction function (8.2) to refute the Lucas critique empirically. Details appear in Hendry (1988).

Eighth, super exogeneity can identify θ by establishing its uniqueness through its invariance with respect to λ. This parallels the classical identification of parameters in a demand function when the demand curve remains fixed in the presence of a shifting supply curve.

Finally, every test of the Lucas critique is subject to the usual caveat of having Type I and Type II errors for the associated hypotheses. Cuthbertson (1991) notes this caveat for test 1, but it applies equally to test 2 and to tests used to confirm the Lucas critique.

In summary, the Lucas critique provides one of several possible explanations for the less-than-satisfactory performance over the last two decades of many macroeconometric models. If the Lucas critique applies, it has ramifications for policy simulations with such models. If economic agents base their decisions on forward-looking expectations and empirical models fail to account for that, then those models will mispredict when policies change and so will generate misleading policy simulations. The Lucas critique is empirically testable, being both confirmable and refutable.

Methodology and the Data

To assess the empirical importance of the Lucas critique, we searched the Social Science Citation Index (SSCI) for articles citing Lucas (1976) and examined the empirical evidence in those articles. This section summarizes how the literature on the Lucas critique was assembled and what the shortcomings of that assemblage are.

The Literature Defined

This subsection discusses the construction of a database on the literature about the Lucas critique. The interest is in obtaining as complete a list as possible of articles discussing the Lucas critique and in categorizing that literature according to various characteristics. The Social Science Citation Index (SSCI) allows searches for occurrences of a particular article as a reference in another article. So, we searched the SSCI for all articles published during 1976–1990 that included Lucas (1976) in their list of references.[3] The resulting citations were obtained in a computer-readable form and formatted as a database in Borland's (1992) *Paradox for Windows*. For each citing article, the initial database included the author, date of publication, title, journal, journal volume and number, and page numbers.

In total, 590 articles cite Lucas (1976). We were able to obtain copies of over 96 percent of those articles. Of those obtained, fifty-six are treated as "bad cites" because they do not cite Lucas (1976) in the text of the article, do not cite Lucas (1976) in the bibliography, are not in English, or are not journal articles. Table 8.1 details the breakdown. This filtering results in 513 articles available with "good cites" to Lucas (1976).

The articles were read and analyzed, and additional information about the articles was added to the database, as described in Table 8.2. A complete listing of the information on the articles appears in Ericsson and Irons (1995b, app.). Briefly, the articles were categorized according to the nature of the article, the context of the article's citation to Lucas (1976), the author's view on whether or not the article's evidence confirmed the Lucas critique, and the sorts of evidence presented on the Lucas cirtique. These categorizations require some additional explanation:

1. The nature of an article is either theoretical, empirical, mixed (both theoretical and empirical), or "other" (book review, survey, or interview). Many articles develop a theory model and illustrate it with an empirical application. Depending on the originality of the theory and the substantiveness of the empirical application, such an article could be considered theoretical, mixed, or empirical.
2. The context of the cite to Lucas (1976) is either tangential, postulated, or substantial. Numerous articles mention the Lucas critique only in passing and are thus considered "tangential." In these articles, Lucas (1976) typically is referenced only in a footnote, in a sentence about previous work

Table 8.1.   Availability, status, and nature of the articles from the SSCI search on Lucas (1976)

Articles available:	
Good cites:	
Empirical	143
Mixed	147
Theoretical	135
Other	88
Subtotal	513
Bad cites:	
Lucas (1976) not cited in the text	24
Lucas (1976) not listed in the bibliography	8
Article not in English	19
Book	5
Subtotal	56
Subtotal	569
Articles not available	21
All articles in the SSCI search	590

in the field, or as a reference for a topic not examined in the paper. In these papers, the Lucas critique does not enter into the discussion substantively, and little is learned about the empirical relevance of the Lucas critique.

Articles categorized as "postulated" typically discuss the Lucas critique in the context of the topic at hand (or of a closely related issue), but they fail to examine the critique itself or its implications in the current context. They recognize the potential importance of the critique as it relates to the topic but do little more than mention that fact. The postulated category also includes articles that motivate their approach by citing the Lucas critique but that never directly deal with the critique. Many articles cite the Lucas critique to justify estimating a rational expectations model but do not compare that model's performance with other sorts of models. Hansen and Sargent (1980) is an example in the "postulated" category.

Articles with "substantial" cites to the Lucas critique not only raise the issue of the Lucas critique but attempt to assess its implications or validity in the context of the paper. Typically, two or three citations of Lucas (1976) are sufficient to categorize a paper as postulated or substantial rather than as tangential.

Table 8.2.   Information compiled on articles citing Lucas (1976)

Information from the SSCI

Author(s) of the article
Date of publication
Title of the article
Journal
Journal volume and number
Page numbers of the article

Information added to the above for "good" articles

1. Nature of the article	Theoretical, empirical, mixed (both theoretical and empirical), other (book review, survey, interview)
2. Context of the citation of Lucas (1976)	Tangential, postulated, substantial
3. Author's view on whether or not the article's evidence confirms the Lucas critique	Yes, no, maybe, assumed, warning, not applicable
4. The type of the model(s) estimated	Conditional, expectational, both
5. Is the estimated model empirically constant?	Yes, no, maybe, not applicable or no test calculated
6. Are the rational expectations cross-equation restrictions statistically acceptable?	Yes, no, maybe, not applicable or no test calculated
7. Are residual-based tests statistically acceptable?	Yes, no, maybe, not applicable or no test calculated

3. The author's views on the applicability of the Lucas critique are categorized as yes, maybe, no, assumed, warning, or not applicable ("NA"). We have tried to preserve the author's own views, as presented in the paper, regardless of the validity or type of test employed. If the author believes that the Lucas critique is empirically relevant, given the evidence presented (whatever that evidence might be), then the article is categorized as "yes." The "yes" and "assumed" categories are sometimes only subtly different. If the author presents any type of evidence, including past cites, the paper is categorized as "yes." If no evidence is presented, yet it is clear that the author thinks the critique is relevant, the paper is classified as "assumed." Some authors take no view on the applicability of the Lucas critique ("NA") or merely cite Lucas (1976) as a "warning" to modelers.

4. The type of the estimated model is either conditional (as in (8.5)) or expectational (as in (8.3)). In some instances, both types of models are estimated.

5–7. The next three categorizations concern the sorts of empirical evidence presented on the Lucas critique and the results obtained. Evidence includes tests of parameter constancy, cross-equation restrictions for rational expectations models, and the residuals' properties. Results are classified as "yes," "maybe," "no," and "not applicable," the last including situations where no test is calculated.

With the augmented database, tabulation by one or more types of classification can shed light on the empirical evidence on the Lucas critique.[4] Before doing so in the fourth section, various shortcomings of the methodology and the data are examined.

Shortcomings of the Methodology and Data

The methodology for gathering and constructing the data is closely related to the data themselves, so shortcomings of the methodology and of the data are considered together. Shortcomings include possible sample selection bias in the SSCI search and in our use of the SSCI search, and fuzziness in categorization.

The SSCI search itself entails sample selection of several sorts. First, the issue of the Lucas critique may appear in an article without Lucas ever being mentioned. Because the Lucas critique was widely discussed well prior to Lucas's own formulation (as in Haavelmo, 1944), relevant articles prior to 1976 are excluded. Second, the Lucas critique may be mentioned explicitly in the text, but Lucas (1976) may not appear in the references. In many circles, "Lucas critique" is a household word, and citation to the paper itself may be missing. Third, the SSCI excludes some publications citing Lucas (1976), such as books and articles appearing in books.

For the first two sources of sample selection, the sins of omission are no doubt great although the direction of bias is unclear. Correcting for those omissions is simply beyond the scope of this paper and the current technology for citation searches. The third source is considered immediately below in conjunction with sample selection in our use of the SSCI.

As implied by Table 8.1, our use of the SSCI entails additional sample selection, which may bias our findings. Most but not all of the articles from the SSCI search were obtained: 569 out of 590. The twenty-one articles "not available" either were not in the libraries accessible to us or were not available in a reasonable amount of time. However, all articles citing Lucas (1976) and appearing in the 130 most cited economic journals are "available."[5] The articles "not available" are in journals very infrequently cited by the economics profession, such as *Potato Research* and *Transportation Research Part B (Methodological)*. Fifty-six of the available articles are "bad" because, for example, they list Lucas (1976) in their references but do not cite Lucas in the body of the paper. The remaining 513 articles are considered "good." Tables 8A.1, 8A.2, and 8A.3 (in the Appendix) respectively list the numbers of good, bad, and unavailable articles by journal. In short, the percentage of articles available is very high, and the articles obtained reflect the core of published economic research.

Categorization is an issue with some articles. In particular, both the nature of the article and the context of the cite to Lucas (1976) can be difficult to decide— for example, as in classifying an article as tangential or postulated. Some fuzziness may exist at the edges of the associated types, but overall this does not appear to be a substantial problem.

Empirical Evidence in Favor of the Lucas Critique

This section summarizes the statistical characteristics of the citation database and examines it for empirical evidence in favor of the Lucas critique. Surprisingly little evidence exists that substantiates the Lucas critique in practice, so this section also considers reasons for that lack of evidence.

The Evidence

The citation database allows sorting of articles according to a given characteristic or characteristics. By eliminating articles that are empirically uninformative on the Lucas critique, the articles remaining provide the essence of evidence on the Lucas critique. That evidence is weak at best and nonexistent at worst.

To start, consider some basic time-series properties of the citations. Figure 8.1 plots the total number of SSCI citations by year, broken down into the categories good, bad, and not available. The growth of new citations is dramatic in the late 1970s, with the frequency of citation remaining relatively constant throughout the 1980s. Figures 8.2, 8.3, and 8.4 decompose the good cites by the nature of the article, the context of the citation, and the view of the author respectively. While citations are dominated by empirically oriented papers, remarkably few are "substantial." Lucas (1976) is often cited without any view towards the empirical relevance of the Lucas critique ("NA" in Figure 8.4), with smaller numbers of cites confirming the Lucas critique. Only six articles prior to 1980 simply assumed that the Lucas critique applied in practice, whereas in the mid-1980s more articles assumed it than provided evidence in its favor.

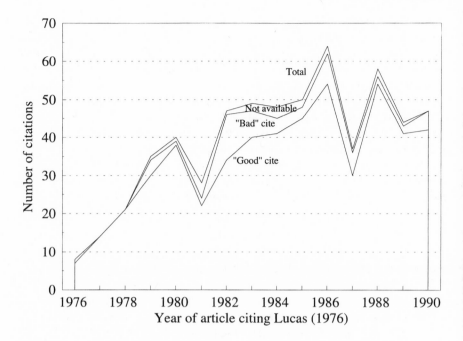

Figure 8.1. Yearly number of citations to Lucas (1976), by availability

Table 8.3 tabulates the joint distribution of cites across the nature of the article, the context of the cite, and the view of the author. While this ignores the time structure in Figures 8.2 through 8.4, Table 8.3 provides the basis for winnowing the citations. Of the 513 good citations, 327 are tangential and 98 are postulated. Of the remaining eighty-eight substantial citations, twenty-nine are purely theoretical and five are surveys or the like, leaving fifty-four empirical or mixed articles that cite Lucas (1976) in a substantive context. Of those, only forty-three find any evidence for the Lucas critique: less than 10 percent of the total citations.

Table 8.4 lists the types of empirical evidence on the Lucas critique provided by those forty-three citations. Each category of evidence and its informativeness on the Lucas critique is now considered.

Eighteen articles show the nonconstancy of a conditional model and five that of a vector autoregression (VAR) or reduced form. As such, this evidence on nonconstancy is uninformative about the empirical validity of the Lucas critique. For instance, a vector autoregression may be nonconstant even while a factorization of the associated joint density of the data may have a constant-parameter conditional equation. The VAR of x_t and y_t from (8.4) and (8.5) could be nonconstant due to changes in λ even if θ is constant and is invariant to λ. Likewise, the

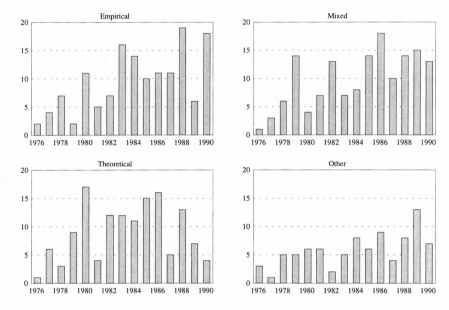

Figure 8.2.   Yearly number of citations to Lucas (1976), by nature of the article

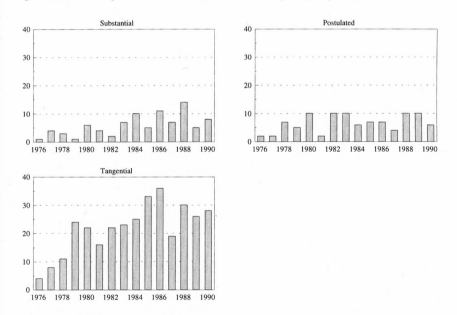

Figure 8.3.   Yearly number of citations to Lucas (1976), by context of the citation

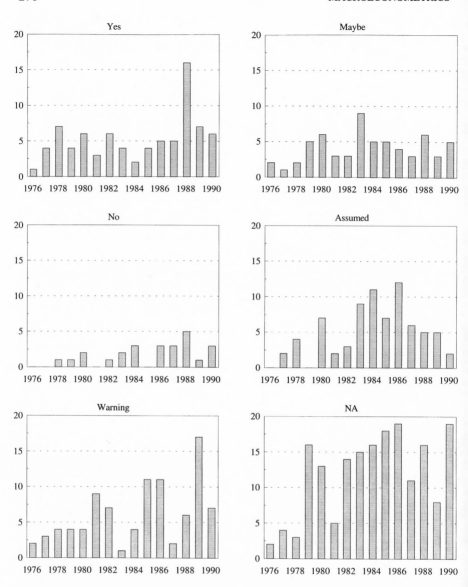

Figure 8.4. Yearly number of citations to Lucas (1976), by view of the author on the empirical validity of the Lucas critique

Table 8.3. Author's view on the empirical applicability of the Lucas critique: By nature of the article and context of the cite

Context of the cite Author's view	Nature of the article				Total
	Empirical	Mixed	Theoretical	Other	
Substantial:					
Yes	19	10	13		42
Maybe	9	5	5		19
No	4	6		1	11
Assumed			8	1	9
Warning		1		1	2
NA			3	2	5
Subtotal	32	22	29	5	88
Postulated:					
Yes	3	8	7	2	20
Maybe	5	4	2	6	17
No	1	1		1	3
Assumed	7	17	12	4	40
Warning	4	2		2	8
NA	2		1	7	10
Subtotal	22	32	22	22	98
Tangential:					
Yes	7	10	1		18
Maybe	8	7	6	5	26
No	5	5	1		11
Assumed	6	11	9		26
Warning	30	24	9	19	82
NA	33	36	58	37	164
Subtotal	89	93	84	61	327
Total	143	147	135	88	513

nonconstancy of a particular conditional model does not preclude some other conditional model from being constant. In the previous example, a regression of y_t on x_{t-2} would obtain a nonconstant, noninvariant coefficient on x_{t-2} (due to dynamic misspecification) even though (8.5) is constant. Simply put, the observed nonconstancy may arise from misspecification other than one involving expectations. Two additional articles show nonconstancy of estimated expectational models, which is certainly not evidence for the Lucas critique.

Two articles find noninvariance of a reduced form or VAR. For the same reasons as with nonconstancy, this evidence is uninformative about the Lucas critique.

Table 8.4. Empirical evidence presented for the Lucas critique: By nature of the article and type of evidence

	Nature of the article				
	Empirical		*Mixed*		
Evidence	*Yes*	*Maybe*	*Yes*	*Maybe*	*Total*
Nonconstancy:					
Conditional model	8	3	4	3	18
Reduced form or VAR	1	2	1	1	5
Rational expectations model		1	1		2
Noninvariance:					
Conditional model					0
Reduced form or VAR	2				2
Rational expectations model					0
Prediction or simulation		1		1	2
Survey data	5	1	1		7
Cross-equation restrictions	2	1	2		5
Constant rational expectations model and nonconstant alternative model	1		1		2
Total	19	9	10	5	43

Note: Articles included above make a substantial cite to Lucas (1976), are either empirical or mixed, and have an author's view of yes or maybe.

Two articles compare prediction or simulation properties of conditional and expectations-based models, concluding that the latter are favored in terms of measures such as mean square forecast error. While this evidence is against the *particular* conditional models examined, it in no way validates the expectations-based models. In any comparison of forecasts, all the models examined might be misspecified and yet one would have the smallest mean square forecast error. Additionally, if strong exogeneity is invalidly assumed, the models' ranking from multistep ahead forecast criteria could be affected, even if the equation of interest is correctly specified in one of the models (see Hendry and Richard, 1982). Finally, by constructing forecast-encompassing tests, the forecasts themselves could be informative about misspecification. See Chong and Hendry (1986), who develop the first such tests, and Ericsson (1992b), who clarifies the information content of mean square forecast errors.

Seven articles use survey data, either to proxy expectations in determining agent behavior or to be modeled itself. Characterizing articles in the first category,

Peek and Wilcox (1987) construct an empirically constant model for the determination of U.S. interest rates over 1952–1984. Their model contains expected prices, which are calculated from the Livingston survey data on inflation expectations, and allows for the effects of changing monetary regimes. While constancy of the model using the expectations data is of economic interest, it does not confirm or disprove the Lucas critique. Rather, its constancy shows the econometric value of the survey data. The measured expectations could be adaptive rather than forward looking or could be derived from a data-based (rather than model-based) predictor. Articles modeling the survey data itself provide no information on the Lucas critique, since *inter alia* the importance of the measured expectations in agents' decisions is not shown.

Five articles corroborate the Lucas critique by finding statistically acceptable cross-equation restrictions in expectational models. As noted in the second section above, those restrictions could be satisfied by a conditional-marginal representation as well.

Each of the final two articles finds an empirically constant expectations model and (on the same data) an empirically nonconstant alternative model. This evidence on the Lucas critique appears more fruitful, so these articles are considered in greater detail.

One of the articles (McNelis and Neftçi, 1982) examines two output supply models for the United States over 1954–1978, one being a conditional equation subsequently published in Fair (1984, p. 132) and the other being Sargent's (1976) "supply-side alternative" involving expectations in prices. The models are estimated with the Kalman filter, allowing for time-varying coefficients, similar to the recursive estimation procedure employed in the fifth section. The estimated parameters of Sargent's equation appear "somewhat more stable over time" (p. 305) than those in Fair's equation. While suggestive, these results can only be taken as tentative. First, *both* models show some apparent nonconstancy, although no formal tests of constancy are calculated, partly from the (then) scarcity of good econometric techniques for doing so. Much better tests are now available (see Hoffman and Pagan, 1989; Ghysels and Hall, 1990; Hansen, 1992; Dufour and Ghysels, 1996). Second, the coefficient on unanticipated price changes in Sargent's model is statistically insignificant for virtually all subsamples and becomes (barely) significant at the 95 percent level at the very end of the sample. The unanticipated price change is the only expectational variable in Sargent's model, so the role of expectations in obtaining constancy in Sargent's model is questionable. Finally, Sargent's model would need to be subjected to the standard battery of diagnostic tests over an extended dataset to establish its empirical viability.

The other article (LaHaye, 1985) accounts for expectations of currency reform in Cagan's model of money demand, using data from hyperinflationary periods in Germany, Poland, and Greece. For all three countries, Cagan's model is empirically constant if expectations of currency reform are incorporated; and for Germany and Greece, the model is nonconstant if those expectations are excluded from it. With expectations of currency reform included, LaHaye's algorithm for estimating Cagan's model in effect treats the date of reform as known (pp. 548–550). Such knowledge may or may not have been available to agents prior to the reform. In any case, a constant expectational model does not necessarily preclude a conditional model that is constant also (see Hendry, 1988; Ericsson and Hendry, 1989).

In summary, the vast majority of articles citing Lucas (1976) are not concerned with testing the Lucas critique *per se*. Those that are provide scant evidence for its empirical basis.

Understanding the Lack of Evidence

In order to understand the lack of empirical evidence for the Lucas critique, it is useful to summarize how authors have dealt with the critique. Three approaches dominate.

In the first, the Lucas critique is ignored, or claims are made that it is of little significance to the problem at hand. For example, many authors argue that, despite the theoretical complications of the Lucas critique, their policy or counterfactual simulations are valid because the policy experiments fall within the range of historical experience and thus do not constitute a regime change. Other authors warn that the results of their policy simulations are not strictly interpretable because of the Lucas critique, but then proceed to calculate and discuss these results, ignoring the Lucas critique. Still others find empirically constant conditional models and thus conclude that the Lucas critique must not be a problem, albeit without checking for changes in the marginal process or determining what those changes are.

In the second approach, the author acknowledges that the Lucas critique may apply. It is then circumvented by avoiding periods of structural change or by including dummies, or the empirical results are used for another purpose. For example, several authors interpret empirical nonconstancy in an equation as indicating that a structural shift occurred in the economic relation being modeled. Here, the Lucas critique is cited in defining a regime change, rather than for using a regime change to investigate the importance of the Lucas critique. Many papers set out to determine whether a regime shift in variable x occurred in year t without examining the effect of such a regime shift on any particular model. Quite commonly, the sample is split according to *a priori* reasoning (for example, in half) or in light of an *ex post* regime shift, and estimation results over the subsamples are then compared. The Lucas critique is used to explain why the estimated parameters may have changed. As discussed in the second section above, the Lucas critique is only *one* explanation for parameter instability: many other types of model misspecification lead to nonconstant parameters as well. Rarely is any attempt made to eliminate alternative explanations of the observed nonconstancy.

In the third approach, the Lucas critique serves to justify introducing expectational models. Lucas (1976) is cited as motivation for abandoning conditional models and explicitly modeling expectations instead, often in a rational expectations framework. Typically, the weaknesses of conditional models are never demonstrated. The empirical nonconstancy of conditional models and the presence of regime shifts in sample are often cited as evidence of the Lucas critique. However, little or no evidence is usually given that all conditional models are nonconstant, that the rational expectations model is constant, or even that the marginal or forcing variable process is actually nonconstant. The Lucas critique is assumed to be empirically valid, and the class of theoretical and empirical models is chosen to avoid the Lucas critique without regard for the data. Blinder (1988, p. 283) poignantly describes in the context of the Phillips curve the profession's "logic" for pursuing this third approach:

> Academic readers of Lucas put two and two together and jumped like lemmings to the wrong conclusion. The facts were (a) that inflation rose and (b) that the correlation between inflation and unemployment changed. The (untested) assertion was that the Lucas critique explained why (b) followed from (a): the government had adopted a more inflationary policy, which in turn had changed [the inflation dynamics].
>
> . . . Rather than seek evidence on this point, partisans of the Lucas critique became econometric nihilists. Theory, not data, was supposed to answer such questions; and theory allegedly said yes.

In a similar vein, the Lucas critique is used to argue for modifications to conditional models. For example, the Lucas critique often motivates including various dummy variables or working with stochastic coefficient models.

None of these three approaches actually provides evidence on the empirical validity of the Lucas critique, as is apparent from analysis of the citation database. However, as the following section documents, numerous examples have accrued in which super exogeneity does exist in a conditional model, in which case the Lucas critique does not apply in practice for that empirical relationship.

Empirical Evidence Against the Lucas Critique

This section examines empirical evidence against the Lucas critique by considering evidence on super exogeneity. It illustrates the procedures for testing super exogeneity with a particular empirical model, Hendry and Ericsson's (1991a, eq. (10)) U.K. money demand function. Then, it examines the evidence on super exogeneity generally, developing and analyzing a citation database for super exogeneity.

An Empirically Constant Conditional Model

The Lucas critique implies that conditional models cannot have super exogenous variables, leading to the two testable implications discussed in the second section above: the constancy of parameters in conditional models and the invariance of those parameters to changes in the marginal process. To clarify the practical application of the associated tests, this section analyzes super exogeneity in Hendry and Ericsson's (1991a) conditional model of annual U.K. money demand. This subsection shows that that model is empirically constant. The following subsections demonstrate the nonconstancy of the marginal processes, thus showing super exogeneity via test 1; extend the marginal models for test 2; calculate test 2, finding super exogeneity for the conditional model and demonstrating the high empirical power of the invariance test on misspecifications of the conditional model; and consider some implications of the conditional model and associated tests.

Using Friedman and Schwartz's (1982) annual data, Hendry and Ericsson (1991a) obtain the following conditional error correction model:

$$\widehat{\Delta(m - p)}_t = 0.45\Delta(m - p)_{t-1} - 0.10\Delta^2(m - p)_{t-2} - 0.60\Delta p_t$$
$$\quad [0.06] \qquad\qquad\quad [0.04] \qquad\qquad\quad [0.04]$$

$$+ \, 0.39\Delta p_{t-1} - 0.021\Delta rs_t - 0.062\Delta_2 rl_t$$
$$\quad [0.05] \qquad\quad [0.006] \qquad\quad [0.021]$$

$$- \, 2.55(\hat{u}_{t-1} - 0.2)\hat{u}_{t-1}^2 + 0.005 + 3.7(D_I + D_{II})_t, \qquad (8.6)$$
$$\quad [0.59] \qquad\qquad\qquad [0.002] \quad [0.6]$$

where

$$T = 93 \ [1878\text{–}1970], \ R^2 = 0.87, \ \hat{\sigma} = 1.424\%.$$

The variables are per capita nominal money M2 (M), real net national product (Z), its deflator (P), short- and long-term nominal interest rates (RS and RL), and dummies for the two world wars (D_I and D_{II}), with logs indicated by lower case. Details of the data appear in Friedman and Schwartz (1982) and Hendry and Ericsson (1991a). The residual $\hat{u}$ is the error correction $m - p - z + 0.309 + 7.00RS$, and it enters (8.6) nonlinearly. White's (1980) heteroscedasticity consistent standard errors are in brackets, Δ is the difference operator, T is the number of observations, R^2 is the squared multiple correlation coefficient, $\hat{\sigma}$ is the estimated equation standard error, and a circumflex ^ indicates least squares estimation.

Hendry and Ericsson (1991a) show that (8.6) passes a battery of diagnostic tests and that it is constant over subsamples prior to and after World War I. Recursive estimation over the entire sample was not undertaken because of the dummy $(D_I + D_{II})_t$ in (8.6). Constancy of the conditional model is central to the

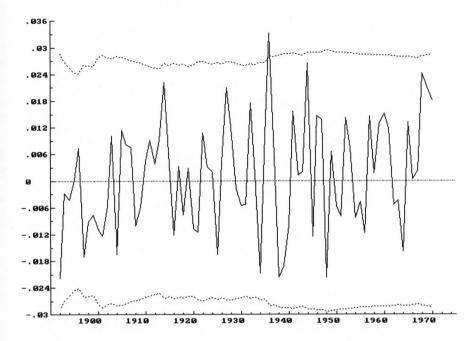

Figure 8.5. One-step residuals (—) from the money demand equation (8.6), with $0 \pm 2\hat{\sigma}_t$ ($\cdots$)

first super exogeneity test, so (8.6) is estimated recursively over the entire sample, taking the full-sample estimate of the coefficient on $(D_I + D_{II})_t$ as known.[6] Figure 8.5 plots the one-step residuals and the corresponding equation standard errors— that is, $\{y_t - \hat{\beta}'_t x_t\}$ and $\{0 \pm 2\hat{\sigma}_t\}$ in a common notation. The equation standard error $\hat{\sigma}$ varies little over time. Figure 8.6 records the "break-point" Chow (1960) statistics for the sequence $\{1893–1970, 1894–1970, \ldots, 1969–1970, 1970\}$. None of the Chow statistics are significant at their one-off 5 percent critical values. Likewise, Hansen's (1992) test against coefficient nonconstancy with an unknown break point is insignificant at the 5 percent level for each coefficient, for the equation error variance, and for the coefficients and equation error variance jointly. Figures 8.7 and 8.8 plot the recursive estimates and standard error bands for coefficients on two central variables, current inflation $[\Delta p_t]$ and the error correction term $[(\hat{u}_{t-1} - 0.2)\hat{u}^2_{t-1}]$. Both coefficients are empirically constant over time; the other coefficients in (8.6) show similar stability. The marked narrowing of the standard error bands in the 1890s and just after World War I reflects the high information content of the data during those periods. Results in the following

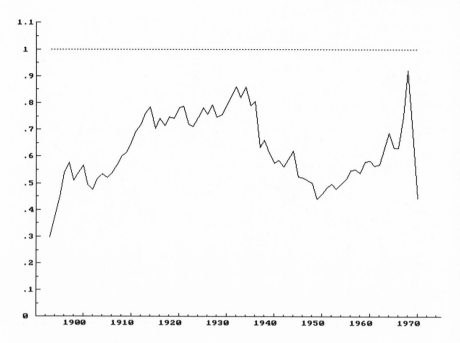

Figure 8.6.   Break-point Chow statistics (—) for the money demand equation (8.6), normalized by their one-off 5 percent critical values (· · ·)

subsections document that some of that information arises from nonconstancy in the marginal processes.

Nonconstant Marginal Models

Inflation and the two interest rates enter (8.6) contemporaneously, so the nonconstancy of their marginal processes is of interest for testing super exogeneity. Figure 8.9 plots the annual inflation rate and the long-term interest rate, while Figure 8.10 plots the two nominal interest rates. Several features of the data are striking. First, inflation deviates wildly from RL during and after World War I, albeit in opposite directions for the two subsamples. Second, the *ex post* real long rate is generally positive but does not appear constant. Third, the short- and long-term nominal interest rates tend to move together, excepting the period 1932–1952. Thus, inflation was modeled as a univariate marginal process, whereas RS and RL were modeled both as univariate processes and as a bivariate marginal process, the latter permitting cointegration between RS and RL. This subsection

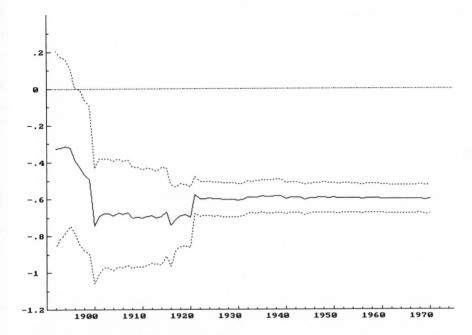

Figure 8.7. Equation (8.6): recursive estimates (—) of the coefficient of inflation Δp_t, with ± 2 estimated standard errors ($\cdots$)

presents Ericsson and Irons's (1995a) marginal process for inflation and develops the univariate marginal models for the interest rates. The next subsection develops the bivariate marginal model for the interest rates.

Starting with a fifth-order autoregressive model of p_t, Ericsson and Irons (1995a) obtain the following generalized random walk:

$$\widehat{\Delta p_t} = 0.65\Delta p_{t-1} + 0.0081, \qquad (8.7)$$
$$[0.18] \qquad\qquad [0.0036]$$

where

$$T = 93 \ [1878\text{--}1970], \ R^2 = 0.43. \ \hat{\sigma} = 4.239\%, \ Inn \ F(4, \ 87) = 1.22.$$

Inn $F(\cdot, \ \cdot)$ is the standard F statistic for testing that the reduction from the more general (fifth-order autoregressive) model is valid. Under the null hypothesis of valid reduction, *Inn* $F(\cdot, \ \cdot)$ is asymptotically distributed as an F statistic with degrees of freedom as given (albeit ignoring the presence of a unit root in p_t). The reduction to (8.7) appears statistically acceptable. Still, (8.7) is highly nonconstant.

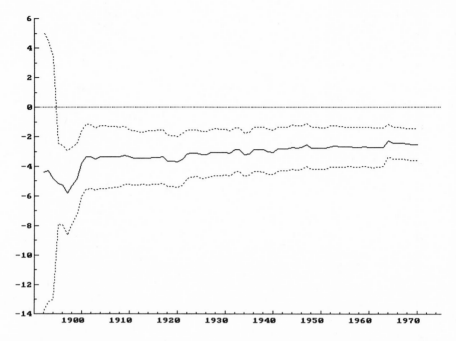

Figure 8.8.   Equation (8.6): recursive estimates (—) of the coefficient of the error correction term $(\hat{u}_{t-1} - 0.2)\,\hat{u}_{t-1}^2$, with ±2 estimated standard errors (· · ·)

Figures 8.11 and 8.12 plot the recursively estimated equation standard errors and the break-point Chow statistics.

A similar picture develops for the interest rates. Starting from univariate fifth-order autoregressive models for RS and RL, the following simple models were obtained:

$$\widehat{\Delta RS}_t = -0.37 \Delta RS_{t-2} + 0.00078, \tag{8.8}$$
$$\quad\quad\quad\quad [0.13] \quad\quad\quad [0.00091]$$

where

$$T = 93\ [1878–1970],\ R^2 = 0.14,\ \hat{\sigma} = 0.862\%,\ Inn\ F(4,\ 87) = 0.49,$$

and

$$\widehat{\Delta RL}_t = 0.45 \Delta^2 RL_{t-1} + 0.23 \Delta_2 RL_{t-3} + 0.00040 \tag{8.9}$$
$$\quad\quad\quad [0.12] \quad\quad\quad\quad [0.08] \quad\quad\quad\quad [0.00025]$$

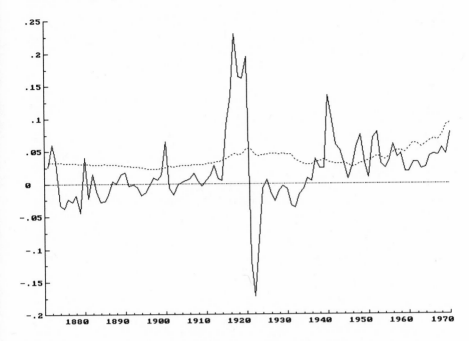

Figure 8.9.   Annual rate of inflation Δp_t (—) and the long-term interest rate RL_t ($\cdot \cdot$)

where

$$T = 93 \; [1878–1970], \; R^2 = 0.29, \; \hat{\sigma} = 0.262\%, \; Inn \; F(3, \; 87) = 0.54.$$

Figures 8.13 through 8.16 plot the recursively estimated equation standard errors
and the break-point Chow statistics for each of (8.8) and (8.9). Equation (8.8) may
be constant, but (8.9) clearly is not. For the latter, Hansen's (1992) joint instability
test is 1.92 with four degrees of freedom, rejecting at the 1 percent level. Using
test 1 from the second section above, super exogeneity of prices and interest rates
in (8.6) follows from the constancy of the conditional model (8.6) and the
nonconstancy of the marginal models (8.7) and (8.9).

Extended Marginal Models

To perform test 2 from the second section above, empirically more constant,
better-fitting marginal models are developed for Δp, RS, and RL. Equations (8.7)
through (8.9) are extended to include dummies, which proxy for shifts in λ over

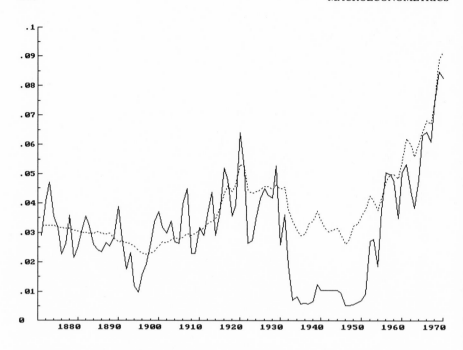

Figure 8.10. The short-term and long-term interest rates, RS_t (—) and RL_t ($\cdots$)

time and which thus are used in the next subsection to test the invariance of the coefficients in (8.6). The major shifts are of several forms, so a notation for dummy variables is convenient. I_{ab} denotes an impulse dummy for the year 19*ab* (that is, being +1 in 19*ab* and zero otherwise). S_{abcd} denotes a step dummy beginning in the year 19*ab* and ending in the year 19*cd* (that is, being +1 for 19*ab*–19*cd* and zero otherwise). Some dummies also interact with the lagged dependent variable or with a time trend (*trend*). The dummies aim to capture the inflationary and deflationary periods during and after World War I (S_{1520}, S_{2123}) and the large deviations between RS and RL for part of the interwar period and during and following World War II (S_{3351}, S_{3945}, I_{32}, I_{33}, I_{52}). Additionally, dummies are included for the remainders of the respective samples (S_{2470}, S_{5270}).

Ericsson and Irons (1995a) model inflation as the first-order autoregressive process (8.7) augmented by three dummies (S_{1520}, S_{2123}, S_{2470}), which enter directly, interactively with inflation, and interactively with the time trend. Aiming to maximize the power of the invariance test, Ericsson and Irons simplify that augmented equation to obtain the following:

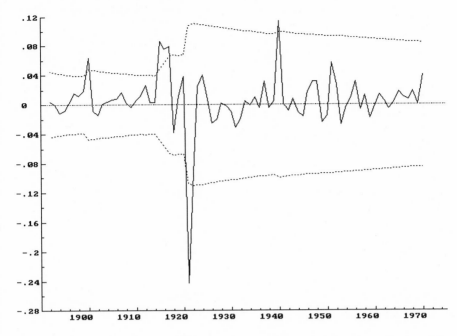

Figure 8.11. One-step residuals (—) from equation (8.7) for Δp_t, with $0 \pm 2\hat{\sigma}_t$ (· · ·)

$$\widehat{\Delta p_t} = 0.31\Delta p_{t-1} + 0.28(S_{2470} \cdot \Delta p)_{t-1} + 0.115S_{1520t} - 4.3S_{2123t}$$
$$\quad [0.11] \qquad (0.15) \qquad\qquad (0.016) \qquad (1.4)$$

$$- 0.009 + 0.00029trend_t + 0.074(S_{2123} \cdot trend)_t, \qquad (8.10)$$
$$[0.006] \quad [0.00010] \qquad (0.024)$$

where

$$T = 93 \ [1878–1970], \ R^2 = 0.83, \ \hat{\sigma} = 2.388\%, \ Inn \ F(5, 81) = 0.97.$$

OLS estimated standard errors (in parentheses) are reported for coefficients on dummy variables, since the dummies often have implausibly small estimated heteroscedasticity consistent standard errors. Equation (8.10) is more constant than (8.7) and has an estimated equation standard error $\hat{\sigma}$ virtually half that of (8.7), indicating the statistical and numerical importance of the additional variables in (8.10).

The interest rates RS and RL are modeled as a bivariate fifth-order VAR in light of their apparent cointegration in Figure 8.10. That VAR is estimated with a

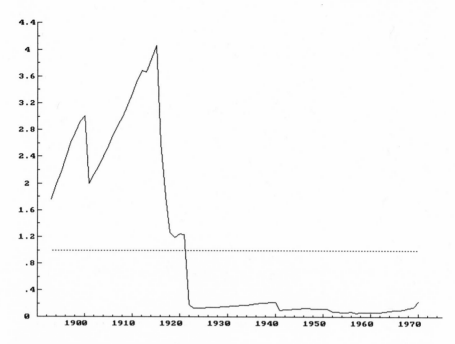

Figure 8.12.   Break-point Chow statistics (—) for equation (8.7) of Δp_t, normalized by their one-off 5 percent critical values ($\cdots$)

constant only (System A), with a constant and S_{3351} (System B), and with a constant and all dummies associated with the interest rates (that is, S_{3351}, S_{3945}, S_{5270}, $S_{5270} \cdot trend$, I_{32}, I_{33}, I_{52}) (System C). The dummies enter the systems unrestrictedly and are allowed to (but not forced to) enter the cointegrating vector, if one exists.

While System A does not appear to be cointegrated, both Systems B and C are: see Table 8.5. Inclusion of S_{3351} appears critical in capturing the temporary deviation between RS and RL around and immediately prior to and after World War II.[7] Using Johansen's (1988, 1991) and Johansen and Juselius's (1990) maximum likelihood procedure, the null hypothesis of no cointegration is rejected at the 1 percent level in favor of one cointegrating vector for Systems B and C. The estimated cointegrating vector is approximately $(1, -0.7)$, and the estimated error correction feedback coefficients in the equations for RS and RL are approximately -0.7 and -0.03, respectively. From Johansen's (1992a, 1992b) test, RL appears weakly exogenous for the cointegrating vector (that is, $-0.03 \approx 0$), whereas RS clearly is not weakly exogenous. Long-run unit homogeneity is marginally rejected in System C, although not when tested jointly with the weak exogeneity of RL.

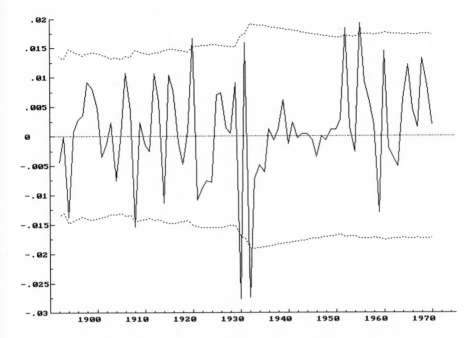

Figure 8.13. One-step residuals (—) from equation (8.8) for RS_t, with $0 \pm 2\hat{\sigma}_t$ $(\cdots)$

With these data features in mind, System C was simplified to the following pair of equations, which are estimated by maximum likelihood:

$$\widehat{\Delta RS_t} = 0.53\Delta RL_{t-1} - 1.19\Delta RL_{t-2} - 0.613(RS - RL)_{t-1} - 0.0006$$
$$\quad\;\; [0.24] \qquad\quad [0.36] \qquad\quad [0.093] \qquad\qquad\quad [0.0011]$$

$$- 0.0158 S_{3351t} + 0.0047 S_{3945t} - 0.025 I_{32t}, \qquad (8.11)$$
$$\;\;(0.0026) \qquad\;\; (0.0028) \qquad\; (0.008)$$

$$\widehat{\Delta RL_t} = 0.33\Delta RL_{t-1} - 0.48\Delta RL_{t-2} + 0.0002 - 0.018 S_{5270t}$$
$$\quad\;\; [0.11] \qquad\quad\;\; [0.15] \qquad\quad\; [0.0002] \quad (0.008)$$

$$+ 0.00022 S_{5270t} \cdot trend - 0.0088 I_{32t} + 0.0035 I_{52t}, \qquad (8.12)$$
$$\quad (0.00009) \qquad\qquad\qquad (0.0024) \qquad (0.0021)$$

where

$$T = 93 \; [1878\text{--}1970], \; \hat{\sigma}_{RS} = 0.743\%, \; \hat{\sigma}_{RL} = 0.238\%, \; \mathrm{corr}(\hat{u}_{RS}, \hat{u}_{RL}) = 0.63,$$
$$Inn \; \chi^2(22) = 30.5 \; [0.11].$$

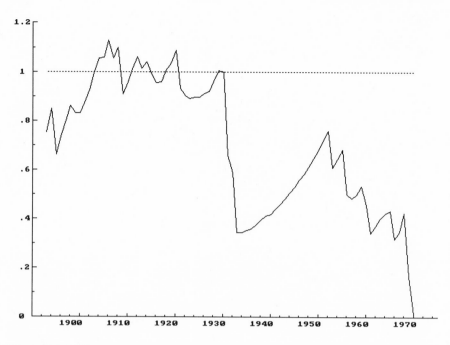

Figure 8.14.   Break-point Chow statistics (—) for equation (8.8) of RS_t, normalized by their one-off 5 percent critical values ($\cdots$)

The statistic corr($\hat{u}_{RS}$, $\hat{u}_{RL}$) is the empirical correlation between the residuals from the two equations, and Inn $\chi^2(22)$ is the likelihood ratio test statistic against the unrestricted System C. Cointegration is readily apparent from the large and highly significant feedback coefficient on $(RS - RL)_{t-1}$ in (8.11), which is statistically close to the corresponding value of -0.81 from the unrestricted VAR in System C. If the error correction term is added to (8.12), it is statistically insignificant and numerically small, in line with RL being weakly exogenous. Lagged changes in the long-term interest rate affect both short- and long-term rates, whereas lags in the short-term rate matter only through the error correction term, which appears in only (8.11). Several of the dummy variables are statistically and numerically highly significant, reflecting their importance in capturing some of the major movements in the series. While (8.11) and (8.12) are more constant and better fitting than (8.8) and (8.9), equations (8.11) and (8.12) still have some residual autocorrelation and heteroscedasticity. An even more general model of interest rates might capture those features of the data: for the present purposes, (8.11) and (8.12) suffice.[8]

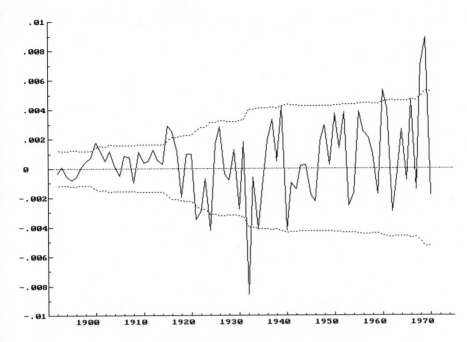

Figure 8.15.   One-step residuals (—) from equation (8.9) for RL_t, with $0 \pm 2\hat{\sigma}_t$
($\cdot \cdot \cdot$)

The Invariance Test for Super Exogeneity

Using equations (8.10) through (8.12), this subsection constructs the second type of super exogeneity test for (8.6) and provides evidence on the empirical power of that test. The column under "(8.6)" in Table 8.6 lists four variants of that test statistic for super exogeneity. The first three variants test for the significance in (8.6) of the right-hand side variables from the marginal models (8.10), (8.11), and (8.12), respectively, with redundant variables excluded from the test. The final statistic (using "all" marginal models) tests for the joint significance of all three marginal models' right-hand side variables. None of the four statistics are significant, even at the 20 percent significance level: asymptotic p-values appear in square brackets. The parameters in (8.6) appear invariant to the changes in the inflation and interest rate processes, so inflation and interest rates are super exogenous in (8.6), precluding a role for model-based expectations of those variables in U.K. money demand.

Power may be an issue for both super exogeneity tests 1 and 2, and their finite sample power can be assessed directly. Hendry and Ericsson (1991a) show that the

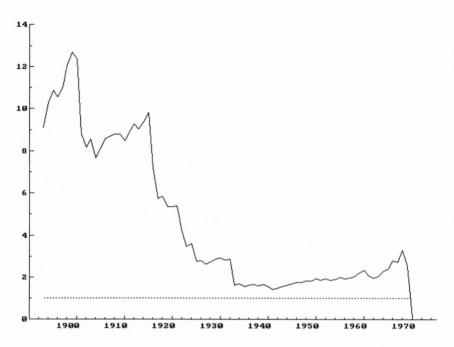

Figure 8.16.   Break-point Chow statistics (—) for equation (8.9) of RL_t, normalized by their one-off 5 percent critical values ($\cdots$)

inversion of (8.6) on inflation is nonconstant, implying high empirical power for test 1. The remainder of this subsection examines the power of test 2 by applying that test to misspecified versions of (8.6).

Misspecification of a conditional model typically generates parameters in the conditional model that are not invariant to changes in λ, even if the parameters in the original conditional model are invariant. Thus, rejection of invariance in the misspecified model provides some measure of power. We consider two classes of misspecification: lagging the marginal variable in (8.6) rather than including it contemporaneously, and omitting the marginal variable from (8.6) entirely. Within each class, we consider four misspecifications by variable: one for each of the three marginal variables and one for all marginal variables together. For a given class of misspecification and a given variable involved in that misspecification, four variants of test 2 are calculated, as for (8.6) above. The last four columns in Table 8.6 list the resulting F statistics, with each column corresponding to a specific type of misspecification by variable.

Rejection almost invariably results when the test statistic utilizes the right-hand side variables from the marginal process of the misspecified variable in (8.6). For

Table 8.5. Cointegration analyses of the short- and long-term interest rates RS and RL

	System A		System B		System C	
Hypotheses	$r = 0$	$r \leq 1$	$r = 0$	$r \leq 1$	$r = 0$	$r \leq 1$
Eigenvalues	0.067	0.018	0.256	0.019	0.239	0.010
λ_{max}	6.4	1.7	27.5**	1.8	25.4**	0.9
λ_{max}^{a}	5.7	1.5	24.5**	1.6	22.7**	0.8
95% critical value	14.1	3.8	14.1	3.8	14.1	3.8
λ_{trace}	8.1	1.7	29.3**	1.8	26.4**	0.9
λ_{trace}^{a}	7.2	1.5	26.1**	1.6	23.5**	0.8
95% critical value	15.4	3.8	15.4	3.8	15.4	3.8

Standardized eigenvectors β'

	RS	RL	RS	RL	RS	RL
	1	−0.30	1	−0.70	1	−0.73
	−0.37	1	−0.27	1	−0.21	1

Standardized adjustment coefficients α

	RS	RL	RS	RL	RS	RL
RS	−0.15	0.10	−0.60	0.08	−0.81	−0.07
RL	0.00	0.05	−0.03	0.05	−0.03	−0.04

Weak exogeneity test statistics

	RS	RL	RS	RL	RS	RL
	2.60	0.00	17.0**	0.28	17.7**	0.24
	[0.11]	[0.95]	[0.000]	[0.59]	[0.000]	[0.62]

Unit homogeneity test statistics

1.80	6.27*	4.71*
[0.18]	[0.012]	[0.030]

Joint test statistics

2.33	7.49*	4.71
[0.31]	[0.024]	[0.095]

* Significant at 5 percent.
** Significant at 1 percent.
Notes:
1. The systems are fifth-order VARs in RS and RL over 1878–1970. All systems include a constant term. In addition, System B includes S_{3351}; and System C includes S_{3351}, S_{3945}, S_{5270}, $S_{5270} \cdot trend$, I_{32}, I_{33}, and I_{52}. Asymptotic p-values appear in square brackets.
2. The statistics λ_{max} and λ_{trace} are Johansen's maximal eigenvalue and trace eigenvalue statistics for testing cointegration. The null hypothesis is in terms of the cointegration rank r and, e.g., rejection of $r = 0$ is evidence in favor of at least one cointegrating vector. The statistics λ_{max}^{a} and λ_{trace}^{a} are the same as λ_{max} and λ_{trace}, but with a degrees-of-freedom adjustment. Critical values are taken from Osterwald-Lenum (1992, table 1).
3. The weak exogeneity test statistics are evaluated under the assumption that $r = 1$ and so are asymptotically distributed as $\chi^2(1)$ if weak exogeneity of the specified variable for the cointegrating vector is valid. The joint test statistic is asymptotically distributed as $\chi^2(2)$ if RL is weakly exogenous and long-run unit homogeneity holds.

Table 8.6. Invariance test statistics for super exogeneity in equation (8.6)

Basis for test		Conditional model				
Marginal model	Null distribution		Variable misspecified in (8.6)			
		(8.6)	Δp	Δrs	$\Delta_2 rl$	all
		Misspecification in lag				
Δp	$F(5, 79)$	0.78	11.9**	0.88	0.78	13.4**
		[0.56]	[0.000]	[0.50]	[0.57]	[0.000]
RS	$F(6, 78)$	0.67	1.49	2.29*	2.81*	5.39**
		[0.67]	[0.19]	[0.044]	[0.016]	[0.000]
RL	$F(6, 78)$	1.12	0.30	1.73	2.83*	2.60*
		[0.36]	[0.93]	[0.13]	[0.015]	[0.024]
All	$F(14, 70)$	1.12	5.22**	2.02*	1.72	8.18**
		[0.35]	[0.000]	[0.028]	[0.07]	[0.000]
	$\hat{\sigma}$	1.424%	2.710%	1.541%	1.500%	3.349%
		Misspecification by omission				
Δp	$F(5, 80)$		9.99**	0.78	0.80	11.0**
			[0.000]	[0.56]	[0.56]	[0.000]
RS	$F(6, 79)$		1.51	2.41*	1.44	4.88**
			[0.19]	[0.034]	[0.21]	[0.000]
RL	$F(6, 79)$		0.31	1.79	1.95	2.01
			[0.93]	[0.11]	[0.08]	[0.07]
All	$F(14, 71)$		4.91**	2.09*	1.10	7.25**
			[0.000]	[0.022]	[0.38]	[0.000]
	$\hat{\sigma}$		2.700%	1.537%	1.508%	3.314%

* Significant at 5 percent.
** Significant at 1 percent.
Notes:
1. The marginal models for Δp, RS, and RL are given by equations (8.10), (8.11), and (8.12). The right-hand side variables in those equations provide the basis for the various invariance tests.
2. Listed degrees of freedom in the F statistic are for (8.6) and for misspecifications involving Δrs or $\Delta_2 rl$. Degrees of freedom for other misspecifications may differ slightly because Δp appears in (8.6) at the first lag as well as current-dated. Asymptotic p-values appear in square brackets.

instance, misspecification in the lag of the short-term interest rate implies replacing Δrs_t in (8.6) by Δrs_{t-1}. The invariance test statistic using the right-hand side variables from (8.11) is $F(6, 78) = 2.29$ with a p-value of 4.4 percent (that is, the second pair of values in the fifth column of Table 8.6). Much stronger rejection results when the role of inflation in (8.6) is misspecified. The rejections in Table

8.6 reflect the power of the test and the high information content in the data. In summary, inflation and interest rates are super exogenous for the parameters in the money demand equation (8.6), and the power of the super exogeneity tests appears high.

Some Implications

A few comments may help clarify the implications of these results. First, both types of super exogeneity tests indicate that inflation and interest rates are super exogenous in the money demand model (8.6). Instrumental variables estimation of (8.6) by Hendry and Ericsson (1991a, p. 30) obtains virtually identical and empirically constant coefficient estimates, thus also supporting valid conditioning. Even with super exogeneity, *data-based* predictors are allowable, so error correction models such as (8.6) can have a forward-looking interpretation (see Hendry and Ericsson, 1991b). Specifically, current and lagged inflation enter (8.6) as $-0.3(\Delta p_t + \Delta^2 p_t)$ (approximately), where $\Delta p_t + \Delta^2 p_t$ is a natural predictor of next period's inflation. Flemming (1976) proposes similar such models for forming expectations about inflation; Campos and Ericsson (1988) and Kamin and Ericsson (1993) generalize the class of predictors and implement them in conditional models of Venezuelan consumers' expenditure and Argentine broad money demand respectively. Super exogeneity is feasible with such a predictor because the predictor does not require estimating λ. That is, the predictor is data-based, not model-based.

Second, conditional models may imply trivial losses in utility relative to an expectational solution. Cochrane (1989) provides numerical comparisons for consumers' expenditure, as do Akerlof (1979), Akerlof and Milbourne (1980), and Hendry (1995, p. 582) for money demand. Data-based predictors may be only slightly less accurate than model-based ones; and the information costs to agents may be high for achieving a model-based predictor that betters a data-based one, particularly in the presence of frequent regime changes to a complicated policy reaction function. A conditional error correction model thus may parallel an optimal decision rule by agents facing such information costs. More generally, Ss-type models provide the economic underpinnings for error correction models such as (8.6): see Akerlof (1979), Akerlof and Milbourne (1980), Milbourne (1983), and Smith (1986) for money demand in particular.

Third, policy can and (in general) does affect agent behavior when super exogeneity holds. Policy does so through the variables entering the conditional model, albeit not through the parameters of that model. Government policy might well affect inflation and interest rates, and so the demand for money. However, under super exogeneity, the precise mechanism that the government adopts for such a policy does not affect agent behavior, except insofar as the mechanism affects actual outcomes.

Fourth, Lucas (1988, p. 162) argues that the long-run money demand function should be stable, even if its short-run behavior is not. The results above show that both long- and short-run aspects of the estimated money demand function are empirically constant and are invariant to the policy changes that occurred.[9] Its empirical constancy is surprising, given Judd and Scadding's (1982) survey of empirical money demand equations for the United States. The empirical constancy of Kamin and Ericsson's (1993) conditional money demand equation for Argentina is even more surprising, since its estimation period spans a sample with inflation rates ranging from under 1 percent to nearly 200 percent per month. Further, the Lucas critique *is* of potential issue for even long-run parameters in conditional money demand models, noting the numerous cites in Laidler (1993) to articles modeling money demand with expectations for each of its right-hand side variables. "Policy" then should also be interpreted in Lucas's (1976, p. 21) broad sense because government agencies are likely to be not the only forces determining income, prices, and interest rates.

Fifth, while the bivariate model of interest rates suffices for the expository purposes of this empirical illustration, a marginal analysis is feasible for interest rates, prices, and income jointly, as in Hendry and Ericsson (1986). More generally, analysis of the system for money, prices, income, interest rates, and (possibly) other variables may offer additional insights for policy, even when super exogeneity holds for the conditional money demand equation. On postwar quarterly U.K. data, Hendry and Mizon (1993) and Hendry and Doornik (1994) find an additional cointegrating vector linking inflation with output relative to trend; and the short-run dynamics of the marginal equations are important for understanding the implied behavior of money. Similarly, Juselius's (1993) system analysis of Danish money data helps clarify the interactions between variables, beyond that obtainable from a single equation approach. By working with subsystems, our analysis of U.K. data bridges Hendry and Ericsson's (1991a) single equation results and an analysis of a closed system.

The Empirical Literature on Super Exogeneity

This subsection analyzes the overall empirical evidence on super exogeneity. To do so, we have conducted an SSCI search for articles that cite any of Engle, Hendry, and Richard (1983), Hendry (1988), and Engle and Hendry (1993). The first reference develops the concept of super exogeneity, and the other two references propose tests 1 and 2 for super exogeneity. Paralleling the third and fourth sections above, the articles in the current SSCI search were categorized and

Table 8.7. Availability, status, and nature of the articles from the SSCI search on the exogeneity papers

Articles available:	
Good cites:	
Empirical	74
Mixed	44
Theoretical	39
Other	24
Subtotal	181
Bad cites:	
Exogeneity papers not cited in the text	9
Exogeneity papers not listed in the bibliography	14
Article not in English	3
Book	4
Subtotal	30
Subtotal	211
Articles not available	5
All articles in the SSCI search	216

examined for their empirical evidence on super exogeneity. Considerable empirical evidence already exists showing super exogeneity for a variety of macroeconomic equations across several countries: the empirical applicability of the Lucas critique is rejected in these instances. Analysis of the SSCI search also indicates directions for future empirical research on the role of expectations in the economy.

The SSCI search obtains 216 articles published during 1980–1993 that cite at least one of the references mentioned above.[10] We were able to obtain copies of all but five articles. Only one of those five articles was published in a journal appearing on Laband and Piette's (1994) list of the 130 most cited economic journals: *Applied Economics*, ranked seventy-sixth. Of those articles obtained, thirty are "bad cites," leaving 181 articles available with "good cites."[11] Table 8.7 details the breakdown.

The articles were read and then categorized according to several characteristics:

- The nature of the article (empirical, mixed, theoretical, and other),
- The author's view on whether or not the article's evidence supported super exogeneity ("yes," "maybe," "no," "only weak exogeneity tested," and "not applicable or not tested"),

Table 8.8.   Author's view on the empirical presence of super exogeneity: By nature of the article

Author's view	Nature of the article				
	Empirical	Mixed	Theoretical	Other	Total
Yes	18	7			25
Maybe	4	2			6
No	4	1			5
Weak exogeneity	4	4			8
NA	44	30	39	24	137
Total	74	44	39	24	181

- The sorts of evidence presented on super exogeneity (test 1 on constancy, test 2 on invariance, and nonconstancy of the inverted equation, the last as discussed in Hendry and Ericsson (1991a, 1991b)), and
- The area of application.

A complete listing of the information on the articles appears in Ericsson and Irons (1995b, app.). Table 8.8 tabulates the joint distribution of cites across the nature of the article and the view of the author. Of the 118 empirical and mixed articles, thirty offer clear evidence in favor of or against super exogeneity.

Table 8.9 analyzes those thirty articles by the area of application, tests calculated, and result obtained. Twenty-five papers find evidence for super exogeneity; only five find evidence against. Models of money demand predominate, perhaps reflecting the initial application of tests 1 and 2 in Hendry (1988) and Engle and Hendry (1993) to money demand equations. Several papers show that the conditional model is constant without demonstrating either the nonconstancy of the marginal process (test 1) or the invariance of the conditional model to changes in the marginal process (test 2). Often, these omissions occur because the nonconstancy of the marginal process is "patently evident" from the data, because the inverted conditional model is nonconstant, or because *other* conditional models are nonconstant. Still, explicit statistical evidence would be helpful.

Additionally, Table 8.9 clarifies just how little evidence exists on super exogeneity for many important macroeconomic relations. For example, only a single article applies these tests to a model of prices, yet price stability and inflation targeting are central issues in the current policy arena. The relatively recent development of the tests is no doubt partly responsible for the lack of applications. Also, some papers implementing super exogeneity tests are not yet published or may not cite any of the three articles in the SSCI search. Even so, much testing and modeling remains for the empirical macro-modeler.

Table 8.9. Empirical evidence presented for and against super exogeneity: By type of test and area of application

Area of application	Type of Test							Total	
		Constancy		Invariance		Inversion			
	Cond.	Yes	No	Yes	No	Yes	No	Yes	No
Consumption	2	1	1	1	1	1		3	1
Expenditure	1							1	
Housing	3							3	
Money demand	4	10	1	7	1	5		15	2
Prices	1							1	
Public finance			1		1				2
Trade		1						1	
Wages		1		1				1	
Total	11	13	3	9	3	6	0	25	5

Note: The column "cond." indicates that the conditional model is empirically constant but that evidence on the marginal process was not presented. Articles where the evidence was mixed or where only weak exogeneity was tested are not included in the table. The two right-hand side columns list the corresponding numbers of articles cited in a given row, which need not be the sums across the row, noting that some articles report more than one of the tests.

Conclusions

This paper shows that the Lucas critique is a possibility theorem, not an existence theorem. An extensive search of the literature reveals virtually no evidence demonstrating the empirical applicability of the Lucas critique. That search clarifies what sort of evidence would constitute support for the Lucas critique: much of the evidence cited in the literature is uninformative because it could arise from more mundane sorts of model misspecification. A case study of U.K. money demand shows how super exogeneity tests can be used to test for and refute the Lucas critique in practice. An additional literature search finds considerable evidence refuting the Lucas critique for specific macroeconomic equations across a number of countries. Model-based expectations may be important for some (other) areas of the economy: that is an empirical issue, and one on which there is currently scant evidence. Equally, rejection of super exogeneity for a particular conditional model does not preclude another conditional model (explaining the same data) from having super exogenous variables.

Refutation of the Lucas critique does not mean that agents are backward looking rather than forward looking. Rather, refutation may imply that agents' formation of expectations is simply not model-based. The conditional model of U.K.

money demand includes a natural data-based predictor of inflation, which illustrates this distinction. Even while such error correction models are conditional and hence "feedback" in an important statistical sense, these models are interpretable economically as forward looking, but not in a model-based formulation.

Appendix. Partitioning of SSCI Journal Citations

Tables 8A.1, 8A.2, and 8A.3, respectively, list the numbers of good, bad, and unavailable articles, by journal.

Table 8A.1. Number of articles in SSCI searches for Lucas (1976) and the exogeneity papers: Article is available and cite is "good"

Lucas	Exogeneity	Journal
1		*Agricultural Economics Research*
1		*Akron Business and Economic Review*
1		*American Behavioral Scientist*
31	5	*American Economic Review*
9		*American Journal of Agricultural Economics*
	1	*American Journal of Political Science*
1	1	*American Political Science Review*
1	1	*American Sociological Review*
1		*Annals of Regional Science*
12	5	*Applied Economics*
	2	*Applied Mathematics and Computation*
4		*Australian Economic Papers*
1		*Australian Journal of Agricultural Economics*
1		*Behavioral Science*
14		*Brookings Papers on Economic Activity*
2	1	*Cambridge Journal of Economics*
11	4	*Canadian Journal of Economics*
		(Revue Canadienne d'Economique)
2		*Canadian Public Policy (Analyse de Politiques)*
8		*Carnegie-Rochester Conference Series on Public Policy*
4		*Cato Journal*
	1	*Climatic Change*
1		*Computers and Mathematics with Applications*
3		*Contemporary Policy Issues*
5	1	*De Economist*
1	5	*Econometric Theory*
11	6	*Econometrica*
2	1	*Economic and Social Review*

Table 8A.1. (continued)

Lucas	Exogeneity	Journal
8		*Economic Inquiry*
13	10	*Economic Journal*
13	3	*Economic Modelling*
9		*Economic Record*
3	2	*Economica*
	1	*Economics and Philosophy*
4	4	*Economics Letters*
11	7	*European Economic Review*
2		*Explorations in Economic History*
1		*Giornale degli Economisti e Annali di Economia*
2		*History of Political Economy*
1		*Housing Finance Review*
1		*Interfaces*
6	4	*International Economic Review*
7	2	*International Journal of Forecasting*
	1	*International Journal of Industrial Organization*
9	2	*International Monetary Fund Staff Papers*
2		*International Regional Science Review*
1	1	*International Statistical Review*
1		*Journal of Accounting Research*
5	4	*Journal of Applied Econometrics*
1	1	*Journal of Banking and Finance*
1		*Journal of Business*
4	3	*Journal of Business and Economic Statistics*
	1	*Journal of Comparative Economics*
1		*Journal of Contemporary Business*
2	1	*Journal of Development Economics*
	1	*Journal of Development Studies*
7	18	*Journal of Econometrics*
13		*Journal of Economic Dynamics and Control*
1		*Journal of Economic Education*
	1	*Journal of Economic Issues*
8		*Journal of Economic Literature*
4	1	*Journal of Economic Perspectives*
1	1	*Journal of Economic Studies*
2		*Journal of Economic Theory*
1		*Journal of Economics and Business*
1		*Journal of Economics (Zeitschrift für Nationalökonomie)*
1		*Journal of Environmental Economics and Management*
3	1	*Journal of Finance*
3	1	*Journal of Forecasting*

Table 8A.1.   (continued)

Lucas	Exogeneity	Journal
	2	*Journal of Industrial Economics*
3		*Journal of International Economics*
10	3	*Journal of International Money and Finance*
2		*Journal of Labor Economics*
7	2	*Journal of Macroeconomics*
41	4	*Journal of Monetary Economics*
29	2	*Journal of Money Credit and Banking*
1		*Journal of Optimization Theory and Applications*
12	15	*Journal of Policy Modeling*
30	1	*Journal of Political Economy*
1		*Journal of Politics*
4		*Journal of Public Economics*
1		*Journal of the American Statistical Association*
	2	*Journal of the Royal Statistical Society, Series A*
1		*Land Economics*
1		*Lloyds Bank Review*
1		*Managerial and Decision Economics*
6	4	*Manchester School of Economic and Social Studies*
3		*National Tax Journal*
	2	*Nationaløkonomisk Tidsskrift*
2		*NBER Macroeconomics Annual*
2	14	*Oxford Bulletin of Economics and Statistics*
7	5	*Oxford Economic Papers—New Series*
1		*Policy Review*
2		*Policy Sciences*
1		*Psychological Bulletin*
1		*Public Finance Quarterly*
3	1	*Public Finance—Finances publiques*
1		*Quarterly Journal of Business and Economics*
5		*Quarterly Journal of Economics*
1		*Quarterly Review of Economics and Business*
1		*Review of Economic Conditions in Italy*
4	4	*Review of Economic Studies*
11	3	*Review of Economics and Statistics*
1		*Revue Economique*
9	2	*Scandinavian Journal of Economics*
1		*Science*
2	3	*Scottish Journal of Political Economy*
	2	*Social and Economic Studies*
2	1	*South African Journal of Economics*
12	2	*Southern Economic Journal*

Table 8A.1.   (continued)

Lucas	Exogeneity	Journal
8	1	*Weltwirtschaftliches Archiv*
1		*World Development*
	1	*World Politics*
1		*Zeitschrift für Nationalökonomie (Journal of Economics)*
513	181	Total

Table 8A.2.   Number of articles in SSCI searches for Lucas (1976) and the exogeneity papers: Article is available and cite is "bad"

Lucas	Exogeneity	Journal
1		*American Economic Review*
1		*Brookings Papers on Economic Activity*
1		*Cahiers Economiques de Bruxelles*
2		*Canadian Journal of Economics*
		(Revue Canadienne d'Economique)
1		*De Economist*
1		*Desarrollo Económico*
1		*Economic Inquiry*
	1	*Economic Journal*
2		*Economic Record*
1		*Economica*
1	3	*Economics Letters*
	1	*European Economic Review*
2	1	*Giornale degli Economisti e Annali di Economia*
2		*International Economic Review*
1		*International Monetary Fund Staff Papers*
2		*Jahrbuch für Sozialwissenschaft*
2		*Jahrbucher für Nationalökonomie und Statistik*
	1	*Journal of Applied Econometrics*
1	1	*Journal of Banking and Finance*
	1	*Journal of Business and Economic Statistics*
	3	*Journal of Econometrics*
1		*Journal of Economic Dynamics and Control*
1		*Journal of Economic Literature*
	1	*Journal of Finance*
	1	*Journal of Forecasting*
1		*Journal of International Economics*
2		*Journal of International Money and Finance*
4		*Journal of Monetary Economics*

Table 8A.2.   (continued)

Lucas	Exogeneity	Journal
1		*Journal of Political Economy*
2		*Journal of Post Keynesian Economics*
3		*Kyklos*
5	4	*Lecture Notes in Economics and Mathematical Systems*
1		*Manchester School of Economic and Social Studies*
1	1	*Nationaløkonomisk Tidsskrift*
	1	*Oxford Bulletin of Economics and Statistics*
2	1	*Oxford Economic Papers—New Series*
1		*Regional Science and Urban Economics*
	1	*Review of Economic Studies*
	2	*Review of Economics and Statistics*
3	1	*Revue Economique*
	1	*Scandinavian Journal of Economics*
	2	*Scottish Journal of Political Economy*
1		*Southern Economic Journal*
3		*Trimestre Económico*
2	1	*Weltwirtschaftliches Archiv*
	1	*World Development*
56	30	Total

Table 8A.3.   Number of articles in SSCI searches for Lucas (1976) and the exogeneity papers: Article is not available

Lucas	Exogeneity	Journal
1		*Agricultural Administration and Extension*
1		*Annual Review of Ecology and Systematics*
	1	*Applied Economics*
1		*Computers and Mathematics with Applications*
	1	*Current Contents / Social and Behavioral Sciences*
2		*De Economist*
	1	*Defence Economics*
1		*Environment and Planning C—Government and Policy*
1		*Giornale degli Economisti e Annali di Economia*
6		*Nationaløkonomisk Tidsskrift*
1		*Potato Research*
	1	*Quality and Quantity*
1		*Resources Policy*
2		*Revista Brasileira de Economia*
2		*Rivista Internazionale di Scienze Economiche e Commerciali*

Table 8A.3.   (continued)

Lucas	Exogeneity	Journal
1		*Transportation Research Part B—Methodological*
	1	*Western Journal of Agricultural Economics*
1		*Zeitschrift für Wirtschafts und Sozialwissenschaften*
21	5	Total

Acknowledgments

The first author is an economist in the Division of International Finance, Federal Reserve Board, Washington, DC. The second author is in the Department of Economics at MIT and was on the staff of the Federal Reserve Board when the initial draft of this paper was prepared. The views expressed in this paper are solely the responsibility of the authors and should not be interpreted as reflecting those of the Board of Governors of the Federal Reserve System or other members of its staff. We are grateful to Cathy Tunis in the Research Library of the Federal Reserve Board for invaluable guidance in using the Social Science Citation Index; to Sebastian Thomas for excellent research assistance while revising the initial draft of this paper; and to David Bowman, Julia Campos, David DeJong, Jon Faust, David Hendry, Eric Leeper, Jaime Marquez, Ed Nelson, and Jean-François Richard for helpful discussions and comments. All numerical results were obtained using Borland's (1992) *Paradox for Windows Version 1.0*, Borland's (1993) *Quattro Pro for Windows Version 5.0*, and Doornik and Hendry's (1994) *PcGive Professional Version 8.0*. We are grateful to Jurgen Doornik and David Hendry for providing us with a prerelease version of *PcGive Professional*.

Notes

1. Constancy need not imply invariance or invariance constancy. A parameter may be time-varying yet still be invariant to policy interventions. Equally, a parameter may lack invariance, yet be constant because policy has remained unchanged over the sample.

2. Loosely speaking, x_t is super exogenous for θ in (8.1) if the parameters of interest can be retrieved from θ alone and if θ does not depend on λ or on the range of λ. See Engle, Hendry, and Richard (1983) for a precise definition of super exogeneity.

3. Searching the SSCI is not entirely straightforward, especially for Lucas (1976). The article whose citation is to be searched is indexed by author, year, and journal, and there is little consensus on the proper citation of Lucas (1976) or the proper way to index the cite. Sample indexes include "Phillips Curve Labor" with 117 entries; "V1, P19, Carnegie-Rochester C . . . " with sixty-three; "J Monetary Ec S" with twenty-one; and dozens more with various permutations, (mis)spellings, hyphenations, and abbreviations.

4. Some additional information on the articles was gathered but is left for future analysis. For each article, the SSCI provides the author's affiliation; and we established the pages on which Lucas (1976) is cited, the article's primary and secondary JEL numbers, whether or not Lucas (1976) motivates the article, whether or not Lucas (1976) is cited in the context of policy analysis, and whether or not the article is about policy.

5. The frequency of journal citation is taken from Laband and Piette's (1994, Table A2) ranking based on impact-adjusted citations per character for 1990 citations to articles published in 1985–1989. Their other rankings make little difference to the distribution between available and unavailable articles for citations to Lucas (1976) occurring in frequently cited journals.

6. Treating that coefficient as known may bias the Chow statistic towards rejection because an extra degree of freedom is assumed. However, this bias did not matter in practice.

7. Other studies also include transients and short-run variables in their cointegration analyses. Johansen and Juselius (1992) include oil price inflation in their analysis of purchasing power parity and uncovered interest rate parity; Hendry and Mizon (1993) and Hendry and Doornik (1994) include various dummies in their models of postwar U.K. money, prices, output, and interest rates; and Juselius (1993) includes both transient dummies and stationary variables in her analysis of Danish money demand. Kremers, Ericsson, and Dolado (1992) show analytically and empirically that accounting for short-run or temporary fluctuations can dramatically improve the power of cointegration tests.

8. Univariate and bivariate models for the interest rates are qualitatively similar if logs of the interest rates are modeled rather than their levels. Levels appear to deliver better-specified equations than logs, so the levels equations are presented.

9. Hendry and Ericsson (1991a) show that the short-run elasticity of RS may have changed with the introduction of Competition and Credit Control in 1971. That change does not obviate the empirical constancy of the model over a near century of data, nor does it provide evidence for the Lucas critique. Rather, the nonconstancy appears to arise from mismeasurement of the opportunity cost of holding money (see Hendry and Ericsson, 1991a, p. 32). Lubrano, Pierse, and Richard (1986) and Steel and Richard (1991) find comparable results in extensive Bayesian analyses of a similar U.K. aggregate (M3); and Hendry and Ericsson's (1991b) model of M1 demand is constant over a period spanning the introduction of Competition and Credit Control.

10. Citations to unpublished versions of the papers are also included, noting that Engle, Hendry, and Richard (1983) and Engle and Hendry (1993) were particularly long in gestation.

11. Fourteen articles in the SSCI search do not include any of the exogeneity papers in their bibliographies, although they do cite other papers by Engle, Hendry, or Richard. Their inclusion in the SSCI search reflects our inability in using the SSCI to specify fully a citation of interest when the citation appeared as a discussion paper in a year different from its year of publication.

References

Akerlof, G.A. (1979). "Irving Fisher on His Head: The Consequences of Constant Threshold-target Monitoring of Money Holdings." *Quarterly Journal of Economics* 93(2), 169–187.

Akerlof, G.A., and R.D. Milbourne. (1980). "Irving Fisher on His Head II: The Consequences of the Timing of Payments for the Demand for Money." *Quarterly Journal of Economics* 95(1), 145–157.

Aldrich, J. (1989). "Autonomy." *Oxford Economic Papers* 41(1), 15–34.

Baba, Y., D.F. Hendry, and R.M. Starr. (1992). "The Demand for M1 in the U.S.A., 1960–1988." *Review of Economic Studies* 59(1), 25–61.

Blinder, A.S. (1988). "The Fall and Rise of Keynesian Economics." *Economic Record* 64, 187, 278–294.

Borland. (1992). *Paradox for Windows Version 1.0: User's Guide.* Scotts Valley, CA: Borland International.

Borland. (1993). *Quattro Pro for Windows Version 5.0: User's Guide.* Scotts Valley, CA: Borland International.

Brodin, P.A., and R. Nymoen. (1992). "Wealth Effects and Exogeneity: The Norwegian Consumption Function 1966(1)–1989(4)." *Oxford Bulletin of Economics and Statistics* 54(3), 431–454.

Campos, J., and N.R. Ericsson. (1988). "Econometric Modeling of Consumers' Expenditure in Venezuela." International Finance Discussion Paper No. 325, Board of Governors of the Federal Reserve System, Washington, DC, June.

Chong, Y.Y., and D.F. Hendry. (1986). "Econometric Evaluation of Linear Macroeconomic Models." *Review of Economic Studies* 53(4), 671–690. Reprinted in C.W.J. Granger (ed.), (1990), *Modelling Economic Series: Readings in Econometric Methodology* (ch. 17, pp. 384–410). Oxford: Oxford University Press.

Chow, G.C. (1960). "Tests of Equality Between Sets of Coefficients in Two Linear Regressions." *Econometrica* 28(3), 591–605.

Cochrane, J.H. (1989). "The Sensitivity of Tests of the Intertemporal Allocation of Consumption to Near-rational Alternatives." *American Economic Review* 79(3), 319–337.

Cuthbertson, K. (1991). "The Encompassing Implications of Feedforward versus Feedback Mechanisms: A Reply to Hendry." *Oxford Economic Papers* 43(2), 344–350.

Doornik, J.A., and D.F. Hendry. (1994). *PcGive Professional 8.0: An Interactive Econometric Modelling System.* London: International Thomson.

Dufour, J.-M., and E. Ghysels (eds.). (1996). *Journal of Econometrics.* Special issue on "Recent Developments in the Econometrics of Structural Change." In press.

Engle, R.F., and D.F. Hendry. (1993). "Testing Super Exogeneity and Invariance in Regression Models." *Journal of Econometrics* 56(1/2), 119–139.

Engle, R.F., D.F. Hendry, and J.-F. Richard. (1983). "Exogeneity." *Econometrica* 51(2), 277–304.

Ericsson, N.R. (ed.). (1992a). *Journal of Policy Modeling,* 14(3) and 14(4). Special issues on "Cointegration, Exogeneity, and Policy Analysis."

Ericsson, N.R. (1992b). "Parameter Constancy, Mean Square Forecast Errors, and Measuring Forecast Performance: An Exposition, Extensions, and Illustration." *Journal of Policy Modeling* 14(4), 465–495.

Ericsson, N.R., and D.F. Hendry. (1989). "Encompassing and Rational Expectations: How Sequential Corroboration Can Imply Refutation." International Finance Discussion Paper No. 354, Board of Governors of the Federal Reserve System, Washington, DC, June.

Ericsson, N.R., and J.S. Irons (eds.). (1994). *Testing Exogeneity.* Oxford: Oxford University Press.

Ericsson, N.R., and J.S. Irons. (1995a). "Book Review of *Applied Econometric Techniques* by Keith Cuthbertson, Stephen G. Hall, and Mark P. Taylor." *Econometric Reviews* 14(1), 121–133.

Ericsson, N.R., and J.S. Irons. (1995b). "The Lucas Critique in Practice: Theory Without Measurement." International Finance Discussion Paper No. 506, Board of Governors of the Federal Reserve System, Washington, DC, March.

Fair, R.C. (1984). *Specification, Estimation, and Analysis of Macroeconometric Models.* Cambridge, MA: Harvard University Press.

Favero, C., and D.F. Hendry. (1992). "Testing the Lucas Critique: A Review." *Econometric Reviews* 11(3), 265–306.

Fischer, S. (1983). "Comment on 'Macroconfusion: The Dilemmas of Economic Policy.' " In J. Tobin (ed.), *Macroeconomics, Prices, and Quantities: Essays in Memory of Arthur M. Okun* (pp. 267–276). Washington, DC: Brookings Institution.

Flemming, J.S. (1976). *Inflation.* Oxford: Oxford University Press.

Friedman, M., and A.J. Schwartz. (1982). *Monetary Trends in the United States and the United Kingdom: Their Relation to Income, Prices, and Interest Rates, 1867–1975.* Chicago: University of Chicago Press.

Frisch, R. (1948). "Repercussion Studies at Oslo." *American Economic Review* 38(3), 367–372.

Ghysels, E., and A. Hall. (1990). "Are Consumption-based Intertemporal Capital Asset Pricing Models Structural?" *Journal of Econometrics* 45(1/2), 121–139.

Gordon, R.J. (1976). "Can Econometric Policy Evaluations Be Salvaged?—A Comment." In K. Brunner and A.H. Meltzer (eds.), *The Phillips Curve and Labor Markets, Carnegie-Rochester Conference Series on Public Policy,* Vol. 1, *Journal of Monetary Economics,* supplementary issue, 47–61.

Haavelmo, T. (1944). "The Probability Approach in Econometrics." *Econometrica* 12 (Supp.), i–viii, 1–118.

Hansen, B.E. (1992). "Testing for Parameter Instability in Linear Models." *Journal of Policy Modeling* 14(4), 517–533.

Hansen, L.P., and T.J. Sargent. (1980). "Formulating and Estimating Dynamic Linear Rational Expectations Models." *Journal of Economic Dynamics and Control* 2(1), 7–46.

Hendry, D.F. (1988). "The Encompassing Implications of Feedback Versus Feedforward Mechanisms in Econometrics." *Oxford Economic Papers* 40(1), 132–149.

Hendry, D.F. (1995). *Dynamic Econometrics.* Oxford: Oxford University Press.

Hendry, D.F., and J.A. Doornik. (1994). "Modelling Linear Dynamic Econometric Systems." *Scottish Journal of Political Economy* 41(1), 1–33.

Hendry, D.F., and N.R. Ericsson. (1986). "Prolegomenon to a Reconstruction: Further Econometric Appraisal of *Monetary Trends in . . . the United Kingdom* by Milton Friedman and Anna J. Schwartz." Mimeo, Board of Governors of the Federal Reserve System, Washington, DC, March.

Hendry, D.F., and N.R. Ericsson. (1991a). "An Econometric Analysis of U.K. Money Demand in *Monetary Trends in the United States and the United Kingdom* by Milton Friedman and Anna J. Schwartz." *American Economic Review* 81(1), 8–38.

Hendry, D.F., and N.R. Ericsson. (1991b). "Modeling the Demand for Narrow Money in the United Kingdom and the United States." *European Economic Review* 35(4), 833–881.

Hendry, D.F., and G.E. Mizon. (1993). "Evaluating Dynamic Econometric Models by Encompassing the VAR." In P.C.B. Phillips (ed.), *Models, Methods, and Applications of Econometrics: Essays in Honor of A.R. Bergstrom* (ch. 18, pp. 272–300). Cambridge, MA: Basil Blackwell.

Hendry, D.F., and J.-F. Richard. (1982). "On the Formulation of Empirical Models in Dynamic Econometrics." *Journal of Econometrics* 20(1), 3–33. Reprinted in C.W.J. Granger (ed.), (1990), *Modelling Economic Series: Readings in Econometric Methodology* (ch. 14, pp. 304–334). Oxford: Oxford University Press.

Hoffman, D., and A.R. Pagan. (1989). "Post-sample Prediction Tests for Generalized Method of Moments Estimators." *Oxford Bulletin of Economics and Statistics* 51(3), 333–343.

Johansen, S. (1988). "Statistical Analysis of Cointegration Vectors." *Journal of Economic Dynamics and Control* 12(2/3), 231–254.

Johansen, S. (1991). "Estimation and Hypothesis Testing of Cointegration Vectors in Gaussian Vector Autoregressive Models." *Econometrica* 59(6), 1551–1580.

Johansen, S. (1992a). "Cointegration in Partial Systems and the Efficiency of Single-equation Analysis." *Journal of Econometrics* 52(3), 389–402.

Johansen, S. (1992b). "Testing Weak Exogeneity and the Order of Cointegration in UK Money Demand Data." *Journal of Policy Modeling* 14(3), 313–334.

Johansen, S., and K. Juselius. (1990). "Maximum Likelihood Estimation and Inference on Cointegration—With Applications to the Demand for Money." *Oxford Bulletin of Economics and Statistics* 52(2), 169–210.

Johansen, S., and K. Juselius. (1992). "Testing Structural Hypotheses in a Multivariate Cointegration Analysis of the PPP and the UIP for UK." *Journal of Econometrics* 53(1/2/3), 211–244.

Judd, J.P., and J.L. Scadding. (1982). "The Search for a Stable Money Demand Function: A Survey of the Post-1973 Literature." *Journal of Economic Literature* 20(3), 993–1023.

Juselius, K. (1993). "VAR Modelling and Haavelmo's Probability Approach to Macroeconomic Modelling." *Empirical Economics* 18(4), 595–622.

Kamin, S.B., and N.R. Ericsson. (1993). "Dollarization in Argentina." International Finance Discussion Paper No. 460, Board of Governors of the Federal Reserve System, Washington, DC, November.

Kremers, J.J.M., N.R. Ericsson, and J.J. Dolado. (1992). "The Power of Cointegration Tests." *Oxford Bulletin of Economics and Statistics* 54(3), 325–348.

Laband, D.N., and M.J. Piette. (1994). "The Relative Impacts of Economics Journals: 1970–1990." *Journal of Economic Literature* 32(2), 640–666.

LaHaye, L. (1985). "Inflation and Currency Reform." *Journal of Political Economy* 93(3), 537–560.

Laidler, D.E.W. (1993). *The Demand for Money: Theories, Evidence, and Problems* (4th ed.). New York: HarperCollins.

Lubrano, M., R.G. Pierse, and J.-F. Richard. (1986). "Stability of a U.K. Money Demand Equation: A Bayesian Approach to Testing Exogeneity." *Review of Economic Studies* 53(4), 603–634.

Lucas, Jr., R.E. (1976). "Econometric Policy Evaluation: A Critique." In K. Brunner and A.H. Meltzer (eds.), *The Phillips Curve and Labor Markets, Carnegie-Rochester Conference Series on Public Policy*, Vol. 1, *Journal of Monetary Economics*, supplementary issue, 19–46.

Lucas, Jr., R.E. (1988). "Money Demand in the United States: A Quantitative Review." In K. Brunner and B.T. McCallum (eds.), *Money, Cycles, and Exchange Rates: Essays in Honor of Allan H. Meltzer, Carnegie-Rochester Conference Series on Public Policy*, Vol. 29, *Journal of Monetary Economics*, supplementary issue, 137–168.

McCallum, B.T. (1989). *Monetary Economics: Theory and Policy*. New York: Macmillan.

McNelis, P.D., and S.N. Neftçi. (1982). "Policy-dependent Parameters in the Presence of Optimal Learning: An Application of Kalman Filtering to the Fair and Sargent Supply-side Equations." *Review of Economics and Statistics* 64(2), 296–306.

Milbourne, R. (1983). "Optimal Money Holding Under Uncertainty." *International Economic Review* 24(3), 685–698.

Neftçi, S.N., and T.J. Sargent. (1978). "A Little Bit of Evidence on the Natural Rate Hypothesis from the U.S." *Journal of Monetary Economics* 4(2), 315–319.

Osterwald-Lenum, M. (1992). "A Note with Quantiles of the Asymptotic Distribution of the Maximum Likelihood Cointegration Rank Test Statistics." *Oxford Bulletin of Economics and Statistics* 54(3), 461–472.

Peek, J., and J.A. Wilcox. (1987). "Monetary Policy Regimes and the Reduced Form for Interest Rates." *Journal of Money, Credit, and Banking* 19(3), 273–291.

Sargent, T.J. (1976). "A Classical Macroeconometric Model for the United States." *Journal of Political Economy* 84(2), 207–237.

Sims, C.A. (1987). "A Rational Expectations Framework for Short-run Policy Analysis." In W.A. Barnett and K.J. Singleton (eds.), *New Approaches to Monetary Economics* (ch. 14, pp. 293–308). Cambridge: Cambridge University Press.

Smith, G.W. (1986). "A Dynamic Baumol-Tobin Model of Money Demand." *Review of Economic Studies* 53(3), 465–469.

Steel, M.F.J., and J.-F. Richard. (1991). "Bayesian Multivariate Exogeneity Analysis: An Application to a UK Money Demand Equation." *Journal of Econometrics* 49(1/2), 239–274.

White, H. (1980). "A Heteroskedasticity-consistent Covariance Matrix Estimator and a Direct Test for Heteroskedasticity." *Econometrica* 48(4), 817–838.

Commentary on Chapter 8

Eric M. Leeper

Introduction

Lucas's (1976) critique of policy evaluation is a theorem about economic behavior: when the process that determines policy changes, private behavior will shift systematically with the changes in policy. One application of this theorem relates to econometric models: a model that fails to incorporate the dependence of private decisions on policy decisions will generate poor predictions of the effects of some kinds of changes in policy.

Stated this way, the critique and its application are indisputably true. They are also empirically vacuous. The theorem is nearly tautological, and by adding the proviso about "some kinds of changes in policy," the application has no general empirical implications.

Ericsson and Irons are correct that the Lucas critique has become something of a mantra for many macroeconomists, who invoke it reflexively as though every contemplated policy exercise necessarily shifts the stochastic structure of econometric models.[1] Thus, it is useful to develop procedures designed to determine whether the expectational behavior that Lucas emphasizes is important for the stability of econometric models. But the authors' claim that "little evidence exists to support the empirical applicability of the Lucas critique" is simply false. Lucas's criticisms gained wide and rapid acceptance in large measure *because* of their empirical applicability. In many economists' minds, the critique provides the most plausible (that is, economically reasonable and empirically consistent) explanation of the empirical breakdown of econometric models in the 1970s.

The instability of the Phillips curve serves as the outstanding example of an empirical breakdown. Lucas, in his critique and in earlier papers, formalized Friedman's (1968) and Phelps's (1970) explanations of why the Phillips curve does not represent a stable tradeoff between inflation and unemployment. Lucas's work also inspired macroeconomists to bring into the modern macro fold and to make concrete the idea developed by the Cowles Commission that a model is "structural" or invariant only with respect to particular classes of interventions.[2] The critique and the subsequent emphasis on dynamic optimizing behavior, therefore, produced two outcomes. First, they provided an answer to the puzzle of why the apparent tradeoff between inflation and unemployment worsened in the 1970s as inflation rates rose. Second, they led to a research program designed to explicitly

313

characterize the class of policy interventions that economic theory predicts will shift private behavior.

Viewing the Lucas critique as a theorem about economic behavior, and its implication for the stability of econometric models as a potential application of the theorem, leads inevitably to the issue of identification. Thus, the central theme of this comment is summarized by the question: In their empirical example of money demand, have Ericsson and Irons *identified* private and policy behavior that supports their conclusion that they can "refute the Lucas critique"? Although Ericsson and Irons liberally use the phrase "refute the Lucas critique," no amount of empirical evidence can disprove the logical proposition. More modestly, and more accurately, the authors have found that a particular empirical relationship remained stable in a particular data sample even though the stochastic processes for the contemporaneous explanatory variables displayed instability.

This comment proposes some interpretations of what the authors found and discusses the usefulness of the authors' procedures for policy analysis. Before turning to these interpretations, I will comment briefly on the literature searches that Ericsson and Irons conduct.

The Literature Searches

Over half of the paper reports results from searches of the *Social Science Citation Index*. Ericsson and Irons search for references to Lucas (1976) and to super exogeneity tests. They focus initially on the fifty-four citations to Lucas that are empirical in nature. Of those, forty-three claim to find evidence supporting the sort of behavior that Lucas emphasizes. The authors then critically evaluate the forty-three articles according to their notions of what constitutes "valid" empirical evidence.[3] The authors' evaluation includes phrases like: "a vector autoregression may be nonconstant even while a factorization of the associated joint density of the data may have a constant-parameter conditional equation," "the nonconstancy of a particular conditional model does not preclude some other conditional model from being constant," "measured expectations could be adaptive rather than forward-looking, or could be derived from a data-based (rather than a model-based) predictor," "statistically acceptable cross-equation restrictions in expectational models . . . could be satisfied by a conditional-marginal representation as well." With such statistical incantations, Ericsson and Irons reduce to two the number of articles containing "fruitful" evidence about the Lucas critique. Ultimately they reject these, too, on similar statistical grounds. Thus, exactly zero papers find empirical support for the Lucas critique.

In contrast, the authors report that twenty-five papers find evidence for super exogeneity and only five find evidence against it. According to Ericsson and Irons,

"Considerable empirical evidence already exists showing super exogeneity for a variety of macroeconomic equations across several countries: the empirical applicability of the Lucas critique is rejected in these instances."

Missing from their evaluation of the literature is any discussion of *economic behavior.* The authors proceed as if all factorizations of the probability distribution of the data are created economically equal. Economic theory could and should be applied to sort the factorizations and select the economically meaningful ones.

The authors refuse to acknowledge the difficulties inherent in the process of drawing economic inferences from data. That process is necessarily impure—both statistically and economically. It is never mechanistic. It is always controversial and rarely decisive.

Ericsson and Iron's statistical sound and fury leaves in its wake bewildered economists who, like me, are struggling in that dirty middle ground between high theory and pure econometrics. These economists are searching for economically coherent explanations of the data and want statistical tools that use data to choose among well-specified theories. I think it is unlikely these tools will be powerful enough to rule out broad classes of behavioral theories, yet this is precisely the claim Ericsson and Irons make for super exogeneity tests.

Lost in the bluster and the ideology that Ericsson and Irons foist on their readers are the obvious points made by their literature search. Private behavioural decisions are probably not nearly as sensitive to shifts in policy as many macroeconomists believe. But this point is not new, as their quotations from Fischer and McCallum underscore. Also lost is the fact that Lucas's paper has had a paralyzing effect on macroeconomic policy analysis. Few academic economists are willing to estimate large-scale econometric models for fear that the work is not intellectually respectable. Yet the demand by governments and businesses for forecasts from such models remains strong and the influence of these forecasts is as pervasive as ever. Revealed preference alone suggests that the academic profession has probably overreacted to Lucas's criticisms.[4]

The substance of Ericsson and Irons's dismissal of existing evidence in favor of the Lucas critique lies in their super exogeneity tests, which are illustrated in the remainder of their paper. I found their assessment of this literature to be almost wholly uncritical. The rest of this comment attempts to regain the balance.

The Rational Expectations Framework for Policy Analysis

Ericsson and Irons embed their empirical tests in the now-standard rational expectations framework for econometric policy evaluation, as articulated by Lucas (1976). Private-sector behavior is summarized by

$$y_{t+1} = F(y_t, x_t, \theta, \varepsilon_t). \tag{1}$$

The function F and the parameter vector θ are derived from dynamic optimizing behavior on the part of private agents, so they represent decision rules. ε_t is a vector of independent, identically distributed random shocks. Policy behavior is characterized by

$$x_t = G(y_t, \lambda, \eta_t), \tag{2}$$

where G is a known function that, coupled with λ, describes the decision rules of the policy authorities, and η_t is a vector of independent, identically distributed disturbances. Substituting equation (2) into (1) yields the model of the economy:

$$y_{t+1} = F(y_t, x_t, \theta(\lambda), \varepsilon_t). \tag{3}$$

The econometric problem is to estimate the function, $\theta(\lambda)$, rather than a set of fixed parameters, θ. Policy evaluation, according to Lucas, consists of considering the effects of various settings of λ, not of forecasting y conditional on different choices of time paths for x.

Ericsson and Irons, drawing on previous work by Hendry (1988) and others, base their test of the empirical importance of the Lucas critique on two procedures:

- *Test 1:* Test if θ is constant in (1) and if λ is constant in (2). If θ is constant but λ is not, θ must not change systematically with λ, implying that private decision rules do not depend on the policy process.
- *Test 2:* Add sufficient variables to make λ constant in (2). Then test for the significance of these other variables in (1). Insignificance in (1) implies θ is invariant to changes in λ.

For equation (1) the authors estimate a relationship whose dependent variable is real money balances $(m - p)$ and whose right variables include lagged real balances, current and lagged inflation (Δp), the short-term interest rate (rs), the long-term interest rate (rl), and a lagged error correction term (u) that depends on real balances, real income (z), and the short rate:

$$\Delta(m - p)_t = F(\Delta(m - p)_{t-1}, \Delta^2(m - p)_{t-2}, \Delta p_t, \Delta p_{t-1},$$

$$\Delta rs_t, \Delta_2 rl_t, u_{t-1}^2, u_{t-1}^3, D), \tag{4}$$

where $u = m - p - z + \alpha \cdot RS + constant$ and D is a vector of dummy variables for world wars and a regression constant. The authors report a final empirical specification for (4) that exhibits constant parameters. They interpret (4) as a money demand function and the vector of estimated elasticities from (4) as θ in (1).

The paper then shows that the stochastic processes for the three variables that enter (4) contemporaneously (inflation, short and long interest rates) exhibit time-varying parameters. The authors interpret these processes as examples of (2) and infer that λ changed. This exercise is meant to implement empirical test 1. The authors interpret the finding to mean that the decision rule for real money balances does not depend on the parameters of the process for policy.

This empirical procedure is self-contradictory. If the authors have found versions of "(2)" in which λ is not constant, then they have not estimated (2). To be internally consistent, (2) is a set of decision rules for policy authorities that come from policy makers solving well-defined optimization problems that make policy choices fixed functions of the state of the economy. An empirical specification that allows parameters to change in arbitrary ways over time is not a description of policy behavior.

An Alternative Framework for Policy Analysis

Ericsson and Irons have run up against the same logical problems that Sargent (1984) discusses and the Cooley, LeRoy, and Raymon (1984), and Sims (1986, 1987) emphasize. If it is reasonable to evaluate changes in policy that are represented as different settings of λ, then it is unreasonable to model policy as if a fixed λ has been in place forever and to assume that private agents expect it to remain fixed forevermore.[5] Sims has developed an alternative framework for policy analysis that requires identifying policy behavior to avoid the logical problems inherent in the rational expectations approach.

As Sims (1987) puts it, if λ can be changed, then it is necessarily a time series, and private agents form expectations over its future values. Subscripting λ by time and substituting (2) into (1) yields

$$y_{t+1} = F(y_t, G(y_t, \lambda_t, \eta_t), \theta(\lambda_t), \varepsilon_t) \equiv F^*(y_t, \lambda_t, \varepsilon_t^*), \tag{5}$$

where $\varepsilon_t^* \equiv (\varepsilon_t, \eta_t)$. F^* has the same functional form as F with λ_t playing the role of x_t.[6] Now the econometric problem is to estimate the unknown parameters in the functional form of $\theta(\lambda_t)$. Sims's point is that there is no logical difference between evaluating policy as changes in λ or as alternative time paths for x.[7]

This argument pertains to Ericsson and Irons's procedures, which rest entirely on the identification that nonconstant marginal processes reflect changes in λ, not merely changes in the time paths of x. Different realizations of the policy disturbance, η_t, and hence in x_t, do not generate changes in θ, according to the rational expectations framework for policy evaluation. But if changes in λ and changes in x are not logically distinct, then according to the model economy in (3), any sort of change in policy destabilizes private behavior, rendering all policy evaluation meaningless. The alternative framework, however, explicitly models the time-varying nature of policy and treats private agents as having probability distributions over λ. Under this framework, changes in λ within some class do not shift private decision rules so, according to (5), it is possible to conduct policy analysis.

Ericsson and Irons pose policy changes as a grander thing than (5) envisions. To execute the test that Ericsson and Irons want to perform, it is crucial to identify the policy function G and periods when λ changed in important ways. The test consists of checking if changes in λ are associated with changes in θ. The only way to perform this test is to identify the aspects of an economic model that produce the F and G functions (and their associated parameter vectors).[8]

Have Ericsson and Irons Identified Economic Behavior?

Solving the identification problem involves separating the private sector's response to policy from policy's response to economic conditions. Otherwise one is likely to make the mistake of interpreting endogenous policy reactions, which do not engender changes in private decision rules, as shifts in policy that do.

Ericsson and Irons perform a battery of statistical tests from which they infer that simultaneity is not a problem, so they do not need to model policy. This inference requires one to believe that money demand disturbances have no effect on short and long interest rates and prices within a year, which is the frequency of the data Ericsson and Irons use. Policy can offset short-term interest rate movements by fully accommodating demand shocks, but then the effects show up instead in prices (possibly with a lag) and in long rates (likely immediately). Thus, Ericsson and Irons's estimation of money demand embodies special and, I believe, implausible identifying assumptions about both policy behavior and the structure of the rest of the economy.

Specifying and estimating the policy function, (2), also distinguishes policy from nonpolicy disturbances. Ericsson and Irons interpret the instability of the marginal processes for inflation and interest rates as stemming entirely from policy behavior. This is a strong identifying assumption, as many factors unrelated to policy can shift the stochastic structure of the economy.[9] Although this point is not important for evaluating the logic of the tests Ericsson and Irons perform, it is crucial for interpreting their findings in the context of policy analysis. Whether a change in the stochastic process for, say, technological innovation shifts the processes for inflation and interest rates depends on how policy reacts to it. Essentially, the function G in Ericsson and Irons's procedure is composed of a G_1 function with parameters λ_1 describing policy and a G_2 function with parameters λ_2 describing all behavior other than policy and money demand. It is impossible to discern from Ericsson and Irons's work whether changes in λ_1 or λ_2 generated the instability of the marginal processes.

Ericsson and Irons also maintain the assumption that *any* instability in the marginal processes should generate instability in (4) if expectational behavior is important. A more moderate view is that "big" changes in the marginal processes should shift private behavior but that small ones will have more modest effects over short horizons, even if individuals form expectations rationally. Because they have confined themselves to the rational expectations framework Lucas laid out, Ericsson and Irons's methodology treats all statistically significant changes in the marginal processes as equally important. But whether a statistically significant change is economically important depends on the economic model under consideration.

What Have Ericsson and Irons Found?

The authors asset that "if the Lucas critique is refuted by tests 1 and 2, the refutation is generic." But the authors do not discuss in detail, much less fully specify, even a single *economic* model that implies the equations they estimate. So exactly what are the authors refuting? This section explores some possible interpretations of Ericsson and Irons's findings.

Without an economic model, the identification of (4) as a money demand function is tenuous. Ericsson and Irons's final empirical specification raises several questions that need to be addressed before many readers are willing to interpret (4) as a behavioral relationship:

- Is there a persuasive economic argument for including lagged real balances and lagged inflation rates in the demand function?
- What role, if any, are expectations playing in the underlying money demand function?
- With short rates, long rates, and inflation appearing as contemporaneous explanatory variables, how are the individual demand elasticities identified?
- How far from a theoretically grounded money demand specification must we stray to obtain a reasonably stable relationship?

If we grant that equation (4) can be interpreted as a money demand function, then Ericsson and Irons's discovery that it is stable over a period when the economic environment shifted is not too surprising from the standpoint of many economic theories. In a model with a wide array of assets, money demand emerges from a no-arbitrage condition between money and other nominal assets. There may be no reason to expect this condition to change with policy. Lucas (1988) goes so far as to argue that when money demand is grounded in a transactions motive, rather than merely portfolio choice, the "long-run" demand function is likely to be relatively stable over time. General equilibrium models that Lucas has in mind imply demand functions of the form

$$\frac{M_t}{P_t} = f(r_t, c_t),\tag{6}$$

where r is the short-term nominal interest rate and c is consumption (or permanent income). Broad classes of monetary models imply specification (6).[10] Because (6) contains no expectations terms, other than those embodied implicitly in current realizations of r and c, the demand elasticities do not depend on the stochastic processes for policy variables. One interpretation of Ericsson and Irons's findings is that they have estimated a transactions-based money demand function that looks like (6) in the long run but includes lags of differenced variables and a dummy to capture more complicated short-run dynamics.

Based on Ericsson and Irons's procedure, we can conclude only that (4) is invariant with respect to the interventions that occurred in sample. So another interpretation is that their findings support Sims's argument that big policy changes are rare events and that using an econometric model to evaluate interventions like the ones that occurred historically will not destabilize the model.[11] This conclusion says nothing about the "generic" importance of the Lucas critique.

Alternatively, one could argue that (4) is not a behavioral relationship at all. Ericsson and Irons seem to believe that if an empirical relationship is stable, then it is necessarily behavioral. This belief confuses the economically distinct notions of a "structural" relationship and a "behavioral" one.[12] The fact that $m - p$ appears on the left side of (4) does *not* make the equation a money demand function. A demand function reports how the quantity demanded by a set of private agents changes when income and a vector of relevant prices change, holding all else fixed. Until the authors connect their estimated equation to some economic theory that predicts a money demand function like (4), the equation is more naturally interpreted as an *equilibrium* relationship among the variables.

Many economists would be surprised by the discovery of a stable equilibrium relationship for real balances, particularly in light of the countless studies that have found simple variations on a specification like (6) to be unstable (see, for example, Goldfeld, 1976). Of course, an equilibrium relationship confounds supply and demand behavior, so it is unclear what implications such a stable relationship has for policy evaluation.

I cannot end a discussion of Ericsson and Irons's empirical work without touching on the possible connection between their discovery of an empirically stable money demand function and the general problem of overfitting. In an interesting new paper, Hess, Jones, and Porter (1994) revisit Baba, Hendry, and Starr's (1992) "stable" demand function for M1 in the United States. This demand function, like Ericsson and Irons's, passed the requisite battery of statistical tests, including super exogeneity. Hess, Jones, and Porter added five years of quarterly data to the original sample and found that the model's specification unambiguously fails the authors' own statistical criteria. Hess, Jones, and Porter then present evidence and a set of arguments that point toward the conclusion that the model's failure is associated with overfitting.

Concluding Remarks

If the past twenty years of macroeconomic research have taught economists anything, it has taught the dangers of fitting (and refitting) empirical specifications that are not solidly grounded in economic theory. All the sophisticated econometric techniques developed in recent years cannot substitute for sound economic reasoning and careful efforts to identify data correlations with economic behavior.

The main fault I find with Ericsson and Irons's work is that it frames policy analysis in black and white terms when, in fact, policy analysis is largely gray. Strategic interdependence of the sort that Lucas emphasizes certainly is present in the actual economy. Its importance surely depends both on the private behavioral relationship of interest and on the type of policy intervention being contemplated. Even believers in the stability of money demand would be unlikely to argue that the same functional form and demand elasticities would remain in effect if inflation rose from 2 percent to 200 percent per year. Likewise, believers in the instability of the Phillips curve probably would not throw out a relationship estimated using data that fluctuated mildly around 2 percent when inflation was contemplated to rise temporarily to $2\frac{1}{2}$ percent.

Ericsson and Irons's methodology views policy analysis in its starkest form: a relationship is stable or unstable; private behavior shifts with policy or it does not; expectations affect behavior or they do not. Such starkness lends itself to statistical testing but misses the subtlety inherent in actual policy analysis. By missing the subtlety, the methodology loses its applicability for policy evaluation.

There is a continuum running from theoretically coherent models to ones that fit data. This is an unfortunate reality. Theoretically coherent models can be understood well because they are simple; empirical models fit the data well because they are not. One is always faced with this unpleasant tradeoff when trying to infer economic behavior from data. Real business-cycle models following Kydland and Prescott (1982), which are "calibrated" to match certain time series statistics, lie on one end of the spectrum; LSE-style empirical work chooses to land at the other end. Ericsson and Irons view the world through statistical glasses, while many followers of Kydland and Prescott see things through the lens of economic theory. Progress in empirical macroeconomics requires bifocals.

Acknowledgments

Jon Faust, Kevin Hoover, and Will Roberds provided useful comments and suggestions.

Notes

1. The alternative treatment among macroeconomists, of course, is to dismiss the critique as being unimportant for their application.
2. Among the Cowles Commission writers on this topic were Marschak (1953), Koopmans and Bausch (1959), and Hurwicz (1962).
3. They present no critical analysis of the eleven citations that do not support the Lucas critique.
4. Another blow against large-scale models was leveled by Sims (1980). Sims argued that the identification of those models and, therefore, their economic interpretations are fragile. The reactions to his criticisms have probably also been overdone.
5. Sargent admits the logical difficulties with the rational expectations approach to policy evaluation. His solution is to treat policy as having been in a single regime historically and to assume that policy behavior was not purposeful during the period. The assumptions about policy allow him to treat changes in policy variables as identifying sources of variation off of which private parameters can be estimated. Policy evaluation, according to Sargent, is a once-and-for-all exercise that consists of solving for the parameters λ that solve the policy authority's optimization problem.
6. In F^* there are no time-invariant aspects of policy choice, but that can be modified easily.
7. Ericsson and Irons's remarks on Sims's views completely miss the point. Sims lays out a framework within which conventional policy analysis, consisting of projecting the effects of alternative time paths of policy variables, does not render unstable the decision rules of rational private agents. His structure makes precise the class of policy interventions that will not destabilize the model.
8. Neftçi and Sargent (1978) and Hoover (1991) conduct tests along these lines.
9. Indeed, the real business-cycle literature launched by Kydland and Prescott (1982) questions whether shifts in policy, especially monetary policy, have any important effects on the economy.
10. For example, Lucas's (1988) cash-in-advance model, McCallum's (1989) shopping-time model, as well as a variety of money-in-the-utility function and transactions cost models. Richer models imply demand specifications that depend on realized values of a vector of asset returns as well as some measure of transactions or wealth, but not on their expected values. In contrast, the money demand behavior emerging from the model in Gordon and Leeper (1995) depends explicitly on expected future monetary and fiscal policy outcomes. Such a demand function shifts with the processes describing policy behavior.
11. See Miller and Roberds (1991), though, for an argument that Sims's econometric policy evaluation procedures are not robust to big changes in policy.
12. A "structural" relationship need not connect the decision variable of a particular group of economic decisionmakers to variables that they take as beyond their control. Conversely, a description of the behavior of some group of decisionmakers need not be invariant or structural.

References

Baba, Yoshihisa, David F. Hendry, and Ross M. Starr. (1992). "The Demand for M1 in the U.S.A., 1960–1988." *Review of Economic Studies* 59, 26–61.

Cooley, Thomas F., Stephen LeRoy, and Neil Raymon. (1984). "Econometric Policy Evaluation: Note." *American Economic Review* 74, 467–70.

Friedman, Milton. (1968). "The Role of Monetary Policy." *American Economic Review* 58, 1–17.

Goldfeld, Stephen. (1976). "The Case of the Missing Money." *Brookings Papers on Economic Activity* 3, 683–730.

Gordon, David B., and Eric M. Leeper. (1995). "A Growth Model of Private Transactions and Velocity." Manuscript, Federal Reserve Bank of Atlanta, February.

Hendry, David F. (1988). "The Encompassing Implications of Feedback Versus Feedforward Mechanisms in Econometrics." *Oxford Economic Papers* 40, 132–149.

Hess, Gregory D., Christopher S. Jones, and Richard D. Porter. (1994). "The Predictive Failure of the Baba, Hendry, and Starr Model of the Demand for M1 in the United States." *Finance and Economics Discussion Series No. 94–34*, Federal Reserve Board, November.

Hoover, Kevin D. (1991). "The Causal Direction Between Money and Prices: An Alternative Approach." *Journal of Monetary Economics* 27, 381–324.

Hurwicz, Leonid. (1962). "On the Structural Form of Interdependent Systems." In Ernest Nagel, Patrick Suppes, and Alfred Tarski (eds.), *Logic and Methodology in the Social Sciences* (pp. 232–239). Stanford: Stanford University Press.

Koopmans, Tjalling C., and Augustus F. Bausch. (1959). "Selected Topics in Economics Involving Mathematical Reasoning." *SIAM Review* 1, 138–148.

Kydland, Finn, and Edward C. Prescott. (1982). "Time to Build and Aggregate Fluctuations." *Econometrica* 50, 1345–1370.

Lucas, Robert E., Jr. (1976). "Econometric Policy Evaluation: A Critique." In Karl Brunner and Allan H. Meltzer (eds.), *The Phillips Curve and Labor Markets, Carnegie-Rochester Conference Series on Public Policy*. Vol. 1, *Journal of Monetary Economics*, supplementary issue, 19–46.

Lucas, Robert E., Jr. (1988). "Money Demand in the United States: A Quantitative Review." In Karl Brunner and Bennett T, McCallum (eds.), *Money, Cycles, and Exchange Rates: Essays in Honor of Allan H. Meltzer, Carnegie-Rochester Conference Series on Public Policy* (Vol. 29) (pp, 137–168). Amsterdam: North-Holland.

Marschak, Jacob. (1953). "Econometric Measurements for Policy and Prediction." In William C. Hood and Tjalling C. Koopmans (eds.), *Studies in Econometric Methods* (pp. 1–26). New York: Wiley.

McCallum, Bennett T. (1989). *Monetary Economics: Theory and Policy*. New York: Macmillan.

Miller, Preston J., and William T. Roberds. (1991). "The Quantitative Significance of the Lucas Critique." *Journal of Business and Economic Statistics* 9, 361–387.

Neftçi, Salih, and Thomas J. Sargent. (1978). "A Little Bit of Evidence on the Natural Rate Hypothesis for the U.S." *Journal of Monetary Economics* 4, 315–319.

Phelps, Edmund S. et al. (1970). *Microeconomic Foundations of Employment and Inflation Theory*. New York: Norton.

Sargent, Thomas J. (1984). "Vector Autoregressions, Expectations, and Advice." *American Economic Review* 74, 408–415.

Sims, Christopher A. (1980). "Macroeconomics and Reality." *Econometrica* 48, 1–48.

Sims, Christopher A. (1986). "Are Forecasting Models Usable for Policy Analysis?" *Quarterly Review* (Federal Reserve Bank) Winter, 2–16.

Sims, Christopher A. (1987). "A Rational Expectations Framework for Short-Run Policy Analysis." In William A. Barnett and Kenneth J. Singleton (eds.), *New Approaches to Monetary Economics* (pp. 293–308). Cambridge: Cambridge University Press.

9 RATIONAL EXPECTATIONS AND THE ECONOMIC CONSEQUENCES OF CHANGES IN REGIME

James D. Hamilton

Many economic variables undergo episodes in which the behavior of the series changes quite dramatically. Sometimes this is caused by events such as wars, financial panics, and economic recessions. Abrupt departures from the historical pattern can also be the result of deliberate policy actions taken by the government. For example, if inflation has become a very serious problem, the government may adopt radical changes to try to bring inflation down quickly. Other sources of abrupt change can be the introduction of new taxes and the elimination of previous government regulations.

How economic variables behave in times of dramatic change is an important area of study. This essay surveys recent research on this topic, with a particular focus on how major changes in the economic environment or government policy can affect the behavior of rational economic agents. For concreteness we begin with a detailed discussion of government policies designed to eliminate high inflation. We will subsequently comment on the ways in which similar considerations apply in a variety of different settings.

The Economics of Hyperinflations

A Simple Model of Money Demand

A good example for discussing the economic consequences of changes in regime is provided by a model of money demand developed by Cagan (1956) and Sargent and Wallace (1973). Let

m_t = natural log of the public's money holdings at date t,
p_t = natural log of the aggregate price level at date t,
y_t = natural log of the level of aggregate real income at date t,
i_t = nominal interest rate at date t (measured as a fraction of one).

A simple model of money demand is given by

$$m_t = d + by_t - ai_t + p_t. \tag{9.1}$$

The coefficient b gives the effect of a change in the log of aggregate real income on the log of desired money holdings—that is, b is the elasticity of money demand with respect to income. The coefficient $-a$ gives the effect of a change in the nominal interest rate on the log of desired money holdings, sometimes called the semi-elasticity of money demand with respect to the interest rate. A higher interest rate makes it more costly to hold money relative to bonds, suggesting that people try to reduce their money holdings as the interest rate rises—hence the parameter a is presumed to be positive. The money demand equation also assumes that, for given values of income and the interest rate, an increase in the price level (p_t) causes an equivalent increase in desired nominal money holdings: if prices of goods double, the public needs twice as much nominal cash to purchase the same amount of goods in real terms.

The inflation rate between dates t and $t + 1$ is approximately equal to the change in the log of the price level, $p_{t+1} - p_t$. Thus if $E_t p_{t+1}$ denotes the public's expectation formed at date t as to the value that p_{t+1} will take on, the public's expectation of the inflation rate would be given by

$$E_t p_{t+1} - p_t.$$

The ex ante real interest rate is defined as the nominal interest rate (i_t) minus expected inflation. If r_t denotes the ex ante real interest rate, then

$$i_t = r_t + (E_t p_{t+1} - p_t).$$

Substituting this expression into equation (9.1) results in

$$m_t = d + by_t - a[r_t + (E_t p_{t+1} - p_t)] + p_t.$$

A hyperinflation is characterized by extremely high rates of inflation—say, in excess of 50 percent per year. In such environments, variability in the price level and expected inflation are so large that they are likely to be far more important in determining money demand than are changes in real income or the real interest rate. In such settings a reasonably good approximation to money demand might be obtained by treating real income and the real interest rate as if they were constant. If y_t is replaced by $\bar{y}$ and r_t is replaced by $\bar{r}$, the result is

$$m_t = d + b\bar{y} - a\bar{r} - a(E_t p_{t+1} - p_t) + p_t$$

or

$$m_t = c - a(E_t p_{t+1} - p_t) + p_t \qquad (9.2)$$

for

$$c = d + b\bar{y} - a\bar{r}.$$

Equation (9.2) explains the public's desired money holdings (m_t) in terms of the current price level (p_t) and the rate of inflation expected by the public $(E_t p_{t+1} - p_t)$. The actual money supply is controlled by the central bank. In equilibrium the public's desired money holdings must equal the money supply. Thus for a given money supply set by the central bank we can think of equation (9.2) as determining the equilibrium price level. Rearranging the equation results in

$$p_t = m_t - c + a(E_t p_{t+1} - p_t). \qquad (9.3)$$

This equation describes the equilibrium price level (p_t) as a function of the money supply set by the government (m_t) and the public's expectation as to future inflation $(E_t p_{t+1} - p_t)$. The greater the rate of inflation expected by the public, the higher will be today's price level. This is because when inflation is high there is a great penalty to holding cash. The public would accordingly try to reduce its cash holdings when higher inflation is expected, by using the cash to buy other assets or commodities that might better hold their value. This increased spending would drive up the current price level p_t.

Thus in this setting the effect of government policy depends not only on what the government has already done (as reflected in the current value of the money supply) but also on expectations about what the government may do in the future (insofar as these affect the expectation $E_t p_{t+1} - p_t$). This makes it a useful example for evaluating the consequences of dramatic changes in government policy.

Rational Expectations Under Permanent Regimes

To complete the model we need a theory of how the public's expectations of inflation are formed. One approach is based on the principle of rational expectations.

This approach was originally proposed by Muth (1961) and developed more fully by Lucas (1973) and Sargent and Wallace (1973). The approach requires the model builder to specify the statistical properties of the exogenous variables. In this case such a specification might take the form of an equation describing m_t in terms of its own past values and some random variable representing changes in money that are impossible to forecast. The model builder then specifies the information on which people in the economy are presumed to base their forecast of endogenous variables, and conjectures a form that this forecast would take. For the model of hyperinflation we would guess a rule that people might use to form a forecast of the future price level, $E_t p_{t+1}$. The final step is to verify that the model is internally consistent—that is, to verify that the conjectured forecasts are indeed rational ones to make given the dynamic properties of the variables that are implied by the model.

For example, suppose that the money–supply process is described by

$$m_{t+1} = m_t + g + e_{t+1}.$$

Here g is a parameter that measures the average growth rate of the money supply. The variable e_{t+1} represents changes in the money supply that are impossible to forecast. We could posit that e_{t+1} is drawn from a $N(0, \sigma_e^2)$ distribution and is independent of previous values of any variable in the economy. This money supply process implies that the government is just as likely to increase the money supply by more than g percent as it is to increase the money supply by less than g percent.

We might conjecture that since the money supply grows by g percent on average, it would be rational for the public to expect g percent inflation:

$$E_t p_{t+1} - p_t = g.$$

Substituting this into the money demand function (9.3) implies that

$$p_t = m_t - c + ag. \tag{9.4}$$

It is easy to verify that this model is internally consistent. If p_t is described by the above equation, them p_{t+1} should be as well:

$$p_{t+1} = m_{t+1} - c + ag.$$

The actual inflation rate would them be

$$p_{t+1} - p_t = (m_{t+1} - c + ag) - (m_t - c + ag)$$

$$= m_{t+1} - m_t$$

$$= g + e_{t+1}.$$

Since e_{t+1} is impossible to forecast and is equal to zero on average, it would be perfectly rational for people in such an economy to expect g percent inflation, as we conjectured.

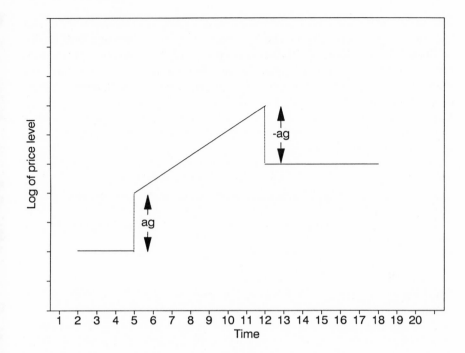

Figure 9.1.   Behavior of the price level under changes in regime that are regarded as permanent

Consider next the effects of a change in policy. Suppose that historically the economy has had zero money growth and stable prices ($g = 0$), but beginning at date T_1 the government allows the money supply to grow rapidly ($g > 0$). Suppose that up until date T_1 the relation between prices and money is given by the pricing equation (9.4) with $g = 0$,

$$p_t = m_t - c \qquad \text{for } t < T_1,$$

whereas after date T_1 the appropriate equation is that for the positive inflation environment,

$$p_t = m_t - c + ag \qquad \text{for } t \geq T_1.$$

The time path followed by prices (under the simplifying assumption that $e_{t+1} = 0$ for all t) is plotted in Figure 9.1. Note that not only does the change in policy cause the average *inflation rate* to move from zero to g percent per year, the change also induces a *one–time surge* in prices at date T_1 in the amount ag. This one–time surge in prices is the result of the flight from money described earlier.

These results point to a difficulty with basing policy predictions on historical correlations. Suppose we had collected data from the zero inflation regime, and used it to estimate the relation between prices and money that held for that historical episode:

$$p_t = m_t - c.$$

As noted by Lucas (1976), this historical relation will not accurately predict the consequences of changing the money growth. The reason is that the historical relation is influenced by the expectations about government policy that people held during the sample. If the government changes its policy, the nature of people's forecasts may change, and this implies a different relation between prices and money—namely,

$$p_t = m_t - c + ag.$$

The earlier historical relation between money and prices, $p_t = m_t - c$, will underpredict the level of prices under the new regime.

If the government were to reform its policy at some later date T_2 and return money growth to zero, the above reasoning applies in reverse. The reform would be accompanied by a one-time drop in the price level in the amount $-ag$ (again see Figure 9.1). Alternatively, if the government could credibly convince the public that *future* money growth was going to be controlled, at the end of the inflation (date T_2) the government could implement a one-time surge in the money supply, increasing m_{T_2} by the amount ag, without any inflationary consequences. Although this scenario might seem farfectched, it in fact describes exactly what seems to have happened at the the end of many historical hyperinflations. If convincing, dramatic monetary reforms are adopted, such as commitment to a fixed exchange rate and a clear institutional separation of the central bank from the fiscal authority, governments often have been able to increase the money supply dramatically at the end of big inflations. This increase does not drive up prices because it simply is meeting the increased demand for money that comes at the end of a hyperinflation. On a more modest scale, some economists have suggested that the U.S. Federal Reserve's demonstrated willingness to tolerate very high interest rates in the early 1980s convinced the public of its seriousness about bringing down inflation. The result was that a large increase in the money supply after 1982 produced little increase in inflation. Auernheimer (1974) argued that analyses that leave out this potential surge in the money supply at the end of a hyperinflation often underestimate the revenue benefits that a government can enjoy by moving to a money supply path with a slower average growth rate.

Rational Expectations and Changes in Regime

While this framework offers some useful insights into hyperinflation, it is not altogether satisfactory for analyzing the dynamic transition between low and high inflation episodes. As emphasized by Cooley, LeRoy, and Raymon (1984), the above analysis is not really true to the principle of rational expectations. Prior to date T_1, the people in the economy were assumed to attach zero probability to the likelihood of an acceleration of money growth—that is, they regarded $g = 0$ as a fixed constant. Yet as events turn out, the parameter g is evidently subject to change.

A model closer in spirt to the ideas of Muth (1961) would carry the analysis one step further and specify a probability distribution governing the value of the average money growth parameter g. The simplest such model might postulate that if the government is currently following the zero inflation regime, there is a probability q that it will continue with the zero inflation regime the next period, and a probability $1 - q$ that it will shift to the regime in which money grows at g percent per year. That is, if the economy is in the zero inflation regime at date t, then

$$m_{t+1} = m_t + e_{t+1} \qquad \text{with probability } q,$$
$$= m_t + g + e_{t+1} \qquad \text{with probability } 1 - q.$$

The rational forecast of the money supply for date $t + 1$ given that the economy is in the zero inflation regime at date t would then be

$$E_t m_{t+1} = m_t + (1 - q)g.$$

Similarly, if the economy is in the high inflation regime at date t, there is a probability w that it will continue in the high inflation regime next period, and a probability $(1 - w)$ that it will return to the zero inflation regime:

$$m_{t+1} = m_t + g + e_{t+1} \qquad \text{with probability } w,$$
$$= m_t + e_{t+1} \qquad \text{with probability } 1 - w.$$

The optimal forecast of the money supply in the high inflation regime would then be

$$E_t m_{t+1} = m_t + wg.$$

Let s_t be a variable representing which regime the economy is in at date t; $s_t = 0$ means that the government was following the zero money growth strategy between dates $t - 1$ and t, while $s_t = 1$ means that the government was allowing the money supply to grow by g percent between dates $t - 1$ and t. Then the forecasts appropriate under the two regimes can be summarized by the following single expression:

$$E_t m_{t+1} = m_t + (1 - q)g + (-1 + w + q)gs_t.$$

In this environment it turns out that a rational expectations description of the price process is provided by

$$p_t = -c + \frac{ag(1 - q)}{(1 - v)} + m_t + \frac{vg}{(1 - v)}s_t, \qquad (9.5)$$

where

$$v = \frac{a(-1 + w + q)}{(1 + a)}.$$

The appendix verifies that equation (9.5) satisfies the internal consistency requirement of rational expectations.

If the economy is currently in the zero inflation regime ($s_t = 0$), then as the probability of remaining in that regime goes to one ($q \rightarrow 1$), equation (9.5) approaches

$$p_t = -c + m_t,$$

which is the earlier equation used for the pure zero inflation economy. Likewise, if the economy is currently in the high inflation regime ($s_t = 1$), then as the probability of staying with high inflation goes to one ($w \rightarrow 1$), the price process can be shown to converge to

$$p_t = -c + m_t + ag,$$

which is the earlier equation used for the pure high inflation economy. Thus as noted by Lucas (1976), the simple model employed in Figure 9.1 can be viewed as a limiting case of a more general framework, the limiting case being one in which people believe that each regime is virtually certain to persist forever. The more general framework also applies to situations in which people's anticipations of future changes in regime can materially affect the current equilibrium.

Econometric Analysis of Changes in Regime

Suppose we have data that may have been characterized by changes in regime. Even though the econometrician may not know when the changes occurred, the observed data can be used to estimate the parameters describing each regime and to form an inference about the most likely dates of changes in regime.

For example, consider a data set consisting only of money growth rates for a series of different dates. Suppose that the term e_{t+1} described above is drawn from a $N(0, \sigma_e^2)$ distribution. If the economy is in the high inflation regime at date t, the

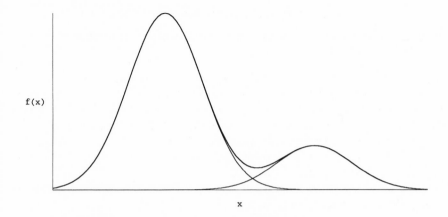

Figure 9.2.   Density of a mixture of two normal variables

probability that the economy will be in the high inflation regime at date $t + 1$ is w. If the economy is in the zero inflation regime at date t, the probability that the economy will be in the high inflation regime at date $t + 1$ is $1 - q$. Consider the simplest case in which the probability of being in the high inflation regime next period is the same regardless of the current regime ($w = 1 - q$). Then a fraction w of the observed money growth changes would likely be drawn from a normal distribution with mean g, and the remaining fraction $1 - w$ would be drawn from a normal distribution with mean zero:

$$m_{t+1} - m_t \sim N(g, \sigma_e^2) \qquad \text{with probability } w,$$

$$m_{t+1} - m_t \sim N(0, \sigma_e^2) \qquad \text{with probability } 1 - w.$$

The density of $(m_{t+1} - m_t)$ is then a weighted average of the two normal densities:

$$f(m_{t+1} - m_t; g, \sigma_e, w) = \frac{w}{\sqrt{2\pi}\sigma_e} \exp\left\{\frac{-(m_{t+1} - m_t - g)^2}{2\sigma_e^2}\right\}$$

$$+ \frac{(1 - w)}{\sqrt{2\pi}\sigma_e} \exp\left\{\frac{-(m_{t+1} - m_t)^2}{2\sigma_e^2}\right\}. \qquad (9.6)$$

Figure 9.2 gives an example of what such a density might look like. This family of densities is described by the parameters g, σ_e, and w. In a more general application, we might allow nonzero means for both regimes and different variances across regimes. This is a fairly rich class of probability distributions and need not be characterized by the bimodal appearance of the example graphed in Figure 9.2;

see Everitt and Hand (1981, pp. 28–29) for other possible shapes this distribution might assume.

Given data on money growth rates $(m_{t+1} - m_t)$ for some sample of size $T(t = 1, 2, \ldots, T)$, the values of the parameters g, σ_e, and w can be estimated by the principle of maximum likelihood. This principle suggests that we use as estimates of g, σ_e, and w those values that would have been most likely to have generated the observed data. Loosely speaking, the maximum likelihood estimate $\hat{w}$ will essentially be the fraction of observations that cluster in a bell–shaped curve centered at some point above zero. The estimate $\hat{g}$ will be the sample mean of this subset of the observations, while σ_e^2 will be based on the average squared deviation of each observation from its nearest mean.[1]

Once we have estimated the population parameters g, σ_e, and w, these can be used to form an inference about which regime was in effect for any given date in the sample. The probability that $s_{t+1} = 1$—that is, the probability that money growth between periods t and $t + 1$ is characterized by the high inflation regime—is given by w. Moreover, if the economy is in regime 1 at date $t + 1$, then $(m_{t+1} - m_t)$ is distributed $N(g, \sigma_e^2)$. Hence the joint probability that (1) $s_{t+1} = 1$ and (2) money growth would equal the observed value $m_{t+1} - m_t$ is given by

$$f(s_{t+1} = 1, m_{t+1} - m_t; g, \sigma_e, w) = \frac{w}{\sqrt{2\pi}\sigma_e} \exp\left\{\frac{-(m_{t+1} - m_t - g)^2}{2\sigma_e^2}\right\}. \quad (9.7)$$

An estimate of this joint probability could be obtained by evaluating equation (9.7) at the maximum likelihood estimates $\hat{g}$, $\hat{\sigma}_e$, and $\hat{w}$. If this joint probability is then divided by the marginal density of $m_{t+1} - m_t$ in (9.6), the result is the probability that $s_{t+1} = 1$ conditional on having observed that money growth for that date was equal to $m_{t+1} - m_t$:

$$\text{Prob}(s_{t+1} = 1 \mid m_{t+1} - m_t; \hat{g}, \hat{\sigma}_e, \hat{w}) = \frac{f(s_{t+1} = 1, m_{t+1} - m_t; \hat{g}, \hat{\sigma}_e, \hat{w})}{f(m_{t+1} - m_t; \hat{g}, \hat{\sigma}_e, \hat{w})}$$

This quantity tells us how likely it is that the government was actually following a high inflation policy between dates t and $t + 1$.

The above description assumed that the current regime ($s_t = 0$ or 1) has no effect on the probability of next period's regime and that the term e_{t+1} is independent and identically distributed across dates. However, the same basic idea can be applied with more general dynamic behavior for both the regime and the error, and is easily extended beyond two possible states (see Hamilton, 1989, 1990, 1994, for details). The maximum likelihood estimate of w essentially turns out to be the fraction of times that regime 1 appeared to be followed by another observation from regime 1, while the maximum likelihood estimate of q is roughly the fraction of times that regime 0 was followed by another observation from regime 0. General dynamic relations can be fit separately to the subset of observations that describe each of the two regimes.

One might think that if a switch in regime only appears to have happened once in a given sample, no reliable inference about the parameters of the process can be drawn. However, this is not the case. The reliability of the inference about the parameters that describe regime 1 depends on the total number of observations that were generated from regime 1 and not on the number of switches between regimes that occur. Every observation generated from regime 1 gives new information about the parameter w; if regime 1 is almost always followed by another observation from regime 1, that is evidence that w is large. If the economy seems to have remained in regime 1 for ten consecutive periods, for example, then we can assert with some confidence that w must be larger than 0.7.[2]

Econometric Analysis and Rational Expectations

We described above how data on exogenous variables such as $m_{t+1} - m_t$ can be used to form an inference about the timing and nature of changes in regime. It is also possible to use data on endogenous variables such as p_t to further refine this inference and to test hypotheses about how the public responds to the perceived changes in regime. For example, if measurement error, represented by the variable u_t, is added to the pricing equation (9.5), then the model implies the following joint description for money and prices:

$$p_t = -c + \frac{ag(1 - q)}{(1 - v)} + m_t + \frac{vg}{(1 - v)} s_t + u_t$$

$$m_t = m_{t-1} + gs_t + e_t.$$

Let $\mathbf{y}_t$ denote the vector

$$\mathbf{y}_t = \begin{bmatrix} p_t - m_t \\ m_t - m_{t-1} \end{bmatrix}.$$

Then the model can be expressed as

$$\mathbf{y}_t \sim N(\boldsymbol{\mu}_0, \boldsymbol{\Sigma}) \qquad \text{when } s_t = 0,$$

$$\mathbf{y}_t \sim N(\boldsymbol{\mu}_1, \boldsymbol{\Sigma}) \qquad \text{when } s_t = 1$$

where

$$\boldsymbol{\mu}_0 = \begin{bmatrix} -c + ag(1 - q)/(1 - v) \\ 0 \end{bmatrix}$$

$$\mu_1 = \begin{bmatrix} -c + ag(1-q)/(1-v) + vg/(1-v) \\ g \end{bmatrix}$$

$$\Sigma = \begin{bmatrix} \sigma_u^2 & 0 \\ 0 & \sigma_e^2 \end{bmatrix}.$$

The parameters c, a, q, w, g, σ_e^2, and σ_u^2 can again be estimated by maximum likelihood on the basis of the observed data on money growth rates and the price level, and hypotheses about the public's behavior can be tested. For an illustration of this approach see Engel and Hamilton (1990).

This specification assumed that, unlike the econometrician, the public knew for certain the regime s_t that the government was following at date t. The same framework can be adapted to the case in which the public's behavior is based on the same inference that the econometrician would use,

$$\text{Prob}(s_t = 1 \mid m_t - m_{t-1}, m_{t-1} - m_{t-2}, \ldots, m_1 - m_0).$$

See Hamilton, 1988a, for an illustration of how this can be done.

Figure 9.3 displays the results obtained by Ruge-Murcia (1992), who used a related approach to analyze Brazilian inflation data. The top panel plots monthly inflation rates in Brazil over the period 1983–1989. Three major attempts at stabilizing prices—the Cruzado plan in 1986, the Bresser plan in 1987, and the Summer plan in 1989—are seen in retrospect to have been purely transitory reforms. In Ruge-Murcia's model, the different regimes for money growth are presumed to be driven by underlying changes in the level of government spending that the government tries to finance by printing new money. Using the specification of money demand described above and a generalization of the regime-switching model that is assumed to describe spending, Ruge-Murcia estimated the model's parameters based on the observed behavior of government spending and prices. The bottom panel of Figure 9.3 plots the variable

$$\text{Prob}(s_t = 1 \mid g_t, g_{t-1}, \ldots, g_1, p_t - p_{t-1}, p_{t-1} - p_{t-2}, \ldots, p_1 - p_0)$$

as a function of t. When this variable is close to one, it means that during period t the government appears to have been engaging in the high-spending regime. This inference is based on both the level of spending and on the behavior of prices, which signal the public's perceptions of high levels of spending through the effect that expectations of inflation are assumed to have on the demand for money.

Other Economic Implications of Changes in Regime

The public's perceptions of current and future changes in regime can have important economic consequences. This possibility was illustrated above in terms of a

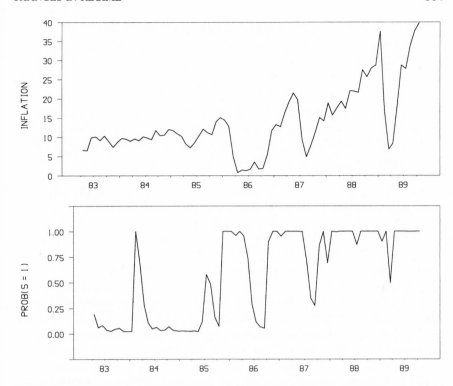

Figure 9.3. Top panel: Monthly inflation rate in Brazil, 1983–1989; bottom panel: Probability that Brazilian fiscal policy is in the high inflation regime
Source: Ruge-Murcia (1992).

simple model of hyperinflation. A related theme appears in a variety of other settings as well.

Balance of Payments and Currency Crises

One important example can occur if a government is trying to maintain a fixed rate of exchange between its currency and some other country's currency. For example, the Mexican government might try to peg its currency (the peso) to the U.S. dollar. It does this by maintaining reserves of dollar-denominated assets. When the public wants to sell pesos in exchange for dollars, the government provides a ready demand for these pesos by buying these pesos with its dollar reserves. Such purchases can keep the peso's value from falling.

The Mexican government is limited in its ability to engage in such stabilization by the quantity of dollar reserves it holds and by the market fundamentals that would determine the dollar-peso exchange rate in the absence of intervention. If speculators form the belief that in the future the Mexican government will be forced to abandon the current exchange rate and devalue the peso, they have an added incentive to convert pesos into dollars today before the pesos lose their value. Hence in this case the perception of a future change in regime can produce a speculative attack on the currency and foment a balance of payments crisis today. Krugman (1979) and Flood and Garber (1984) provided theoretical analyses of this phenomenon.

Such destabilizing effects of the possibility of future changes in regime may have made a material contribution to the severity of the Great Depression of 1929–1933.[3] In the late 1920s the world returned to an international gold standard, in which each country tried to maintain a fixed rate of exchange between its currency and gold. Uncertainties about monetary and fiscal policies and misalignment of currencies in many European countries left the system vulnerable to the kind of speculative attack described by Krugman, Flood, and Garber. Up until 1931 the Depression could have been described as a severe recession similar to earlier downturns. In 1931, doubts developed about the abilities of countries to maintain gold parity, and many countries (including the United States) experienced speculative attacks. These attacks exacerbated the climate of business and financial uncertainty and generated volatile flows of capital between different countries and different classes of assets. In the case of the United States, the attacks were abated by a tightening of monetary policy, which further contributed to the depth of the Depression. Individual countries began recovering from the Depression at different times, but the general pattern is that recovery began only after the gold standard was abandoned (see Eichengreen and Sachs, 1985; Bernanke and James, 1991). By going off the gold standard, countries were able to eliminate the incentives for speculation that arose from uncertainty about future changes in regime.

A related potential consequence of the public's expectation about future changes in regime was discussed by Rodrik (1992). Many developing countries have tried to liberalize markets and open up their economies to foreign trade. However, if the public has doubts about the longevity of the regime of liberalization, there are incentives to go on an import buying binge for the period in which the regime lasts. Such purchases can undermine the success of the reforms.

Dating Turning Points and the Business Cycle

Another application of the approach described above to inferring changes in regime is in the identification of "turning points" in the behavior of a given series.

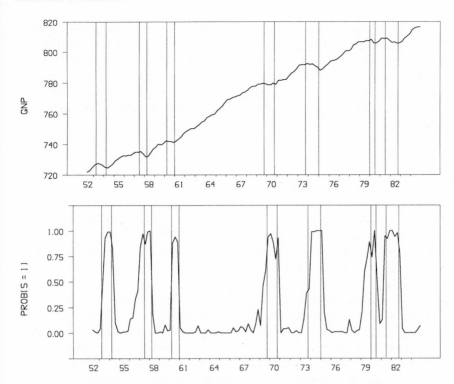

Figure 9.4. Top panel: 100 times the log of U.S. real GNP, 1951–1984; bottom panel: Probability that the U.S. economy is in the recessionary regime
Source: Hamilton (1989).

The top panel of Figure 9.4 graphs the log of quarterly real GNP for the United States over 1951–1984. The general upward trend is occasionally interrupted by short episodes in which GNP actually falls, known as economic recessions. The dates at which the National Bureau of Economic Research believes that recessions began and ended are indicated with vertical lines on the top panel. These dates are based on *ex post* judgmental examination of a number of economic indicators.

When GNP growth rates are viewed as having come from two different dynamic regimes, the maximum likelihood estimates suggest that one of the regimes is associated with rising GNP and the other with falling GNP. The bottom panel of Figure 9.4 (taken from Hamilton, 1989) graphs the probability that the economy was in the falling GNP regime at any given historical date. This designation is remarkably similar to that arrived at by the National Bureau of Economic Research based on qualitative judgment.

This basic approach has been generalized by a number of researchers. Phillips (1991) extended this approach to a two-country setting to examine the transmission mechanism of business cycles across countries. Filardo (1994) allowed the transition probabilities between the expansion and recession regimes to be functions of other observed variables. Lam (1990) proposed an alternative specification in which some shocks have permanent effects and others have temporary effects.

Changes in Regime and Financial Markets

The world's market economies have experienced a number of financial panics during the past century; Friedman and Schwartz (1963), Kindleberger (1989), and Mishkin (1991) have provided useful descriptions of these crises. These episodes are marked by a sudden increase in interest rates and plunge in stock prices. Schwert (1989, 1990) has used the regime-switching specification described above to provide a useful descriptive summary of this phenomenon.

In an effort to explain this phenomenon in terms of economic fundamentals, Cecchetti, Lam, and Mark (1990a) fit a regime-switching model to one hundred years of observations on real dividends for the United States. Typically dividends grow at around three percent per year in real terms. At roughly twenty-year intervals, however, real dividends plunge by 35 percent per year. This pattern of rare but large outliers has important implications both for how investors would price stocks and for the reliability of econometric inference that does not take this non-normal distribution of returns into account. When the apparent process for dividends is factored in to conventional asset pricing formulas, several previous apparent anomalies in the behavior of stock prices can be explained.

Other investigations of financial markets using this approach include Cecchetti, Lam, and Mark (1990b), Engel and Hamilton (1990), Garcia and Perron (1989), and Turner, Startz, and Nelson (1989).

Summary

The dynamic behavior of many economic time series can sometimes change dramatically from the previous historical pattern. The public's expectations about future changes have important implications for how the economy behaves today. Using a statistical model to describe these changes in regime offers a useful approach for analyzing their effects on rational economic agents.

Appendix: Rational Expectations Solution of the Money Demand Model

Notice that according to the conjectured solution (9.5),

$$
p_{t+1} - p_t = m_{t+1} + \frac{vg}{(1-v)}s_{t+1} - m_t - \frac{vg}{(1-v)}s_t
$$

$$
= (m_t + gs_{t+1} + e_{t+1}) + \frac{vg}{(1-v)}s_{t+1} - m_t - \frac{vg}{(1-v)}s_t
$$

$$
= e_{t+1} + \left\{ \frac{(1-v)}{(1-v)} + \frac{v}{(1-v)} \right\} gs_{t+1} - \frac{vg}{(1-v)}s_t
$$

$$
= e_{t+1} + \frac{g}{(1-v)}s_{t+1} - \frac{vg}{(1-v)}s_t,
$$

from which the public's expected inflation is

$$
E_t p_{t+1} - p_t = \frac{g}{(1-v)}E_t(s_{t+1}) - \frac{vg}{(1-v)}s_t.
$$

Recalling that

$$
E_t(s_{t+1}) = (1-q) + (-1+w+q)s_t,
$$

it follows that

$$
E_t p_{t+1} - p_t = \frac{g(1-q)}{(1-v)} + \frac{g(-1+w+q)}{(1-v)}s_t - \frac{vg}{(1-v)}s_t
$$

$$
= \frac{g(1-q)}{(1-v)} + \frac{g}{(1-v)}(-1+w+q-v)s_t. \qquad (9A.1)
$$

But since

$$
-1+w+q-v = (-1+w+q) - \frac{a(-1+w+q)}{(1+a)}
$$

$$
= \left\{ \frac{(1+a)}{(1+a)} - \frac{a}{(1+a)} \right\}(-1+w+q)
$$

$$
= \frac{(-1+w+q)}{(1+a)},
$$

expression (9A.1) becomes

$$
E_t p_{t+1} - p_t = \frac{g(1-q)}{(1-v)} + \frac{g(-1+w+q)}{(1-v)(1+a)}s_t.
$$

Substituting this into the money demand equation (9.3) results in

$$p_t = m_t - c + a(E_t p_{t+1} - p_t)$$

$$= m_t - c + \frac{ag(1-q)}{(1-v)} + \frac{ag(-1+w+q)}{(1-v)(1+a)} s_t$$

$$= m_t - c + \frac{ag(1-q)}{(1-v)} + \frac{vg}{(1-v)} s_t$$

as claimed in (9.5).

In the special case when $s_t = 1$ this implies

$$p_t = m_t - c + \frac{g[a(1-q)+v]}{(1-v)} . \qquad (9A.2)$$

Under the further restriction that $w = 1$ we have

$$[a(1-q)+v] = a(1-q) + \frac{aq}{(1+a)}$$

$$= a\left\{1 - \frac{(1+a)}{(1+a)}q + \frac{q}{(1+a)}\right\}$$

$$= a\left\{1 - \frac{aq}{(1+a)}\right\}$$

$$= a(1-v),$$

in which case equation (9A.2) would be

$$p_t = m_t - c + \frac{ag(1-v)}{(1-v)}$$

$$= m_t - c + ag,$$

reproducing the earlier result (9.4) for the pure high inflation regime as a special case.

Acknowledgments

The author is Professor of Economics, University of California at San Diego, La Jolla, CA 92093-0508. I thank the National Science Foundation for financial support under grant number SBR93-08301.

Notes

1. See Everitt and Hand (1981, pp. 36–37) for a more formal characterization of the maximum likelihood estimates.
2. This statement is based on the observation that $0.7^{10} = 0.028$, which means the probability of observing such a run if the true value of w were 0.7 or smaller would be less than 3 percent.
3. This argument is developed in Hamilton (1988b).

References

Auernheimer, Leonardo. (1974). "The Honest Government's Guide to the Revenue from the Creation of Money." *Journal of Political Economy* 82, 598–606.

Bernanke, Ben, and Harold James. (1991). "The Gold Standard, Deflation, and Financial Crisis in the Great Depression: An International Comparison." In R. Glenn Hubbard (ed.), *Financial Markets and Financial Crises* (pp. 33–68). Chicago: University of Chicago Press.

Cagan, Phillip. (1956). "The Monetary Dynamics of Hyperinflation." In Milton Friedman (ed.), *Studies in the Quantity Theory of Money* (pp. 25–117). Chicago: University of Chicago Press.

Cecchetti, Stephen G., Pok-sang Lam, and Nelson C. Mark. (1990a). "Evaluating Empirical Tests of Asset Pricing Models: Alternative Interpretations." *American Economic Review* 80, 48–51.

Cecchetti, Stephen G., Pok-sang Lam, and Nelson C. Mark. (1990b). "Mean Reversion in Equilibrium Asset Prices." *American Economic Review* 80, 398–418.

Cooley, Thomas F., Stephen F. LeRoy, and Neil Raymon. (1984). "Econometric Policy Evaluation: Note." *American Economic Review* 74, 467–470.

Eichengreen, Barry, and Jeffrey Sachs. (1985). "Exchange Rates and Economic Recovery in the 1930s." *Journal of Economic History* 45, 925–946.

Engel, Charles M., and James D. Hamilton. (1990). "Long Swings in the Dollar: Are They in the Data and Do Markets Know It?" *American Economic Review* 80, 689–713.

Everitt, B.S., and D.J. Hand. (1981). *Finite Mixture Distributions*. New York: Chapman and Hall.

Filardo, Andrew. (1994). "Business Cycle Phases and Their Transitional Dynamics." *Journal of Business and Economic Statistics* 12, 299–308.

Flood, Robert P., and Peter M. Garber. (1984). "Gold Monetization and Gold Discipline." *Journal of Political Economy* 92, 90–107.

Friedman, Milton, and Anna J. Schwartz. (1963). *A Monetary History of the United States, 1867–1960*. Princeton, NJ: Princeton University Press.

Garcia, Rene, and Pierre Perron. (1989). "An Analysis of the Real Interest Rate Under Regime Shifts." Mimeo, University of Montreal.

Hamilton, James D. (1988a). "Rational-Expectations Econometric Analysis of Changes in Regime: An Investigation of the Term Structure of Interest Rates." *Journal of Economic Dynamics and Control* 12, 385–423.

Hamilton, James D. (1988b). "The Role of the International Gold Standard in Propagating the Great Depression." *Contemporary Policy Issues* 6, 67–89.

Hamilton, James D. (1989). "A New Approach to the Economic Analysis of Nonstationary Time Series and the Business Cycle." *Econometrica* 57, 357–384.

Hamilton, James D. (1990). "Analysis of Time Series Subject to Changes in Regime." *Journal of Econometrics* 45, 39–70.

Hamilton, James D. (1994). *Time Series Analysis.* Princeton NJ: Princeton University Press.

Kindleberger, Charles P. (1989). *Manias, Panics, and Crashes: A History of Financial Crises* (2nd ed.). New York: Basic Books.

Krugman, Paul. (1979). "A Model of Balance-of-Payments Crises." *Journal of Money, Credit, and Banking* 1, 311–325.

Lam, Pok-sang. (1990). "The Hamilton Model with a General Autoregressive Component: Estimation and Comparison with Other Models of Economic Time Series." *Journal of Monetary Economics* 26, 409–432.

Lucas, Robert E., Jr. (1973). "Some International Evidence on Output-Inflation Trade-Offs." *American Economic Review* 63, 326–334.

Lucas, Robert E., Jr. (1976). "Econometric Policy Evaluation: A Critique." In Karl Brunner and Allen H. Meltzer (eds.), *The Phillips Curve and Labor Markets.* Vol. 1, *Carnegie-Rochester Conference Series on Public Policy,* 19–46.

Mishkin, Frederic S. (1991). "Asymmetric Information and Financial Crises: A Historical Perspective." In R. Glenn Hubbard (ed.), *Financial Markets and Financial Crises* (pp. 69–108). Chicago: University of Chicago Press.

Muth, John F. (1961). "Rational Expectations and the Theory of Price Movements." *Econometrica* 29, 315–335.

Phillips, Kerk L. (1991). "A Two-Country Model of Stochastic Output with Changes in Regime," *Journal of International Economics* 31, 121–142.

Rodrik, Dani. (1992). "The Limits of Trade Policy Reform in Developing Countries." *Journal of Economic Perspectives* 6, 87–105.

Ruge-Murcia, Francisco. (1992). "Government Credibility in Heterodox Stabilization Programs." Ph.D. dissertation, University of Virginia.

Sargent, Thomas J., and Neil Wallace. (1973). "Rational Expectations and the Dynamics of Hyperinflation." *International Economic Review* 14, 328–350.

Schwert, G. William. (1989). "Business Cycles, Financial Crises, and Stock Volatility." In Karl Brunner and Allen H. Meltzer (eds.), *IMF Policy Advice, Market Volatility, Commodity Price Rules, and Other Essays.* Vol. 31, *Carnegie-Rochester Conference Series on Public Policy,* Autumn 83–125.

Schwert, G. William. (1990). "Stock Volatility and the Crash of '87." *Review of Financial Studies* 3, 77–102.

Turner, Christopher M., Richard Startz, and Charles R. Nelson. (1989). "A Markov Model of Heteroskedasticity, Risk, and Learning in the Stock Market." *Journal of Financial Economics* 25, 3–22.

Commentary on Chapter 9

Glenn D. Rudebusch

- How do rational economic agents identify and react to major changes in their economic environment?
- How do econometricians identify and conduct inference in the presence of such structural changes?
- What are the causes and mechanisms of such structural changes?

Finding answers to these questions has been a robust research enterprise in economics in the past decade, and James Hamilton has been a prolific and insightful contributor to this literature, as evidenced by his latest work in this volume. Here, I provide some comments to elucidate two broad themes. First, I discuss in some detail the Lucas critique, which stresses the links between rational expectations and structural change and is the impetus underlying Hamilton's work in this volume. Second, I discuss a few aspects of the specific regime-switching model that Hamilton popularized in his earlier work and that he uses here so effectively.

The Lucas Critique

Lucas (1976) criticized traditional macroeconometric models for their failure to account explicitly for agents' expectations of future variables. He argued that the coefficients of the behavioral equations of these models depended, in part, on the parameters describing the formation of agents' expectations; furthermore, under rational expectations, the expectations parameters reflect agents' understanding of the underlying economic structure. Accordingly, if there were a structural change in the laws of motion for the exogenous variables, the coefficients of the models' equations could not be expected to remain stable. The basic thrust of the Lucas critique—that the coefficients of reduced-form models are not invariant to structural changes—had been acknowledged well before 1976. As Lucas points out, Marschak (1953) and Tinbergen (1956) raised similar criticisms. However, Lucas's version of this critique, which stressed the crucial role of expectations, was widely viewed as a devastating indictment of traditional consumption, wage-price, and investment equations.

Lucas's charge that the coefficients of most empirical models were reduced-form, "shallow" parameters that were subject to change resulted in a major reorientation of econometric modeling. The subsequent research program of rational expectations econometrics has attempted to estimate the underlying parameters of taste and technology governing objective functions. In particular, much research has focused on the estimation of the stochastic first-order conditions for optimal choice by a rational, forward-looking representative agent. Indeed, this "Euler equation" modeling strategy has dominated empirical work in consumption (following Hall, 1978) and investment (following Abel, 1980).

Although Euler equations have become a very popular approach, there has been surprisingly little examination of their empirical adequacy and, in particular, their structural stability. For modeling investment spending, many authors have estimated the first-order conditions of the firm's intertemporal optimization problem given production and adjustment cost functions, and they generally view the resulting estimates as shedding light on stable "deep" parameters. To provide some specification tests of this investment Euler equation, Oliner, Rudebusch, and Sichel (1995, 1996) examine its structural stability. There are two different types of tests available in the literature that they employ.

First, there are *split-sample* tests that separate the whole sample into two parts and compare model parameters estimated from each part. The simplest split-sample test for structural stability is the usual F-test for structural change in a linear regression discussed by Chow (1960). The general case for this type of test is described in Andrews and Fair (1988). These tests assume that if structural change has occurred, it took place on a known breakpoint date. However, recent advances have been made in split-sample testing for structural change at an unknown breakpoint. In particular, Andrews (1993) describes the distribution of the maximum value of a *sequence* of test statistics from all possible breakpoints.

Second, there are *subsample* tests (often called "recursive" tests in the literature) that are based on the sequence of model estimates obtained by starting with a small set of observations and progressively enlarging the estimation sample one observation at a time. (Dufour, 1982, provides a useful survey.) This sequence of subsample estimates provides direct evidence concerning parameter drift and out-of-sample forecast performance.

Oliner, Rudebusch, and Sichel (1995, 1996) find that both types of tests indicate that the standard investment Euler equation exhibits substantial parameter instability. This is not an indictment of the Lucas critique but is instead an indication of the adequacy of the Euler equation response to that critique.

It is one thing to detect structural change empirically; it is a separate enterprise to explain that change. The source of much of the structural instability exhibited by empirical equations is often unclear. For example, whether indeed the instability demonstrated by a traditional accelerator investment equation reflects the response of expectations of rational agents (as in Lucas's critique) or some other model misspecification has not been determined.

Regime-Switching Models

In Hamilton's example, the application of the Lucas critique implies that the equation that appears to adequately describe rational agents' money demand during a zero-inflation regime breaks down with a change in the policy regime. The reduced form relationship between prices and money changes from one regime to the other. What is unsatisfactory about this analysis, as pointed out by Hamilton as well as Sims (1982) and fully developed by Cooley, LeRoy, and Raymon (1984) and by LeRoy's work in this volume, is that it has the rational agents treat the structural change as a change in a parameter. That is, the change is treated as unforeseen and permanent. More plausibly in most cases, the object that changes should be treated as a variable and incorporated in the model. Hamilton provides a useful example of how a change in policy can be incorporated as a probabilistic element in a larger model. In his model, the agent with rational, or model-consistent, expectations correctly recognizes and takes into account the probability that the policy regime may change.

Of course, not all potential structural changes can be fruitfully incorporated into a complete, all-encompassing model that is understood by rational agents. Indeed, an interesting literature has developed that continues to treat the structural change as an unforeseen, permanent parameter shift. However, this literature is sensible because it relaxes the assumption of the rationality of the economic agents and introduces explicitly the notion that some learning about the new structure must take place. For example, Sargent (1993) provides a useful introduction to the literature and centers his analysis on the "bounded rationality" of agents with respect to structural change. Thus, rather than treating a change in a parameter as something rational agents seamlessly adapt to (as did Lucas), the literature with learning permits agents to slowly adjust their behavior to new situations in which their previous experience is not entirely informative. For example, understanding the economic actions of those in the newly emerging market economies of Eastern Europe, who face unprecedented changes, realistically requires an understanding of transitional learning dynamics.

In any case, to return to Hamilton's analysis, where there is an explicit process generating the structural change, the next question he addresses is how to conduct an econometric analysis of the changes in regime. Hamilton's model in this paper is based on his pioneering work examining series whose time-series dynamics depend on an unobservable state that is governed by a first-order Markov process. There have been numerous applications of this specific regime-switching model— perhaps the best known is the use in a business-cycle context for dating turning points between recessions and expansions.[1]

One shortcoming of almost all of these applications is that they make no attempt to statistically test the hypothesis of regime switching against the hypothesis of a constant structure. The infrequency of testing for regime switching reflects the difficult, nonstandard econometrics involved. The difficulty lies in the Markov probabilities governing the transition, which are not identified under the hypothesis that there is no regime switching. Hansen (1992) proposes a valid but computational burdensome test. Diebold and Rudebusch (1994) describe and implement a closely related but tractable test, and they find striking support for a two-state regime switching process governing business cycles.

Finally, with respect to "explaining" regime switching, Diebold and Rudebusch (1994) survey some interesting models that can be construed as supporting regime switching in a business-cycle context. These are models in which there is a "strategic" element to an agent's economic actions. These strategic elements or externalities can arise, for example, in a model of search; in essence, search is more desirable when other agents are also searching because it is likely to be more productive. These externalities can produce multiple equilibria, and the dynamic transition between these equilibria may be fruitfully modeled by a regime-switching model.

Acknowledgments

The views expressed are those of the author and are not necessarily shared by the Federal reserve Bank of San Francisco or the Federal Reserve System.

Note

1. Note that Hamilton's process can be used in real time by an agent to discern turning points. A different real-time procedure to uncover turning points that also treats expansions and contraction as different probabilistic objects is analyzed in Diebold and Rudebusch (1989, 1991).

References

Abel, A. (1980). "Empirical Investment Equations: An Integrative Framework." In Karl Brunner and Allan H. Meltzer (eds.), *On the State of Macroeconomics*, Carnegie-Rochester Conference Series on Public Policy 12, 39–91.

Andrews, D. (1993). "Tests for Parameter Instability and Structural Change with Unknown Change Point." *Econometrica* 61, 821–856.

Andrews, D., and R. Fair. (1988). "Inference in Nonlinear Econometric Models with Structural Change." *Review of Economic Studies* 55, 615–640.

Chow, G. (1960). "Tests of Equality Between Sets of Coefficients in Two Linear Regressions." *Econometrica* 28, 591–605.

Cooley, T., S. LeRoy, and N. Raymon. (1984). "Econometric Policy Evaluation: Note." *American Economic Review* 74, 467–470.

Diebold, F., and G. Rudebusch. (1989). "Scoring the Leading Indicators." *Journal of Business* 62, July, 369–391.

Diebold, F., and G. Rudebusch. (1991). "Turning Point Prediction With the Composite Leading Index: An Ex Ante Analysis." In K. Lahiri and G.H. Moore (eds.), *Leading Economic Indicators: New Approaches and Forecasting Records* (pp. 231–256). Cambridge: Cambridge University Press.

Diebold, F., and G. Rudebusch. (1994). "Business Cycles: A Modern Perspective." *Review of Economics and Statistics*, forthcoming.

Dufour, J. (1982). "Recursive Stability Analysis of Linear Regression Relationships." *Journal of Econometrics* 19, 31–76.

Hall, R. (1978). "Stochastic Implication of the Life Cycle-Permanent Income Hypothesis: Theory and Evidence." *Journal of Political Economy* 86, 971–987.

Hansen, B. (1992). "The Likelihood Ratio Test Under Non-Standard Conditions: Testing the Markov Trend Model of GNP." *Journal of Applied Econometrics* 7, S61–S82.

Lucas, Robert E. (1976). "Econometric Policy Evaluation: A Critique." In K. Brunner and A.H. Meltzer (eds.), *The Phillips Curve and Labor Markets*. Carnegie-Rochester Conference Series on Public Policy (Vol. 1) (pp. 19–46). Amsterdam: North-Holland.

Marschak, J. (1953). "Econometric Measurements for Policy and Prediction." In William C. Hook and Tjalling G. Koopmans (eds.), *Studies in Econometric Method* (pp. 1–26). Cowles Commission Monograph 14. New York: Wiley.

Oliner, S., G. Rudebusch, and D. Sichel. (1995). "New and Old Models of Business Investment: A Comparison of Forecasting Performance." *Journal of Money, Credit, and Banking*, forthcoming.

Oliner, S., G. Rudebusch, and D. Sichel. (1996). "The Lucas Critique Revisited: Assessing the Stability of Empirical Euler Equations for Investment." *Journal of Econometrics*, forthcoming.

Sargent, T. (1993). *Bounded Rationality in Macroeconomics*. Oxford: Clarendon Press.

Sims, C. (1982). "Policy Analysis With Econometric Models." *Brookings Papers on Economic Activity* 1, 107–152.

Tinbergen, J. (1956). *Economic Policy: Principles and Design*. Amsterdam: North-Holland.

10 HISTORICAL MACROECONOMICS AND AMERICAN MACROECONOMIC HISTORY

Charles W. Calomiris
Christopher Hanes

Introduction

We take macroeconometrics to be the application of statistical models to questions posed by macroeconomic theory. Macroeconomic facts and theories relate to two sets of issues usually viewed as separable: long-term variations in economic growth across decades or countries and short-term (high-frequency) variations in employment and output, usually referred to as business cycles. Empirical research can help one judge among competing theories and can establish facts that join the list of patterns to be explained by new theories.

The vast majority of macroeconometric studies rely on data for the period since World War II. There can be good reasons for focusing only on postwar data: some data useful for describing the macroeconomy and discriminating among macroeconomic theories were not collected in earlier years or were collected in less reliable ways. What can macroeconomic history—the study of the macroeconomy before World War II—offer to macroeconomists and macroeconometricians? History may offer some opportunities to apply macroeconomic theory to explain events that are interesting in themselves—the Great Depression, for example. But that is merely a matter of applying macroeconomic theory and empirical methods to history, not using history to inform macroeconomics or macroeconometrics.

Our focus in this essay is to highlight the factual, theoretical, and econometric implications of historical research on American business cycles.

Sometimes the past has been used simply to extend time-series data to permit tests of questions of current interest. The data and methods of such studies will change over time as new paradigms are introduced by macroeconomists. Perhaps the most famous and influential example of this approach is Friedman and Schwartz's (1963) *Monetary History of the United States*. This was arguably the first and most influential test of the monetarist proposition that money and nominal income are closely related. The authors' argument was based largely on the robustness of the association over a long span of time.[1] More recently, macroeconomists in search of longer time series have turned to historical data to resolve debates between the "new Keynesian" and "new classical" schools, which often translate into debates about the cyclical properties of wages, prices, and technological change.

In some cases, macroeconomists have been drawn to particular data from historical periods because those data are of better quality than any postwar data on the same subject—for example, surveys of wage rate changes from the 1890s and 1930s (as we discuss below). More important, some interwar and prewar events may constitute shocks to the economy that are more dramatic, and possibly more informative, than any shocks that occurred in the postwar period. The Great Depression is a case in point. As Milton Friedman noted long ago, "The major defect of the data on which economists must rely—data generated by experience rather than deliberately contrived experiment—is the small range of variation they encompass" (1952, p. 612).

The past can also be useful as a source of unique "historical experiments" that can shed light on questions of current interest to macrotheorists or policy makers. For example, Calomiris and Hubbard (1994a) use observed marginal tax rates paid by firms subject to the short-lived undistributed profits tax of 1936–1937 (which taxed retained earnings with a progressive marginal tax schedule) to measure the shadow cost of external finance to firms and to show how differences in the shadow cost of finance affect investment behavior. Some of history's natural experiments take on new importance in light of later experience and policy issues. The high-inflation episodes of the 1970s renewed interest in past experiences with hyperinflation, and in the question of whether policy regime changes in the past that ended high inflation were associated with major contractions in real activity (Sargent, 1981a, 1981b). During the 1980s, controversies over rising federal deficits prompted new research on extreme historical examples of high deficits in the past and their links to inflation and interest rates (Smith, 1985a, 1985b; Calomiris, 1988a, 1988b; Evans, 1985; Barro, 1987).

But we will argue that macroeconomic history offers more than long strings of data and special examples. It suggests an *historical definition* of the macroeconomy, which has important implications for macroeconometric methods. Historical macro-economics is not the application of standard macroeconomic tools to data from the distant past or the selective exploration of the past to discover interesting experiments; it is "thinking historically" about macroeconomic change—an alternative approach to analyzing data both from the recent and distant past.[2]

The defining characteristic of the historical view of the macroeconomy is its emphasis on *path-dependence*.[3] Historical path dependence does not refer to the serial correlation properties of time-series data. Indeed, the historical view runs counter to the mainstream macroeconomist's interpretation of historical time series as the realizations of a changing, but essentially homogeneous, stochastic process resulting from optimization rules that relate macroeconomic outcomes to exogenous changes in utility functions, endowments, and information sets of agents. Mainstream macroeconometric studies assume that variations in data are generated by exogenous shocks acting on a fixed macroeconomic structure. Patterns in the data can reveal the nature of that structure, including the values of its underlying parameters. The structure may change over time, but structural changes occur independently of the exogenous shocks. Historical path dependence, in contrast, explores ways in which the *cumulative* past of the economy, including the history of shocks and their effects, change the structure of the economy.

Path dependence manifests itself in a variety of ways: decision rules change as a result of learning; institutional innovations (private and public) change the constraints of agents. Some events have permanent importance for the future of the economy through their influence on the way decision rules and institutions change.

"Structural" differences between today's economy and the economies of the past—which are sometimes viewed as a reason to avoid historical data—are in fact what make historical data uniquely useful to macroeconomists. The features that make up the modern economy—everything from the body of knowledge that constitutes technology to the rules and behaviors that define institutions—developed over time. If understanding and taking account of such structural change is part of the job of macroeconomics—and we believe it is—then there is no avoiding the past.

Given the tenets of the historical view of the macroeconomy, it is not surprising that macrocliometricians often ask different questions than their mainstream counterparts and use different methods to answer those questions. In particular, they explore the origins of institutional change (the particular events that result in change), and measure the consequences of these changes. This often requires looking closely at specific moments, and relying on panel data and cross-sections, analysis of nonquantitative information, and good story-telling rather than long strings of time series to argue a point.

Our goals in this essay are two. First, we provide a selective review of American macroeconomic history to illustrate the potential uses of historical data for a

354   MACROECONOMETRICS

variety of purposes—to increase sample size for testing models, to address questions of current interest with unique experiments from the past, and to demonstrate the uses of the historical view of the economy (in particular, the importance of institutional change). Second, we emphasize and draw out methodological issues that arise in these examples and their implications for econometric modeling.

Our review of American macroeconomic history begins with an overview of the salient facts about the U.S. macroeconomy during the nineteenth and twentieth centuries, which focusses on continuity and change in patterns of covariation among macroeconomic time series. The next section discusses the uses of these and other data for discriminating among models of high-frequency macroeconomic fluctuations. We focus on uses of historical data to distinguish between "new Keynesian" and "new classical" paradigms and to distinguish among new Keynesian explanations for wage and price rigidities. We argue that Keynesian models can account for the most obvious cyclical patterns in macroeconomic variables in all historical periods, while new classical models cannot. New classical models are also inconsistent with historical evidence on the nature of technological change. It seems unlikely, therefore, that historical data will prove to offer much support for real business-cycle theory, at least in its current form. We also argue that nominal wage rigidity (which has been deemphasized by macroeconomists in response to the "Barro critique") was important historically in generating layoffs and that some models of nominal wage rigidity and its allocative costs receive more support from history than others.

With respect to low-frequency fluctuations, neither the new-classical emphasis on exogenous technological change nor Keynesian nominal rigidities offers a complete account. Here historical evidence can be particularly useful for defining the interesting unit of observation (the Kuznets cycle) and pointing to plausible explanations for "long swings" by focusing on common historical patterns (city building, frontier settlement, waves of immigration, and endogenous technological change).

The final two sections discuss evidence of the importance of institutions, regulations, and beliefs for macroeconomic outcomes, consider how important changes in these variables have occurred (using the Great Depression as an example), and offer conclusions.

From the standpoint of the methodological lessons we seek to draw out of our review, each of these sections makes distinct but related points. The following section focuses on problems of constructing consistent time series over long periods of time, and analyzing those data in the presence of shifting historical regimes (particularly, shifts in the time series process of prices). The next two sections criticize both prominent macroeconometric frameworks for ignoring sets of facts inconsistent with their models. In particular, we emphasize the failure of real business-cycle theorists to consider historical evidence on the pace of technological innovation and diffusion, and the failure of neo-Keynesian macro-economists to come to grips with long swings in the economy.

In both cases, those shortcomings are reflected in assumptions about the identification of supply and demand shocks in the economy. Both Keynesian and new-classical approaches share the tendency to view low-frequency change as exogenous to demand—an assumption grossly at odds with the historical literature on the Kuznets cycle. The history of the Kuznets cycle is largely a history of aggregate demand shocks that produced endogenous changes in aggregate supply. Economies of scale, learning effects, and convergences of expectations—many within the *spatial* contexts of city building and frontier settlement—seem to have been especially important. Put differently, aggregate supply historically has been *path-dependent*.

Once one begins to focus on low-frequency changes and on the persistent effects of particular events and shifts in institutional regimes, other methodological criticisms follow. First, the true number of observations in time-series data may be smaller than annual time-series data suggest. Second, the occupation of estimating the parameters of a supposedly fixed economic "structure" with long runs of time-series data is of questionable value. This can be thought of as a more general version of the so-called Lucas critique (Lucas, 1976): the economy's "fundamentals" as well as agents' expectations change with experience. Third, alternative approaches to testing macroeconomic models—those that exploit cross-sectional variation as well as time-series variation—may be desirable. Panel or cross-sectional studies are useful both as a means to isolate spatial or sectoral characteristics of relevance to the history of long swings, and as a means to gain numbers of observations without assuming structural constancy over long periods of time.

The Cyclical Behavior of Macroeconomic Variables

As of ten years ago, most research had indicated two big historical changes in cyclical patterns. First, output and employment were much less volatile after World War II than before World War I or in the interwar period. Second, nominal wages and prices were less "flexible" in the postwar period than in earlier periods, in the sense that wage and price inflation had become less sensitive to deviations from trend in output and employment levels. This evidence was cited to support theoretical conclusions and even recommendations for policy (for an example see DeLong and Summers, 1986). Since then careful attention to the nature of historical time series has somewhat modified these stylized facts.

Cyclical Volatility of Output and Employment

Comparisons between historical periods require series that are consistent across the periods: constructed in the same way from the same kinds of data. Otherwise one may mistake differences in the way the series were constructed for changes over time in economic behavior. If consistent data are not available, one must take account of the inconsistencies and adjust one's conclusions accordingly. Economists largely ignored this point until Christina Romer (1986a, 1986b) asserted that standard output and employment series for the late nineteenth and early twentieth centuries had been constructed in ways that "exaggerated" cyclical movements. Romer accepted the conventional wisdom that the Great Depression had been much more severe than any postwar cycle, but she argued that otherwise "the relative stabilization of the postwar economy is a figment of the data. . . . the severity of economic fluctuations on both sides of the Great Depression are roughly equal" (1986b, p. 333).

Others have challenged Romer's results (for a review, see Zarnowitz, 1992, ch. 3). David Weir (1986, 1992) concluded: "To the simple question of whether cyclical fluctuations around trend in GNP and unemployment have become smaller since World War II the data are more than adequate to deliver a definitive answer: yes" (1986, p. 365). Nathan Balke and Robert Gordon (1989) constructed historical series for real GNP that indicate "substantially greater volatility before 1929 than after 1946" (p. 81). The standard deviation of deviation from trend in the log of the series is about 70 percent greater over 1869–1908 or 1869–1928 than in postwar periods. Indeed, Romer's own prewar real GNP series (1989) is more volatile than the postwar series, with a standard deviation of deviation from trend that is 30 percent greater over 1869–1928 than 1947–1985. In Romer's view this means the prewar series is "only slightly more volatile" than the postwar data (p. 35). Others might judge the difference to indicate an important stabilization of output.

Unfortunately, no employment or GNP series for prewar years can be truly comparable to postwar series. Annual data on many sectors of the economy were simply not collected before the 1920s. Historical estimates must be built on debatable assumptions. In the words of Susan Carter and Richard Sutch (1990), the process is like "inferring the shape of some long-extinct animal from bones collected in an ancient tar pit" (p. 294). It appears unlikely that we will reach a consensus any time soon. One might put more faith in results using data that are more consistent and directly comparable, if less comprehensive. Romer (1986b) compares the behavior of the best prewar series on industrial production, Edwin Frickey's index of manufacturing output (1947), to a couple of very similar postwar series on industrial production. She finds the standard deviation of deviation from trend to be 10 to 14 percent greater over 1866–1914 than 1947–1982—a clear decrease in volatility but smaller than that indicated by anyone's real GNP series.

The difference between results from series on real GNP and industrial production raises an issue that has been more or less ignored in the literature. Simon
Kuznets (1951) observed that sectors vary in their sensitivity to business cycles.
The cyclical behavior of aggregate output and employment might change over
time as a result of shifts in the relative importance of different sectors, even if
"there are no marked secular shifts within each sector in responsiveness to business cycles. . . . For example, a decline in the weight of agriculture, combined
with a lack of responsiveness of agricultural output to business cycles, would
mean, other conditions being equal, a widening of business cycle amplitudes"
(p. 159). It made sense to focus on agriculture, for National Bureau researchers
like Wesley Mitchell and Arthur Burns had found farming to be a uniquely acyclical
sector: "the basic industry of growing crops does not expand and contract in
unison with mining, manufacturing, trading, transportation, and finance" (Mitchell,
1951, p. 56). Farm output and employment "undergo cyclical movements, but they
have little or no relation to business cycles" (Burns, 1951, pp. 7, 8). This was
especially obvious in the interwar period. From 1930 to 1932 employment fell in
every nonagricultural sector, including trade and services. Aggregate employment
fell by 14 percent. Meanwhile farm employment *increased* by 3 percent.[4] But it
was also true before World War I. Edwin Frickey (1942, p. 229) found that from
the 1870s through 1914 "agricultural production patterns traced out short-term
fluctuations bearing little resemblance to those for other major production groups.
The causal relationships between the agricultural and non-agricultural groups
certainly did not express themselves in the form of any simple correlation." This
is not to say that agricultural *incomes* are acyclical; that depends on the cyclical
pattern in the relative price of farm output.

As Table 10.1 shows, the twentieth century saw an enormous shift of resources
out of agriculture, while the share of manufacturing in employment or output did
not fall until the 1970s. Most of the balance went to services. Services output and
employment are less cyclical than manufacturing but more cyclical than agriculture. By itself, the sectoral shift should have tended to decrease the cyclicality of
nonagricultural GNP but increase the cyclicality of real GNP including agriculture. Both the Romer and Balke and Gordon series for real GNP purport to measure the latter. It seems odd that both indicate a larger decline in volatility than the
consistent manufacturing production series examined by Romer.

Suppose, however, that one had reliable historical series for both real GNP and
manufacturing output. Which would be appropriate to indicate changes in cyclical
behavior? In comparing cyclical "volatility" over long periods, should one hold
sectoral weights fixed or, equivalently, look at individual sectors? This issue is
especially important for comparisons of cyclical volatility across different periods
within the nineteenth century, before and after the War Between the States, for
example. John James (1993) found that Robert Gallman's unpublished real GNP

Table 10.1. Agriculture and manufacturing in the economy

Census year	Output % of GNP		Employment % of total labor force	
	Farm gross product	Manufacturing value added	Agriculture	Manufacturing
1840	47	16	63	9
1850	37	19	55	15
1860	36	20	53	14
1870	31	20	53	19
1880	32	21	51	19
1890	22	27	43	19
1900	21	28	40	20
1910			31	22
1920			26	27
1930	9	30	22	20
1940	7	27	17	20
1950	7	29	12	24
1960	4	33	8	23
1970	3	33	4	23
1980	2	27	3	19
1990	2	25	3	15

Sources: Employment and labor force 1840–1960 from Lebergott (1964, table 1). Employment and labor force 1970–1990 from U.S. Council of Economic Advisers (1993). Farm gross product 1840–1900 from Towne and Rasmussen (1960). Manufacturing value-added 1839–1859 from Gallman (1960, p. 43). GNP 1839–1859 from Gallman (1966, p. 26); 1869–1899 from Balke and Gordon (1989, table 10). All other series from U.S. Bureau of the Census (1975): GNP 1929–1969 series F1; farm gross product 1929–1969 series K220-239; manufacturing value-added 1929–1969 series P1–12. Remaining years from issues of *Statistical Abstract of the United States*.

series (described in Gallman, 1960) indicates "a substantial increase in the degree of business-cycle severity or economic fluctuations" (p. 710) from 1834–1859 to 1869–1909. Calomiris and Hanes (1994) show that consistent series on industrial production are if anything less volatile in the postbellum period. These two results are not necessarily inconsistent with each other: given the rapid growth of manufacturing relative to agriculture over the nineteenth century, it is quite possible that real GNP became more volatile even as manufacturing output became less volatile.

Historical changes in the timing of business cycles—duration from peak to trough, and trough to peak—have also been the subject of recent studies. Francis Diebold and Glenn Rudebusch (1992, p. 1003) show that the standard NBER chronology suggests "a postwar shift toward longer expansions and shorter contractions" with "no evidence for a postwar shift in the distribution of whole-cycle durations." Geoffrey Moore and Victor Zarnowitz (1986) made the same observation but noted that the comparison was tricky because the NBER peak-trough dates for the prewar period were not chosen in the same way as interwar and postwar dates. Mark Watson (1994) and Christina Romer (1994) present evidence that the change in timing of NBER cycles indeed reflects changing definitions rather than changing economic behavior. They argue that contractions and expansions were of about the same length in both the prewar and postwar periods.

Overall, the conclusion to draw from these various studies seems to be that business-cycle severity has fallen over time while the duration and frequency of cycles has not significantly changed across historical eras, excluding the interwar period. The extent of the decline in cycle variance depends on assumptions both about how to measure output comparably over time and whether to focus on manufacturing or the whole economy.

Cyclical Movements in Nominal Wages and Prices

The cyclical behavior of nominal wages or prices is often described in terms of a *Phillips curve*: an estimated relation between the rate of change of wages (prices) and the current (or recent) output or employment level, given the rate of change of wages (prices) in the recent past. The relation is often assumed to be linear, giving an estimated coefficient on output or employment and a coefficient on lagged inflation. A number of studies compared prewar and postwar periods using the standard real GNP or employment series criticized by Romer and various series for wages or prices, including Albert Rees's (1961) series for average hourly earnings in manufacturing over 1890–1914, GNP deflators and wholesale price series. Most studies found smaller coefficients on output and larger coefficients on lagged inflation in the postwar period, concluding that there had been a decrease over time in cyclical "flexibility" (Cagan, 1975; Sachs, 1980). More recently, Steven Allen (1992) has shown that the Rees earnings series have a strong procyclical bias as a measure of true average hourly earnings. Taking account of that bias, Allen found an increase in the coefficient on lagged inflation but "no discernable change in the response of nominal wages to the output gap." Hanes (1993) found a similar pattern using consistent data on wage rates rather than hourly earnings. Robert Gordon (1990) observed a similar pattern in prices, as measured by a newly constructed GNP deflator: "The sole change between pre–World War I and post–World War II was an increase in the inertia coefficient" (p. 1130)— that is, the coefficient on lagged inflation.

Some studies have described price behavior in other terms. David Backus and Patrick Kehoe (1992) measure the relation between deviation from trend in output and deviation from trend in the price level. They find that the price level is procyclical over 1869–1914 and 1920–1939 and countercyclical over 1950–1983. Thomas Cooley and Lee Ohanian (1991) observe the same pattern and also estimate the correlation between the rate of price inflation and the rate of growth in output. The latter is positive over 1870–1900 and 1900–1946, negative over 1949–1975.

Table 10.2 reproduces the general results of these studies using standard whole-sale price indices (that constructed by Warren and Pearson, 1932, linked to the BLS "All items" index) and the most consistent output series, the Frickey index and the Federal Reserve Board Materials Production Index (Romer, 1986b), to compare 1869–1914 and 1949–1990. Trends are defined using the Hodrick-Prescott filter (following Kydland and Prescott, 1990). We omit the interwar period because there is no clearly consistent output series to compare it with both of the others. Several studies have suggested that price behavior was very unusual in the oil shock of the early 1970s, so we also present results excluding 1974 from the postwar sample. Specification (1) shows the pattern found by Allen, Gordon, and Hanes: the Phillips curve coefficient on output deviation from trend is stable but that on lagged inflation increases considerably. Specification (2) shows the pattern found by Backus and Kehoe and Cooley and Ohanian: price and output deviations from trend are positively correlated in the early period, negatively correlated in the later period. Specification (3) shows the pattern found by Cooley and Ohanian: change in inflation and change in output are positively related in the early period, negatively related in the later period. The postwar correlation between inflation and output growth is very weak and becomes positive if 1974 is excluded from the sample. None of the other results are much affected when 1974 is excluded.

Some of the seemingly contradictory conclusions drawn by these studies can be reconciled by distinguishing price-output correlation from *inflation*-output correlation. As Alogoskoufis and Smith (1991), Allen (1992), and Obstfeld (1993, pp. 242–246) point out, changes in the persistence of the inflation process will be reflected in a reduced sensitivity of inflation to the output gap, but this does not imply a reduced correlation between the output gap and the level of wages or prices. Allen judges that the stability in his Phillips curve output coefficient indicates that "wages 100 years ago were no more sensitive to the business cycle than they are today" (1992, p. 137). That conclusion may be correct with respect to wage *level* adjustment, but the increase in the *persistence* of inflation reflected in the coefficient on lagged price change implies a considerable decrease in the response of *inflation* to a cyclical downturn. Specification (4) demonstrates this point, showing that the ratio of the change in inflation to the change in the output deviation in NBER downturns. (Dates are taken from Moore and Zarnowitz, 1986.) The ratio is much smaller in the later period, even excluding 1974.

Cooley and Ohanian interpret the observed weakness of the association be-tween inflation and output growth to imply the absence of a correlation between

Table 10.2.   Changes in price behavior

p	Log wholesale price index	
y	Log industrial production: 1869–1914 Frickey Manufacturing Output, 1949–1990 FRB Materials Production	
$\hat{x}$	Hodrick-Prescott trend in variable	

Specifications

(1) Inflation on output deviation, lagged inflation

$$(p_t - p_{t-1}) = \alpha + \beta(y_t - \hat{y}_t) + \gamma(p_{t-1} - p_{t-2})$$

(2) Price deviation on output deviation

$$p_t - \hat{p}_t = \delta(y_t - \hat{y}_t)$$

(3) Inflation change on output change

$$p_t - p_{t-1} = \alpha + \varepsilon(y_t - y_{t-1})$$

(4) Ratio, inflation change over change in output deviation, NBER downturns

$$\zeta = \frac{(p_t - p_{t-1}) - (p_{t-1} - p_{t-2})}{(y_t - \hat{y}_t) - (y_{t-1} - \hat{y}_{t-1})}$$

(5) Inflation change on output deviation

$$(p_t - p_{t-1}) - (p_{t-1} - p_{t-2}) = \alpha + \eta(y_t - \hat{y}_t)$$

Historical patterns, pre-1914 versus post-1947

	(1) β	γ	(2) δ	(3) ε	(4) ζ	(5) η
			(t-statistics)			
1869–1914	0.3501	0.0987	0.4505	0.2844	0.772	0.2171
	(3.630)	(0.738)	(5.306)	(3.293)		(1.622)
1949–1990	0.3516	0.5790	−0.2211	−0.0039	0.047	0.3929
	(3.998)	(5.065)	(−1.289)	(−0.039)		(3.929)
1949–1990	0.3189	0.4932	−0.2328	0.0327	0.196	0.3828
(excluding 1974)	(3.790)	(4.336)	(1.337)	(0.361)		(3.790)

the *change* in the rate of inflation and the output gap, and hence they argue their results are inconsistent with the notion of a Phillips curve. In fact, that is not the case. Specification (5) shows that the correlation between the change in inflation and output deviation is in fact positive in both periods. The correlation is larger in the later period—from a Phillips curve point of view, an artifact of constraining the coefficient on lagged inflation to be one.

A few studies have used changes in the Phillips curve to measure changes in the covariation of output with wage and price changes *within* the prewar period, rather than between the prewar and postwar periods. Hanes (1993) presents evidence of a change around 1890: the Phillips curve coefficient on output is larger and the coefficient on lagged inflation is smaller in the 1870s and 1880s than the 1890s and 1900s. Hanes's result is consistent with James's (1989) study of price behavior over 1837 to 1909: "the American economy earlier characterized by rapid (or instantaneous) price adjustment to clear markets evolved into one marked by gradual price adjustment (and one in which markets do not clear instantaneously) in the last part of the 19th century. . . . the movement toward increasingly sluggish price adjustment was most pronounced between 1880 and 1890" (p. 126).

But historical patterns of output-price correlations over time are clearer to document that to interpret. Despite the tendency in many studies to use Phillips curve coefficients to measure wage and price rigidity, we argue below that this is not a straightforward exercise. In particular, there are many pitfalls in inferring wage- and price-setting behavior from Phillips curve coefficients and in using Phillips curves to measure the unemployment consequences of wage and price rigidity.

Cyclical Patterns in Other Variables

Backus and Kehoe (1992) measure historical patterns in a number of other variables for the United States and some other countries, comparing prewar, interwar, and postwar periods. For all countries, in all periods, consumption appears "uniformly procyclical" and investment is "strongly procyclical." Net exports have "generally been countercyclical"; for the United States net exports appear countercyclical in all periods.

Bernanke and Powell (1986) compare the cyclical behavior of employment, weekly hours, average hourly earnings, and physical labor productivity in a fixed set of industries across the interwar and postwar periods. They find that "the interrelation of productivity, hours, output, and employment is essentially stable between the prewar and postwar periods" (p. 597), though they do observe "an increased reliance in the postwar period on layoffs, rather than short workweeks, as a means of reducing labor input." The real consumption value of hourly earnings—an imperfect measure of "real wages"—was "procyclical (essentially coincident) in the postwar period but 'half out of phase' (usually lagging)" in the interwar (p. 617). They find no change in the cyclical behavior of labor productivity. "Procyclical labor productivity . . . appears to be present in every industry, in both . . . periods" (p. 617). The lack of comparable employment data makes it hard to say whether labor productivity was also procyclical before 1919. Some evidence suggests that labor productivity was *not* procyclical over the depression of the 1890s (Weir, 1986; Carter and Sutch, 1990).

Cyclical patterns in a few other variables are of particular interest for our discussion below. One is the rate at which a domestic producer could exchange output for foreign goods—that is, the terms of international trade net of domestic tariffs. Robert Lipsey (1963) presents an annual series of terms of trade for the United States beginning in 1879. Unfortunately the series is not a true index; it is based on values per unit in fairly broad categories of goods and thus affected by variations in the composition of goods as well as prices (p. 93). In the postwar period terms of trade excluding tariffs can be roughly measured by the GNP deflator for exports divided by that for imports; these series begin with 1959. Tariff rates are even more of a problem, since the usual measure, tariff revenue divided by the value of imports, varies with shifts among commodities as well as changes in rates. Indices of tariff rates for interwar years have been constructed by E. Lerdau (1957) and Mario Crucini (1994). Crucini presents indices with both fixed and changing commodity weights. There are no tariff rate series for earlier years, but we may at least note that Frank Taussig (1931) describes no general rate changes preceding prewar downturns.

We regress the terms of trade gross or net of tariffs on industrial production, with both expressed as deviations of logs from the Hodrick-Prescott trend. Results are in Table 10.3. In the prewar period the terms of trade are procyclical but the relation is not very strong. In the interwar period the terms of trade excluding tariffs are strongly countercyclical. The difference between the prewar and interwar periods was noted by Lipsey (1963, p. 15): "In the short-run behavior of U.S. terms of trade, a sharp shift may be noted. In the prewar years . . . they moved with prices and were roughly inverse to the terms of trade of the U.K. and [industrialized Europe]. . . . After World War I, when U.S. terms of trade became inverse to price changes, they conformed well to both British and [European] terms of trade. It might be said that the trade pattern matured, developing from one that is characteristic of a primary goods exporter to one characteristic of a nation exporting manufactured products." In the postwar period terms of trade excluding tariffs are weakly procyclical if 1974 (the year of the oil price shock) is included in the sample, otherwise weakly countercyclical. The interwar pattern in terms of trade including tariffs depends on the tariff index. Using Lerdau's index they appear weakly countercyclical; with Crucini's indices they appear weakly procyclical.

Table 10.3 also shows the cyclical pattern in (gross) investment in capital for household production—that is, the flow of consumer durables. Shaw (1947) presents an annual series for this variable from 1889 through 1939. It is independent of both the prewar and interwar industrial production indices. Deviation from trend in durables consumption appears strongly procyclical before and after World War I. Indeed, examination of the Shaw series shows that an absolute decline in

Table 10.3.   Cyclical patterns in terms of trade consumer durables investment (all variables in logs)

$p_{EXPORTS} - p_{IMPORTS}$	Terms of trade or terms of trade divided by tariff index
$c_{DURABLES}$	Flow of consumer durables (gross)
y	Index of industrial production
$\hat{x}$	Hodrick-Prescott trend in variable

Terms of trade: $(p_{EXPORTS} - p_{IMPORTS}) - (\widehat{p_{EXPORTS} - p_{IMPORTS}}) = \beta(y - \hat{y})$

	β (*t statistic*) Excluding tariffs	Including Lerdau tariff index	Including Crucini variable-weight tariff index	Including Crucini constant-weight tariff index
1879–1914	0.0772 (0.73)			
1919–1940	−0.3439 (−5.03)	−0.1334 (−0.61)	0.0124 (0.0987)	0.0673 (0.4254)
1959–1990	0.2006 (0.86)			
1959–1973	−0.1992			
1975–1990	(−1.13)			

Durables consumption: $c_{DURABLES} - \hat{c}_{DURABLES} = \beta(y - \hat{y})$

	β (*t statistic*)
1889–1914	2.9097 (91.57)
1919–1940	6.052 (81.60)

Sources: Terms of trade 1879–1940 from Lipsey (1963, table H1); terms of trade 1959–1990 export price deflator divided by import price deflator, U.S. Council of Economic Advisers (1993, p. 353). Tariff indices 1919–1940 from Lerdau (1957, p. 235) and Crucini (1994). Production of consumer durables from Shaw (1947). Industrial production 1879–1914 is Frickey (1947) manufacturing production index, 1919–1990 Federal Reserve Board index of industrial production.

household capital investment accompanied every downturn in the Gordon real GNP series, with two exceptions: 1919, the end of World War I, and 1896, when durables consumption showed no growth over the previous year.

To summarize, the general patterns of business-cycle history appear to be the following. Prewar business cycles were larger than postwar cycles, in terms of deviation from trend output and employment, but not more frequent. They were

associated with the same patterns in most real variables—consumption, investment (including household investment), and the trade balance—that appear in
postwar cycles. The interwar Great Depression was an extreme case of standard
patterns. On the other hand, there are obvious differences between prewar and
postwar periods in the cyclical behavior of nominal variables. Described in terms
of a conventional Phillips curve, the coefficient on past inflation was larger in the
postwar period than in the prewar period, though the coefficient on output deviation was more or less the same. Some of the disagreement among macroeconomists
over the historical stability of the Phillips curve can be resolved by noting that
changes in the inflation process altered the relationship between innovations in
inflation and output.

Confronting Theory with History

These patterns and other research in economic history bear on many issues in
business-cycle theory. Here we focus on the debate between the two major schools
of thought in macroeconomics at present: the new classical or real business-cycle
approach versus the Keynesian approach and modern new Keynesian attempts to
fill in the holes in the old Keynesian model. We judge the plausibility of each
school's models in light of historical experience. Along the way we point out some
important open questions for empirical study.

New Classical (Real Business-Cycle) Models

What Causes Business Cycles?   New classical models assume that cyclical-
frequency variations in output and employment are caused by shocks to real
preferences and constraints: "no matter how monetary policy is conducted, the
behavior of real quantities is determined by real shocks to the economy" (Manuelli,
1986). Such shocks might include temporary changes in the government's demand
for goods and services (as in Barro, 1981; Christiano and Eichenbaum, 1992) or
changes in the expected return to saving and investment. However, assuming conventional household utility functions, either of these would cause consumption to
move in the opposite direction from output and employment.[5] Since consumption
appears decidedly procyclical in all historical periods, new classical models must
rely on another sort of real shock: procyclical fluctuations in the return to employment versus leisure (Barro and King, 1984; Mankiw, 1989). If wages reflect the
return to employment and the return to leisure is fixed, then the models imply that
real consumption wages must be procyclical. The failure of most empirical studies
to find such a pattern has been taken as evidence against new classical models

(David Romer, 1993). Barro and King (1984) speculate that real wages need not reflect the return to employment if employment relations are long-term and firms smooth real wages to insure employees against cyclical shocks. A study of real consumption wages over pre-1914 business cycles could be useful here, and is a conspicuous gap in the literature. Before World War I most workers' attachments to firms were not long term: turnover was much higher, employment spells much shorter, and a laid-off worker much less likely to be rehired by his old firm than in later decades (Jacoby, 1985; Jacoby and Sharma, 1992). Prewar data on wage rates and prices of consumption goods ought to show the underlying pattern in the return to employment even if postwar data do not.

What might be the exogenous source of short-run fluctuations in the return to employment? Procyclical variations in the rate at which domestic output can be exchanged for foreign goods would do the trick (Mendoza, 1991). But they would presumably appear as a procyclical pattern in the terms of trade and the trade balance. As noted above, there is no strong procyclical pattern in the terms of trade in any historical period, and the trade balance appears countercyclical in all periods.

Exogenous Shocks to Technology. That leaves cyclical-frequency shocks to technology—that is, physical factor productivity—as the fundamental cause of business cycles under new classical assumptions. To account for the absolute decreases in output and employment that occur in cyclical downturns, models that assume a fixed utility value of leisure (as in Plosser, 1989) require absolute deteriorations of total factor productivity. Models that assume leisure includes home production as well as true leisure and that the technology of the home sector, like that of the market sector, is subject to rapid changes do not require such absolute deteriorations: improvements in home technology relative to market technology can cause a reallocation of time to home production, reducing market-sector employment and output (Benhabib, Rogerson, and Wright, 1991). The latter class of new classical model appears implausible if only because, as noted above, investment in household capital (consumer durables) is and always has been procyclical, just like investment in capital for market production. Household investment is *negatively* correlated with time allocated to household production. The hypothesized improvements in home technology would have to be associated with decreases in investment in the associated capital stock, the opposite of the relation observed in the market sector.

In any case, new classical models require exogenous shocks to economywide factor productivity to explain the patterns in consumption, investment, and the trade balance that appear in all historical periods. The shocks must be fast enough to create cyclical frequencies and large enough to account for cyclical amplitudes. At least for the postwar period that seems to mean movements from one year to the next on the order of 2 or 3 percent of total GDP (see, for example, Plosser, 1989).

Aggregate total factor productivity is determined by the productivity of individual producers, firms, or households. Changes in aggregate productivity reflect changes in the technologies applied by those producers, as existing firms (households) apply new technologies or old firms (households) are replaced by new ones utilizing new techniques. The behavior over time of aggregate total factor productivity is determined by the process generating technological innovations, the speed with which innovations are implemented by producers, the magnitude of the savings in input requirements associated with each innovation, and the importance in total final output of the sector or sectors utilizing that innovation.

New classical business-cycle theory thus rests on a hypothesis about technological innovation and diffusion. Individual innovations must be large and rapidly diffused to create significant quarter-to-quarter variations in aggregate productivity. Many small innovations diffused slowly could not deliver the magnitude of sudden shocks required by new classical models unless they came in bunches, for reasons *exogenous* to aggregate demand or the expected return on investment.

Technology Shocks in History. One can test the new classical hypothesis about technological change against the considerable body of research on technological innovation and diffusion, much of which has taken place within the context of economic history. One aspect of the cliometric revolution was the careful dating and quantification of observations about technological changes, including estimates of their effects on total factor productivity. Economic history is also useful here because long hindsight allows one to identify the innovations that might be big enough to make a difference in the aggregate and hence provide appropriate tests of the new classical hypothesis.

Three innovations that have attracted the attention of economic historians, precisely because they appear so overwhelmingly important, are steam-powered railroads, stationary steam engines (to power machinery), and electric motors. Railroads were introduced to the United States in the 1830s, with more than 2,000 miles of way in operation by 1840 (U.S. Bureau of the Census, 1975, series Q321). Robert Fogel (1964) and Albert Fishlow (1965) described the effect of railroads on total factor productivity in terms of "social savings." They compared aggregate output in certain years to estimates of what annual output would have been in the absence of railroads using the next-best transportation technologies and the same stocks of land, labor, and capital. Fogel guessed that railroad freight service alone had increased total factor productivity by 4 to 5 percent as of 1890. Fishlow estimated that both freight and passenger service had increased factor productivity by 5 percent as of 1859. Either estimate implies that railroads increased total factor productivity by a negligible amount from one year to the next, for no single year saw a significant fraction of the rail network put in place, and there were gradual improvements in railroad technology all along.

G.N. von Tunzelmann (1978, p. 286) presents an estimate along these lines for the effect of the steam engine on British GNP growth in the early nineteenth century: "For Boulton and Watt engines alone (including their pirates) the social savings over atmospheric engines can be put at about 0.11 percent of national income in 1800. If total real output was then growing at its average rate for the take-off years, the level of national income reached on 1 January 1801 would not have been attained much before 1 February 1801 without James Watt. If all steam engines, Watt and atmospheric alike, were hypothetically replaced with other means of motive power (a combination of water and wind would be optimal), the setback would have been about two months. These are upward-biassed figures." There is no similar estimate for the effect of steam engines on American GNP growth, but it could scarcely have been greater. Steam engines replaced waterpower at a very gradual rate. It was not until the 1860s that steam produced more horse-power (Atack, Bateman, and Weiss, 1980, p. 282).

The subsequent replacement of steam engines by electric motors was also slow. "Steam power prevailed at the turn of the century. . . . By 1920, electricity had replaced steam as the major source of motive power, and in 1929—just 45 years after their first use in a factory—electric motors represented about 78 percent of total capacity for driving machinery" (Devine, 1983, p. 349). Paul David (1990, p. 359) guesses that the adoption of the electric motor accounts for "approximately half of the 5 percentage point acceleration recorded in the aggregate TFP growth rate of the U.S. manufacturing sector during 1919–29 (compared with 1909–19)." That does not translate into much of an effect on total factor productivity within a period relevant for business cycles.

The rates of diffusion for these particularly important technological innova-tions were not unusually slow. Edwin Mansfield's (1961, p. 744) study of interwar and postwar innovations found that "the diffusion of a new technique is generally a rather slow process. Measuring from the date of the first successful commercial application, it took 20 years or more for all the major firms to install centralized traffic control, car retarders, by-product coal ovens, and continuous annealing. Only in the case of the pallet-loading machine, tin container, and continuous mining machine did it take 10 years or less for all the major firms to install them." "The empirical picture is clear. Research from a wide variety of disciplines has shown that new technologies are not diffused instantaneously into the prevailing economic and social structure and that the pattern of diffusion can vary greatly across technologies and industries, in some cases being drawn out over decades" (Metcalfe, 1990, p. 17). Salter (1960, pp. 95–99) reviewed the history of the diffusion of new technologies in many industries, in the United States and United Kingdom, for the nineteenth and twentieth centuries. He argued that the slow dif-fusion of technological change is largely attributable to the physical embodiment of technological change in fixed capital, and the slow replacement of fixed capital in response to new technologies. Salter showed that embodied changes in technology that cut costs in half often coexisted with older technologies embodied in earlier vintages of capital. The adjustment of the capital stock, in some cases, is measured in decades. Average-practice techniques often deviate significantly from best practice.

We conclude that the diffusion of any one technological innovation could not increase aggregate factor productivity by more than a trivial amount from one year to the next. If no single innovation can make much of a difference, it seems extremely unlikely that the aggregate rate of improvement could vary *exogenously* over cyclical frequencies to an important degree.

What, then, explains procyclical labor productivity, which is strongly apparent in aggregate and industry-level data in both the interwar and postwar periods? Before the advent of new classical macroeconomics, the standard explanation of this phenomenon was that measured employment does not exactly correspond to labor input. Firms "hoard labor" when output is low because it is cheaper to keep idle workers on hand than to fire them and hire new ones when product demand picks up. Robert Solow (1968) presents a model of this phenomenon. Another explanation is that some employment is a fixed input—"overhead labor"; "the aggregate hours worked by some kinds of employees counted as 'production and related workers,' e.g., watchmen, are not likely to increase or decrease as fast as production" (Hultgren, 1960, p. 27).[6]

Historical evidence is quite consistent with these old-fashioned explanations. Bernanke and Parkinson (1991) point out that if one takes the postwar pattern as evidence in favor of productivity shocks, the very similar pattern over the interwar period must be evidence that "changes in industrial technologies caused the Depression" (p. 457). "No one, including the real business cycle school, seriously maintains that the great Depression was caused primarily by technological shocks to industry production functions" (p. 448). Along the same lines, Mankiw (1989) notes that "the increase in output associated with the World War II buildup is most plausibly a demand-driven phenomenon. Yet from 1939 to 1944 measured total factor productivity grew an average of 7.6 percent per year. (By contrast, the most productivity has grown in any year since then is 5.2 percent in 1950)" (p. 85). We mentioned the possibility that labor productivity was not procyclical in the prewar period, based on evidence for the depression of the 1890s (Weir, 1986; Carter and Sutch, 1990). This evidence runs counter to the new classical premise that technology shocks caused cyclical variation, especially if one can argue that overhead labor and labor hoarding were less important before World War I than in later periods. Solid evidence of a general pattern of acyclical productivity during this period has yet to be produced.

So far we have not discussed the phenomenon of technological regress, which most new classical models rely on to explain cyclical downturns. Technological regress does not appear to correspond to any event in Western economic history since the fall of the Roman Empire. Two proponents of the new classical approach, Gary Hansen and Edward Prescott (1993), recently admitted as much. "Although the rate at which inventions and discoveries are made may vary over time, the stock of knowledge should not decrease. Thus, these variations are not likely to account for the negative growth rates sometimes observed." Hansen and Prescott suggest that "changes in the legal and regulatory system within a country often induce negative as well as positive changes in technology" (p. 281). The effect of institutions on economic performance is an important focus of economic history (see, for example, North, 1990). The burst of growth in West Germany after the monetary reform of 1948 was as large and rapid as a cyclical recovery. But one would be hard-pressed to identify such events in American history, and certainly one could not imagine a string of such events to account for experienced downturns and upturns.

An emphasis on changes in regulatory policy, fiscal policy, or institutional change as a source of "technology" shocks works against the real business-cycle paradigm. Prior to World War I, when regulation, fiscal policy, and government institutions were far less prevalent (Hughes, 1991), and when changes in such policies were relatively infrequent, business cycles were *more* pronounced. The post-World War II era has seen dramatic increases in government activism, and a much greater frequency of change in fiscal and regulatory policies, while business cycles dampened.

Output Variations as a Cause of Technological Change.   While it is impossible to argue that exogenous changes in the rate of aggregate productivity growth cause business cycles, there is plenty of evidence for an effect the other way around: cyclical-frequency variations in output and employment affect the rate of technological innovation and diffusion and the average productivity of operating firms. Demand-driven business cycles can have long-run effects on the economy through aggregate factor productivity as well as investment.

Mansfield (1983) examines the correlation between technological innovation (measured by the patent rate) and cyclical variation in capacity utilization. He finds evidence of a positive correlation between the two but that at high rates of capacity utilization the correlation turns negative. Sokoloff (1988) and Khan and Sokoloff (1993) provide much stronger evidence of the procyclicality of patenting for the antebellum period.

Paul David (1975) studies several examples of demand-induced technological change. He argues that permanent productivity improvements came from endogenous technological innovation and diffusion and that these can be traced to economies of scale or learning effects. In the case of the cotton textile industry, early growth (due to the isolation produced by the Napoleonic Wars and subsequent tariff protection) made possible lasting technological improvements through learning. In the case of the reaper (which greatly reduced the cost of harvesting wheat), the temporarily high international demand for grain during the Crimean War promoted an expansion of farm acreage and encouraged the rapid diffusion of the new technology in the American Middle West.

Bresnahan and Raff (1991) analyze technological change in the automobile industry during the Depression. They find that the collapse of demand forced the permanent closure of old-fashioned production plants and thereby hastened the advance of technological change and increased average productivity during the recovery from the Depression.

The notion that demand shocks can cause permanent increases in output is squarely at odds with many recent macroeconometric attempts to identify aggregate-demand and technology shocks (Blanchard and Quah, 1988; Shapiro and Watson, 1988). These studies assume that aggregate-demand shocks are transitory and that aggregate-demand shocks are uncorrelated with shifts in aggregate supply and conclude that aggregate-demand shocks explain little cyclical variation. But it may be that much of cyclical-frequency variation in output is produced by demand shocks that induce long-run changes in productivity.

Technological change is only one of the mechanisms linking shifts in aggregate demand and supply. For example, Bernanke (1983) argues that bank failures and reductions in the net worth of banks and their borrowers, which resulted from the aggregate-demand shocks of 1929–1933, shifted aggregate supply by reducing the effectiveness of capital markets in linking ultimate suppliers of funds to worthwhile uses of funds (see also Bernanke and James, 1991; Calomiris, 1993c; and Bernanke, 1994). Other examples of endogenous supply shifts produced by aggregate-demand disturbances can be found in the voluminous literature on Kuznets cycles (economic fluctuations associated with cycles of roughly eighteen-year average duration), which we discuss below. A consistent theme of that literature has been that persistent changes in supply related to immigration and capital flows may have been triggered by aggregate-demand fluctuations.

Keynesian Models

What Causes Business Cycles?   The IS-LM model following John Maynard Keynes (1936) and John R. Hicks (1937) is based on two assumptions: real money balances are substitutes for capital assets, and nominal wages, prices, and debt obligations underadjust to aggregate shocks. At least in the short run—say, from one month to the next—they are "sticky." Keynes, Hicks, and most of their American followers believed that wage rates were the main source of nominal rigidities. Nominal price rigidities followed because prices were set as mark-up over marginal cost. Since the 1970s textbook Keynesian models have combined the IS-LM model with an aggregate-supply function that allows for exogenous price shocks (supply shocks) from agriculture and foreign trade and have allowed for nominal rigidities in product prices *per se*. A new Keynesian literature has attempted to derive the features of the old Keynesian model from standard utility functions and more fundamental constraints. Many new Keynesian models describe nominal rigidities in prices with no special reference to wage rates or even an assumption that nominal wages adjust to clear labor markets. So far the similar puzzle of fixed nominal debt contracts, also an important part of the old Keynesian story, has attracted surprisingly little attention.

Purely monetary shocks, like changes in the aggregate money-demand function or changes in the rate of growth of the money supply, have no (or minimal) real effects in new classical models. In Keynesian models monetary shocks cause variations in employment and real output, procyclical movements in consumption and investment (both market and household), and countercyclical movements in the trade balance. Monetary shocks affect real variables in three ways that operate together but are theoretically distinct.

First, the production level chosen by a profit-maximizing firm varies when the nominal product demand schedule shifts relative to sticky prices of products or factors. When demand falls, for example, a firm that is constrained from cutting the nominal wage rates it pays for given jobs will lay off employees, though the workers' marginal revenue product remains greater than the value of their best alternative opportunity: low-value underemployment, a search for another job, even involuntary unemployment.

Second, whether or not wages and prices are sticky, changes in demand affect the size of existing nominal debt obligations relative to debtors' nominal incomes. In the presence of some plausible capital-market imperfections the real burden of existing debt affects investment and consumption as described by Ben Bernanke (1983). Keynes himself was confused on this point, arguing that a fall in aggregate demand would increase debt burdens only if it were associated with a fall in wages and prices (1936, p. 264). In fact, the real burden of a fixed nominal debt depends on the size of the contracted payments relative to the debtor's nominal income or wealth. Real income and wealth fall with aggregate demand even if wages and prices are rigid.

Third, since wages and prices are not *absolutely* rigid, changes in nominal aggregate demand should be associated with changes in expected inflation rates. Changes in expected inflation affect the expected real return to holding money balances and the demand for real assets. This implies that during the wage and price adjustment process, a higher expected inflation rate will offset somewhat the expansionary effect of a temporary increase in real balances produced by sticky prices. DeLong and Summers (1986) show that for some price- and wage-setting rules this effect even can make business-cycle volatility an *increasing* function of the degree of price flexibility because greater price flexibility increases the rate of expected inflation during the adjustment process.

In Keynesian models, aggregate real shocks like changes in government spending or changes in the expected return to investment have effects quite different from those predicted by new classical models. As Keynesian IS shocks, all can be associated with procyclical movements in consumption and investment and countercyclical movements in the trade balance. Also unlike new classical models, Keynesian models have no necessary implication for the real return to employment. Real wages may be countercyclical, acyclical, or procyclical depending on the relative rigidity of prices versus wages (Barro, 1979, p. 59; Mankiw, 1990, p. 1657). Real wages could be procyclical even if firms were free to choose prices subject to sticky nominal wage rates, as long as profit-maximizing price mark-ups over marginal cost were countercyclical (Dunlop, 1938; Keynes, 1939; Tobin, 1993). Countercyclical mark-ups can be derived from a number of different assumptions about the structure of product markets (for examples, see Bils, 1989; Rotemberg and Woodford, 1991).

Keynesian Models and Business Cycles Before World War II

The predictions of Keynesian models are consistent with the cyclical patterns in real variables that appear in the prewar and interwar periods as well as the postwar period. Perhaps more important, they point to specific causes of most business cycles in terms of observable events. Narratives like those of Friedman and Schwartz (1963) and Rendigs Fels (1959) present a long catalogue of plausible monetary (LM) and spending (IS) shocks to account for almost every upturn and downturn as defined by the NBER—an embarrassment of riches that has only been carefully studied for the case of the interwar Great Depression (for example, Temin, 1989).

The macroeconomic events of 1929–1941 pose no special problems for Keynesian theory, unlike new classical theories. As Robert Barro (1979, p. 58) has noted, "From a reduced-form perspective that relates business fluctuations to prior monetary disturbances, the contraction from 1930 to 1933 seems well in line with other experiences. The unprecedented monetary collapse over this period accords quantitatively with the drastic decline in economic activity." Christina Romer (1993, p. 24) argues that "the path of output and employment in the United States in the 1930s is, contrary to common perception, very well understood" in terms of a standard Keynesian model: "The United States slipped into recession in mid-1929 because of tight domestic monetary policy aimed at stemming speculation on the U.S. stock market. The Great Depression started in earnest when the stock market crash in the United States caused consumers and firms to become nervous and therefore to stop buying irreversible durable goods. The American Depression worsened when banking panics swept undiversified and overextended rural banks and the Federal Reserve failed to intervene. Finally, the American Depression ended when the Roosevelt administration chose to increase the money supply tremendously after 1933" (p. 37). The increase in the money supply "had exactly the effect on the U.S. economy that a traditional aggregate supply-aggregate demand model would lead one to predict . . . real interest rates plummeted in response to the gold inflows . . . followed fairly quickly by a recovery of interest-sensitive spending, such as construction spending and consumer purchases of durable goods" (p. 36). While Romer's description of the Great Depression may attach too little weight to long-lived disruptions (supply-side shifts) that followed the severe aggregate-demand shocks of 1929–1933, she is on firm ground in her claim that the downturns and upturns of 1929–1941 are associated with the movements in monetary variables predicted by the Keynesian model.

Nominal Wage Rigidity in History.   No one who makes payments on a mortgage or student loan would quarrel with the assumption that some intertemporal contracts fix payments in nominal terms. It is no less clear that some product prices are held fixed for months at a time even in cyclical downturns, as was noted before World War II (Means, 1935) and has been amply documented in the postwar period (for example, Carlton, 1986). Underadjustment of nominal wage rates is harder to discern, especially in an inflationary environment. In the postwar period the upward trend in real wages together with the absence of absolute decreases in prices and nominal aggregate demand even in downturns means that nominal wage rates for most jobs are increased every year. Adjusting a wage rate to an economywide shock or relative to other wages is a matter of a larger or smaller increase. There are also problems of constructing consistent data to measure wages. Over most of the postwar period no agency collected comprehensive time-series data on wage rates. The best proxies have been series on average hourly earnings. These are affected by cyclical patterns in the composition of employment among low- and high-wage sectors, firms within a sector, and workers within a firm (U.S. Bureau of Labor Statistics, 1969). Average hourly earnings series could vary considerably over a business cycle even if all nominal wage rates were held fixed.

   The nature of wage and price adjustment might be easier to observe in data from earlier periods. Average nominal wage rates rose very little over the late 1920s (U.S. Bureau of the Census, 1975, series D802) and from the 1870s through the late 1890s (see Long, 1960, p. 67; Rees, 1961, p. 38). Most important, before World War II most cyclical downturns saw absolute declines in the money supply and prices with relatively little change in wages. This was certainly true in the downturns of 1893, 1907, and 1929. In all three downturns the money supply, wholesale prices, and consumer prices fell along with industrial production, real GNP, and employment (according to anyone's series).[7]

Fortunately, each of these downturns left behind records of changes in wage rates paid by firms for given jobs that are quite consistent with the notion that wage rigidity was associated with significant layoffs during business-cycle downturns in the face of falling aggregate demand and falling prices. The NBER dates the 1893 depression as a peak in January 1893 and a trough in June 1894. In 1894 the state labor bureaus of New York, Ohio, Connecticut, and Maine surveyed establishments as to whether they had cut wage rates over the calendar year 1893 or in a period from early 1893 through summer 1894. The Ohio bureau continued its surveys through the 1900s, covering the NBER peak in May 1907 and trough in June 1908. These state surveys are described by William Sundstrom (1990, 1992), Carter and Sutch (1990), and Hanes (1993). In every survey, many establishments reported cuts in wage rates for some or all occupations. This is consistent with available time series on average wage rates or hourly earnings, which show decreases over the same years. But in all but one survey, most establishments reported they had not cut wage rates for any occupation, even though they had cut employment by large percentages. The Ohio 1894 survey did not ask about employment, but other data show that employment fell a lot in the same sectors and geographic area (Sundstrom, 1990). The exception is the Connecticut 1894 survey, which includes the longest period after the downturn (through August 1894). In that survey slightly more than half of the establishments reported wage cuts (Carter and Sutch, 1990, p. 17). In the early 1930s the U.S. Bureau of Labor Statistics collected similar (but not directly comparable) information on wage rate changes. These data show that many establishments held wage rates fixed until more than a year after the downturn from the NBER peak in August 1929, long after they had cut employment (Shister, 1944; Mitchell, 1985).

There is no way to be sure that the behavior of the firms in these samples was representative of firms in general, but the surveys' results are certainly consistent with other information about firms' wage rate changes in these downturns. Robert Ozanne's (1968) study of International Harvester, originally the McCormick Reaper Company, shows that the firm cut employment early in each of the three depressions. But in 1893 the company "cut only the [wages of] skilled workers and those on piece rates. Eventually, three years after the depression began, the McCormick firm cut [wages for] common labor 1 cent" (Ozanne, p. 32). After the 1907 downturn International Harvester did not cut wages until the beginning of 1908 (p. 37). After 1929 "the company took no action to cut wages. . . . Finally, in October, 1931, the first production worker wage cuts of 15 percent were instituted" (p. 52). In 1908 U.S. Steel and other large steel producers refrained from wage cuts despite deep reductions in employment (Shergold, 1975, p. 181). After 1929 U.S. Steel held its common labor wage fixed until October 1931. Other firms appear to have followed the same policy. "If we believe the newspapers, magazines, trade publications, and academic journals of the time, money wages in manufacturing were not cut until the fall of 1931" (O'Brien, 1989, pp. 720, 721; see also Jacoby, 1985, pp. 216, 217). There can be no reasonable doubt that in each of these downturns, months after wholesale and consumer prices had begun to fall, establishments accounting for a significant fraction of aggregate employment and output held their nominal wages absolutely fixed as they cut production and laid off workers.[8]

Note that all of this evidence is in regard to wages in just one sector—manufacturing. It is important to note that nominal wage rigidity in the manufacturing sector need not have had the same effects on aggregate output and employment in the prewar and interwar periods as in the postwar period. As we have already mentioned, agriculture is an acyclical sector, and it was much more important before World War II. Unlike manufacturing wages, farm wages appear to have adjusted quickly to aggregate shocks (Goldin and Margo, 1992), and at least in the nineteenth century, workers moved between the manufacturing and farm sectors at seasonal and cyclical frequencies (Dawley, 1976; Keyssar, 1986; Goldin and Engerman, 1993).

The decline in the intersectoral substitution of labor is also related to the decline in labor turnover within manufacturing over time. Margo (1990a, 1990b, 1991) shows that the duration of unemployment spells in the manufacturing sector was relatively short prior to the Great Depression, and that long-duration unemployment became much more common during and after the 1930s. Some of the high historical turnover rate (short unemployment spell duration) in manufacturing likely reflected substitution into agriculture during cyclical and seasonal lulls in manufacturing.[9] The elasticity of labor substitution across sectors, and the turnover of labor, was reduced in the early twentieth century (Jacoby and Sharma, 1992).

The relative ease with which labor moved across sectors before World War I, combined with the smaller size of the manufacturing sector relative to farming, the acyclicality of agricultural production, and the more rapid adjustment of nominal wages in agriculture than manufacturing all made it easier for displaced manufacturing workers to be absorbed in agriculture. Thus, a cyclical downturn in manufacturing and other sticky-wage sectors could have pushed workers into agricultural underemployment rather than unemployment.

Wage Rigidity and the Phillips Curve.   In our discussion of wage rigidity, we have so far avoided reference to results of the Phillips curve studies referred to earlier. That is because none of those studies makes much effort to relate the coefficients of estimated relations to an underlying model of the system of setting prices, wages, and output. Under any reasonable assumptions, the estimated relations are at best reduced forms of much more complex systems, and interpretation of estimated coefficients is not straightforward. Hanes (1994) shows that changes in estimated Phillips curve coefficients can reflect changes in the volatility of shocks to aggregate demand as well as changes in wage and price setting behavior.

Moreover, as discussed above and as noted by Alogoskoufis and Smith (1991), Calomiris (1993a), Obstfeld (1993), and Hanes (1994), changes in the persistence of forcing processes to which wages are responding (like monetary growth and inflation) can affect the correlations between price and output change and therefore affect the interpretation of correlations between price and output processes.

Finally, factors other than wage and price rigidity can account for correlations between nominal price change and real output or employment. Calomiris and Hubbard (1989), in their study of monthly data for the period 1894–1909, argue that the Phillips curve does not necessarily reflect the lack of market clearing in labor or product markets or measure the degree of price and wage rigidity. Instead, aggregate output-price correlations may reflect the contractionary effects of aggregate-demand shocks operating through debt deflation. Calomiris and Hubbard (1989) find that much of the comovement between the wholesale price index and output over the business cycle reflects changes that originate as price innovations. Such innovations could have real effects either due to rigid nominal wages or through predetermined financial contracts (debt deflation). The relative weights of wage rigidity, debt deflation, and other factors in explaining wage, price, and output correlations in manufacturing remains an open issue for future research.

History and New Keynesian Models

Menu Costs. The most general explanation of nominal wage and price rigidity offered by new Keynesian models is the notion of menu costs. Menu cost models show that a firm's incentive to adjust prices to shifts in nominal aggregate demand can be small if its product market is less than perfectly competitive (Mankiw, 1985). As Robert Gordon (1990) and David Romer (1993) point out, the menu-cost argument also applies to wages, whether they are set by firms or monopoly unions. The less elastic is product demand, the smaller the increase in profit resulting from a decrease in marginal cost and hence the smaller the firm's incentive to cut wages. The firm's derived demand for labor is also less elastic, so allowing a wage cut gives workers a relatively small increase in employment (a small decrease in the probability of being laid off).

If the benefit of adjusting prices or wages is small, a small "menu" cost of adjustment itself is enough to cause the setter to hold them fixed. It is not clear, however, what these menu costs might be. So far proponents of these models have invoked various forms of transactions and administrative costs. "Taken literally, these menu costs are the resources required to post new price lists. More metaphorically, these menu costs include the time taken to inform customers, the customer annoyance caused by price changes, and the effort required even to think about a price change" (Mankiw, 1990, p. 1657). But failing to adjust prices brings on administrative costs of adjusting output and employment—costs of cutting production, laying off workers (with the associated turnover costs), closing down plants altogether—which seem larger, if anything.

What kind of costs could apply to wage and price changes alone? The Great Depression offers an example: public disapproval, government pressure and regulations. Anthony O'Brien (1989, p. 724) argues that in the 1920s it was generally believed that wage and price deflation made depressions worse, or even caused them: "By the mid-1920s many manufacturing firms had publicly announced that wage rates would not be reduced during the next downturn." Shortly after the stock-market crash President Hoover called a conference of large employers to encourage them to maintain nominal wage rates. Most promised to do so. Thus "cutting wage rates at the onset of the depression" would have been a "public relations debacle" (p. 729). In 1933 the National Industrial Recovery Act created minimum wages and other forms of regulation that raised nominal wages and prices after deflation had set in and before any considerable upturn in employment. Michael Weinstein (1981, p. 279) points out that "the economy could not have recovered in historically expected ways as long as the NIRA wage and price regulations were effective."

These policies were peculiar to the 1930s, of course, but it may be useful to consider the reasons that rational government and business administrators came to adopt such policies, and whether they have general implications. Olmstead and Rhode (1985) argue that similar "social pressures" were important in restricting gasoline price increases during the California gasoline famine of 1920. Gasoline sellers voluntarily chose to ration fuel rather than increase its price to the market clearing level, which Olmstead and Rhode argue reflected their fears of violent public reactions to price increases.

Long-Term Contracts. As mentioned above, old Keynesian models assumed that the price of labor is the most important source of nominal "stickiness" in the economic system and that firms chose employment levels to equalize the marginal revenue product of labor to the sticky marginal cost of labor implied by wage rates. Marginal labor costs would include other costs contingent on the number of workers employed, like pension contributions and health insurance. Such costs were negligible before World War II.

The old Keynesian view of wages and employment appeared to be undermined by early work in the microeconomic theory of optimal contracts (following Azariadis, 1975). If firms were bound to workers in some kind of long-term relationship, employment and earnings might follow the terms of an explicit or implicit state-contingent contract that set employment at the optimal level, where the marginal revenue product of labor equaled its opportunity cost and stipulated payments to workers so as to equalize the marginal utility of income across states. Under such an agreement the nominal or real "wage rate" prevailing at any point in time would be nothing more than the state-contingent payment divided by the state-contingent quantity of labor supplied. It would not be a price in the ordinary sense and would have no direct relation to employment (Barro and King, 1984).

This argument seems to have been accepted by some new Keynesians, contributing to the recent emphasis on price rather than wage rigidity, though it applies just as well to product prices: firms can also have long-term relationships with suppliers of raw materials and with consumers of final products. Fortunately, later work following Calvo and Phelps (1977) showed that the neutrality argument depends on an implausible assumption that workers know as much as firms about the value of labor's product. If a firm has private information and is willing to trade off some amount of expected profit for a reduction in its variance—a consequence of the same financial-market imperfections that generate real effects of a debt burden—then the optimal contract leaves the firm free to choose the employment level subject to positive marginal costs of labor (Azariadis, 1983), just as in the old Keynesian story. Thus, the problem becomes one of accounting for the underadjustment of marginal labor costs—that is, wage rates (and employment-contingent benefits)—to aggregate shocks.

Many Keynesian models of the late 1970s accounted for the underadjustment of nominal wage rates with an assumption that wages were set by long-term contracts before the realization of aggregate shocks. This was often justified as a depiction of American union labor contracts, which set nominal wage rates for one to three years with little or no indexing. The relation between union contracts and nominal wage rigidity seemed to be confirmed by the earliest studies of wage and price behavior based on standard historical series for output, prices, and average hourly earnings. As we mentioned above, Cagan (1975) and Sachs (1980) showed changes in Phillips curve coefficients on output and lagged inflation from prewar or interwar periods to the postwar period. That matched up nicely to the timing of the spread of unions and long-term wage contracts across the manufacturing sector. Robert Gordon (1986, p. 20) summarized the conventional wisdom: "The greater postwar persistence of wages and prices is generally attributed to two factors. First, the increased importance of labor unions since the late 1930s has led to centralized wage bargaining, and high perceived costs of negotiation have made it economical to establish three-year contracts in many industries. That today's wage changes were in many cases agreed upon last year or the year before tends to insulate wage changes from current market forces and to increase their dependence on what has happened previously. Second, the greater confidence of private agents in the willingness of monetary and fiscal policy to reduce the severity of recessions lessens their need to reduce wages and prices quickly and increases their incentive to wait for the expected prompt return of prosperity."

But pointing to union contracts or any other long-term price arrangements did not amount to an explanation of nominal rigidity. Why should workers and firms fail to adjust the marginal cost of labor, determined by the terms of the contract, to aggregate shocks that both sides should be able to observe? Wage bargainers should adjust rates set by a long-term contract to those shocks, either by renegotiating the contract or indexing its terms in advance. As Robert Barro (1979, p. 54) put it, "Long-term labor agreements do not imply a failure of employment to increase when all parties to the agreements perceive that they could be made better off by such a change." Perfect indexation of a long-term contract may be impossible, if only because published price indices are very noisy measures of true changes in the price level (Meltzer, 1994; Bullard, 1994). But it is hard to account for a total lack of indexation in a three-year contract or a failure to renegotiate a contract in the face of a general recession.

More important, wage rates display nominal rigidity in the absence of any kind of long-term contract. The historical association between union contracts and wage rigidity has not held up to further scrutiny. Recall that better wage and price series used in more recent studies of the Phillips curve show no decrease in the Phillips curve coefficient on output (Allen, 1992; Hanes, 1993). The coefficient on lagged inflation still appears larger in the postwar period, but as we have argued, that did not reflect a change in the association between wages or prices and deviations of output from trend. Most important, the microeconomic historical evidence we have discussed indicates that many firms refrained from cutting wages in prewar and interwar depressions like 1893, 1907, and 1929 though few faced formal unions and none was constrained by a contract. Before the 1930s courts did not enforce wage contracts between firms and worker groups even if they were written down.

Insider-Outsider Models. The lack of a historical correlation between formal contracts and nominal wage or price rigidity poses less of a problem for insider-outsider models like those described by Assar Lindbeck and Dennis Snower (1988). These have always emphasized that one source of union workers' bargaining power, the employer's costs of replacing its incumbent workforce, is present in nonunion firms as well. An informal group of workers (or even an individual worker) might be able to threaten a withdrawal of effort or "cooperation" and force the firm to pay wages greater than the value of alternative employment (or a search for alternative employment). Organization of a formal union might add to workers' bargaining power but might be more a signal of bargaining power that had been there all along. If so, the fixed nominal wages set by union contracts may be an extreme version of a more general characteristic of wages set by bargaining.

Many patterns in postwar data are consistent with the ideas in the insider-outsider literature. Some nonunion firms appear to pay wage premia that resemble those in unionized firms—in excess of compensating differentials for unpleasant work conditions or differentials associated with an employee's human-capital characteristics and paid to workers in virtually all the firm's jobs. High-wage firms are usually found in industries with certain characteristics: large establishments, firms with high capital-labor ratios, and firms that enjoy greater product market power (those with high profits and market shares). For example, wages are higher in manufacturing than in agriculture and higher in machine tool manufacture than in textiles. Establishment size, capital-intensity, and market-power indicators are highly correlated across sectors, so it is hard to identify which might bear a causal relation to wage premia (Dickens and Katz, 1987), but the latter two correlations are certainly "consistent with the idea that labor can extract rents which depend on how much damage it could do by temporarily stopping the firm from producing. Production interruptions are more costly for capital-intensive firms and those earning high profits than for other firms" (Katz and Summers, 1989, p. 241). Postwar data also suggest an association between high wages and nominal wage rigidity. Wage differentials across sectors and firms are countercyclical: wages in high-wage sectors fall less in recessions and rise less in booms (Wachter, 1970). But since firms in high-wage sectors are also more likely to be unionized, it is hard to say whether this pattern holds for high-wage nonunion firms.

Historical evidence allows one to separate the effects of workers' bargaining power and industry characteristics from those of formal unions and long-term contracts, since unions were rare before the late 1930s, even in manufacturing. Such evidence makes it clear that worker groups can threaten firms even in the absence of formal organization. In the late nineteenth century nonunion workers were capable of withdrawing effort in the most spectacular way, by going on strike (Hanes, 1993). Large-scale strikes by nonunion workers against cuts in nominal wages and threatened cuts continued through the 1920s (Wright, 1981), and it was observed that nonunion workers would slack off and damage machinery if they felt they had been treated "unfairly" (Mathewson, 1931). The firm characteristics that are associated with wage premia and unions in the postwar period were associated with strikes in the late nineteenth century (Hanes, 1993) and wage premia in the 1900s and 1920s, *before* the spread of unions (Krueger and Summers, 1987).

They were also associated with nominal wage rigidity. In the downturn after 1929 firms in industries with less competitive product markets and high capital-labor ratios were the last to cut wages (Shister, 1944). In the depression of 1893 firms were less likely to cut wages if their industries had suffered especially large numbers of strikes in earlier years (Hanes, 1993). Recall that the general historical pattern in the cyclical behavior of nominal wages and prices appears (at present) to be an increase in rigidity in the late nineteenth century, followed by no clear change to the postwar period. That would make sense if nominal rigidity were linked to the technologies and product-market structures associated with high wages, rather than with unionization *per se*. In America, firms with those characteristics came into being with the rise of mass production in the postbellum period. By most accounts, the 1870s, 1880s, and 1890s saw historically unique increases in establishment size, capital intensity, and product-market concentration (Chandler, 1977; Spencer, 1977; Lamoreaux, 1985; Jacoby, 1985; O'Brien, 1988).

None of this is to suggest that current versions of insider-outsider models provide a theoretical explanation for nominal wage rigidity. Such models face exactly the same problem as models of formal long-term contracts: in either case, workers with bargaining power should adjust their wage demands to observable aggregate shocks. Insiders should not force the firm to pay wage rates that cause them to be laid off and become outsiders.

Efficiency Wages. The basic assumptions of most efficiency-wage models resemble those of insider-outsider models: a firm loses profit if its employees choose to reduce effort or if it must replace incumbent workers (Stiglitz, 1986). But in efficiency-wage models the workers do not take *strategic* advantage of their ability to harm the firm: the workers do not make threats and bargain. The firm need only worry that employees will quit for nonstrategic reasons or will "shirk" to enjoy leisure on the job. Employees are less likely to quit or shirk if the firm's wage is higher than the value of workers' alternative employment, so a firm may choose to pay wage premia to reduce turnover and raise effort on the job. Sectors in which firms face especially large costs of turnover and monitoring will pay persistently high wages. The problems that would cause firms to pay efficiency wages should also cause firms to promise employees *future* rewards in the form of pensions, promotions, and raises by seniority if they do not quit and are not caught slacking off on the job (Lazear, 1981). Such policies are generally referred to as *bureaucratic* or *internal labor market* employment patterns.

The phenomena described by efficiency-wage models have implications for nominal wage rigidity in that a firm's incentive to cut its wage when outside wages fall or unemployment rises is smaller if the cost of maintaining an unnecessarily high wage is partly offset by the benefit of lower turnover and less shirking. Thus, a small menu cost of changing wage rates could cause the firm to hold them fixed.

In some ways, efficiency-wage models are a complement to insider-outsider models (Krueger and Summers, 1987). Efficiency-wage effects on the behavior of individual workers reduce the cost to the firm of giving in to a group's demands. In general, however, efficiency-wage and strategic-threat models are substitutes, offering alternative explanations of the same features of employment and wage setting.

Historical evidence suggests that strategic threats and bargaining have been more important. Daniel Raff (1988, p. 398) has examined Henry Ford's adoption of the "five-dollar day" in 1914, a clear example of a policy to pay wages in excess of workers' alternative opportunities: "None of the three canonical efficiency wage theories—turnover costs, adverse selection, and moral hazard—speaks to a plausible central motive. A desire to buy the peace seems far more consistent with the facts. Ford was alone in his industry in paying such wages when he did because he was alone in his method of making automobiles." Ford faced "the specter of the sit-down strike. Ford's single-minded focus on a dedicated capital stock and economies of scale made the company peculiarly vulnerable. Its profits left the opportunity cost of such action to the owners of the company relatively high. . . . The Wobblies had been in Detroit in the late springtime of 1913" (p. 396).

Sanford Jacoby (1985) describes the origins of the internal labor-market policies that should be related to the payment of premium wages, if efficiency-wage models are correct. Jacoby finds that "the new bureaucratic approach to employment did not gradually take hold in an ever-growing number of firms" (p. 8), as one might expect if it were a profit-maximizing managerial innovation. Instead, "the growth of internal labor markets in large firms was erratic, occurring chiefly during World War I and the Great Depression" (p. 280). At the same time firms came to see turnover as a bad thing, but "the new concern with turnover was not attributable to any increase in separation costs associated with technological change of a firm-specific character. In fact, manufacturing technology was becoming less firm-specific and idiosyncratic than it had been in the nineteenth century" (p. 122). "The historical record indicates that the employment reforms introduced during World War I and after 1933 were attributable not so much to competitive market forces as to the growing power of the unions and the ascendance of the personnel department over other branches of management. . . . With the benefit of forty years' hindsight, we may observe that these policies often enhanced efficiency by reducing turnover and increasing morale, or by stimulating programs to upgrade the work force. But this effect was by no means obvious to the managers of firms in transition, who were skeptical that internal labor market arrangements would lower costs. Efficiency incentives were neither strong enough nor obvious enough to produce the modern internal labor market" (pp. 277, 278).

Moreover, "personnel managers can be viewed as mere conduits for union threat effects in that many of their ideas were borrowed from the unions and their influence often rested on the imminence of labor unrest" (p. 281). The firms that adopted internal labor-market policies in the 1900s did so to "divert industry's skilled workers from the unions by means of quasi-pecuniary incentives, including profit-sharing, pension, and home ownership plans" (p. 52). When unions spread during World War I: "Personnel management reduced the potential for unionization by replicating within the firm some of the union's protective structures"

(p. 164). After unions were crushed in the early 1920s personnel departments lost influence, but in the 1930s, after the NIRA and the Wagner Act: "The strategy of using employment reforms to deter unionism was given new life" (p. 242). Personnel managers cared about turnover because "the same conditions that gave rise to quits and low morale in the present might lead to strikes or worse in the future. If these conditions could be identified and remedied, they reasoned, morale would improve, quits would fall, and the possibility of industrial revolt would be greatly lessened" (p. 120).

Historical Lessons for New Keynesians. On the whole, historical experience suggests that nominal wage rigidity is associated with bilateral monopoly and bargaining between firms and groups of workers, whether or not the workers are organized in a formal union and the bargain takes the form of a formal contract.

The missing link between bargaining and nominal rigidity may perhaps be found in a set of ideas that has been more or less ignored in new Keynesian theory: agents' information about current levels of nominal demand may not be good enough to allow perfect adjustment of their behavior to monetary shocks. Lucas (1972) and Lucas and Woodford (1993) show the effects of such information problems in economies made up of preindustrial producer households. Gordon (1981, 1990) and Meltzer (1994) point out some reasons information can be imperfect in complex economies with many buyer-seller relationships, many commodities, and long lags in the availability of reliable statistics on the aggregate price level. Such ignorance should affect the outcomes of bargaining between firms and groups of workers in negotiations of new long-term agreements or series of short-term agreements. "Insiders" may *wish* to adjust their wage demands to nominal shocks but lack the information to do so. The difficulty of indexing a long-term agreement to subsequent shocks is a related problem.

One need not assume that bargainers have *no* information about aggregate shocks, only that their information is less than perfect. In addition, the experience of the Great Depression suggests that violation of social norms may be a part of the cost of adjusting wages downward, and prices upward, in response to aggregate shocks.

Rediscovering Long Swings

A theme of business-cycle research that is receiving increasing attention is that many disturbances to economic activity have long lives. The Great Depression is one prominent example, as is the "Eurosclerosis" of the 1980s. More generally, however, simple statistical decompositions that divide economic shocks into short-lived and long-lived disturbances find that a large proportion of variation in economic activity is attributable to long-lived shocks (Blanchard and Quah, 1988; Shapiro and Watson, 1988).

Persistent swings in output and employment pose an important challenge to explanations of business cycles that posit wage and price rigidities. Models of wage and price rigidity may have a difficult time explaining the persistence of economic disturbances, despite some attempts to do so (Blanchard and Summers, 1988). Clearly, menu cost models will not be capable of generating significant long swings. But even models that posit institutional rigidities (as in insider-outsider stories) must face the following dilemma. Any contracting friction that creates significant unemployment of resources should also spur the development of competing producers to make use of those idle resources.

As we noted before, one way of explaining the persistence of high-frequency disturbances is to argue that demand shocks can have persistent effects, a common assumption in a wide variety of endogenous-growth models and a point of view about the economy that goes back at least as far as Schumpeter (1939). In theory, endogenous persistence of demand shocks may be due to a variety of factors. One of the dangers of the new growth literature is that once one relaxes the simple neo-classical framework—with constant returns to scale and without externalities—it may be difficult to choose among the wealth of alternative possible explanations for endogenous persistence. An historical view of the economy, however, can help to give specific meaning to the notion of long swings and distinguish among various possible explanations for them.

It is worth noting that economic historians (and macroeconomists over the age of fifty) have been thinking about endogenous growth for a long time. The notion that aggregate-demand disturbances have sometimes been associated with persistent growth or decline underlay a large literature on long swings, which largely went out of fashion by the late 1960s.

The phenomenon of long-duration Kuznets cycles—of roughly sixteen to eighteen years—is central to American macroeconomic history. Indeed, anyone attempting to describe concisely the history of American economic development will find himself essentially plotting out Kuznets cycles. Kuznets cycles are not just a convenient means of organizing a long time series into clumps. Each cycle coincides with identifiable eras of fundamental change in the economy that are central to the story of how America developed. There is the era of canal building and canal bankruptcy, the period of rapid railroad building in the Middle West during the 1850s and the demise of the railroad boom prior to the Civil War, and the postbellum railroad booms and busts.

The Kuznets cycle literature did more than make notions of endogenous growth credible by identifying moments of persistent takeoff and collapse in the economy. It provided a descriptive body of evidence that can help macroeconomists choose from the number of plausible theoretical models that might explain long swings. Similar patterns of phenomena within each cycle suggest a common mechanism. The phases of the Kuznets cycle are remarkably common across the various cycles and are associated with similar sequences of activities—most notably, the construction of transportation networks and structures and massive waves of immigration. These similarities led proponents of the Kuznets cycle to describe long swings as *building cycles* (see Abramovitz, 1964; the review of this vast literature in Hughes, 1990, ch. 8 and 16; Solomou, 1987; Zarnowitz, 1992).

There is widespread disagreement about how such cycles began—with possible triggers ranging from immigration shocks to financial or political factors that set the stage for expansion.[10] There is similar disagreement about the factors that brought such cycles to an end.[11] Whatever the answers to those questions, it is clear that land settlement, canal building, and railroad speculation on the frontier were central to the booms of the nineteenth century, and reversals in these processes were associated with rapid declines in migration westward and investment. For example, migration westward in April of 1857 resulted in the arrival of 1,000 people per day into Kansas alone. Railroads—which were speculating heavily in land and building new lines in anticipation of a transcontinental trunk line—encouraged the migration by lowering the cost of passage by as much as 25 percent. Land prices soared, mortgage lending grew, and speculative railroad stocks boomed. Adverse political news in the middle of 1857 (associated with the conflict over slavery in the territories, and its consequences for timely construction of a transcontinental line) seems to have been responsible for a collapse of speculative land and railroad securities prices, and the end of rapid immigration (Calomiris and Schweikart, 1991). This experience illustrates the importance of expectations for migration decisions and land and railroad construction, and the potential for bootstrapping effects (mutually reinforcing expectations and investments). As Brinley Thomas (1954) notes, supply-side and demand-side forces often reinforced each other in producing economic growth, as international and interregional migration responded to differences in standards of living across locations. Analysis of the timing and location of persistent bursts of economic growth also show that long swings were closely tied to specific locations in which economic development was occurring very rapidly.

The common *spatial* patterns of long-run cycles historically in the United States suggest that a model of endogenous growth capable of explaining the Kuznets cycles must begin with a spatial conceptual framework for modeling economic activity (e.g., Murphy, Shleifer, and Vishny, 1989; Krugman, 1991). Waves of American economic development were associated with three related spatial phenomena—the settlement of an expanding frontier, the establishment of a transportation and communication network within the boundaries of that frontier, and the creation of high concentrations of population and economic activity that served as nodes within that network. Epochs of great expansion were times when large investments in transportation and communication occurred, removing preexisting barriers to the flow of capital and labor and allowing the reorganization of the production and distribution process within the economy (Chandler, 1977). These investments promoted massive flows of capital and labor, which chose to move to new locations and often to concentrate in large cities.

This spatial interpretation of the Kuznets cycle suggests four related features of the spatial economy that seem essential to explaining moments of sudden change followed by persistent expansion or contraction. First, the decision to bear fixed costs is central to the suddenness of economic expansion that characterizes Kuznets cycles. Entrepreneurs must be willing to pay fixed costs necessary to the establishment of transportation and communication facilities that substantially reduce the marginal cost of settlement. Once the initial barriers are breached, that sets the stage for a prolonged expansion—a free lunch for followers and, of course, some rents for leaders.

Second, the expectations of entrepreneurs are central to the beginning of this process. That does not mean that visionary entrepreneurs "make it all happen" (for example, see Fishlow's, 1965, analysis of patterns of settlement and railroad construction in the antebellum period). But it does mean that rapid settlement must be occurring, or expected to occur soon, to justify large expenditures of resources on infrastructure. Moments of expansion are focal points when immigrants, land speculators, infrastructure builders, and external owners of capital agree that rents can be had from moving quickly into new areas to build and populate them or to connect them to preexisting areas in new ways. The frontier always beckoned as the obvious point of future expansion, but the timing of the great push was unknown. Clearly, the origins of long waves cannot be attributed to exogenous technological changes. The technologies for building canals and railroads or for harvesting the vast prairies of the Midwest were developed long in advance of their application. Demand-side explanations for origins (including financial and political events, domestically or abroad) are more plausible as focal points for starting or stopping long waves, but it would be hard to argue that uniquely large shocks started long waves. Convergent expectations—often associated with dramatic aggregate-demand shocks (like wars)—seem to be a key ingredient to explaining why some shocks helped to trigger great pushes of economic activity or great collapses. Of course, the precise timing of convergent (perhaps mutually fulfilling) expectations is intrinsically hard to explain convincingly.

Third, in addition to the removal of fixed costs of settlement, persistence of growth seems to be related to economies of agglomeration (city building). Location-specific factor market and product market externalities are the defining characteristic of cities (David and Rosenbloom, 1990). Without such externalities, diseconomies of congestion would prevent cities from ever having formed. Economies of agglomeration fed long waves by creating locations of increasing returns that attracted capital and labor after the initial stage of frontier settlement. Specific historical examples of economies of agglomeration include Boston in the early nineteenth century, which served as a focal point for the financing and operation of early American industry (Hekman, 1980), and Chicago, which acted as a production and distribution gateway connecting the East and West (David and Rosenbloom, 1990).

Fourth, network economies created opportunities for growth within preexisting frontiers for entrepreneurs who found efficient means of combining activities across production and distribution nodes. During the canal-building ear, entrepreneurs who owned anthracite coal fields in Eastern Pennsylvania profited handsomely by financing the construction of a canal to bring those resources in touch with the existing network of transportation and production (Chandler, 1972). In the postbellum era, the construction of railroad trunk lines linking distant points on the map revolutionized the production and distribution of industrial output and the organization of industrial enterprises (Chandler, 1977). The revolutions in production, distribution, and marketing during this period, and the creation of the modern corporate form of hierarchical management, were largely a *spatial* revolution in the economy. Large geographical scope changed the definition of the economy from a collection of local and regional economies to a single national economy, with firms that operated throughout the nation. This transformation largely reflected the economies of operating networks emphasized by Chandler (1977)—achieving more efficient larger production scale and high "throughput" by improving management, distribution, and nationwide marketing (Field, 1983, 1987).

Of course, opening new frontiers and building transportation networks and cities were not the only contributing factors in producing long swings. As discussed above, endogenous technological change may have been important as well— particularly in the cases of the textile industry in the early nineteenth century and agricultural growth in the 1850s. Looking to the future, in an economy with closed geographical boundaries and well-developed transportation networks and urban centers, the relative importance of technological factors is likely to be even greater. Conceivably, the new frontier in the American economy may be technological rather than spatial, with new construction defined in terms of the information superhighway. To the extent that convergent expectations and network externalities are important preconditions for realizing technological breakthroughs, Kuznets cycles of the future may be describable more in terms of redesigning existing technologies or networks of communication.

Econometric Lessons

What are the methodological implications of historical long swings for macro-econometrics? First, as already noted, demand shocks often set in motion long-run changes in aggregate supply, and thus it is wrong to view long-run shifts in supply as independent of momentary demand disturbances. Second, the importance of spatial concepts like cities and frontiers suggest advantages from disaggregation across locations for understanding macroeconomic change. Third, the number of observations of business cycles may be few, even though the number of calendar years of data are many. Once one defines the cycle of interest to be of eighteen-year duration, that substantially limits the number of cycles. This suggests further advantages from disaggregation. By relying on panel data (for states and towns, enterprises and individuals), one can exploit cross-sectional variation in the data when testing hypotheses. As we show in the subsequent discussion, recognition of institutional nonneutrality reinforces these same methodological implications.

Institutional Nonneutrality

Macroeconomic stability and growth may be affected by institutional innovations as well as by more conventionally defined supply and demand shocks. A discussion of institutional change presumes a definition of institutions. For our purposes we define *institutions* to include entities that make decisions or regulate and enforce contracts (such as governments, banks, labor unions, and courts), as well as decision rules and coalitions that may not be embodied in a physical location, formal association, or contract. The most interesting institutions, from the standpoint of macroeconomic history, are those that influence information, resources, tastes, and technology rather than simply reflect them. As Alexander Field (1981) has argued, despite the historian's instinct to explain institutional change as a purposeful choice, often institutions, once formed, take on a life of their own. Indeed, Field argues that at any point in time an organized market economy must take as given most of its most important institutional parameters (for example, what constitutes an enforceable contract); otherwise chaos would result.

Labor Markets

In addition to basic legal and ethical principles on which a market economy must be founded, other institutions play an active role in determining outcomes. In labor contracting, for example (discussed at length above), some macroeconomists and historians have placed great weight on technological changes and the development of unions in affecting the bargaining power of workers, the distribution of wealth, and the rigidity of wages. Changes in the integration of labor markets have also been emphasized as important preconditions to the settlement of the frontier and the transfer of workers from relatively unproductive occupations to more productive regions and jobs (Field, 1978; Wright, 1979, 1981, 1986; Hatton and Williamson, 1991; Goldin and Sokoloff, 1984; Rosenbloom, 1988, 1990; Sundstrom and Rosenbloom, 1993; Margo, 1994; Simkovich, 1994). Such changes were important determinants of the cross-regional distribution of wealth and were necessary conditions for rapid expansion phases of the Kuznets cycle.

Capital Markets, Bank Regulation, and Monetary Policy Regimes

Financial institutional change also had important (largely unintended) effects on the economy. North (1961) argues that the early concentration of capital among New England merchants provided the financing for early industrialization. Special chartering of banks to serve the needs of favored borrowers—the mercantilistic approach of creating rents to spur development—may also have helped to concentrate resources in the hands of early industrialists. Davis (1957, 1960) and Lamoreaux (1994) show that New England's manufacturers relied heavily on loans from the banks they controlled as a supplement to retained earnings in financing rapid expansion. Carosso (1970) and Neal (1994) argue—from the financial histories of the United States and Britain, respectively—that the development of networks of investment bankers and dealers (often spurred by dramatic events, such as the government's need to finance wars with debt) had long-lived benefits for private costs of external finance. In a similar vein, Calomiris and Raff (1994) argue that the growth of U.S. pension funds and mutual funds in the 1950s and 1960s—largely an unintended benefit of tax policy and demographic changes in the economy—significantly reduced the cost to industrial corporations of raising external funds by reducing the costs of selling common stock.

The literature on the role of bank financing during the postbellum second industrial revolution emphasizes the shortcomings of bank regulation—especially restrictions on branching and consolidation within the banking system—and the way restrictions on American banking hindered interregional capital flows, slowed capital accumulation, and promoted instability. The earliest work in this literature (Davis, 1963, 1965; Sylla, 1969; James, 1978; Snowden, 1984) established that American capital markets were highly segmented. Compared to other countries, which operated nationwide branch banking systems, interest rates and profit rates differed greatly across regions and sectors. Interregional profit rate differentials widened in the latter half of the nineteenth century as the geographic scope of the economy and the minimum efficient scale of production expanded rapidly (Chandler, 1977; Calomiris, 1993b; Bodenhorn, 1992; Atack and Bateman, 1994). Small unit banks were unable to meet the needs of the new generation of large firms operating production and distribution networks throughout the country. The participation of banks in industrial finance was relatively small, as banks came to specialize more in financing commercial enterprises. The costs of industrial finance in the United States were much higher than in the concentrated, universal banking system of Germany, where large-scale banking permitted greater diversification, as well as the reaping of network and scope economies in placing traded securities, managing trust accounts, and participating in corporate finance and governance of large-scale industrial firms (Calomiris, 1994).[12] Higher financing costs not only retarded industrial expansion, but also led industrial producers to favor less fixed-capital intensive production processes (Field, 1983, 1987; Wright, 1990; Calomiris, 1994).

Access to bank services in rural areas was also restricted by unit banking laws. Unit banking reduced the profitability of establishing high-overhead banks in sparsely populated areas, which would have been better served by low-overhead branches (Evanoff, 1988). Furthermore, after episodes of local or regional financial distress, states with unit banking laws found it much harder to rebuild their banking systems through acquisitions of failed banks or the establishment of new offices (Calomiris, 1990, 1992, 1993b).

While the mortgage market—which was able to rely on insurance companies for financing—apparently overcame some of the barriers to integration posed by unit banking laws, Snowden (1993) and Snowden and Abu-Saba (1994) argue that the fragmentation of the national mortgage market (a by-product of unit banking laws) exacerbated agency problems between mortgage financiers (insurance companies) and local brokers and promoted inefficient allocation of mortgage credit.

The greater instability of the unit banking system—which saw much higher failure rates and a unique propensity for banking panics in comparison with other countries—was also a result of the fragmentation of the financial system that unit banking entailed. Times of trouble for banks both reflected adverse economic conditions and propagated cyclical disturbances through contractions in the availability of credit (Calomiris and Hubbard, 1989; Calomiris and Gorton, 1991; Grossman, 1993). Other countries enjoyed the benefits of the diversification of risk *ex ante*, and the coordination of the banking system's response to adversity *ex post*, which a banking system with a small number of large banks made possible (Calomiris and Gorton, 1991; Calomiris and Schweikart, 1991; Calomiris, 1993b). In addition, unit banking supporters eager to achieve banking stability without allowing branching pushed for the establishment of deposit insurance, which further undermined the stability of the system by encouraging excessive risk taking by banks (White, 1983; Calomiris, 1993b; Calomiris and White, 1994; Wheelock and Kumbhakar, 1994).

Despite the potential benefits of relaxing unit banking restrictions, special interests succeeded in blocking branch banking legislation (White, 1984; Calomiris, 1993b; Calomiris and White, 1994). Historical "path dependence" played an important role here. Prior to the 1870s, branch banking was not a contentious issue, and the costs of unit banking were arguably small, since the minimum efficient scale of industrial firms and the geographic scope of the economy were limited up to that point. During the second industrial revolution, as unit banking increasingly became a costly constraint on the economy, the existing special interests of unit bankers and their allies limited the adaptation of the banking system to the new needs of industry, agriculture, and commerce.

The consequences of unit banking laws for the financial system helped set the stage for the creation of the Federal Reserve in 1913. Like most changes in government financial regulation, the Fed was created in the wake of a crisis—the Panic of 1907—as a brainchild of the National Monetary Commission, which brought together politicians, bankers, and many of the most prominent financial economists of the time to redesign the American banking system. Given the politics of unit banking, however, the Federal Reserve Act avoided dealing with the fragmentation of the banking system, which was understood to be the fundamental source of instability in the system. Instead, the Fed was designed to stabilize the banking system by limiting interbank lending and reducing the seasonal volatility of interest rates.

The Fed was conceived essentially as a microeconomic intervention into the reserve market. It was intended to remedy, first and foremost, the absence of an elastic supply of reserves at seasonal frequency. Given seasonal fluctuations in loan demand—linked to the needs to finance planting, harvesting, and marketing of agricultural produce—banks in the aggregate were forced to choose between allowing seasonal fluctuations in their loan-to-reserve ratio or importing and exporting gold in large quantities in response to seasonal fluctuations in loan demand.[13] Gold was costly to import and export (it cost roughly 0.5 percent of the value of gold to bring it across the Atlantic) (Officer, 1986). Thus there were strong incentives to allow loan-to-reserve ratios to fluctuate with demand. Seasonal increases in the loan ratio placed banks at greater risk of defaulting on their deposits and therefore resulted in the comovement of loan interest rates and loan demand. Thus peak-time borrowers were forced to compensate bankers for the greater portfolio risk to banks during peak periods. Clark (1986), Miron (1986), Barsky et al. (1988), Calomiris and Gorton (1991), and Calomiris and Hubbard (1994b) discuss evidence that prior to the founding of the Fed seasonal fluctuations in U.S. loan demand produced important seasonal fluctuations in U.S. and foreign interest rates, and in flows of foreign capital and gold. The Fed's discount window was intended to provide an elastic supply of reserves at seasonal frequency, thus obviating the need for seasonal interest rate fluctuations or gold flows.

The other main goal of the Fed was to restructure the market for reserves to eliminate reserve pyramiding in the banking system (White, 1983). Under unit banking, banks outside of the Eastern financial centers would lend funds to money-center banks during periods of low local loan demand. These funds were used, among other things, to finance the underwriting and trading of securities. Critics of this arrangement argued that it placed the reserves of the entire banking system at excessive risk, since problems in securities markets, which sometimes produced losses for investment bankers and money-center banks that lent money to them, could threaten the ability of all banks to repay their depositors. This was not an unwarranted concern. For example, during the Panic of 1857, and in all the other major financial panics of the national banking era, security market losses in the financial center played an important role in destabilizing the system. Crises during the national banking era tended to be transmitted through the system from the top of the pyramid down (Calomiris and Gorton, 1991; Calomiris and Schweikart, 1991).[14]

The twelve Federal Reserve Banks were intended to substitute as repositories for interbank reserves. The hope was that banks would decide to keep funds with these regional Feds and forego lending to money-center banks. But the Fed failed to accomplish this goal due to two crucial flaws in the design of the system. First, costly regulations of Fed member banks discouraged banks from joining (which became referred to as the membership problem). Small banks found that they could reap the advantages of access to the discount window by borrowing from large banks that were Fed members, and so it did not pay them to join the Fed system and pay the high regulatory costs of membership. In this respect, White (1983) argues, the creation of the Fed may have reinforced rather than undermined reserve pyramiding. Second, the Fed did not pay interest on reserves. If it had done so, then large regional member banks would have been willing to deposit funds with the Fed rather than in New York banks. But without an incentive to deposit reserves at the Fed, banks continued their practice of concentrating funds in the East during times of slack local loan demand.

More generally, despite its apparent success in reducing the seasonal volatility of interest rates, the Fed failed as a mechanism to insulate the macroeconomy from deflationary international shocks and disruptive banking collapses, as several waves of banking failures during the 1930s illustrated.[15] The core problems that made the U.S. banking system so fragile—lack of diversification within, and coordination among, banks—were products of unit banking, and were not addressed by the founding of the Fed. The Fed is a good example of an institution that was designed to accomplish clear objectives but that was hampered by flaws in its design and by the constraints posed by special interests. The Fed is also a good example of Field's (1981) argument that institutions come to take on a life of their own independent of the reasons they came into being. Countercyclical monetary policy, which came to be the Fed's primary occupation, was not one of the principal objectives that gave rise to the Fed.

Do Governments Learn? Institutional Change and the Great Depression

One way to approach the economic history of the period leading up to and following the Great Depression is to consider it as a case study in institutional adaptation to changing circumstances. The emphasis of much of the literature on the period 1929–1939 is that learning was occurring—about appropriate monetary policy rules, about the macroeconomic consequences of wage rigidity, about the costs of adherence to the gold standard, and about the remaining weaknesses in the banking system. Interestingly, the recent literature on institutional learning during the Depression does not suggest that, as a general proposition, learning led to improvement in policy. Rather, the record is mixed. In some respects, the right lessons seem to have been learned—particularly with respect to monetary policy rules, the disadvantages of rigid wages, and the potential costs of adherence to the gold standard. In other respects—notably, bank regulatory policy and fiscal policy— recent research suggests that major institutional changes resulting from government intervention were ill-advised and based on false interpretations of the Depression.

On the positive side, the Fed's approach to monetary policy seems to have changed for the better. The increased concentration of Fed authority in Washington, and greater coordination of decision making within the Fed, which Marriner Eccles championed through his support for the Banking Act of 1935 and his stewardship as Fed chairman, transformed the Fed into a more effective (though not perfect) maker of monetary policy. Friedman and Schwartz (1963) provided the seminal analysis of policy errors by the Federal Reserve during the Depression, which has been substantially updated by recent research (see the review in Calomiris, 1993c). Friedman and Schwartz argued that Fed money-supply contractions produced the Great Depression and that those errors would not have occurred if Benjamin Strong had remained at the helm of the New York Fed. The thrust of much of the recent work on Fed policy during the interwar period casts doubt on these arguments. Despite strong evidence that monetary policy was contractionary in 1929 (which was not the focus of Friedman and Schwartz's argument), later episodes of monetary contraction seem likely not to have resulted from money-supply shocks. Moreover, Fed policy was constrained by adherence to the gold standard and by concerns over gold outflows, which limited its reactions to adverse shocks originating elsewhere in the economy (Eichengreen, 1992, pp. 117–119, 296–298). With respect to alleged changes in Fed targeting rules, Wheelock (1989, 1990) has shown that the reaction function of the Fed was essentially unchanged before and after the departure of Strong. This reaction function was based on targeting rules of thumb that had proved useful in the past but that misled the Fed during the Depression. It may be that the Fed's reaction function and its adherence to the gold standard were disastrous during the Depression; however, as Temin (1989) argues, it is hard to blame the Fed for not learning the lessons of the Great Depression before it happened.

The abandonment of the gold standard was another important component of Great Depression learning in many countries. Adherence to the gold standard was one of the central tenets of classical economic policy (Temin, 1989). The classical approach—whose influence over central banking policy can be traced at least as far as the Peel Act of 1844 in England (Helms, 1939; Wood, 1939)—emphasized the benefits of rules over discretion. A related classical tenet was that recessions were necessary means of forcing resources out of relatively unproductive, older firms, and into new technologies—recessions were the occasional growing pains of capitalism. While these tenets may have merit, slavish adherence to simplistic rules, or the belief that recessions are always good for the economy, can have drastic adverse consequences: this was an important lesson of the Great Depression. Countries that abandoned gold in 1931 to halt the free fall in their economies avoided the worst of the collapse of the Great Depression, while those that retained their ties to gold suffered worsening deflation, bankruptcy, and economic disaster (Eichengreen and Sachs, 1985, 1986; Temin, 1989; Bernanke and James, 1991; Eichengreen, 1992; Bernanke, 1994). Ironically, in some cases (notably Germany) earlier experience with hyperinflation had led government to establish new mechanisms in the 1920s to prevent discretionary relaxation of the gold standard (Eichengreen, 1992, pp. 125–152, 273–277). This illustrates the difficulty of applying lessons from history. The shocks of the future are not always the same as those of the past.

Eichengreen (1992) argues that the lesson of the interwar collapse under the gold standard was not that the gold standard per se is a bad system but, rather, that the successful maintenance of the gold standard requires coordination among countries to prevent destabilizing exchange market disequilibrium. According to this view, the classical (pre-World-War-I) gold standard operated well largely because of coordination among the major central banks of Europe—in Britain, France, and Germany—who acted together to reinforce each other's actions. This lent credibility to any one country's policies and discouraged private capital from taking positions opposite central banks (that is, engaging in speculative attacks on a currency). This may have been an important contributor to the ease of international capital flows and the small differences in money-market interest rates across countries (Calomiris and Hubbard, 1994b).

While the postwar Bretton Woods system claimed to offer the possibility of both adherence to rules and (contrary to the gold standard) the flexibility of controlling the overall supply of the unit of account (that is, the dollar), it did not provide effective checks and balances to coordinate monetary policy among the participants. The lack of discipline of U.S. monetary policy, in particular, turned out to be an important omission, which led to the demise of the system (Bordo and Eichengreen, 1993). In that sense, the lessons of the collapse of the gold standard were not learned: in retrospect, the classical gold standard of the pre-World-War-I era remains the most successful example of how flexibility in response to crises can be combined with long-run adherence to rules in an international monetary system (Bordo and Kydland, 1990; Eichengreen, 1992). In this respect, history has been regressive.

One example of progress in economic thinking and economic policy after the 1930s—which may have reflected the experience of the Depression—is the demise of the doctrine of high wages, which seems to have no adherents currently. According to this doctrine, resisting wage cuts during recessions is a desirable macroeconomic policy because it keeps workers' consumption high (O'Brien, 1989). This argument is logically flawed: while it may be beneficial for individual firms to maintain high wages in the face of a declining demand for labor (as in some new Keynesian arguments about efficiency wages), in the aggregate this will have a *negative* effect on output, not the positive effect claimed by supporters of the doctrine of high wages. Nevertheless, this doctrine was widely believed as late as the 1930s.

The Depression may have illustrated problems with some existing policy rules and prescriptions, but it also provided fertile political ground for flawed economic analyses and policies. Two prominent examples include the many changes in the regulation of banks and the taxation of corporations. In the latter case, the surtax on undistributed profits of 1936 is a prime example. Berle and Means (1932) suggested that lack of discipline over corporate management could lead to wasteful use of shareholders resources. Some proponents of the classical view of business cycles carried that argument further and argued that declining industries had contributed to the Depression by refusing to pay out their earnings to stockholders, which limited resources available to finance new, more productive enterprises. The proposed solution was the surtax on undistributed profits, which taxed firms up to a marginal surtax rate of 27 percent on retained earnings (defined as net earnings less dividends, calculated after the payment of normal corporate taxes). Corporations opposed the tax from the beginning. Ironically, the most bitter opponents of the tax were corporations in high-growth sectors, which tended to face high costs of raising external funds. For these firms, taxation of retained earnings imposed a large cost on their primary means for financing growth (Calomiris and Hubbard, 1994a). Compared to the presumed gains from enhancing corporate discipline, these costs were enormous. Fully 20 percent of taxpaying firms—typically small, growing firms in high-growth industries—chose to pay marginal surtax rates of at least 22 percent to be able to retain earnings. The opposition to the surtax effectively won repeal of the measure after only two years.

The attack on the banking system, based on what proponents claimed were lessons from the Depression, was much more far-reaching and long-lived. The Banking Act of 1933 fundamentally changed the structure of financial institutions, and its key provisions remained essentially unchanged for six decades.[16] Many of the changes in 1933 were policies that had long been contemplated and rejected by Congress (like federal deposit insurance). Others were variations on old themes. For example, the separation between commercial and investment banking, and Regulation Q, were the brainchildren of Senator Carter Glass. Glass echoed decades of previous arguments about bank instability when he argued that banks' involvement in the securities market and the pyramiding of reserves had promoted the banking collapse and the Depression of the 1930s. There were also accusations of fraud or conflict of interest in commercial bank marketing of the securities they underwrote. In addition to the separation of commercial and investment banking, Glass argued for Regulation Q (which prohibited the payment of interest on demand deposits) as a way to discourage banks from depositing funds in other banks. Ironically, recent empirical evidence points to stabilizing effects from combining commercial and investment banking prior to the Depression, and there is no evidence of conflict of interest in doing so (Kroszner and Rajan, 1994). White (1986) found that banks with securities affiliates had lower probabilities of failure and enjoyed greater diversification of earnings. Kroszner and Rajan (1994) found that the *ex post* performance of investments in securities underwritten by banks were at least as good as for other securities. Benston (1989) argues that there was never really any evidence unearthed by Congress that pointed to a destabilizing influence from underwriting or to a pattern of conflict of interest. Congress never bothered with the evidence. The coincidence of the banking collapse of 1931–1933 and the stock market collapse of 1929 provided all the evidence Congress needed to make its decision.

While Glass did not support the creation of federal deposit insurance, his Senate Banking Committee's Pecora hearings served to buttress the case for deposit insurance made by his opponents, Congressman Henry Steagall and Senator Huey Long. They used the Pecora hearings as evidence that a banking system based on large-scale banks was prone to crisis, arguing that commercial banks in financial centers were the source of excessive speculation that had led to the Depression. Unit bankers, in contrast, were—like the public—portrayed as the victims of speculative excess. Steagall, Long, and their allies succeeded in making banking reform a central issue in the forum of public debate. Despite the enormous losses and evidence of moral-hazard problems in state-level deposit insurance systems of the 1920s (White, 1983; Calomiris, 1990, 1992, 1993b), and despite the opposition of Glass, Roosevelt, the Federal Reserve, and the Treasury, advocates of deposit insurance, and capital assistance to banks through the Reconstruction Finance Corporation, pushed though legislation resuscitating unit banks and effectively restricting bank consolidation (Flood, 1991; Calomiris and White, 1994). Steagall's success was one of the most impressive examples of legislative maneuvering in the history of congressional politics.

To sum up, economic doctrine and regulation are important state variables for determining macroeconomic outcomes. The Great Depression illustrates how false beliefs and wrong-headed policies can emerge during times of crisis. Crisis-induced changes often are not clearly thought through and may reflect motives that have more to do with political opportunism than with social welfare. Ill-advised institutional changes can have large and persistent costs because of the difficulty of reversing them. The persistence of inefficient institutions can reflect the opera-tion of special interests that defend the institution (as in unit banking) or the protracted process of social learning about the costs of institutions (as in Fed targeting in the interwar period, and the rigid adherence to gold standard rules in many countries during 1929–1933).

Econometric Lessons

The methodological message of institutional nonneutrality for econometrics is similar to that of the Lucas critique, which was formulated as a criticism of macro-economic modeling that does not take proper account of changes in behavior that follow from changes in policy. Institutional changes are another dimension of behavioral response to policy but much more. They also alter decision making in manners similar to monetary and fiscal policy, and they define and constrain the realms in which decisions are made.

Institutions have been important in economic history, both as sources of distur-bance and as propagators of shocks that originate elsewhere, and it is likely that institutional effects have been particularly important in explaining low-frequency economic change. Institutional change has been associated with changes in the averages of important macroeconomic variables (like inflation or unemployment) over long periods of time, as well as the variance-covariance structure of macro-economic variables at cyclical and seasonal frequency. Some of the clearest examples are the changes in seasonal credit patterns associated with the creation of the Federal Reserve System and the changes in the inflation process that have accompanied different monetary regimes (the gold standard, the greenback suspension, and the current fiduciary standard). Less clearcut, more gradual institutional changes have been important as well—for example, Fed learning about monetary targeting during the Great Depression, and the movement away from a unit banking system in the 1980s and 1990s.

The institutional history of a nation is difficult to define as an aggregate variable, much less to control for when analyzing time series aggregates. Such a task is particularly difficult given the frequent changes in institutions that take place. But in disaggregated data, and in comparisons across countries, one can exploit cross-sectional variation to test for, and control for, the importance of institutional effects. In this respect, the methodological lessons of institutional non-neutrality are quite similar to those of long swings.

Conclusion

In what ways do the facts of the past confirm and challenge macroeconomists' existing models of the economy today? Available statistical evidence on the cyclical properties of prices, wages, and other variables, as well as historical evidence on the pace of technological change, are consistent with traditional explanations of business cycles that revolve around shocks to aggregate demand as the most important sources of economic fluctuation.

That does not mean that mainstream macroeconomic models based on sticky wages and prices, or statistical analyses of time-series aggregates suggested by those models, provide a complete explanation of American macroeconomic history. Perhaps surprisingly, the new frontiers of macroeconomics remain the old frontiers that have been beckoning for half a century. In particular, economists should devote more effort to understanding the history of low-frequency cycles and severe, long-lived depressions.

Despite all that we have learned about the history of the economy and about the sources of shocks during the 1930s in particular, macroeconomists still lack a fully satisfying explanation of the protracted duration of high unemployment and excess capacity during the Depression. More generally, standard macroeconomic analysis, which focuses on high-frequency cycles produced by transitory demand shocks, has neglected the phenomena surrounding Kuznets cycles—cycles of eighteen-year duration that are associated with waves of new settlement, construction activity, city building, and migration.

The lack of attention to low-frequency cycles is an important gap in our knowledge about the economy. Anyone attempting to provide a concise summary of American economic development will find himself essentially plotting out the Kuznets cycle. During the nineteenth and early twentieth centuries, especially, as America pushed back the physical frontier westward, building cycles were central to the process of territorial expansion and industrialization. Migration, construction, and other related investment depended on each other and were prone to sustained progress, as well as rapid reversal.

New work in the endogenous growth literature has led macroeconomists back to the threshold of studying long swings by emphasizing the long duration of disturbances to economic activity, and it is likely that models of economic growth that consider product and factor market externalities and nonconvexities in production may be useful for understanding long-duration cycles. Perhaps the main contribution an historical view of the economy can make to this research program is to suggest the importance of spatially and sectorally defined processes, as well as institutional change, for understanding long swings. For example, economies of agglomeration (city building) provide a natural way to think about endogenous growth that maps nicely into the history of the expansion of the American frontier and the construction cycle. Such economies should show themselves in particular places and particular sectors at particular points in time. Aggregate time-series analysis, therefore, should be supplemented with analysis of specific historical circumstances when judging the applicability of new models of economic growth to American history.

Other factors suggested by Schumpeter (1939)—who practically invented the idea that shocks to aggregate demand can lead to irreversible changes in long-run growth—are likely to be important, as well. Such irreversibilities may include migration of laborers, the creation or destruction of banks and the destruction of firms' net worth (which can be thought of as changes in financial technology, as argued by Bernanke, 1983), or demand-induced irreversible changes in production technology (such as the shake-out associated with the closing of factories). Severe contractions in demand may produce long-lasting structural unemployment of resources as well as technological change—as in the automobile industry in the 1930s (Bresnahan and Raff, 1991).

For all these reasons, we believe that economists interested in low-frequency change are likely to find it useful to disaggregate time series data to examine the behavior of particular locations, sectors, and types of workers over the business cycle. The answers to important questions like "What shocks prompt business cycles?" or "What sorts of environments produce greater wage rigidity?" are not likely to come from the latest econometric twist in analyzing the same old time-series data. We think it is more likely that answers will come from constructing new data designed to answer specific questions (with a panel dataset), from appeal to simple examples (for example, when considering the likely importance of exogenous technological change in producing high-frequency variation in output), and from historically informed comparisons across well-defined regimes (as we argued in our analysis of labor market rigidities).

The work of Eichengreen and Sachs (1985, 1986), Bernstein (1987), Margo

(1993), Wallis (1989), Bresnahan and Raff (1991), Bernanke and James (1991), Calomiris and Hubbard (1994), and Bernanke (1994) on the Great Depression exemplify such a research agenda. All of these papers have in common the use of cross-sectional variation to identify important macroeconomic shocks and propagators during the Depression. Margo and Wallis focus on the question of how employment supply shifted in response to New Deal programs. Bresnahan and Raff show how the Depression produced important endogenous technological responses to the collapse of aggregate demand. Bernstein argues that cross-sectional variation in the performance of different sectors is consistent with significant changes in consumer demand brought on by the Depression. Bernanke and James and Calomiris and Hubbard use cross-country and cross-firm differences to link debt deflation and capital market constaints to the collapse of investment.

Macroeconomic history also teaches us that economic institutions are an integral part of macroeconomic history and important contributors to path-dependent economic change. The Federal Reserve System is a particularly important example. Like other important changes in institutions, its origins can be traced to an adverse macroeconomic event. The Fed fell short of achieving the objectives it was designed to achieve because its powers and the structure of the banking system were constrained by other institutional arrangements—the gold standard and preexisting unit banking. Over time, and in response to other events, the structure or operating rules of the Fed have changed dramatically (for example, in 1935, 1951, and 1979), often with significant macroeconomic consequences.

Trying to model and measure the impact of institutional change, and test explanations of institutional change, are challenges that have mainly been ignored by macroeconomists and macroeconometricians. "Endogenizing" institutions and tracing the long-run macroeconomic implications of specific institutional changes pose formidable challenges to macroeconomic theory and measurement; but the alternative—pretending that institutional change is an irrelevant sideshow—has nothing to recommend it except the bliss of ignorance.

Donald McCloskey sometimes argues that Ph.D. students are the only audience of economists worth addressing. With that advice in mind, we conclude with a list of recommendations for students willing to brave the frontiers of macroeconomic history. (1) Interesting questions about macroeconomic history often flow from an understanding of the lives of real people. It does not hurt to become acquainted with facts other than statistics. (2) Research that addresses questions posed by models is not usually as interesting as research that addresses questions posed by historical data or events. (3) Searching history for controlled experiments to test models is a fine occupation, so long as the history surrounding the experiments is not viewed as incidental to the exercise. (4) Scholars should not be afraid to tell and defend stories on grounds of plausibility. Stories are no substitute for logic or facts, but without them, economics is a rudderless ship. Researchers should look to the past as a check against intellectual fads, as a source of controlled experiments, and as a fountain of wisdom about how economies develop in real time.

Acknowledgments

The authors thank Barry Eichengreen, Kevin Hoover, Robert Margo, Allan Meltzer, Kenneth Snowden, Peter Temin, and Jeffrey Williamson for helpful discussions.

Notes

1. Despite Friedman and Schwartz's comprehensive coverage of financial institutional history, ironically, the message of their treatise is that institutions matter only through their effect on the money stock. Other work, discussed below, is at odds with that view.

2. The distinction between historical macroeconomics and macroeconomic history is also emphasized in a precursor to this article, Eichengreen (1987).

3. See David (1991) for a review of the theoretical literature on path dependence and its applicability to economic history.

4. United States Bureau of the Census (1975): nonagricultural sectoral employment series D127–141, total employment series D5, farm employment series K174.

5. Greenwood, Hercowitz, and Huffman (1988) show that one *can* construct utility and production functions that allow consumption to move procyclically in response to a change in the expected productivity of investment, but this appears to be a knife-edge result.

6. Another explanation for procyclical productivity is endogenous technological improvement in response to aggregate-demand shocks. We argue that endogenous technological improvement through increasing returns, learning, and shake-out of low-productivity firms were important historically over long periods of time and were relevant for understanding Kuznets cycles. But given the long lags of technological change, endogenous technological improvement was likely not very important for year-to-year fluctuations.

7. Money supply (currency held by the public plus bank deposits) from Friedman and Schwartz (1963, table A-1). Wholesale prices from Warren and Pearson (1932, table 1). Consumer prices from Rees (1961, table 22) and U.S. Bureau of Labor Statistics (1992).

8. Interestingly, similar evidence for the nineteenth century (reported in Bowley, 1904) was cited by Keynes (1931, p. 165) and formed the basis for his view that nominal wage rigidity was greater than nominal price rigidity: "It is the decade from 1886 to 1896 with which I am concerned, and chiefly with the years of declining prices from 1890 to 1896. Between 1890 and 1896 Sauerbeck's Wholesale Index fell about 18 per cent, and the *Economist*'s about 14 percent. . . . But there was no evidence of Income Deflation. On the contrary, rates of money wages were moving slightly upwards, and other money-incomes were also on the up-grade, apart from a slight sagging in 1892–93 owing to the very severe unemployment in those years" (pp. 164–165).

9. Intersectoral substitution is not the only explanation for higher historical labor turnover in manufacturing. Margo (1990a) argues that some of the relatively short duration of historical employment can be attributed to changes in the composition of the workforce and changes in unemployment relief policies in the 1930s.

10. In one fascinating account, Harley (1982) argues that the collapse of railroad cartels helped to set in motion the railroad and construction boom of the 1880s. According to this argument, so long

as the railroads were able to cooperate, it was profitable for development to follow a regular, deliberate process. Once cooperation broke down, the only way to seize market share was to build ahead of demand.

11. Even more fundamentally, scholars disagree over whether long swings reflected an endogenous cyclical process—in which cycles of similar duration repeated naturally—or a shock-and-propagation process, in which the timing and duration of the cycles reflected unique and unpredictable disturbances. Easterlin's (1966) emphasis on immigration led him to argue that "echo effects" may have explained the average duration of the cycle—a wave of immigrants would produce a new generation of frontier builders roughly at eighteen-year intervals.

12. That is not to say that investment banking was unimportant in the United States as a means of financing industry. But despite the efforts and successes of investment banks in reducing some firms' costs of external finance (DeLong, 1991), such financing was confined to the largest, most mature firms in the economy, and new issues typically were restricted to senior claims against those firms (bonds and preferred stock) because of the high cost of placing common stock (Calomiris and Raff, 1994).

13. To some extent, especially in New York, deposits on foreign banks, wired via the trans-Atlantic cable, may have been a cheaper means to introduce reserves to the U.S. banking system. But as Calomiris and Hubbard (1994b) point out, there were limitations to the substitutability between foreign bank balances and gold, particularly given the risk of runs on banks.

14. This was not true of the waves of banking failures and bank runs during the Great Depression (Wicker, 1993). These began with regional problems in the South and Midwest, associated with severe deflation and exposure by those regions' banks to loan losses. Only later did problems spread to financial centers in the East and abroad. Great Depression banking problems also occurred near a business-cycle trough, while national banking era panics coincided with cyclical peaks.

15. It is important to note that many, possibly most, bank failures during the 1930s did not coincide with runs or panics. Many banks failed as the result of isolated insolvencies in the wake of continuing deterioration in their *particular* assets. Panics or runs did occur, nationally and regionally, during the 1930s, but only as occasional punctuation points in the general trend of asset value decline and failure. Thus it would be premature, and probably incorrect, to attribute most of the bank failures of the 1930s to panic episodes. For recent research trying to measure the importance of general runs on banks for producing bank failure, see Wicker (1993) and Calomiris and Mason (1994).

16. In the face of new competitive pressures on American banks, and the failures of many banks and thrifts in the 1980s, branching limitations and limits on the powers of commercial banks have been relaxed recently. In many ways, this process mirrors the branching and merger wave in banking during the 1920s. This illustrates how regulatory reform typically requires extreme circumstances.

References

Abramovitz, Moses. (1964). *Evidence of Long Swings in Aggregate Construction since the Civil War*. New York: Columbia University Press.

Allen, Steven G. (1992). "Changes in the Cyclical Sensitivity of Wages in the United States, 1891–1987." *American Economic Review* 82, March, 122–140.

Alogoskoufis, George S., and Smith, Ron. (1991). "The Phillips Curve, the Persistence of Inflation, and the Lucas Critique: Evidence from Exchange-Rate Regimes." *American Economic Review* 81, December, 1254–1275.

Atack, Jeremy, and Fred Bateman. (1994). "Did the United States Industrialize Too Slowly?" Working Paper, Vanderbilt University, July.

Atack, Jeremy, Fred Bateman, and Thomas Weiss. (1980). "The Regional Diffusion and Adoption of the Steam Engine in American Manufacturing." *Journal of Economic History* 40, June, 281–308.

Azariadis, Costas. (1975). "Implicit Contracts and Underemployment Equilibria." *Journal of Political Economy* 83, December, 1183–1202.

Azariadis, Costas. (1983). "Implicit Contracts and Fixed Price Equilibria." *Quarterly Journal of Economics* 98, Supplement, 1–22.

Backus, David K. and Patrick J. Kehoe. (1992). "International Evidence on the Historical Properties of Business Cycles." *American Economic Review* 82, September, 864–888.

Balke, Nathan S. and Robert J. Gordon. (1989). "The Estimation of Prewar Gross National Product: Methodology and New Evidence." *Journal of Political Economy* 97, February, 38–92.

Barro, Robert J. (1979). "Second Thoughts on Keynesian Economics." *American Economic Review* 69, May, 54–59.

Barro, Robert J. (1981). "Output Effects of Government Purchases." *Journal of Political Economy* 89, December, 1086–1121.

Barro, Robert J. (1987). "Government Spending, Interest Rates, Prices, and Budget Deficits in the United Kingdom, 1701–1918." *Journal of Monetary Economics* 20, September, 221–248.

Barro, R.J., and R.G. King. (1984). "Time-Separable Preferences and Intertemporal Substitution Models of the Business Cycle." *Quarterly Journal of Economics* 99, November, 817–839.

Barsky, Robert B., N. Gregory Mankiw, Jeffrey A. Miron, and David N. Weill. (1988). "The Worldwide Change in the Behavior of Interest Rates and Prices in 1914." *European Economic Review* 32, 1123–1154.

Benhabib, Jess, Richard Rogerson, and Randall Wright. (1991). "Homework in Macroeconomics: Household Production and Aggregate Fluctuations." *Journal of Political Economy* 99, 1166–1187.

Benston, George J. (1989). *The Separation of Commercial and Investment Banking: The Glass-Steagall Act Revisited and Reconsidered*. Norwell, MA: Kluwer.

Berle, Adolph A., and Gardiner Means. (1932). *The Modern Corporation and Private Property*. New York: Columbia University Press.

Bernanke, Ben S. (1983). "Nonmonetary Effects of the Financial Crisis in the Propagation of the Great Depression." *American Economic Review* 73, June, 257–276.

Bernanke, Ben S. (1994). "The Macroeconomics of the Great Depression: A Comparative Approach." NBER Working Paper No. 4814, August.

Bernanke, Ben S., and Harold James. (1991). "The Gold Standard, Deflation, and Financial Crisis in the Great Depression." In R. Glenn Hubbard (ed.), *Financial Markets and Financial Crises* (pp. 33–68). Chicago: University of Chicago Press.

Bernanke, Ben S., and Martin L. Parkinson. (1991). "Procyclical Labor Productivity and Competing Theories of the Business Cycle: Some Evidence from Interwar U.S. Manufacturing Industries." *Journal of Political Economy* 99, 439–459.

Bernanke, Ben S. and James L. Powell. (1986). "The Cyclical Behavior of Industrial Labor Markets: A Comparison of the Prewar and Postwar Eras." In Robert J. Gordon (ed.), *The

American Business Cycles: Continuity and Change (pp. 583–638). Chicago: University of Chicago Press.

Bernstein, Michael A. (1987). *The Great Depression: Delayed Recovery and Economic Change in America 1929–1939.* Cambridge: Cambridge University Press.

Bils, Mark. (1989). "Pricing in a Customer Market." *Quarterly Journal of Economics* 104, November, 699–718.

Blanchard, Olivier, and Nobuhiro Kiyotaki. (1987). "Monopolistic Competition and the Effects of Aggregate Demand." *American Economic Review* 77, September, 647–666.

Blanchard, Olivier J., and Danny Quah. (1988). "The Dynamic Effects of Aggregate Demand and Supply Disturbances." Working Paper, Massachusetts Institute of Technology.

Blanchard, Olivier J., and Lawrence H. Summers. (1988). "Why Is Unemployment So High in Europe? Beyond the Natural Rate Hypothesis." *American Economic Association Papers and Proceedings*, May, 182–187.

Bodenhorn, Howard. (1992). "Capital Mobility and Financial Integration in Antebellum America." *Journal of Economic History* 52, September, 585–610.

Bordo, Michael D., and Barry Eichengreen (eds.). (1993). *A Retrospective on the Bretton Woods System: Lessons for International Monetary Reforms.* Chicago: University of Chicago Press.

Bordo, Michael D., and Finn Kydland. (1990). "The Gold Standard as a Rule." Working Paper, Rutgers University.

Bowley, A.L. (1904). "Tests of National Progress." *Economic Journal* 14, September, 457–465.

Bresnahan, Timothy F., and Daniel M.G. Raff. (1991). "Intra-industry Heterogeneity and the Great Depression: The American Motor Vehicles Industry, 1929–1935." *Journal of Economic History* 51, June, 317–331.

Bullard, James B. (1994). "How Reliable Are Inflation Reports?" *Monetary Trends*, Federal Reserve Bank of St. Louis, February.

Burns, Arthur F. (1951). "Mitchell on What Happens During Business Cycles." In *Conference on Business Cycles* (pp. 3–33). New York: National Bureau of Economic Research.

Cagan, Phillip. (1975). "Changes in the Recession Behavior of Wholesale Prices in the 1920s and Post–World War II." *Explorations in Economic Research* 2, Winter, 54–104.

Calomiris, Charles W. (1988a). "Institutional Failure, Monetary Scarcity, and the Depreciation of the Continental." *Journal of Economic History* 48, March, 47–68.

Calomiris, Charles W. (1988b). "Price and Exchange Rate Determination During the Greenback Suspension." *Oxford Economic Papers* 40, December, 719–750.

Calomiris, Charles W. (1990). "Is Deposit Insurance Necessary? A Historical Perspective." *Journal of Economic History* 50, June, 283–295.

Calomiris, Charles W. (1992). "Do 'Vulnerable' Economies Need Deposit Insurance: Lessons from the U.S. Agriculture in the 1920s." In Philip L. Brock (ed.), *If Texas Were Chile: A Primer on Banking Reform* (pp. 237–315, 450–458). San Francisco: Institute for Contemporary Studies.

Calomiris, Charles W. (1993a). "Greenback Resumption and Silver Risk: The Economics and Politics of Monetary Regimes Change in the United States, 1862–1900." In M.D.

Bordo and Forrest Capie (eds.), *Monetary Regimes in Transition* (pp. 86–132). Cambridge: Cambridge University Press.

Calomiris, Charles W. (1993b). "Regulation, Industrial Structure, and Instability in U.S. Banking: An Historical Perspective." In Michael Klausner and Lawrence J. White (eds.), *Structural Change in Banking* (pp. 19–116). Homewood, IL: Business-One Irwin.

Calomiris, Charles W. (1993c). "Financial Factors in the Great Depression." *Journal of Economic Perspectives* 7, Spring, 61–85.

Calomiris, Charles W. (1994). "The Costs of Rejecting Universal Banking: American Finance in the German Mirror, 1870–1914." In Naomi Lamoreaux and Daniel Raff (eds.), *Coordination and Information: Historical Perspectives on the Organization of Enterprise*. Chicago: University of Chicago Press.

Calomiris, Charles W., and Gary Gorton. (1991). "The Origins of Banking Panics: Models, Facts, and Bank Regulation." In R. Glenn Hubbard (ed.), *Financial Markets and Financial Crises* (pp. 109–173). Chicago: University of Chicago Press.

Calomiris, Charles W., and Christopher Hanes. (1994). "Consistent Output Series for the Antebellum and Postbellum Periods: Issues and Preliminary Results." *Journal of Economic History* 54, June, 409–422.

Calomiris, Charles W., and R. Glenn Hubbard. (1989). "Price Flexibility, Credit Availability, and Economic Fluctuations: Evidence from the United States, 1894–1909." *Quarterly Journal of Economics* 104, February, 429–452.

Calomiris, Charles W., and R. Glenn Hubbard. (1994a). "Internal Finance and Investment: Evidence from the Undistributed Profits Tax of 1936–1937." *Journal of Business*, forthcoming.

Calomiris, Charles W., and R. Glenn Hubbard. (1994b). "International Adjustment under the Classical Gold Standard: Evidence from the U.S. and Britain, 1879–1914." In Bayoumi and Eichengreen (eds.), *Modern Perspectives on the Gold Standard*, Cambridge: Cambridge University Press, forthcoming.

Calomiris, Charles W., and Joseph R. Mason. (1994). "Contagion and Bank Failures during the Depression: The June 1932 Chicago Banking Panic." NBER/No. 4934, November. Working Paper.

Calomiris, Charles W., and Raff, Daniel M.G. (1994). "The Evolution of Market Structure, Information, and Spreads in American Investment Banking." In M.D. Bordo and R. Sylla (eds.), *Anglo-American Finance*. Homewood, IL: Irwin.

Calomiris, Charles W., and Larry Schweikart. (1991). "The Panic of 1857: Origins, Transmission, and Containment." *Journal of Economic History* 51, December, 807–834.

Calomiris, Charles W., and Eugene N. White. (1994). "The Origins of Federal Deposit Insurance." In Claudia Goldin and Gary D. Libecap (eds.), *The Regulated Economy: A Historical Approach to Political Economy* (pp. 145–188). Chicago: University of Chicago Press.

Calvo, Guillermo A. and Edmund S. Phelps. (1977). "Employment-Contingent Wage Contracts." *Journal of Monetary Economics*, Supplement, 160–168.

Carlton, Dennis W. (1986). "The Rigidity of Prices." *American Economic Review* 76, September, 637–658.

Carosso, Vincent, P. (1970). *Investment Banking in American: A History*. Cambridge, MA: Harvard University Press.

Carter, Susan B. and Richard Sutch. (1990). "The Labour Market in the 1890's: Evidence from Connecticut Manufacturing." In Erik Aerts and Barry Eichengreen (eds.), *Unemployment and Underemployment in Historical Perspective*. Studies in Social and Economic History, Vol. 12. City: Leuven University Press.

Chandler, Alfred D. (1972). "Anthracite Coal and the Beginnings of the Industrial Revolution in the United States." *Business History Review* 46, Summer, 141–181.

Chandler, Alfred D. (1977). *The Visible Hand: The Managerial Revolution in American Business*. Cambridge, MA: Harvard University Press.

Christiano, Lawrence J., and Martin Eichenbaum. (1992). "Current Real-Business-Cycle Theories and Aggregate Labor-Market Fluctuations." *American Economic Review* 82, June, 430–450.

Clark, Truman A. (1986). "Interest Rate Seasonals and the Federal Reserve." *Journal of Political Economy* 94, February, 76–125.

Cooley, Thomas F., and Lee E. Ohanian. (1991). "The Cyclical Behavior of Prices." *Journal of Monetary Economics* 28, August, 25–60.

Crucini, Mario J. (1994). "Sources of Variation in Real Tariff Rates: The United States, 1900–1940." *American Economic Review* 84, June, 732–744.

David, Paul A. (1975). *Technical Choice, Innovation, and Economic Growth: Essays on American and British Experience in the Nineteenth Century*. New York: Cambridge University Press.

David, Paul A. (1990). "The Dynamo and the Computer: An Historical Perspective on the Modern Productivity Paradox." *American Economic Review* 80, May, 355–361.

David, Paul A. (1991). "Economic History Association Presidential Address." Working Paper, Stanford University.

David, Paul A., and Joshua L. Rosenbloom. (1990). "Marshallian Factor Market Externalities and the Dynamics of Industrial Location." *Journal of Urban Economics* 28, 349–370.

Davis, Lance E. (1957). "Sources of Industrial Finance: The American Textile Industry, A Case Study." *Explorations in Entrepreneurial History* 9, 190–203.

Davis, Lance E. (1960). "The New England Textile Mills and the Capital Markets: A Study of Industrial Borrowing." *Journal of Economic History* 20, 1–30.

Davis, Lance, E. (1963). "Capital Immobilities and Finance Capitalism: A Study of Economic Evolution in the United States." *Explorations in Entrepreneurial History* 15, Fall, 88–105.

Davis, Lance E. (1965). "The Investment Market, 1870–1914: The Evolution of a National Market." *Journal of Economic History* 25, September, 355–393.

Dawley, Allen. (1976). *Class and Community: The Industrial Revolution in Lynn Massachusetts*. Cambridge, MA: Harvard University Press.

DeLong, J. Bradford. (1991). "Did J.P. Morgan's Men Add Value? An Economist's Perspective on Financial Capitalism." In Peter Temin (ed.), *Inside the Business Enterprise: Historical Perspectives on the Use of Information* (pp. 205–236). Chicago: University of Chicago Press.

DeLong, J. Bradford, and Lawrence Summers. (1986) "The Changing Cyclical Variability of Economic Activity in the United States." In Robert J. Gordon (ed.), *The American Business Cycle: Continuity and Change* (pp. 679–732). Chicago: University of Chicago Press.

Devine, Warren D. (1983). "From Shafts to Wires: Historical Perspectives on Electrification." *Journal of Economic History* 43, June, 347–372.

Dickens, William T., and Lawrence F. Katz. (1987). "Inter-Industry Wage Differences and Industry Characteristics." In Kevin Lang and Jonathan S. Leonard (eds.), *Unemployment and the Structure of Labor Markets* (pp. 48–49). New York: Basil Blackwell.

Diebold, Francis X., and Glenn D. Rudebusch. (1992). "Have Postwar Economic Fluctuations Been Stabilized?" *American Economic Review* 82, September, 993–1005.

Dunlop, John. (1938). "The Movement of Real and Money Wage Rates." *Economic Journal* 48, September, 413–434.

Easterlin, Richard. (1966). "Economic-Demographic Interactions and Long Swings in Economic Growth." *American Economic Review* 56, December, 1063–1104.

Eichengreen, Barry. (1987). "Macroeconomics and History." In Alexander Field (ed.), *The Future of Economic History* (pp. 43–90). Boston: Kluwer Nijhoff.

Eichengreen, Barry. (1992). *Golden Fetters: The Gold Standard and the Great Depression, 1919–1939.* Oxford: Oxford University Press.

Eichengreen, Barry, and Jeffrey Sachs. (1985). "Exchange Rates and Economic Recovery in the 1930s." *Journal of Economic History* 45, December, 925–946.

Eichengreen, Barry, and Jeffrey Sachs. (1986). "Competitive Devaluation in the Great Depression: A Theoretical Reassessment." *Economic Letters* 22, 67–71.

Evanoff, Douglas D. (1988). "Branch Banking and Service Accessibility." *Journal of Money, Credit and Banking* 20, May, 191–202.

Evans, Paul. (1985). "Do Large Deficits Produce High Interest Rates." *American Economic Review* 75, March, 68–87.

Fels, Rendigs. (1959). *American Business Cycles, 1865–1897.* Chapel Hill: University of North Carolina Press.

Field, Alexander J. (1978). "Sectoral Shift in Antebellum Massachusetts: A Reconsideration." *Explorations in Economic History* 15, April, 146–171.

Field, Alexander J. (1981). "The Problem with Neoclassical Institutional Economics: A Critique with Special Reference to the North/Thomas Model of Pre-1500 Europe." *Explorations in Economic History* 18, April, 174–198.

Field, Alexander J. (1983). "Land Abundance, Interest/Profit Rates and Nineteenth-Century American and British Technology." *Journal of Economic History* 42, June, 405–431.

Field, Alexander J. (1987). "Modern Business Enterprise as a Capital-Saving Innovation." *Journal of Economic History* 46, June, 473–485.

Fishlow, Albert. (1965). *American Railroads and the Transformation of the Ante-Bellum Economy.* Cambridge, MA: Harvard University Press.

Flood, Mark D. (1991). "The Great Deposit Insurance Debate." *Federal Reserve Bank of St. Louis Review* 74, July–August, 51–77.

Fogel, Robert William. (1964). *Railroads and American Economic Growth: Essays in Econometric History.* Baltimore: Johns Hopkins Press.

Frickey, Edwin. (1942). *Economic Fluctuations in the United States.* Cambridge, MA: Harvard University Press.

Frickey, Edwin. (1947). *Production in the United States 1860–1914.* Cambridge, MA: Harvard University Press.

Friedman, Milton. (1952). "Price, Income and Monetary Changes in Three Wartime Periods." *American Economic Review*, May, – .

Friedman, Milton, and Anna Jacobson Schwartz. (1963). *A Monetary History of the United States 1867–1960*. Princeton, NJ: Princeton University Press.

Gallman, Robert. (1960). "Commodity Output, 1839–1899." In *Trends in the American Economy in the Nineteenth Century*, NBER Studies in Income and Wealth (Vol. 24) (pp. 13–71). New York: Columbia University Press.

Gallman, Robert. (1966). "Gross National Product in the United States, 1834–1909." In *Output, Employment and Productivity in the United States After 1800*, NBER Studies in Income and Wealth (Vol. 30) (pp. 3–90). New York: Columbia University Press.

Goldin, Claudia, and Stanley Engerman. (1993). "Seasonality in Nineteenth Century American Labor Markets." In Donald Schaefer and Thomas Weiss (eds.), *Economic Development in Historical Perspective*. Stanford, CA: Stanford University Press.

Goldin, Claudia, and Robert Margo. (1992). "Wages, Prices, and Labor Markets Before the Civil War." In Claudia Goldin and Hugh Rockoff (eds.), *Strategic Factors in Nineteenth Century American Economic Development*. Chicago: University of Chicago Press.

Goldin, Claudia, and Kenneth Sokoloff. (1984). "The Relative Productivity Hypothesis of Industrialization: The American Case, 1820 to 1850." *Quarterly Journal of Economics* 69, August, 461–487.

Gordon, Robert J. (1981). "Output Fluctuations and Gradual Price Adjustment." *Journal of Economic Literature* 19, June, 493–530.

Gordon, Robert J. (1986). "Introduction: Continuity and Change in Theory, Behavior, and Methodology." In Robert J. Gordon (ed.), *The American Business Cycle: Continuity and Change* (pp. 1–33). Chicago: University of Chicago Press.

Gordon, Robert J. (1990). "What Is New-Keynesian Economics?" *Journal of Economic Literature* 28, September, 1115–1171.

Greenwood, Jeremy Z. Hercowitz, and G.W. Huffman. (1988). "Investment, Capacity Utilization, and the Real Business Cycle." *American Economic Review* 78, June, 402–417.

Grossman, Richard S. (1993). "The Macroeconomic Consequences of Bank Failures Under the National Banking System." *Explorations in Economic History* 30, July, 294–320.

Hanes, Christopher. (1993). "The Development of Nominal Wage Rigidity in the Late Nineteenth Century." *American Economic Review* 83, September, 732–756.

Hanes, Christopher. (1994). "Changes in the Cyclical Behavior of Nominal Prices, 1869–1990." Working Paper, University of Pennsylvania.

Hansen, Gary D., and Edward C. Prescott. (1993). "Did Technology Shocks Cause the 1990–1991 Recession?" *American Economic Review* May, 280–286.

Harley, C. Knick. (1982). "Oligopoly Strategy and the Timing of American Railroad Construction." *Journal of Economic History* 42, December, 797–824.

Hatton, Timothy J., and Jeffrey G. Williamson. (1991). "Wage Gaps Between Farm and City: Michigan in the 1890s." *Explorations in Economic History* 28, October, 381–408.

Hekman, John S. (1980). "The Product Cycle and New England Textiles." *Quarterly Journal of Economics* 95, June, 697–717.

Helms, Lloyd A. (1939). *The Contributions of Lord Overstone to the Theory of Currency and Banking*. Urbana: University of Illinois Press.

Hicks, John R. (1937). "Mr. Keynes and the 'Classics': A Suggested Interpretation." *Econometrica* 5, 147–159.

Hughes, Jonathan. (1990). *American Economic History* (3rd ed.). Glenview, IL: Scott, Foresman.

Hughes, Jonathan. (1991). *The Governmental Habit Redux: Economic Controls from Colonial Times to the Present.* Princeton, NJ: Princeton University Press.

Hultgren, Thor. (1960). "Changes in Labor Cost During Cycles in Production and Business." National Bureau of Economic Research Occasional Paper 74.

Jacoby, Sanford. (1985). *Employing Bureaucracy: Managers, Unions, and the Transformation of Work in American Industry, 1900–1945.* New York: Columbia University Press.

Jacoby, Sanford and Sunil Sharma. (1992). "Employment Duration and Industrial Labor Mobility in the United States, 1880–1980." *Journal of Economic History* 52, March, 161–179.

James, John A. (1978). *Money and Capital Markets in Postbellum America.* Princeton, NJ: Princeton University Press.

James, John A. (1989). "The Stability of the Nineteenth-Century Phillips Curve Relationship." *Explorations in Economic History* 26, April, 117–134.

James, John A. (1993). "Changes in Economic Instability in Nineteenth-Century America." *American Economic Review* 83, September, 710–731.

Katz, Lawrence F., and Lawrence H. Summers. (1989). "Industry Rents: Evidence and Implications." *Brookings Papers: Microeconomics*, 209–290.

Keynes, John Maynard. (1931/1953). *A Treatise on Money.* Vol. 2, *The Applied Theory of Money.* London: Macmillan.

Keynes, John Maynard. (1936/1964). *The General Theory of Employment, Interest, and Money.* New York: Harcourt Brace Jovanovich.

Keynes, John Maynard. (1939). "Relative Movements of Real Wages and Output." *Economic Journal* 49, March, 35–51.

Keyssar, Alexander. (1986). *Out of Work: The First Century of Unemployment in Massachusetts.* New York: Cambridge University Press.

Khan, B. Zorina, and Kenneth L. Sokoloff. (1993). " 'Schemes of Practical Utility': Entrepreneurship and Innovation Among 'Great Inventors' in the United States, 1790–1865." *Journal of Economic History* 53, June, 289–307.

Kindleberger, Charles P. (1973). *The World in Depression, 1929–1939.* Barkeley: University of California Press.

Kroszner, Randall S., and Raghuram Rajan. (1994). "Is the Glass-Steagall Act Justified? A Study of the U.S. Experience with Universal Banking Before 1933." *American Economic Review* 84, September, 810–832.

Krueger, Alan B., and Lawrence H. Summers. (1987). "Reflections on the Inter-industry Wage Structure." In Kevin Lang and Jonathan S. Leonard (eds.), *Unemployment and the Structure of Labor Markets* (pp. 17–47). New York: Basil Blackwell.

Krugman, Paul. (1991). "Increasing Returns and Economic Geography." *Journal of Political Economy* 99, June, 483–499.

Kuznets, Simon. (1951). "Comment on Joseph Schumpeter." In *Conference on Business Cycles* (pp. 155–162). New York: National Bureau of Economic Research.

Kydland, Finn, and Edward Prescott. (1990). "Business Cycles: Real Facts and a Monetary Myth." *Federal Reserve Bank of Minneapolis Quarterly Review* 14, Spring, 3–18.

Lamoreaux, Naomi R. (1985). *The Great Merger Movement in American Business, 1895–1904.* Cambridge: Cambridge University Press.

Lamoreaux, Naomi R. (1994). *Insider Lending: Banks, Personal Connections, and Economic Development in Industrial New England.* Cambridge: Cambridge University Press.

Lazear, Edward. (1981). "Agency, Earnings Profiles, Productivity and Hours Restrictions." *American Economic Review* 71, June, 606–620.

Lebergott, Stanley. (1964). *Manpower in Economic Growth: The American Record Since 1800.* New York: McGraw-Hill.

Lerdau, E. (1957). "On the Measurement of Tariffs: The U.S. Over Forty Years." *Economia Internazionale* 10, May, 232–244.

Lindbeck, Assar, and Dennis J. Snower. (1988). *The Insider-Outsider Theory of Employment and Unemployment.* Cambridge, MA: MIT Press.

Lipsey, Robert E. (1963). *Price and Quantity Trends in the Foreign Trade of the United States.* Princeton, NJ: Princeton University Press.

Long, Clarence D. (1960). *Wages and Earnings in the United States, 1860–1890.* Princeton, NJ: Princeton University Press.

Lucas, Robert E. (1972). "Expectations and the Neutrality of Money." *Journal of Economic Theory* 4, April, 103–124.

Lucas, Robert E. (1976). "Econometric Policy Evaluation: A Critique." *Carnegie-Rochester Series on Public Policy* 1.

Lucas, Robert E., and Michael Woodford. (1993). "Real Effects of Monetary Shocks in an Economy with Sequential Purchases." NBER Working Paper No. 4250, January.

Mankiw, N. Gregory. (1985). "Small Menu Costs and Large Business Cycles: A Macroeconomic Model of Monopoly." *Quarterly Journal of Economics* 100, May, 529–539.

Mankiw, N. Gregory. (1989). "Real Business Cycles: A New Keynesian Perspective." *Journal of Economic Perspectives* 3, Summer, 79–90.

Mankiw, N. Gregory. (1990). "A Quick Refresher Course in Macroeconomics." *Journal of Economic Literature* 28, December, 1645–1660.

Mansfield, Edwin. (1961). "Technical Change and the Rate of Imitation." *Econometrica* 29, October, 741–766.

Mansfield, Edwin. (1983). "Long Waves and Technological Innovation." *American Economic Association Papers and Proceedings* 73, May, 141–145.

Manuelli, Rodolfo E. (1986). "Modern Business Cycle Analysis: A Guide to the Prescott-Summers Debate." *Federal Reserve Bank of Minneapolis Quarterly Review* 10, Fall, 3–8.

Margo, Robert A. (1990a). "Unemployment in 1910: Some Preliminary Findings." In Erik Aerts and Barry Eichengreen (eds.), *Unemployment and Underemployment in Historical Perspective,* Studies in Social and Economic History Vol. 12. City: Leuven University Press.

Margo, Robert A. (1990b). "The Incidence and Duration of Unemployment: Some Long-Term Comparisons." *Economics Letters* 32, January, 217–220.

Margo, Robert A. (1991). "The Microeconomics of Depression Unemployment." *Journal of Economic History* 51, June, 333–341.

Margo, Robert A. (1993). "Employment and Unemployment in the 1930s." *Journal of Economic Perspectives* 7, Spring, 41–60.

Margo, Robert A. (1994). "Labor Market Integration Before the Civil War: New Evidence." Working Paper, Vanderbilt University, June.

Mathewson, Stanley B. (1931). *Restriction of Output Among Unorganized Workers.* New York: Viking.

Means, Gardiner C. (1935). "Industrial Prices and Their Relative Inflexibility." U.S. Senate Document 13, 74th Cong., 1st Sess., Washington, DC.

Meltzer, Allan. (1994). "Information, Sticky Prices, and Macroeconomic Foundations." Working Paper, Carnegie-Mellon University, October.

Mendoza, Enrique. (1991). "Real Business Cycles in a Small Open Economy." *American Economic Review* 81, September, 797–818.

Metcalfe, Stan. (1990). "On Diffusion, Investment and the Process of Technological Change." In Enrico Deiaco, Erik Hornell, and Graham Vickery (eds.), *Technology and Investment: Crucial Issues for the 1990s* (pp. 17–38). London: Pinter.

Miron, Jeffrey A. (1986). "Financial Panics, the Seasonality of the Nominal Interest Rate, and the Founding of the Fed." *American Economic Review* 76, March, 125–140.

Miron, Jeffrey A., and Christina D. Romer. (1990). "A New Monthly Index of Industrial Production, 1884–1940." *Journal of Economic History* 50, June, 321–332.

Mitchell, Daniel J.B. (1985). "Wage Flexibility: Then and Now." *Industrial Relations* 24, Spring, 266–279.

Mitchell, Wesley C. (1951). *What Happens During Business Cycles: A Progress Report.* New York: National Bureau of Economic Research.

Moore, Geoffrey H., and Victor Zarnowitz. (1986). "The Development and Role of the National Bureau of Economic Research's Business Cycle Chronologies." In Robert J. Gordon (ed.), *The American Business Cycle: Continuity and Change* (pp. 735–779). Chicago: University of Chicago Press.

Murphy, Kevin M., Andrei Shleifer, and Robert W. Vishny. (1989). "Industrialization and the Big Push." *Journal of Political Economy* 97, October, 1003–1026.

Neal, Larry. (1994). "Why Crowding Out Did Not Occur and Crowding In Did: A New Look at the History of the British National Debt." Working Paper, University of Illinois.

North, Douglass C. (1961). *The Economic Growth of the United States, 1790–1860.* Englewood Cliffs, NJ: Prentice-Hall.

North, Douglass C. (1990). *Institutions, Institutional Change and Economic Performance.* Cambridge: Cambridge University Press, 1990.

O'Brien, Anthony Patrick. (1988). "Factory Size, Economies of Scale, and the Great Merger Wave of 1898–1902." *Journal of Economic History* 48, September, 639–649.

O'Brien, Anthony Patrick. (1989). "A Behavioral Explanation for Nominal Wage Rigidity During the Great Depression." *Quarterly Journal of Economics* 104, November, 719–735.

Obstfeld, Maurice. (1993). "The Adjustment Mechanism." In Michael D. Bordo and Barry Eichengreen (eds.), *A Retrospective on the Bretton Woods System: Lessons for International Monetary Reforms* (pp. 201–256). Chicago: University of Chicago Press.

Officer, Lawrence H. (1986). "The efficiency of the Dollar-Sterling Gold Standard." *Journal of Policial Economy* 94, October, 1038–1073.

Olmstead, Alan, and Paul, Rhode. (1985). "Rationing Without Government: The West Coast Gas Famine of 1920." *American Economic Review* 75, December, 1044–1055.

Ozanne, Robert. (1968). *Wages in Practice and Theory: McCormick and International Harvester, 1860–1960.* Madison, WI: University of Wisconsin Press.

Plosser, Charles I. (1989). "Understanding Real Business Cycles." *Journal of Economic Perspectives* 3, Summer, 51–77.

Raff, Daniel M.G. (1988). "Wage Determination Theory and the Five-Dollar Day at Ford." *Journal of Economic History* 48, June, 387–399.

Ransom, Roger, Richard Sutch, and Susan Carter. (1992). "Reestimating the Annual Unemployment Rate Series for the United States, 1890–1940." *Research in Economic History* 14, 293–299.

Rees, Albert. (1961). *Real Wages in Manufacturing, 1890–1914.* Princeton, NJ: Princeton University Press.

Romer, Christina. (1986a). "Spurious Volatility in Historical Unemployment Data." *Journal of Political Economy* 94, February, 1–37.

Romer, Christina. (1986b). "Is the Stabilization of the Postwar Economy a Figment of the Data?" *American Economic Review* 76, June, 314–334.

Romer, Christina. (1989). "The prewar Business Cycle Reconsidered: New Estimates of Gross National Product, 1869–1908." *Journal of Political Economy* 97, February, 1–37.

Romer, Christina. (1993). "The Nation in Depression." *Journal of Economic Perspectives* 7, Spring, 19–39.

Romer, Christina. (1994). "Remeasuring Business Cycles." *Journal of Economic History* 54, September, 573–609.

Romer, David. (1993). "The New Keynesian Synthesis." *Journal of Economic Perspectives* 7, Winter, 5–22.

Rosenbloom, Joshua L. (1988). "Labor Market Institutions and the Geographic Integration of Labor Markets in the Late Nineteenth Century United States." Ph.D. Dissertation, Stanford University.

Rosenbloom, Joshua L. (1990). "One Market or Many? Labor Market Integration in the Late Nineteenth-Century United States." *Journal of Economic History* 50, March, 85–107.

Rotemberg, Julio J., and Michael Woodford. (1991). "Markups and the Business Cycle." In Olivier Jean Blanchard and Stanley Fischer (eds.), *NBER Macroeconomic Annual 1991.* Cambridge, MA: MIT Press.

Sachs, Jeffrey. (1980). "The Changing Cyclical Behavior of Wages and Prices: 1890–1976." *American Economic Review* 70, March, 78–90.

Salter, W.E.G. (1960). *Productivity and Technical Change.* Cambridge: Cambridge University Press.

Sargent, Thomas J. (1981a). "The Ends of Four Big Inflations." Working Paper, University of Minnesota.

Sargent, Thomas J. (1981b). "Stopping Moderate Inflations: The Methods of Poincare and Thatcher." Working Paper, University of Minnesota.

Schumpeter, Joseph A. (1939). *Business Cycles: A Theoretical, Historical and Statistical Analysis of the Capitalistic Process.* New York: McGraw-Hill.

Shapiro, Matthew D., and Mark W. Watson. (1988). "Sources of Business Cycle Fluctuations." *NBER Macroeconomics Annual 1988*, 111–156.

Shaw, William Howard. (1947). *Value of Commodity Output Since 1869*. New York: National Bureau of Economic Research.

Shergold, Peter R. (1975). "Wage Rates in Pittsburgh During the Depression of 1908." *Journal of American Studies* 9, August 163–188.

Shister, Joseph. (1944). "A Note on Cyclical Wage Rigidity." *American Economic Review* 34, March, 111–116.

Simkovich, Boris A. (1994). "Agriculture and Industry in the New Republic: Explaining America's Structural Transformation, 1800–1860." Working Paper, Harvard University, July.

Smith, Bruce D. (1985a). "Some Colonial Evidence on Two Theories of Money: Maryland and the Carolinas." *Journal of Political Economy* 93, December, 1178–1211.

Smith, Bruce D. (1985b). "American Colonial Monetary Regimes: The Failure of the Quantity Theory of Money and Some Evidence in Favor of an Alternate View." *Canadian Journal of Economics* 18, August, 531–565.

Snowden, Kenneth. (1984). "Three Essays on the American Capital Market, 1870–1913." Ph.D. Dissertation, University of Wisconsin-Madison.

Snowden, Kenneth. (1993). "The Evolution of Interregional Mortgage Lending Channels, 1870–1940." Working Paper, Harvard University.

Snowden, Kenneth, and Nidal Abu-Saba. (1994). "Why Did Late Nineteenth Century American Mortgage Banking Fail?" Working Paper, Harvard University.

Sokoloff, Kenneth L. (1988). "Inventive Activity in Early Industrial America: Evidence from Patent Records, 1790–1846." *Journal of Economic History* 48, December, 813–850.

Solomou, Solomos. (1987). *Phases of Economic Growth, 1850–1973: Kondratieff Waves and Kuznets Swings*. Cambridge: Cambridge University Press.

Solow, Robert M. (1968). "Distribution in the Long and Short Run." In Jean Marchal and Bernard Ducros (eds.), *The Distribution of National Income*. New York: St. Martin's Press.

Spencer, Austin. (1977). "Relative Downward Industrial Price Flexibility, 1870–1921." *Explorations in Economic History* 14, January, 1–19.

Stiglitz, Joseph D. (1986). "Theories of Wage Rigidities." In J. Butkiewicz (ed.), *Keynes' Economic Legacy: Contemporary Economic Theories*. New York: Praeger.

Sundstrom, William A. (1990). "Was There a Golden Age of Flexible Wages? Evidence from Ohio Manufacturing, 1892–1910." *Journal of Economic History* 50, June, 309–320.

Sundstrom, William A. (1992). "Rigid Wages or Small Equilibrium Adjustments? Evidence from the Contraction of 1893." *Explorations in Economic History* 29, October, 430–455.

Sundstrom, William A., and Joshua L. Rosenbloom. (1993). "Occupational Differences in the Dispersion of Wages and Working Hours: Labor Market Integration in the United States, 1890–1903." *Explorations in Economic History* 30, October, 379–408.

Sylla, Richard. (1969). "Federal Policy, Banking Market Structure, and Capital Mobilization in the United States, 1863–1913." *Journal of Economic History* 29, December, 657–686.

Taussig, Frank William. (1931). *A Tariff History of the United States*. New York: Putnam's.

Temin, Peter. (1989). *Lessons from the Great Depression*. Cambridge, MA: MIT Press.

Thomas, Brinley. (1954). *Migration and Economic Growth*. Cambridge: Cambridge University Press.

Tobin, James. (1993). "Price Flexibility and Output Stability: An Old Keynesian View." *Journal of Economic Perspectives* 7, Winter, 45–65.

Towne, Marvin W., and Wayne D. Rasmussen. (1960). "Farm Gross Product and Gross Investment in the Nineteenth Century." In *Trends in the American Economy in the Nineteenth Century* (pp. 255–315). NBER Studies in Income and Wealth, Vol. 24. New York: Columbia University Press.

United States Bureau of Labor Statistics. (1969). "Summary of Manufacturing Production Workers Earnings Series, 1939–1968." Bulletin 1616, Washington, DC.

United States Bureau of Labor Statistics. (1992). "Consumer Price Index Detailed Report." March 1992.

United States Bureau of the Census. (1975). *Historical Statistics of the United States*. Washington, DC: U.S. Government Printing Office.

United States Council of Economic Advisers. Various years. *Economic Report of the President*. Washington, DC: U.S. Government Printing Office.

von Tunzelmann, G.N. (1978). *Steam Power and British Industrialization to 1860*. Oxford: Oxford University Press.

Wachter, Michael. (1970). "Cyclical Variation in the Interindustry Wage Structure." *American Economic Review* 60, March, 75–84.

Wallis, John J. (1989). "Employment in the Great Depression: New Data and Hypotheses." *Explorations in Economic History* 26, January, 45–72.

Warren, G.F., and F.A. Pearson. (1932). "Wholesale Prices in the United States for 135 Years, 1797 to 1932." Cornell University Agricultural Experiment Station, Memoir 142, November.

Waston, Mark W. (1994). "Business-Cycle Durations and Postwar Stabilization of the U.S. Economy." *American Economic Review* 84, March, 24–46.

Weinstein, Michael M. (1981). "Some Macroeconomic Impacts of the National Industrial Recovery Act, 1933–1935." In Karl Brunner (ed.), *The Great Depression Revisited*. Rochester Studies in Economics and Policy Issues, Vol. 2.

Weir, David R. (1986). "The Reliability of Historical Macroeconomic Data for Comparing Cyclical Stability." *Journal of Economic History* 46, June, 353–365.

Weir, David R. (1992). "A Century of U.S. Unemployment, 1890–1990: Revised Estimates Evidence for Stabilization." *Research in Economic History* 14, 301–346.

Wheelock, David C. (1989). "The Strategy, Effectiveness, and Consistency of Federal Reserve Monetary Policy, 1924–1933." *Explorations in Economic History* 26, October, 453–476.

Wheelock, David C. (1990). "Member Bank Borrowing and the Fed's Contractionary Monetary Policy During the Great Depression." *Journal of Money, Credit and Banking* 22, November, 409–426.

Wheelock, David C., and Subal C. Kumbhakar. (1994). "'The Slack Banker Dances': Deposit Insurance and Risk-Taking in the Banking Collapse of the 1920s." *Explorations in Economic History* 31, July, 357–375.

White, Eugene N. (1983). *The Regulation and Reform of the American Banking System, 1900–1929*. Princeton, NJ: Princeton University Press.

White, Eugene N. (1984). "Voting for Costly Regulation: Evidence from Banking Referenda in Illinois, 1924." *Southern Economic Journal* 51, 1084–1098.

White, Eugene N. (1986). "Before the Glass-Steagall Act: An Analysis of the Investment Banking Activities of National Banks." *Explorations in Economic History* 23, January, 33–55.

Wicker, Elmus. (1993). "A Reconstruction of the Gold and Banking Crises in 1931." Working Paper, Indiana University, October.

Wood, Elmer. (1939). *English Theories of Central Banking Control, 1819–1858*. Cambridge, MA: Harvard University Press.

Wright, Gavin. (1979). "Cheap Labor and Southern Textiles Before 1880." *Journal of Economic History* 39, September, 655–680.

Wright, Gavin. (1981). "Cheap Labor and Southern Textiles, 1880–1930." *Quarterly Journal of Economics* 96, November, 605–629.

Wright, Gavin. (1986). *Old South, New South*. New York: Basic Books.

Wright, Gavin. (1990). "The Origins of American Industrial Success, 1879–1940." *American Economic Review* 80, September, 651–668.

Zarnowitz, Victor. (1992). *Business Cycles: Theory, History, Indicators, and Forecasting*. Chicago: University of Chicago Press.

Commentary on Chapter 10

Steven N. Durlauf

Introduction

Charles Calomiris and Christopher Hanes have written a masterful survey of the contribution of recent work in American economic history to our understanding of macroeconomic theory. Underlying the various empirical analyses of the paper is the argument that this work in macroeconomic history requires macroeconomists to shift away from the standard conceptualization of macroeconomic data as the realization of a time invariant stochastic process toward one that accounts for the way in which the "*cumulative* past of the economy, including the history of shocks and their effects, change the structure of the economy."

This comment is designed to complement Calomiris and Hanes by describing what path dependence means from the perspective of statistics and economic theory. The discussion is organized as follows. The following section provides a couple of definitions of path dependence that represent ways of formally defining the role of history in contemporaneous fluctuations. These definitions illustrate how historical exercises of the type Calomiris and Hanes propose are an important supplement to standard econometric exercises. The next two sections describe recent work in macroeconomics which provides theoretical underpinnings for Calomiris and Hanes's arguments on empirical methodology and extend the discussion of relevant economic theory to the notion of institutional evolution that Calomiris and Hanes consider. The final section concludes.

Defining Path Dependence

Much of the motivation for Calomiris and Hanes's analysis stems from the belief that history matters: "Some events have permanent importance for the future of the economy." The idea that initial conditions, or some finite set of individual events, can have long-run consequences for aggregate activity, which is often called *path dependence*, may be given a rigorous probabilistic formulation. One possible formal definition of path dependence is the following. Suppose that aggregate output in the economy, Y_t, is an asymptotically stationary stochastic process with a well-defined limit Y_∞. Without loss of generality, Y_t can be taken to be a function of the history of some underlying set of exogenous innovations X_i; denote the history of these innovations as F_t, so that $Y_t = \Psi(F_t)$. Finally, let

Prob(*x* | *z*) denote the conditional probability measure of *x* given information *z*. Aggregate output exhibits path dependence with respect to the history F_T if

$$Prob(Y_\infty \mid F_T) \neq Prob(Y_\infty \mid F_0). \tag{1}$$

This definition says that something in the history of the economy between 0 and *T* has an effect on the long-run stochastic process characterizing aggregate activity. Equivalently, if aggregate output is path dependent according to this definition, then the process is nonergodic. Nonergodicity means that the limits of the sample moments of the output process will depend on the particular sample path realization of the economy. Since initial conditions can always be included in $F_T - F_0$, this definition represents a stochastic generalization of the sorts of multiple equilibria which arise in deterministic models.

On the other hand, the ideas of positive feedbacks and self-reinforcing behavior extend to a far larger set of models than those that exhibit path dependence as defined by equation (1). For example, suppose that we take an economy that exhibits multiple deterministic equilibria and superimpose on this model a selection mechanism that picks one of the equilibria each period based on the realization of some random process. It is straightforward to see that all sample paths generated by the model will have the same moments so long as the selection mechanism is itself ergodic. Such an economy would not, by equation (1), be path dependent, since the selection mechanism would now be part of the model. Distinguishing between the deterministic and stochastic versions of the model would seem to be undesirable as both models possess the fundamental feature of self-reinforcing behavior.

Such considerations suggest a second definition of path dependence that distinguishes models on the basis of whether shocks are or are not self-correcting. Again, suppose that Y_t is a measurable function of some set of exogenous innovations. Further, suppose that the stochastic process characterizing the exogenous variables has the property that for all $t > T$, all innovations are equal to zero, which means that no new shocks affect the economy after *T*. Aggregate output is path dependent when the realized history of innovations affects the behavior of Y_∞ with positive probability—that is,

$$Prob(Y_\infty \mid F_T) \neq Prob(Y_\infty \mid F_0) \text{ if } X_t = 0 \text{ if } t > T. \tag{2}$$

In other words, *when all future innovations equal zero*, then the realized sample path of the economy can have long-run effects.

This definition of path dependence distinguishes those models in which the history of shocks will eventually work their way out of an economy from those models in which the history of shocks is not self-correcting. This definition incorporates stationary, nonergodic economies as well as economies that shift between self-reinforcing regimes and therefore seems useful in characterizing the extent to which history matters. Such a definition seems particularly useful in thinking about models that can generate phenomena similar to the Great Depression in the United States, where the output declines of 1929–1932 do not seem to have been self-correcting, yet the New Deal and World War II were able to shift the economy away from sustained low-production. Finally, observe that economies that fail to exhibit self-correction will possess the feature that is fundamental to the work by Arthur (1989, 1990), David (1986, 1988), and others that history matters. It is straightforward to show that for economies that are path dependent under our second definition, the effects of particular shocks can be arbitrarily long-lasting, depending on the probability distribution of shocks to the economy.

What are the implications for econometric practice of economies whose stochastic processes are path dependent as defined by equations such as (1) and (2)? No ready answers will exist which are independent of the particular form of the stochastic process. For example, if Y_t is path dependent in the sense of equation (1) due to the presence of a unit root, then parameters of the process such as its ARMA structure may still be consistently estimated, although the asymptotic theory for inferences will, of course, be nonstandard. On the other hand, if the process obeys a finite state Markov chain with multiple absorbing states, then much of the structure of the economy cannot be consistently identified by a single sample path realization of the process. This is an obvious case where macroeconomic history can, either through within- or across-country analysis, augment standard macroeconometric analyses.

Similar possibilities exist for economies that are path dependent in the sense of equation (2). Suppose that one starts with an economy with multiple absorbing states of the sort described above and adds to it an additional white noise shock that throws the economy out of these absorbing states when its takes on a nonzero value. This economy will be path dependent by equation (2) although not by equation (1). The parameters of this economy (namely, the associated Markov transition matrix) can be consistently estimated from the data. However, the convergence rate of estimates of these parameters will be very slow, most obviously in the case where there are some states of the economy where the probability of staying in the state is near 1, which will occur if this additional shock takes on nonzero values with very low probability. This will be the case for the city-building example of Calomiris and Hanes, where one can interpret these bursts of migration as infrequent nonzero realizations of our additional shock. This is the sense in which path dependence can imply strong limitations on the ability of time-series analyses to yield firm evidence on macroeconomic theories, as is the case with the Kuznets cycle discussion of Calomiris and Hanes. At the same time, it is important to recognize that these inference difficulties are due to specific features of the example, rather than path dependence per se, as can readily be seen if one allows the additional shocks to take on nonzero values with high probability.

Theories of Path Dependence

Calomiris and Hanes's arguments in favor of the role of historical processes in understanding current economic behavior are consistent with much recent research in economic theory, particularly in macroeconomics. This literature, which started with Peter Diamond's search model (Diamond, 1982) and John Bryant's productivity spillover model (Bryant, 1985), has focused on the consequences of incomplete markets and coordination failure for aggregate behavior. Much of this research has been motivated by the desire to explain phenomena such as the persistent disparities in per capita incomes across developed and underdeveloped economies or regions and the episodes of boom and depression observed within developed economies.

The incomplete-markets and coordination-failure approach to macroeconomics, which is very well surveyed in Cooper and John (1988), studies economies that are distinguished by two fundamental characteristics. First, agents in the economy are assumed to be linked by strong positive feedbacks. In particular, the desirability of high production on the part of one agent is taken to be an increasing function of the level of production of other agents. Second, markets are assumed to be incomplete as agents cannot individually or collectively coordinate decisions. This inability to coordinate means that the aggregate economy is characterized by a noncooperative equilibrium. As a result, high and low levels of aggregate activity can represent internally self-reinforcing equilibria for the same economy. Consequently, the microeconomic specification of technology and preferences does not uniquely determine the long-run behavior of the aggregate system; depending on the model, the long-run behavior of the economy will be determined by initial conditions and expectations about which equilibrium will prevail. Dynamic and stochastic versions of these models can exhibit path dependence as characterized above.

The work on incomplete-markets and coordination-failure models has considered a wide range of sources for positive spillovers. In papers such as Cooper (1987), Heller (1986), and Murphy, Shleifer, and Vishny (1989), the emphasis has been on the implications of demand spillovers between firms or industries in economies with imperfect competition. These analyses have demonstrated how imperfect competition renders the level of aggregate output sensitive to changes in the level of aggregate demand in ways far different from a competitive economy, due to strategic behavior by individual firms. Alternatively, a number of authors have considered economies in which productivity spillovers exist either between individuals or between firms. In Romer (1986), Lucas (1988), and Azariadis and Drazen (1990), economies are studied where the individual accumulation of physical or human capital increases the productivity of other agents throughout the economy. Such models imply that a form of "social" increasing returns to scale holds for the aggregate production function. In a third strand of this literature,

Diamond (1982) and Durlauf (1994b) have analyzed economies characterized by imperfect communication where the willingness of each agent to seek out trading and coordination opportunities is affected by the number of other agents who do so.

The incomplete markets approach to macroeconomics has implications for both the long-run level of activity as well as the properties of the business cycle. As shown in papers such as Murphy, Shleifer, and Vishny (1989) for demand spillovers across industries and in papers such as Azariadis and Drazen (1990) for productivity spillovers across individuals, incomplete markets can, through the presence of multiple equilibria, help explain why some economies appear to be in underdevelopment traps. In Durlauf (1994b), it has further been shown that when spillover effects are intertemporal, these effects represent a potentially powerful transmission mechanism for business cycles. It is possible to construct models (see Durlauf, 1994a, for an example) where aggregate output obeys a white-noise process under complete markets, whereas aggregate output exhibits substantial intertemporal persistence when incomplete markets make production coordination impossible.

Finally, many of the recent path dependent models, such as Arthur (1989, 1990), Durlauf (1993, 1994a), and Krugman (1991, 1993, 1994), by emphasizing the stochastic and dynamic aspects to economic behavior in space between large populations of agents as well as time, have shown that path dependence is much more likely to occur in economies with complex cross-section as well as intertemporal dependence, as opposed to the representative agent models conventionally used to motivate macroeconometric work. These papers thus reinforce the importance attached by Calomiris and Hanes to historical epochs such as city building in which important cross-section as well as intertemporal interactions are occurring, in order to understand the determinants of aggregate activity in the long run. Indeed, these papers call into question the use of aggregate time series to draw structural inferences about the economy. Historical analyses of the type done by Calomiris and Hanes are an important step in addressing some of the limitations of conventional aggregate time-series analyses. In addition, an important paper by Brock (1993) develops a number of formal methods for formulating cross-section interactions that permit the application of formal econometrics to complex economies of this type.

Institutional Evolution in the Presence of Spillovers

One important feature of Calomiris and Hanes paper that has relevance for economic theory concerns the endogeneity of institutions. Specifically, the authors argue that a fundamental feature of economic development is the way in which institutions such as the government learn to respond to differing economic circumstances, of which the evolution of monetary policy during the Depression is a striking example.

From the perspective of theories of path dependence, the idea of institutional evolution is an important one for two reasons. First, institutional evolution can have a first-order effect on the degree of path dependence, however measured, in an economy. As the authors argue, learning on the part of the Federal Reserve presumably reduced the degree of persistence of the Depression, whereas the learning mistakes associated with Gold Standard exacerbated it. Institutional evolution is thus a route by which path dependence can be made an endogenous feature of an economy. Second, the idea of institutional evolution as described by Calomiris and Hanes is an example of a more general weakness of many models of incomplete markets and spillovers—namely, the assumption that the spillover structure between agents is exogenous and time invariant. In other words, spillover models have paid inadequate attention to the ways in which economic agents respond to the presence of different spillovers, especially in respect to the evolution of economic institutions when interpreted to include organizations in general.

Some work on the effects of different spillover structures, as manifested in the ways in which individual agents are organized into different types of coalitions, has been done in the context of income distribution models. In Bénabou (1993, 1994) and Durlauf (1994c, 1994d), positive spillovers exist between the distribution of occupations among parents within a community and the resulting human capital acquisition of children. These forces lead to economic segregation of families by income by neighborhood and provide a theory of ghetto formation. Kremer and Maskin (1994) develop similar results in the context of worker allocation to firms. Spillover effects between workers of different types can lead to segregation by skill and will affect the equilibrium size of firms. Dynamic versions of these models embody institutional evolution in the sense that allocation of families and workers will depend sensitively on the cross-section distribution of character traits as well as the state of technology.

An important area for future theoretical work is the extension of spillover models of business cycles to incorporate the endogenous evolution of interactions. Part of the role of macroeconomic history in informing economic theory is the identification of areas where this endogeneity has been important. One obvious area suggested by the Calomiris and Hanes study is the evolution of credit markets in economies with aggregate demand externalities.

Conclusions

Path dependence represents an important organizing principle for macroeconomics. Path-dependent models have emerged in the study of questions ranging from economic growth to business cycles to the emergence of ghettos. This recent work in economic theory has, in turn, clarified the sort of path dependence that is likely to emerge in data. Calomiris and Hanes provide a very valuable contribution to our understanding of the empirical relevance of this theoretical work, as well as an important challenge to traditional methods of empirical work in macroeconomics by demonstrating the importance of research in macroeconomic history in complementing standard statistical analyses.

Acknowledgments

Support from the National Science Foundation is gratefully acknowledged.

References

Arthur, W.B. (1989). "Increasing Returns, Competing Technologies and Lock-in by Historical Small Events: The Dynamics of Allocation Under Increasing Returns to Scale." *Economic Journal* 99, 116–131.
Arthur, W.B. (1990). "Silicon Valley Locational Clusters: When Do Increasing Returns Imply Monopoly?" *Mathematical Social Sciences* 19, 235–251.
Azariadis, C., and A. Drazen. (1990). "Threshold Externalities and Economic Development." *Quarterly Journal of Economics* 105, 501–526.
Bénabou, R. (1993). "Workings of a City: Location, Education, and Production." *Quarterly Journal of Economics* 108, 619–652.
Bénabou, R. (1994). "Education, Income Distribution, and Growth: The Local Connection." Working Paper No. 4798, National Bureau of Economic Research.
Brock, W. (1993). "Pathways to Randomness in the Economy: Emergent Nonlinearity in Economics and Finance." *Estudios Economicos* 8, 3–55.
Bryant, J. (1985). "A Simple Rational Expectations Keynes-Type Model." *Quarterly Journal of Economics* 98, 525–529.
Cooper, R. (1987). "Dynamic Behavior of Imperfectly Competitive Economies with Multiple Equilibria." Working Paper No. 2388, National Bureau of Economic Research.
Cooper, R., and A. John. (1988). "Coordinating Coordination Failures in Keynesian Models." *Quarterly Journal of Economics* 103, 441–465.
David, P. (1986). "Understanding the Economics of QWERTY: The Necessity of History." In W. Parker (ed.), *Economic History and the Modern Economist*. Oxford: Basil Blackwell.
David, P. (1988). "Path Dependence: Putting the Past in the Future of Economics." Working Paper, Stanford University.
Diamond, P. (1982). "Aggregate Demand in Search Equilibrium." *Journal of Political Economy* 90, 881–894.
Durlauf, S.N. (1993). "Nonergodic Economic Growth." *Review of Economic Studies* 60, 349–366.

Durlauf, S.N. (1994a). "Path Dependence in Aggregate Output." *Industrial and Corporate Change* 3, 173–198.

Durlauf, S.N. (1994b). "An Incomplete Markets Theory of Business Cycle Fluctuations." Working Paper, University of Wisconsin at Madison.

Durlauf, S.N. (1994c). "A Theory of Persistent Income Inequality." Working Paper, University of Wisconsin at Madison.

Durlauf, S.N. (1994d). "Neighborhood Feedbacks, Endogenous Stratification, and Income Inequality." In W. Barnett, G. Gandolfo, and C. Hillinger (eds.), *Dynamic Disequilibrium Modelling: Proceedings of the Sixth International Symposium on Economic Theory and Econometrics.* Cambridge: Cambridge University Press.

Heller, W.P. (1986). "Coordination Failure Under Complete Markets with Applications to Effective Demand." In W.P. Heller, R.M. Starr, and D.A. Starrett (eds.), *Essays in Honor of Kenneth J. Arrow* (Vol. 2). Cambridge: Cambridge University Press.

Kremer, M., and E. Maskin. (1994). "Segregation of Workers by Skill and the Rise in Inequality." Working Paper, Massachusetts Institute of Technology.

Krugman, P. (1991). "Increasing Returns and Economic Geography." *Journal of Political Economy* 99, 483–499.

Krugman, P. (1993). "On the Number and Location of Cities." *European Economic Review* 37, 293–298.

Krugman, P. (1994). "Fluctuations, Instability, and Agglomeration." Working Paper, Stanford University.

Lucas, R.E. (1988). "On the Mechanics of Economic Development." *Journal of Monetary Economics* 22, 3–42.

Murphy, K., A. Shleifer, and R. Vishny. (1989). "Industrialization and the Big Push." *Journal of Political Economy* 97, 1003–1026.

Romer, P. (1986). "Increasing Returns and Long Run Growth." *Journal of Political Economy* 94, 1002–1037.

III FRONTIERS OF MACROECONOMETRICS

11 MODELING VOLATILITY DYNAMICS

Francis X. Diebold
Jose A. Lopez

Introduction

Good macroeconomic and financial theorists, like all good theorists, want to get the facts straight before theorizing; hence, the explosive growth in the methodology and application of time-series econometrics in the last twenty-five years. Many factors fueled that growth, ranging from important developments in related fields (see Box and Jenkins, 1970) to dissatisfaction with the "incredible identifying restrictions" associated with traditional macroeconometric models (Sims, 1980) and the associated recognition that many tasks of interest, such as forecasting, simply do not require a structural model (see Granger and Newbold, 1979). A short list of active subfields includes vector autoregressions, index and dynamic factor models, causality, integration and persistence, cointegration, seasonality, unobserved-components models, state-space representations and the Kalman filter, regime-switching models, nonlinear dynamics, and optimal nonlinear filtering. Any such list must also include models of volatility dynamics. Models of autoregressive conditional heteroskedasticity (ARCH), in particular, provide parsimonious approximations to volatility dynamics and have found wide use in macroeconomics and finance.[1] The family of ARCH models is the subject of this chapter.

Economists are typically introduced to heteroskedasticity in cross-sectional contexts, such as when the variance of a cross-sectional regression disturbance depends on one or more of the regressors. A classic example is the estimation of Engel curves by weighted least squares, in light of the fact that the variance of the disturbance in an expenditure equation may depend on income. Heteroskedasticity is equally pervasive in the time-series contexts prevalent in macroeconomics and finance. For example, in Figures 11.1 and 11.2, we plot the log of daily deutsche-mark/dollar and Swiss franc/dollar spot exchange rates, as well as the daily returns and squared returns, 1974–1991. Volatility clustering (that is, contiguous periods of high or low volatility) is apparent. However, models of cross-sectional heteroskedasticity are not useful in such cases because they are not dynamic. ARCH models, on the other hand, were developed to model such time-series volatility fluctuations. Engle (1982) used them to model the variance of inflation, and more recently they have enjoyed widespread use in modeling asset return volatility.

Exhaustive surveys of the ARCH literature already exist, including Engle and Bollerslev (1986), Bollerslev, Chou, and Kroner (1992), Bera and Higgins (1993) and Bollerslev, Engle and Nelson (1994), and it is not our intention to produce another. Rather, we shall provide a selective account of certain aspects of conditional volatility modeling that are of particular relevance in macroeconomics and finance. In the following section we sketch the rudiments of a rather general univariate time-series model, allowing for dynamics in both the conditional mean and variance. We introduce the ARCH and generalized ARCH (GARCH) models there. Then we provide motivation for the models, discuss the properties of the models in depth, and discuss issues related to estimation and testing. Finally, we detail various important extensions and applications of the model and conclude with speculations on productive directions for future research.

A Time-Series Model with Conditional Mean and Variance Dynamics

Wold's (1938) celebrated decomposition theorem establishes that any covariance stationary stochastic process $\{x_t\}$ may be written as the sum of a linearly deterministic component and a linearly indeterministic component with a square-summable, one-sided moving average representation.[2] We write $x_t = d_t + y_t$, where d_t is linearly deterministic and y_t is a linearly regular (or indeterministic) covariance stationary stochastic process (LRCSSP) given by

$$y_t = B(L)\varepsilon_t,$$

$$B(L) = \sum_{i=0}^{\infty} b_i L^i, \quad \sum_{i=0}^{\infty} b_i^2 < \infty, \quad b_0 = 1,$$

Daily Spot DM/$ (1974-1991)

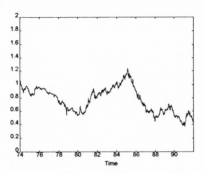

Daily DM/$ Returns (1974-1991)

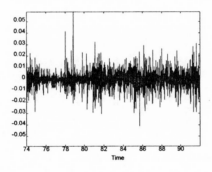

Squared DM/$ Returns (1974-1991)

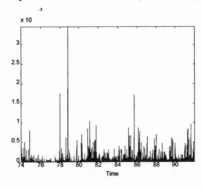

Figure 11.1.   Daily logged deutschemark/dollar exchange rates (1974–1991) along
with the corresponding daily returns and squared daily returns

Daily Spot SF/$ (1974-1991)

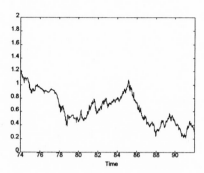

Daily SF/$ Returns (1974-1991)

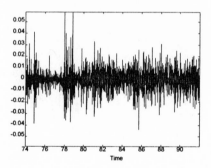

Squared SF/$ Returns (1974-1991)

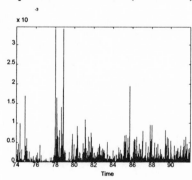

Figure 11.2. Daily logged swiss franc/dollar exchange rate (1974–1991) along with the corresponding daily returns and squared daily returns

$$E[\varepsilon_t \varepsilon_\tau] = \begin{cases} \sigma_\varepsilon^2 < \infty, & \text{if } t = \tau \\ 0, & \text{otherwise.} \end{cases}$$

The uncorrelated innovation sequence $\{\varepsilon_t\}$ need not be Gaussian and therefore need not be independent. Nonindependent innovations are characteristic of nonlinear time series in general and conditionally heteroskedastic time series in particular.

In this section, we introduce the ARCH process within Wold's framework by contrasting the polar extremes of the LRCSSP with independent and identically distributed (iid) innovations, which allows only conditional mean dynamics, and the pure ARCH process, which allows only conditional variance dynamics. We then combine these extremes to produce a generalized model that permits variation in both the first and second conditional moments. Finally, we introduce the generalized ARCH (GARCH) process, which is very useful in practice.

Conditional Mean Dynamics

Suppose that y_t is a LRCSSP with iid, as opposed to merely white-noise, innovations.[3] The ability of the LRCSSP to capture conditional mean dynamics is the source of its power. The *unconditional* mean and variance are $E[y_t] = 0$ and $E[y_t^2]$ $= \sigma_\varepsilon^2 \sum_{i=0}^{\infty} b_i^2$, which are both time invariant. However, the *conditional* mean is time varying and is given by $E[y_t \mid \Omega_{t-1}] = \sum_{i=1}^{\infty} b_i \varepsilon_{t-i}$, where the information set is $\Omega_{t-1} = \{\varepsilon_{t-1}, \varepsilon_{t-2}, \ldots\}$.

Because the volatility of many economic time series seems to vary, one would hope that the LRCSSP could capture conditional variance dynamics as well, but such is not the case for the model as presently specified. The conditional variance of y_t is constant at $E[(y_t - E[y_t \mid \Omega_{t-1}])^2 \mid \Omega_{t-1}] = \sigma_\varepsilon^2$. This potentially unfortunate restriction manifests itself in the properties of the k-step-ahead conditional prediction error variance. The least-squares forecast is the conditional expectation

$$E[y_{t+k} \mid \Omega_t] = \sum_{i=0}^{\infty} b_{k+i} \varepsilon_{t-i},$$

and the associated prediction error is

$$y_{t+k} - E[y_{t+k} \mid \Omega_t] = \sum_{i=0}^{k-1} b_i \varepsilon_{t+k-i},$$

which has a conditional prediction error variance of

$$E[(y_{t+k} - E[y_{t+k} \mid \Omega_t])^2 \mid \Omega_t] = \sigma_\varepsilon^2 \sum_{i=0}^{k-1} b_i^2.$$

As $k \to \infty$, the conditional prediction error variance converges to the unconditional variance $\sigma_\varepsilon^2 \sum_{i=0}^{\infty} b_i^2$. Note that for any k, the conditional prediction error variance depends only on k and not on Ω_{t-1}; thus, readily available and potentially useful information is discarded.

Conditional Variance Dynamics

By way of contrast, we now introduce a pure ARCH process, which displays *only* conditional variance dynamics. We write

$$y_t = \varepsilon_t,$$

$$\varepsilon_t \mid \Omega_{t-1} \sim N(0, h_t),$$

$$h_t = \omega + \gamma(L)\varepsilon_t^2,$$

$$\omega > 0, \quad \gamma(L) = \sum_{i=1}^{\infty} \gamma_i L^i, \quad \gamma_i \geq 0 \; \forall \; i, \quad \gamma(1) < 1.$$

The process is parameterized in terms of the conditional density of $\varepsilon_t \mid \Omega_{t-1}$, which is assumed to be normal with a zero conditional mean and a conditional variance that depends linearly on past squared innovations. Note that even though the ε_t's are serially uncorrelated, they are not independent. The stated conditions are sufficient to ensure that the conditional and unconditional variances are positive and finite as well as that y_t is covariance stationary.

The unconditional moments are constant and are given by $E[y_t] = 0$ and $E[(y_t - E[y_t])^2] = \dfrac{\omega}{1 - \gamma(1)}$. As for the conditional moments, by construction, the conditional mean of the process is zero, and the conditional variance is potentially time varying. That is, $E[y_t \mid \Omega_{t-1}] = 0$ and $E[(y_t - E[y_t \mid \Omega_{t-1}])^2 \mid \Omega_{t-1}] = \omega + \gamma(L)\varepsilon_t^2$.

Conditional Mean and Variance Dynamics

We can incorporate *both* conditional mean and conditional variance dynamics by introducing ARCH innovations into the standard LRCSSP. We write

$$y_t = B(L)\varepsilon_t,$$

$$\varepsilon_t \mid \Omega_{t-1} \sim N(0, h_t),$$

$$h_t = \omega + \gamma(L)\varepsilon_t^2,$$

subject to the conditions discussed earlier. Both the unconditional mean and variance are constant—that is, $E[y_t] = 0$ and

$$E[(y_t - E[y_t])^2] = \left(\sum_{i=0}^{\infty} b_i^2\right) E[\varepsilon_t^2] = \frac{\omega}{1 - \gamma(1)} \sum_{i=0}^{\infty} b_i^2.$$

However, the conditional mean and variance are time-varying—that is,

$$E[y_t \mid \Omega_{t-1}] = \sum_{i=1}^{\infty} b_i \varepsilon_{t-i},$$

$$E[(y_t - E[y_t \mid \Omega_{t-1}])^2 \mid \Omega_{t-1}] = \omega + \gamma(L)\varepsilon_t^2.$$

Thus, this model treats the conditional mean and variance dynamics in a symmetric fashion by allowing for movement in each, a common characteristic of economic time series.

The Generalized ARCH Process

In the previous subsections, we used an infinite-ordered ARCH process to model conditional variance dynamics. We now introduce the GARCH process, which we shall subsequently focus on almost exclusively. The finite-ordered GARCH model approximates infinite-ordered conditional variance dynamics in the same way that finite-ordered ARMA models approximate infinite-ordered conditional mean dynamics.[4]

The GARCH (p, q) process, introduced by Bollerslev (1986), is given by

$$y_t = \varepsilon_t,$$

$$\varepsilon_t \mid \Omega_{t-1} \sim N(0, h_t),$$

$$h_t = \omega + \alpha(L)\varepsilon_t^2 + \beta(L)h_t,$$

$$\alpha(L) = \sum_{i=1}^{p}\alpha_i L^i, \quad \beta(L) = \sum_{i=1}^{q}\beta_i L^i,$$

$$\omega > 0; \quad \alpha_i \geq 0, \quad \beta_i \geq 0 \; \forall i; \quad \alpha(1) + \beta(1) < 1.$$

The stated conditions ensure that the conditional variance is positive and that y_t is covariance stationary.[5] The ARCH model of Engle (1982) emerges when $\beta(L) = 0$. If *both* $\alpha(L)$ and $\beta(L)$ are zero, then the model is simply iid noise with variance ω. The GARCH (p, q) model can be represented as a restricted infinite-ordered ARCH model:

$$h_t = \frac{\omega}{1 - \beta(1)} + \frac{\alpha(L)}{1 - \beta(L)}\varepsilon_t^2 = \frac{\omega}{1 - \beta(1)} + \sum_{i=1}^{\infty}\delta_i\varepsilon_{t-i}^2 .$$

The first two unconditional moments of the pure GARCH model are constant and given by $E[y_t] = 0$ and

$$E[(y_t - E[y_t])^2] = \frac{\omega}{1 - \alpha(1) - \beta(1)}$$

The conditional moments are $E[y_t \mid \Omega_{t-1}] = 0$ and

$$E[(y_t - E[y_t \mid \Omega_{t-1}])^2 \mid \Omega_{t-1}] = \omega + \alpha(L)\varepsilon_t^2 + \beta(L)h_t.$$

Motivating GARCH Processes

GARCH models have been used extensively in macroeconomics and finance because of their attractive approximation-theoretic properties. However, these models do not arise directly from economic theory, and various efforts have been made to imbue them with economic rationale. Here, we discuss both approximation-theoretic and economic motivations for the GARCH framework.

Approximation-Theoretic Considerations

The primary and most powerful justification for the GARCH model is approximation-theoretic. That is, the GARCH model provides a flexible and parsimonious approximation to conditional variance dynamics, in exactly the same way that ARMA models provide a flexible and parsimonious approximation to conditional mean dynamics. In each case, an infinite-ordered distributed lag is approximated as the ratio of two finite, low-ordered lag operator polynomials. The power and usefulness of ARMA and GARCH models come entirely from the fact that ratios of such lag operator polynomials can accurately approximate a variety of infinite-ordered lag operator polynomials.[6] In short, ARMA models with GARCH innovations offer a natural, parsimonious, and flexible way to capture the conditional mean and variance dynamics observed in a time series.

Economic Considerations

Economic considerations may also lead to GARCH effects, although the precise links have proved difficult to establish. Any of the myriad economic forces that produce *persistence* in economic dynamics may be responsible for the appearance of GARCH effects in volatility. In such cases, the persistence happens to be in the conditional second moment rather than the first.

To take one example, conditional heteroskedasticity may arise in situations in which "economic time" and "calendar time" fail to move together. A well-known example from financial economics is the subordinated stochastic process model of Clark (1973). In this model and its subsequent extensions, the number of trades occurring per unit of calendar time (I_t) is a random variable, and the price change per unit of calendar time (ε_t) is the sum of the I_t intraperiod price changes (δ_i), which are assumed to be normally distributed:

$$\varepsilon_t = \sum_{i=1}^{I_t} \delta_i, \quad \delta_i \overset{\text{i.i.d.}}{\sim} N(0, \eta).$$

Using a simple transformation, ε_t can be written more directly as a function of I_t,

$$\varepsilon_t = (\eta I_t)^{1/2} z_t, \quad z_t \overset{\text{i.i.d.}}{\sim} N(0, 1).$$

Thus, ε_t is characterized by conditional heteroskedasticity linked to trading volume. If the number of trades per unit of calendar time displays serial correlation, as in Gallant, Hsieh, and Tauchen (1991), the serial correlation induced in the conditional variance of returns (measured in calendar time) results in GARCH-like behavior. Similar ideas arise in macroeconomics. The divergence between economic time and calendar time accords with the tradition of "phase-averaging" (see Friedman and Schwartz, 1963) and is captured by the time-deformation models of Stock (1987, 1988).

Several other explanations for the existence of GARCH effects have been advanced, including parameter variation (Tsay, 1987), differences in the interpretability of information (Diebold and Nerlove, 1989), market microstructure (Bollerslev and Domowitz, 1991), and agents' "slow" adaptation to news (Brock and LeBaron, 1993). Currently, a consensus economic model producing persistence in

GARCH(1,1) Realization   Sample Autocorrelation Function

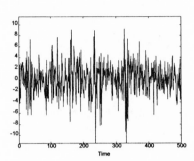 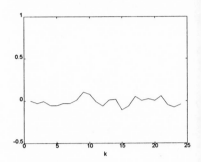

Figure 11.3. GARCH(1, 1) realization and its sample autocorrelation function

conditional volatility does not exist, but it would be foolish to deny the existence of such persistence; measurement is simply ahead of theory.

Properties of GARCH Processes

Here we highlight some important properties of GARCH processes. To facilitate the discussion, we generate a realization of a pure GARCH(1, 1) process of length 500 that we will use repeatedly for illustration.[7] The parameter values are $\omega = 1$, $\alpha = .2$, and $\beta = .7$, and the underlying shocks are $N(0, 1)$.[8] This parameterization delivers a persistent conditional variance and has finite unconditional variance and kurtosis.[9] We plot the realization and its first twenty-five sample autocorrelations in Figure 11.3. The sample autocorrelations are indicative of white noise, as expected.

The Conditional Variance is a Serially Correlated Random Variable

The conditional variance associated with the GARCH model is

$$h_t = \omega + \alpha(L)\varepsilon_t^2 + \beta(L)h_t.$$

Recall that the unconditional variance of the process is given by

$$\sigma_y^2 = \frac{\omega}{1 - \alpha(1) - \beta(1)}.$$

Conditional Variance   Sample Autocorrelation Function

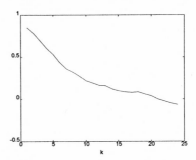

Figure 11.4. Conditional variance of the GARCH(1, 1) realization and its sample autocorrelation function

Replacing ω with $\sigma_y^2(1 - \alpha(1) - \beta(1))$ yields

$$h_t = \sigma_y^2(1 - \alpha(1) - \beta(1)) + \alpha(L)\varepsilon_t^2 + \beta(L)h_t,$$

so that

$$h_t - \sigma_y^2 = \alpha(L)\varepsilon_t^2 - \sigma_y^2\alpha(1) + \beta(L)h_t - \sigma_y^2\beta(1)$$
$$= \alpha(L)(\varepsilon_t^2 - \sigma_y^2) + \beta(L)(h_t - \sigma_y^2).$$

Thus, the conditional variance is itself a serially correlated random variable.

We plot the conditional variance of the simulated GARCH(1, 1) process and its sample autocorrelation function in Figure 11.4. The high persistence of the conditional variance is due to the large sum of the coefficients, $\alpha + \beta = 0.90$.

ε_t^2 Has an ARMA Representation

If ε_t is a GARCH(p, q) process, ε_t^2 has the ARMA representation

$$\varepsilon_t^2 = \omega + [\alpha(L) + \beta(L)]\varepsilon_t^2 - \beta(L)v_t + v_t,$$

where $v_t = \varepsilon_t^2 - h_t$ is the difference between the squared innovation and the conditional variance at time t. To see this, note that, by supposition, $h_t = \omega + \alpha(L)\varepsilon_t^2 + \beta(L)h_t$. Adding and subtracting $\beta(L)\varepsilon_t^2$ from the right side gives

$$h_t = \omega + \alpha(L)\varepsilon_t^2 + \beta(L)\varepsilon_t^2 - \beta(L)\varepsilon_t^2 + \beta(L)h_t$$
$$= \omega + [\alpha(L) + \beta(L)]\varepsilon_t^2 - \beta(L)[\varepsilon_t^2 - h_t].$$

Squared GARCH(1,1) Realization

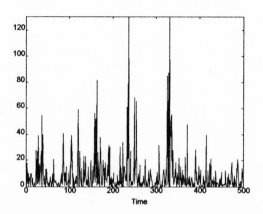

Figure 11.5.   Squared GARCH(1, 1) realization

Adding ε_t^2 to each side gives

$$h_t + \varepsilon_t^2 = \omega + [\alpha(L) + \beta(L)]\varepsilon_t^2 - \beta(L)[\varepsilon_t^2 - h_t] + \varepsilon_t^2,$$

so that

$$\varepsilon_t^2 = \omega + [\alpha(L) + \beta(L)]\varepsilon_t^2 - \beta(L)[\varepsilon_t^2 - h_t] + [\varepsilon_t^2 - h_t],$$

$$= \omega + [\alpha(L) + \beta(L)]\varepsilon_t^2 - \beta(L)v_t + v_t.$$

Thus, ε_t^2 is an ARMA($[\max(p, q)]$, p) process with innovation v_t, where $v_t \in [-h_t, \infty)$, and it is covariance stationary if the roots of $\alpha(L) + \beta(L) = 1$ are outside the unit circle.

The square of our GARCH(1, 1) realization is presented in Figure 11.5; the persistence in ε_t^2, which is essentially a proxy for the unobservable h_t, is apparent. *Differences* in the behavior of ε_t^2 and h_t are also apparent, however. In particular, ε_t^2 appears "noisy." To see why, use the multiplicative form of the GARCH model, $\varepsilon_t = h_t^{1/2} z_t$ with $z_t \sim N(0, 1)$. It is easy to see that ε_t^2 is an unbiased estimator of h_t,

$$E[\varepsilon_t^2 \mid \Omega_{t-1}] = E[h_t \mid \Omega_{t-1}]E[z_t^2 \mid \Omega_{t-1}] = E[h_t \mid \Omega_{t-1}],$$

because $z_t^2 \mid \Omega_{t-1} \sim \chi_{(1)}^2$. However, because the median of a $\chi_{(1)}^2$ is .455, $P\left(\varepsilon_t^2 < \frac{1}{2} h_t\right)$ $> 1/2$. Thus, the ε_t^2 proxy introduces a potentially significant error into the analysis of small samples of h_t, $t = 1, \ldots, T$, although the error diminishes as T increases.

The Conditional Prediction Error Variance Depends on the
Conditioning Information Set

Because the conditional variance of a GARCH process is a serially correlated
random variable, it is of interest to examine the optimal k-step-ahead prediction,
prediction error and conditional prediction error variance. Immediately, the k-
step-ahead prediction is $E[y_{t+k} \mid \Omega_t] = 0$, and the prediction error is

$$y_{t+k} - E[y_{t+k} \mid \Omega_t] = \varepsilon_{t+k}.$$

This implies that the conditional variance of the prediction error,

$$E[(y_{t+k} - E[y_{t+k} \mid \Omega_t])^2 \mid \Omega_t] = E[\varepsilon_{t+k}^2 \mid \Omega_t],$$

depends on both k *and* Ω_t because of the dynamics in the conditional variance.
Simple calculations reveal that the expression for the GARCH(p, q) process is
given by

$$E[\varepsilon_{t+k}^2 \mid \Omega_t] = \omega \left[\sum_{i=1}^{k-1} [\alpha(1) + \beta(1)]^i \right] + [\alpha(1) + \beta(1)]^{k-1} h_{t+1}.$$

In the limit, this conditional variance reduces to the unconditional variance of the
process,

$$\lim_{k \to \infty} E[\varepsilon_{t+k}^2 \mid \Omega_t] = \frac{\omega}{1 - \alpha(1) - \beta(1)}.$$

For finite k, the dependence of the prediction error variance on the current
information set Ω_t can be exploited to produce better interval forecasts, as illustrated in Figure 11.6 for $k = 1$. We plot the one-step-ahead 90 percent conditional
and unconditional interval forecasts of our simulated GARCH(1, 1) process along
with the actual realization. We construct the conditional prediction intervals using
the conditional variance

$$E[\varepsilon_{t+1}^2 \mid \Omega_t] = h_{t+1} = \omega + \alpha \varepsilon_t^2 + \beta h_t = 1 + .2 \varepsilon_t^2 + .7 h_t;$$

thus, the conditional prediction intervals are $\left\{ \pm 1.64 \sqrt{h_t} \right\}_{t=1}^{500}$. The 90 percent unconditional interval, on the other hand, is simply $[f_{.05}, f_{.95}]$, where f_α denotes the
α percentile of the unconditional distribution of the GARCH process. The ability
of the conditional prediction intervals to adapt to changes in volatility is clear.

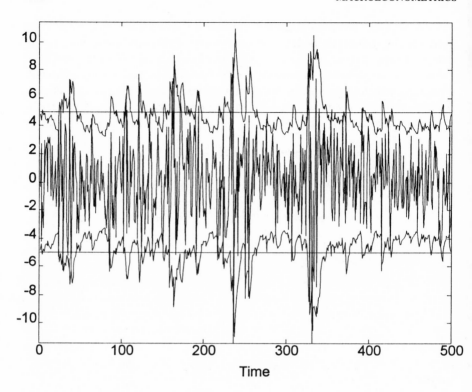

Figure 11.6.   GARCH(1, 1) realization with one-step-ahead 90 percent conditional and unconditional confidence intervals

The Implied Unconditional Distribution is Symmetric and Leptokurtic

The moment structure of GARCH processes is a complicated affair. In addition to the earlier-referenced surveys, Milhoj (1985) and Bollerslev (1988) are good sources. However, straightforward calculation reveals that the unconditional distribution of a GARCH process is symmetric and leptokurtic, a characteristic that agrees nicely with a variety of financial market data. The unconditional leptokurtosis of GARCH processes follows from the persistence in conditional variance, which produces the clusters of low-volatility and high-volatility episodes associated with observations in the center and in the tails of the unconditional distribution.

GARCH processes are not constrained to have finite unconditional moments, as shown in Bollerslev (1986). In fact, the only conditionally Gaussian GARCH process with unconditional moments of all orders occurs when $\alpha(L) = \beta(L) = 0$, which is the degenerate case of iid innovations. Otherwise, depending on the precise parameterization, unconditional moments will cease to exist beyond some point. For example, most parameter estimates for financial data indicate an infinite fourth moment, and some even indicate an infinite second moment. Our illustrative process has population mean 0, variance 10, skewness 0, and kurtosis 5.2.

Temporal Aggregation Produces Convergence to Normality

Convergence to normality under temporal aggregation is a key feature of much economic data and is also a property of covariance stationary GARCH processes. The key insight is that a low-frequency change is simply the sum of the corresponding high-frequency changes; for example, an annual change is the sum of the internal quarterly changes, each of which is the sum of its internal monthly changes, and so forth. Thus, if a Gaussian central limit theorem can be invoked for sums of GARCH processes, convergence to normality under temporal aggregation is assured. Such theorems can be invoked so long as the process is covariance stationary, as shown by Diebold (1988) using a central limit argument from White (1984) that requires only the existence of an unconditional second moment. Drost and Nijman (1993) extend Diebold's result by showing that a particular generalization of the GARCH class is closed under temporal aggregation and by characterizing the precise way in which temporal aggregation leads to reduced GARCH effects.[10]

Estimation and Testing of GARCH Models

Following the majority of the literature, we focus primarily on maximum-likelihood estimation (MLE) and associated testing procedures.[11]

Approximate Maximum Likelihood Estimation

As always, the likelihood function is simply the joint density of the observations,

$$L(\theta; y_1, \ldots, y_T) = f(y_1, \ldots, y_T; \theta).$$

This joint density is non-Gaussian and does not have a known closed-form expression, but it can be factored into the product of conditional densities,

$$L(\theta; y_1, \ldots, y_T) = f(y_T \mid \Omega_{T-1}; \theta)f(y_{T-1} \mid \Omega_{T-2}; \theta) \ldots$$
$$f(y_{p+1} \mid \Omega_p; \theta)f(y_p, \ldots, y_1; \theta),$$

where, if the conditional densities are Gaussian,

$$f(y_t \mid \Omega_{t-1}; \theta) = \frac{1}{\sqrt{2\pi}} h_t(\theta)^{-1/2} \exp\left[-\frac{1}{2} \frac{y_t^2}{h_t(\theta)} \right].$$

The $f(y_p, \ldots, y_1; \theta)$ term is often ignored because a closed-form expression for it does not exist and because its deletion is asymptotically inconsequential. Thus, the approximate log likelihood is

$$\ln L(\theta; y_{p+1}, \ldots, y_T) = -\frac{T-p}{2} \ln(2\pi) - \frac{1}{2} \sum_{t=p+1}^{T} \ln h_t(\theta) - \frac{1}{2} \sum_{t=p+1}^{T} \frac{y_t^2}{h_t(\theta)}.$$

It may be maximized numerically using iterative procedures and is easily generalized to models richer than the pure univariate GARCH process, such as regression models with GARCH disturbances. In that case, the likelihood is the same with $\varepsilon_t \equiv y_t - E[y_t \mid \Omega_{t-1}; \theta]$ in place of y_t. The unobserved conditional variances $\{h_t(\theta)\}_{t=p+1}^{T}$ that enter the likelihood function are calculated at iteration j using $\theta^{(j-1)}$, the estimated parameter vector at iteration $j-1$. The necessary initial values of the conditional variance are set at the first iteration to the sample variance of the observed data and at all subsequent iterations to the sample variance of a simulated realization with parameters $\theta^{(j-1)}$.

The assumption of conditional normality is not always appropriate. Nevertheless, Weiss (1986) and Bollerslev and Wooldridge (1992) show that even when normality is inappropriately assumed, the resulting quasi-MLE estimates are asymptotically normally distributed and consistent if the conditional mean and variance functions are specified correctly. Bollerslev and Wooldridge (1992), moreover, derive asymptotic standard errors for the quasi-MLE estimates that are robust to conditional nonnormality and are easily calculated as functions of the estimated parameters and the first derivatives of the conditional mean and variance functions.

Exact Maximum Likelihood Estimation

Diebold and Schuermann (1993) propose a numerical procedure for constructing the exact likelihood function of an ARCH process using simulation techniques in conjunction with nonparametric density estimation, thereby retaining the information contained in $\{y_p, \ldots, y_1\}$.[12] Consider the ARCH(p) process, $y_t = \varepsilon_t$, where $\varepsilon_t \mid \Omega_{t-1} \sim N(0, h_t)$, $h_t = \omega + \alpha_1 \varepsilon_{t-1}^2 + \ldots + \alpha_p \varepsilon_{t-p}^2$, $\omega > 0$, $\alpha_i \geq 0$, $\forall\, i = 1, \ldots, p$, and $\sum_{i=1}^{p} \alpha_i < 1$. The conditional normality assumption is adopted only because it is the most common; alternative distributions can be used with no change in the procedure. Let $\theta = (\omega, \alpha_1, \ldots, \alpha_p)$.

The initial likelihood term $f(y_p, \ldots, y_1; \theta)$ for any given parameter configuration θ is simply the unconditional density of the first p observations evaluated at $\{y_p, \ldots, y_1\}$, which can be estimated to any desired degree of accuracy using well-known techniques of simulation and consistent nonparametric density estimation. At any iteration j, a current "best guess" of the parameter vector $\theta^{(j)}$ exists. Therefore, a very long realization of the process with parameter vector $\theta^{(j)}$ can be simulated and the value of the joint unconditional density evaluated at $\{y_p, \ldots, y_1\}$ can be consistently estimated and denoted as $\hat{f}(y_p, \ldots, y_1; \theta^{(j)})$. This estimated unconditional density can then be substituted into the likelihood where the true unconditional density appears. By simulating a large sample, the difference between $\hat{f}(y_p, \ldots, y_1; \theta^{(j)})$ and $f(y_p, \ldots, y_1; \theta^{(j)})$ is made arbitrarily small, given the consistency of the density estimation technique. The full conditionally Gaussian likelihood, evaluated at $\theta^{(j)}$, is then

$$L(\theta^{(j)}; y_T, \ldots, y_1) \approx \hat{f}(y_p, \ldots, y_1; \theta^{(j)}) \times$$

$$\prod_{t=p+1}^{T} \left[\frac{1}{\sqrt{2\pi}} h_t(\theta^{(j)})^{-1/2} \exp\left[-\frac{1}{2} \frac{y_t^2}{h_t(\theta^{(j)})} \right] \right],$$

which may be maximized with respect to θ using standard numerical techniques.

Testing

Standard likelihood-ratio procedures may be used to test the hypothesis that no ARCH effects are present in a time series, but the numerical estimation required under the ARCH alternative makes that a rather tedious approach. Instead, the Lagrange-multiplier (LM) approach, which requires estimation only under the null, is preferable. Engle (1982) proposes a simple LM test for ARCH under the assumption of conditional normality that involves only a least-squares regression of squared residuals on an intercept and lagged squared residuals. Under the null of no ARCH, TR^2 from that regression is asymptotically distributed as $x_{(q)}^2$, where q is the number of lagged squared residuals included in the regression.

A minor limitation of the LM test for ARCH is the underlying assumption of conditional normality, which is sometimes restrictive.[13] A more important limitation is that the test is difficult to generalize to the GARCH case. Lee (1991) and Lee and King (1993) present such a generalization, but as discussed in Bollerslev, Engle, and Nelson (1994), the GARCH parameters cannot be separately identified in models close to the null—the LM test for GARCH(1, 1) is the same as that for ARCH(1).

Thus, less formal diagnostics are often used, such as the sample autocorrelation function of squared residuals. McLeod and Li (1983) show that under the null hypothesis of no nonlinear dependence among the residuals from an ARMA model, the vector of normalized sample autocorrelations of the squared residuals,

$$\sqrt{T}\hat{\rho}_{\varepsilon^2}(\tau) = \sqrt{T}\frac{\sum_{t=\tau+1}^{T}(\hat{\varepsilon}_t^2 - \hat{\sigma}^2)(\hat{\varepsilon}_{t-\tau}^2 - \hat{\sigma}^2)}{\sum_{t=1}^{T}(\hat{\varepsilon}_t^2 - \hat{\sigma}^2)^2},$$

where $\hat{\sigma}^2$ is the estimated residual variance and $\tau = 1, \ldots, m$, is asymptotically distributed as a multivariate normal with a zero mean and a unit covariance matrix. Moreover, the associated Ljung-Box statistic,

$$\hat{Q}_{\varepsilon^2}(m) = T(T+2)\sum_{\tau=1}^{m}\frac{\hat{\rho}_{\varepsilon^2}(\tau)^2}{T - \tau},$$

is asymptotically $\chi^2_{(m)}$ under the null. If the null is rejected, then nonlinear dependence, such as GARCH, may be present.[14]

After fitting a GARCH model, it is often of interest to test the null hypothesis that the standardized residuals are conditionally homoskedastic. Bollerslev and Mikkelsen (1993) argue that one may use the Ljung-Box statistic on the squared standardized residual autocorrelations, but that the significance of the statistic should be tested using a $\chi^2_{(m-k)}$ distribution, where k is the number of estimated GARCH parameters. This adjustment is necessary due to the deflation associated with fitting the conditional variance model.

A related testing issue concerns the effect of GARCH innovations on tests for *other* deviations from classical behavior. Diebold (1987, 1988) examines the impact of GARCH effects on two standard serial correlation diagnostics, the Bartlett standard errors and the Ljung-Box statistic. As is well-known, in the large-sample Gaussian white-noise case,

$$\hat{\rho}(\tau) \overset{\text{i.i.d.}}{\sim} N\left[0, \frac{1}{T}\right], \tau = 1, 2, \ldots$$

and

$$\hat{Q}(m) = T(T+2)\sum_{\tau=1}^{m}\frac{1}{(T-\tau)}\hat{\rho}(\tau)^2 \overset{a}{\sim} \chi^2_{(m)},$$

where $\hat{\rho}(\tau)$ denotes the sample autocorrelation at lag τ. In the GARCH case, however, an adjustment must be made,

$$\hat{\rho}(\tau) \overset{\text{i.i.d.}}{\sim} N\left(0, \frac{1}{T}\left[1 + \frac{\gamma_{y^2}(\tau)}{\sigma^4}\right]\right), \tau = 1, 2, \ldots,$$

where $\gamma_{y^2}(\tau)$ denotes the autocovariance function of y_t^2 at lag τ and σ^4 is the squared unconditional variance of y_t. The adjustment is largest for small τ and decreases monotonically as $\tau \to \infty$ if the process is covariance stationary. Similarly, the robust Ljung-Box statistic is

$$\hat{Q}(m) = T(T + 2)\sum_{\tau=1}^{m} \frac{1}{(T - \tau)}\left[\frac{\sigma^4}{\sigma^4 + \gamma_{y^2}(\tau)}\right]\hat{\rho}(\tau)^2 \overset{a}{\sim} \chi^2_{(m)}.$$

The formulas are made operational by replacing the unknown population parameters with the usual consistent estimators.

It is important to note that the standard error adjustment serves to *increase* the standard errors; failure to perform the adjustment results in standard error bands that are "too tight." Similarly, failure to adjust the Ljung-Box statistic causes empirical test size to be larger then nominal size—often *much* larger, due to the cumulation of distortions through summation. Thus, failure to use robust serial correlation diagnostics for GARCH effects may produce a spurious impression of serial correlation.

A more general approach that yields robust sample autocovariances and related statistics is obtained by adopting a generalized method of moments (GMM) perspective, as proposed by West and Cho (1994).[15] Define $X_t = (\varepsilon_t^2, \varepsilon_t \varepsilon_{t-1}, \ldots, \varepsilon_t \varepsilon_{t-m})'$, $\theta = (E[\varepsilon_t^2], E[\varepsilon_t \varepsilon_{t-1}], \ldots, E[\varepsilon_t \varepsilon_{t-m}])'$ and $g_t(\theta) = X_t - \theta$ as $((m + 1) \times 1)$ vectors and $\hat{\theta}_{GMM}$ as the value of θ that satisfies the condition

$$\frac{1}{T - m}\sum_{t=m+1}^{T} g_t(\hat{\theta}_{GMM}) = 0.$$

Note that, because there are as many parameters being estimated as there are orthogonality conditions, GMM simply yields the standard point estimates of the autocovariances. Their standard errors and related test statistics are asymptotically robust, because as shown by Hansen (1982) under general conditions allowing for heteroskedasticity and serial correlation of unknown form, $\sqrt{T}(\hat{\theta}_{GMM} - \theta) \, \mathbf{a} \, N(0, V)$ where

$$V = \left\{E\left[\frac{\partial g_t(\hat{\theta}_{GMM})}{\partial \theta}\right]S^{-1}E\left[\frac{\partial g_t(\hat{\theta}_{GMM})}{\partial \theta}\right]'\right\}^{-1}$$

and S is the spectral density matrix of $g_t(\theta)$ at frequency zero. This expression for V is made operational by replacing all population objects with consistent estimates. The GMM-estimated autocovariances of y_t and their standard errors will be robust to possible conditional heteroskedasticity in ε_t, as will the Ljung-Box statistic computed using the GMM-estimated autocovariances.

Applications and Extensions

There are numerous applications and extensions of the basic GARCH model. In this section, we highlight those that we judge most important in macroeconomic and financial contexts. It is natural to discuss applications and extensions simultaneously because many of the extensions are motivated by applications.

Functional Form and Density Form

Numerous alternative functional forms for the conditional variance have been suggested in the literature.[16] One of the most interesting is Nelson's (1991) exponential GARCH(p, q) or EGARCH(p, q) model,

$$y_t = \varepsilon_t = h_t^{1/2} z_t,$$

$$z_t \overset{\text{i.i.d.}}{\sim} N(0, 1),$$

$$ln(h_t) = \omega + \sum_{i=1}^{p} \alpha_i g(z_{t-i}) + \sum_{i=1}^{q} \beta_i ln(h_{t-i}),$$

$$g(z_t) = \theta z_t + \gamma(|z_t| - E[|z_t|]).$$

The log specification ensures that the conditional variance is positive, and the model allows for an asymmetric response to the z_t innovations depending on their sign. Thus, the effect of a negative innovation on volatility may differ from that of a positive innovation. This allowance for asymmetric response has proved useful for modeling the "leverage effect" in the stock market described by Black (1976).[17]

With respect to density from, non-Gaussian conditional distributions are easily incorporated into the GARCH model. This is important, because it is commonly found that the Gaussian GARCH model does not explain all of the leptokurtosis in asset returns. With this in mind, Bollerslev (1987) proposes a conditionally student-t GARCH model, in which the degrees-of-freedom is treated as another parameter to be estimated. Alternatively, Engle and González-Rivera (1991) propose a semiparametric methodology in which the conditional variance function is parametrically specified in the usual fashion, but the conditional density is estimated nonparametrically.

GARCH-M: Time-Varying Risk Premia

Consider a regression model with GARCH disturbances of the usual sort, with one additional twist: the conditional variance enters as a regressor, thereby affecting the conditional mean. Write the model as

$$y_t = x_t'\beta + \gamma h_t + \varepsilon_t,$$

$$\varepsilon_t \mid \Omega_{t-1} \sim N(0, h_t).$$

This GARCH-in-Mean (GARCH-M) model is useful in modeling the relationship between risk and return when risk (as measured by the conditional variance) varies. Engle, Lillien, and Robins (1987) introduce the model and use it to examine time-varying risk premia in the term structure of interest rates.

IGARCH: Persistence in Variance

A special case of the GARCH model is the integrated GARCH (IGARCH) model, introduced by Engle and Bollerslev (1986). A GARCH(p, q) process is integrated of order one in variance if $1 - \alpha(L) - \beta(L) = 0$ has a root on the unit circle. The IGARCH process is potentially important because, as an empirical matter, GARCH roots near unity are common in high-frequency financial data.

The earlier ARMA result for the squared GARCH process now becomes an ARIMA result for the squared IGARCH process. As before, $\varepsilon_t^2 = \omega + [\alpha(L) + \beta(L)]\varepsilon_t^2 - \beta(L)v_t + v_t$; thus, $[1 - \alpha(L) - \beta(L)]\varepsilon_t^2 = \omega - \beta(L)v_t + v_t$. When the autoregressive polynomial contains a unit root, it can be rewritten as

$$[1 - \alpha(L) - \beta(L)]\varepsilon_t^2 = \phi(L)(1-L)\varepsilon_t^2 = \omega - \beta(L)v_t + v_t.$$

Thus, the differenced squared process is of stationary ARMA form.

Unlike the conditional prediction error variance for the covariance stationary GARCH process, the IGARCH conditional prediction error variance does not converge as the forecast horizon lengthens; instead, it grows linearly with the length of the forecast horizon. Formally, $E[\varepsilon_{t+k}^2 \mid \Omega_t] = (k - 1)\omega + h_{t+1}$ so that $\lim_{k \to \infty} E[\varepsilon_{t+k}^2 \mid \Omega_t] = \infty$. Thus, the IGARCH process has an infinite unconditional variance.

Clearly, a parallel exists between the IGARCH process and the vast literature on unit roots in conditional mean dynamics (see Stock, 1994). This parallel, however, is partly superficial. In particular, Nelson (1990b) shows that the IGARCH(1, 1) process (with $\omega \neq 0$) is nevertheless strictly stationary and ergodic, which leads one to suspect that likelihood-based inference may proceed in the standard fashion. This conjecture is verified in the theoretical and Monte Carlo work of Lee and Hansen (1994) and Lumsdaine (1992, 1995).

Although conditional variance dynamics are often empirically found to be highly persistent, it is difficult to ascertain whether they are actually integrated. (Again, this difficulty parallels the unit root literature.) Circumstantial evidence against IGARCH arises from several sources, such as temporal aggregation. Little is known about the temporal aggregation of IGARCH processes, but due to the infinite unconditional second moment, we conjecture that a Gaussian central limit theorem is unattainable. (To the best of our knowledge, no existing Gaussian central limit theorems are applicable.) If so, this bodes poorly for the IGARCH model, because actual series displaying GARCH effects seem to approach normality when temporally aggregated. It would then appear likely that highly persistent covariance-stationary GARCH models, not IGARCH models, provide a better approximation to conditional variance dynamics.

The possibility also arises that some findings of IGARCH may be due to misspecification of the conditional variance function. In particular, Diebold (1986) suggests that the appearance of IGARCH could be an artifact resulting from failure to allow for structural breaks in the unconditional variance, if in fact such breaks exist. This is borne out in various contexts by Lastrapes (1989), Lamoureux and Lastrapes (1990), and Hamilton and Susmel (1994). Accordingly, Chu (1993) suggests procedures for testing parameter instability in GARCH models.

Stochastic Volatility Models

A simple first-order stochastic volatility model is given by

$$\varepsilon_t = \sigma_t z_t = \exp\left[\frac{h_t}{2}\right] z_t,$$

$$z_t \sim N(0, 1),$$

$$h_t = \omega + \beta h_{t-1} + \eta_t,$$

$$\eta_t \sim N(0, \sigma_\eta^2).$$

Thus, as opposed to standard GARCH models, h_t is not deterministic conditional on Ω_{t-1}; the conditional variance evolves as a first-order autoregressive process driven by a separate innovation. Moreover, the exponential specification ensures that the conditional variance remains positive. It is clear that the stochastic volatility model is intimately related to Clark's (1973) subordinated stochastic process model: in fact, for all practical purposes, it *is* Clark's model. For further details, see Harvey, Ruiz, and Shephard (1994), and for alternative approaches to estimation, which can be challenging, see Jacquier, Polson, and Rossi (1994) and Kim and Shephard (1994). Although there has been substantial recent interest in stochastic volatility models, their empirical success relative to GARCH models has yet to be established.

Multivariate GARCH Models

Cross-variable interactions are key in macroeconomics and finance. Multivariate GARCH models are used to capture cross-variable conditional volatility interactions. The first multivariate GARCH model, developed by Kraft and Engle (1982), is a multivariate generalization of the pure ARCH model. The multivariate GARCH (p, q) model is proposed in Bollerslev, Engle, and Wooldridge (1988). The N-dimensional Gaussian GARCH(p, q) process is $\varepsilon_t \mid \Omega_{t-1} \sim N(0, H_t)$, where H_t is the $(N \times N)$ conditional covariance matrix given by

$$\text{vech}(H_t) = W + \sum_{i=1}^{q} A_i \text{vech}(\varepsilon_{t-i}\varepsilon_{t-i}') + \sum_{j=1}^{p} B_i \text{vech}(H_t),$$

vech(.) is the vector-half operator that converts $(N \times N)$ matrices into $(N(N+1)/2 \times 1)$ vectors of their lower triangular elements, W is an $(N(N+1)/2 \times 1)$ parameter vector, and A_i and B_j are $((N(N+1)/2) \times (N(N+1)/2))$ parameter matrices. Likelihood-based estimation and inference are conceptually straightforward and parallel the univariate case. The approximate log likelihood function for the conditionally Gaussian multivariate GARCH(p, q) process, aside from a constant, is

$$\ln L(\theta; \varepsilon_j, \ldots, \varepsilon_T) = -\frac{1}{2}\sum_{t=j}^{T} \ln|H_t| - \frac{1}{2}\sum_{t=j}^{T} \varepsilon_t' H_t^{-1} \varepsilon_t \,; j \geq 1.$$

In practice, however, two complications arise. First, the conditions needed to ensure that H_t is positive definite are complex and difficult to verify. Second, the model lacks parsimony; an unrestricted parameterization of H_t is too profligate to be of much empirical use. As written above, the model has $(N(N+1)/2)[1 + (p + q)N(N+1)/2] = O(N^4)$ parameters, which makes numerical maximization of the likelihood function extremely difficult, even for low values of N, p, and q.

Various strategies have been proposed to deal with the positive definiteness and parsimony complications. Engle and Kroner (1993) propose restrictions that

guarantee positive definiteness without entirely ignoring these cross-variable interactions. Bollerslev, Engle, and Wooldridge (1988) enforce further parsimony by
requiring that the A_i and B_i matrices be diagonal, reducing the number of parameters to $(N(N + 1)/2)[1 + p + q] = O(N^2)$. However, the parsimony of this
"diagonal" model comes at potentially high cost because much of the potential
cross-variable volatility interaction, a key point of multivariate analysis, is assumed away.

Common Volatility Patterns: Multivariate Models with Factor Structure

Multivariate models with factor structure, such as the latent-factor GARCH model
(Diebold and Nerlove, 1989) and the factor GARCH model (Engle, 1987; Bollerslev
and Engle, 1993), capture the idea of commonality of volatility shocks, which
appears empirically relevant in systems of asset returns in the stock, foreign
exchange, and bond markets.[18] Models with factor structure are also parsimonious
and are easily constrained to maintain positive definiteness of the conditional
covariance matrix.

In the latent-factor model, movements in each of the N time series are driven
by an idiosyncratic shock and a set of $k < N$ common latent shocks or "factors."[19]
The latent factors display GARCH effects, whereas the idiosyncratic shocks are
i.i.d. and orthogonal at all leads and lags. The one-factor model is important in
practice, and we describe it in some detail. The model is written as $\varepsilon_t = \lambda F_t + v_t$,
where ε_t, λ, and v_t are $(N \times 1)$ vectors and F_t is a scalar. F_t and v_t have zero
conditional means and are orthogonal at all leads and lags. The factor F_t follows
a GARCH(p, q) process,

$$F_t \mid \Omega_{t-1} \sim N(0, h_t)$$

$$h_t = \omega + \alpha(L)F_t^2 + \beta(L)h_t,$$

so that the conditional distribution of the observed vector is

$$\varepsilon_t \mid \Omega_{t-1} \sim N(0, H_t),$$

$$H_t = \lambda\lambda'h_t + \Gamma,$$

where $\Gamma = \text{cov}(v_t) = \text{diag}(\gamma_1, \ldots, \gamma_N)$. Thus, the jth time-t conditional variance is

$$H_{jj,t} = \lambda_j^2 h_t + \gamma_j = \lambda_j^2\left[\omega + \sum_{i=1}^{p}\alpha_i F_{t-i}^2 + \sum_{i=1}^{q}\beta_i h_{t-i}\right] + \gamma_j,$$

and the j, k^{th} time-t conditional covariance is

Factor-GARCH Series 1   Factor-GARCH Series 2

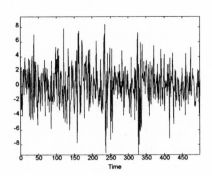

Figure 11.7. The two factor-GARCH series

$$H_{jk,t} = \lambda_j \lambda_k \, h_t = \lambda_j \lambda_k \left[\omega + \sum_{i=1}^{p} \alpha_i F_{t-i}^2 + \sum_{i=1}^{q} \beta_i h_{t-i} \right].$$

Note that the latent factor F_t is unobservable and not directly included in $\Omega_{t-1} = \{\varepsilon_{t-1}, \ldots, \varepsilon_1\}$. Effectively, the latent-factor model is a stochastic volatility model.

In general, the number of parameters in the k-factor model is $N(k + 1) + k^2(1 + p + q) = O(N)$, so the number of parameters in the one-factor case is $2N + (1 + p + q)$, a drastic reduction relative to the general multivariate case. Moreover, the conditional covariance matrix is guaranteed to be positive definite, so long as the conditional variances of the common and idiosyncratic factors are constrained to be positive.

A simulated realization from a bivariate model with one common GARCH(1, 1) factor is shown in Figures 11.7, 11.8, and 11.9. The model is parameterized as

$$\begin{bmatrix} \varepsilon_{1t} \\ \varepsilon_{2t} \end{bmatrix} = \begin{bmatrix} 0.6 \\ 0.9 \end{bmatrix} F_t + \begin{bmatrix} v_{1t} \\ v_{2t} \end{bmatrix},$$

$$F_t \mid \Omega_{t-1} \sim N(0, h_t),$$

$$h_t = 1 + .2F_{t-1}^2 + .7h_{t-1},$$

$$(v_{1t}, v_{2t})' \overset{\text{i.i.d.}}{\sim} N(0, I).$$

The realization of the common factor underlying the system is precisely the one presented in our earlier discussion of univariate GARCH models. The latent-factor GARCH series exhibit the volatility clustering present in the common factor. As

Factor-GARCH Series 1 Squared   Factor-GARCH Series 2 Squared

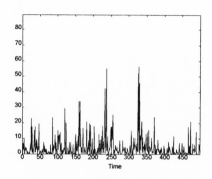   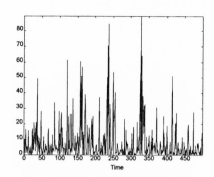

Figure 11.8.   The squared factor-GARCH series

before, the squared realizations of the two series indicate a degree of persistence in volatility. Furthermore, as expected, the conditional second moments of the two series are similar to that of F_t because, as shown above, they are simply multiples of h_t.

Diebold and Nerlove (1989) suggest a two-step estimation procedure. The first step entails performing a standard factor analysis—that is, factoring the unconditional covariance matrix as $H = \lambda \lambda' \sigma^2 + \Gamma$, where σ^2 is the unconditional variance of F_t, and extracting an estimate of the time series of factor values $\{\hat{F}_t\}_{t=1}^T$. The second step entails estimating the latent-factor GARCH model treating the extracted factor series $\hat{F}_t$ as if it were the actual series F_t.

The Diebold-Nerlove procedure is clearly suboptimal relative to fully simultaneous maximum likelihood estimation because the $\hat{F}_t$ series is not equal to the F_t series, even asymptotically. Harvey, Ruiz, and Sentana (1992) provide a better approximation to the exact likelihood function that involves a correction factor to account for the fact that the F_t series is unobservable.[20] For example, using an ARCH(1) specification, the conditional variance of the latent factor F_t in the Diebold-Nerlove model is

$$h_t = \text{var}(F_t \mid \Omega_{t-1}) = \omega + \alpha F_{t-1}^2 = \omega + \alpha E[F_{t-1}^2 \mid \Omega_{t-1}].$$

Using the identity $F_{t-1} = \hat{F}_{t-1} + (F_{t-1} - \hat{F}_{t-1})$,

$$E[F_{t-1}^2 \mid \Omega_{t-1}] = E[(\hat{F}_{t-1} + (F_{t-1} - \hat{F}_{t-1}))^2 \mid \Omega_{t-1}] = E[\hat{F}_{t-1}^2 \mid \Omega_{t-1}] + p_{t-1}$$

$$= \hat{F}_{t-1}^2 + p_{t-1},$$

Conditional Variance of Series 1

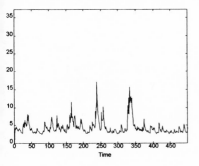

Sample Autocorrelation Function

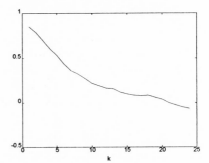

Conditional Variance of Series 2

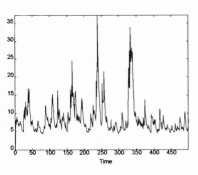

Sample Autocorrelation Function

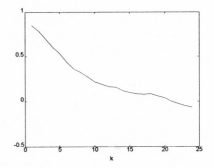

Conditional Covariance

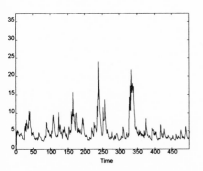

Sample Autocorrelation Function

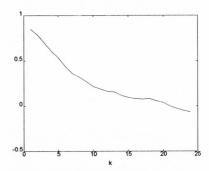

Figure 11.9. The conditional variance of the two factor-GARCH series and their conditional covariance as well on the corresponding sample autocorrelation functions

where p_{t-1} is the correction factor. Thus, h_t is expressed as $h_t = \omega + \alpha(\hat{F}_{t-1} + p_{t-1})$. The correction factor can be constructed using the appropriate elements in the conditional covariance matrix of the state vector estimated by the Kalman filter.

Finally, we note that recently developed Markov-chain Monte Carlo techniques facilitate exact maximum-likelihood estimation of the latent-factor model (or, more precisely, approximate maximum-likelihood estimation with the crucial distinction that the approximation error is under the user's control and can be made as small as possible). For details see Kim and Shephard (1994).

Optimal Prediction Under Asymmetric Loss

Volatility forecasts are readily generated from GARCH models and used for a variety of purposes, such as producing improved interval forecasts, as discussed previously. Less obvious but equally true is the fact that, under asymmetric loss, volatility dynamics can be exploited to produce improved *point* forecasts, as shown by Christoffersen and Diebold (1994). If, for example, y_{t+k} is normally distributed with conditional mean $\mu_{t+k} \mid \Omega_t$ and conditional variance $h_{t+k} \mid \Omega_t$ and $L(e_{t+k})$ is any loss function defined on the k-step-ahead prediction error $e_{t+k} = y_{t+k} - \hat{y}_{t+k}$, then the optimal predictor is $\hat{y}_{t+k} = \mu_{t+k} \mid \Omega_t + \alpha_t$, where α_t depends only on the loss function and the conditional prediction error variance $\text{var}(e_{t+k} \mid \Omega_t) = \text{var}(y_{t+k} \mid \Omega_t) = h_{t+k} \mid \Omega_t$. The optimal predictor under asymmetric loss is *not* the conditional mean, but rather the conditional mean shifted by a time-varying adjustment that depends on the conditional variance. The intuition for this is simple: when, for example, positive prediction errors are more costly than negative errors, a negative conditionally expected error is desirable and is induced by setting the bias $\alpha_t > 0$. The optimal amount of bias depends on the conditional prediction error variance of the process. As the conditional variation around $\mu_{t+k} \mid \Omega_t$ grows, so too does the optimal amount of bias needed to avoid large positive prediction errors.

To illustrate this idea, consider the linlin loss function, so-named for its linearity on each side of the origin (albeit with possibly different slopes):

$$L(y_{t+k} - \hat{y}_{t+k}) = \begin{cases} a \mid y_{t+k} - \hat{y}_{t+k} \mid, \text{ if } y_{t+k} - \hat{y}_{t+k} > 0 \\ b \mid y_{t+k} - \hat{y}_{t+k} \mid, \text{ if } y_{t+k} - \hat{y}_{t+k} \leq 0. \end{cases}$$

Christoffersen and Diebold (1994) show that the optimal predictor of y_{t+k} under this loss function is

$$\hat{y}_{t+k} = \mu_{t+k} \mid \Omega_t + (h_{t+k} \mid \Omega_t)^{1/2} \Phi^{-1} \left[\frac{a}{a+b} \right],$$

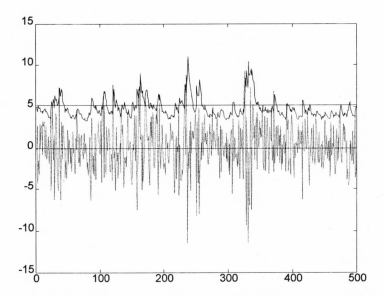

Figure 11.10.   GARCH(1, 1) realization with linlin optimal, pseudo-optimal, and conditional mean predictors
Notes: The linlin loss parameters are set to a = .95 and b = .05, so that a/(a + b) = .95. The GARCH(1, 1) parameters are set to α = .2 and β = .70. The dotted line is the GARCH(1, 1) realization. The horizontal line at zero is the conditional mean predictor, the horizontal line at 1.65 is the pseudo-optimal predictor, and the time-varying solid line is the optimal predictor.

where Φ is the Gaussian cumulative density function. In contrast, a pseudo-optimal predictor, which accounts for loss asymmetry but not conditional variance dynamics, is

$$\hat{y}_{t+k} = \mu_{t+k} \mid \Omega_t + \sigma_k \Phi^{-1}\left[\frac{a}{a+b}\right],$$

where σ_k^2 is the unconditional variance of y_{t+k}.

In Figure 11.10, we show our GARCH(1,1) realization together with the one-step-ahead linlin-optimal, pseudo-optimal, and conditional mean predictors for the loss parameters $a = .95$ and $b = .05$. Note that the optimal predictor injects more bias when conditional volatility is high, reflecting the fact that it accounts for both loss asymmetry and conditional heteroskedasticity. This conditionally optimal amount of bias may be more or less than the constant bias associated with the pseudo-optimal predictor. Of course, the conditional-mean predictor injects no bias, as it accounts for neither loss asymmetry nor conditional heteroskedasticity.

Evaluating Volatility Forecasts

Although volatility forecast accuracy comparisons are often conducted using mean-squared error, loss functions that explicitly incorporate the forecast user's economic loss function are more relevant and may lead to different rankings of models. West, Edison, and Cho (1993) and Engle et al. (1993) make important contributions along those lines, proposing economic loss functions based on utility maximization and profit maximization, respectively.

Lopez (1995) proposes a volatility forecast evaluation framework that sub-sumes a variety of economic loss functions. The framework is based on transform-ing a model's volatility forecasts into probability forecasts by integrating over the distribution of ε_t. By selecting the range of integration corresponding to an event of interest, a forecast user can incorporate elements of her loss function into the probability forecasts. For example, given $\varepsilon_t \mid \Omega_{t-1} \sim D(0, h_t)$ and a volatility forecast $\hat{h}_t$, an options trader interested in the event $\varepsilon_t \in [L_{\varepsilon,t}, U_{\varepsilon,t}]$ would generate the probability forecast

$$P_t = Pr(L_{\varepsilon,t} < \varepsilon_t < U_{\varepsilon,t}) = Pr\left(\frac{L_{\varepsilon,t}}{\sqrt{\hat{h}_t}} < z_t < \frac{U_{\varepsilon,t}}{\sqrt{\hat{h}_t}}\right) = \int_{l_{\varepsilon,t}}^{u_{\varepsilon,t}} f(z_t) dz_t,$$

where z_t is the standardized innovation, $f(z_t)$ is the functional form of the distribu-tion $D(0, 1)$, and $[l_{\varepsilon,t}, u_{\varepsilon,t}]$ is the standardized range of integration. In contrast, a forecast user such as a portfolio manager or a central bank interested in the behavior of $y_t = \mu_t + \varepsilon_t$, where $\mu_t = E[y_t \mid \Omega_{t-1}]$, would generate the probability forecast

$$P_t = Pr(L_{y,t} < y_t < U_{y,t}) = Pr\left(\frac{L_{y,t} - \hat{\mu}_t}{\sqrt{\hat{h}_t}} < z_t < \frac{U_{y,t} - \hat{\mu}_t}{\sqrt{\hat{h}_t}}\right) = \int_{l_{y,t}}^{u_{y,t}} f(z_t) dz_t,$$

where $\hat{\mu}_t$ is the forecasted conditional mean and $(l_{y,T+t}, u_{y,T+t})$ is the standardized range of integration.

The probability forecasts so-generated can be evaluated using statistical tools tailored to the user's loss function. In particular, probability scoring rules can be used to assess the accuracy of the probability forecasts, and the significance of differences across models can be tested using a generalization of the Diebold-Mariano (1995) procedure. Moreover, the calibration tests of Seillier-Moiseiwitsch and Dawid (1993) can be used to examine the degree of equivalence between an event's predicted and observed frequencies of occurrence within subsets of the probability forecasts specified by the user.

Directions for Future Research

Fifteen years ago, little attention was paid to conditional volatility dynamics in modeling macroeconomic and financial time series; the situation has since changed dramatically. GARCH and related models have proved tremendously useful in modeling such dynamics. However, perhaps in contrast to the impression we may have created, we believe that the literature on modeling conditional volatility dynamics is far from settled and that complacency with the ubiquitous GARCH(1, 1) model is not justified.

Almost without exception, low-ordered (and hence potentially restrictive) GARCH models are used in applied work. For example, among hundreds of empirical applications of the GARCH model, almost all casually and uncritically adopt the GARCH(1, 1) specification. EGARCH applications have followed suit with the vast majority adopting the EGARCH(1, 1) specification. Similarly, applications of the stochastic volatility model typically use an AR(1) specification. However, recent findings suggest that such specifications—as well as the models themselves, regardless of the particular specification—are often too restrictive to maintain fidelity to the data.

It appears, for example, that the conditional volatility dynamics of stock market returns (as well as certain other asset returns) contain long memory. Ding, Engle, and Granger (1993) find positive and significant sample autocorrelations for daily S&P 500 returns at up to 2,500 lags and that their rate of decay is slower than exponential. A model consistent with such long-memory volatility findings is the fractionally integrated GARCH (FIGARCH) model developed by Baillie, Bollerslev, and Mikkelsen (1993), building on earlier work by Robinson (1991). FIGARCH is a model of fractionally integrated conditional variance dynamics, in parallel to the well-known fractionally integrated ARMA models of conditional mean dynamics (see Granger and Joyeux, 1980). The FIGARCH model implies a hyperbolic rate of decay for the autocorrelations of the squared process that is slower than exponential.

To motivate the FIGARCH process, begin with the GARCH(1, 1) process,

$$y_t = \varepsilon_t,$$

$$\varepsilon_t \mid \Omega_{t-1} \sim N(0, h_t),$$

$$h_t = \omega + \alpha(L)\varepsilon_t^2 + \beta(L)h_t.$$

Autocorrelation Function-S&P
$|\epsilon|$ - Jan 28 to May 90

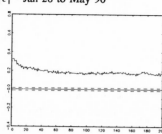

Autocorrelation Function-S&P
ϵ^2 - Jan 28 to May 90

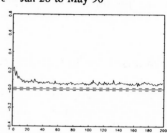

Figure 11.11. Autocorrelation function—S&P ($|\varepsilon|$ Jan. 1928 to May 1990), and autocorrelation function—S&P (ε^2, Jan. 1928 to May 1990)

Rearranging the conditional variance into ARMA form, the FIGARCH (p, d, q) equation is

$$[1 - \alpha(L) - \beta(L)]\varepsilon_t^2 = \phi(L)(1 - L)^d \varepsilon_t^2 = \omega + (1 - \beta(L))v_t.$$

That is, the $[1 - \alpha(L) - \beta(L)]$ polynomial can be factored into a stationary ARMA component and a long-memory difference operator. If $0 < d < 1$, the process is FIGARCH(p, d, q). If $d = 0$, then the standard GARCH(p, q) model obtains; if $d = 1$, then the IGARCH(p, q) model obtains. Bollerslev and Mikkelsen (1993) conjecture that the coefficients in the ARCH representation of a FIGARCH process $(d < 1)$ are dominated by those of an IGARCH process. If so, then FIGARCH $(d < 1)$ would be strictly stationary (though not covariance stationary) because IGARCH is strictly stationary.

Long memory is only one of many previously unnoticed features of volatility. Interestingly, as we study volatility more carefully, more and more anomalies emerge. Volatility patterns turn out to differ across assets, time periods, and transformations of the data. The complacency with the "standard" CARCH model is being shattered, and we think it unlikely that any one consensus model will take its place. The implications of this development are twofold. First, real care must be taken in tailoring volatility models to the relevant data, as in Engle and Ng (1993). Second, because all volatility models are likely to be misspecified, care should be taken in assessing models' robustness to misspecification.

To illustrate the deviations from classical GARCH models that turn out to be routinely present in real data, we present in Figure 11.11 the sample autocorrelation functions of the absolute and squared change in the log daily closing value of the S&P 500 stock index, 1928–1990. The autocorrelation functions are shown to displacement $\tau = 200$ in order to assess the evidence for long memory, and dashed lines indicate the Bartlett 95 percent confidence interval for white noise. Note that

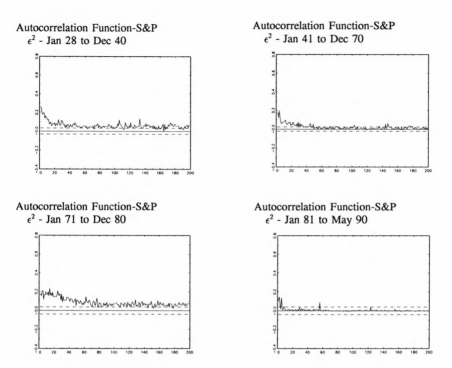

Autocorrelation Function-S&P
ϵ^2 - Jan 28 to Dec 40

Autocorrelation Function-S&P
ϵ^2 - Jan 41 to Dec 70

Autocorrelation Function-S&P
ϵ^2 - Jan 71 to Dec 80

Autocorrelation Function-S&P
ϵ^2 - Jan 81 to May 90

Figure 11.12.   Autocorrelation function—S&P (ε^2, Jan. 1928 to Dec. 1940), auto-correlation function—S&P(ε^2, Jan. 1941 to Dec. 1970), autocorrelation function—S&P (ε^2, Jan. 1971 to Dec. 1980), and autocorrelation function—S&P (ε^2, Jan. 1981 to May 1990)

substantially more persistence is found in absolute returns than in squared returns, in keeping with Ding, Engle, and Granger (1993), and that both absolute and squared returns appear too persistent to accord with any of the "standard" volatility models. In addition, these patterns are different over time. In Figure 11.12, we show squared returns over various subperiods: 1928–1940, 1941–1970, 1971–1980, and 1981–1990. It seems clear that most of the long memory is driven by the 1928–1940 period. To the extent that there is any long memory in the post-1940 period, it seems to be coming from the 1970s. Interestingly, there seems to be *no* GARCH effects in the 1980s as shown by the negligible autocorrelations for ε_t^2.

Other assets, including interest rates, foreign exchange rates, and other stock indexes, display a bewildering variety of volatility patterns, as discussed in Mor (1994). Sometimes there seems to be long memory; sometimes not. Sometimes the autocorrelation patterns of ε_t^2 match those of $|\varepsilon_t|$, and sometimes the autocorrelation patterns of $|\varepsilon_t|$ appear much more persistent. The patterns differ across assets and often seem to indicate structural change. For example, the long memory seemingly present in exchange rate volatility seems concentrated in the 1970s, while long memory in interest rate volatility is typically concentrated in the 1980s. These observed phenomena, as well as occasional long-horizon spikes in autocorrelations and the appearance of oscillatory autocorrelation behavior, are again inconsistent with standard specifications.

An additional illustration of the inadequacies of GARCH models is provided by West and Cho (1994). Using weekly exchange rates, they show that for horizons longer than one week, out-of-sample GARCH volatility forecasts loose their value, even though volatility seems highly persistent. The good in-sample performance of GARCH models breaks down rapidly out-of-sample.[21] In addition, standard tests of forecast optimality, such as regressions of realized squared returns on an intercept and the GARCH forecast, strongly reject the null of the optimality of the GARCH forecast with respect to available information. West and Cho (1994) suggest time-varying parameters and discrete shifts in the mean level of volatility as possible explanations.

In light of the emerging evidence that GARCH models are likely misspecified and the unlikely occurrence of happening upon a "correct" specification, it is of interest to consider whether GARCH models might still perform adequately in tracking and forecasting volatility—that is, whether their good properties are robust to misspecification. In a series of papers (Nelson, 1990a, 1992, 1993; Nelson and Foster, 1991, 1994), Nelson and Foster find that the usefulness of GARCH models in volatility tracking and short-term volatility forecasting is robust to a variety of types of misspecification; thus, in spite of misspecification, GARCH models can consistently extract conditional variances from high-frequency time series. More specifically, if a process is well approximated by a continuous-time diffusion, then broad classes of GARCH models provide consistent estimates of the instantaneous conditional variance as the sampling frequency increases. This occurs because the sequence of GARCH(1, 1) models used to form estimates of next period's conditional variance average increasing numbers of squared residuals from the increasingly recent past. In this way, a sequence of GARCH(1, 1) models can consistently estimate next period's conditional variance despite potentially severe misspecification.

Acknowledgments

Helpful comments were received from Richard Baillie, Tim Bollerslev, Pedro de Lima, Wayne Ferson, Kevin Hoover, Peter Robinson, and Til Schuermann. We gratefully acknowledge the support of the National Science Foundation, the Sloan Foundation, and the University of Pennsylvania Research Foundation.

Notes

1. ARCH is short for autoregressive conditional heteroskedasticity.

2. A process is linearly deterministic if it can be predicted to any desired degree of accuracy by linear projection on sufficiently many past observations.

3. Recall that the defining characteristic of white noise is a lack of serial correlation, which is a weaker condition than serial independence.

4. The obvious empirically useful approximation to an LRCSSP (which is an infinite-ordered moving average) with infinite-ordered ARCH errors is an ARMA process with GARCH errors. See Weiss (1984), who studies ARMA processes with finite-ordered ARCH errors. (The GARCH process had not yet been invented.)

5. Nelson and Cao (1992) show that, for higher-order GARCH processes, the nonnegativity constraints are sufficient, but not necessary, for the conditional variance to be positive.

6. See, for example, Jorgenson (1966).

7. Setting $y_0 = 0$ and $h_0 = E(y_t^2)$, we generate 1,500 observations, and we discard the first 1,000 to eliminate the effects of the start-up values.

8. The parameter values for α and β are typical of the parameter estimates reported in the empirical literature.

9. For a precise statement of the necessary and sufficient condition for finite kurtosis, see Bollerslev (1986).

10. Their results, however, require a finite fourth unconditional moment, a condition likely to be violated in financial contexts.

11. Alternative approaches may of course be taken. Geweke (1989), for example, discusses Bayesian procedures.

12. Generalization to the GARCH case has not yet been done.

13. However, Bollersley, and Wooldridge (1992) introduce a modified LM test robust to non-normal conditional distributions.

14. As always, rejection of the null does not imply acceptance of the alternative. Tests for conditional heteroskedasticity, for example, often have power against alternatives of serial correlation as well; see Engle, Hendry, and Trumble (1985).

15. Robinson (1991) also treats the issue of robustness by proposing general classes of heteroskedasticity-robust serial correlation tests and serial correlation-robust heteroskedasticirty tests.

16. In fact, Robinson (1987) goes so far as to propose nonparametric estimation of the conditional variance function, thereby eliminating the need for parametric specification of functional form.

17. Negative shocks appear to contribute more to stock market volatility than do positive shocks. This phenomenon is called the leverage effect, because a negative shock to the market value of equity increases the aggregate debt-equity ratio (other things the same), thereby increasing leverage.

18. Models of "copersistence" in variance and cointegration in variance are based on similar ideas (see Bollerslev and Engle, 1993).

19. Despite the similarity in their names, the latent-factor GARCH model discussed here is different from the factor GARCH model. In the latent-factor GARCH case, the observed variables are linear combinations of latent GARCH processes, whereas in the factor GARCH case, linear combinations of the observed variables follow univariate GARCH processes. As pointed out by Sentana (1992), the difference between the two models is similar to the difference between standard factor analysis and principal components analysis.

20. See also King, Sentana, and Wadhwani (1994), Demos and Sentana (1991), and Sentana (1992).

21. Note, however, that West and Cho (1994) evaluate volatility forecasts using the mean-squared error criterion, which may not be the most appropriate. For further discussion, see Bollerslev, Engle, and Nelson (1994) and Lopez (1995).

References

Baillie, R.T., T. Bollerslev, and H.O. Mikkelsen. (1993). "Fractionally Integrated Generalized Autoregressive Conditional Heteroskedasticity." Manuscript, J.L. Kellogg School of Management, Northwestern University.

Bera, A.K., and M.L. Higgins. (1993). "ARCH Models: Properties, Estimation and Testing." *Journal of Economic Surveys* 7, 305–362.

Black, F. (1976). "Studies of Stock Price Volatility Changes." *Proceedings of the American Statistical Association, Business and Economic Statistic Section* (pp. 177–181).

Bollerslev, T. (1986). "Generalized Autoregressive Conditional Heteroskedasticity." *Journal of Econometrics* 31, 307–327.

Bollerslev, T. (1987). "A Conditional Heteroskedastic Time Series Model for Speculative Prices and Rates of Return." *Review of Economics and Statistics* 69, 542–547.

Bollerslev, T. (1988). "On the Correlation Structure for the Generalized Autoregressive Conditional Heteroskedastic Process." *Journal of Time Series Analysis* 9, 121–131.

Bollerslev, T., R.Y. Chou, and K.F. Kroner. (1992). "ARCH Modeling in Finance: A Selective Review of the Theory and Empirical Evidence." *Journal of Econometrics* 52, 5–59.

Bollerslev, T., and I. Domowitz. (1991). "Price Volatility, Spread Variability and the Role of Alternative Market Mechanisms." *Review of Futures Markets* 10, 78–102.

Bollerslev, T., and R.F. Engle. (1993). "Common Persistence in Conditional Variances." *Econometrica* 61, 166–187.

Bollerslev, T., R.F. Engle, and D.B. Nelson. (1994). "ARCH Models." In R.F. Engle and D. McFadden (eds.), *Handbook of Econometrics* (Vol. 4). Amsterdam: North-Holland.

Bollerslev, T., R.F. Engle, and J.M. Wooldridge. (1988). "A Capital Asset Pricing Model with Time Varying Covariances." *Journal of Political Economy* 95, 116–131.

Bollerslev, T., and H.O. Mikkelsen. (1993). "Modeling and Pricing Long Memory in Stock Market Volatility." Manuscript, J.L. Kellogg School of Management, Northwestern University.

Bollerslev, T., and J.M. Wooldridge. (1992). "Quasi-Maximum Likelihood Estimation and Inference in Dynamic Models with Time-Varying Covariances." *Econometric Reviws* 11, 143–179.

Box, G.E.P., and G.W. Jenkins. (1970). *Time Series Analysis Forecasting and Control.* Oakland: Holden-Day.

Brock, W.A., and B.D. LeBaron. (1993). "Using Structural Modeling in Building Statistical Models of Volatility and Volume of Stock Market Returns." Manuscript, Department of Economics, University of Wisconsin, Madison.

Christoffersen, P.F., and F.X. Diebold. (1994). "Optimal Prediction under Asymmetric Loss." Technical Working Paper 167, National Bureau of Economic Research.

Chu, C.-S.J. (1993). "Detecting Parameter Shifts in Generalized Autoregressive Conditional Heteroskedasticity Models." Manuscript, Department of Economics, University of Southern California.

Clark, P.K. (1973). "A Subordinated Stochastic Process Model with Finite Variance for Speculative Prices." *Econometrica* 41, 135–156.

Demos, A., and E. Sentana. (1991). "An EM-Based Algorithm for Conditionally Heteroskedastic Latent Factor Models." Manuscript, Financial Markets Group, London School of Economics.

Diebold, F.X. (1986). "Modeling the Persistence of Conditional Variances: Comment." *Econometric Reviews* 5, 51–56.

Diebold, F.X. (1987). "Testing for Serial Correlation in the Presence of ARCH." *Proceedings of the American Statistical Association, Business and Economic Statistics Section, 1986* (pp. 323–328). Washington, DC: American Statistical Association.

Diebold, F.X. (1988). *Empirical Modeling of Exchange Rate Dynamics.* New York: Springer-Verlag.

Diebold, F.X., and R.S. Mariano. (1995). "Comparing Predictive Accuracy." *Journal of Business and Economic Statistics* 13, 253–264.

Diebold, F.X., and M. Nerlove. (1989). "The Dynamics of Exchange Rate Volatility: A Multivariate Latent-Factor ARCH Model." *Journal of Applied Econometrics* 4, 1–22.

Diebold, F.X., and T. Schuermann. (1993). "Exact Maximum Likelihood Estimation of ARCH Models." Manuscript, Department of Economics, University of Pennsylvania.

Ding, Z., R.F. Engle, and C.W.J. Granger. (1993). "A Long Memory Property of Stock Market Returns and a New Model." *Journal of Empirical Finance* 1, 83–106.

Drost, F.C., and T.E. Nijman. (1993). "Temporal Aggregation of GARCH Processes." *Econometrica* 61, 909–927.

Engle, R.F. (1982). "Autoregressive Conditional Heteroskedasticity with Estimates of the Variance of U.K. Inflation." *Econometrica* 50, 987–1008.

Engle, R.F. (1987). "Multivariate GARCH with Factor Structures—Cointegration in Variance." Manuscript, Department of Economics, University of California, San Diego.

Engle, R.F., and T. Bollerslev. (1986). "Modeling the Persistence of Conditional Variances." *Econometric Reviews* 5, 1–50.

Engle, R.F., and G. González-Rivera. (1991). "Semiparametric ARCH Models." *Journal of Business and Economic Statistics* 9, 345–359.

Engle, R.F., D.F. Hendry, and D. Trumble. (1985). "Small-Sample Properties of ARCH Estimators and Tests." *Canadian Journal of Economics* 18, 66–93.

Engle, R.F., C.-H. Hong, A. Kane, and J. Noh. (1993). "Arbitrage Valuation of Variance Forecasts with Simulated Options." In D. Chance and R. Tripp (eds.), *Advances in Futures and Options Research.* Greenwich, CT: JIA Press.

Engle, R.F., and K.F. Kroner. (1993). "Multivariate Simultaneous Generalized ARCH." *Econometric Theory,* forthcoming.

Engle, R.F., D.M. Lillien, and R.P. Robins. (1987). "Estimating Time-Varying Risk Premia in the Term Structure: The ARCH-M Model." *Econometrica* 55, 391–408.

Engle, R.F., and V.K. Ng. (1993). "Measuring and Testing the Impact of News on Volatility." *Journal of Finance* 48, 1749–1778.

Friedman, M., and A.J. Schwartz. (1963). *A Monetary History of the United States, 1867–1960*. Princeton, NJ: Princeton University Press.

Gallant, A.R., D.A. Hsieh, and G. Tauchen. (1991). "On Fitting a Recalcitrant Series: The Pound-Dollar Exchange Rate, 1974–1983." In W.A. Barnett, J. Powell, and G. Tauchen (eds.), *Nonparametric and Semiparametric Methods in Econometrics and Statistics*. Cambridge: Cambridge University Press.

Geweke, J. (1989). "Bayesian Inference in Econometric Models Using Monte Carlo Integration." *Econometrica* 57, 1317–1339.

Granger, C.W.J., and R. Joyeux. (1980). "An Introduction to Long-Memory Time Series Models and Fractional Differencing." *Journal of Time Series Analysis* 1, 15–39.

Granger, C.W.J., and P. Newbold. (1979). *Forecasting Economic Time Series*. New York: Academic Press.

Hamilton, J.D., and R. Susmel. (1994). "Autoregressive Conditional Heteroskedasticity and Changes in Regime." *Journal of Econometrics* 64, 307–333.

Hansen, L.P. (1982). "Large Sample Properties of the Method of Moment Estimators." *Econometrica* 50, 1029–1054.

Harvey, A., E. Ruiz, and E. Sentana. (1992). "Unobserved Component Time Series Models with ARCH Disturbances." *Journal of Econometrics* 52, 129–158.

Harvey, A., E. Ruiz, and N. Shephard. (1994). "Multivariate Stochastic Variance Models." *Review of Economic Studies* 61, 247–264.

Jacquier, E., N.G. Polson, and P.E. Rossi. (1994). "Bayesian Analysis of Stochastic Volatility Models." *Journal of Business and Economics Statistics* 12, 371–389.

Jorgenson, D.W. (1966). "Rational Distributed Lag Functions." *Econometrica* 34, 135–149.

Kim, S., and N. Shephard. (1994). "Stochastic Volatility: Likelihood Inference and Comparison with ARCH Models." Manuscript, Nuffield College, Oxford University.

King, M., E. Sentana, and S. Wadhwani. (1994). "Volatility and Links Between National Stock Markets." *Econometrica* 62, 901–933.

Kraft, D., and R.F. Engle. (1982). "Autoregressive Conditional Heteroskedasticity in Multiple Time Series Models." Discussion Paper 82–23, Department of Economics, University of California, San Diego.

Lamoureux, C.G., and W.D. Lastrapes. (1990). "Persistence in Variance, Structural Change and the GARCH Model." *Journal of Business and Economic Statistics* 8, 225–234.

Lastrapes, W.D. (1989). "Exchange Rate Volatility and U.S. Monetary Policy: An ARCH Application." *Journal of Money, Credit and Banking* 21, 66–77.

Lee, J.H.H. (1991). "A Lagrange Multiplier Test for GARCH Models." *Economics Letters* 37, 265–271.

Lee, J.H.H., and M.L. King. (1993). "A Locally Most Mean Powerful Based Score Test for ARCH and GARCH Regression Disturbances." *Journal of Business and Economics Statistics* 11, 17–27.

Lee, S.-W., and B.E. Hansen. (1994). "Asymptotic Theory for the GARCH (1, 1) Quasi-Maximum Likelihood Estimator." *Econometric Theory* 10, 29–52.

Lopez, J.A. (1995). "Evaluating the Predictive Accuracy of Volatility Models." Manuscript, Department of Economics, University of Pennsylvania.

Lumsdaine, R.L. (1992). "Asymptotic Properties of the Quasi-Maximum Likelihood

Estimator in GARCH(1, 1) and IGARCH(1, 1) Models." Manuscript, Department of Economics, Princeton University.

Lumsdaine, R.L. (1995). "Finite Sample Properties of the Maximum Likelihood Estimator In GARCH(1, 1) and IGARCH(1, 1) Models: A Monte Carlo Investigation." *Journal of Business and Economic Statistics* 13, 1–10.

McLeod, A.I., and W.K. Li. (1983). "Diagnostic Checking of ARMA Time Series Models Using Squared Residual Autocorrelations." *Journal of Time Series Analysis* 4, 269–273.

Milhoj, A. (1985). "The Moment Structure of ARCH Processes." *Scandinavian Journal of Statistics* 12, 281–292.

Mor, N.M. (1994). "Essays on Nonlinearity in Exchange Rates." Doctoral dissertation, Department of Economics, University of Pennsylvania.

Nelson, D.B. (1990a). "ARCH Models as Diffusion Approximations." *Journal of Econometrics* 45, 7–39.

Nelson, D.B. (1990b). "Stationarity and Persistence in the GARCH(1, 1) Model." *Econometric Theory* 6, 318–334.

Nelson, D.B. (1991). "Conditional Heteroskedasticity in Asset Returns: A New Approach." *Econometrica* 59, 347–370.

Nelson, D.B. (1992). "Filtering and Forecasting with Misspecified ARCH Models: I." *Journal of Econometrics* 52, 61–90.

Nelson, D.B. (1993). "Asymptotic Filtering and Smoothing Theory for Multivariate ARCH Models." Manuscript, Graduate School of Business, University of Chicago.

Nelson, D.B., and C.Q. Cao. (1992). "Inequality Constraints in the Univariate GARCH Model." *Journal of Business and Economic Statistics* 10, 229–235.

Nelson, D.B., and D.P. Foster. (1991). "Filtering and Forecasting with Misspecified ARCH Models: II." *Journal of Econometrics*, forthcoming.

Nelson, D.B., and D.P. Foster. (1994). "Asymptotic Filtering Theory for Univariate ARCH Models." *Econometrica* 62, 1–41.

Robinson, P.M. (1987). "Adaptive Estimation of Heteroskedastic Econometric Models." *Revista de Econometria* (Rio de Janeiro) 7, 5–28.

Robinson, P.M. (1991). "Testing for Strong Serial Correlation and Dynamic Conditional Heteroskedasticity in Multiple Regression." *Journal of Econometrics* 47, 67–84.

Sentana, E. (1992). "Identification and Estimation of Multivariate Conditionally Heteroskedastic Latent Factor Models." Manuscript, Financial Markets Group, London School of Economics.

Seillier-Moiseiwitsch, F., and A.P. Dawid. (1993). "On Testing the Validity of Sequential Probability Forecasts." *Journal of the American Statistical Association* 88, 355–359.

Sims, C.A. (1980). "Macroeconomics and Reality." *Econometrica* 48, 1–48.

Stock, J.H. (1987). "Measuring Business Cycle Time." *Journal of Political Economy* 95, 1240–1261.

Stock, J.H. (1988). "Estimating Continuous-Time Processes Subject to Time Deformation: An Application to Postwar U.S. GNP." *Journal of the American Statistical Association* 83, 77–85.

Stock, J.H. (1994). "Unit Roots and Trend Breaks." In R.F. Engle and D. McFadden (eds.), *Handbook of Econometrics*, Vol. 4. Amsterdam: North-Holland.

Tsay, R.S. (1987). "Conditional Heteroskedastic Time Series Models." *Journal of the American Statistical Association* 82, 509–604.

Weiss, A.A. (1984). "ARMA Models with ARCH Errors." *Journal of Time Series Analysis* 5, 129–143.

Weiss, A.A. (1986). "Asymptotic Theory for ARCH Models: Estimation and Testing." *Econometric Theory* 2, 107–131.

West, K.D., and D. Cho (1994). "The Predictive Ability of Several Models of Exchange Rate Volatility." Technical Working Paper 152, National Bureau of Economic Research.

West, K.D., H.J. Edison and D. Cho (1993). "A Utility-Based Comparison of Some Models of Exchange Rate Volatility." *Journal of International Economics* 35, 23–45.

White, H. (1984). *Asymptotic Theory for Econometricians*. New York: Academic Press.

Wold, H.O. (1938). *The Analysis of Stationary Time Series*. Uppsala: Almquist and Wicksell.

Commentary on Chapter 11

Douglas G. Steigerwald

Frank Diebold and Jose Lopez have written an excellent primer on conditional heteroskedasticity (CH) models and their use in applied work. A principal motivation for CH models, as outlined in Diebold and Lopez, is their ability to parsimoniously capture the observed characteristics of many financial time series. By far the most widely used CH model, in part because of the fact that estimators for the model are simple to construct, is the generalized autoregressive conditional heteroskedasticity (GARCH) specification of order (1, 1) with normal innovations (henceforth termed the normal GARCH (1, 1) model). Despite its widespread use, the normal GARCH(1, 1) model does not account for important features in many financial time series. For example, assuming that the GARCH innovations have a normal density generates far fewer outliers than are typically observed in asset prices, while assuming that the order of the GARCH model is (1, 1) fails to account for the variety of dynamic patterns observed in the conditional heteroskedasticity of asset prices.

As Diebold and Lopez note in describing avenues for future research, it is important to consider alternative CH models that do account for such features of asset prices. Two alternatives to a normal GARCH(1, 1) model, which are mentioned by Diebold and Lopez and for which estimators are also simple to construct, are (1) to allow for nonnormal innovations that have a thicker tailed density, thereby accounting for a larger number of outliers and (2) to allow for orders other than (1, 1) by developing powerful test statistics for selection of order in GARCH models, thereby accounting for a wider variety of dynamic patterns. I discuss each of these alternatives in turn, in an effort to bring them within the set of commonly used methods for estimation and testing of CH models.

Unknown Density

Let y_t be a period-t variable (such as an exchange rate) that has conditional mean $x_t\beta$ where $x_t\varepsilon\Re^k$ and the period-t regressors include a constant. The normal GARCH(1, 1) model for y_t is

$$y_t = x_t\beta + h_t u_t, \tag{1}$$

where the period-t conditional variance is

467

$$h_t^2 = \omega + \alpha_1(y_{t-1} - x_{t-1}\beta)^2 + \gamma_1 h_{t-1}^2, \tag{2}$$

with period-t innovation u_t and where $(\beta', \omega, \alpha_1, \gamma_1)$ are parameters to be estimated. The sequence $\{u_t\}_{t=1}^T$ is a sequence of independent and identically distributed (iid) normal random variables with mean zero and variance one.[1]

Because the normal GARCH(1, 1) model does not adequately account for outliers in asset prices such as exchange rates, researchers constructing CH models of exchange rates often assume that the density of u_t has thicker tails than a normal density. For example, Baillie and Bollerslev (1989) use both an exponential-power and a t density to model exchange rates.

Although the use of thicker-tailed parametric innovation densities does account for a larger number of outliers, it also raises the issue of the properties of the estimators if the selected density is misspecified. Virtually all researchers that estimate CH models also use a quasi-maximum likelihood estimator (QMLE). If the assumed density is normal, the QMLE is consistent for the parameters of the conditional variance. If the assumed density is nonnormal, then consistency of the QMLE depends on the specification of the conditional mean. For a nonnormal GARCH(1, 1) model, which is given by (1) and (2) together with the assumption that u_t has a nonnormal density, Newey and Steigerwald (1994) show that a nonnormal QMLE is not generally consistent.[2]

An alternative estimator that also accounts for a larger number of outliers is a semiparametric estimator. A semiparametric estimator of the parameters in a GARCH(1, 1) model is constructed under the assumption that the innovation density is any member within a class of densities, and uses a nonparametric estimator of the density. Steigerwald (1994) shows that a semiparametric estimator is consistent for general GARCH(p, q) models.

Given that a semiparametric estimator accounts for a larger number of outliers and consistently estimates the parameters of (1) and (2), attention turns to finite sample performance. The finite sample performance of a semiparametric estimator depends on the bandwidth used to construct the nonparametric density estimator. The bandwidth, in turn, depends on the conditional variance parameterization. For the conditional variance parameterization (2), the regularity conditions given in Steigerwald require that the bandwidth used to construct the nonparametric density estimator be smaller than the optimal bandwidth. Such a restriction on choice of bandwidth may lead to a poor estimate of the density, thereby reducing the gains of a semiparametric estimator.

A reparameterization of the conditional variance, which allows the optimal bandwidth to be used to estimate the density, is to let the variance of u_t be restricted only to be finite and to reparameterize the conditional variance as

$$h_t^2 = e^\omega[1 + \alpha_1(y_{t-1} - x_{t-1}\beta)^2] + \gamma_1 h_{t-1}^2. \tag{3}$$

Linton (1993) develops this reparameterization for ARCH models, Drost and Klaasen (1993) and Steigerwald extend the reparameterization to GARCH models.[3]

A guide to the finite sample performance of semiparametric estimators for the two conditional variance parameterizations is provided by the simulations contained in Engle and Gonzalez-Rivera (1991) and Steigerwald. Both studies compare the performance of a semiparametric estimator with a normal QMLE. For a sample size of 2,000, Engle and Gonzalez-Rivera report essentially no gain in efficiency for a semiparametric estimator of the parameters in (1) and (2) when the density of u_t is a t density with 5 degrees of freedom. Steigerwald, using a different nonparametric estimator, reports more favorable results for a semiparametric estimator of the parameters in (1) and (2), finding some efficiency gains with a sample of only fifty observations when the density for u_t is a t density with 5 degrees of freedom. The efficiency gains increase dramatically if (3) replaces (2), indicating that the parameterization of the conditional variance is important for applied work.

Testing for Order

All discussion in the preceding section considers a fixed order (1, 1) for the conditional variance. As is noted in the introduction, the (1, 1) order specification fails to account for the variety of dynamic patterns in many time series. In response, I turn to extending the GARCH(1, 1) specification to general order (p, q).

To extend the GARCH(1, 1) specification to GARCH(p, q) requires a test statistic for choosing correct order. To keep the following discussion of test statistics clear, I consider two distinct testing problems. The first problem is to test the null hypothesis that the conditional variance is ARCH(p) against the univariate alternative hypothesis that the conditional variance is ARCH($p + 1$). The second problem is to test the null hypothesis that the conditional variance is ARCH(p) against the multivariate alternative hypothesis that the conditional variance is ARCH($p + k$), where $k > 1$. In particular, the two problems can be viewed as testing the null hypothesis of homoskedasticity against the alternative either of ARCH(1) or ARCH(p).[4]

Engle (1982) develops Lagrange multiplier (LM) test statistics for the univariate testing problem in a normal ARCH model. The test is two sided, the null hypothesis that a specific conditional variance parameter equals zero is tested against the alternative that the parameter is nonzero. Yet to ensure that the conditional variance is always positive, the parameter of the conditional variance must be nonnegative. Therefore, more powerful test statistics can be constructed that are one sided. For the univariate testing problem, the signed square-root of the LM test statistic provides such a one-sided test. For the multivariate testing problem, there is no uniformly best one-sided test because the region over which the power function is evaluated spans more than one dimension. Lee and King (1993) propose a one-sided test statistic, termed an LBS test statistic, for the multivariate testing problem that maximizes the average slope, over all directions, of the power function in a neighborhood of the null hypothesis. They show that their one-sided test can be more powerful in finite samples than a two-sided LM test statistic.

Both the LM test statistic and the LBS test statistic are constructed under the assumption that the innovation density is normal. Fox (1994a) develops semiparametric versions of both test statistics. He finds that incorporating a nonparametric estimator of the density can have important finite sample consequences. Specifically, for samples of 100 observations the semiparametric test statistics achieve size-adjusted power gains of as much as 20 percent over their parametric counter-parts. Linton and Steigerwald (1994) extend the semiparametric tests to the reparameterization of the conditional variance in (3) and show that the semiparametric tests are optimal in that they maximize the average slope of the power function in a neighborhood of the null hypothesis for any innovation density in a general class. Fox also finds that testing for correct order is important in estimation, incorrect order specification can lead to substantial bias in the estimators of the conditional variance parameters.

Empirical Implementation

To demonstrate the potential importance of semiparametric methods in testing and estimation, I construct a model for the dollar per pound exchange rate. The data are collected at noon on the New York foreign exchange market and span the period January 2, 1985 to September 30, 1993 yielding 2,185 observations. As is commonly done, I model the first difference of the logarithm of the exchange rate rather than the exchange rate itself. The initial model is

$$y_t = \beta + h_t u_t,$$

where y_t is the period-t value of the change in the logarithm of the exchange rate and the conditional variance specification is given by

$$h_t^2 = e^\omega[1 + \alpha_1(y_{t-1} - \beta)^2] + \gamma_1 h_{t-1}^2.$$

Estimates of the parameters are reported in Table 11.1. (Standard errors are reported in parentheses below each estimate.) Although the magnitude of the normal QML and semiparametric estimates differ only slightly, the asymptotic standard errors of the semiparametric estimator are typically about half the size of the asymptotic standard errors for the normal QMLE. In addition, as Fox (1994b)

Table 11.1. Parameter estimates for an exchange-rate model

Parameter	Normal QML	Semiparametric
Beta	−.0231	−.0227
	(.6744)	(.3887)
Alpha	.0693	.0702
	(.3540)	(.1533)
Gamma	.8884	.8876
	(.5638)	(.2742)

notes, apparently small differences in the point estimates of the conditional variance parameters can have important economic consequences. He shows that optimal portfolio weights based on the estimated conditional variance process differ markedly for two sets of estimates that differ only slightly, as do those in Table 11.1. The portfolio weights implied by the semiparametric estimators are better, in the sense that the risk associated with a portfolio that provides a fixed expected return is reduced by 8 to 10 percent out-of-sample.

Although the GARCH(1, 1) specification is common in the empirical finance literature, it may not adequately account for the dynamic pattern in the data. To test for incorrect order specification, I test the null hypothesis that the conditional variance is GARCH(1, 1) against the alternative hypothesis that the conditional variance is GARCH(2, 1). I construct both parametric and semiparametric versions of the LM test statistic and the King and Lee test statistic. Both the parametric and semiparametric LM test statistics, which are two-sided tests, fail to reject the null hypothesis. The parametric King and Lee test statistic also fails to clearly reject the null hypothesis. Only the semiparametric King and Lee test statistic clearly rejects the null hypothesis. It appears that if the true dynamic process is richer than a GARCH(1, 1), the power gains available from both a nonparametric density estimator and a one-sided alternative are needed to detect it.

In summary, recent advances in econometric methodology have provided researchers with powerful tools to move beyond the restrictive framework of a normal GARCH(1, 1) model. Semiparametric estimators and test statistics are available and provide alternatives that more flexibly account for the wide variety of patterns in financial time series.

Notes

1. The variance of u_t is assumed to equal one because $(\omega, \alpha_1, \gamma_1)$ and the scale of u_t are not separately identified.

2. To ensure that the likelihood has a unique maximum, which is a necessary condition for consistent estimation, the set of regressors must include the conditional standard deviation.

3. In (3) the parameter ω cannot be separately identified because the variance of u_t is restricted only to be finite, so only ratios of the parameters (namely $e^{\omega}\alpha_1$ and $e^{\omega}\gamma_1$) are identified.

4. Considering only ARCH processes is not restrictive, as Lee and King (1993) note testing a null hypothesis of homoscedasticity against an alternative hypothesis of ARCH(p) is equivalent to testing against an alternative of GARCH(p, q).

References

Baillie, R., and T. Bollerslev. (1989). "The Message in Daily Exchange Rates: A Conditional-Variance Tale." *Journal of Business and Economic Statistics* 7, 297–305.

Drost, F., and C. Klaasen. (1993). "Adaptivity in Semiparametric GARCH Models." Manuscript, Tilburg University.

Engle, R. (1982). "Autoregressive Conditional Heteroscedasticity with Estimates of the Variance of U.K. Inflation." *Econometrica* 50, 987–1008.

Engle, R., and G. Gonzalez-Rivera. (1991). "Semiparametric ARCH Models." *Journal of Business and Economic Statistics* 9, 345–360.

Fox, S. (1994a). "Semiparametric Testing of Generalized ARCH Processes." Manuscript, University of California, Santa Barbara.

Fox, S. (1994b). "Hedge Estimation Using Semiparametric Methods." Manuscript, University of California, Santa Barbara.

Linton, O., and D. Steigerwald. (1994). "Efficient Testing in GARCH Models." Manuscript, Yale University.

Lee, J., and M. King. (1993). "A Locally Mean Most Powerful Score Based Test for ARCH and GARCH Disturbances." *Journal of Business and Economic Statistics* 11, 17–27.

Linton, O. (1993). "Adaptive Estimation in ARCH Models." *Econometric Theory* 9, 539–569.

Newey, W., and D. Steigerwald. (1994). "Consistency of Quasi-Maximum Likelihood Estimators in Models with Conditional Heteroskedasticity." Manuscript, University of California, Santa Barbara.

Steigerwald, D. (1994). "Efficient Estimation of Financial Models with Conditional Heteroskedasticity." *Econometric Theory*, forthcoming.

12 DYNAMIC SPECIFICATION AND TESTING FOR UNIT ROOTS AND COINTEGRATION

Anindya Banerjee

Introduction

In the field of modeling economic time series, the 1980s might easily be described as the decade of cointegration. During this decade, theoretical and applied econometricians alike invested a great deal of effort in dealing with the theoretical and empirical implications of Nelson and Plosser's (1982) central observation that time series of important economic variables such as consumption and *per capita* GNP may have statistical properties quite distinct from those that would warrant the use of standard tools, such as normal, *t*-, and *F*-tables, of inference and estimation.

The results of this research have given rise to an unmanageably vast literature on almost every aspect of estimation and inference in the presence of nonstationary series. It is therefore impossible, in the space available, to provide a complete account of this field. The case for writing a formal survey is in any case rather limited, given the several surveys that have already appeared (see, for example, Stock and Watson, 1988; Dolado, Jenkinson, and Rivero, 1990; Campbell and Perron, 1991). The purpose of this paper is instead to focus on specific issues that, in my view, are important in any evaluation of this literature. In particular, I will attempt to address, at least partially, the issue of the extent to which our notions of what constitutes good or appropriate modeling practice have changed as a result of the research on unit roots.

The mathematical and statistical tools on which the econometrics literature on unit roots depends, date back at least to the 1920s, 1930s, and 1940s, notably to the work of Wiener, Lévy, Doob, and many others. Thus no claim for mathematical or statistical originality can be made, *per se*, on behalf of this literature. Rather, I will argue that econometricians have brought the highly developed theory on stochastic processes into the realm of every-day econometric modeling and, by applying it to problems particular to econometrics, have added considerably to our store of knowledge of the very special properties of nonstationary series and the implications of these properties for estimation and inference.

However, I will also argue that while a greater realization of how things can go wrong when dealing with these series has had an important effect on our econometric consciousness, this does not lead us necessarily to a fundamental reevaluation of modeling practice, in particular of dynamic modeling. For example, it will be shown that some of the inferential problems that arise may be overcome by suitable transformations and appropriate augmentation of equations. These methods will often allow us to return to using standard tables for inference.

In the next section, two examples are presented that illustrate the fundamental differences that could arise between the treatments of unit root and non-unit root processes. The differences emerge particularly because the critical values of standard tests, such as t- or F- tests, are affected by the presence or absence of unit roots. In the third section it is shown how these differences can, in some circumstances, be eliminated by a proper reformulation of the model. However, there are cases where such reformulations are not possible, and it therefore becomes very important, before proceeding to the formal task of econometric modeling, to classify the variables of interest by their orders of integration. This is a task that is by no means an easy one to accomplish, even with our fairly advanced understanding of the asymptotic theory, given the low powers of most available tests for unit roots. I propose a conservative testing strategy to allow for the possibility of incorrect classification and also deal with the issue of estimating cointegrating relationships in single equations, dealing with, in particular, the two-step method proposed by Engle and Granger (1987) and suggesting a simple alternative. This is linked with the issue of *testing* for cointegration and unit roots, an area that has generated considerable interest in the literature. Finally, I consider single-equation versus systems methods of estimation and show that the choice between these two methods can be made and understood within the familiar concepts of exogeneity. The final section concludes. Since frequent reference is made in the text to the concepts of weak and strong exogeneity, an appendix contains a discussion, based on Engle, Hendry, and Richard (1983), of these concepts.

Spurious and Inconsistent Regressions

Spurious regressions

While Nelson and Plosser's paper provided one of the early surprising insights in the literature on unit roots, Yule (1926) had already alerted the profession to the potential dangers of undertaking stationary inference in an environment with nonstationary variables. He termed the phenomenon "nonsense" regressions and showed how regressing one variable that followed a random walk on another totally unrelated random walk led to findings of significant correlations between the two series. Granger and Newbold (1974) returned to the Yule example, and their formulation of the problem forms the starting point for our analysis. Granger and Newbold called such regressions "spurious," and this has come to be regarded as the more commonly accepted terminology.

Granger and Newbold considered the following data-generation process (DGP) for the data series $\{x_t\}_{t=1}^T$, $\{y_t\}_{t=1}^T$:

$$y_t = y_{t-1} + u_t, \ u_t \sim IID(0, \ \sigma_u^2), \tag{12.1}$$

$$x_t = x_{t-1} + v_t, \ v_t \sim IID(0, \ \sigma_v^2), \tag{12.2}$$

$$E(u_t v_s) = 0 \ \forall \ t, \ s; \ E(u_t u_{t-k}) = E(v_t v_{t-k}) = 0 \ \forall \ k \neq 0.$$

Thus x_t and y_t are uncorrelated random walks. Before proceeding to the formal details of the example some important features of the data generation process may be noted. The process generates two variables, each with a unit root. This terminology can be understood more readily by rewriting the DGP in lag polynomial operator form:

$$(1 - \rho_1 L)y_t = u_t, \tag{12.1'}$$

$$(1 - \rho_2 L)x_t = v_t, \tag{12.2'}$$

where the processes generating $\{u_t\}$ and $\{v_t\}$ remain unchanged and L is the lag operator such that $L^j x_t = x_{t-j}$, $L^j y_t = y_{t-j}$.

The "unit root" in the $\{x_t\}$ and $\{y_t\}$ processes refers to the value of unity for the coefficients ρ_1 and ρ_2. Values of ρ_1 and ρ_2 such that $|\rho_1| < 1$, and $|\rho_2| < 1$ correspond to "stationary roots." In the terminology of Engle and Granger (1987), (12.1) and (12.2) are called processes "integrated of order 1", denoted I (1)—that is, they need to be differenced once to achieve stationarity.[1]

It is interesting to compare the properties of the series $\{x_t\}$ and $\{y_t\}$ when $\rho_1 = \rho_2 = 1$ with the properties of the series generated by values of $|\rho_1| < 1$ and $|\rho_2| < 1$. In the former case both series have unconditional variances that grow with time (at rate t) while the series have time-invariant finite variances in the latter.

The autocorrelation function $r_i = E(z_t z_{t-i})/[\text{var}(z_t)\text{var}(z_{t-i})]^{1/2}$, $z = y$, x, is an exponentially declining function of i when $|\rho_1| < 1$, $|\rho_2| < 1$—that is, the past of the series becomes increasingly less important. When the processes have unit roots, however, the correlations persist at significantly large values even when the observations are substantially far apart.

It is this property of persistence that drives many of the properties of spurious regressions. Each time series is growing but for entirely different reasons and by increments that are uncorrelated. Hence a correlation, induced simply by persistent but *independent* growth, cannot be interpreted in the way that it could be if it arose among stationary series.

Granger and Newbold showed that if standard normal tables were used to conduct tests of significance on the t-ratio $t_{\beta_1=0}$, in the regression

$$y_t = \beta_0 + \beta_1 x_t + \varepsilon_t, \tag{12.3}$$

the tests would reject the null of $\beta_1 = 0$, on average, between 50 and 70 percent of the time (at a nominal significance level of 5 percent)! Thus the use of standard tables would be grossly misleading in the presence of integrated processes.

A question that might well be asked is whether the misleading inferences arise simply because the two integrated series are unrelated with each other and if we considered two integrated but related series whether the problem would disappear. Unfortunately, this too happens to be untrue. In a regression such as (12.3) the finite and asymptotic distributions of both β_0 and β_1 are non-normal even when y_t and x_t are linked by some hypothesized equilibrium relationship (say, y is income and x is consumption). The tools of inference are, in general, nonstandard. However, as we shall show in a later section, it is possible to reparameterize and extend (12.3) such that at least some of the inferences can be undertaken using standard tables.

A detailed theoretical analysis of the spurious regression problem was undertaken by Phillips (1986). He showed that the t-statistic diverged asymptotically. Thus the inferential problem would become worse as the sample size increased and therefore, in the limit, to avoid making spurious inferences, infinitely large t-values would be needed to reject the null $\beta_1 = 0$. The asymptotic distribution of the R^2 of the regression would also have substantial weight at the ends of its support (-1 and 1) and values well away from zero would therefore be very likely. For stationary series however, none of these problems would arise. In particular, β_1 would tend in probability to zero.

It is possible to provide a good intuition for some of the rather dramatic results described above. In (12.3), both the null hypothesis $\beta_1 = 0$ and alternative $\beta_1 \neq 0$ lead to false models, since the true DGP is not nested within (12.3). It is therefore not surprising that the null hypothesis, implying that $y_t = \varepsilon_t$—in other words, that $\{y_t\}$ is a white-noise process—is rejected: the persistence in $\{y_t\}$ is projected onto

$\{x_t\}$, also a random walk and therefore also highly persistent, and spurious correlations arise. Further, the use of the normal table asymptotically is based on the assumption that $\{\varepsilon_t\}$ is a white-noise process under H_0. This is clearly false and it follows then that the t-statistic is not asymptotically normally distributed.

Phillips (1986) also demonstrated an important feature of the Durbin-Watson statistic (DW) calculated from the residuals of (12.3). When the regression is spurious, $DW \rightarrow 0$ in probability. This is a consequence of precisely the property discussed in the previous paragraph. Under H_0, $\{\varepsilon_t\}$ far from being a white-noise process is instead highly correlated and this is revealed in a low value of DW. When the two series are genuinely related, the DW statistic converges to a nonzero value and the behavior of the DW statistic therefore provides a way of discriminating between genuine and spurious regressions. We will return to this issue in a later section.

Inconsistent Regressions

Another example of the dangers involved in using standard distributions for inference when there are nonstationary variables present was highlighted by Mankiw and Shapiro (1985, 1986) in their discussion of what have come to be called "inconsistent" or "unbalanced" regressions.

In this terminology, a regression is said to inconsistent (unbalanced) if the regressand is not of the same order of integration as the regressors or any linear combination of the regressors. The inconsistency (imbalance) refers to the disparity in the orders of integration of the variables on the two sides of the regression. Thus the problem occurs if, say, the regressand is an I(0) variable while the regressors, individually *and* in combination, are I(1). The problem also appears if the regressors are only near-integrated—that is, ρ_1 in (12.1') is close to, but not equal to, one in absolute value. Mankiw and Shapiro's analysis, which we describe below, concentrates on these near-integrated cases, but their results apply equally well to integrated series.

The difficulty with these inconsistent regressions can be understood in the context of spurious regressions. An I(0) variable cannot be related in any meaningful sense to an I(1) variable (where the I(1) variable may be taken to be a linear combination or composite of several I(1) variables), given their very different statistical properties and behavior over time. Thus an inconsistent or near-inconsistent (if only near-integrated variables appear) regression may be regarded as a special kind of spurious regression. The use of standard tables will therefore lead to misleading inferences on the significance of estimates of parameters.

This discussion has considerable economic interest since tests for rational expectations, in consumption (Flavin, 1981) or the stock market (Fama and French,

1989), typically give rise to such regressions. For example, Flavin's (1981) test of Hall's (1978) random walk hypothesis for consumption takes the form of regressing differenced consumption ($(1 - L)c_t = \Delta c_t$) on lagged income (y_{t-1}). If both consumption and income are I(1) variables, this regression is inconsistent. Under the null hypothesis, that consumption follows a random walk, the coefficient on the lagged income term should not be significantly different from zero. However, given the form of the regression, the t-statistic for the coefficient estimate on lagged income does not have the standard t-distribution and use of the t-table will lead to spurious findings of significance and hence rejections of the random walk hypothesis.

Mankiw and Shapiro (1986) consider the following DGP for hypothetical $\{c_t\}$ and $\{y_t\}$ series:

$$\Delta c_t = v_t,$$

$$y_t = \theta y_{t-1} + \varepsilon_t,$$

$$E_{t-1}(v_t) = E_{t-1}(\varepsilon_t) = 0,$$

$$\text{corr}(v_t, \varepsilon_t) = \rho,$$

$$\text{corr}(\varepsilon_{t+j}, v_t) = 0 \; \forall \; j \neq 0. \tag{12.4}$$

E_{t-1} is the expectation, conditional on information available at time $t - 1$, of the value of variables dated in the future. The model is given by

$$\Delta c_t = d_1 + d_2 y_{t-1} + u_t. \tag{12.5}$$

The null hypothesis is given by $H_0: d_2 = 0$ and Mankiw and Shapiro use Monte Carlo simulations to tabulate the *actual* rejection frequencies of $H_0: d_2 = 0$, when standard t-critical values are used, for a range of specified values for θ, ρ, and T (the size of the samples generated). Table 12.1 gives some of their results for model (12.5) and also for a model with a linear time trend,[2]

$$\Delta c_t = d_1 + d_2 y_{t-1} + d_3 t + u_t. \tag{12.6}$$

Table 12.1 has several interesting features. First, the size distortions are an increasing function of the value of the autoregressive parameter. Critical values given by Mankiw and Shapiro show that this arises from a leftward (from zero) shift of the t-density for values of θ close to 1. The closer θ is to 1, the greater the shift and the more likely the occurrence of values in excess of—2, leading to a higher probability of rejection of the true null and hence giving rise to greater size distortions. Because of the nature of the alternative hypothesis $H_A: d_2 < 0$, rejections of the null hypothesis all take place in the lower tail. In fact, because $d_2 > 0$ implies an explosive (or exponentially growing) process, two-sided critical values are not significantly different from one-sided critical values, giving the scarcity of

Table 12.1. Percentage rejection frequencies in standard t-tests at nominal 5 percent level[3]

$\theta \backslash \rho \rightarrow$ $\downarrow$	Model (12.5)					Model (12.6)				
	1.0	0.9	0.8	0.5	0.0	1.0	0.9	0.8	0.5	0.0
$T = 50$										
0.999	30	24	20	11	7	60	45	36	16	6
0.99	26	20	15	10	7	54	40	33	15	6
0.98	22	17	15	8	7	50	37	30	14	5
0.95	17	12	10	7	6	38	30	25	12	6
0.90	12	9	8	6	6	28	22	19	10	6
0.00	5	6	6	5	5	6	7	7	5	6
$T = 200$										
0.999	29	23	20	10	5	61	48	38	18	5
0.99	18	15	13	8	4	41	32	27	13	5
0.98	13	10	9	7	5	29	24	20	11	6
0.95	9	7	7	6	5	17	14	12	7	6
0.90	7	6	6	6	6	10	9	8	6	7
0.00	5	4	4	5	5	5	5	4	5	5

Notes: DGP: (12.4); sample size = T; number of replications = 1,000.

rejections in the upper tail of the density. For values of θ well within the unit circle, the size distortions disappear.

Second, the distortions are a decreasing function of T although this holds only when the series are near-integrated. For $\theta = 1$, there will be no reductions in size distortions when the sample size increases.

Finally, the distortions are an increasing function of the number of *nuisance* parameters (such as constant or trend) estimated. Thus the distortions in model (12.6) are higher than those in model (12.5). This is again a characteristic feature of such densities.

In summary, the results in this section again show the dangers of conducting inference using standard tables when unit roots are present. This leads naturally to the conclusion that tests of economic hypotheses of interest, such as the excess sensitivity of consumption to income, crucially depend on a preclassification of the variables of interest by their orders of integration, as this determines what critical values should be used for inference. Incorrect preclassifications will lead to an inappropriate choice of critical values and thus lead to incorrect inferences.

For most of the next section we duck this issue of possible incorrect classification and proceed conditionally on a classification of the orders of integration of the variables. We ask the question whether, given that some of the variables have been classified as I(1), it is possible under any circumstances to return to using standard tools of inference and whether such a return has any other practical benefits such as unbiased or efficient estimation. We then return briefly to the issue of ameliorating the consequences of incorrect classification by being conservative in our testing strategy.

Dynamic Regressions

Overview

The fundamental point, which is the first major theme of this survey, emerging from the discussion above is the striking difference that may arise between the critical values required to conduct inference in a stationary environment and those required when unit roots are present, and, as a corollary, the mistakes that can occur if incorrect critical values are used.

The classification of time series by their integration properties, say, into I(0) and I(1), is an area fraught with difficulty. There is a vast literature just on *testing* for unit roots, with a wide variety of tests proposed. Each of these tests may have satisfactory power properties against a given set of alternative hypotheses but may be powerless against a range of other alternatives.

However, given that the classification has been properly made, series integrated, say, of order one and *related* to each other seem to offer a special advantage to the applied econometrician. The asymptotic property that confers this advantage is called *superconsistency*, and discussion of this property takes us to the second important theme of the literature on I(1) processes—namely, the modelling of long-run economic relationships by means of static regressions.

Engle and Granger (1987) introduced the notion of *cointegration* to the mainstream of applied and theoretical econometric research. The idea is simple yet very powerful and can be understood by looking at a simple DGP (taken from Engle and Granger):

$$y_t + \beta x_t = u_t \tag{12.7a}$$

$$y_t - \alpha x_t = e_t \tag{12.7b}$$

$$u_t = u_{t-1} + \varepsilon_{1t} \tag{12.7c}$$

$$e_t = \rho e_{t-1} + \varepsilon_{2t}, \text{ with } |\rho| < 1. \tag{12.7d}$$

$(\varepsilon_{1t}, \varepsilon_{2t})'$ is distributed identically and independently as a bivariate normal with zero means, finite variances, and zero covariance.

From (12.7a) and (12.7b), x_t and y_t can be expressed as linear combinations of the error processes u_t and e_t (where the weights in the linear combinations are functions of α and β). Thus, both x_t and y_t are weighted sums of an I(1) variable and an I(0) variable and are therefore both I(1). Yet a linear combination of x_t and y_t, given by (12.7b), is I(0). In the terminology of Engle and Granger the two series x_t and y_t are said to be *cointegrated* with each other. In slightly more formal terms, two I(d) series are said to be cointegrated with each other if a linear combination of these two series is integrated of order $d - b$, where $b > 0$—that is, linearly combining the two series leads to a series of a lower order of integration. In the example above, x_t and y_t are said to be cointegrated of order 1 and 1, denoted CI (1, 1), where the first 1 gives the order of the component series and the second the reduction in the order of integration. Thus two series are CI(d, b) if each series is individually I(d) while the linear combination is I($d - b$).

For the most part in this chapter we will focus on reductions from I(1) to I(0). The concept of cointegration applies to multivariate (greater than two) systems of variables where the nonuniqueness of the cointegrating relationship becomes an important issue.

The concept of cointegration gains importance from the fact that the statistical properties of the composite variable (which is I(0)) are so dramatically different from the properties of the component series (both of which are I(1)). Thus series growing stochastically over time are said to be linked together in the long-run or cointegrated if a linear combination of these series remains bounded in a statistical sense.[4] Cointegration captures the notion of long-run relationships in economics, such as consumption being a fraction of permanent income or purchasing power parity, which are testable on data sets albeit with nonstandard tools. Cointegration allows for possibly extensive divergences in the short-run, but because a stable relationship among variables cannot be meaningfully said to exist if these divergences persist in the long-run, it uses the criterion of stationarity in a series such as $\{e_t\}$ in (12.7b), or its estimated counterpart $\{\hat{e}_t\}$, to define the existence of a long-run or equilibrium relationship. Tests for cointegration therefore reduce to testing for unit roots in the estimated series $\{\hat{e}_t\}$, introducing all the difficulties in testing for unit roots into the literature on testing for cointegration.

In an important sense, the concept of cointegration is the natural opposite to the concept of spurious regressions. If, say, a bivariate static regression is spurious, there does not exist a stationary linear combination of the variables. If a stationary linear combination does exist the regression is the cointegrating regression.

Looking more closely at the asymptotic properties of a cointegrating regression, the difficulty of non-standard distributions remains. However, the nonstandardness has several important implications.

First, consider estimating (12.7b) as the cointegrating regression. Then,

$$(\hat{\alpha} - \alpha) = \left[\sum_{t=1}^{T} x_t^2\right]^{-1} \left[\sum_{t=1}^{T} x_t e_t\right]. \qquad (12.8)$$

Earlier in the chapter we noted that the variance of x_t, if x_t is generated by a unit root process, grows with t. From this, and from the properties of e_t, it is possible to see after some tedious manipulation that the variance of the numerator of (12.8) is of order T^2 while the denominator has variance of order T^4. Thus to prevent explosive (or degenerate) behavior of both the numerator and the denominator, they need to be scaled by T and T^2, respectively.[5] Simplifying, it is then clear that $T(\hat{\alpha} - \alpha)$ has a nondegenerate distribution.

The scaling is one important way in which the presence of unit roots alters the asymptotic theory of the distributions of estimators even in models as simple as (12.8). $\hat{\alpha}$ tends in probability to α, denoted $\hat{\alpha} \xrightarrow{p} \alpha$ at rate T, instead of the usual $T^{1/2}$,[6] the rate of convergence of consistent estimators in stationary asymptotic theory. This is known as *super-* or *T-consistency*, as distinct from $T^{1/2}$-consistency.

The integratedness of the series feeds into the distribution of the estimator in another important respect. The denominator of (12.8) does not tend in probability to a finite limit but has an asymptotic distribution. Similarly, the distribution of the numerator of (12.8) is not asymptotically normal. Standard central limit theorems do not apply because of the nonstationarity of x_t.

Finally, consider taking the Cochrane-Orcutt transform of (12.7b). This yields

$$y_t = \alpha x_t + \rho(y_{t-1} - \alpha x_{t-1}) + \varepsilon_{2t}. \qquad (12.9)$$

Equation (12.8) differs from (12.9) only in the former's omission of an I(0) term given by $(y_{t-1} - \alpha x_{t-1})$ (I(0) because y_t and x_t are cointegrated), which thereby enters the residual of the regression in (12.8). Nevertheless, a remarkable consequence of *T*-consistency is that the omission of I(0) terms in the model does not affect the consistency of the coefficient estimator on an I(1) variable. Thus, with a long data series, a static regression such as (12.8) is enough to obtain a consistent estimate of the long-run relationship between the variables. However, the finite-sample and asymptotic distributions of the coefficient estimator is affected by the presence of unmodeled terms, an observation that is of some importance in our later discussion. This is also a point taken up by Zivot in his comment, which follows this chapter.

Engle and Granger's paper emphasized the value of static regressions in an environment where the processes are integrated of order 1 and recommended modeling such integrated processes in two stages. In the first stage, the long-run relationship is estimated *via* static regressions. At the second state, the dynamics of the model, all parameterized as I(0) variables, are estimated. Thus in an I(1) environment, static regressions formed, according to this line of argument, an important part of good modeling practice. How much of this recommendation still holds true, in the light of subsequent research, is a matter of some debate. Several interlinked issues are important in any evaluation of this point. These include, in particular, issues concerning the distributions of the coefficient estimators, biases in these estimates and tests for cointegration based on these estimates. We address all these issues in turn.

Asymptotic Theory

The nonstandardness of the distributions, both in spurious and nonspurious regressions, arises, in the main, from the coefficient of interest being a coefficient on a variable integrated of order 1 (or higher). From this follows a central observation, due to Sims, Stock, and Watson (1990) *inter alia* (for related analysis, see Banerjee and Dolado, 1988, and Stock and West, 1988) that if the coefficients of interest can be written as coefficients on I(0) variables, by means of suitable linear transformations of the variables in the original regression equation, then standard asymptotic tools can be used to conduct inference. In essence this implies that the regression equation is rich enough to allow transformations such as differencing of the variables and linearly combining lagged levels of the variables—that is, a sufficiently rich dynamic specification is required.

Consider a test of the permanent income hypothesis of the form given by (12.5) but augmented to include lags of y_t and c_t, where c_t is consumption in period t and y_t is disposable income. If the permanent income hypothesis is correct, y_t is cointegrated with c_t and since c_t has a unit root, so does y_t. Further, in the regression equation

$$\Delta c_t = \beta c_{t-1} + \pi_1 y_{t-1} + \pi_2 y_{t-2} + \ldots + \pi_p y_{t-p} + u_t, \qquad (12.10)$$

the permanent income hypothesis, which is taken to be the null hypothesis implies, first, that $\beta = 0$ and, second, that $\pi_i = 0$ $(i = 1 \ldots p)$. Take the latter as the main hypothesis of interest, and to simplify matters further, suppose that β is correctly imposed at its true value of 0. Thus, as in (12.5), we are interested in testing for the excess sensitivity of consumption to income. Then *a* rewriting of (12.10) yields

$$\Delta c_t = (\pi_1 + \pi_2 + \ldots + \pi_p)k + (\pi_1 + \pi_2 + \ldots + \pi_p)c_{t-1} + \pi_1(y_{t-1} - c_{t-1} - k)$$

$$+ \ldots + \pi_p(y_{t-p} - c_{t-p} - k) + u_t,$$

$$= m + \phi c_{t-1} + \pi_1(y_{t-1} - c_{t-1} - k) + \ldots + \pi_p(y_{t-p} - c_{t-p} - k) + u_t,$$

where k is the intercept of the long-run consumption function, possibly equal to 0, $m = k\sum_{i=1}^{p}\pi_i$, and $\phi = \sum_{i=1}^{p}\pi_i$. In this rewriting, the coefficients on all the disposable income variables, $\pi_1, \ldots, \pi_p$, have been expressed as coefficients on I(0) variables (given that y_t and c_t are cointegrated). Because it is possible to achieve this rewriting, the distributions of the coefficient estimators of $\pi_1, \ldots,$ π_p, denoted $\hat{\pi}_1, \ldots, \hat{\pi}_p$, are individually and jointly asymptotically normally distributed. Thus standard normal tables can be used to test for significance of the individual $\hat{\pi}_i s$ while F-tables can be used to conduct tests of joint significance (asymptotically). This therefore represents a considerable simplification of the process of inference although it is based, importantly, on a proper classification of the integration and cointegration properties of the variables concerned. This analysis alone is enough to reinstate the use of dynamic regressions and should lead to a focus away from static regressions. But there are at least two other important reasons—the first concerning biases in estimates of the cointegrating relation and the second linked with the issue of testing for cointegration.

Biases

The discussion in this section is based on the important, but clearly not always realistic, assumption that single-equation methods are statistically valid (and efficient) for estimating the parameters of interest. The parameters of interest include those describing short-run behavior and also those giving the long-run relationships among the variables. The claim in this section is that, even when single-equation estimation methods suffice,[7] both the long-run and the short-run parameters are better estimated using dynamic methods. Thus the important notion, that the errors should form a martingale difference sequence[8] in a well-specified model, continues to hold true when dealing with nonstationary series. Therefore, in finite samples, the biases in the estimates of the long-run parameters, introduced by not explicitly modeling the dynamic I(0) terms, which thus enter the residuals of a static regression, are considerable.[9]

We illustrate the argument with an example taken from Banerjee, Dolado, Galbraith, and Hendry (1993) (referred to henceforth as Banerjee et al., 1993). While an important charge that can be made against any example is that the DGP is too special, the results here are representative of a large number of Monte Carlo results (Hendry and Neale, 1987; Stock, 1987; Phillips and Hansen, 1990).

Suppose the series $\{y_t\}$ and $\{x_t\}$ are generated by the following process:

$$y_t = \gamma_1 y_{t-1} + \gamma_2 x_t + \gamma_3 x_{t-1} + \varepsilon_{1t} \tag{12.11a}$$

$$x_t = x_{t-1} + \varepsilon_{2t}; \tag{12.11b}$$

$$\varepsilon_{1t} \sim NID(0, \sigma_1^2), \; \varepsilon_{2t} \sim NID(0, \sigma_2^2), \; \text{cov}(\varepsilon_{1t}, \varepsilon_{2s}) = 0, \; \forall \; t, s;$$

$$\gamma_1 + \gamma_2 + \gamma_3 = 1.$$

Table 12.2. Biases in static models

	Sample size (T)				
	25	50	100	200	400
$\gamma_1 = 0.9,\ \gamma_2 = 0.5$ $\sigma_1/\sigma_2 = 3$	−0.39	−0.25	−0.15	−0.07	−0.04
$\gamma_1 = 0.9,\ \gamma_2 = 0.5$ $\sigma_1/\sigma_2 = 1$	−0.32	−0.22	−0.14	−0.08	−0.04
$\gamma_1 = 0.5,\ \gamma_2 = 0.1$ $\sigma_1/\sigma_2 = 3$	−0.23	−0.13	−0.07	−0.03	−0.02
$\gamma_1 = 0.5,\ \gamma_2 = 0.1$ $\sigma_1/\sigma_2 = 1$	−0.21	−0.12	−0.06	−0.03	−0.02

Source: Banerjee *et al.* (1993, table 7.3).

Notes: *DGP*: (12.11a) + (12.11b); 5,000 replications. Standard errors of these estimates vary widely, but the estimated biases are in almost all cases significantly different from zero. The biases do not decline at rate T but they do decline more quickly than $T^{1/2}$. The simulations used GAUSS. The mean biases are computed as $[(5,000)^{-1}\sum_{i=1}^{5,000}(\hat{\alpha}_i - 1)]$, where i is the index for the replications for each parameter configuration.

Thus, both $\{y_t\}$ and $\{x_t\}$ are I(1) series and are CI(1, 1), with a long-run multiplier of 1 linking the two series.[10] Further, $\{x_t\}$ is strongly exogenous for the regression parameters.

Consider now estimating the long-run by means of the static regression:

$$y_t = \alpha x_t + u_t. \qquad (12.12)$$

The omitted dynamic I(0) terms are given by $(y - x)_{t-1}$ and Δx_t[11] and are included in the residual u_t, which, in general, is therefore serially correlated. The data are generated using the specification in (12.11) above. The strong exogeneity of x_t is ensured by drawing the $\{\varepsilon_{1t}\}$ and $\{\varepsilon_{2t}\}$ series from uncorrelated pseudonormal distributions. The γ_is are chosen to preserve homogeneity and sample sizes ranging from 25 to 400 are considered. The ratio of the standard deviations of ε_{1t} and ε_{2t} are also varied and each parameter configuration is run 5,000 times and the results noted. Table 12.2, taken from Banerjee *et al.* (1993), summarizes the estimated mean biases in the static model.

The significance of the results reported in Table 12.2 become clear when these are compared with the biases arising from estimating a dynamic model corresponding to (12.12)—say, regressing y_t not only on x_t but also on y_{t-1} and x_{t-1}—which, expressed in error-correction form,[12] is given as (12.13) below:

$$\Delta y_t = b\Delta x_t + c(y_{t-1} - x_{t-1}) + dx_{t-1} + v_t. \qquad (12.13)$$

The extra lagged term is included to avoid imposing homogeneity on the relation between y and x. Although homogeneity would be a valid restriction in this case— that is, $d = 0$, the extra term allows for the possible ignorance of the investigator and, as results reported in Banerjee, Galbraith, and Dolado (1990) show, does not affect the estimate of the short-run adjustment coefficient c. The estimate of the long-run multiplier is deduced from (12.13) as $(1 - \hat{d}/\hat{c})$.[13] For the same configuration of parameters given in Table 12.2, the biases in the estimate of the long-run parameter derived from (12.13) are all insignificantly different from zero.

It is possible to extend this set of experiments to allow for weakly exogenous x_t. The results carry through in this case. However, as we show in a later section, if weak exogeneity fails to hold, the usefulness of estimates from dynamic single equations is reduced substantially and the comparison between static and dynamic estimates becomes ambiguous. Systems estimation is the main route to consider in the absence of weak exogeneity and Monte Carlo evidence here (see, for example, Gonzalo, 1994) again supports the claim of substantial inferiority, in general, of estimates derived from static regressions.

Finally, it is important to note that it is possible to derive analytical expressions that explain the difference in the accuracy of the estimates using alternative methods. From these analytical expressions, it is possible to derive the parameter configurations or DGP specifications for which, say, static regressions are likely to outperform (or perform as well as) dynamic regressions or *vice versa* (see Kremers, Ericsson, and Dolado, 1992).

Testing for Cointegration

This paper has taken as its main theme the importance of dynamic regressions in a nonstationary environment. This theme has been emphasized via several sub-themes discussing the particular benefits of conducting estimation and testing in a dynamic setting. This section discusses the third sub-theme of this line of argument, testing for cointegration and discusses first using a specific simple example and then more generally tests of cointegration in dynamic models.

A large class of tests for cointegration (Phillips and Ouliaris, 1990) takes as its starting point a static regression such as (12.12) and tests for unit roots in the estimated residual series $\hat{u}_t$. A popular test in this category is known as the augmented Dickey-Fuller test and consists of estimating the regression

$$\Delta \hat{u}_t = (c_0) + \beta(t) + \rho \hat{u}_{t-i} + \sum_{i=1}^{\ell} \delta_i \Delta \hat{u}_{t-i} + \omega_t, \qquad (12.14)$$

and testing for the significance of the estimate of ρ. A significant $\hat{\rho}$, according to appropriate critical values, constitutes a rejection of the null of a unit root in the residual series and hence provides *prima facie* evidence of the existence of cointegration.

The critical values used for this test are essentially modified Dickey-Fuller critical values. The unmodified critical values, given in Fuller (1976), apply to testing for unit roots in raw series. These critical values have to be adjusted for size when the series to be tested for a unit root is constructed or derived from a regression such as (12.12). Naturally this implies that the critical values are sensitive to the number of variables in the cointegrating regression and to the existence of a constant or a trend in the regression.[14] An extensive set of tables is provided by MacKinnon (1991), while Engle and Granger (1987) and Engle and Yoo (1987) provide a more limited set.

Return now to the experiment described in (12.11). The parameter configuration given by $\gamma_1 = 1$, $\gamma_2 = \gamma_3 = 0$ generates the case where y_t and x_t are not cointegrated. Equation (12.11a) can be written in error correction form as

$$\Delta y_t = \gamma_2 \Delta x_t + (\gamma_1 - 1)(y_{t-1} - x_{t-1}) + \varepsilon_{1t}. \qquad (12.15)$$

Thus a test for cointegration can be based on the t-statistic for $\hat{c}$ in (12.13) because under the usual null hypothesis of "no cointegration", $c = 0$ from (12.15). The distribution of this test statistic is nonstandard because under H_0, $(y_{t-1} - x_{t-1})$ is I(1) while both differenced terms are I(0) and the regression, in the terminology discussed above, is inconsistent. However, the test is straightforward and would be useful if it had good power properties.

It is interesting to remark that under the alternative hypothesis of cointegration, $t_{c=0}$ is asymptotically normally distributed. This follows from the property that in this case c is a coefficient on an I(0) variable and the arguments discussed above apply.

The $t_{c=0}$ test is a simple example of what Boswijk and Franses (1992) call a Wald test for cointegration and is based on a dynamic regression model with a constant included. It is instructive to compare the power properties of this test with an $ADF(1)$[15] test based on the residuals of the static model (12.12). The critical values for both these tests are derived by simulating the model under the null (that is, $\gamma_1 = 1$, $\gamma_2 = \gamma_3 = 0$, $s = \sigma_1/\sigma_2 = 1$ in (12.11a) and (12.11b)) for 5,000 replications. These critical values are then used for deriving the test powers, when the null hypothesis of no cointegration is false, of the $t_{c=0}$ test and the $ADF(1)$ test. Critical values are reported in Table 12.3 while powers of the tests are given in Table 12.4. Both tables are taken from Banerjee *et al.* (1993) and the simulations used PC-NAIVE (Hendry, Neale, and Ericsson, 1990).[16]

Several issues may now be noted. First, the most significant divergences in the powers of the two tests appear in the last three blocks of Table 12.4 and may be understood in terms of the common-factor restriction imposed by an $ADF(1)$ type of test. The $ADF(1)$ test involves testing $\gamma_1 = 1$ in the regression

Table 12.3. Fractiles of $t_{c=0}$ in (12.13) and *ADF* (1) in (12.14)

	Fractiles of $\mathrm{t}_{c=0}$			*Fractiles of* ADF *(1)*		
T	0.10	0.05	0.01	0.10	0.05	0.01
25	−2.99	−3.42	−4.22	−3.15	−3.51	−4.30
50	−2.95	−3.33	−4.06	−3.10	−3.41	−4.08
100	−2.93	−3.28	−3.95	−3.09	−3.39	−4.00

Notes: *DGP*: (12.11a) + (12.11b) with $\gamma_1 = 1$, $\gamma_2 = \gamma_3 = 0$, $s = \sigma_1/\sigma_2 = 1$; 5,000 replications.

$$\Delta(y_t - \alpha x_t) = (\gamma_1 - 1)(y_{t-1} - \alpha x_{t-1}) +$$
$$\delta\Delta(y_{t-1} - \alpha x_{t-1}) + \omega_t, \qquad (12.16)$$

where α, which here has a true value of unity, may be replaced by its estimate $\hat{\alpha}$ from the first-step regression of y_t on x_t. In (12.16), therefore, the dynamics of the model implicitly impose the short-run elasticity to equal its long-run value of 1. In (12.13), however, the coefficient on Δx_t is unrestricted. When the common-factor restriction is far from being satisfied (γ_2 is very different from 1), as in the last three blocks of the table, the performance of the ADF statistic, relative to $t_{c=0}$, is very poor.

Second, calculations in Banerjee *et al.* (1993) provide estimates of the non-centrality of both test statistics for fixed alternatives. For $T = 25$, these are given in Table 12.5 and show that the noncentralities of the ECM test are substantially greater, in most cases, than the corresponding noncentralities for the *ADF*(1) test. The relative magnitudes of the noncentralities help further to explain the performances of the two tests and again provide reasons for not modeling dynamics restrictively, both in general and where common factor restrictions are likely to be violated.

Third, to illustrate the issue of a conservative testing strategy, consider the choice of critical values to test for significance of $\hat{c}$ in (12.13) using the ECM test. In Table 12.3 we require *t*-statistics greater than, roughly, 3.5 in absolute magnitude to reject the null of no cointegration at the 5 percent confidence level. Let us call these the I(1) critical values. If the variables in the regression had been integrated of order 0, *t*-values in excess of 2.0 in absolute value would have sufficed. An I(0) critical value is therefore given by 2.0. Four possible situations are evident, labeled S1 to S4, when H_0: $c = 0$ is true (see Table 12.6). A conservative strategy would be one that sets the *maximum* of the rejections probability of the true null equal to the nominal confidence level of the test (here 5 percent). Looking at Table 12.6, this requires the use of the I(1) critical values, although this may entail a loss of power (if the variables are I(0)).

The conservative strategy may be adopted as a crude device to minimize the

Table 12.4. Test rejection frequencies in ECMs and ADFs

	Estimated power at given fractile		
	0.10 $t_{c=0}$/ADF	0.05 $t_{c=0}$/ADF	0.01 $t_{c=0}$/ADF
$\gamma_1 = 0.9$, $\gamma_2 = 0.5$, $\sigma_1/\sigma_2 = 3$			
$T = 25$	0.13/0.13	0.06/0.06	0.01/0.01
50	0.21/0.17	0.10/0.10	0.02/0.02
100	0.44/0.31	0.26/0.20	0.07/0.05
$\gamma_1 = 0.9$, $\gamma_2 = 0.5$, $\sigma_1/\sigma_2 = 1$			
$T = 25$	0.14/0.11	0.06/0.05	0.01/0.01
50	0.21/0.15	0.10/0.09	0.02/0.02
100	0.49/0.30	0.30/0.19	0.08/0.04
$\gamma_1 = 0.9$, $\gamma_2 = 0.5$, $\sigma_1/\sigma_2 = 1/3$			
$T = 25$	0.13/0.10	0.07/0.05	0.02/0.01
50	0.24/0.13	0.12/0.07	0.03/0.01
100	0.59/0.24	0.40/0.14	0.13/0.03
$\gamma_1 = 0.5$, $\gamma_2 = 0.1$, $\sigma_1/\sigma_2 = 3$			
$T = 25$	0.66/0.35	0.45/0.20	0.16/0.05
50	0.99/0.84	0.97/0.72	0.78/0.34
100	1.00/1.00	1.00/1.00	1.00/0.97
$\gamma_1 = 0.5$, $\gamma_2 = 0.1$, $\sigma_1/\sigma_2 = 1$			
$T = 25$	0.79/0.31	0.66/0.18	0.29/0.04
50	1.00/0.80	1.00/0.67	0.94/0.28
100	1.00/1.00	1.00/1.00	1.00/0.96
$\gamma_1 = 0.5$, $\gamma_2 = 0.1$, $\sigma_1/\sigma_2 = 1/3$			
$T = 25$	0.94/0.23	0.87/0.12	0.64/0.03
50	1.00/0.75	1.00/0.60	1.00/0.22
100	1.00/1.00	1.00/1.00	1.00/0.94

Notes: *DGP*: (12.11a) + (12.11b); model: (12.13), (12.14); 5,000 replications.

Table 12.5. Noncentrality (*NC*) of $t_{c=0}$ and *ADF* (1)

Case	(a)	(b)	(c)	(d)	(e)	(f)
NC_{ADF}	−1.15	−1.15	−1.15	−2.89	−2.89	−2.89
NC_{ECM}	−1.19	−1.28	−1.52	−3.25	−3.88	−5.32

Notes: *DGP*: (12.11a) + (12.11b); 5,000 replications.

Table 12.6.

	Order of integration	Critical values used	Rejection of $H_0(\%)$
S1	I(1)	I(1)	5
S2	I(1)	I(0)	> 5
S3	I(0)	I(0)	5
S4	I(0)	I(1)	< 5

consequences of *incorrect* classifications. However it is not a strategy that attacks the preclassification issue directly. Papers by Elliott and Stock (1992), Stock (1992), and Phillips and Ploberger (1991) propose Bayesian methods of classification and inference in models when the orders of integration of the variables are unknown. A description of these methods is beyond the scope of this paper.

Finally, the logic of the argument in favor of the ECM test generalizes to cases where the regressors are only weakly exogenous for the parameters of interest. Boswijk and Franses (1992) propose a Wald test for cointegration identical in spirit to the one developed above. In the simplest case, they consider the case where there is at most one cointegration vector and the vector $\mathbf{x}_t$ is weakly exogenous for the cointegration parameters. Boswijk and Franses's test involves writing a conditional error correction model for the dependent variable y_t given $\mathbf{x}_t$ (where linearity of the conditional model follows from the assumption of normality of the joint distribution of $\mathbf{z}_t = (y_t:\mathbf{x}_t')'$):

$$\Delta y_t = c_0 + \phi_0'\Delta\mathbf{x}_t + \lambda(y_{t-1} - \theta'\mathbf{x}_{t-1}) + \sum_{j=1}^{p-1}(\psi_j\Delta y_{t-j} + \phi_j'\Delta\mathbf{x}_{t-j}) + \eta_t$$

$$= c_0 + \phi_0'\Delta\mathbf{x}_t + \pi'\mathbf{z}_{t-1} + \sum_{j=1}^{p-1}(\psi_j\Delta y_{t-j} + \phi_j'\Delta\mathbf{x}_{t-j}) + \eta_t, \tag{12.17}$$

where $\pi' = \lambda(1, -\theta')$. Equation (12.17) is a generalization of the test given in (12.15). As before, $\lambda = 0$ implies that there is no cointegration while if $\lambda \neq 0$, (12.17) can be reparameterized as an autoregressive distributed lag model of order p with y_t and $\mathbf{x}_t$ cointegrated. If θ were known, a test for cointegration could be based on a t-test of $\lambda = 0$. In general, this test is not implementable because θ is not known but must be estimated. Thus the regression must either be reparameterized as

$$\Delta y_t = c_0 + \phi_0'\Delta\mathbf{x}_t + \lambda(y_{t-1} - \iota'\mathbf{x}_{t-1}) + \xi'\mathbf{x}_{t-1}$$

$$+ \sum_{j=1}^{p-1}(\psi_j\Delta y_{t-j} + \phi_j'\Delta\mathbf{x}_{t-j}) + \eta_t, \tag{12.18}$$

where ι is a vector (of dimension equal to the dimension of $\mathbf{x}_t$) whose elements are all equal to 1 and $\xi = \lambda(\iota' - \theta')$, and the t-test now based on the t-statistic for $\hat{\lambda}$ in (12.18), or, using the result that $\lambda = 0$ implies $\pi = \mathbf{0}$, based on a Wald-type statistic of the form

$$\text{Wald} = \hat{\pi}'[\hat{\mathbf{V}}(\hat{\pi})]^{-1}\hat{\pi}, \tag{12.19}$$

where $\hat{\pi}$ is the OLS estimator of π in (12.17), with estimated variance matrix $\hat{\mathbf{V}}(\hat{\pi})$. Boswijk and Franses's results suggest that a test of the form (12.19) is likely to have better statistical properties than the one given by (12.18).

Boswijk and Franses present power calculations comparing the power of the Wald test with an ADF test based on the residuals of static regression. In this framework, selection of lag length becomes an issue of some importance. For underparameterized models, relative to the DGP, the Wald test may have incorrect size (too many rejections of the true null hypothesis at any nominal confidence level) while overparameterization leads to loss in power of the test. Using various "optimal" lag-length selection criteria, Boswijk and Franses show that the Wald test is superior to the ADF test (and to a test based on Johansen's (1988) procedure discussed below). Also, because both λ and θ can be retrieved from the estimate of π, after suitable transformation, the evidence from the simpler DGP (12.11(a) and (12.11b)) suggests that the long-run is also likely to be better estimated in a dynamic model such as (12.17).

Systems Estimation

It is natural to ask, given that the discussion above has focused exclusively on single-equation estimation techniques, how the arguments generalize to estimation in systems. In essence, this is equivalent to asking what happens when the regressors are not weakly exogenous for the cointegrating parameters. Based on our discussion so far, it should not be surprising to observe that the long-run relation is poorly estimated not only in static regressions but that single-equation dynamic models in general do not perform much better.

There are at least four interrelated issues in single-equation estimation that are worth highlighting. First, the presence of unit roots introduces nonstandard distributions of the coefficient estimates. Second, the errors may be processes that are autocorrelated. Third, in a multivariate setting, there can exist several cointegrating relations and there is no longer a natural ordering of the variables (which dependent and which independent) in a static regression.[17] Finally, the explanatory variables in the single equation may not be weakly exogenous for the parameters of interest.

In some of the discussion above, we have provided examples of how dynamic regressions can overcome some of the problems posed by the first two effects. However, for most purposes of empirical modeling the question ultimately boils down to a discussion of the circumstances in which only systems-estimation provides efficient and unbiased estimates.

The answer in this nonstationary world is not dramatically different from the answer one would have given, say, fifteen years ago—when weak-exogeneity is violated, estimating only the conditional model is suboptimal, leading to biased, inconsistent, and inefficient estimates. Thus the debate that raged in the 1970s on the need to have *at least* weakly exogenous regressors to conduct estimation and inference in single-equation models remains an issue of considerable importance.

A discussion of estimating cointegrated systems requires us first to provide a formal statement of a cointegrated system (Engle and Granger, 1987):

Definition: The components of the vector $\mathbf{x}_t$ are said to be cointegrated of order d, b, denoted $\mathbf{x}_t \sim CI(d, b)$ if (1) each component of $\mathbf{x}_t$ is $I(d)$ and (2) there exists a nonzero vector α such that $\alpha'\mathbf{x}_t \sim I(d - b)$, $d > b \geq 0$. The vector α is called the cointegrating vector.

As we have stated before, if $\mathbf{x}_t$ has $n > 2$ components, then it is possible for r linearly independent (equilibrium) relationships to govern the evolution of the variables. It may be shown that $0 \leq r \leq n - 1$. The r linearly independent cointegrating vectors can be gathered into an $n \times r$ matrix α with rank r.

The Granger representation theorem (Engle and Granger, 1987) shows that a cointegrated system can be written in several equivalent forms (see Engle and Granger, 1987; Banerjee *et al.*, 1993). We focus on one of these forms, the ECM form, to illustrate the importance of estimation in systems. In ECM form, the system can be written as

$$\mathbf{A}(L)(1 - L)\mathbf{x}_t = -\gamma\mathbf{z}_{t-1} + \omega_t, \tag{12.20}$$

where ω_t is a stationary multivariate disturbance, $\mathbf{A}(L)$ is a stationary lag-polynomial matrix, with $\mathbf{A}(0) = \mathbf{I}_n$ and $\mathbf{A}(1)$ finite, $\mathbf{z}_t = \alpha'\mathbf{x}_t$ and γ is a nonzero matrix with rank r.

Thus, because α is also a reduced-rank matrix of rank r, the reduced rank (r) of $\pi = \gamma\alpha'$ is the restriction implied by cointegration in the system given by (12.20).

Consider the case where $n = 2$ and $r = 1$, let $\alpha' = (1, -\kappa)$, and let the system be given by

$$x_{1t} - kx_{2t} = u_{1t},$$

$$\Delta x_{2t} = u_{2t}, \tag{12.21}$$

where $(u_{1t}, u_{2t})'$ follow a jointly stationary process. Then, in ECM form, the system can be written as

$$\Delta x_{1t} = d_{12}(L)\Delta x_{2t} + d_{11}(L)\Delta x_{1t-1} + \gamma_1(x_{1t-k} - \kappa x_{2t-k}) + e_{1t},$$

$$\Delta x_{2t} = d_{21}(L)\Delta x_{1t} + d_{22}(L)\Delta x_{2t-1} + \gamma_2(x_{1t-k} - \kappa x_{2t-k}) + e_{2t}. \quad (12.22)$$

Weak exogeneity will be violated in (12.22) if, say, $\gamma_1\gamma_2 \neq 0$,[18] and thus the error-correction term (which Engle and Granger proposed estimating at the first step by a static regression) enters both equations. The x_2 process therefore contains information about the process generating x_1 and therefore, in the absence of *a priori* information of the form, say, $\gamma_1\gamma_2 = 0$,[19] systems-based methods of estimation are essential. Hendry (1992) provides several examples of how violations of weak exogeneity leads to problems of bias in single-equation-based estimators.

It is impossible, in the space available, to provide an account of the various methods proposed of estimating cointegrated systems. Two main methods of estimation have been proposed, one due to Phillips (1991) that uses the triangular or canonical form of the system given by (12.21) and the other due to Johansen (1988) that estimates the model in the ECM form given by (12.22).[20] Estimation focuses on several issues, especially the cointegrating rank given by the rank of π (or equivalently the number of cointegrating vectors), the economic interpretability of the linear equilibrium relationships and the testing of any special economic hypotheses of interest, where the latter are given by restrictions on the parameters of the equilibrium relationships. As in the usual analysis of simultaneous equation systems, it is also necessary to take account of restrictions that serve to identify the system.

Conclusion

We have taken as our main theme of this paper the observation that the fundamental methods *per se* of econometric modeling, for specification and estimation, remain unaltered in the new world of nonstationary econometrics. Some of the dramatic simplifications that appeared possible, in terms of, say, modeling the long-run and short-run separately, or focusing primarily on the long-run properties of and interrelationships between series, seem eventually to be fraught with difficulties of tests having low powers and estimators having large biases.

We have also argued that, even for modeling the long run or testing for cointegration, dynamic models provide the most effective way of obtaining information. Where weak exogeneity is violated, single-equation estimation techniques are, in general, inadequate, and systems-based methods are optimal. Thus the importance of this literature lies rather in the new awareness we have of the properties of common time series and of the consequent need to take account of these properties in estimation and to modify, wherever necessary, the tools required to conduct inference.

Appendix: Concepts of Exogeneity

Econometric analysis often proceeds by using a single-equation model of a process of interest. In basing inference on single-equation methods, we implicitly assume that knowledge of the processes generating the explanatory variables carries no information relevant to the parameters of the process of interest. Engle, Hendry, and Richard (1983) provide conditions (concepts of exogeneity) relating to the circumstances in which this assumption is valid. Rather than refer to particular variables as exogenous in general, however, Engle *et al.* refer to a variable as exogenous *with respect to a particular parameter* if knowledge of the process generating the exogenous variable contains *no* information about that parameter.

Three different concepts are introduced by Engle et al. and correspond to three different ways in which a parameter estimate may be used: inference, forecasting based on forecasts of the exogenous variables, and policy analysis. These different uses require that increasingly stringent conditions be met for exogeneity (that is, for the irrelevance of the regressor process to a parameter of interest). These conditions can be examined with the following definitions.

Let $\mathbf{x}_t = \begin{bmatrix} y_t \\ z_t \end{bmatrix}$ be generated by the process with conditional density function $D(\mathbf{x}_t \mid \mathbf{X}_{t-1}, \boldsymbol{\lambda})$ where $\mathbf{X}_{t-1}$ denotes the history of the variable X: $\mathbf{X}_{t-1} = (\mathbf{x}_{t-1}, \mathbf{x}_{t-2}, \dots \mathbf{x}_0)$. Let the set of parameters $\boldsymbol{\lambda}$ be partitioned into ($\boldsymbol{\lambda}_1, \boldsymbol{\lambda}_2$) such that

$$D(\mathbf{x}_t \mid \mathbf{X}_{t-1}, \boldsymbol{\lambda}) = D(y_t \mid z_t, \mathbf{X}_{t-1}, \boldsymbol{\lambda}_1) D(z_t \mid \mathbf{X}_{t-1}, \boldsymbol{\lambda}_2).$$

The first element of the product on the right side of the equality is known as the *conditional* density (or model), while the second element is the marginal density. In the simple case where $\mathbf{x}_t$ is bivariate normal, the conditional model leads to a bivariate regression with y_t as the dependent variable and z_t the regressor.

Suppose our parameter of interest is given by ψ (in the conditional model). Weak exogeneity of z_t for ψ requires that (1) ψ is a function of $\boldsymbol{\lambda}_1$ alone and (2) there are no cross-restrictions between $\boldsymbol{\lambda}_1$ and $\boldsymbol{\lambda}_2$. The essential element of weak exogeneity is that $\boldsymbol{\lambda}_2$ contains no information relevant to discovering $\boldsymbol{\lambda}_1$. Inference concerning ψ can be made conditional on z_t with no loss of information relative to what could be obtained using the joint density of y_t and z_t.

Strong exogeneity requires that z_t is weakly exogenous for ψ and

$$D(z_t \mid \mathbf{X}_{t-1}, \boldsymbol{\lambda}_2) = D(z_t \mid \mathbf{Z}_{t-1}, y_0, \boldsymbol{\lambda}_2),$$

so that Y does not Granger-cause Z. (That is, Y does not enter the process generating Z. In a simple regression model this implies that the equation generating z_t does not contains any lags of y_t.) Strong exogeneity is necessary for forecasting that proceeds by forecasting future z's and then forecasting y's conditional on the predicted z's.

Finally, z_t is superexogenous for ψ if and only if z_t is weakly exogenous for ψ and $d\lambda_1/d\lambda_2 = 0$. Superexogeneity is necessary where models will be used for policy analysis, in which the investigator is interested in predicting the derivative of the dependent variable with respect to a change that can be made in an explanatory variable; a change made to the value of the explanatory variable by an external actor is in effect a change in the parameters of the process governing that variable's evolution.

Acknowledgments

This paper is part of a program of research with which I have been associated for several years. During this period I have benefited greatly from discussions with my colleagues Juan Dolado, John Galbraith, and David Hendry. While absolving them of any responsibility for the views expressed in this paper, it is a pleasure to acknowledge their help. The financial assistance of the Economic and Social Research Council (UK) under grant R231184 is also gratefully acknowledged.

Notes

1. This definition can be extended to cover variables integrated of order $d > 1$. Roughly speaking, a series is said to be integrated of order d if it is stationary after differencing d times but is not stationary after differencing only $d - 1$ times.

2. An issue of some interest is which of model (12.5) or (12.6) is appropriate. The advantage of using a model such as (12.6) lies, generally, not in its plausibility but rather in making the critical values appropriate for testing the null $H_0 : d_2 = 0$ invariant to the presence or absence of a constant in the process generating c_t. If this *DGP* has a constant, say, $\Delta c_t = d + v_t$, the critical values of the t-test in (12.5), used for testing H_0, are sensitive to the value of d whereas this is not the case in model (12.6). A related problem concerns what critical values should be used. West (1988) shows that if $d \neq 0$, $t_{d_2=0}$ is asymptotically normally distributed in (12.5) while it has a nonstandard distribution in (12.6). In the absence of *a priori* knowledge of whether or not there is a constant in the *DGP*, invariance of the critical values is a useful property and I would argue in favor of using the more general model, and hence nonstandard critical values, given by (12.6).

3. Source: Mankiw and Shapiro (1986, table 2). The standard errors of each of the entries a_{ij}, expressed as a fraction, is given by $[(a_{ij})(1 - a_{ij})/N]^{1/2}$ where N is the number of replications in the Monte Carlo ($N = 1,000$ for this table).

4. Work on nonlinear cointegration, although mathematically more complex, shares this main idea of some function of the component series being bounded statistically.

5. By order T^k we mean that the variance grows at rate T^k. For example, for a random walk process such as (12.1), it may be shown that variance $(y_T) = T\sigma_u^2$ and thus $k = 1$ in the terminology given above. Thus if we define a variable $z_T = T^{-1/2}y_T$, variance $(z_T) = \sigma_u^2$ which is finite, bounded away from zero and remains constant with time. Scalings such as these are important in deriving the asymptotic theory because it ensures that the asymptotic distributions of the *scaled* expressions are neither nondegenerate (do not collapse on a single value) nor explosive (have infinitely large variances).

6. That is, it is $T(\hat{\alpha} - \alpha)$, which has a nondegenerate, nonexplosive distribution asymptotically rather than $T^{1/2}(\hat{\alpha} - \alpha)$. The latter is the scaling appropriate for estimators based on stationary processes.

7. It is important to make this qualification in order not to mislead the reader. There are many circumstances, some described below, especially under failure of weak exogeneity, when single-equation dynamic models also provide badly biased estimates. However, this does not run counter to our main assertion here that static regressions are hardly ever desirable and thus two-step methods based on first estimating the long-run and then modeling the short-run have severe limitations. For estimation and inference, the two steps are best accomplished together.

8. A martingale difference sequence (MDS) generalizes the concept of an identically and independently distributed sequence of random variables, by allowing for some amount of dynamic dependence among the elements of the sequence. An MDS is defined with respect to an information set $\mathcal{I}_{t-1}$ of data realized by time $t - 1$. A sequence $\{y_t, t = 1, 2, \ldots\}$ is defined to be a MDS with respect to $\{\mathcal{I}_t, t = 1, 2, \ldots\}$ if $E\{|y_t|\} < \infty \ \forall \ t$ and that $E\{y_t \mid \mathcal{I}_{t-1}\} = 0 \ \forall \ t$. In words, we require that the expectation of the absolute value of y_t be finite and that the expectation of y_t *conditional on the past* be zero. For the purposes of the analysis that follows, the reader will not lose by thinking of the simpler special case of serially uncorrelated, mean zero, variables.

9. There is a literature on correcting, nonparametrically, the estimates derived from a static regression in order to account for the effects of the omitted dynamic terms (see, for example, Phillips and Hansen, 1990). Provided single-equation estimation is valid, dynamic specification and nonparametric correction of the estimates from a static regression are asymptotically equivalent procedures. Comparisons in finite samples are usually ambiguous and depend on the particular specifications of the DGP.

10. The long-run multiplier is derived by setting $y_t = y^*$, $x_t = x^* \ \forall \ t$ and ε_{1t} to its expected value of 0. Thus, $y^* = \gamma_1 y^* + (\gamma_2 + \gamma_3)x^*$, which implies that $(1 - \gamma_1)y^* = (\gamma_2 + \gamma_3)x^*$. Under the restriction that $\gamma_1 + \gamma_2 + \gamma_3 = 1$, it follows that $y^* = x^*$ in the long-run.

11. This may be seen by rewriting (12.11a), using the homogeneity restriction, as $y_t = x_t + \gamma_1(y - x)_{t-1} + (\gamma_2 - 1)\Delta x_t + \varepsilon_{1t}$.

12. Error-correction models (ECMs) are the focus of an extensive literature, starting wih Sargan (1964), Hendry and Anderson (1977) and Davidson, Hendry, Srba, and Yeo (1978). They are a way of capturing adjustments in a dependent variable that may depend not only on the level of some explanatory variable but also on the extent of the deviation of the explanatory variable from an *equilibrium* relationship with the dependent variable. Thus, if the equilibrium relationship is given by $y^* = \theta x^*$, the error-correction term is given by $(y_t - \theta x_t)$. In (12.13) $\theta = 1$. The estimate of the coefficient on the error-correction term, given above by c, provides an estimate of the short-run adjustment to equilibrium.

13. If it is necessary to have estimates of the standard error of this multiplier estimate, (12.13) can be estimated more conveniently in a linearly transformed form that gives the long-run multiplier directly. This is known as the Bewley transform and the estimates derived from this transform are numerically equivalent to those obtained from (12.13).

14. See footnote 2.

15. ADF(1) refers to an augmented Dickey-Fuller test with $\ell = 1$ in (12.14).

16. Critical values for the $t_{c=0}$ test for the case where (12.13) includes a constant and $\mathbf{x}_t$ is a vector (at most of dimension 5) are given by Banerjee, Dolado, and Mestre (1993). These critical values depend on the dimension of the system (number of regressors). Hansen (1992) provides an ECM test

that is invariant to dimension, but the test imposes a common factor restriction. Where this restriction is violated, the losses of power involved are important. Banerjee, Dolado, and Mestre (1993) provide a full discussion of this issue.

17. Techniques that rely on rotating the dependent variable in sequence are in general unsatisfactory.

18. Naturally, this is only a *sufficient* condition for such a violation. To derive all the necessary conditions for weak exogeneity would require us to look at the properties of the error process $(e_{1t}, e_{2t})'$.

19. To emphasize the point made in the earlier footnote, this is clearly only a necessary condition for weak exogeneity since the parameters of the two equations may be linked in other ways.

20. For details of the first method, see Phillips and Hansen (1990), Phillips and Loretan (1991), and Phillips (1991). For the second method, in addition to the original account contained in Johansen (1988), also see Banerjee and Hendry (1992) and Banerjee *et al.* (1993).

References

Banerjee, A., and J. Dolado. (1988). "Tests of the Life-Cycle-Permanent Income Hypothesis in the Presence of Random Walks: Asymptotic Theory and Small Sample Interpretations." *Oxford Economic Papers* 40, 610–633.

Banerjee, A., J. Dolado, J.W. Galbraith, and D.F. Hendry. (1993). *Co-integration, Error Correction and the Econometric Analysis of Non-stationary Data.* Oxford: Oxford University Press.

Banerjee, A., J. Dolado, and R. Mestre. (1993). "On Some Tests for Co-integration: The Cost of Simplicity." Manuscript.

Banerjee, A., J.W. Galbraith, and J. Dolado. (1990). "Dynamic Specification with the General Error-Correction From." *Oxford Bulletin of Economics and Statistics* 52, 95–104.

Banerjee, A., and D.F. Hendry. (1992). "Testing Integration and Co-integration." *Oxford Bulletin of Economics and Statistics* 54, 225–235.

Boswijk, H.P., and P.H. Franses. (1992). "Dynamic Specification and Cointegration." *Oxford Bulletin of Economics and Statistics* 54, 369–381.

Campbell, J.Y., and P. Perron. (1991). "Pitfalls and Opportunities: What Macroeconomists Should Know About Unit Roots." In O.J. Blanchard and S. Fischer (eds.), *NBER Economics Annual 1991.* Cambridge, MA: MIT Press.

Davidson, J.E.H., D.F. Hendry, F. Srba, and S. Yeo. (1978). "Econometric Modelling of the Aggregate Time-Series Relationship Between Consumers' Expenditure and Income in the United Kingdom." *Economic Journal* 88, 661–692.

Dolado, J., T.J. Jenkinson, and S.-S. Rivero. (1990). "Cointegration and Unit Roots." *Journal of Economic Surveys* 4, 249–273.

Elliott, G., and J.H. Stock. (1992). "Inference in Time Series Regression When the Order of Integration of a Regressor Is Unknown." Technical Working Paper No. 122, *National Bureau of Economic Research.*

Engle, R.F., and C.W.J. Granger. (1987). "Co-integration and Error Correction: Representation, Estimation and Testing." *Econometrica* 55, 251–276.

Engle, R.F., D.F. Hendry, and J.-F. Richard. (1983). "Exogeneity." *Econometrica* 55, 277–304.

Engle, R.F., and B.S. Yoo. (1987). "Forecasting and Testing in Cointegrated Systems." *Journal of Econometrics* 35, 143–159.

Fama, E.F., and K.R. French. (1989). "Business Conditions and Expected Returns on Stocks and Bonds." *Journal of Financial Economics* 25, 23–49.

Flavin, M.A. (1981). "The Adjustment of Consumption to Changing Expectations About Future Income." *Journal of Political Economy* 89, 974–1009.

Fuller, W.A. (1976). *Introduction to Statistical Time Series.* New York: Wiley.

Gonzalo, J. (1994). "Five Alternative Methods of Estimating Long-Run Equilibrium Relationships." *Journal of Econometrics* 60, 203–233.

Granger, C.W.J., and P. Newbold. (1974). "Spurious Regressions in Econometrics." *Journal of Econometrics* 2, 111–120.

Hall, R.E. (1978). "Stochastic Implications of the Life-Cycle Permanent Income Hypothesis." *Journal of Political Economy* 86, 971–987.

Hansen, B.E. (1992). "A Powerful Simple Test for Cointegration Using Cochrane-Orcutt." Working Paper No. 230, Department of Economics, University of Rochester.

Hendry, D.F. (1992). "On the Interactions of Unit Roots and Exogeneity." Manuscript, Nuffield College, Oxford.

Hendry, D.F., and G.J. Anderson. (1977). "Testing Dynamic Specification in Small Simultaneous Models: An Application to a Model of Building Society Behaviour in the United Kingdom." In M.D. Inrilligator (ed.), *Frontiers of Quantitative Economics* (ch. 8c, pp. 361–383). Amsterdam: North-Holland.

Hendry, D.F., and A.J. Neale. (1987). "Monte Carlo Experimentation Using PC-NAIVE." In T. Fomby and G. Rhodes (eds.), *A Century of Economics* (Vol. 6) (pp. 91–125). Greenwich, CT: JAI Press.

Hendry, D.F., A.J. Neale, and N.R. Ericsson. (1990). *PC-NAIVE: An Interactive Program for Monte Carlo Experimentation in Econometrics.* Oxford: Institute of Economics and Statistics, Oxford University.

Johansen, S. (1988). 'Statistical Analysis of Cointegration Vectors." *Journal of Economic Dynamics and Control* 12, 231–254.

Kremers, J.J.M., N.R. Ericsson, and J. Dolado. (1992). "The Power of Co-integration Tests." *Oxford Bulletin of Economics and Statistics* 54, 325–348.

MacKinnon, J.G. (1991). "Critical Values for Co-integration Tests." In R.F. Engle and C.W.J. Granger (eds.), *Long-Run Economic Relationships* (pp. 267–276). Oxford: Oxford University Press.

Mankiw, N.G., and M.D. Shapiro. (1985). "Trends, Random Walks and Tests of the Permanent Income Hypothesis." *Journal of Monetary Economics* 16, 165–174.

Mankiw, N.G., and M.D. Shapiro. (1986). "Do We Reject Too Often? Small Sample Properties of Tests of Rational Expectations Models." *Economics Letters* 20, 139–145.

Nelson, C.R., and C.I. Plosser. (1982). "Trends and Random Walks in Macro-Economic Time Series: Some Evidence and Implications." *Journal of Monetary Economics* 10, 139–162.

Phillips, P.C.B. (1986). "Understanding Spurious Regressions in Econometrics." *Journal of Econometrics* 33, 311–340.

Phillips, P.C.B. (1991). "Optimal Inference in Co-integrated Systems." *Econometrica* 59, 282–306.

Phillips, P.C.B., and B.E. Hansen. (1990). "Statistical Inference in Instrumental Variables Regression with I(1) Processes." *Review of Economic Studies* 57, 99–125.

Phillips, P.C.B., and M. Loretan. (1991). "Estimating Long-Run Economic Equilibria." *Review of Economic Studies* 58, 407–436.

Phillips, P.C.B., S. Ouliaris. (1990). "Asymptotic Properties of Residual Based Tests for Cointegration." *Econometrica* 58, 165–193.

Phillips, P.C.B., and W. Ploberger. (1991). "Time Series Modelling with a Bayesian Frame of Reference: I. Concepts and Illustrations." Manuscript, Yale University.

Sargan, J.D. (1964). "Wages and Prices in the United Kingdom: A Study in Econometric Methodology." In P.E. Hart, G. Mills, and J.K. Whitaker (eds.), *Econometric Analysis for National Economic Planning*. London: Butterworth. Reprinted in D.F. Hendry and K.F. Wallis (eds.), *Econometrics and Quantitative Economics*. Oxford: Basil Blackwell, 1984.

Sims, C.A., J.H. Stock, and M.W. Watson. (1990). "Inference in Linear Time Series with Some Unit Roots." *Econometrica* 58, 113–144.

Stock, J.H. (1987). "Asymptotic Properties of Least-Squares Estimators of Co-integrating Vectors." *Econometrica* 55, 1035–1056.

Stock, J.H. (1992). "Deciding Between I(0) and I(1)." Technical Working Paper No. 121, National Bureau of Economic Research.

Stock, J.H., and M.W. Watson. (1988). "Variable Trends in Economic Time Series." *Journal of Economic Perspectives* 2, 147–174.

Stock, J.H., and K.D. West. (1988). "Integrated Regressors and Tests of the Permanent Income Hypothesis." *Journal of Monetary Economics* 21, 85–96.

West, K.D. (1988). "Asymptotic Normality When Regressors Have a Unit Root." *Econometrica* 56, 1397–1418.

Yule, G.U. (1926). "Why Do We Sometimes Get Nonsense Correlations Between Time Series? A Study in Sampling and the Nature of Time Series." *Journal of the Royal Statistical Society* 89, 1–64.

Commentary on Chapter 12

Eric Zivot

Introduction

An important issue in the modeling of integrated variables addressed by Banerjee concerns the circumstances under which the static cointegrating regression can be augmented or modified so that OLS on the modified equation yields an estimator of the cointegrating vector that is free of asymptotic and finite sample biases and asymmetries so that conventional test statistics, like t-ratios and F-ratios, can be used for inference about the cointegrating vector. Banerjee focusses on the use of single-equation dynamic regression equations (dynamic specifications) to achieve this aim, and he illustrates some situations when such regressions work and are appropriate and the situations when problems arise. The key condition required for valid inference on the cointegrating vector in a single equation dynamic speci-fication is the weak exogeneity of the right-side integrated variables for the cointe-grating vector. If this condition fails, then a dynamic specification for the full system must be estimated, for example, as in Johansen (1988). Given the difficul-ties in specifying a complete system and the dangers of misspecification errors, testing for weak exogeneity in cointegrating models can be an important modeling issue.

To better understand the sources of asymptotic and finite sample biases in the estimation of cointegrating relationships, and the issue of weak exogeneity and its relationship to the efficient estimation of a cointegrating vector, it is helpful to view the dynamic specifications used by Banerjee as conditional regression models derived from a cointegrated triangular system of equations. Then the results of Phillips (1991), on efficient estimation in the presence of cointegration, can be applied to succinctly characterize the asymptotic properties of cointegrating re-gressions. It turns out that the appropriateness of a dynamic specification rests on the validity of the conditioning process used to derive the dynamic specification from the triangular system. In this regard, failure of weak exogeneity is equivalent to the failure of valid conditioning from the system to the dynamic specification. We elaborate on this point below with several examples.

Dynamic specification is not the only method one can use to modify a static cointegrating regression to improve the estimation of the cointegrating vector and allow conventional test statistics to be used for inference.[1] In fact, asymptotically efficient estimation (in the sense of being equivalent to MLE on the full system)

501

of the cointegrating vector in a static single-equation model and valid inference using conventional test statistics can be achieved by semiparametric modification of the static regression model. This technique, developed by Phillips and Hansen (1990), is called *fully modified ordinary least squares* (FM-OLS). A related procedure, called *canonical cointegrating regression*, is developed by Park (1992). As we illustrate below, there is a close connection between the parametric corrections made by dynamic specifications and the semiparametric corrections made by FM-OLS. FM-OLS has one advantage over dynamic specification, however, in that the former technique remains valid if the condition of weak exogeneity fails whereas the latter technique does not.

Semiparametric procedures, like FM-OLS, are attractive single-equation alternatives to dynamic specifications for the estimation of long-run equilibrium relationships. If the parameters describing the short-run adjustment to the long-run equilibrium are also of interest, then a two-step estimation procedure may be employed to estimate the short-run parameters. The procedure works in exactly the same way as the Engle-Granger two-step procedure except that in the first step an efficient semiparametric procedure is used to estimate the cointegrating vector. Since the semiparametric estimator of the cointegrating vector eliminates the asymptotic biases that plague the static OLS estimator, the short-run parameters estimated in the second step should be more accurate than if the Engle-Granger procedure is used. Semiparametric procedures can also be used in a two-step framework to test for weak exogeneity. We elaborate on these procedures in the examples below.

Regarding testing for cointegration, Banerjee demonstrates that, when appropriate, tests based on a dynamic error correction model (ECM) have higher power than the commonly used two-step Engle-Granger procedure whose first step is based on a static regression and second step on a residual autoregression. The ECM test has higher power because it is based on a correctly specified model under the alternative of cointegration whereas the Engle-Granger test, in general, is not. To complete Banerjee's discussion of ECM tests for cointegration, we suggest an alternative two-step residual-based ECM test for cointegration in the spirit of the Engle-Granger test. This residual-based ECM test turns out to have the same asymptotic null distribution and similar power properties as Banerjee's ECM test.

The remainder of this comment is organized as follows. First, we sketch the asymptotic theory necessary to understand the sources of the biases in OLS estimation of cointegrating vectors from static regressions and outline the FM-OLS procedure in detail. Then we present three examples to illustrate the connections between cointegrated systems of equations, dynamic specifications, weak exogeneity and efficient estimation of long-run parameters. Finally; we briefly outline an Engle-Granger style two-step residual-based ECM test for cointegration.

Asymptotic Biases in Static Cointegrating Regression[2]

Let $y_t' = (y_{1t}, y_{2t})$ be a two-dimensional I(1) process and $u_t' = (u_{1t}, u_{2t})$ be a stationary and ergodic I(0) process. We assume that y_t is cointegrated with a triangular structural representation

$$y_{1t} = \beta y_{2t} + u_{1t}, \tag{1a}$$

$$y_{2t} = y_{2t-1} + u_{2t}. \tag{1b}$$

Equation (1a) may be thought of as a stochastic representation of the long-run equilibrium relationship $y_{1t} = \beta y_{2t}$, with u_{1t} representing stationary deviations away from equilibrium. Equation (1b) is a reduced-form representation for y_{2t}, relating the evolution of y_{2t} to the driving process u_{2t}.

We assume that u_t has a moving average representation of the form $u_t = \Psi(L)\varepsilon_t = \sum_0^\infty \Psi_k \varepsilon_{t-k}$ with $\varepsilon_t \sim$ iid $(0, \Sigma)$. We may think of u_t as absorbing all of the short-run dynamic in the system (1a) and (1b). Later on we make explicit the relationship between the dynamic behavior of u_t and the dynamic specification regression models used by Banerjee. The long-run covariance matrix of u_t is given by $\Omega = \Psi(1)\Sigma\Psi(1)' = \sum_{-\infty}^\infty E[u_0 u_k']$, which is also the spectrum of u_t evaluated at frequency zero. It will be useful to write $\Omega = \Delta + \Gamma'$ with $\Delta = \Gamma_0 + \Gamma$, $\Gamma_0 = E[u_0 u_0']$ and $\Gamma = \sum_1^\infty E[u_0 u_k']$. Also, we partition Ω and Δ conformably with u_t so that

$$\Omega = \begin{bmatrix} \omega_{11} & \omega_{12} \\ \omega_{21} & \omega_{22} \end{bmatrix}, \Delta = \begin{bmatrix} \Delta_{11} & \Delta_{12} \\ \Delta_{21} & \Delta_{22} \end{bmatrix}.$$

Let $B(r) = (B_1(r), B_2(r))'$ denote a two-dimensional Brownian motion for $r \in [0, 1]$ with covariance matrix Ω.[3] Define $\xi_t = \sum_0^t u_j$, with $\xi_0 = 0$. Then under mild restrictions on $\Psi(L)$, the following convergence results hold (see Hamilton, 1994, ch. 18):

$$T^{-1/2} \sum_1^{[Tr]} u_t \Rightarrow B(r), T^{-3/2} \sum_1^T \xi_t \Rightarrow \int_0^1 B(r)dr,$$

$$T^{-2} \sum_1^T \xi_t \xi_t' \Rightarrow \int_0^1 B(r)B(r)'dr, T^{-1} \sum_1^T \xi_t u_t' \Rightarrow \int_0^1 B(r)dB(r)' + \Delta,$$

where $[Tr]$ denotes the integer part of Tr and $\Rightarrow$ denotes weak convergence (the function space equivalent of convergence in distribution).

Our interest is on the efficient estimation of β in the system (1a) and (1b). Let $\hat{\beta}$ denote the ordinary least squares (OLS) estimator of β using (1a) as a regression model. Then it can be shown that

$$T(\hat{\beta} - \beta) = \left(T^{-2} \sum_1^T y_{2t}^2 \right)^{-1} T^{-1} \sum_1^T y_{2t} u_{1t}$$

$$\Rightarrow \left(\int_0^1 B_2(r)^2 dr \right)^{-1} \left(\int_0^1 B_2(r) dB_1(r) + \Delta_{21} \right). \tag{2}$$

This result demonstrates that $\hat{\beta}$ converges to the true value β at rate T instead of the usual rate $T^{1/2}$ and that $\hat{\beta}$ scaled by T converges to a nonnormal random variable.

The expression for the limiting distribution in (2) is not very convenient for analysis since the Brownian motions $B_2(r)$ and $B_1(r)$ are correlated (Ω is nondiagonal). Phillips (1989) shows, however, that we may orthogonalize $B_2(r)$ and $B_1(r)$ through the relation

$$B_1(r) = \omega_{21}\omega_{22}^{-1}B_2(r) + B_{1\cdot2}(r) = \psi\omega_{22}^{1/2}W_2(r) + \omega_{11\cdot2}^{1/2}W_{1\cdot2}(r), \tag{3}$$

where $\psi = \omega_{21}\omega_{22}^{-1}$ and $B_{1\cdot2}(r)$ is a scalar Brownian motion, independent of $B_2(r)$, with variance $\omega_{11\cdot2} = \omega_{11} - \omega_{21}^2\omega_{22}^{-1}$. Using (3) we may decompose the limit distribution in (2) into three parts:

$$\left(\int_0^1 B_2(r)^2 \right)^{-1} \int_0^1 B_2(r)dB_{1\cdot2} + \psi \left(\int_0^1 B_2(r)^2 \right)^{-1} \int_0^1 B_2(r)dB_2(r) + \left(\int_0^1 B_2(r)^2 \right)^{-1} \Delta_{21}. \tag{4}$$

To gain some insight into the above expression, consider separately the three terms in (4). The first integral term is a mean zero and symmetric "mixture normal" random variable. That is,

$$\left(\int_0^1 B_2(r)^2 dr \right)^{-1} \int_0^1 B_2(r)dB_{1\cdot2}(r) \sim N\left(0, \omega_{11\cdot2}\omega_{22}^{-1} \cdot \left(\int_0^1 W_2(r)^2 dr \right)^{-1} \right),$$

where $W_2(r)$ is a standard Brownian motion on $[0, 1]$. In other words, the first integral term is a normally distributed random variable with a random variance determined by $W_2(r)$. The second integral term has a unit root or Dickey-Fuller distribution. As is well known, this distribution is left skewed from the origin and will, in general, produce a downward bias in $\hat{\beta}$ if ψ is positive. From (4), it can be seen that this unit root term arises from the nondiagonal nature of the long-run covariance matrix of u_t and thus the endogeneity of y_{2t} in (1a). If $\omega_{21} = 0$, this unit root term disappears from (4). The last term is a bias arising from the long-run contribution of the contemporaneous correlation between u_{1t} and u_{2t} given by Δ_{21}.

The decomposition of the limiting distribution in (4) highlights the fact that even though $\hat{\beta}$ converges at rate T to β ($\hat{\beta}$ is superconsistent), the asymptotic distribution of $\hat{\beta}$ is polluted by asymmetries, nuisance parameters (ω_{21}, ω_{22}) and a bias term (Δ_{21}). The presence of these effects makes the asymptotic distribution of $\hat{\beta}$ nonnormal and invalidates the use of conventional test statistics (e.g., t and F tests) and tables for inference about β.

In the special diagonal case

$$\psi(L) = \begin{bmatrix} \psi_{11}(L) & 0 \\ 0 & \psi_{22}(L) \end{bmatrix}, \; \Sigma = \begin{bmatrix} \sigma_{11} & 0 \\ 0 & \sigma_{22} \end{bmatrix}$$

so that y_{2t} is strictly exogenous, it is easily shown that $\omega_{21} = \Delta_{21} = 0$ and the limit distribution in (4) simplifies to the mixture-normal random variable

$$\left(\frac{\omega_{11.2}}{\omega_{22}}\right)^{1/2} \cdot \left(\int_0^1 W_2(r)^2 \, dr\right)^{-1} \int_0^1 W_2(r) \, dW_{1.2}(r), \tag{5}$$

where $W_2(r)$ and $W_{1.2}(r)$ are independent standard Brownian motions and $\omega_{11.2} = \omega_{11}$. Since the distribution in (5) is mixture-normal, standard test statistics can be used for inference about β.[4] Moreover, in this special case, the limit distribution (5) is the same as that obtained from applying full systems maximum likelihood estimation (MLE) on (1a) and (1b) that explicitly incorporates the short-run dynamics embodied in $\Psi(L)$.[5] We have the interesting result that when y_{2t} is strictly exogenous, OLS on the static regression model (1a), which ignores the short-run dynamics in u_{1t}, produces an estimate of β that is asymptotically equivalent to full systems MLE.

Fully Modified OLS

As was mentioned above, dynamic specification is not the only method available to augment the static cointegrating regression to improve inference. We now illustrate how the technique of FM-OLS works to correct the static regression equation. FM-OLS corrects the static regression for the long-run endogeneity between y_{2t} and y_{1t} and for the contribution of the serial correlations in the error terms u_{1t} and u_{2t} to the long-run covariance of u_t so that when OLS is applied to the corrected static regression the second and third terms of the nonnormal limiting distribution in (4) are eliminated and the (mixture) normal limiting distribution (5) obtains. Simple modifications of conventional test statistics can then be made so that inference about β can proceed using standard tables.

The modification of the static regression proceeds in two steps. First, the long-run endogeneity between y_{2t} and y_{1t} is purged through the transformation

$$y_{1t}^+ = y_{1t} - \psi\Delta y_{2t}, \; u_{1t}^+ = u_{1t} - \psi u_{2t}, \tag{6}$$

where $\psi = \omega_{21}\omega_{22}^{-1}$, which creates a diagonal long-run covariance matrix for the random vector $(u_{1t}^+, u_{2t})'$. Second, any remaining asymptotic bias due to residual correlation between u_{1t}^+ and u_{2t} is captured by constructing

$$\Delta_{21}^+ = \sum_{k=0}^{\infty} E[u_{20}u_{1k}^+] = [\Delta_{21}, \Delta_{22}] \begin{bmatrix} 1 \\ -\omega_{21}\omega_{22}^{-1} \end{bmatrix} = \Delta_{21} - \psi\Delta_{22}. \tag{7}$$

The FM-OLS estimator is defined to be

$$\beta^+ = \left(\sum_{1}^{T} y_{2t}^2 \right)^{-1} \left(\sum_{1}^{T} y_{1t}^+ y_{2t} - T\Delta_{21}^+ \right). \tag{8}$$

Phillips and Hansen (1990) show that

$$T(\beta^+ - \beta) \Rightarrow \left(\frac{\omega_{11\cdot2}}{\omega_{22}} \right)^{1/2} \cdot \left(\int_0^1 W_2(r)^2 \right)^{-1} \int_0^1 W_2(r)dW_{1\cdot2}(r), \tag{9}$$

which is the asymptotic distribution of the full systems MLE (5). It is important to note that this result holds regardless of whether y_{2t} is weakly exogenous for β.

The usefulness of the convergence result (9) is that inference about β can proceed with standard test statistics with a simple modification to take account of the long-run variance $\omega_{11\cdot2}$. For example, a modified t-ratio has the form

$$t^+ = \frac{\beta^+ - \beta_0}{s^+}, \quad (s^+)^2 = \omega_{11\cdot2} \cdot \left(\sum_{1}^{T} y_{2t}^2 \right)^{-1},$$

and this ratio has an asymptotic $N(0,1)$ distribution.

To make the FM-OLS procedure operational, the values ω_{21}, ω_{22}, Δ_{21}, and Δ_{22} in (6) and (7) need to be replaced with consistent estimates. In practice one would use nonparametric kernel estimates for Ω and Δ of the form

$$\hat{\Omega} = \sum_{j=-T+1}^{T-1} w\left(\frac{j}{K} \right) \hat{\Gamma}(j), \quad \hat{\Delta} = \sum_{j=0}^{T-1} w\left(\frac{j}{K} \right) \hat{\Gamma}(j), \quad \hat{\Gamma}(j) = T^{-1} \sum_{t=j+1}^{T} \hat{u}_t \hat{u}_{t-j}',$$

where $w(\cdot)$ is a kernel function, K is a lag truncation or bandwidth parameter and $\hat{u}_t$ is constructed from static OLS on (1a). Newey and West (1987), Andrews (1991), and Andrews and Monahan (1992) give suggestions for the choices of kernel functions and bandwith parameters. Park and Ogaki (1991) discuss the performance of various nonparametric estimators of the long-run covariance terms.

FM-OLS attacks the problem of biases and asymmetries in the asymptotic distribution of β in the static regression by performing nonparametric corrections to the regression whereas a dynamic specification tackles the problem using parametric corrections. FM-OLS has an asymptotic advantage over dynamic specification if y_{2t} is not weakly exogenous for β, since FM-OLS explicitly corrects for long-run endogeneities. However, dynamic specification may have a finite sample advantage over FM-OLS in situations where weak exogeneity holds due to its parametric structure. This is due to the fact that a dynamic specification estimates parametrically the short-run dynamics as well as the long-run coefficient β while the FM-OLS procedure only corrects for the impact of the short-run dynamics on the structure of the long-run covariance matrix. The simulation evidence reported in Phillips and Hansen (1990), Hansen and Phillips (1990), Phillips and Loretan (1991), and Stock and Watson (1993) generally support these claims.

Some Examples of Biases in Estimating Cointegrating Vectors[6]

Consider a special case of the triangular cointegrated model (1a) and (1b) where we assume a stable first order VAR structure for u_t: $C(L)u_t = \varepsilon_t$, $\varepsilon_t \sim$ iid $N(0, \Sigma)$, $C(L) = I - CL$ and C has elements $c_{i,j}$ $(i, j = 1, 2)$. In this case, we may write $u_t = (I - CL)^{-1}\varepsilon_t = \Psi(L)\varepsilon_t$. The long-run covariance matrix of u_t is given by $\Omega = \Psi(1)\Sigma\Psi(1)' = (I - C)^{-1}\Sigma(I - C')^{-1}$. More explicitly,

$$\Omega = \begin{bmatrix} \omega_{11} & (c_{21}\omega_{11} + \pi)(1 - c_{22})^{-1} \\ (c_{21}\omega_{11} + \pi)(1 - c_{22})^{-1} & (c_{21}^2\omega_{11} + 2c_{21}\pi + \sigma_{22})(1 - c_{22})^{-2} \end{bmatrix}, \quad (10)$$

where $\omega_{11} = \sigma_{11}(1 - c_{11})^{-2}$ and $\pi = \sigma_{12}(1 - c_{11})^{-1}$. Notice that y_{2t} is strictly exogenous, and Ω is diagonal, only if $\sigma_{12} = c_{21} = 0$. It will be shown later that y_{2t} is weakly exogenous for β if $c_{21} = 0$. Notice that weak exogeneity does not imply a diagonal long-run covariance matrix.

We consider three special cases of this model, corresponding to specific restrictions on the elements of C and Σ (and, hence, Ω), to illustrate the construction of the dynamic specification as a conditional model and to compare and contrast the dynamic specification to the FM-OLS procedure. In what follows, let I_{t-1} denote the set of all relevant information available at time $t - 1$.

Case 1: $c_{12} = c_{21} = c_{22} = 0$; Σ nondiagonal

Here, $u_{1t} = c_{11}u_{1t-1} + \varepsilon_{1t}$, $u_{2t} = \varepsilon_{2t}$, so that only u_{1t} is serially correlated but u_{1t} and u_{2t} are contemporaneously correlated. To derive the single equation dynamic specification for this model we must reduce the system (1a) and (1b) by conditioning (1a) on y_{2t} and I_{t-1}. First we rewrite (1a), using (1b), to produce the system

$$y_{1t} = \beta(1 - c_{11})y_{2t-1} + c_{11}y_{1t-1} + v_t,$$

$$y_{2t} = y_{2t-1} + \varepsilon_{2t},$$

where $v_t = \varepsilon_{1t} + \beta\varepsilon_{2t}$. This system has error structure

$$\begin{bmatrix} v_t \\ \varepsilon_{2t} \end{bmatrix} \sim i.i.d.\ N\left(\begin{pmatrix} 0 \\ 0 \end{pmatrix}, \begin{pmatrix} \sigma_{11}^* & \sigma_{12}^* \\ \sigma_{12}^* & \sigma_{22} \end{pmatrix}\right) \tag{11}$$

with $\sigma_{11}^* = \sigma_{11} + \beta^2\sigma_{22} + 2\beta\sigma_{12}$ and $\sigma_{12}^* = \sigma_{12} + \beta\sigma_{22}$. Then, using properties of the bivariate normal distribution, it is easy to show that

$$y_{1t} \mid y_{2t}, I_{t-1} \sim N(c_{11}y_{1t-1} + (\beta + \phi)y_{2t} - (\beta c_{11} + \phi)y_{2t-1}, \sigma_{11.2}), \tag{12}$$

where $\phi = \sigma_{12}\sigma_{22}^{-1}$ and $\sigma_{11.2} = \sigma_{11} - \sigma_{12}^2\sigma_{22}^{-1}$. From this conditional distribution we may write the dynamic specification for y_{1t} in several forms by defining the residual $\eta_t = y_{1t} - E[y_{1t} \mid y_{2t}, I_{t-1}] \sim N(0, \sigma_{11.2})$. One representation is the autoregressive distributed lag (ADL) model

$$y_{1t} = \gamma_1 y_{1t-1} + \gamma_2 y_{2t} + \gamma_3 y_{2t-1} + \eta_t, \tag{13}$$

where $\gamma_1 = c_{11}$, $\gamma_2 = \beta + \phi$, $\gamma_3 = -(\beta c_{11} + \phi)$. Notice that (13) is consistent with the long-run equilibrium $y_{1t} = \beta y_{2t}$ since $(\gamma_2 + \gamma_3)/(1 - \gamma_1) = \beta$.

Using $\beta = (\gamma_2 + \gamma_3)/(1 - \gamma_1)$, we may also write the dynamic specification as

$$y_{1t} = \beta y_{2t} + \gamma_1(y_1 - \beta y_2)_{t-1} + \phi\Delta y_{2t} + \eta_t. \tag{14}$$

Equation (14) is the static regression equation (1a) augmented with the lagged cointegrating term $(y_1 - \beta y_2)_{t-1}$ and Δy_{2t}. Both of these terms are I(0) (i.e., stationary) and serve as parametric corrections for the long-run endogeneity of y_{2t} and the serial correlation in u_{1t}. However, due to the nonlinear restrictions on β in (14), OLS cannot be used to estimate β.

We may also express the dynamic specification as the error correction model (ECM):

$$\Delta y_{1t} = -(1 - \gamma_1)(y_1 - \beta y_2)_{t-1} + \gamma_2\Delta y_{2t} + \eta_t. \tag{15}$$

From (15) we see that if $\gamma_1 = 1$, there is no error correction term and the model is expressed in first differences so that y_{1t} and y_{2t} are I(1) and not cointegrated. Banerjee discusses how OLS on (15) can be used to both test for cointegration and to estimate β.

Equations (13), (14), or (15) together with (1b) produces an orthogonal system with error structure

$$\begin{pmatrix} \eta_t \\ \varepsilon_{2t} \end{pmatrix} \sim i.i.d.\ N\left(\begin{pmatrix} 0 \\ 0 \end{pmatrix}, \begin{pmatrix} \sigma_{11.2} & 0 \\ 0 & \sigma_{22} \end{pmatrix}\right). \tag{16}$$

Notice that η_t is uncorrelated with ε_{2t} by construction.

To determine if y_{2t} is weakly exogenous for β, so that efficient estimation of β can proceed from the conditional model, we must be able to recover β from the parameters of the conditional model without any information from the marginal model for y_{2t}. Since $c_{12} = c_{21} = c_{22} = 0$, from (1b) we get directly that

$$y_{2t} \mid I_{t-1} \sim N(y_{2t-1}, \sigma_{22}).$$

From inspection of the conditional model (12), the only parameter common to both distributions is σ_{22}. Clearly, the marginal model for y_{2t} contains no additional information about β beyond what is available in the conditional model (12) and so y_{2t} is weakly exogenous for β.

With $c_{12} = c_{21} = c_{22} = 0$, the OLS estimate of β from the static equation (1a) has the asymptotic distribution given in (4) with $\psi = \phi(1 - c_{11})^{-1}$ and $\Delta_{21} = \sigma_{21}(1 - c_{11})^{-1}$, so that this estimate suffers from asymptotic asymmetry and bias. Notice that these effects are caused by the nonzero value of σ_{12}, the contemporaneous correlation between u_{1t} and u_{2t}. On the other hand, since the dynamic specification (14) is a valid conditional model the (nonlinear) least squares estimate of β from (14) is asymptotically equivalent to the full systems MLE. In addition, since the short-run dynamics are explicitly estimated conventional test statistics can be used to test hypotheses about β without modification.

If the data are in logs, we can interpret the coefficient on Δy_{2t} in (15), γ_2, as the short-run elasticity with respect to y_{1t} and β as the long-run elasticity. Notice that since $\gamma_2 = \phi + \beta$, $\gamma_2 = \beta$ only if $\sigma_{12} = 0$. In this case (1a) reduces to the common factor model

$$(1 - c_{11}L)y_{1t} = (1 - c_{11}L)y_{2t} + \varepsilon_{1t}$$

where ε_{1t} is independent of ε_{2t}.[7] As noted above, in this case y_{2t} is strictly exogenous and OLS on the static regression model (1a) is asymptotically equivalent to full systems MLE.

This special case of the triangular representation helps shed some light on the biases in $\hat{\beta}$ from the static regressions reported in Table 12.2 from Banerjee. In this simulation experiment, Banerjee used the ADL model (13) as the DGP and in all configurations of the parameters reported in Table 12.2 the common factor restriction is violated. Therefore, the OLS estimate of β from the static regression (1a) when the DGP is (13) will suffer from both asymptotic and finite sample biases. Further, since $\gamma_2 = \phi + \beta$, the magnitude of the bias should increase with the magnitude of ϕ (that is, with the difference between the short-run and long-run elasticities) and the simulation results confirm this observation.

The FM-OLS estimator is easily constructed in this case. Since $\psi = \pi\sigma_{22}^{-1}$, the first step modification, which makes u_{1t} long-run uncorrelated with u_{2t}, is simply

$$y_{1t}^+ = y_{1t} - \pi\sigma_{22}^{-1}\Delta y_{2t}, \ u_{1t}^+ = u_{1t} - \pi\sigma_{22}^{-1}u_{2t}.$$

Notice that the bias correction is not needed since

$$\Delta_{21}^+ = \sum_{k=0}^{\infty} E[u_{20}u_{1k}^+] = -\sigma_{12}(1 - c_{11})^{-1} + \sigma_{12}\cdot\sum_{k=0}^{\infty} c_{11}^k = 0.$$

Consequently, the FM procedure is asymptotically equivalent to OLS on the modified regression

$$y_{1t} = \beta y_{2t} + \pi\sigma_{22}^{-1}\Delta y_{2t} + u_{1t}^+.$$

This regression is similar to the dynamic specification (14). The dynamic specification, however, includes a lagged error correction term that eliminates the first-order serial correlation in u_{1t}, whereas the FM regression ignores the short-run effects of the serial correlation. In addition, in the dynamic specification η_t is uncorrelated with u_{2t} by construction but in the FM regression u_{1t}^+ is only long-run uncorrelated with u_{2t}. Thus there might be some finite sample biases in the FM-OLS estimator, relative to the dynamic specification estimator, of β due to short-run correlation and endogeneity effects.

Case 2: $c_{11} = c_{12} = c_{21} = 0$; Σ nondiagonal

In this example, $u_{1t} = \varepsilon_{1t}$ and $u_{2t} = c_{22}u_{2t-1} + \varepsilon_{2t}$, so that only u_{2t} is serially correlated but u_{1t} and u_{2t} are contemporaneously correlated. To determine the conditional model for y_{1t}, substitute $(1 - c_{22}L)u_{2t} = \varepsilon_{2t}$ into (1b) and rearrange to get the system

$$y_{1t} = \beta y_{2t-1} + \beta c_{22}\Delta y_{2t-1} + v_t,$$

$$y_{2t} = y_{2t-1} + c_{22}\Delta y_{2t-1} + \varepsilon_{2t},$$

where v_t is defined as in Case 1 above. A straightforward calculation then gives the conditional distribution

$$y_{1t} \mid y_{2t}, I_{t-1} \sim N(\beta y_{2t} + \phi\Delta y_{2t} - c_{22}\phi\Delta y_{2t-1}, \sigma_{11.2}). \tag{17}$$

The dynamic specification can then be written as the system

$$y_{1t} = \beta y_{2t} + \phi\Delta y_{2t} - c_{22}\phi\Delta y_{2t-1} + \eta_t, \tag{18}$$

$$y_{2t} = y_{2t-1} + c_{22}\Delta y_{2t-1} + \varepsilon_{2t}, \tag{19}$$

where $\eta_t = y_{1t} - E[y_{1t} \mid y_{2t}, I_{t-1}]$ and is uncorrelated with ε_{2t} by construction. In (18), the effects of the serial correlation in u_{2t} is removed by the addition of the regressors Δy_{2t} and Δy_{2t-1} to (1a).

In levels, (18) becomes the simple distributed lag model

$$y_{1t} = \gamma_2 y_{2t} + \gamma_3 y_{2t-1} + \gamma_4 y_{2t-2} + \eta_t, \tag{20}$$

where $\gamma_2 = \beta + \phi$, $\gamma_3 = -(1 + c_{22})\phi$, $\gamma_4 = c_{22}\phi$. Notice that (20) is consistent with the long-run equilibrium $y_{1t} = \beta y_{2t}$ since $\gamma_2 + \gamma_3 + \gamma_4 = \beta$. The ECM form is given by

$$\Delta y_{1t} = -(y_1 - \beta y_2)_{t-1} + \gamma_2 \Delta y_{2t} - \gamma_4 \Delta y_{2t-1} + \eta_t. \tag{21}$$

Again, the short-run elasticity γ_2 is equal to the long-run elasticity β only if $\sigma_{12} = 0$. In this case, however, $\gamma_3 = \gamma_4 = 0$ and the model reverts to (1a) with y_{2t} strictly exogenous.

From (19), the marginal model for y_{2t} is

$$y_{2t} \mid I_{t-1} \sim N(y_{2t-1} + c_{22}\Delta y_{2t-1}, \ \sigma_{22}),$$

and we see immediately from inspection of the conditional distribution (18) that y_{2t} is weakly exogenous for β. Thus the OLS estimate of β in (18) will be asymptotically equivalent to full systems MLE and standard test statistics can be used without modification for inference.

OLS on the static regression equation (1a) is asymptotically biased since $\psi = \phi(1 - c_{22})$ and $\Delta_{21} = \sigma_{12}$. As in Case 1, this bias is caused by the contemporaneous correlation between u_{1t} and u_{2t}. If $\sigma_{12} = 0$, then OLS on (1a) is asymptotically equivalent to full-systems MLE, but standard test statistics need to be adjusted for the long-run variance of u_{2t} before they can be used for inference about β.

To determine the FM-OLS estimator we first form

$$y_{1t}^+ = y_{1t} - \phi(1 - c_{22})\Delta y_{2t}, \quad u_{1t}^+ = u_{1t} - \phi(1 - c_{22})u_{2t}. \tag{22}$$

In this case, however, the modification to diagonalize the long-run covariance matrix is not sufficient to remove the asymptotic bias since

$$\Delta_{21}^+ = \sum_{k=0}^{\infty} E[u_{20}u_{1k}^+] = \sigma_{12}[1 - (1 - c_{22}^2)^{-1}]. \tag{23}$$

The FM-OLS estimator is then given by substituting (22) and (23) into (8).

It is interesting to compare the FM-OLS procedure to the dynamic specification (18). In (18), the addition of Δy_{2t} and Δy_{2t-1} to the static regression (1a) are sufficient to remove the asymptotic bias terms. The modification in (22) involves only Δy_{2t} and so the bias correction term in (23) is needed to pick up the effects of Δy_{2t-1}.

Case 3: $c_{12} = c_{22} = 0$; Σ nondiagonal

In this last example, $u_{1t} = c_{11}u_{1t-1} + \varepsilon_{1t}$, $u_{2t} = c_{21}u_{1t-1} + \varepsilon_{2t}$ so that u_{1t} and u_{2t} are both serially and contemporaneously correlated but the serial correlation in u_{2t} arises from the feedback from u_{1t-1}. As we shall see, the presence of this feedback causes y_{2t} to not be weakly exogenous for y_{1t} and thus biases will occur in the estimation of β from the conditional dynamic specification.

To determine the conditional and marginal models we first solve the system (1a) and (1b) using the specified dynamics for u_t:

$$y_{1t} = \beta y_{2t-1} + (\beta c_{21} + c_{11})(y_1 - \beta y_2)_{t-1} + v_t,$$

$$y_{2t} = y_{2t-1} + c_{21}(y - \beta y_2)_{t-1} + \varepsilon_{2t},$$

where v_t is defined as in Case 1 above. Again, straightforward calculations yield the conditional model

$$y_{1t} \mid y_{2t}, I_{t-1} \sim N(\beta y_{2t} + \phi\Delta y_{2t} + (c_{11} - c_{21}\phi)(y_1 - \beta y_2)_{t-1}, + \sigma_{11.2}), \quad (22)$$

and we may write the dynamic specification as the system

$$y_{1t} = \beta y_{2t} + (c_{11} - c_{21}\phi)(y_1 - \beta y_2)_{t-1} + \phi\Delta y_{2t} + \eta_t, \quad (23)$$

$$y_{2t} = y_{2t-1} + c_{21}(y_1 - \beta y_2)_{t-1} + \varepsilon_{2t}, \quad (24)$$

where η_t and ε_{2t} are uncorrelated by construction. Interestingly, the conditional model (23) has the same form as the conditional model (14) for Case 1, where there is no feedback from u_{1t-1} to u_{2t}. This result suggests that (23) does not take into consideration the feedback between the errors in (1a) and (1b). However, the marginal model for y_{2t}, (24), is different from that in Case 1 since (24) retains the feedback from u_{1t-1} to u_{2t} through the lagged error correction term.

The levels specification of (23) is the ADL model

$$y_{1t} = \gamma_1 y_{1t-1} + \gamma_2 y_{2t} + \gamma_3 y_{2t-1} + \eta_t, \quad (25)$$

where $\gamma_1 = c_{11} - c_{21}\phi$, $\gamma_2 = \beta + \phi$, $\gamma_3 = -(\phi + \beta\gamma_1)$ and the ECM form is

$$\Delta y_{1t} = -(1 - \gamma_1)(y_1 - \beta y_2)_{t-1} + \gamma_2\Delta y_{2t} + \eta_t. \quad (26)$$

The marginal distribution for y_{2t}, from (24), is

$$y_{2t} \mid I_{t-1} \sim N(y_{2t-1} + c_{21}(y_1 - \beta y_2)_{t-1}, + \sigma_{22}). \quad (27)$$

Clearly, from (27), β directly affects the marginal distribution of y_{2t} through the error correction term unless $c_{21} = 0$. This means an estimate of β from conditional model (24) does not use all of the information in the system regarding β and will be less efficient than an estimate utilizing all information in the conditional and marginal models. Therefore, y_{2t} is not weakly exogenous for β.

In this example, we have the interesting result that $c_{21} \neq 0$ implies that the error-correction term enters the marginal model for y_{2t}, which results in the failure of weak exogeneity of y_{2t} for β. More generally, Urbain (1993) shows that the absence of the error correction term in the marginal model of the conditioning variables turns out to be a necessary and sufficient condition for valid inference on the long-run parameters using a single equation conditional model derived from a cointegrated system.

The bias terms in the asymptotic distribution of $\hat{\beta}$ are given by

$$\psi = (c_{21}\omega_{11} + \pi)(c_{21}^2\omega_{11} + 2c_{21}\pi + \sigma_{22})^{-1}, \tag{28}$$

$$\Delta_{21} = c_{21}\sigma_{11}c_{11}[(1 - c_{11})(1 - c_{11}^2)]^{-1} + \pi. \tag{29}$$

These effects are caused by two factors: the contemporaneous correlation between u_{1t} and u_{2t} captured by σ_{12}; and the feedback from u_{1t-1} to u_{2t} caused by c_{21}. In particular, the conditioning process used to derive (23) removes the correlation between u_{1t} and u_{2t} so that $\sigma_{21} = 0$ (see (16)) but it does not remove the feedback from u_{1t-1} to u_{2t}. In other words, the conditioning process fails to diagonalize the long-run covariance matrix Ω. Therefore the asymptotic distribution of the (nonlinear) least squares estimate of β from (23) is given by (4) with $\psi = c_{21}\omega_{11}(c_{21}^2\omega_{11} + \sigma_{22})^{-1}$ and $\Delta_{21} = \pi$. As long as $c_{21} \neq 0$ (y_{2t} is not weakly exogenous for β), estimation of β from the dynamic specification is asymptotically biased.

The FM-OLS estimate of β is asymptotically unbiased even though y_{2t} may not be weakly exogenous for β. This result occurs because the FM procedure works directly to diagonalize the long-run covariance matrix and therefore asymptotically eliminates both σ_{12} and c_{21}. The modification in this case is straightforward but messy and not very illuminating beyond what is presented in Cases 1 and 2 so we do not present it.

Since weak exogeneity necessitates the absence of the error correction mechanism from the marginal model of y_{2t}, the FM-OLS procedure can be used to construct a simple single equation test for weak exogeneity within a two-step framework. In the first step, FM-OLS is used to efficiently estimate β and form the estimate of the error correction term $(y_1 - \beta^+ y_2)_{t-1}$. The second step involves estimating the regression

$$\Delta y_{2t} = c_{21}(y_1 - \beta^+ y_2)_{t-1} + \varepsilon_{2t}$$

and testing the hypothesis that $c_{21} = 0$ using the conventional t-ratio.

Banerjee argues that the Engle-Granger two-step procedure is inferior to dynamic specification because of the biases in the first step OLS estimate of the cointegrating parameters. This suggests that if the biases in the first step can be eliminated or mitigated then the Engle-Granger procedure may perform better in finite samples. The use of FM-OLS in the first stage is one way of mitigating the OLS biases. The error-correction term constructed from the FM-OLS regression can then be used as a regressor in the second stage. For example, in case I above a modified two-step procedure to estimate the short-run parameters in the ECM (15) is based on the regression

$$\Delta y_{1t} = \alpha_0 + \alpha_1 z_{t-1} + \alpha_2 \Delta y_{2t} + e_t,$$

where $z_{t-1} = y_{1t-1} - \beta^+ y_{2t-1}$ and β^+ is the FM-OLS estimate of β. This type of modification to the Engle-Granger two-step procedure has been suggested by Phillips and Loretan (1991) and Stock and Watson (1993), but we know of no published studies that evaluate such procedures. We believe that more research into this area is needed.

A Residual-based ECM Test for Cointegration

Banerjee illustrates how a test for non-cointegration based on the significance of an error-correction term in a dynamic regression can have higher power (against the alternative of cointegration) than a unit root test based on the residuals of a static cointegration regression (Engle-Granger test). As Banerjee points out, the residual-based autoregression imposes a potentially invalid common factor restriction on the short-run dynamics whereas the dynamic ECM does not.

The logic of the ECM test is based on the result, due to Engle and Granger (1987), that cointegration implies and is implied by an ECM representation of the data. Using Banerjee's notation, if $z_t' = (y_t, x_t')$ is cointegrated and generated by a finite-order vector autoregression with normal errors and if x_t is weakly exogenous for the long-run parameter θ then, conditional on Δx_t, Δy_t has the error correction representation

$$\Delta y_t = c + \phi_0' \Delta x_t + \lambda(y_{t-1} - \theta' x_{t-1}) + \sum_1^{p-1} (\psi_j \Delta y_{t-j} + \phi_j' \Delta x_{t-j}) + \eta_t \quad (30)$$

or

$$\Delta y_t = c + \phi_0' \Delta x_t + \lambda(y_{t-1} - \iota' x_{t-1}) + \zeta' x_{t-1} + \sum_1^{p-1} (\psi_j \Delta y_{t-j} + \phi_j' \Delta x_{t-j}) + \eta_t, (31)$$

where $\zeta = \lambda(\iota - \theta)$. Banerjee's proposed test for no-cointegration with unknown θ is based on the t-ratio for λ in (31). However, if θ is unknown it seems plausible to construct a test by replacing $w_{t-1} = y_{t-1} - \theta' x_{t-1}$ in (30) with $\hat{w}_{t-1} = y_{t-1} - \hat{\theta} x_{t-1}$, where $\hat{\theta}$ is estimated from a preliminary static cointegrating regression, and then test for the significance of $\hat{w}_{t-1}$ using a standard t-ratio. In fact, Zivot (1994) shows that the t-ratio for the coefficient on $\hat{w}_{t-1}$ has the same asymptotic null distribution and similar power properties as the t-ratio for λ in (31). This result suggests that the biases in the first stage cointegrating regression have a smaller effect on the power of residual-based tests for cointegration than the proper specification of the second step ECM regression.

Acknowledgments

The author acknowledges financial support from the University of Washington Graduate Research Fund.

Notes

1. Banerjee mentions some of these other methods in note 6.

2. The presentation given in this section is a simplified and abbreviated version of the results given in Phillips and Loretan (1991).

3. An n-dimensional standard Brownian motion $W(.)$ is a continuous time process associating each date $r \in [0,1]$ with the $(n \times 1)$ vector $W(r)$ satisfying: (a) $W(0) = 0$; (b) for any dates $0 \le r_1 < \ldots < r_k \le 1$, the increments $W(r_2) - W(r_1), \ldots, W(r_k) - W(r_{k-1})$ are independent multivariate normal with $W(s) - W(r) \sim N(0, (s - r)I_n)$; (c) for any given realization, $W(r)$ is continuous with probability 1. An n-dimensional Brownian motion with covariance matrix Ω is defined as $B(r) = P^*W(r)$, where $\Omega = PP'$.

4. However, standard test statistics constructed from the OLS regression have to be modified to allow for the serial correlation in u_{1t}, by using an estimate for the long-run variance $\omega_{11.2}$, before standard tables can be used for statistical inference. Only in the special case when $\Psi_{11}(L) = 1$, so that u_{1t} is not serially correlated, can standard test statistics and tables be used without modification for inference about β.

5. Full systems MLE refers to maximum likelihood estimation of β using the error-correction model representation of (1a) and (1b). See Phillips (1991) for full details.

6. A more extensive analysis similar to the one in this section is given in Hendry (1994).

7. In terms of the parameters of the ADL representation (13), the common-factor restriction is usually specified as the nonlinear restriction $\gamma_3 = -\gamma_2\gamma_1$.

References

Andrews, D.W.K. (1991). "Heteroskedasticity and Autocorrelation Consistent Covariance Matrix Estimation." *Econometrica* 59, 817–858.

Andrews, D.W.K., and J.C. Monahan. (1992). "An Improved Heteroskedasticity and Autocorrelation Consistent Covariance Matrix Estimator." *Econometrica* 60, 953–966.

Banerjee, A., J. Dolado, J.W. Galbraith, and D.F. Hendry. (1993). *Co-Integration, Error-Correction, and the Econometric Analysis of Non-Stationary Data*. Oxford: Oxford University Press.

Hamilton, J.D. (1994). *Time Series Analysis*. Princeton, NJ: Princeton University Press.

Hansen, B.E., and P.C.B. Phillips. (1990). "Estimation and Inference in Models of Cointegration: A Simulation Study." *Advances in Econometrics* 8, 225–248. JAI Press.

Hendry, D.F. (1994). "On the Interactions of Unit Roots and Exogeneity." *European University Institute Working Paper ECO No.* 94/4, Florence.

Johansen, S. (1988). "Statistical Analysis of Cointegration Vectors." *Journal of Economic Dynamics and Control* 12, 231–254.

Newey, W.K., and K.D. West. (1987). "A Simple, Positive Semi-Definite Heteroskedasticity and Autocorrelation Consistent Covariance Matrix." *Econometrica* 55, 703–708.

Park, J. (1992). "Canonical Cointegrating Regressions." *Econometrica* 60, 119–143.

Park, J.Y., and M. Ogaki. (1991). "Inference in Cointegrated Models Using VAR Prewhitening to Estimate Shortrun Dynamics." Rochester Center for Economic Research Working Paper No. 281, University of Rochester.

Phillips, P.C.B. (1988). "Reflections on Econometric Methodology." *The Economic Record* 64, 344–359.

Phillips, P.C.B. (1989). "Partially Identified Econometric Models." *Econometric Theory* 5, 181–240.

Phillips, P.C.B. (1991). "Optimal Inference in Cointegrated Systems." *Econometrica* 59, 282–306.

Phillips, P.C.B., and B.E. Hansen. (1990). "Statistical Inference in Instrumental Variables Regression with I(1) Processes." *Review of Economic Studies* 57, 99–125.

Phillips, P.C.B., and M. Loretan. (1991). "Estimating Long-run Economic Equilibria." *Review of Economic Studies* 58, 407–436.

Stock, J.H., and M.W. Watson. (1993). "A Simple Estimator of Cointegrating Vectors in Higher Order Systems." *Econometrica* 61, 783–820.

Urbain, J.P. (1993). *Exogeneity in Error Correction Models.* Lecture Notes in Economics and Mathematical Systems 398. Springer-Verlag.

Zivot, E. (1994). "Single Equation Conditional Error Correction Model Based Tests for Cointegration." Institute for Economic Research Discussion Paper 94-12, Department of Economics, University of Washington.

13 NONLINEAR MODELS OF ECONOMIC FLUCTUATIONS

Simon M. Potter

Introduction

The modern study of economic fluctuations rests on stylized facts produced by the use of linear time-series models.[1] There are certainly important controversies concerning the best type of linear models and the interpretation of stylized facts from these linear models as illustrated by some of the other chapters of this book. However, as a class linear models have a number of serious shortcomings for the study of economic fluctuations.[2] They impose a symmetry of the effect of shocks across stages of the business cycle and signs and magnitude of shocks. All fluctuations produced by linear models are generated by exogenous forces and typically these exogenous forces appear to be large. Nonlinear models have the advantage of being able to capture asymmetries over the business cycle and in allowing the internal dynamics of the economy itself to be one of the ultimate sources of fluctuations.

Economists are often taught that "there is no such thing as a free lunch," thus it must be the case that nonlinear models have some disadvantages. Indeed, the very disadvantages of nonlinear models are the advantages of linear models. Nonlinear models are difficult to specify and estimate, and perhaps more important, once estimated it is hard to directly pin down their important dynamics. Linear models can all be derived from one common specification and have widely available estimation programs, and their global and local dynamics can be obtained directly by reference to the dynamics contained in their impulse response functions and variance decompositions. The first purpose of this chapter is to clearly exposit the tradeoffs between linear and nonlinear models.

If one takes a purely statistical view of the tradeoff between linear and nonlinear models, then the choice between them should be based on the result of a statistical comparison. An alternative way of stating this is that since linear models are the dominant tool used in economics, then "evidence for nonlinearity" is required before nonlinear models become a commonly used tool. The second purpose of this chapter is to discuss at a nontechnical level some of the issues involved in testing for nonlinearities. Readers requiring a more technical discussion are directed to Brock and Potter (1993) and Granger and Terasvirta (1993).

The chapter then proceeds to discuss a general class of parametric nonlinear time-series models—endogenous delay threshold autoregression—that are proving useful in describing asymmetries in economic variables over the business cycle. In the last few years a number of univariate nonlinear models have been proposed and estimated for U.S. output. The most well-known is due to Hamilton (1989), but the concentration will be on the recent models due to Beaudry and Koop (1993) and Pesaran and Potter (1994). The latter two is a member of the endogenous delay threshold autoregression (EDTAR) class and works off the intuition of floor and ceiling effects in the economy producing nonlinearities.

The chapter concludes by providing a guide to the use of impulse response functions and variance decompositions for nonlinear models. Techniques from Potter (1996) are described and applied to the floor and ceiling model. Thus, the third and final purpose of this chapter is to give the reader some idea of existing and potential future results using nonlinear models.

The Tradeoffs Between Linear and Nonlinear Models

Background

Frisch's seminal Cassel paper outlined a framework of impulses and propagation mechanism for the analysis of economic time series. It is well summarized by the following quote used by Frisch (1933, p. 198, quoting Wicksell): "If you hit a wooden rocking horse with a club, the movement of the horse will be very different to the movement of the club".

The impulses (club movements) are the exogenous forces that disturb the economy from its steady-state growth path. The propagation mechanism (rocking horse) turns the random impulses into persistent fluctuations or cycles of economic time series around a general upward drift. Frisch's article culminated a line of criticism started in the classic articles of Yule (1927) and Slutzky (1927) of earlier econometric work that had modeled business cycles by assuming that the economy was driven by a periodic process with the same time-series properties as the economy itself. Jevons's (1884) sunspot theory of the business cycle is the standard example. In criticizing this work all three (Yule, Slutzky, and Frisch) had made use of the properties of linear difference equations driven by random disturbances. They found that such statistical models were very capable of producing simulated time series that mimicked the behavior of the actual business cycle. After World War II the linear time-series techniques they promoted came to dominate the study of economic time series. The dominance was produced by the relative sophistication of these new techniques in conjuction with the new feasibility of computation. Further, with the Keynesian revolution in macroeconomics it was easy to interpret the impulses as "animal spirits" and the propagation mechanism as the acclerator-multiplier mechanism.

The Wold Representation. Five years after Frisch's Cassell paper, Wold (1938) showed an interesting theoretical property of all time series that are covariance stationary. It is possible to decompose these series into two components: one component that was perfectly *linearly* predictable from the past of the time series; a second component that is a weighted sum of random variables that cannot be linearly predicted from the past history of the time series. This second component is often called the Wold representation by economists. Thus, if $\{Y_t\}$ is a time series with no perfectly predictable components, its Wold representation has the following form:

$$Y_t = \sum_{i=0}^{\infty} \psi_i U_{t-i},$$

where $E[U_t] = 0$, $E[U_t^2] = \sigma_u$, $E[U_t U_{t-i}] = 0$ if $i \neq 0$, $\psi_0 = 1$ and $\sum_{i=0}^{\infty} \psi_i^2 < \infty$.

Some intuition for the Wold representation can be gained from the following informal argument. Define the linear predictor of Y_{t+N} at time t (using p observations):

$$L_{p,t}[Y_{t+N} \mid Y_t = y_t, \ldots, Y_{t-p+1} = y_{t-p+1}],$$

as the solution to the following prediction problem:

$$\min_{a,\{b_i\}} E\left[\left(Y_{t+N} - a - \sum_{i=0}^{p-1} b_i y_{t-i}\right)^2\right].$$

for abitrary $(y_t, \ldots, y_{t-p+1})$

One can express Y_t as follows by adding and subtracting linear predictions of Y_t from the previous period:

$$Y_t = L_{p,t}[Y_t] - L_{p,t-1}[Y_t] + L_{p,t-1}[Y_t],$$

since $L_{p,t}[Y_t] = Y_t$. Note that the exact conditioning information is surpressed for notational convenience.

Continuing in this way for N periods, one obtains

$$Y_t = L_{p,t}[Y_t] - L_{p,t-1}[Y_t] + L_{p,t-1}[Y_t] - \cdots - L_{p,t-N}[Y_t] + L_{p,t-N}[Y_t]. \quad (13.1)$$

For example, if Y_t is a linear AR(1),

$$Y_t = \phi Y_{t-1} + V_t,$$

then

$$L_{1,t-j}[Y_t] = \phi^j Y_{t-j},$$

and

$$Y_t = Y_t - \phi Y_{t-1} + \phi Y_{t-1} - \phi^2 Y_{t-2} + \cdots + \phi^{N-1} Y_{t-N-1} - \phi^N Y_{t-N} + \phi^N Y_{t-N},$$

which simplifies to

$$Y_t = V_t + \phi V_{t-1} + \cdots + \phi^{N-1} V_{t-N-1} + \phi^N Y_{t-N}.$$

Under the assumption of covariance stationarity and the lack of any purely deterministic components in Y_t the use of an abitrary finite p in the definition of the linear predictor will approximate (in the mean square convergence sense) the optimal predictor over the infinite past (see Brockwell and Davis, 1987, for more formal statements). Thus, as $p \to \infty$ one could write Y_t as a sum of linear prediction errors based on forecasting using information in the infinite past,

$$Y_t = \sum_{i=0}^{\infty} \{L_{t-i}[Y_t] - L_{t-i-1}[Y_t]\}, \quad (13.2)$$

where $L_{t-i}[Y_t] = L_{t-i}[Y_t \mid Y_{t-i}, Y_{t-i-1}, \dots]$. Alternatively, one could follow the intuition of the AR(1) example above, and attempt to find an equivalent expression in the one step ahead forecast errors, $L_{t-i}[Y_{t-i}] - L_{t-i-1}[Y_{t-i}]$. The Wold representation is just such a expression, where the sequence of one-step forecast errors are multiplied by coefficients given by a simple Fourier transformation to provide optimal linear predictions of Y_t. The power of the Wold representation is that no form was assumed for the time series other than the properties of covariance stationarity and the lack of deterministic linear components. The latter feature can be incorporated by adding a deterministic sequence that is covariance stationary to the Wold representation.

At first it might appear as if the Wold representation is only of theoretical interest since it involves an infinite number of coefficients $\{\psi_i\}$; however, in many cases these coefficients can be obtained from a much smaller number of parameters as in the AR(1) example above. Thus, in practice parsimonious linear models are estimated and then "inverted" to obtain the Wold representation, which contains all the linear information on the dynamics of the time series.

There is also a Wold representation for vector valued time series:

$$\mathbf{Y}_t = \sum_{i=0}^{\infty} \mathbf{\Psi}_i \mathbf{U}_{t-i},$$

where $E[\mathbf{U}_t] = 0$, $E[\mathbf{U}_t \mathbf{U}_t'] = \Sigma_{\mathbf{u}}$, $E[\mathbf{U}_t \mathbf{U}_{t-i}'] = \mathbf{0}_k$ if $i \neq 0$, $\mathbf{\Psi}_0 = \mathbf{I}_k$ and $\sum_{i=0}^{\infty} \| \mathbf{\Psi}_i \|_2 < \infty$.

Nonlinear Representation. Unlike the case of the linear predictor there is no general underlying representation of all time series in terms of nonlinear predictors. Recall that linear predictors are guaranteed to be the same as the nonlinear predictors only if the random variables involved are Gaussian. Further, while the linear prediction problem is easy to solve, the general problem of finding a function $NL_{N,p}(y_t, \ldots, y_{t-p+1})$ that

$$\min_{NL_{N,p}(\cdot)} E[(Y_{t+N} - NL\{y_t, \ldots, y_{t-p+1}\})^2],$$

is far more difficult to solve. There are two main difficulties. First, there is no general theory for developing the nonlinear predictor. Second, the nonlinear predictor is indexed by N above to indicate that the nonlinear predictor for $N = 2$ cannot necessarily be obtained from the nonlinear predictor for $N = 1$. For the moment I write the solution to this problem for emphasis as $NL[\cdot]$, but later I will use the conditional expectation notation, $E[\cdot]$. Only in the case of a linear model will the linear predictor agree with the conditional expectation.

For the first problem, one possibility is to restrict attention to a particular class of nonlinear models:

$$NL_{N,p}(Y_t, \ldots, Y_{t-p}) = g_N(Y_t, \ldots, Y_{t-p}; \gamma),$$

where γ is finite dimensional parameter vector. This approach is discussed at length below for the endogenous delay threshold class. Alternatively one might use some type of flexible nonparametric methods as, for example, in Gallant, Rossi, and Tauchen (1993) or White (1993) that have approximating properties for the conditional expectation as the number of terms in the approximation (not the necesarily the number of lags) goes to infinity.

The second problem does not occur in the case of linear models because of the simplifications produced in the linear case by the chain rule of forecasting. Suppose we have available $L_t[Y_{t+n}]$, $n = p, \ldots, N - 1$. Then, using the linear predictor we have

$$L_t[Y_{t+N}] = a + \sum_{i=1}^{p} b_i L_t[Y_{t+N-i}].$$

With a nonlinear predictor, the chain rule of forecasting still applies but it does not lead to any simplifications. In the case that Y_t has a Markov property—that is, the conditional distribution of Y_t depends on a finite number of the past values of the time series—it is possible to generate the n step ahead forecasts from the one-step ahead conditional distributions. For example, suppose

$$Y_t = g(Y_{t-1}) + V_t.$$

Then

$$NL[Y_{t+1} \mid Y_t = y_t] = \int (g(y_t) + v_{t+1}) f_v dv_{t+1},$$

$$NL[Y_{t+2} \mid Y_t = y_t] = \int \left[\int (g(y) + v_{t+2}) f_v dv_{t+2} \right] f_{y|y_t} dy,$$

where f_v is the density of the innovation V_t and the conditional density $f_{y|y_t}$ is equal to f_v with all values translated by the value of $g(y_t)$:

$$NL[Y_{t+N} \mid Y_t = y_t] = \int \left[\int (g(y_{t+N-1}) + v_{t+N}) f_v dv_{t+N} \right] f_{y+N-1|yt} dy_{t+N-1}$$

$$= \int \left[\int \left[\int (g(g(y_{t+N-2}) + v_{t+N-2}) \right. \right.$$
$$\left. \left. + v_{t+N}) f_v dv_{t+N} \right] f_v dv_{t+N-1} \right] f_{yt+N-2|yt} dt$$

$$= \int \cdots \int (g \cdots (g(y_t) + v_{t+1}) \cdots) + v_{t+N}) \prod_{n=1}^{N} f_v dv_{t+N} \cdots dv_{t+1},$$

where $f_{y_{t+n}|y_t}$ is the conditional density of y_{t+n} given y_t.

There were two elements in the development of the Wold representation above. The first was the use of a linear predictor over the infinite past. The second was a representation of the time series as a weighted sum of one-step-ahead forecast errors from this predictor. Equation (13.2) is still valid if one replaces the linear predictor of the infinite past with the nonlinear predictor over the finite past:

$$Y_t = \sum_{i=0}^{\infty} \{NL_{i,p}[Y_t] - NL_{i-1,p}[Y_t]\}. \tag{13.3}$$

In the case that Y_t has a Markov property of order p, then the nonlinear predictors in (13.3) will contain all the relevant information about the dynamics of nonlinear models in a similar manner to the way the linear predictors in the Wold representation contains all the relevant information about linear models. If Y_t does not have a Markov property, then it is not obvious how to construct unique measures of the dynamics. The above considerations lead to the condition that the analysis of nonlinear models be restricted to those satisfying a Markov property.

Advantages of Linear Models and Disadvantages of Nonlinear Models

The dynamics of estimated linear models are mainly evaluated by the use of impulse response functions and variance decompositions.

The Univariate Case. There are four possible conceptual experiments one can go through to generate the impulse response function of a linear model:

- Compare two realizations of the same covariance stationary time series from time t onwards. One realization, $\{\hat{Y}_t\}$, is hit by an "impulse" u_t at time t and no impulses thereafter. The other realization, $\{\bar{Y}_t\}$, is hit by a zero impulse at time t and no impulses thereafter. Using the Wold representation one has

$$\hat{Y}_{t+N} = \sum_{i=N}^{\infty} \psi_i u_{t+N-i},$$

$$\bar{Y}_{t+N} = \sum_{i=N+1}^{\infty} \psi_i u_{t+N-i},$$

$$\hat{Y}_{t+N} - \bar{Y}_{t+N} = \psi_N u_t.$$

- The difference between two linear predictions of the series with one information set perturbed from the other by the shock u at time t. Again using the Wold representation:

$$L(Y_{t+N} \mid Y_t = y_t + u, \ldots) = \psi_N u + \sum_{i=N}^{\infty} \psi_i u_{t+N}$$

$$L(Y_{t+N} \mid Y_t = y_t, \ldots) = \sum_{i=N}^{\infty} \psi_i u_{t+N},$$

$$L(Y_{t+N} \mid Y_t = y_t + u, \ldots) - L(Y_{t+N} \mid Y_t = y_t, \ldots) = \psi_N u.$$

- The difference between two linear predictions of the series one from time t the other from time $t - 1$:

$$L(Y_{t+N} \mid Y_t = y_t, \ldots) = \sum_{i=N}^{\infty} \psi_i u_{t+N_i}$$

$$L(Y_{t+N} \mid Y_{t-1} = y_{t-1}, \ldots) = \sum_{i=N}^{\infty} \psi_i u_{t+N_i},$$

$$L(Y_{t+N} \mid Y_t = y_t, \ldots) - L(Y_{t+N} \mid Y_{t-1} = y_{t-1}, \ldots) = \psi_N u_t.$$

- Finally, the derivative of the linear predictor of Y_{t+N} at time t:

$$\frac{\partial L(Y_{t+N} \mid Y_t = y_t, \ldots)}{\partial y_t} = \psi_N.$$

After suitably scaling, the impulse response function of a univariate time series is given directly by the coefficients of its Wold representation using any one of the four possible definitions given above. In the case of models estimated using a non-linear predictor, the situation is far more complicated.

The linear predictor can be obtained by setting all future shocks to their mean value of zero in the Wold representation. This is not possible for nonlinear models because it is not possible to pass the expectations operator through the nonlinear functions (recall that expectations are linear operators). In order to form the non-linear predictor (more than one step ahead) one must integrate out over the future as shown above. The first definition of an impulse response function is no longer directly useful since with the minor exceptions noted in Potter (1996) it is no longer the same across all the future realizations. Thus, the whole probability distribution of the shocks rather then just its mean value (zero) is relevant for the dynamic responses.

If one replaces the linear predictor in the second through fourth definitions with the nonlinear predictor, then it is not the case that the information produced is the same across the three definitions after a suitably scaling. Following Potter (1996) we have

$$nlirf_n(v, y_t, y_{t-1}, y_{t-p+1}) = NL(Y_{t+n} \mid Y_t = y_t + v, \ldots) - NL(Y_{t+N} \mid Y_t = y_t, \ldots),$$

$$nludf_n(y_t, y_{t-1}, y_{t-2}, y_{t-p}) = NL(Y_{t+n} \mid Y_t = y_t, \ldots) - NL(Y_{t+N} \mid Y_{t-1} = y_{t-1}, \ldots),$$

$$dnlirf_n(y_t) = \frac{\partial NL(Y_{t+n} \mid Y_t = y_t, \ldots)}{\partial y_t},$$

Potter (1996) shows that the derivative measure does not necessarily converge to zero even though the first two definitions do. As well as the difficulty about choosing between measures of the dynamics of the system there is the further difficulty that now history and shocks matter. This leads to a reporting problem. It is possible to find histories and shocks that can generate arbitrary responses. Below I discuss ways of reporting representative information on dynamic responses in stochastic nonlinear models.

The Multivariate Case. In economics much research concentrates on estimating vector autoregressive representations and then inverting them to find the multivariate Wold representation. In the vector linear time-series case the dynamics are harder to read off directly from the Wold representation since there is a composition problem. At any time the vector of shocks $\{\mathbf{U}_t\}$ could feed directly into all the variables, and the underlying shocks can be recovered only by some identification restrictions. Even after the underlying shocks have been recovered, there is still the question of how to perturb the system to obtain dynamics. One possibility would be to look at the cases where all but one of the shocks was set equal to zero. However, in the nonlinear model case this does not lead to representative dynamics.

Three possible alternative solutions are to

- Use prior information to identify some underlying shocks that are independent of each other and set all but one shock to zero,
- Orthogonalize the shocks using a Cholesky factorization and set all but one shock to zero, and
- Integrate out over all the shocks but one as described below. This method will work for nonlinear models as well.

Without going into the details of any of the procedures, it is the case that the result of all of them is a $K \times 1$ pertubation vector v_k for each shock and the ($K \times 1$) impulse response function of the kth shock is then given by

$$\mathbf{\Psi}_n v_k.$$

Once the method of combining shocks is decided the impulse response function is uniquely determined in the linear case. In a vector time-series model it is also of interest to ask which shock is causing the most variability in each variable. The technique used to answer this question is a variance decomposition. A variance decomposition decomposes the forecast error variance of each variable into contributions from each of the K shocks in the model. Using the Wold representation again one can write the forecast error variance as

$$V(\mathbf{Y}_{t+n} - L_t[\mathbf{Y}_{t+n}]) = \sum_{i=1}^{n} \mathbf{\Psi}_n \Sigma_u \mathbf{\Psi}_n'.$$

Once again there is a composition problem in attributing variation in initial shocks to variables. In this case it is necessary to find some underlying orthogonal shocks so that the forecast variance can be written as

$$V(Y_{t+n} - L_t[Y_{t+n}]) = \sum_{n=1}^{N} \sum_{k=1}^{K} \Psi_n^* \Delta_{kk} \Psi_n^{*\prime},$$

where Δ_{kk} is a $K \times K$ matrix with all zero elements except for $\delta_{kk} = 1$, Ψ^* is a transformation of the moving average matrices such that

$$\Psi \Sigma_u \Psi' = \sum_{k=1}^{K} \Psi_n^* \Delta_{kk} \Psi_n^{*\prime}$$

It is also possible to relate the variance decomposition to the information contained in the impulse response functions by adding and subtracting linear predictors as in (13.2):

$$VAR(\mathbf{Y}_{t+N} - L_t[\mathbf{Y}_{t+N}]) = VAR(\mathbf{Y}_{t+N}[\mathbf{Y}_{t+N}] - L_{t+N-1}[\mathbf{Y}_{t+N}]) + VAR(L_{t+N-1}[\mathbf{Y}_{t+N}]$$

$$- L_{t+N-1}[\mathbf{Y}_{t+N}]) + \ldots + VAR(L_{t+2}[\mathbf{Y}_{t+N}] - L_{t+1}[\mathbf{Y}_{t+N}])$$

$$+ VAR(L_{t+1}[\mathbf{Y}_{t+N}] - L_t[\mathbf{Y}_{t+N}]).$$

Hence, the variance decomposition of the linear model gives information on the relative importance of the impulse response functions defined by particular combinations of the underlying shocks. As shown in the fifth section such a relation is not true for the nonlinear case.

Disadvantages of Linear Models and Advantages of Nonlinear Models

> *An initiating impulse, when it comes into play, operates upon a certain complex of industrial and monetary conditions. Given the impulse, these will determine the nature of the effect that it produces, and are, in this sense, causes of industrial fluctuations. The impulse is the dropping of a match: the consequences are determined by the nature of the material with which it comes in contact*
>
> —Acemoglu and Scott (1993, quoting A.C. Pigou,
> *Industrial Fluctuations*, 1928, p. 8).

In order to illustrate the differences between nonlinear and linear cases a Volterra series expansion is introduced. This is a special form of nonlinear moving average that allows one to give some intuition for the additional effects present in nonlinear models. In order to keep the discussion tractable only the univariate case is examined:

$$Y_t = \sum_{i=0}^{\infty} \psi_i V_{t-i} + \sum_{i=1}^{\infty}\sum_{j=1}^{\infty} \psi_{ij} V_{t-i} V_{t-j} + \sum_{i=1}^{\infty}\sum_{j=1}^{\infty}\sum_{k=1}^{\infty} \psi_{ijk} V_{t-i} V_{t-j} V_{t-k} \cdots, \quad (13.4)$$

with V_t iid symmetrically distributed and the coefficients ψ_{ij}, ψ_{ijk} also have a symmetry property.

I will concentrate on the third order expansion and assume that the innovation sequence $\{V_t\}$ is directly observed. Thus, in this special case the nonlinear predictor is given by

$$NL_{t-n}[Y_t] = \sum_{i=0}^{\infty} \psi_i E_{t-n}[V_{t-i}] + \sum_{i=1}^{\infty}\sum_{j=1}^{\infty} \psi_{ij} E_{t-n}\left[V_{t-i}V_{t-j}\right]$$

$$+ \sum_{i=1}^{\infty}\sum_{j=1}^{\infty}\sum_{k=1}^{\infty} \psi_{ijk} E_{t-n}\left[V_{t-i}V_{t-j}V_{t-k}\right],$$

which simplifies to

$$NL_{t-n}[Y_t] = \sum_{i=n}^{\infty} \psi_i v_{t-i} + \sum_{i=n}^{\infty}\sum_{j=n}^{\infty} \psi_{ij} v_{t-i} v_{t-j} + \sum_{i=n}^{\infty}\sum_{j=n}^{\infty}\sum_{k=n}^{\infty} \psi_{ijk} v_{t-i} v_{t-j} v_{t-k}$$

$$+ \sum_{i=1}^{n-1} \psi_{ii} \sigma^2 + 3 \sum_{i=1}^{n-1}\sum_{j=n}^{\infty} \psi_{iij} \sigma^2 v_{t-j}.$$

Asymmetries and Stabilizers. Above it was shown using the Wold representation that the effect of any arbitrary shock at an arbitrary time period can be summarized by the coefficient in the Wold representation perhaps scaled by a function of the variance covariance matrix of the innovations to the time series in the vector case. Although this is a major advantage in terms of the simplicity of reporting task (the composition problem not withstanding), it is also a major restriction on the type of dynamics that can be captured by using linear methods. Most of the early business-cycle researchers believed that the business cycle was asymmetric: expansions were different from contractions. Linear models restrict the effect of impulses to be the same at each stage of the cycle. Thus, their ease of use comes with a large price: recessions must have the same dynamics as booms.

Nonlinear models do not restrict positive and negative shocks to have the same effect for a particular initial condition. Further, they do not restrict the same impulse to have the same effect for different initial conditions. In order to illustrate these characteristics, consider the *nlirf* for the Volterra series expansion above:

$$nlirf_n(v, v_t, v_{t-1}, v_{t-2}, \ldots) = v\psi_n + v^2\psi_{nn} + v^3\psi_{nnn} + 2v\sum_{j=n+1}^{\infty}\psi_{nj}v_{t-j+N}$$

$$+ 3v^2\sum_{j=n+1}^{\infty}\psi_{nnj}v_{t-j+n} + 3v\sum_{j=n+1}^{\infty}\sum_{k=n+1}^{\infty}\psi_{njk}v_{t-j+n}v_{t-k+n}$$

$$+ 3v\sigma^2\sum_{j=1}^{n-1}\psi_{njj}.$$

This expression illustrates three possible asymmetries:

- The magnitude of the shock for the same history will produce asymmetries because of the presence of v^2, v^3.
- The response to v will not be the same as $-v$ because of the v^2 terms.
- The same shock will have differing effects depending on the sequence of v_t, $v_{t-1}, \ldots$.

In order to illustrate the possibility of an intrinsic stabilizer, consider the *dnlirf* of the cubic Volterra series expansion:

$$dnlirf_n(v_t, v_{t-1}, v_{t-2}, \ldots) = \psi_n + 2v_t\psi_{nn} + 3v_t^2\psi_{nnn} + 2\sum_{j=n+1}^{\infty}\psi_{nj}v_{t-j+N}$$

$$+ 6v_t\sum_{j=n+1}^{\infty}\psi_{nnj}v_{t-j+n} + 3\sum_{j=n+1}^{\infty}\sum_{k=n+1}^{\infty}\psi_{njk}v_{t-j+n}v_{t-k+n}$$

$$+ 3\sigma^2\sum_{j=1}^{n-1}\psi_{njj}.$$

Assume that $v_t \ll 0$. It is possible for certain histories that the direct negative effect is outweighed by the squared term and the terms not involving v_t.

Endogenous Fluctuations.   All fluctuations in linear models are produced by the impulses to the system. This is not the case for nonlinear models. The fifth section develops this aspect of nonlinear models from a technical perspective; for the moment the discussion will be more informal. Consider two claims in economics:

- Asset prices sometimes fluctuate a great deal after the announcement of news that had been predicted.
- Stabilization policy can only have a second-order effect at best on the welfare of the representative consumer (see Lucas, 1987).

In the first case it is often assumed that the price of a stock depends on expectation of future dividends and interest rates. Assume that the interest rate is constant. The change in the value of a stock is given by

$$P_t - E_{t-1}[P_t] = \sum_{n=1}^{\infty} \beta^n \{ E_t[D_{t+n}] - E_{t-1}[D_{t+n}] \},$$

where P_t is the ex-dividend price of the stock, D_t is the dividend, and $0 < \beta < 1$ is the discount factor.

Suppose that dividends follow an integrated process. If

$$\Delta D_t = \phi \Delta D_{t-1} + V_t,$$

then

$$P_t - E_{t-1}[P_t] = \sum_{n=1}^{\infty} \beta^n \frac{1 - \phi^{n+1}}{1 - \phi} v_t .$$

Hence, in the case that v_t is small, the change in stock price is small and zero if v_t is zero. If alternatively the change in the dividend is described by the cubic Volterra model, then simple calculations lead to the updating function:

$$nludf_n(v_t, v_{t-1}, \ldots) = v_t \psi_n + (v_t^2 - \sigma^2) \psi_{nn} + v_t^3 \psi_{nnn}$$

$$+ 2v_t \sum_{j=n+1}^{\infty} \psi_{nj} v_{t-j+n} \; 3(v_t^2 - \sigma^2) \sum_{j=n+1}^{\infty} \psi_{nnj} v_{t-j+n}$$

$$+ 3v_t \sum_{j=n+1}^{\infty} \sum_{k=n+1}^{\infty} \psi_{njk} v_{t-j+n} v_{t-k+n} + 3v_t \sigma^2 \sum_{j=1}^{n-1} \psi_{njj}$$

In the special case that $v_t = 0$ and $v_{t-s} = 0$, $s > 0$, we would have for the unanticipated movement in the stock price

$$P_t - E_{t-1}[P_t] = \sigma^2 \sum_{n=1}^{\infty} \beta^n \sum_{i=1}^{n} \psi_{ii} .$$

The asset price has an unanticipated movement even though the current change in dividend was perfectly predicted. In the nonlinear case, there is "news" in this perfect prediction that a linear predictor cannot extract.

Lucas (1987) considers the value of stabilization policy by asking how much initial consumption a representative agent would be prepared to give up to remove fluctuations in consumption around "trend" for the rest of time. He finds that the amount is second order compared to the consumer's willingness to pay for an increase in the growth rate with initial consumption. For linear models, Lucas's experiment can be interpreted as reducing the variance of the time-series innovation in the consumption stochastic process to zero. Suppose instead that the change in the logarithm of consumption is actually generated by the cubic Volterra series model. First note that the average growth rate of consumption will be approximately given by the mean of this process:

$$E[\Delta ln C_t] = \sigma^2 \sum_{i=1}^{\infty} \psi_{ii}.$$

Next assume that the growth rate is positive. Reducing the variance of the innovation V_t would decrease growth and therefore reduce welfare of the representative agent. Depending on the relative importance of σ^2 versus $\sum_{i=1}^{\infty} \psi_{ii}$ for the value of the mean, this could have a large effect on welfare even for small changes in the variance.

Testing Linear Versus Nonlinear Specifications

If we return to the two prediction problems discussed in the previous section, then the choice between linear models and nonlinear models at first appears obvious. Choose the nonlinear model if the minimized value of the quadratic loss function is smaller than that of the linear predictor. A major difficulty is that the linear functions are a potential choice under the minimization of $NL(\cdot)$. Thus, the loss of the linear predictor is an upper bound on the loss for the unrestricted predictor. A similar problem occurs in deciding the order of an autoregression. By increasing the lag length one can always reduce the squared loss.

There are three main solutions to the question of order selection for linear time series models:

- Check the residuals of the estimated model for evidence of further linear structure. For example, one might calculate a Box-Lung statistic for the residuals.
- Penalize the loss function for the number of parameters that must be estimated relative to the number of observations.

- Test if additional terms are statistically significant at a conventional level. For example, one can estimate an AR(10) and perform a Wald test on the coefficients of lags 6 to 10.

The analogs in the case of evaluating linear models versus nonlinear models are as follows:

- The residuals of linear models are checked for evidence of nonlinear dependence. There are two main ways of doing this:

  Use a nonparametric approach such as the BDS test (see Brock, Hsieh, and LeBaron, 1991).

  Use a test function that looks for specific departures from the assumption of linearity. For example, one common approach is to see if the residuals are correlated with polynomial functions of the regressors (see Tsay, 1986).

- Many order selection criterion are based on penalizing general likelihood functions, therefore the traditional penalties could be used. However, their efficacy in the nonlinear case is not known and experience with some criterion suggests that they are biased to parsimonious models (that is, linear models).
- Test for the significance of the nonlinear effects in the model using the linear model as the null. As we discuss below this is not as easy as it might first appear.

Many economists believe that tests of the significance of the nonlinear terms are crucial in deciding whether nonlinear models are worth using. Since economists have a great deal of sunk capital in linear models, there is much to support this position despite the possible advantages of nonlinear models in capturing business cycles dynamics. Note that a statistical test does not give any information on whether the dynamics of a nonlinear model are economically interesting.

The testing solution has a less direct connection with the problem of overparameterization in linear time-series modeling. In order to understand the difficulties consider the likelihood ratio test in the case where for the linear and nonlinear models a Gaussian innovation is assumed and the linear model is nested within the nonlinear model. Then the likelihood ratio test statistic for a sample of size T is

$$T(\ln(\hat{\sigma}_L) - \ln(\hat{\sigma}_{NL})).$$

If the linear model is obtained from the nonlinear model by restricting all parameters that are not shared, then the likelihood ratio statistic will have a chi-squared distribution in large samples under the null hypothesis. However, if there are some parameters in the nonlinear model that are not restricted in the linear model then the likelihood ratio statistic will not have the standard properties.

Consider the following simple example to illustrate these points:

$$Y_t = \phi Y_{t-1} + \theta F(Y_{t-1}; \gamma) + V_t.$$

A linear model can be obtained from the nonlinear model be restricting $\theta = 0$, but this does not restrict γ. However, for the nonlinear model, γ is an important parameter to be estimated. Thus, suppose that there are two values of γ that imply different values of θ and lead to different inferences. That is, one leads to the rejection of the null linear model and the other does not. To make things even more concrete suppose γ is restricted to [0, 1] and the two values of γ are given by the maximum and minimum of the likelihood ratio over this interval. Which test result should one report?

Clearly a believer in linear models would tend to want to report the smallest test statistic and a believer in nonlinear models the largest test statistic. One compromise would be to take an average of the two, but what would be the appropriate distribution to compare this test statistic to? Consider whether either of the test statistics could have a chi-squared distribution. Recall that under the null the likelihood ratio should have an approximate chi-squared distribution with one degree of freedom for an arbitrary value of γ. However, in our experiment we took the maximum and the minimum over γ. Thus, one needs to know the maximum and minimum of a chi-squared distribution to obtain the appropriate distribution. If the test statistics calculated at different values of γ were independent, this would not be a difficult task given modern computer technology. Unfortunately the test statistics are far from independent since the same time series is used for each calculation of the test statistic.

The conclusion is that to provide a correct distribution for any test statistic whether it be at a single value of γ or some average one needs to calculate a function of collection of dependent chi-squared random variables. Fortunately, in an important paper Bruce Hansen (1993) has developed a simulation approach to solve this problem. Although the paper relies on some sophisticated empirical process arguments, the actual approach is relatively simple. Consider how one might use a computer to simulate the distribution of the maximum of a chi-squared random variable. One would generate realizations by squaring and summing the appropriate number of standard normal random variables from a random number generator. Next one would find the maximum of this set of realizations. Repeating the process would allow one to obtain an empirical distribution. Of course, one could also find the distribution of other functions of the realizations such as the average.

Now in order to deal with the dependence across values Hansen's method uses the empirical distribution of the time series itself, as it is used in the formation of the test statistic, to appropriately link the realizations of the computer simulated chi-squared random variables. This leaves one unresolved question: what test statistic or combination of test statistics are the best to use? In recent work Andrews and Ploberger (1994) show that in addition to the commonly used maximum statistic, various weighted averages have good statistical properties.

Nonlinear Models for Economic Time Series

Nonlinear Models of U.S. Output

Nonlinear time-series models of U.S. output share the common theme of regime switching to model possible nonlinearities. Further, the regimes are taken to represent different phases of the business cycle providing a connection with the notion of business-cycle asymmetry. The standard form of regime-switching model was introduced by Tong and Lim (1980).

Let $\{X_t: t = -\infty, \ldots, -1, 0, 1, \ldots,\}$ be a time series and let J_t be an indicator random variable taking values in the set $\{1, 2, \ldots, K\}$. Then the canonical threshold autoregression is defined by

$$X_t = \alpha^{(J_t)} + \phi^{(J_t)}(L)X_{t-1} + \sigma^{(J_t)}V_t, \tag{13.5}$$

where V_t is an iid sequence of standardized random variables with zero means and unit variances; and for $J_t = j$, $\alpha^{(j)}$ is a constant, $\phi^{(j)}(L)$ is a finite-order polynomial in the lag operator L.

The main characteristic of the TAR class is its use of piecewise linear dynamic models over regimes classified by the value of an index variable J_t. In Hamilton (1989) the regime switching is exogenously generated by an unobserved Markov chain. In the threshold autoregression models of Potter (1995) and Tiao and Tsay (1994) the regime switching is endogenously generated by a fixed lag or lags of output growth. In the model of Beaudry and Koop (1993) an additional variable enters the autoregression that is only nonzero when output is below its previous maximum. Thus, Beaudry and Koop's model contains two regimes with endogenous switching. We start by working with Beaudry and Koop's model because of its simplicity compared to the others and its direct economic interpretation.

Beaudry and Koop construct a variable they call the current depth of recession variable, CDR_t:

$$CDR_t = X_t - \max(X_t, X_{t-1}, \ldots, X_0),$$

where X_t is the logarithm of output and X_0 is the level of output in 1947Q1.

The first difference of the logarithm of output (approximately the growth rate) is then modeled as the Beaudry and Koop model:

$$Y_t = \alpha + \phi_p(L)Y_{t-1} + \theta\, CDR_{t-1} + V_t.$$

where $Y_t = X_t - Y_{t-1}$ and $\phi_p(L) = \phi_1 L + \ldots \phi_p L^p$.

Beaudry and Koop find a statistically significant negative coefficient on the current depth of recession variable. Since they do not estimate any nuisance parameters under the alternative hypothesis, a simple t-test is valid in this case. More important, the estimated θ is negative, indicating that the previous maximum of output acts as a ratchet effect. The ideas of floors or ratchets in output growth was very common in the 1950s but has fallen out of favor more recently (see Gordon and Klein, 1965, for a review of the most important articles). To see exactly why the negative coefficient represents a ratchet effect we consider the following scenario: current output growth is negative, thus next period the current depth of recession variable has a *positive* effect on output growth. Suppose that this upward pressure on the growth rate is outweighed by a further negative output shock. Now the current depth of recession variable has a larger magnitude and represents more upward pressure on the growth rate. This upward pressure on the growth rate will remain in force until output exceeds the previous maximum.

The dynamics found by Beaudry and Koop are similar to those of the threshold autoregression model of Potter (1995) and Tiao and Tsay (1994). The dynamics of output suggest that the economy tends to have an in-built stabilizer that prevents recessions from lasting as long as implied by the forecasts of linear models. Further, the growth in the recovery phase is higher the deeper was the recession, the more negative the CDR_t variable. A stylized fact that is supported by other nonparametric methods. One feature that the model of Beaudry and Koop does not contain, found in previous work particularly Hamilton (1989), is a sharp drop into recession. The construction of Beadry and Koop's model does not allow for such effects. In the more general floor and ceiling model of Pesaran and Potter (1994) this effect is allowed as well as pairing the floor of Beaudry and Koop with a ceiling. In order to do this we return to the canonical formulation of the threshold autoregression model above.

Endogenous Delay Threshold Autoregression

Most applications of threshold autoregressions have simplified the problem of choice of the index variable by choosing a lag of the observed time series d, known as the delay variable, and a series of thresholds $\{r_i, i = 1, \ldots, K - 1\}$ to construct J_t. An example would be

$$X_t = \begin{cases} \alpha_1 + \phi_1(L)X_{t-1} + \sigma_1 V_t & \text{if } X_{t-d} < r_1, \\ \alpha_1 + \phi_2(L)X_{t-1} + \sigma_2 V_t & \text{if } r_1 \leq X_{t-d} < r_2, \\ \quad\vdots & \qquad\vdots \\ \alpha_K + \phi_K(L)X_{t-1} + \sigma_K V_t & \text{if } X_{t-d} > r_{K-1}. \end{cases} \quad (13.6)$$

Since the index variable is constructed from the location of observable lags of the time series, the specification is relatively easy to estimate, test, and evaluate as exemplified in Tong (1990). For example, in Potter (1995) the second lag of quarterly output growth, Y_{t-2}, is used as the delay variable with the threshold at zero growth to define a two-regime model. Although the model fits the data well and significantly better than a linear model, it is difficult to give a convincing economic rationale why only the second lag should be so crucial. Further, the specification of abrupt changes in behavior based on the value of output growth at a two-quarter lag is difficult to reconcile with nonlinear theoretical models where one would expect the most recent output growth rate, Y_{t-1}, to have nonlinear effects on Y_t as well. Tiao and Tsay (1994) go some way toward dealing with this criticism by introducing two regimes conditional on $Y_{t-2} < 0$: (1) one regime where output growth continues to worsen, $Y_{t-1} < Y_{t-2}$ and (2) a second regime where output growth improves in the most recent quarter, $Y_{t-1} > Y_{t-2}$.

One can continue in the manner of Tiao and Tsay and introduce further regimes. For example, it is possible to further split the two contractionary regimes above depending on whether $Y_{t-3} < 0$ or not. However, this is not a parsimonious approach, and in applying it one could soon run out of degrees of freedom when analyzing most macroeconomic time series. One possible method of avoiding this difficulty is to utilize parameter restrictions across the various regimes. The EDTAR class provides a natural method of generating such restrictions by an endogenous generation of the index variable defining the regimes and a recursive construction of additional variables to be added to the autoregression.

Potter (1996) contains a description of the general class. For expositional purposes we concentrate on a somewhat simpler form here which is extended below for the case of the floor and ceiling model of Pesaran and Potter (1994). We also introduce a generalization of the indicator function, the squashing function. Squashing functions take on values in [0, 1] as does the indicator function, but they allow for a smooth transition between the value of 0 to 1.

First, a collection of M index variables, called endogenous delay variables $\{I_{mt}, m = 1, \ldots, M\}$ or $\{N_{mt}, m = 1, \ldots, M\}$, is generated by a feedback relationship among past values of the time series. The form of feedback relationship has some similarities to recurrent neural networks (see White, 1993, for an overview of neural networks). Note that in what follows, X_t will be the generic time series from the start of this section:

$$I_{mt} = \sum_{j=0}^{\infty} \left\{ \prod_{s=0}^{j} 1(X_{t-s} \in A_m) \right\}, \text{ for } m = 1, \ldots, M, \qquad (13.7)$$

or in the case of a squashing function

$$N_{mt} = \sum_{j=0}^{\infty} \delta_m^j \left\{ \prod_{s=0}^{j} F(\beta_m(X_{t-s} - r_m)) \right\}, \text{ for } m = 1, \ldots, M, \qquad (13.8)$$

where $1(A)$ is the indicator function taking the value of unity if the event A occurs and zero otherwise, A_m are nonoverlapping intervals on the line and $F(\cdot)$ is the logistic function:

$$\frac{1}{1 + \exp(-\beta_m(X_{t-s} - r_m))}.$$

Notice that as $\beta_m \to \infty$ that the logistic function is equal to 0 if $X_{t-s} < r_m$, 1/2 if $X_{t-s} = r_m$, and 1 if $X_{t-s} > r_m$.

The collection of endogenous delay indicator variables can then be used to recursively define new variables. In the indicator function case,

$$Z_{mt} = 1(I_{mt} > 0)[Z_{mt-1} + X_t], \text{ for } m = 1, \ldots, M. \qquad (13.9)$$

In the squashing function case,

$$W_{mt} = F(\gamma_{m1} N_{mt} - \gamma_{m0})[W_{mt-1} + X_t], \text{ for } m = 1, \ldots, M. \qquad (13.10)$$

The first the lag of Z_{mt} can be rewritten as

$$Z_{mt-1} = \sum_{j=1}^{\infty} \left\{ \prod_{s=1}^{j} 1(I_{mt-s} > 0) \right\} X_{t-j}, \qquad (13.11)$$

and the first lag of W_{mt} as

$$W_{mt-1} = \sum_{j=1}^{\infty} \left\{ \prod_{s=1}^{j} F(\gamma_{m1} N_{mt-s} - \gamma_{m0}) \right\} X_{t-j}. \qquad (13.12)$$

Potter (1996) discusses conditions required to ensure that the maximum possible lag length in the recursion is finite in the case of the indicator function and the sum itself converges in the squashing function case (see below for some brief details). Intuitively the conditions relate to the stationarity of the series being modeled. If the time series is stationary, then it should not remain in one location for a long time. Thus, the consecutive time periods spent in any of the regions defined by the thresholds will be finite. The squashing function version of the model clearly gives a more flexible lag structure, but this comes at the expense of significantly more parameters to be estimated.

Given M endogenous delay variables $\{I_{1t}, I_{2t}, \ldots, I_{Mt}\}$ and the recursive variables Z_{mt} they generate when applied to the time series $\{X_t\}$, we can define the EDTAR(p, M) model by

$$X_t = \alpha + \phi_p(L)X_{t-1} + \sum_{m=1}^{M} \theta_m Z_{mt-1} + \left\{\sum_{m=0}^{M} \sigma_m 1(I_{mt-1} > 0)\right\} V_t,$$

where $I_{0t} = 1(\sum_{m=1}^{M} I_{mt} = 0)$ and $\phi_p(L)$ is a pth order polynomial in the lag operator.

Alternatively, one can use the recursive variables W_{mt} to define the smooth endogenous delay threshold autoregression, SEDTAR(p, M), model by

$$X_t = \alpha + \phi_p(L)X_{t-1} + \sum_{m=1}^{M} \theta_m W_{mt-1} + \sigma V_t.$$

One advantage that the EDTAR model has over the SEDTAR model is that heteroskedasticity in the error term can be modeled using the endogenous delay variables. It is possible to use the endogenous delay variables from the SEDTAR to model conditional heteroscedasticity but it requires more parameters.

The EDTAR model can be reexpressed to show a more direct relationship to the TAR using (13.11):

$$X_t = \begin{cases} \alpha + \phi_p(L)X_{t-1} + \sigma_0 V_t & \text{if } I_{0t-1} = 1, \\ \alpha + \phi_p(L)X_{t-1} + \theta_1 V_{t-1} + \sigma_1 V_t & \text{if } I_{1t-1} > 0 \text{ and } I_{2t-2} = 0 \\ \quad\vdots & \quad\vdots \\ \alpha + \phi_p(L)X_{t-1} + \theta_1 \sum_{s=1}^{j} X_{t-s} + \sigma_1 V_t & \text{if } \prod_{s=1}^{j} I_{1t-s} > 0 \text{ and } I_{1j-1} = 0, \\ \quad\vdots & \quad\vdots \\ \alpha + \phi_p(L)X_{t-1} + \theta_m X_{t-1} + \sigma_m V_t & \text{if } I_{mt-1} > 0 \text{ and } I_{mt-2} = 0 \\ \quad\vdots & \quad\vdots \\ \alpha + \phi_p(L)X_{t-1} + \theta_m \sum_{s=1}^{j} X_{t-s} + \sigma_m V_t & \text{if } \prod_{s=1}^{j} I_{mt-s} > 0 \text{ and } I_{mj-1} = 0, \\ \quad\vdots & \quad\vdots \\ \alpha + \phi_p(L)X_{t-1} + \theta_M X_{t-1} + \sigma_M V_t & \text{if } I_{Mt-1} > 0 \text{ and } I_{Mt-2} = 0 \\ \quad\vdots & \quad\vdots \\ \alpha + \phi_p(L)X_{t-1} + \theta_M \sum_{s=1}^{j} X_{t-s} + \sigma_M V_t & \text{if } \prod_{s=1}^{j} I_{Mt-s} > 0 \text{ and } I_{Mt-j-1} = 0, \\ \quad\vdots & \quad\vdots \end{cases}$$

$$(13.13)$$

The above extended description of the EDTAR model shows that it has the ability to parsimoniously capture a large number of possible regimes. The cost is the restricted way that lags enter the different regimes. The SEDTAR model allows the lags to enter in a less restricted manner.

The additional flexibility of the SEDTAR model can be illustrated by using (13.12) to give

$$X_t = \alpha + \phi_p(L)X_{t-1}$$

$$+ \sum_{m=0}^{M}\theta_m \sum_{k=1}^{\infty}\left[\prod_{\tau=1}^{k}F\left(\left\{\gamma_{m1}\sum_{j=\tau}^{\infty}\delta_m^j\prod_{s=1}^{j}F(\beta_m(X_{t-s}-r_m))\right\}-\gamma_{m0}\right)\right]X_{t-k} + \sigma V_t.$$

Formally, the SEDTAR model can be interpreted as approximating the co-efficients in an exact first order Taylor series expansion of a general nonlinear autoregression with a two hidden layer recurrent $\Sigma\Pi$ neural network. White (1993) provides an extended discussion of the excellent approximation capabilities of somewhat simpler networks hence one would expect this formulation to be successful in practice.

Unlike other nonlinear time series models, EDTAR and SEDTAR have obvious generalizations to the vector time series case. For given functions I_{mt} and N_{mt} the recursions defined in equations (13.7) and (13.8) can be defined in terms of more than one time series. Thus, if X_t is a K-dimensional time series, one would define

$$Z_{kmt-1} = \sum_{j=1}^{\infty}\left\{\prod_{s=1}^{j}1(I_{mt-s}>0)\right\}X_{t-j} \text{ for } m=1,\ldots,M \text{ and } k=1,\ldots,K, \quad (13.14)$$

and

$$W_{kmt-1} = \sum_{j=1}^{\infty}\left\{\prod_{s=1}^{j}F(\gamma_{km1}N_{mt-s}-\gamma_{km0})\right\}X_{kt-j}$$

$$\text{for } m=1,\ldots M \text{ and } k=1,\ldots K. \quad (13.15)$$

Thus, vector time-series versions of the EDTAR and SEDTAR models are given by

$$X_t = a + \Phi_p(L)X_{t-1} + \sum_{m=1}^{M}\Theta_m Z_{mt-1} + \left\{\sum_{m=0}^{M}H_m 1(I_{mt-1}>0)\right\}V_t,$$

where $\Phi_p(L)$ is a pth order matrix polynomial in the lag operator, Θ_m, H_m are $K \times K$ matrices, a is a $K \times 1$ vector and $Z_{mt}=(Z_{1mt},\ldots,Z_{Kmt})'$. The vector SEDTAR model is

$$\mathbf{X}_t = \mathbf{a} + \Phi_{\mathbf{p}}(\mathbf{L})\mathbf{X}_{t-1} + \sum_{m=1}^{M} \Theta_m \mathbf{W}_{mt-1} + H\mathbf{V}_t.$$

$\mathbf{W}_{mt} = (W_{1mt}, \ldots, W_{Kmt})'$ and HH' scales the identity variance matrix of $\mathbf{V}_t$.

Estimation and Testing. Both of these models are very parsimonious compared to other possible extensions of nonlinear time series models to the vector time series case. Further, once the Z_{kmt}, W_{kmt} variables are known in any of the models, they can be estimated by linear least squares. This is especially important in the vector time-series case where the total number of parameters is large. For the EDTAR models the main difficulty in estimation is the need to evaluate the model at all possible threshold values to form estimates. The lack of smoothness of the indicator function form of the nonlinearity prevents the use of gradient descent type algorithms to estimate the thresholds. The SEDTAR can be estimated by traditional gradient descent methods or the neural network technique of backpropagation.

In order to test for the significance of the nonlinear terms one must deal with the nuisance parameter problem. In the EDTAR case the nuisance parameters are the thresholds defining the sets A_m, and the Hansen simulation method can be applied to the grid used for the estimation. In the SEDTAR case there are more nuisance parameters, and the Hansen approach requires very large computer resources to apply. One possibility is to consider the EDTAR model for testing and then check whether the SEDTAR version of the model has superior properties. An alternative testing approach for the EDTAR model discussed in Pesaran and Potter (1994) is to use a likelihood ratio test of a linear heteroscedastic model against the full nonlinear model. When the heteroscedasticity is described by the endogenous delay variables this test has a conventional chi-squared distribution.

A Markov Representation of the EDTAR Model. It is possible to write the EDTAR and SEDTAR models in a Markov form. For simplicity, I only consider the univariate EDTAR model here, with $\alpha = 0$.

Define the $p + M$ vector time series, $\mathbf{Y}_t = (X_t, X_{t-1}, \ldots, X_{t-p+1}, Z_{1t}, Z_{2t}, \ldots, Z_{Mt})'$, and $p + M$ innovation sequence $\mathbf{U}_t = (V_t, 0, \ldots, 0, V_t, \ldots, V_t)'$. Let the matrix $\mathbf{A}_t$ be given by

$$\begin{bmatrix} I_p & 0_{p \times M} \\ 0_{M \times p} & F_t \end{bmatrix},$$

where $\mathbf{I}_p$ is the indentity matrix, 0 is a matrix of zeros with the given dimensions, and the $M \times M$ matrix $\mathbf{F}_t$ is given by

$$
\begin{bmatrix}
1(I_{1t} > 0) & 0 & \cdots & & 0 \\
0 & 1(I_{2t} > 0) & \cdots & & \vdots \\
\vdots & 0 & \ddots & & 0 \\
0 & & \cdots & 0 & 1(I_{Mt} > 0)
\end{bmatrix},
$$

Let the $(p + M) \times (p + M)$ matrix $\mathbf{B}$ be given by

$$
\begin{bmatrix}
\phi_1 & \cdots & \phi_p & \theta_1 & \cdots & \theta_M \\
1 & 0 & 0 & 0 & \cdots & 0 \\
0 & 1 & \cdots & \cdots & \cdots & \vdots \\
\vdots & \cdots & \ddots & \cdots & \cdots & \vdots \\
\phi_1 & \cdots & \phi_p & 1 + \theta_1 & \cdots & \theta_M \\
\ddots & \cdots & \vdots & \cdots & \ddots & \vdots \\
\phi_1 & \cdots & \phi_p & \theta_1 & \cdots & 1 + \theta_M
\end{bmatrix},
$$

and the $(p + M) \times (p + M)$ matrix $\mathbf{H}_{t-1}$ by

$$
\begin{bmatrix}
h_t & 0 & 0 & \cdots & \cdots & \cdots & 0 \\
0 & 0 & \ddots & \ddots & \ddots & \ddots & \vdots \\
0 & \ddots & \ddots & \ddots & \ddots & \ddots & \vdots \\
\vdots & \ddots & \ddots & 0 & \ddots & \ddots & \vdots \\
0 & \ddots & \ddots & 0 & h_t & 0 & 0 \\
\vdots & \ddots & \ddots & \ddots & \ddots & \ddots & 0 \\
0 & \cdots & \cdots & \cdots & 0 & 0 & h_t
\end{bmatrix},
$$

where $h_t = \{\sum_{m=0}^{M} \sigma_m 1(I_{mt-1} > 0)\}$

Using the above matrices one can write the EDTAR model in a first-order Markov form as

$$
\mathbf{Y}_t = \mathbf{A}_t(\mathbf{B}\mathbf{Y}_{t-1} + \mathbf{H}_{t-1}\mathbf{U}_t).
$$

The Markov representation can be used to give an expression for the time series N periods ahead in terms of the innovations between $t + 1$ and $t + N$:

$$
\mathbf{Y}_{t+N} = \left\{ \prod_{n=1}^{N} \mathbf{A}_{t+n} \mathbf{B} \right\} \mathbf{Y}_t + \sum_{n=1}^{N} \left\{ \prod_{i=n}^{N} \mathbf{A}_{t+i} \mathbf{B} \right\} \mathbf{H}_{t-1+n} \mathbf{U}_{t+n}
$$

Notice that if the innovations are zero after time t, the "stability" of the time series is determined by $\{\prod_{n=1}^{N} \mathbf{A}_{t+n}\mathbf{B}\}$ As shown in Potter (1996) this expression goes to zero under certain conditions on the first row of $\mathbf{B}$. Using results from

Markov chain theory it is possible to show that this condition is sufficient to ensure stationarity of the time series.

A Floor and Ceiling Model of U.S. Output

Consider the following reformulation of the CDR_t variable of Beaudry and Koop:

$$F_t = \sum_{j=1}^{\infty} \left\{ 1 - \prod_{s=1}^{j} 1(X_t - X_{t-s} > 0) \right\}, \tag{13.16}$$

$$CDR_t = 1(F_t > 0)(CDR_{t-1} + Y_t), \tag{13.17}$$

Although at first this might have appeared to have unduly complicated the approach of Beaudry and Koop, one can now introduce a threshold parameter into their model, r_F:

$$F_t = \sum_{j=1}^{\infty} \left\{ 1 - \prod_{s=1}^{j} 1(X_t - X_{t-s} > r_F) \right\}. \tag{13.18}$$

Although not included in the EDTAR class described above, the variable F_t constructed above is contained within the more general formulation in Potter (1996).

One difficulty noted above was that Beaudry and Koop's model failed to capture the initial strong downward movement in recessions. By amending the recursion defining the CDR_t variable one can capture this effect. This is done by including the floor threshold value in the recursion defining CDR_t for the first time that the floor regime is activated:

$$CDR_t = \begin{cases} 1(F_t > 0)(CDR_{t-1} + Y_t - r_F) & \text{if } F_{t-1} > 0 \text{ and } F_{t-2} = 0 \\ 1(F_t > 0)(CDR_{t-1} + Y_t) & \text{otherwise.} \end{cases} \tag{13.19}$$

Next consider the notion of a ceiling by isolating periods when the economy becomes "overheated." A simple way of defining this phenomenon is to look at periods when output growth has been above a threshold level of "sustainable growth" for at least two consecutive quarters and the floor regime is not active. In a similar manner to the current depth of recession, a variable that measures the total growth above the average can be recursively constructed. Such a variable as shown by Pesaran and Potter tends to predict future output declines:

$$C_t = 1(F_t = 0) \sum_{j=1}^{\infty} \left\{ \prod_{s=0}^{j} 1(Y_{t-s} > r_C) \right\}, \tag{13.20}$$

$$OH_t = 1(C_t > 0)(OH_{t-1} + Y_t - r_c). \qquad (13.21)$$

The regime where neither the floor or ceiling variables are activated is given the name of the corridor. The residual variances are also allowed to change between regimes (as in EDTAR model above).

Thus, we have the following nonlinear floor and ceiling model:

$$Y_t = \alpha + \phi_p(L)Y_{t-1} + \theta_1 CDR_{t-1}\,(\gamma) + \theta_2 OH_{t-1}\,(\gamma) + h_t(\gamma)V_t,$$

$$h_t = \sigma_0 1(COR_{t-1} = 0) + \sigma_1 1(F_{t-1} > 0) + \sigma_2 1(C_{t-1} > 0)$$

where $COR_t = F_t + C_t$.

The floor and ceiling model can also be written model in expanded form as a threshold autoregression by recursing back on the expressions for CDR_t, OH_t:

$$Y_t = \begin{cases} \alpha + \phi(L)Y_{t-1} + \sigma_0 V_t & \text{if } COR_{t-1} = 0, \\ \alpha + \phi(L)Y_{t-1} + \theta_1(Y_{t-1} - r_f) + \sigma_1 V_t & \text{if } F_{t-1} > 0 \\ \quad\vdots & \quad\vdots \\ \alpha + \phi(L)Y_{t-1} + \theta_1\left(\sum_{s=1}^{j} Y_{t-s} - r_f\right) + \sigma_1 V_t & \text{if } \prod_{s=1}^{j} F_{t-s} > 0 \text{ and } F_{t-j-1} \\ & = 0. \\ \quad\vdots & \quad\vdots \\ \alpha + \phi(L)Y_{t-1} + \theta_2(Y_{t-1} - r_c) + \sigma_2 V_t & \text{if } C_{t-1} > 0 \text{ and } C_{t-2} = 0, \\ \quad\vdots & \quad\vdots \\ \alpha + \phi(L)Y_{t-1} + \theta_2 \sum_{s=1}^{j}(Y_{t-s} - r_c) + \sigma_2 V_t & \text{if } \prod_{s=1}^{j} C_{t-s} > 0 \text{ and } C_{t-j-1} \\ & = 0, \\ \quad\vdots & \quad\vdots \end{cases}$$

$$(13.22)$$

showing once again the flexibility of the EDTAR class.

Pesaran and Potter test for the nonlinear effects in this model using the approach of Hansen described above and find statistically significant evidence in favor of the nonlinear model—that is, the null hypothesis that $\theta_1 = \theta_2 = 0$ is rejected. The model is estimated by a grid search technique: all the possible values of output growth and s-differences of the log level of GDP over certain ranges are used as possible estimates of the the thresholds. For each of these possible threshold values the model is estimated by weighted least squares. The grid point (that is, combination of r_f, r_c) with the largest likelihood value is then chosen as the estimate of the thresholds.

Pesaran and Potter find statistical evidence, with $p = 2$, that the autoregressive coefficients sum to one and that the intercept term can be restricted to be zero. This leads them to the following estimated floor and ceiling model in second differences:

$$\Delta^2 X_t = -.46\Delta^2 X_{t-1} - .86CDR_{t-1} + -.16OH_{t-1}$$

$$+ \{.92(COR_{t-1} = 0) + 1.17(F_{t-1} > 0) + .69(C_{t-1} > 0)\} V_t,$$

where $\Delta^2 X_t = X_t - 2X_{t-1} + X_{t-2}$, and with $\hat{r}_F = -.876$ and $\hat{r}_C = 0.539$.

Initial estimates of the SEDTAR version of the floor and ceiling model indicate that the unconditional residual variance decreases to around 0.68 versus 0.76 for the restricted EDTAR model (unrestricted versions have residual variance of .735). Since the SEDTAR model contains eight more parameters from the the construction of W_{1t}, W_{2t}, it is not clear whether the improvement is sufficient to justify the extra complexity. For vector versions of the floor and ceiling model the tradeoff appears to be more favorable disposed to the SEDTAR version.

The implied dynamics of this estimated model are quite different from those of linear models estimated on the output data. In particular, in the case that neither the floor nor ceiling regime is in effect the *growth rate* contains a unit root. Consider the following thought experiment to illustrate the importance of this point:

- At time t output has just entered the corridor regime from either the floor or ceiling regimes.
- Assume that for all $s > t$ that $V_s = 0$.
- Assume that Y_{t+1} is in the corridor regime.

Then we will have the following expression for future values of output growth:

$$Y_{t+n} = Y_t + \frac{-.46(1 - (-.46)^n)}{1.46}\Delta Y_t.$$

Thus, under this scenario the long-run growth rate inside the corridor regime will be given by the entering growth rate and approximately one third of the entering change in the growth rate. This simplifies to two thirds of Y_t and one third of Y_{t-1}.

These values are themselves mainly determined by the behavior of the overheating and current depth of recession variables. Under the conditions of this experiment the long-run growth rate could be anywhere in the interval $[-.876, 0.539]$.

The validity of this experiment crucially depends on the assumption that all future shocks are set to zero. As noted in the second section this can be very misleading in describing the dynamics of nonlinear models, and this is particularly true in the current case. In the case of the floor and ceiling model the standard deviation of shocks in the corridor regime is estimated to be large compared to the width of the estimated corridor regime. One would, therefore, expect movements within the corridor regime in the short run as well as a high probability of exit from

Table 13.1.

Model Types	Conceptual Problems
Univariate linear	None
All nonlinear models	Choice of definition
Univariate nonlinear	History and shock dependence
Multivariate linear	Composition dependence
Multivariate nonlinear	History, shock, composition dependence

the regime in the medium term. Pesaran and Potter contain an extended discussion of the dynamics of the floor and ceiling model using some of the techniques discussed in the next section.

Impulse Response Function Analysis for Nonlinear Models

This sections reviews some of my own work, Potter (1996) and Koop, Pesaran, and Potter (1995) (KPP hereafter) on the extension of the usual linear tools of impulse response functions and variance decompositions to nonlinear models. For impulse response functions one can proceed in the same manner as the linear case except one replaces the linear predictor with the conditional expectation operator as discussed in the second section. Variance decompositions require a different approach. A summary of the issues developed in that section is in table 13.1 taken from KPP.

Generalized Impulse Response Functions

The generalized impulse response function (GI) is designed to solve the problems categorized in Table 13.1. It represents a choice of the updating definition of the impulse response function given in the second section. Let ω_{t-1} be the set containing information used to forecast Y_t. Under a Markov assumption a sufficient set of information would be the realizations of Y_t from $t = t - 1, t - 2, \ldots, t - p$, or for the floor and ceiling model the set of realizations would be $\{x_{t-1}, x_{t-2}, x_{t-3}, cdr_{t-1}, oh_{t-1}\}$. The convention that lowercase values represent realizations and uppercases random variables is maintained with ω_{t-1} being used to denote a particular realization of Ω_{t-1}, the set of all possible realizations. If a lowercase letter is superscripted by 0, then it means the actual observed realization; thus, ω_{t-1}^0 is the actual observed time series, v_t^0 would be the observed innovations—that is, the residuals of the estimated model. The realization of the random variable at time $t + n$, y_{t+n}, will depend on ω_{t-1} and $\{v_t, \ldots, v_{t+n}\}$. Finally, to emphasize the difference between a conditional expectation evaluated at a point in the sample space (that is, a particular realization) and a conditional expectation as a random variable we use $E[Y_{t+n} \parallel \Omega_{t-1}]$ for the latter.

First consider the GI for the case of an arbitrary current shock, v_t, and history, ω_{t-1}:

$$GI_Y(n, v_t, \omega_{t-1}) = E[Y_{t+n} \mid v_t, \omega_{t-1}] - E[Y_{t+n} \mid \omega_{t-1}], \text{ for } n = 0, 1, \ldots \quad (13.23)$$

The GI in this case is a function of v_t and ω_{t-1}. It is natural to treat v_t and ω_{t-1} as realizations from the same stochastic process that generates the realizations of $\{Y_t\}$. Thus, we can consider the GI defined above to be the realization of a random variable defined by

$$GI_Y(n, V_t, \Omega_{t-1}) = E[Y_{t+n} \parallel V_t, \Omega_{t-1}] - E[Y_{t+n} \parallel \Omega_{t-1}]. \quad (13.24)$$

Equation (13.24) is the difference between two conditional expectations which are themselves random variables. Denote this random variable simply by GI_Y.

Various conditional versions of the generalized impulse response function can be defined. For example, one could condition on a particular shock and treat the variables generating the history—namely, $Y_{t-1}, Y_{t-2}, \ldots, Y_{t-p}$ in the case of the Markov model as random:

$$GI_Y(n, v_t, \Omega_{t-1}) = E[Y_{t+n} \parallel v_t, \Omega_{t-1}] - E[Y_{t+n} \parallel \Omega_{t-1}]. \quad (13.25)$$

Or one could condition on a particular history, ω_{t-1}, and treat the GI as a random variable in terms of V_t:

$$GI_Y(n, V_t, \omega_{t-1}) = E[Y_{t+n} \parallel V_t, \omega_{t-1}] - E[Y_{t+n} \mid \omega_{t-1}]. \quad (13.26)$$

The Composition Problem

All the measures defined in (13.23) to (13.26) produce the same information from the generalized impulse response functions when applied to linear univariate models. For the linear model

$$Y_t = \sum_{n=0}^{\infty} \psi_n V_{t-n}, \quad (13.27)$$

using (13.24), we have

$$GI(n, V_t, \Omega_{t-1}) = \psi_n V_t,$$

which is independent of Ω_{t-1}. The dependence of GI on V_t, the size of the current shock, is proportional and can be readily dealt with by appropriate scaling of the GI function. Once the GI function is scaled by V_t, it is equivalent to the outcomes of the various definitions of the linear impulse response function given in the second section.

In the vector case, recall the infinite moving average form:

$$\mathbf{Y}_t = \sum_{n=0}^{\infty} \mathbf{\Psi}_n \mathbf{V}_{t-n}.$$

For this case,

$$GI_\mathbf{Y}(n, \mathbf{V}_t, \Omega_{t-1}) = \mathbf{\Psi}_n \mathbf{V}_t,$$

and, once again does not depend on the history, Ω_{t-1}. However, since $\mathbf{V}_t$ is now a vector, its effect on the generalized impulse response function cannot be eliminated by an "appropriate" scaling of the variables. Hence, the impulse response analysis is subject to the composition problem. One solution to the problem would be to view the GI as a function of the random variable, $\mathbf{V}_t$, and derive its probability density function in terms of the density function of $\mathbf{V}_t$. For example, in the case where $\mathbf{V}_t \sim N(0, \Sigma_v)$, then $GI(n, \mathbf{V}_t, \Omega_{t-1}) \sim N(0, \mathbf{\Psi}_n \Sigma_v \mathbf{\Psi}_n')$, and the impulse response function is fully characterised by the variances, $\mathbf{\Psi}_n \Sigma_v \mathbf{\Psi}_n'$, $n = 0, 1, 2, \ldots$. These variances measure the effect of shocking the system at time t, by a random vector $\mathbf{V}_t$, and then averaging the resultant densities across all such systemwide shocks. This solution deals with the composition problem by ignoring it through focussing on the effect of system-wide shocks.

The GI also lends itself naturally to a solution to the compositional problem without the use of *a priori* theory in both the case of linear and nonlinear models. We can define the generalized impulse response function to be conditional not on all the shocks at time t but on just one of them. That is, we can consider fixing one of the shocks, V_{it}, from the vector of all shocks, $\mathbf{V}_t$, and then integrating out the effects of the other shocks at time t given its value, v_{it}:

$$GI_\mathbf{Y}(n, V_{it} = v_{it}, \Omega_{t-1}) = E[\mathbf{Y}_{t+n} \| V_{it} = v_{it}, \Omega_{t-1}] - E[\mathbf{Y}_{t+n} \| \Omega_{t-1}], \quad (13.28)$$

where $E[\mathbf{Y}_{t+n} \| V_{it} = v_{it}, \Omega_{t-1}]$ means that one is taking the expectations conditional on each of the realizations in Ω_{t-1} for fixed values of the ith shock at time t while averaging out all other contemporaneous and future shocks.

In order to illustrate this use of the generalized impulse response function, consider the Gaussian case from KPP. Assume that the vector of random shocks, $\mathbf{V}_t$ is jointly normally distributed with zero means and the covariance matrix Σ_v. Under this assumption

$$E[\mathbf{V}_t \mid V_{it} = v_{it}] = \eta_i \sigma_{ii}^{-1} v_{it},$$

where $\sigma_{ii} = E[V_{it}^2]$ and $\eta_i = E[\mathbf{V}_t V_{it}] = (\sigma_{1i}, \sigma_{2i}, \ldots, \sigma_{Ki})'$, and the generalized impulse response of the effect of a shock to the ith disturbance term at time t, on Y_{t+n} for the multivariate linear model is given by

$$GI_\mathbf{Y}(n, v_{it}, \Omega_{t-1}) = \left(\frac{\mathbf{\Psi}_n \eta_i}{\sqrt{\sigma_{ii}}} \right) \left(\frac{v_{it}}{\sqrt{\sigma_{ii}}} \right).$$

Scaling the GI by $v_{it}/\sqrt{\sigma_{ii}}$, we obtain the effect of a "unit" shock to the ith disturbance term on Y_{t+n}—namely,

$$\frac{\mathbf{\Psi}_n \eta_i e_i}{\sqrt{\sigma_{ii}}}$$

where e_i is a selection vector with its ith element equal to unity and zeros elsewhere. This impulse response function appropriately takes account of the historical patterns of correlations between the different shocks as characterized by Σ_v. Also, unlike the orthogonalized impulse responses obtained using a Cholesky decomposition of Σ_v, the GI responses

$$\frac{\mathbf{\Psi}_n \eta_i e_i}{\sqrt{\sigma_{ii}}}$$

are unique and are not affected by reordering of the variables in $\mathbf{Y}_t$.

Model-based Conditional Generalized Impulse Response Functions

Although the measures discussed above have a wide range of uses, in many cases the nonlinear model under analysis suggests a particular set of conditioning events. For example, many nonlinear models used in economics imply that impulse responses in recessionary times are different to those in expansionary times. Attempts to average out over recessionary and expansionary regimes could produce misleading information. For example, suppose that negative shocks are attentuated in recessionary times but magnified in expansionary times. And positive shocks are attentuated in expansionary times but magnified in recessionary times. Then averaging over histories to compare the effect of positive and negative shocks will tend to weaken the asymmetries.

For example, in the univariate model of PP above there are three regimes that output can be in: floor (recession), ceiling (fast growth) and corridor (normal times). One can then define generalized impulse response functions conditional on being in one of these regimes at $t-1$ for a particular set of shocks. Figure 13.1

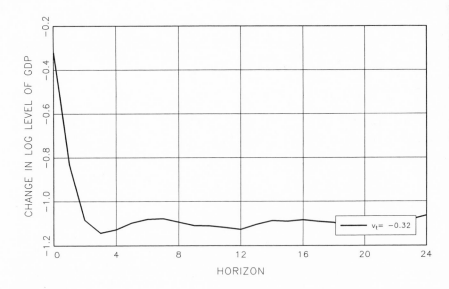

Figure 13.1a

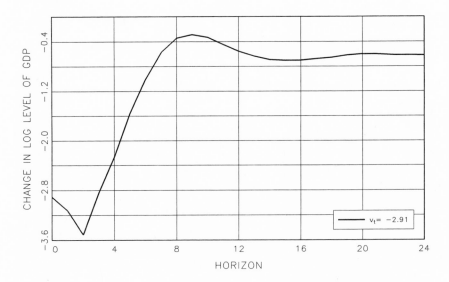

Figure 13.1b

Figure 13.1.   Generalized impulse response function a. Baseline: 1958Q4 in the Ceiling Regime b. Baseline: 1980Q1 in the Corridor Regime c. Baseline: 1990Q3 in the Corridor Regime d. Baseline: 1992Q3 in the Ceiling Regime

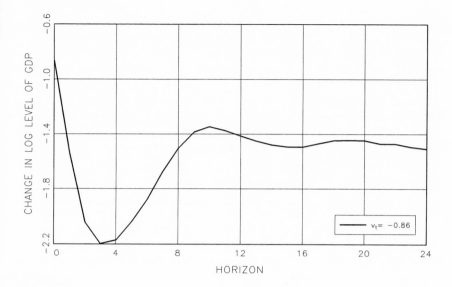

Figure 13.1c

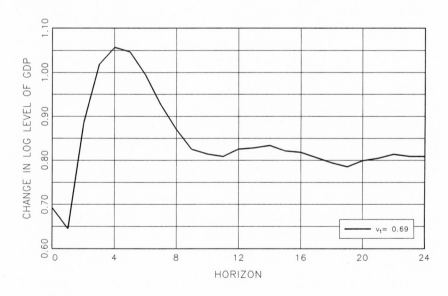

Figure 13.1d

shows the individual realizations of generalized impulse response functions for four separate dates in the post-Korean war sample using the actual shocks produced by the economy at these times. Figure 13.1a shows that the relatively small shock of $v^0_{1959Q1} = -.32$ in the ceiling regime produces a predicted response of approximately -1.1. This is a shock magnification of almost four times. Whereas, the much more negative shock, $v^0_{1980Q2} = -2.91$, is diminished by a factor of 0.2 in Figure 13.1b for a baseline in the corridor regime. This gives some evidence that negative shocks tend to be propagated more strongly in the ceiling regime than in the corridor regime. However, Figure 13.1c provides slightly different information for a baseline of 1990Q3 and a shock, $v^0_{1990Q4} = -0.86$. Recall that 1990Q4 was the start of a recession that had an unusually weak recovery and this is reflected in the GI.

I now turn to examining whether positive shocks are more persistent than negative shocks. It is possible to find further examples as in Figure 13.1 where negative shocks are more persistent than positive shocks and vice versa depending on the particular initial condition and shock. Hence, in order to provide robust information on the persistence of negative versus positive shocks we consider various "average" responses to positive and negative shocks in our sample of generalized impulse response functions. Figures 13.2a is constructed by splitting the sample of generalized impulse response functions produced by the in-sample shocks into two subsamples where $v_t > 0$ and $v_t \leq 0$ and then forming the median of the responses within each subsample. These average responses are then normalized so that the initial shock has an absolute value of one. In this unconditional case the average responses show evidence of asymmetry but of the opposite type found in previous work: on average negative shocks are more persistent than positive shocks across the three regimes.

The two subsamples were then further split into three according to the regime of the baseline forecast. Then, within each of these subsamples the responses were averaged and normalized. Figure 13.2b shows that for the corridor regime both negative and positive shocks are more than persistent than the other two regimes with negative shocks being the most persistent on average. Figure 13.2c shows the behavior in the floor regime where neither positive or negative shocks persist on average. Finally, Figure 13.2d shows the average normalized responses in the ceiling regime. These are similar to the corridor regime but the relative asymmetry between the positive and negative shocks is even more pronounced.

In the multivariate context the possibilities are even richer since the covariance matrices of the innovations (H_m in the vector EDTAR case) vary across regimes. This can imply different contemporaneous relationships between the variables under study.

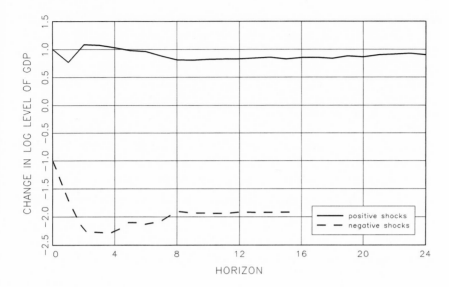

Figure 13.2a

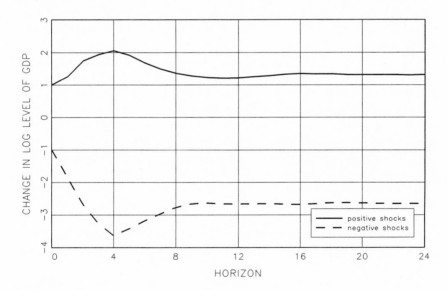

Figure 13.2b

Figure 13.2. Median of Normalized Generalized Impulse Response Function a. Unconditional b. Corridor Regime c. Floor Regime d. Ceiling Regime

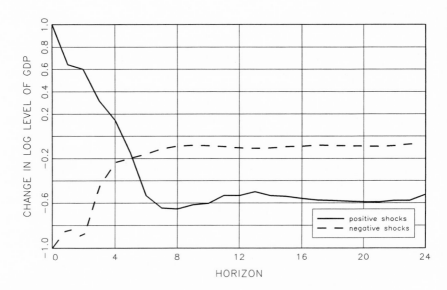

Figure 13.2c

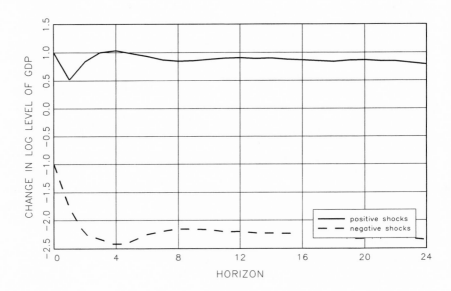

Figure 13.2d

Some Measures of Persistence

In order to define measures of persistence we concentrate on the dispersion of the generalized impulse response function when viewed as a random variable. As shown in Potter (1996) the dispersion of the *GI* is related to a notion of unconditional persistence of the time series. In particular if the time series is integrated of order zero then as the horizon goes to infinity the *GI* converges to zero (with probability one). That is, under stationarity the baseline forecast and perturbed forecast converge to the same value for any realization used to condition on. The unconditional measure can hide much interesting behavior when an integrated series is examined in its first differences but the responses are cumulated up to provide information on the response of the level of the series. Thus, conditional measures of persistence must be used to determine if, for example, "positive shocks are more persistent than negative shocks." One can assess the persistence of shocks for a particular history ω_{t-1}, the persistence of a particular shock v_t for all possible histories or for a particular subset of histories and shocks.

There is no unambiguous measure of dispersion but in cases where random variables have mean zero, second order stochastic dominance applied to their distribution functions has useful properties. One distribution function has more dispersion than another in second-order stochastic dominance sense if it crosses the other distribution exactly once from above. If a time series is not persistent, then the distribution function of its *GI* should quickly narrow to an indicator function at zero. Thus, the distribution function of the *GI* as the horizon gets large is second-order stochastically dominated by the *GI* at the initial horizon. Time series that are persistent will have *GI*s whose distribution functions show dispersion at all horizons. In particular if the propagation mechanism magnifies shocks then the distribution function of the *GI* at future horizons will second order stochastically dominate the distribution function of the *GI* at horizon zero.

I calculated the distribution functions of the *GI* for output growth from the floor and ceiling model at various horizons. A three-dimensional plot of the distribution functions by horizon is presented in Figure 13.3. Notice how the distribution functions quickly converge to a spike indicating that even though the floor and ceiling model is estimated on the second difference of output, output growth is stationary.

Variance Decompositions

In the case of linear models there is a relationship between the variance decomposition and impulse response functions when the Cholesky orthogonalization approach is used. Often the intuition is given as measuring the size of the effect

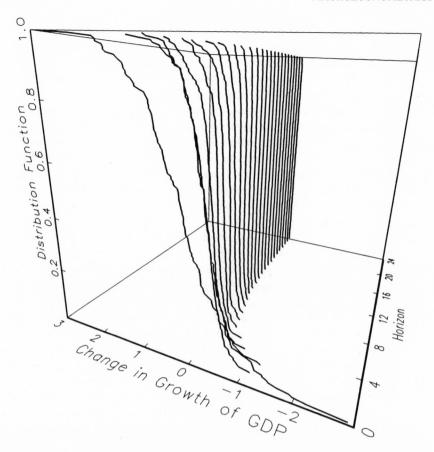

Figure 13.3.   Distribution functions of generalized impulse response function growth
rate of GDP

of shock i under the assumption that all other shocks are zero from time t onward.
For nonlinear models such a treatment of the future doesn't make sense. The
nonlinearity implies that adding up the individual terms produced by such an
experiment does not give a realization of the original series.

A Forecast Error Decomposition for Nonlinear Models.   Instead of proceeding in the standard linear way of determining the variance decomposition consider
a quite different approach. First express the realization of $\mathbf{Y}_t$ at time $t + N$ as

$$\mathbf{Y}_{t+N} = Y(\mathbf{V}_{t+N}, \ldots, \mathbf{V}_{t+1}; \mathbf{Y}_t),$$

where we return to our standard convention that $E[\mathbf{V}_t, \mathbf{V}'_t] = \mathbf{I}_K$. Next consider a particular realization of the shocks from time $t + 1$ to time $t + N$, $(\mathbf{v}^*_{t,N}, \ldots, \mathbf{v}^*_{t,1})$, with the special property that

$$E_t[\mathbf{Y}_{t+N}] = Y(\mathbf{v}^*_{t,N}, \ldots, \mathbf{v}^*_{t,1}; \mathbf{Y}_t), \qquad (13.29)$$

where $E_t[\mathbf{Y}_{t+N}] = E[\mathbf{Y}_{t+N} \mid \mathbf{v}_t, \omega_{t-1}]$. Now use $(\mathbf{v}^*_{t,N}, \ldots, \mathbf{v}^*_{t,1})$ as a point around which to approximate the random variable $\mathbf{Y}_{t+N}$ in a first-order Taylor Series expansion with a remainder term:

$$\mathbf{Y}_{t+N} = Y(\mathbf{v}^*_{t,N}, \ldots, \mathbf{v}^*_{t,1}; \mathbf{Y}_t) + \sum_{n=1}^{n} \boldsymbol{\psi}_t(N, n)(\mathbf{V}_{t+v} - \mathbf{v}^*_{t,n})$$

$$+ R(\mathbf{V}_{t+N}, \ldots, \mathbf{V}_{t+1}; \mathbf{Y}_t), \qquad (13.30)$$

where the $K \times K$ Jacobian matrices $\boldsymbol{\Psi}_t(N, n)$ are given by

$$\begin{bmatrix} \dfrac{\partial y_{1,t+N}}{\partial v_{1,t+j}} & \cdots & \dfrac{\partial y_{1,t+N}}{\partial v_{K,t+j}} \\[2ex] \dfrac{\partial y_{2,t+N}}{\partial v_{1,t+j}} & \cdots & \dfrac{\partial y_{2,t+N}}{\partial v_{K,t+j}} \\[1ex] \vdots & \vdots & \vdots \\[1ex] \dfrac{\partial y_{K,t+N}}{\partial v_{1,t+j}} & \cdots & \dfrac{\partial y_{K,t+N}}{\partial v_{K,t+j}} \end{bmatrix},$$

and are evaluated at $\{\mathbf{v}^*_{t,1}, \ldots, \mathbf{v}^*_{t,N}\}$, and $R(\mathbf{V}_{t+N}, \ldots, \mathbf{V}_{t+1}; \mathbf{Y}_t)$ is the $K \times 1$ remainder vector from the first-order Taylor series expansion.

The $\boldsymbol{\Psi}_t(N, n)$ matrices and the vectors $\mathbf{v}^*_{t,n}$ are fixed at time t and are not correlated with the future realizations of the time series. Using this fact and using the conditional expectation operator, $E_t[\cdot]$ on both sides of (13.30), it can be shown that

$$E_t[\mathbf{R}(t, N)] = \sum_{n=1}^{N} \boldsymbol{\Psi}_t(N, n)\mathbf{v}^*_{t,n},$$

where $\mathbf{R}(t, N) = R(\mathbf{V}_{t+N}, \ldots, \mathbf{V}_{t+1}; \mathbf{Y}_t)$,
Thus, one can reexpress (13.30) as

$$\mathbf{Y}_{t+N} - E_t[\mathbf{Y}_{t+N}] = \sum_{n=1}^{N} \boldsymbol{\Psi}_t(N, n)\mathbf{V}_{t+j} + (\mathbf{R}(t, N) - E_t[\mathbf{R}(t, N)]). \quad (13.31)$$

The forecast error has been decomposed into three factors:

- The heteroskedasticity in the error process. This is captured by $\Psi_t(N, N)$, the differential with respect to $\mathbf{v}_{t+N}$ evaluated along the $\{\mathbf{v}^*(t, n)\}$ sequence. For the vector EDTAR model from the fourth section above this can be written as

$$\sum_{m=0}^{M} 1(I^*_{mt+N-1} > 0) H_m,$$

a weighted average of the variance covariance matrix in each regime, with the weights being given by the probability that the $\{\mathbf{v}^*(t, n)\}$ sequence is in a particular regime N periods ahead. As in the case of a structural linear VAR it is assumed that each $H_i H_i'$ has a recursive triangular structure allowing us to uniquely identify the effect of each underlying shock on the system from the estimated variance/covariance matrices. The ordering of this recursive triangular structure could change between regimes, as well as the variance covariance matrix varying between regimes.
- The piecewise linearity. This is contained in the sequence $\{\Psi_t(N, n), n = 1, \ldots, N\}$ of matrices. Consider the derivative with respect to $\mathbf{v}_{t+N-1}$ for the vector EDTAR model:

$$\Psi_t(N, N-1) = \left\{ \Phi_1 + \sum_{m=1}^{M} \Theta_m 1\left(I^*_{mt+N-2} > 0\right) \right\} \Psi_t(N-1, N-1),$$

Notice how the previous period's regime matters both in terms of the derivative of $\mathbf{Y}_{t+N}$ with respect to $\mathbf{Y}_{t+N-1}$ and in terms of the initial propagation of the shock at time time $t + N - 1$ as represented by the $\Psi_t(N-1, N-1)$ matrix.

As N increases relative to the point in time at which the derivative is taken, the familar recursion for generating the moving average representation of a linear VAR is obtained. The differences are the presence of the additional $\{\Theta_m\}$ matrices for the various regimes that could be activated along the $\{\mathbf{v}^*(t, n)\}$ sequence and the importance of the particular regime in place when the shock, $\mathbf{v}^*(t, n)$ occurs. Note that the direct effect $\Psi_t(N, n)$ does not have to die out as $(N - n) \to \infty$ even if the underlying series is stationary. Since the $\{\mathbf{v}^*(t, n)\}$ sequence might imply that the time series becomes stuck in one of the regimes as N becomes large. For example, this would happen in the floor and ceiling model of output if the long run-mean of the growth rate of output is outside the corridor regime. The remainder in the expansion would cancel out this effect for a stationary time series.

- The global nonlinearity of the system as represented by the deviation of the remainder term in the Taylor series expansion from its mean value.

For a linear model the third term is zero, and the first and second terms are usually assumed to be constant across the business cycle. That is, in the linear case the shocks are propagated by the same moving average matrices for each possible time period t.

A Relationship with the Generalized Impulse Response Function.   Recall the definition of a realization of the GI:

$$GI(N, \mathbf{v}_t, \omega_{t-1}) = E[\mathbf{Y}_{t+N} \mid \mathbf{v}_t, \omega_{t-1}] - E[\mathbf{Y}_{t+N} \mid \omega_{t-1}],$$

by subtracting and adding the realized value of $\mathbf{Y}_{t+N}$ one obtains

$$GI(N, \mathbf{v}_t, \omega_{t-1}) = E[\mathbf{Y}_{t+N} \mid \omega_t] - \mathbf{Y}_{t+N} + \mathbf{Y}_{t+N} - E[\mathbf{Y}_{t+N} \mid \omega_{t-1}]$$

$$= FE(t - 1, N + 1) - FE(t, N)$$

$$= \mathbf{\Psi}_{t-1}(N + 1, 1)\mathbf{v}_t + \sum_{n=1}^{N}\{\mathbf{\Psi}_{t-1}(N + 1, n + 1) - \mathbf{\Psi}_t(N, n)\}\mathbf{V}_{t+n}$$

$$+ \overline{\mathbf{R}}(t - 1, N + 1) - \overline{\mathbf{R}}(t, N).$$

Since the generalized impulse response function does not depend on the values of the innovations after time t it is possible to set these future values to unit vectors under the understanding that the remainder term depends on this particular realization (signified by the use of a lower case, $\mathbf{r}$):

$$GI(N, \mathbf{v}_t, \Omega_{t-1}) = \mathbf{\Psi}_{t-1}(N + 1, 1)\mathbf{v}_t + \sum_{n=1}^{N}\{\mathbf{\Psi}_{t-1}(N + 1, n + 1) - \mathbf{\Psi}_t(N, n)\}$$

$$+ \overline{\mathbf{r}}(t - 1, N + 1) - \overline{\mathbf{r}}(t, N).$$

Returning to the case of endogenous fluctuations from the second section we can see that even if $\mathbf{v}_t$ is a zero vector the generalized impulse response function might not be a zero vector because of the difference in the remainder terms and through differences in $\mathbf{\Psi}_{t-1}(N + 1, n + 1)$, $\mathbf{\Psi}_t(N, n)$.

A Variance Decomposition for Nonlinear Models.   Taking variances in (13.31) one obtains

$$E_t[(\mathbf{Y}_{t+N} - E_t[\mathbf{Y}_{t+N}])(\mathbf{Y}_{t+N} - E_t[\mathbf{Y}_{t+N}])'] =$$

$$\sum_{j=n}^{N} \mathbf{\Psi}_t(N, n)\mathbf{I}_k\mathbf{\Psi}_t(N, n)' + E_t[\mathbf{R}(t, N)\mathbf{R}(t, N)' - E_t[\mathbf{R}(t, N)]E_t[\mathbf{R}(t, N)]']$$

$$+ 2E_t\left[\left(\sum_{n=1}^{N} \mathbf{\Psi}_t(N, n)\mathbf{V}_{t+n}\right)(\mathbf{R}(t, N) - E_t[\mathbf{R}(t, N)])'\right].$$

The effect of shock k on the forecast error variance of the ith variable is given by

$$e_i\left(\sum_{n=1}^{N} \mathbf{\Psi}_t(N, n)e_k'e_k\mathbf{\Psi}_t'(N, n) + 2E_t[(\mathbf{V}_{t+n} \odot e_k')(\mathbf{R}(t, N) - E_t[\mathbf{R}(t, N)])']\right)e_i',$$

where e_k is a $1 \times K$ (selection) vector of zeros except for the kth component, which is one, and $\odot$, which is the Hadamard product (that is, $A \odot B = C$, $c_{ij} = a_{ij}b_{ij}$).

The first term is similar to those found in the linear variance decomposition, but the second term is different and measures the covariance between the kth shock and the random remainder term in the first-order Taylor series expansion. It is possible for the shock to have a negative contribution to the overall forecast error variance of one or more of the variables if the covariance is sufficiently negative. One way of thinking of this phenomenon is that if the covariance is negative, then the shock interacting with the nonlinear system has a dampening effect on the variable and if it is positive then the interaction has an amplifying effect on the variable. Such possibilities are not present in the linear case because of the strict positivity of each of the individual contributions.

After accounting for the importance of each individual shock at each time t, one must also take into account the variance of the remainder term from the Taylor series expansion,

$$E_t[\mathbf{R}(t, N)\mathbf{R}(t, N)' - E_t[\mathbf{R}(t, N)]E_t[\mathbf{R}(t, N)]'].$$

Intuitively if the remainder term accounts for a large fraction of the forecast variance for a particular history then this is a sign of a large nonlinearity in the system.

One could define a collection of variance decompositions by looking at all possible histories. Indeed because the individual contributions are all between [0, 1] the analysis is a little easier. For example, one would say that shock k for variable i is the most important if it first-order stochastically dominates the contribution of all other variables or more weakly if its average effect over all histories is the largest. Alternatively, if the contribution of the remainder term first-order stochastically dominates all the other shocks then this would represent a case where nonlinearity was the main cause of fluctuations.

Acknowledgments

This paper has benefited greatly from discussions with Woon Gyu Choi, Gary Koop, and Hashem Pesaran on related issues. Financial support from the NSF under grant SES 9211726 and the Center for Computable Economics at UCLA is gratefully acknowledged.

Notes

1. Throughout the chapter the following notational conventions will be used. Uppercase letters will represent random variables; lowercase letters will be realizations of these random variables. Boldface will indicate matrices or vectors. V_t, $\mathbf{V}_t$ will be reserved to represent the random (independent and identically distributed) innovation to a time-series model. In the case of the scalar V_t the innovations have mean zero and unit variance. In the case of the random vector $\mathbf{V}_t$, each component of the vector has mean zero and unit variance. The individual components of $\mathbf{V}_t$ are mutually independent of each other unless specifically noted to the contrary.

2. Note that by *linear models* we mean a property of the model itself rather than of the estimation technique for the model. In particular ARMA models are linear in the sense used in this paper but require nonlinear estimation techniques.

References

Acemoglu, D., and A. Scott. (1993). "Asymmetries in the Cyclical Behavior of U.K. Labor Markets." Mimeo, MIT.

Andrews, D., and W. Ploberger. (1994). "Optimal Tests When a Nuisance Parameter Is Present Only Under the Alternative." *Econometrica* 62, 1383–1414.

Beaudry, P., and G. Koop. (1993). "Do Recessions Permanantly Affect Output?" *Journal of Monetary Economics* 31, 149–163.

Brock, W., D. Hsieh, and B. LeBaron. (1991). *Nonlinear Dynamics, Chaos and Instability.* Cambridge, MA: MIT Press.

Brock, W., and S. Potter. (1993). "Nonlinear Time Series and Macroeconometrics." In Maddala, Rao, and Vinod (eds.), *Handbook of Statistics XI.* Amsterdam: Elesevier.

Brockwell, P., and R. Davis. (1987). *Time Series: Theory and Methods.* New York: Springer.

Christiano, L. (1990). "Solving a Particular Growth Model by Linear Quadratic Approximation." Manuscript.

Frisch, R. (1933). "Propagation Problems and Impulse Problems in Dynamic Economics." In *Economic Essays in Honor of Gustav Cassell.* London: Allen and Unwin.

Gallant, R., P. Rossi, and G. Tauchen. (1993). "Nonlinear Dynamic Structures." *Econometrica* 61, 871–908.

Gordon, R., and L. Klein. (1965). *American Economic Association Readings in Business Cycles.* Homewood, IL: Irwin.

Granger, C., and T. Terasvirta. (1993). *Modeling Nonlinear Dynamic Relationships.* Oxford: Oxford University Press.

Hamilton, J. (1989). "A New Approach to the Economic Analysis of Nonstationary Time Series and the Business Cycle." *Econometrica* 57, 357–384.

Hansen, B. (1993). "Inference When a Nuisance Parameter Is Not Identified Under the Null Hypothesis." Mimeo, Department of Economics, University of Rochester.

Jevons, W. (1884). *Investigations in Currency and Finance.* London: MacMillan.

Koop, G., H. Pesaran, and S. Potter. (1995). "Impulse Response Analysis in Nonlinear Multivariate Models." *Journal of Econometrics*, forthcoming.

Lucas, R. (1987). *Models of Business Cycles.* New York: Blackwell.

Pesaran, M., and S. Potter. (1994). "A Floor and Ceiling Model of U.S. Output." Working Paper, Department of Economics, UCLA.

Potter, S. (1990). *Nonlinear Time Series and Economic Fluctuations.* Ph.D thesis, University of Wisconsin.

Potter, S. (1995). "A Nonlinear Approach to U.S. GNP." *Journal of Applied Econometrics.*

Potter, S. (1996). *Nonlinear Time Series and Macroeconomic Flactuations.* London: World Scientific.

Slutzky, E. (1927). "The Summation of Random Causes as the Source of Cyclical Processes." In *The Problems of Economic Conditions.* Moscow: Conjecture Institute.

Tiao, G., and R. Tsay. (1994). "Some Advances in Nonlinear and Adaptive Modeling in Time Series Analysis." *Journal of Forecasting* 13, 109–131.

Tong, H. (1983). *Threshold Models in Non-linear Time Series Analysis.* New York: Springer-Verlag.

Tong, H. (1990). *Non-linear Time Series: A Dynamical Systems Approach.* Oxford: Oxford University Press.

Tong, H., and K. Lim. (1980). "Threshold Autoregression, Limit Cycles and Cyclical Data." *Journal of the Royal Statistical Society Series B*, 42, 245–292.

Tsay, R. (1986). "Nonlinearity Tests for Time Series." *Biometrika* 73, 461–466.

White, H. (1993). *Artificial Neural Networks.* Oxford: Blackwell.

Wold, H. (1938). *A Study in the Analysis of Stationary Time Series.* Uppsale, Sweden: Almqvist and Wiksell.

Yule, G. (1927). "On a Method of Investigating Periodicities in Disturbed Series." *Transactions of Royal Society, London*, Series A 226, 267–298.

Commentary on Chapter 13

Daniel E. Sichel

Introduction

Simon Potter's chapter is an excellent review of some recent developments in nonlinear models of macroeconomic fluctuations, providing several useful extensions and generalizations. Much of the chapter deals with methodological issues, including subtleties of testing for nonlinearities, the use of impulse response functions and variance decompositions for nonlinear models, and a general presentation of endogenous delay threshold autoregressive (EDTAR) models. I have little new to say about this material, which is self-contained and well done.

Instead, I will focus on how to make nonlinear results about economic fluctuations—like those in this paper—more useful for the broader macroeconomics community. As those of us who have toiled in the vineyards of nonlinear testing and modeling know, generating broad interest in nonlinear results can be a challenge. In my judgment, this difficulty arises because nonlinear practitioners and macroeconomists have a different view of the relative benefits and costs of linear and nonlinear models. Nonlinear practitioners point to the benefits of richer nonlinear dynamics, while some macroeconomists may wonder whether much is gained from the greater complexity. In this comment, I argue that macroeconomics ought to incorporate more of the large body of evidence that macroeconomic fluctuations exhibit nonlinearities. But I also argue that nonlinear practitioners should focus more on questions of interest to macroeconomics and go the extra mile to explain the implications of their results for macroeconomics.

I start by reviewing the reasons that nonlinear results are important for macroeconomists and policymakers. Then, to highlight the tradeoffs between linear and nonlinear models, I focus on three papers that have had important impacts on macroeconomics: Neftçi (1984), Hamilton (1989), and Beaudry and Koop (1993). I argue that these three papers were successful because they answered important questions at reasonable cost.

Finally, I turn to the specific nonlinear EDTAR model estimated in this chapter, which neatly summarizes several important nonlinearities in fluctuations. To highlight the importance of nonlinearities for macroeconomics, I draw out one of the broad implications of these nonlinearities. In particular, I show that a key feature of Potter's model implies that fluctuations are primarily lapses beneath sustainable levels of production. This view of fluctuations contrasts sharply from that implied by a random walk with drift or from symmetric movements around a linear trend.

561

Before jumping in, a few preliminaries. In this comment, I focus almost exclusively on the empirical side of this literature. Moreover, most of this research has examined univariate models of broad macroeconomic indicators, such as gross domestic product and unemployment. I will do the same.

Five Reasons That Macroeconomists Should be Interested in Nonlinear Fluctuations

Put simply, the empirical evidence for nonlinearity in macroeconomic fluctuations is compelling.[1] The advance of knowledge in economics requires that this information be used elsewhere within the field. Five more specific reasons are listed below.

Establishing Benchmarks

Benchmarks, or stylized facts, provide simple summary statistics describing key features of fluctuations. For example, what rate of change is typical for a recession and the quarters following a recession? Is behavior in a particular period unusual? Because there is compelling evidence that fluctuations are nonlinear, benchmarks based on linear models could be misleading.

Improving Macroeconomic Theory

Evidence of nonlinearity can highlight features of the economy that theoretical macroeconomic models must capture if they are to accurately represent the true pattern of fluctuations.

Identifying Nonlinear Dynamic and Structural Features

Certain important dynamic (and maybe structural) features of the economy can be captured only by a fully parameterized nonlinear model. Hamilton's (1989) regime-switching model and Beaudry and Koop's (1993) nonlinear transfer function model are important examples, as discussed more fully below.

Improving Forecasts

Because economic fluctuations are nonlinear, modeling the nonlinearity should improve forecasts of the economy. The forecasting criterion is important, not only for the sake of improving forecasts but also because forecast performance on data not used to estimate the model is one of the most rigorous diagnostics to which a nonlinear model can be subjected.

Methodological Advances

Econometric tools and techniques for nonlinear modeling only come to life when applied to data. Although some applications may not generate important new facts about economic fluctuations, they may nevertheless help build a tool box that will prove useful later.

The Tradeoffs Between Linear and Nonlinear Models and Three Papers That Made a Difference

As Simon Potter points out, the key benefit of nonlinear models is the richness of possible dynamics, while the principle cost is the additional complexity. Different assessments of these costs and benefits will lead to different judgments about the importance of particular research. Nonlinear practitioners may see large benefits in richer dynamics, but general macroeconomists may see high costs from needless complexity. To reduce these costs, nonlinear practitioners may well need to focus less on technique and more on what the nonlinearities teach us about the economy.

To see this, consider three papers generating nonlinear results that were published in top journals and have had a large impact on macroeconomics: Neftçi (1984), Hamilton (1989), and Beaudry and Koop (1993).

Neftçi's paper examined the fundamental question of whether economic processes differ in expansions and contractions. Specifically, Neftçi looked for asymmetry in upward and downward movements in the unemployment rate by examining the matrix of Markov probabilities for transitions between these phases.[2] His use of standard Markov chains was quite novel and was very intuitive and transparent.

With a fully specified dynamic model, Hamilton examined the same fundamental issue as Neftçi. Hamilton demonstrated that output growth is well described by an exogenous sequence of shifting regimes of different average growth rates and dynamics that roughly correspond to NBER business cycle phases. Although estimation of Hamilton's model is somewhat involved, the basic structure of the model is very intuitive.

Beaudry and Koop tapped into the long-standing debate about persistence of shocks to output growth. They provided evidence that negative shocks are reversed fairly quickly, while positive shocks are much more persistent. This result implies that recessions may indeed be transitory at the same time that output is not trend stationary. Beaudry and Koop's model for output growth is just an ARMA model with some simple terms added that allow negative shocks—like recessions—to be reversed fairly quickly.[3]

These papers succeeded because they each examined a question of importance to economists, using straightforward techniques that avoided needless complexity. To state this position in stronger terms, nonlinear models in and of themselves will not capture much attention in the profession. Simply establishing that one nonlinear model outperforms another—or outperforms a linear model—is unlikely to generate much interest, just as there is little interest in establishing whether a particular variable is best modeled as an ARMA (2, 2) or an ARMA (3, 2). In any case, with about 200 observations in the postwar quarterly history, the true univariate nonlinear model likely will remain elusive.

A Key Implication of Potter's Floor and Ceiling Model of Output

Although much of this chapter is methodological, Potter also presents estimates of a floor and ceiling version of the EDTAR nonlinear model. To provide an example of the importance of nonlinear features of economic fluctuations, I draw out the macroeconomic implications of one feature of Potter's model. In particular, I focus on the implications of Potter's floor regime, which covers periods of significant downturns and recovery from these contractions.

The distinct dynamics of this regime arise from the variable measuring the current depth of recession (CDR). In Beaudry and Koop, this variable measures how far the *level* of output has fallen below it prior peak and is zero if output is above its prior peak. This setup implies that CDR is nonzero during a downturn and is nonzero during the recovery period until output has returned to its prior peak. In Potter's specification, CDR is nonzero only when the level of output has fallen a certain distance below its prior peak. He estimates this threshold to be 0.88 percent less than output's prior peak and Potter's version of CDR measures the distance below this threshold.

Because CDR is defined to be negative when output is in the floor regime, its negative coefficient implies a positive boost to output growth when output has dropped into this regime. The further output is below its prior peak, the larger is the positive boost to output growth from the CDR term. Thus, output tends to bounce back after large negative shocks, like recessions. In addition to Beaudry and Koop, other papers also have found evidence of this bounceback in output, including Sichel (1994) and Balke and Wynne (1992).

Beaudry and Koop, of course, draw out the implications of the bounceback for the persistence of positive and negative shocks to output.[4] Sichel (1994) draws out another important implication for macroeconomics—namely, that this bounceback of output after recessions strongly supports the output-gap view of fluctuations of DeLong and Summers (1988) and the plucking-model view in Friedman (1969, 1993). Both of these papers argued that output generally grows along a trend (either stationary or nonstationary) and that fluctuations are primarily lapses beneath the sustainable level of production implied by the rising trend.[5] DeLong and Summers refer to these lapses beneath trend as "output gaps," while Friedman identifies them as "plucks." Friedman's terminology makes clear his view (which is also implicit in DeLong and Summers) that output bounces back after it is pulled down from its sustainable level. This pattern of contraction and bounceback is precisely that implied by the dynamics of the floor regime in Potter's model.

Conclusion

This comment underscores several reasons why economists should be interested in nonlinear results. Although the profession may understate the benefits accruing from nonlinear tests and models in some cases, nonlinear modelers may underestimate the costs of complexity associated with nonlinear results. Nonlinear techniques, by themselves, are unlikely to generate broad interest among macroeconomists unless they answer questions economists are interested in.

It is, of course, difficult to foresee which nonlinear applications will have big payoffs for macroeconomics. It may be that the gains have largely been exhausted from identifying and characterizing nonlinearity in broad measures of real activity. Perhaps more work could be done on identifying the sources of nonlinearities. For example, in what part of the economy do nonlinearities arise?[6] Perhaps additional search for nonlinear dynamics in nominal quantities would prove fruitful. For example, in what ways do the dynamics of inflation and interest rates differ over the cycle?[7] Do prices move up more easily than they move down? Are there distinct policy regimes that can be identified in these variables? Are there important asymmetries in the impact of policy?[8] If nonlinear testers and modelers are able to find the interesting questions in economics, then the prospects of spreading nonlinear techniques and models into the profession will surely brighten.

Acknowledgments

I thank William Gale and Gregory Hess for helpful comments.

Notes

1. There is too much research for all of it to be cited here. Potter reviews some of this literature. Also see the references listed in Sichel (1993) and Diebold and Rudebusch (1994).

2. Neftçi provides evidence that the probability of exiting from a contraction exceeds the probability of exiting from an expansion, implying that unemployment rises faster in a contraction than it falls during an expansion. Sichel (1989) identified an error in Neftçi's empirical results. However, Rothman (1991) showed that Neftçi's original results are resurrected if a first-order Markov process is used for unemployment rather than the second-order Markov process used in Neftçi's paper.

3. Iwata and Hess (1994) suggest that standard inference is inappropriate for the extra terms added by Beaudry and Koop. Their results raise questions about the significance of the nonlinear terms.

4. Sichel (1994) demonstrated that the bounceback in output reflects the dynamics of inventory investment; that is, real final sales—output less inventory investment—do not exhibit bounceback dynamics. Furthermore, that paper shows that inventory investment and the inventory-sales ratio are stationary variables. This fact provides further evidence that output has an important transitory component because changes in inventory investment account for so much of the variance of output growth at business cycle frequencies.

5. Sichel (1993) shows that output exhibits "deepness." That is, dips below trend tend to be deeper than rises above trend. This stylized fact also supports the view implicit in DeLong and Summers' and Friedman's work.

6. As indicated earlier, Sichel (1994) showed that inventories play a key role in the nonlinear behavior of output. French and Sichel (1993) find evidence that nonlinearities arise in durable goods output and structures, but not in services. Rothman (1991) looking at unemployment, demonstrated that asymmetry arises in the manufacturing sector.

7. For some examples, see Ball and Mankiw (1991), Hamilton (1988), and Cecchetti, Lam, and Mark (1990).

8. James Cover (1992) provides evidence that output responds more to negative money shocks than to positive money shocks.

References

Balke, N., and M. Wynne. (1992). "The Dynamics of Recoveries." Mimeo, Federal Reserve Bank of Dallas.

Ball, Lawrence, and Gregory Mankiw. (1991). "Asymmetric Price Adjustments and Economic Fluctuations." Manuscript, Harvard University.

Beaudry, Paul, and Gary Koop. (1993). "Do Recessions Permanently Change Output?" *Journal of Monetary Economics*, 149–163.

Cecchetti, S.G., P. Lam, and N.C. Mark. (1990). "Mean Reversion in Equilibrium Asset Prices." *American Economic Review* 80, 398–418.

Cover, James P. (1992). "Asymmetric Effects of Positive and Negative Money-Supply Shocks." *Quarterly Journal of Economics* November, 1261–1282.

DeLong, Bradford, and Lawrence Summers. (1988). "How Does Macroeconomic Policy Affect Output?" *Brookings Papers on Economic Activity* 1988(2), 433–494.

Diebold, Francis X., and Glenn D. Rudebusch. (1994). "Measuring Business Cycles: A Modern Perspective." Mimeo, Federal Reserve Board and University of Pennsylvania.

Friedman, Milton. (1969). "Monetary Studies of the National Bureau." In *The Optimum Quantity of Money and Other Essays* (ch. 12, pp. 261–284). Chicago: Aldine.

Friedman, Milton. (1993). "The 'Plucking Model' of Business Fluctuations Revisited." *Economic Inquiry*, 171–177.

French, Mark W., and Daniel E. Sichel. (1993). "Cyclical Patterns in the Variance of Economic Activity." *Journal of Business and Economic Statistics* 11(1), 113–119.

Hamilton, James D. (1988). "Rational-Expectations Econometric Analysis of Changes in Regime: An Investigation of the Term Structure of Interest Rates." *Journal of Economic Dynamics and Control* 12, 385–423.

Hamilton, James D. (1989). "A New Approach to the Economic Analysis of Nonstationary Time Series and the Business Cycle." *Econometrica* 57, 357–384.

Iwata, Shigeru, and Gregory D. Hess. (1994). "Asymmetric persistence in GDP? A Deeper look at Depth." Mimeo, University of Kansas.

Neftçi, Salih N. (1984). "Are Economic Time Series Asymmetric Over the Business Cycle?" *Journal of Political Economy* 92(2), 307–328.

Rothman, Philip. (1991). "Further Evidence on the Asymmetric Behavior of Unemployment Rates Over the Business Cycle." *Journal of Macroeconomics* 13, 291–298.

Sichel, Daniel E. (1989). "Are Business Cycles Asymmetric: A Correction." *Journal of Political Economy* 97(5), 1255–1260.

Sichel, Daniel E. (1993). "Business Cycle Asymmetry: A Deeper Look." *Economic Inquiry* 31, 224–236.

Sichel, Daniel E. (1994). "Inventories and the Three Phases of the Business Cycle." *Journal of Business and Economic Statistics* 12(3), 269–277.

Subject Index

Author Index